Theory and Practice

of American

Foreign Policy

Theory and Practice of American Foreign Policy

MORTON GORDON

Assistant Professor of Political Science
Tulane University

and

KENNETH N. VINES

Assistant Professor of Political Science
Tulane University

THOMAS Y. CROWELL COMPANY
New York - 1955

MANUFACTURED IN THE UNITED STATES OF AMERICA

Dr. Handler
gift

Preface

THE AIM OF this book is to present a balanced and comprehensive account of the problems and processes of American foreign policy. Although the literature on this subject is now extensive and of increasing richness and variety, most of it is highly specialized, treating of particular aspects or problems. We have attempted to combine theory with practice, to connect institution with constitution, and to relate values to behavior by collecting and organizing some of the scattered literature. Our purpose in collecting these readings has been to facilitate the study of a difficult subject by imposing an orderly and logical outline upon a vast literature. This outline embodies the point of view that American foreign policy is the result of the interaction of a large number of individually complex factors.

Each of the six chapters of this book deals with an important problem in the study of American foreign policy, and each is preceded by an introduction whose dual purpose is to sketch the background of the problem and to relate it to the larger subject of American foreign policy.

The chapters are arranged in sequence from theory to practice and from the general to the particular. Thus, the selections in Chapter One explain the methods and concepts that are involved in the study of foreign policy. Chapter Two treats the theoretical aspects of American foreign policy, which are fundamental to an understanding of the subject.

The responsible student of American foreign policy must be concerned with more than learning what it is and acquiring the ability to discuss intelligently its successes and failures. He must also understand how American policies are formulated and executed and where the power to make foreign policy decisions resides. Therefore the selections in Chapter Three deal with the forces that shape decisions, and Chapters Four and Five treat the formation and the expression of American foreign policy. The concluding chapter traces the contemporary design of American policies and presents several critical views of some of them.

We wish to acknowledge our appreciation and indebtedness to the authors and publishers without whose permission the compilation of this book would have been impossible.

MORTON GORDON
KENNETH N. VINES

Contents

Theory and Practice
of American
Foreign Policy

CHAPTER ONE

Patterns in International Politics

IN THIS VOLUME, we shall attempt to develop some understanding of the principles of American foreign policy, its theoretical basis, its process of formation, and its content. Understanding alone cannot resolve conflicts arising out of substantial differences of interest between states, nor will it necessarily lead to a solution of problems of American foreign policy. But if we know more about the nature of the East-West conflict, the concept of the national interest of the United States, and the processes by which American foreign policy decisions are made, we shall be able to progress toward the development of a sophisticated and confident attitude toward our problems.

What are American foreign policies for? What are they supposed to accomplish? Ex-President Harry S. Truman has described the roots of our policy in terms so broad that probably few Americans would disagree with his formulations. He said:

Policies are the courses of action taken by a nation in the interests of the welfare of its people. The roots of a democratic nation's policies lie in the values cherished by its people. Here are some of the values which have lasted through all our history.

We are an independent nation, and we want to keep our independence.

We attach the highest importance to individual freedom, and we mean to keep our freedom.

We are a peaceful people, and we want to see the time when war and the threat of war are abandoned as instruments of policy by all nations.

We are a friendly people. We have no traditional "enemies." We want to settle our differences with other peoples as "good neighbors."

We believe in justice. A peace based on justice is the only peace which can endure.

Some students of American foreign policy would contend that Mr.

Truman's statement is a description of our aims in terms of universal moral principles. To speak of peace, justice, and individual freedom as ends in themselves, unrelated to American national interests and to the facts of contemporary international affairs, is to moralize. Although there is nothing wrong with moralizing as such, the penchant of high officials of our government to act on the basis of morality alone, and the concomitant inclination of the American people to support policies that can be explained and defended in "idealist" terminology have tended to obscure the nature of international politics and to produce errors of judgment that derive from distorted perspectives about the ends and means of foreign policy.

This "realist" criticism may not be completely valid, but it serves to indicate the necessity of analyzing the content of general pronouncements on foreign policy and of relating that content to the concrete world situation; and to indicate further that problems may be created by the terms in which foreign policy objectives are understood and described.

Confusion and disillusionment may result when we find that policies we regard as the application of the principles of "justice" or of "the importance of human freedom" conflict with the principles of the foreign policy of another power. Because of our belief in these principles, we are unalterably opposed to the forced communization of Poland, with all that it has meant to the Polish people in loss of individual freedom and of justice. Now it has been a cardinal principle of Russian foreign policy that the security of Russian territory depended, in large measure, upon the control of Poland. This was what Czar Alexander I meant when, at the Congress of Vienna in 1815, he placed his hand upon a map of Poland and insisted that the country had to be his. This was what Stalin meant more than one hundred years later, when he said that Poland was a matter of life and death for the Soviet Union. This insistence upon a friendly or even a subservient Poland does not stem from any peculiar and unreasoning facet of the Russian national character, but from the elementary facts of geography. There are no natural barriers, no rivers, no mountains, between Russian and Polish territory. It may seem simple "justice," therefore, to Russian rulers to have a "friendly" government in control of Polish affairs. In that view, it is our position which is at best unjust and unreasonable, at worst "imperialist" and "warmongering."

This example suggests that we cannot define our national interests without considering the values, traditions, and aspirations of other nations. It also indicates the dangers that lie in adopting foreign policies that do not take fully into account the policies which other nations have adopted and will adopt in pursuit of their interests. In a world where the technological conquest of distance has made nations dependent upon each other, the objectives of peace and security can be attained only by cooperation with powers whose objectives are similar or complementary to our own, and by reconciliation with powers whose policies conflict with our own. Without cooperation, we shall be isolated from the rest of the world; and isolation, by the definition of current problems, has now become impossible for the United States. And without reconciliation, war may be the only means left to defend our interests.

International politics has been variously studied in the past as diplomatic history, as current events, or as adherence to or deviation from international law and organizations. More recently, political aspects have been emphasized, and international politics has been analyzed in terms of the struggle for power among states. Each of these approaches has something to contribute to the comprehension of foreign policy, but no one of them can explain all of it.

We have already commented on the dangers that result from conceiving American foreign policy in purely moral and legal terms. There are equal dangers, however, that derive from conceiving international politics purely in terms of power relationships, unrelated to historical context, and distinct from the governmental processes by which foreign policy decisions are made. American policy in Indo-China, for example, is sometimes conceptualized simply in terms of the East-West conflict, the spread of Communist influence in Asia, and the balance of power. All of these are doubtless important; but much more than power relationships are involved. Colonialism, nationalism, American domestic politics, and the constitutional position of the American President, among other factors, have much to do with the formation of American policy in Indo-China.

In this volume, the authors have chosen to conceive of American foreign policy as the result of the many factors involved in complex relationships.

Before we can analyze American foreign policy, however, we must take cognizance of two aspects of international politics: first, the nature of our world at mid-Twentieth Century, and especially the major developments in international politics during the past fifty years; and second, the theoretical approaches that have been adopted by statesmen and scholars in their attempt to understand the problems of international politics, and to work out solutions for them. American foreign policy is practiced within the framework of international politics; theories of American foreign policy derive, in large measure, from theories of international politics.

Chapter One begins with a description of our world at mid-century, and continues with a short exposition of three theories of international politics. That theories in this area have been formulated at all is surely a sign of that maturity of viewpoint which is so badly needed at present. International politics is not a science, but it is something more than an amorphous body of knowledge, without any apparent order, that cannot now or ever be understood by man. As we learn more about the matter and become able to discover recurring patterns of behavior in the relations between states, our present theories of international politics will be refined and become more accurate. Perhaps, in the future, we shall be able to predict developments with some assurance that our predictions will be more than mere guesses.

Chapter Two is devoted to theories of American foreign policy, that is, to an analysis of American approaches to international politics: isolationism, idealism, and realism.

Chapter Three considers the role of the various forces that shape foreign policy decisions. In the instance cited above of Russian policies toward Poland, we have already noted the impact of one of these forces, geography, upon the development of Russian foreign policy. Other significant forces in the formation of American foreign policy are: external pressures; national character; public opinion, political parties, pressure groups, and propaganda; natural resources and the national economy; and science and technology.

Chapter Four deals with the constitutional and institutional framework within which foreign policy is formulated and executed.

Chapter Five presents several illustrations of the manner in which our policies are made known to the world: by official pronouncements; at international conferences; and in the texts of executive agreements and treaties.

In Chapter Six, the final chapter, we turn our attention to the contemporary design and content of American foreign policy—to the nature of the East-West conflict and the major theaters of American-Soviet tension, and to our general objectives and policies. This chapter closes with a critique of these policies.

---

1. The Past Fifty Years and the Next *

Much has been written about the fact that our world is very different from that of our fathers and grandfathers. Mr. Howe

* Quincy Howe, *Saturday Review of Literature,* November 7, 1953. The author is a prominent radio commentator on world affairs and author of *World History of*

describes some of the developments in international affairs during this century. He notes the influence of nationalism and internationalism, and the accomplishments, positive and negative, of Wilson, Lenin, Hitler, and Stalin. "As Asia has gone up in the world," he says, "Europe has gone down." Only the United States and the Soviet Union have the facilities to carry on modern war. Our world has been one of speed, violence, and extremism. The former optimistic view of human nature and human destiny has given way to pessimism. The prospects for world unity look very dim. What, then, is the best we can expect in the next fifty years? "Some new, if temporary, balance of power based at worst on fear, at best on hope."

Mr. Howe's views are certainly not cheerful. But they serve to introduce us to some of the problems of the present through an analysis of past developments.

The record of the past fifty years justifies at least two predictions concerning the next half century. We cannot bring back the vanished world of 1900. Neither can we expect present trends to continue forever. At the turn of the century more and more people in every land assumed that the material progress of the previous hundred years would continue onward and upward for many hundred years to come. Nor did they stop there. Faith in material progress bred faith in human progress. Science had not only enabled man to harness the forces of the universe to his own use. Science had also given man the power to change and improve his own nature. H. G. Wells expressed the hopes of millions when he foresaw twentieth-century science promoting the health, wealth, and happiness of all mankind.

World War I did more than demonstrate the power of modern science. It ended with two mighty efforts to assure the triumph of human progress. Drawing their inspiration from nineteenth-century Europe, taking for granted the limitless scope of scientific advance and human perfectibility, Wilson and Lenin set themselves up as world messiahs who offered universal programs of peace and plenty for all. But the League of Nations that Wilson inspired did not prevent World War II. The Russian Revolution that Lenin led did not sweep the world. Wilson's self-righteous refusal to compromise his principles made cynics of the liberals. Lenin's cynical compromise of every principle made gangsters of the radicals. Hitler then appealed to both cynics and gangsters, proving—even in defeat—that the spirit of nationalism which both Wilson and Lenin tried to transcend had more vitality than the spirit of

---

Our Own Times, a three-volume work of which two volumes have already been published.

internationalism which both Wilson and Lenin tried to evoke. Neither Hitler's cynicism nor his nationalism led to his defeat. Hitler failed because he appealed to only one nation and because that nation lay in Europe. And the chief force that finally laid Hitler low was not the Christian, democratic West; it was Stalin's Russia—more atheistic, more totalitarian than Nazi Germany itself.

By the end of World War II the world of 1900 had vanished altogether. Civilization, on which H. G. Wells was betting at the turn of the century, seemed sure to lose its race to catastrophe. Few prophets at mid-century foresaw much health, wealth, or happiness for mankind. George Orwell's *Nineteen Eighty-Four* carried more conviction. Reversing the last two figures of the year in which he wrote the book—1948—he produced a great satire of his own time, not a preview of the 1980's. But the contemporary historian who merely predicts more unreason and less freedom, more conformity and less progress, risks repeating the mistake of the historian of fifty years ago who assumed that all the major trends of 1900 would continue to run in the same direction for an indefinite period.

If it is the function of the modern satirist to shock us with a picture of a totalitarian world, it is the function of the modern historian to point out that the events of the past fifty years have shaken the optimism of 1900. Not Darwin and Whitman but Nietzsche and Dostoievsky fore-saw today's world. Freud revealed dark, human impulses that Marx attributed to environment. To most of the English-speaking world the defeat of Hilter signified the defeat of the racial and national doctrines he sought to impose on mankind. The dark-skinned majority of the human race takes a different view. Although the British have made noble, honest efforts to live down Kipling's superiority complex toward lesser breeds without the law, and although Americans have made noble, honest efforts to end discrimination, the peoples of Asia see no great difference between Hitler and Kipling or between Nazi stormtroopers and a lynch mob in the American South. Advocates of white superiority, even of white supremacy, in the Western world have encouraged Asian and African demagogues to advocate colored superiority and even colored supremacy. The Gandhis and the Schweitzers, of course, reject all doctrines of racial supremacy, but nationalist and Communist dema-gogues prefer to appeal to prejudice and emotion.

As Asia has gone up in the world Europe has gone down. Nationalist leaders and movements have triumphed in Turkey, India, China, Japan. More than once religions originating in Asia have conquered or converted Europe. Today the religion of nationalism which originated in Europe has gripped Asia. This new force hit America between the eyes at Pearl

Harbor. It struck again, more successfully and on a gigantic scale, when the Communists conquered China. Britain bowed to this force in India, Holland in Indonesia. France tries to fight it in Indo-China. The United States tries to come to terms with it in Korea. Since Lenin's time the Russian Communists have tried with varying success to exploit the force of Asian nationalism, but all history argues that they cannot hope to bend it permanently to their purposes.

Because only Russia and the United States have the facilities required to wage a modern war, it is assumed they must eventually fight and that the victor will rule the world. But if a Soviet-American conflict does materialize what an opportunity for the revolutionary movement in Asia. Already interested parties in various Asian countries seek Russian or American backing for their various enterprises, as Asian Communists cry out against American imperialism and Asian anti-Communists cry out against Russian aggression. A China threatened with civil war or an India threatened with Communism might well set off World War III. But the vast costs and uncertain outcome make for caution in both Washington and Moscow. Atomic weapons give the United States and Russia the power to destroy each other. They do not give either Russia or the United States the power to conquer or control any substantial part of Asia. Just the opposite. The destruction that atomic war could create in Russia, Europe, and the United States would make the world safe for Asia for centuries to come.

The death of Stalin and the election of Eisenhower have reduced the immediate threat of Russian-American conflict. Stalin's successors have had to cope with unrest in the satellite lands and have purged Beria. Although they inherited a state many times stronger than the state Stalin inherited from Lenin, they at once felt it necessary to make substantial concessions to their own people who want something better than Stalin gave them and who believe they can get it. Beyond the Iron Curtain the new rulers of Russia are spreading the word that the time has come to settle the Cold War by negotiation—and it's a word that millions of Europeans and Asians want to believe. Although President Eisenhower and most Americans remain skeptical of Russian good faith and good will, the fear of immediate war has measurably abated. The truce in Korea has made the prospects for peace look a little brighter. The June 17 riots in East Germany have encouraged the hope that the Russian regime will collapse from the inside. This American belief may prove just as groundless as Europe's belief that we can do business with Malenkov, but it is no less passionately held.

How Stalin insulated the Russian people from all ideas and information that he did not want them to receive is an old and familiar story. Only now are we discovering that he and his heirs and assigns wore the same self-imposed blinders. Since Stalin's death the new rulers of Russia have shown themselves somewhat more sensitive to public opinion at home and abroad, but it is difficult to fathom their real beliefs or to forecast the decisions to which these beliefs will lead them. Although no man-made Iron Curtain separates the American people from the rest of the world, the experiences they have gone through—and the experiences they have missed—have created wide gulfs between them and the peoples of Europe and Asia. This might not have mattered if Americans had continued to live by themselves, alone in the world, but it hardly prepared them for global leadership. Having known neither Communism nor Fascism at first hand, having escaped the ravages of war and revolution, many Americans still cling to assumptions that the rest of the world has steadily discarded since 1900. President Eisenhower believes in enlightened self-interest as firmly as he believes in God—and there is every indication that the mass of his fellow citizens believe as he does. The wars of class and race that have ravaged so much of the world never spread to the United States. Although these wars have weakened Europe in many respects, they have given the people of Europe an experience and even a wisdom that most Americans lack. And, even though the power of Europe no longer spreads through the world as it did fifty years ago, Europe's decline may take the same slow course as Europe's rise.

The United States, on the other hand, has come up in the world so fast that it could go down the same way. The British historian D. W. Brogan has warned against "the illusion of American omnipotence," which the Spanish-American War encouraged and which two world wars have not dispelled. Yet a review of the record of the past half-century leads to a paradoxical conclusion. Insofar as the United States continues to expand its power and prestige it will hasten its own doom. Insofar as the United States begins to limit its commitments it will preserve its power and prestige. While the revolt of Europe's masses which Ortega y Gasset analyzed more than twenty years ago may have run its course, the revolt of Asia's masses has only just begun. There lie the forces most likely to shape the great events of the next fifty years. They are forces with which some Americans have worked constructively. But they are forces over which the United States cannot hope to exercise real control.

Nearly every historian of stature who has tried to look into the near future predicts that the rise of Asia will continue to overshadow whatever else this century may bring forth. Henry Adams sensed the possibility at the turn of the century. Spengler and Toynbee have speculated along the same lines. The rise of Asia not only entails the decline of Europe. Because Europe in the past has preached and practiced the doctrine of white supremacy, racial tensions will continue to play a major part in the affairs of our planet. In Europe itself the smaller states will move toward continental unity, but the French poet Paul Valéry missed the mark when he predicted more than twenty years ago, *"Le temps du monde fini commence."* And Wilson's dream of a League of Nations, Lenin's dream of world revolution, Roosevelt's Four Freedoms, and Willkie's One World will have to wait for another century to materialize. The world is not becoming one. The world is dividing into a few great continental groupings, each of which will tend to have its own culture and character, with the Western powers favoring a sort of welfare-warfare economy, Russia continuing its totalitarian system, Asia stressing nationalism. When Willkie returned from his trip around the world in 1942 he concluded that the One World era had arrived. Eleven years later another defeated candidate for the Presidency returned from a similar journey with the news that we are living in three worlds—the Communist world, the free world, and the uncommitted world. And Adlai Stevenson was not one of those who doubted Roosevelt's crusade for the Four Freedoms or rejected the Willkie program of One World in our time. But, even though Roosevelt's crusade has gone the way of Wilson's, everywhere the state encroaches upon the areas once monopolized by the traditional religions.

It is, of course, true that the past decade has witnessed a widespread return to the traditional religions. Church membership in the United States stands at an all-time high. Not since the period of the Protestant Reformation has the Roman Catholic Church wielded such power or enjoyed such prestige in Western Europe. The Moslem faith has taken a new lease on life in its endorsement of nationalism and its opposition to Communism. But the past several centuries of material progress have secularized the traditional religions and given birth to new substitute religions—Communism, Fascism, Nationalism.

The century of material progress between the Battle of Waterloo and World War I encouraged an increasingly optimistic view of human nature and human destiny. Service to society became the highest of ideals and not a mere means to the end of saving one's own soul. But the years between the wars saw the prospects of a worldly Utopia go glimmering. Isaac Deutscher has contrasted the "revolutionary optimism" of Lenin and Trotzky with the "revolutionary pessimism" of Stalin. In like fashion the doubts and vacillations of Nehru follow the spiritual serenity of Gandhi. The dreams of Dr. Sun Yat-sen bring forth the opportunism of Chiang Kai-shek and the cynicism of Mao Tse-tung.

If the aspiration to build a better world in the here and now enlisted some of the same enthusiasm that gave the great religions their positive appeal, the defeat of that aspiration has revived interest in the doctrine of original sin.   But the children of a generation which lost its belief in a life after death have not recaptured their ancestors' belief in eternal damnation. Unable to establish a kingdom of heaven on earth, they have discovered only that man can make his own hell.

The speed and violence of our times have given the extremist a deceptive authority.   The extreme internationalist gives way to the extreme nationalist.   Revolution when it does not provoke reaction devours its own children.   As the second half of our century begins to run its course the older democracies turn to regional solutions abroad and to the welfare state at home while the newer nations that have risen in Asia cultivate the national spirit at the expense of freedom for the individual.   Standards of living and education remain so different in different areas that a world community has even less chance today than it had in Wilson's time.   For the preponderance of power that Wilson proposed held out more hope to mankind than the balance of power which had led to World War I.   But neither Wilson nor Lenin nor Hitler was able to create a preponderance of power to replace the balance of power that sustained the world of 1900 and as matters now stand, in the divided world of 1953, the prospects for world unity within our present century look dim indeed.   The most that we can expect for another fifty years—and perhaps for another five hundred—is for the various nations, regions, and continents to strike some new, if temporary, balance of power based at worst on fear, at best on hope.

2. THEORIES OF INTERNATIONAL POLITICAL BEHAVIOR *

Mr. Quincy Howe has pointed to some of the important changes which have occurred in the world during this century, and has, so to speak, set the stage in which international politics operates.

In attempting to understand the significance and meaning of recurring patterns of international political behavior, students of international politics have developed certain theoretical frameworks which they believe will aid them to explain the past, offer a useful guide to statesmen of our own day, and, with some degree of reliability, predict the probable courses of future developments in

* Kenneth W. Thompson, "The Study of International Politics: A Survey of Trends and Developments," *The Review of Politics,* Notre Dame, Indiana, October, 1952, pp. 433-467.   The author is Associate Professor of Political Science, Northwestern University.

international affairs. Professor Thompson explains and analyzes three theories of international political behavior, those of political idealism, political realism, and eclecticism.

. . . . .

It is frequently said that one test of the independent character of a discipline or field of study is the presence in the field of theories contending for recognition by those engaged in thinking and writing. It may be significant that underlying the study of contemporary international politics are two general theories of human nature and politics. Moreover, there are already the first signs of the origin of a third way of conceiving the nature of international affairs. At this time, however, political idealism and political realism are the major competitors for recognition as the theory of international behavior. In the past there has been no coherent political theory evolved from the ancients which deliberately sets forth to explain politics within a system that is not ordered and controlled by an all-powerful central authority. Indeed idealism and realism as conceived and defined in political theory from Greek times to the present have little in common with the assumptions and premises of the two philosophies of contemporary international politics. Each in its sphere has its own tacit or explicit assumptions. In world politics, the philosophy of idealism or utopianism so-called includes most of the thinking which was done in the intervening years between the two World Wars. The philosophy of realism which had prevailed throughout most of the eighteenth and nineteenth centuries has been revived both in theory and practice especially in the years following World War II. The currently most useful and original literature has been contributed primarily by those concerned with testing the assumptions of realism. Yet it is fashionable, especially in circles of older scholars, to proclaim that the distinctions between realism and idealism are unreal and exaggerated. Moreover, there are many who contend that both terms are fraught with emotions and value judgments and thereby are disqualified from use in social studies. In contrast, great diplomats in the West including the most distinguished representatives in 1952 have rarely been seized by such fears and doubts. Our wisest diplomats and statesmen have taken idealism and realism for granted. For example, the most learned and perceptive of American diplomats and the recent Ambassador to Moscow, Mr. George F. Kennan, has declared: "I see the most serious fault of our past policy formulations to lie in something that I might call the legalistic-moralistic approach to international problems. This approach runs like a red skein through our foreign policy of the last fifty years. . . . It is the belief that it should be possible to suppress the chaotic and dangerous aspirations of governments in the international field by the acceptance of some system of legal rules and restraints. . . . It is the essence of this belief that instead of taking the awkward conflicts of national interest and dealing with them on their merits with the view to finding the solutions least unsettling to the stability of international life, it would be better to find some formal criteria of a judicial nature by which the permissible behavior of states could be defined." Mr. Kennan concludes his estimate of the philosophy of utopianism by pointing to the beliefs and attitudes in the United States which have made this viewpoint meaningful and creditable. "Behind all of this, of course, lies the American assumption that the things for which other peoples in this world are apt to contend are for the most part neither creditable nor important and might justly be expected to take second place behind the desirability of an orderly world, untroubled by international violence. To the American mind, it is unplausible that people should have positive aspirations, and ones that they regard as legitimate, more important to them than the peacefulness and orderliness of international life."

Another wise statesman, a young Conservative Member of Parliament, Captain Peter Thorneycroft, who in 1951 was to become the youngest member of Prime Minister Churchill's Cabinet, voiced on February 28, 1945, essentially the same beliefs that Mr. Kennan was to express in 1951. In a debate in the House of Commons on the issues arising from the Polish settlement agreed to by Prime Minister Churchill, President Roosevelt and Premier Stalin at the Crimean Conference, Captain Thorneycroft chose the occasion to cast his specific comments in the mold of general principles of international politics.

I believe the real difficulty in which my hon. Friends find themselves is not so much Poland at all. I believe it is in the apparent conflict between documents like the Atlantic Charter and the facts of the European situation. We talk to two different people in two different languages. In the East we are talking to the Russians. The Russians are nothing if not realists. . . . I believe that the Russian Foreign Office is perhaps more in tune with the advice which would be given to the Tsars than to the potentates of the twentieth century. In such circumstances we talk in language not far removed from power politics. In the West we are faced by the Americans. They are nothing if not idealists. To them we talk in the polite language of the Atlantic Charter. Somehow or other we have to marry those two schools of thought. If I could persuade the Americans, particularly in the Middle West, to have something of the Russian realism in international relations, and persuade the Russians to have the idealism that exists on the East coast of America, we might get somewhere, but let us face the fact that the process will be a long and painful one. You do not move suddenly from a world in which there are international rivalries into a world where there is international cooperation. It is the world that we are in that the Prime Minister has to deal with. We could not come back from Yalta with a blueprint for a new Utopia. . . . The rights of small nations are safeguarded by a mixture of diplomacy and military power. . . .

These two expressions of an American and British conception of the nature of international politics are significant because of the strong clear light they throw on the two opposing theories. They indicate that professional diplomats and statesmen are unable to indulge themselves the luxury of shying away from the facts of international life. The assumptions underlying the two points of view may be enumerated in relatively simple terms. For the political realist, rivalry and some form of strife among nation-states is the rule and not a mere accident of backwardness in the past. There are harmonies as well as disharmonies to be sure but the failure of every scheme for world peace in the past must be sought in the conditions which have created the disharmonies and not through comparisons with a blueprint of a commonwealth of absolute world harmonies. In all social groups, whether in states or in smaller more intimate communities, a contest for influence and power goes on unceasingly. On the international scene, however, rivalries among states are uncontrolled by effective law or government. The business of statesmanship and diplomacy under the conditions of present-day international society is to limit the struggles and restrict their extent and scope. The means available in the absence of government are the unceasing pursuit of new balances of power and rough equilibriums among contending parties. The aims include adjustment and accommodation on the basis of mutual recognition that an equilibrium does exist. The realist strives to mitigate the rivalries among nations, through checks and balances and by compromise and bargaining. Abstract moral principles may be the ultimate object and purpose of the bargain or agreement but an abstract principle is not an essential part of the bargain itself. Realism would prepare the student of international politics for the tragic and stubborn discrepancy of means and ends in international politics. It accepts for the guide and premise of its thought the permanence and ubiquity of the struggle for power. But it strives unceasingly through every means at its disposal to contain and limit concentrations of power and to compose and relieve tensions which could lead to a situation of war.

The utopian philosophy has little in common with political realism nor has it shown much patience or understanding for this brand of thinking. It chooses to abjure the toils of power politics since at most they are considered an abnormal and passing historic phase. In fact, with the creation of one universal society, so primitive and barbaric a form of international politics, if not indeed politics itself, will be eliminated. Political realism, it is claimed, is a distortion and cynical corruption of the true meaning of history. It is claimed by the spokesmen of political idealism that if there have been group controversies throughout history, these struggles have centered not in political rivalries for influence and power but in the clash between incompatible ideals and principles. A concrete example which is offered is the aggression of fascism against democracy. At such time, therefore, as fascism and the other philosophies whose aims have made conflict inevitable have been permanently smashed and destroyed, power politics and war will disappear. Historically, utopianism has offered three alternatives for moral nations confronting the practical problems of survival in a world of archaic power politics. Ultimately, power politics must be eliminated through instituting a universal world government. Practically, power politics will be abolished when their main exemplars, the totalitarian states have been erased from the face of the earth. Provisionally, their evil influence will be progressively and decisively undermined by the example of moral and upright nations forswearing relations with corrupted, power-seeking nations, pursuing neutrality policies and abstaining from all forms of traditional power politics.

In practice, moreover, the nations of good will who have accepted the philosophy of utopianism have pursued foreign policies reflecting precisely these three alternatives. It is not by accident that the United States as the nation over recent decades that has yielded most readily to utopianism has pursued a foreign policy that has vacillated between these three possibilities. For in these terms we can account for the neutrality policy of the United States before both World Wars. In each pre-war period, we tried to abstain and withdrew from the impure and corrupted power politics of the European continent. Any concession in terms of territorial guaranties against German expansion would have been unworthy of the philosophy we espoused. Any intervention in the affairs of Europe for the purpose of bolstering and strengthening the Weimar Republic would have weakened our moral position. When at length we were driven by the inherent logic of utopianism to justify our role in World War II, we turned from neutrality to a holy crusade against the evil incarnate in fascism. When through no fault of our own war became unavoidable—for had we not meticulously avoided any political action that could have invited the conflict—we gave unstintingly of our resources and our principles. We engaged in the world struggle not selfishly or for political advantage but in order to end conflict in the West and destroy and eliminate those evil men and ideals who had been responsible. These wars were not ordinary struggles for more territorial adjustments, new balances of power or specified political gains but were crusades for advancing the spread of democracy. They were holy wars of "unconditional surrender" against solitary infidels and troublemakers. For these men and ideas had caused the catastrophies; therefore, with their elimination, aggrandizement and rivalry would disappear.

The third stage in the utopian journey, however, has been for us the most basic, fateful and far-reaching. After the war, it was clearly essential that what had been undertaken and achieved in war be sealed and perfected in peace. The agents of power politics lay mortally wounded; now the climate in which their nefarious policies had thrived must be cleansed and transformed and international organization substituted for politics. In this new commonwealth, the problem of power would disappear. What this meant in concrete terms was that the *status quo* with its prevailing lawfulness based on the relative satisfaction of the victorious powers must be made permanent through the regularized procedures of new international organizations. Thus through our policies of neutrality, moralistic crusades and the substitution of organization for anarchic world politics, we have consistently pursued in recent times the aims of political idealism.

Hence the crucial difference and the real point at which political idealism and political realism diverge is with respect to the positions they take regarding the problem of power. Power is an attribute of an archaic and transitory international situation for idealists who have chosen not to recognize it as enduring. Power for the realist is the single most stubborn social psychological factor by which international behavior is influenced. Only through understanding this phenomenon can man hope to improve the melancholy status of his present situation. There is a third general approach or theory, however, which departs explicitly from both of these theories of politics. A viewpoint which is perhaps best designated *eclectic* has been asserted to represent a new synthesis. Thus in the second revised edition of George Schwarzenberger's voluminous *Power Politics,* the author rejects both idealism and realism as unscientific. Neither, he claims, has seen fit to state its major premise which he finds on the one hand in the case of realism to be that of pessimism and on the other hand with idealism that of optimism. Mr. Schwarzenberger concludes: "What is actually required is a primarily empirical approach to international affairs." Eclecticism in these terms asks the student to start without any *a priori* assumptions in making his inquiries in the field. The eclectic point of view has shown a preference for a sociological approach to the problems of world politics. There would appear to be three reasons alleged for this practicality. First, only present-day sociology with its separation of facts and values and its resistance to *a priori* judgments is equipped with a tradition of having pursued truly empirical studies. Also, the sole catholic and inclusive approach to the study of international politics is that of sociology. For example, in the case of tariff legislation, the international lawyer can discuss the legal and normative implications of treaties and treaty observance; the economist can assess the purely economic aspects of the problem; and the political scientist will contribute to an understanding of the political conflicts going on within a certain nation. Yet the only discipline which will cover all these separate facets under the enveloping umbrella of a single conceptual framework is sociology. Thirdly, sociology alone is capable of providing tests or clues by which to separate subject matter that is clearly international in character from what is essentially domestic in nature. It finds this test in the general principle of whether or not a given issue or episode affects the growth or the disintegration of international society. A new unity called the international society which by definition falls short of a true community but in effect exceeds a condition of anarchy is the guidepost by which we must measure whether a thing is international or not. At the present stage of development international society is an emerging embryonic movement that is measurable. Any event must be examined and assessed in light of its effect on the degree of integration and disintegration in international society. In American foreign policy, for example, the scientific way in which to think about the Truman Doctrine or the Marshall Plan would be to estimate their effects on the integration or disintegration of international society.

Of the three approaches or theories of international politics, eclecticism has come on to the scene most recently. Its claim that it forswears the espousal of one viewpoint or another regarding human nature and politics is hardly substantiated in concrete studies by scholars like Professor Schwarzenberger. For that author, after disclaiming the assumption of realism that man is competitive and possesses a lust for power as well as the belief of idealism that he is rational and good, actually proceeds throughout most of his analysis to employ the working concepts of political realism. Indeed the illusion of much of contemporary social science that the student can in fact approach his inquiry with a *tabula rasa* is hardly supported by the undertakings of Schwarzenberger or any of his colleagues. Yet this view is central to eclecticism as a theory of international politics. If this assumption is false, then much of the work of this approach will in all likelihood be seriously undermined. At this stage, however, the presence of three separate theories each avowing qualitatively distinct assumptions tends to give to the study of world politics the character of something approaching a discipline.

CHAPTER TWO

The American Approach to International Politics

IT IS NOW A COMMONPLACE to say that the American people have forsaken the comforts of isolationism and assumed the responsibilities of world leadership. One important result of the assumption of these new burdens has been the awakening of interest in international affairs throughout the nation. Slowly, and with mixed feelings of anxiety, frustration, and the determination to achieve peace and security, Americans have become aware that the problems of contemporary international life are complex.

The world does seem too much with us. How much happier we would be if we could disregard the "alarums and excursions" of the world ouside and devote our energies to pleasurable private pursuits! How fine it would be to say, "A plague on all your houses," and yet remain safe, free, and comfortable! But this will not do. Neutralism and isolationism are the policies that pronounce a plague on all contenders. Both policies have been tried and, in this century at least, both have been found wanting in the most important respect in which such policies may be judged successful or unsuccessful: that of maintaining our security and keeping us out of war.

At the end of World War II, all but two of the powers were exhausted and defeated. Some of the victors—such as France and Britain—were hardly better off than the vanquished. Only the United States remained strong, confident, and energetic. When one world split in two, the leadership of one part of it was summarily thrust upon us.

What choice, then, is left to the United States? Clearly, we must probe the complexities of international politics and search for solutions to international problems. We were unable to avoid war and threats to our national security by refraining from involvement and entanglement.

18

We now believe that the attainment of peace and security will require an active American participation in world politics.

What is American foreign policy all about? Any answer to this question must begin by noting that our foreign policy operates within the larger framework of international politics. Understanding the nature of international politics, therefore, is the first step in achieving comprehension of the nature of American foreign policy.

The vast majority of our citizens, who secure their information from the mass media of communications, tend to seek specific solutions to particular problems. However fervent their aspirations may be for a peaceful, orderly, and uncomplicated world, their horizons of thought are limited to the immediate past, present, and future. How to settle the Korean War with honor, how to prevent the communization of Western Europe, how to strengthen the free world against the threat of aggressive totalitarianism—such is the range of problems considered by our people. It is noteworthy that these problems are generally described in terms connoting action, an indication that the American approach to foreign policy is activist rather than passivist. This preference for activism demonstrates that the American people make certain basic assumptions about the nature of international politics and American foreign policy. In other words, our activist orientation is based upon our acceptance of a theory, or theories, of foreign policy.

Three theories of international politics have already been described (Selection 2). Two of these, realism and idealism, have many adherents among practitioners and students of American foreign policy. Realists and idealists have different views regarding the ends and means of foreign policy. Which views are correct and most useful is not nearly as important, however, as the fact that the realist-idealist debate has stirred considerable interest in governmental and lay circles—a sign that Americans are becoming more accustomed to thinking about foreign policy in broader, more theoretical terms, and are showing some concern for the development of long-term policy as opposed to *ad hoc* improvisation. This growing maturity is reflected in specific action by the Government.

On May 5, 1947, the Policy Planning Staff of the State Department was established, and Mr. George F. Kennan, a career diplomat of many years' service, was designated as its first Director. The State Department regulation which set up the new agency stated that the purpose of the Staff was "to assure the development, within the Department, of long-range policy which will serve as a framework for program-planning and a guide for current policy decisions and operations." As one of its major functions, the Staff was to advise and assist the Under Secretary of State in "formulating and developing, for the consideration and approval of appropriate officials of the Department, a long-term program for the achievement of American foreign policy objectives."

The creation of the Policy Planning Staff was generally approved. Congressional and press comment indicated that there was a widespread belief that the new and exalted position of the United States in world affairs brought with it a heavy responsibility for achieving a just and lasting peace. This peace could not be won by happy accident or "in a fit of absentmindedness." In the late spring of 1947, the optimistic view of the future engendered by wartime cooperation between the United States and the Soviet Union had not yet been fully dissipated, but there were already signs that the close collaboration of the World War II alliance had broken up, perhaps beyond repair. It seemed clear, therefore, that winning the peace would not come easily, that a considerable amount of working and planning for peace would be required; attaining the foreign policy objectives of the United States would be a long-term problem, one which would call for long-range planning. The Policy Planning Staff seemed to be an admirable tool to serve that purpose.

But what are the foreign policy objectives of the United States? Many people would immediately assert that peace is undoubtedly our most important objective. After a moment's reflection, however, it becomes apparent that peace is not enough. A nation can always have peace if it is willing to accept it on any terms. But a difficulty arises when one asks the question: What are the terms which the United States must accept to buy peace? No great nation can accept peace unless and until its vital national interests have been safeguarded. In other words, we must have security along with peace. But how can the United States achieve security in the face of the threat of Soviet aggression? To what extent does our security depend upon our relations with Great Britain, France, China, and other states?

If we formulate the important questions of American foreign policy in terms of the specific relations between the United States and other states —and not in terms of a generalized search for peace, freedom, or democracy—we are led to a consideration of first principles: the first step that must be taken by policy planners is the determination of the nature of international politics.

But what is the nature of international politics? Does it involve the pursuit of peace, security, democracy, power, or something else? This important question must be answered, for the delineation of the objectives of our foreign policy, and the means employed to attain these objectives, will be strongly influenced by the assumptions we make about the true nature of international politics.

The record of American foreign policy since the beginning of World War II has not been particularly good. Indeed, the bitter criticism directed at some of the unhappy results of that policy might lead one to suppose that, since 1941, we have witnessed a series of calamitous defeats unrelieved by any success. Such a conclusion would be unwarranted, however. American policy has been successful in a least two important respects. The Marshall Plan has prevented the threatened economic collapse of Western Europe and, by doing so, forestalled the immediate danger that, because of the disintegration of economic life, the Communist Parties of those states would be able to seize power with the apathetic acquiescence if not the enthusiastic approval of the masses. The North Atlantic Treaty served notice upon the Soviet Union that the United States would regard an attack upon any of the other signatories as an attack upon herself. The seizure of countries, one by one, in the manner practiced by Hitler, was thus closed to the Soviet Union. To this date, largely because of American policy, no country in Western Europe has been in any imminent peril of Communist subversion from within or Soviet aggression from without.

Elsewhere in the world, however, many serious errors were committed. Some of these will not be undone easily. Since the end of World War II, statesmen and scholars have devoted considerable thought and effort to examining the record of the foreign policy of the United States, in order not only to expose the errors that were committed, but, more important, to lay bare the fundamental theoretical bases from which these errors proceeded. This type of inquiry rests upon a belief that miscalculations have occurred frequently because of a failure to adopt a "scientific" approach to international politics, and, contrariwise, because of an inclination among Americans to view the problems of foreign policy in terms of universal moral principles alone. Much research remains to be done along these lines, but the accumulation of speculation about the ends and means of foreign policy based upon morality divorced from reality is being swept away. And if we do not yet have a theory that can explain the past and offer a consistent guide for the future, we can say that we are on our way toward the realization of that goal.

The American approach to foreign policy has usually been characterized by realist and idealist assumptions concerning the nature of international politics. Some of our greatest statesmen have been realists; Alexander Hamilton would certainly be put in this group. Others, such as Woodrow Wilson and Secretary of State Cordell Hull, have adopted an approach which was primarily idealist. Often a policy statement was made or a course of action taken which betrayed a realist or idealist orientation without any apparent consciousness on the part of the author of the policy that he had accepted one or the other view of the nature of international politics.   Much criticism has been directed against several American presidents on the grounds that they were blinded by their own idealist view of the world in which they lived, and were therefore easily duped by the realist policies pursued by their opposite numbers in foreign countries, especially when these policies were presented and defended in idealist terminology.

Idealism is at the present time under attack in the United States.   It is argued that we must adopt a new method of statecraft—that of realism. It is said that our task is somewhat simplified by the fact that we have merely to relearn something we once knew and have now forgotten.   The founders of this nation were realists and were extremely successful.   We must recapture their wisdom.   Although the realist attack has been strong and many have adopted the realist position, the idealist approach still has its adherents.

Americans, then, have thought about foreign policy in realist or idealist terms, or in some combination of the two.   In the earliest days of our history as a nation, the great powers were primarily concerned with maintaining and improving their positions *vis à vis* each other. The United States was months away, a vast wilderness peopled with savages and scattered groups of transplanted Europeans.   We were weak militarily, having secured our independence less by our own power than through a desire on the part of France to utilize the colonists' struggle for freedom as a means to humble her enemy, Britain.   Washington and Jefferson initially welcomed the assistance of France, but when independence had been won, they understood that our greatest danger lay in becoming involved in the power politics of the European states.   Since we were too weak to play a major role, we would be useful only as a pawn in these conflicts.   Under the peculiar circumstances of the times, the thing to do, it seemed, was to have as few dealings with the big powers as possible, especially on any permanent basis.   The policy of isolationism was born of a realist appraisal of the situation by our early leaders.

Isolationism, although it is not a theory about the nature of international politics and American foreign policy (Mr. Albert K. Weinberg says it is a theory about a theory of foreign policy), has been important as an approach to international politics throughout much of our history, and there are still some in our day who would have us return to isolationism.   For these reasons, we have thought it desirable to include several examples of isolationism (Selections 3 and 4) and an explanation of the content of the policy of non-entanglement (Selection 5), a discussion of the relative merits of isolationism and interventionism (Selection

6), and finally an example of the most recent type of isolationism, neo-isolationism (Selection 7).

Idealist theory is represented by a speech of President Wilson (Selection 8), his war message to Congress (Selection 9), the *Four Freedoms* address of President Franklin D. Roosevelt (Selection 10), and an historical account of moralism in American foreign policy (Selection 11).

Realist theory is expounded by two of its best known proponents, Mr. George F. Kennan and Professor Hans J. Morgenthau (Selections 12 and 13). There follow two attacks on realism (Selections 14 and 15), and finally, Professor Morgenthau's reply to these criticisms, explaining the realist position at length (Selection 16).

Isolationism

3. No ENTANGLING ALLIANCES — WASHINGTON'S FAREWELL ADDRESS

President Washington's address is one of the most widely known and least understood orations in the annals of American history. It would be impossible to prove that he intended his advice to be followed by his countrymen for all time to come. His suggestions were based upon his own recent experiences as President, and were probably meant to be applied to the immediate future. The isolationist doctrine he preached, however, has been influential in shaping our foreign policy for more than one hundred and fifty years. His isolationism rested primarily upon the fact of the geographic isolation of the United States from Europe. Yet, as late as 1949, when Europe was closer to the United States than Boston had been to Philadelphia in Washington's day, opponents of the ratification of the North Atlantic Treaty cited Washington's advice to steer clear of entangling alliances.

. . . Observe good faith and justice toward all nations. Cultivate peace and harmony with all. Religion and morality enjoin this conduct. And can it be that good policy does not equally enjoin it? It will be worthy of a free, enlightened, and at no distant period a great nation to give to mankind the magnanimous and too novel example of a people always guided by an exalted justice and benevolence. Who can doubt that in the course of time and things the fruits of such a plan would richly repay any temporary advantages which might be lost by a steady adherence to it? Can it be that Providence has not connected the permanent felicity of a nation with its virtue? The experiment, at least, is recommended by every sentiment which ennobles human nature. Alas! is it rendered impossible by its vices?

In the execution of such a plan nothing is more essential than that permanent, inveterate antipathies against particular nations and passionate attachments for others should be excluded, and that in place of them just and amicable feelings toward all should be cultivated. The nation which indulges toward another an habitual hatred or an habitual fondness is in some degree a slave. It is a slave to its animosity or to its affection, either of which is sufficient to lead it astray from its duty and its interest. Antipathy in one nation against another disposes each more readily to offer insult and injury, to lay hold of slight causes of umbrage, and to be haughty and intractable when accidental or trifling occasions of dispute occur.

Hence frequent collisions, obstinate, envenomed, and bloody contests. The nation prompted by ill will and resentment sometimes impels to war the government contrary to the best calculations of policy. The government sometimes participates in the national propensity, and adopts through passion what reason would reject. At other times it makes the animosity of the nation subservient to projects of hostility, instigated by pride, ambition, and other sinister and pernicious motives. The peace often, sometimes perhaps the liberty, of nations has been the victim.

So, likewise, a passionate attachment of one nation for another produces a variety of evils. Sympathy for the favorite nation, facilitating the illusion of an imaginary common interest in cases where no real common interest exists, and infusing into one the enmities of the other, betrays the former into a participation in the quarrels and wars of the latter without adequate inducement or justification. It leads also to concessions to the favorite nation of privileges denied to others, which is apt doubly to injure the nation making the concessions by unnecessarily parting with what ought to have been retained, and by exciting jealousy, ill will, and a disposition to retaliate in the parties from whom equal privileges are withheld; and it gives to ambitious, corrupted, or deluded citizens (who devote themselves to the favorite nation) facility to betray or sacrifice the interests of their own country without odium, sometimes even with popularity, gilding with the appearances of a virtuous sense of obligation, a commendable deference for public opinion, or a laudable zeal for public good the base of foolish compliances of ambition, corruption, or infatuation.

As avenues to foreign influence in innumerable ways, such attachments are particularly alarming to the truly enlightened and independent patriot.

How many opportunities do they afford to tamper with domestic factions, to practice the arts of seduction, to mislead public opinion, to influence or awe the public councils! Such an attachment of a small or weak toward a great and powerful nation dooms the former to be the satellite of the latter. Against the insidious wiles of foreign influence (I conjure you to believe me, fellow-citizens) the jealousy of a free people ought to be *constantly* awake, since history and experience prove that foreign influence is one of the most baneful foes of republican government. But that jealousy, to be useful, must be impartial, else it becomes the instrument of the very influence to be avoided, instead of a defense against it. Excessive partiality for one foreign nation and excessive dislike of another cause those whom they actuate to see danger only on one side, and serve to veil and even second the arts of influence on the other. Real patriots who may resist the intrigues of the favorite are liable to become suspected and odious, while its tools and dupes usurp the applause and confidence of the people to surrender their interests.

The great rule of conduct for us in regard to foreign nations is, in extending our commercial relations, to have with them as little *political* connection as possible. So far as we have already formed engagements let them be fulfilled with perfect good faith. Here let us stop.

Europe has a set of primary interests which to us have none or a very remote relation. Hence she must be engaged in frequent controversies, the causes of which are essentially foreign to our concerns. Hence, therefore, it must be unwise in us to implicate ourselves by artificial ties in the ordinary vicissitudes of her politics or the ordinary combinations and collisions of her friendships or enmities.

Our detached and distant situation invites and enables us to pursue a different course. If we remain one people, under an efficient government, the period is not far off when we may defy material injury from external annoyance; when we may take such an attitude as will cause the neutrality we may at any time resolve upon to be scrupulously respected; when belligerent nations, under the impossibility of making acquisitions upon us, will not lightly hazard the giving us provocation; when we may choose peace or war, as our interest, guided by justice, shall counsel.

Why forego the advantages of so peculiar a situation? Why quit our own to stand upon foreign ground? Why, by interweaving our destiny with that of any part of Europe, entangle our peace and prosperity in the toils of European ambition, rivalship, interest, humor, or caprice?

It is our true policy to steer clear of permanent alliances with any portion of the foreign world, so far, I mean, as we are now at liberty to do it. . . .

Taking care always to keep ourselves by suitable establishments on a respectable defensive posture, we may safely trust to temporary alliances for extraordinary emergencies. . . .

4. HEMISPHERIC ISOLATION —
LETTER FROM THOMAS JEFFERSON TO PRESIDENT MONROE

> In this letter Ex-President Jefferson urges President Monroe to cooperate with Great Britain in order to prevent the intervention of European powers (the Holy Alliance) in American affairs, "North and South." Jefferson extends Washington's dictum that the United States has different interests from Europe and should therefore keep aloof from Europe's wars and troubles. Washington had warned against European intervention in the affairs of the United States; Jefferson proposes that we pursue a policy which would seek the same objective in South America as well.

The question presented by the letters you have sent me, is the most momentous which has ever been offered to my contemplation since that of Independence. That made us a nation, this sets our compass and points the course which we are to steer through the ocean of time opening on us. And never could we embark on it under circumstances more auspicious. Our first and fundamental maxim should be, never to entangle ourselves in the broils of Europe. Our second, never to suffer Europe to intermeddle with cis-Atlantic [on this side of the Atlantic] affairs. America, North and South, has a set of interests distinct from those of Europe, and peculiarly her own. She should therefore have a system of her own, separate and apart from that of Europe. While the last is laboring to become the domicile of despotism, our endeavor should surely be to make our hemisphere that of freedom.

One nation, most of all, could disturb us in this pursuit; she now offers to lead, aid, and accompany us in it. By acceding to her proposition, we detach her from the bands, bring her mighty weight into the scale of free government, and emancipate a continent at one stroke, which might otherwise linger long in doubt and difficulty. Great Britain is the nation which can do us the most harm of any one, of all on earth; and with her on our side we need not fear the whole world. With her then, we should most sedulously cherish a cordial friendship; and nothing would tend more to knit our affections than to be fighting once more, side by side, in the same cause. Not that I would purchase even her amity at the price of taking part in her wars. But the war in which the present proposition might engage us, should that be its consequence, is not her war, but ours. Its object is to introduce and establish the American system, of keeping out of our land all foreign powers, of never permitting those of Europe to intermeddle with the affairs of our nations. It is to maintain our own principle, not to depart from it. And if, to facilitate this, we can effect a division in the body of the European powers, and draw over to our side its most powerful member, surely we should do it. But I am clearly of Mr. Canning's opinion, that it will prevent instead of provoking war. For how would they propose to get at either enemy without superior fleets? Nor is the occasion to be slighted which this proposition offers, of declaring our protest against the atrocious violations of the rights of nations, by the interference of any one in the internal affairs of another, so flagitiously begun by Bonaparte, and now continued by the equally lawless Alliance, calling itself Holy. . . .

I could honestly, therefore, join in the declaration proposed, that we aim not at the acquisition of any of those possessions, that we will not stand in the way of any amicable arrangement between them and the mother country; but that we will oppose, with all our means, the forcible interposition of any other power, as auxiliary, stipendiary, or under any other form or pretext, and most especially, their transfer to any power by conquest, cession, or acquisition in any other way. I should think it, therefore, advisable, that the Executive should encourage the British government to a continuance in the dispositions expressed in these letters, by an assurance of his concurrence with them as far as his authority goes; and that as it may lead to war, the declaration of which requires an act of Congress, the case shall be laid before them for consideration at their first meeting, and under the reasonable aspect in which it is seen by himself. . . .

5. Principles of Non-Entanglement *

Two examples of isolationist sentiment have been presented in the two preceding selections. One referred, in part, to the desirability of preventing European intervention in the affairs of the United States, the other to a similar policy with regard to European intervention in South American affairs.

* Albert K. Weinberg, "The Historical Meaning of the American Doctrine of Isolation," *American Political Science Review,* June, 1940, pp. 541-547. The author was a member of the Institute for Advanced Study, Princeton, N. J.

In the present selection, Mr. Weinberg analyzes the concept of isolationism as an ideology. He notes that non-entanglement, "freedom from foreign mortgage upon America's life," became an end in itself. He lists eight principles of non-entanglement. Evidently concerned that the reader will be brought to believe that these seemingly all-inclusive prohibitions leave the United States no freedom of action in international affairs at all, he points out that the list of prohibitions leaves "at least as much outside as within," and cites the kind of policies which could be pursued even under a strict interpretation of the principles of non-entanglement.

. . . The conception of alliances as entanglements appeared as early as 1775 in the nationalistic and wary thought of John Adams, who, though yielding later to necessity, was apprehensive that an alliance with France would destroy our "real" independence in both domestic and foreign affairs. But the most influential warning against such relationships in terms of entanglement was in the Farewell Address, which posed the rhetorical question: "Why, by interweaving our destiny with that of any part of Europe, entangle our peace and prosperity in the toils of European ambition, rivalship, interest, humor, or caprice?" Because "Europe has a set of primary interests which to us have none or a very remote relation," that is, interests rooted in aggressiveness or imperilment and foreign to a nation of "detached and distant situation," permanent alliances committed America to "frequent controversies, the causes of which are essentially foreign to our concerns." At the same time, such alliances injured what was primary in our concern, the interest of true independence. In the youth of the nation, peace alone would permit uninterrupted progression to "that degree of strength and consistency which is necessary to give it, humanly speaking, the command of its own fortunes." This self-determination included not only the ability to choose peace or war according to interest, but also freedom from foreign influence and interference—values heightened by the traumatic experiences of the French alliance and by the danger of a tightening of that alliance.

Washington had given forth an idea that, while garbed originally in the meager rule of avoiding permanent alliances, was destined to outgrow its breeches. As the forms of international relationship increased and as new issues presented themselves, Americans became aware that the attribute of entanglement was not peculiar to alliances, but must be watched for throughout international life. Thus, abstracted from its multiplying applications, the counsel of Washington and Jefferson became known as the principle of avoiding foreign entanglements, or more briefly as the doctrine of non-entanglement. Though all the applications of the principle consist of prohibitions, its positive aspect was described by Senator Borah, typically and with approximate accuracy, as "freedom of action."

That the definition falls short of complete accuracy is shown by isolationists themselves when they support neutrality legislation that is a self-restriction. What is really envisaged in non-entanglement is freedom of action in so far as it is preserved through the avoidance of certain relationships with others. However, though all treaties are restrictive, by no means are all regarded as sources of entanglement. The reason is that the true criterion of entanglement is the seriousness of the limitation of freedom from the viewpoint of what is considered vital. While this criterion permits of many commitments, it at the same time forbids certain actions that do not rest upon any commitment. International action frequently entails moral obligations or compulsive external consequences by virtue of which, to quote an early isolationist, "without any formal compact, a nation may find itself as completely entangled . . . as by a solemn treaty stipulation." In sum, non-entanglement is the absence of voluntarily incurred relationships, formal or informal, which remove the substantial control of the nation's action, or even of its experience, from its own choice by placing it in the will, influence, or career of other nations.

This ideal first gained acceptance, not as a sentimentalization of freedom, but rather as a theory of national interest which held that all vital interests, and especially peace, flourish best when detached, in so far as possible through maintaining freedom of action, from the fate of the interests of the others. While some of Washington's arguments lost pertinence in changed conditions, broader grounds were suggested to Americans by all elements of their shrewdness and folly as they observed both a national history that seemed to prosper through independent action and a course of world politics that often shocked and never reassured them. Basic assumptions were America's relative self-sufficiency, the greater or less divergence between its uniquely determined interests and those of others, and its superiority, estimated from slight to tremendous, in respect to goodness, good sense, or at least good fortune.

In a later phase, first prominent with John Quincy Adams' justification of non-intervention in foreign wars for freedom, the principle became also a sincere, or at least professed, theory of national duty. It maintained that America could save the world only if it remained free to save itself, and, in respect to service more active than radiating moral influence, if it maintained its liberty to select time, place, and method. Finally, with the maturity or hypertrophy of American nationalism, which like all nationalism has mystical elements beyond both interest and virtue, a new emphasis became prominent: non-entanglement as an end in itself.   Freedom from foreign mortgage upon America's life was identified with the dignity, the glory, and, in the case of numerous amateur jurists, even the full sovereignty, of the nation.

To be sure, isolationists have motives as far removed from this ideal as is the determination of some fiercely proud senator to take vengeance upon President Wilson for being more successful than himself in both politics and literary style.   But from the viewpoint of isolationism as an ideology, the policies of reserve are the successively emerging and developing embodiments of non-entanglement, an ideal that is incarnated only in its aversions:

1. *Entangling alliances with none.*   Leaving Washington in the position of semi-isolationist, a progressive caution interdicted successively American as well as European permanent alliances, temporary alliances, informal alliances, implicit alliances, and, though not until 1920, a type of engagement that Wilson considered "disentangling" because it was made with all nations in behalf of world peace.   The pervasive objection to all commitments to the use of force was that "every alliance is . . . entangling which places our peace on the discretion or movements of any other government."

2. *Non-intervention.*   Exceeding greatly the prohibitions of international law, this policy forbids not merely participation in foreign conflicts, but any trespass upon the external or internal sovereignty of others that is not warranted by defense of serious national rights.   Intrusive force was regarded as a boomerang that endangered America's own sovereignty or chosen way of life in either or both of two ways: the provocation of counter-intervention, especially feared in our early history, or the plunging of the nation into a swift and uncontrollable current of foreign life that carries it away from the moorings of all its values.

3. *Non-interference and non-participation in European politics.*   While the principle of non-intervention is merely intensified, a novel element is the prohibition of even peaceful and neutral action in matters pertaining wholly or primarily to the politics of Europe or to their ramifications in other areas.   Connected in its origin with the rise of the Spanish-American republics, the policy centered in an ideal of hemispheric self-determination: in return for our abnegation in relation to the Old World, Europe was to refrain from participation as well as intervention in American affairs, and thus leave unimpaired not only this nation's security but also its freedom of action in its own hemisphere.

4. *Avoidance of joint action.*   Such action, which, as distinguished from coincident or concerted action, has an aspect of unity, is forbidden

both in relations with other Powers and in the exercise of administrative obligations. Examples are commonly subscribed interposition or intervention, international maintenance of the Monroe Doctrine, and *condominia* over backward regions or an isthmian canal. All partnership, even that which is *ad hoc* or lacking in formal obligation, is considered entangling because it involves moral obligations, a pooling of interests, and responsibility for the partner's acts.

5. *No entangling commitments.* The principle of freedom of action in unknown contingencies, first associated with the no-alliance rule, became a criterion applied to all commitments and prohibited those which impaired future self-determination too greatly or which lay in spheres where circumstances are especially variable. In its procedural phase, the policy led earlier American statesmen to shrink from indissoluble, long-term, multi-partite, and not quite essential treaties. In its substantive phase, largely still extant, the principle was manifested in reluctance to bind the future in issues with such changing contexts as expansion, arbitration, and the commitment to support or oppose other Powers in any way.

6. *Non-limitation of "essential" rights of sovereignty.* Jurisdictional control and self-defense, while rights claimed by all sovereignty, have had in American interpretation a scope reflecting, not conventional jurisprudence or prudence, but an extreme reluctance to fetter action upon more or less important interest. American reserve towards self-limitation in joint or collective interest, however lessened in recent times, has been manifested in unwillingness to permit any alien determination of what domestic questions and self-defense (or the Monroe Doctrine) are; in exclusions of immigration and tariff policies from the range of international agreement; and in disapproval of the League commitments to suspend resort to war and to limit national control over armament and the trade in arms.

7. *Independence of any political "super-authority."* The blind commitment to accept the authority of any political body, whether the League of Nations, its alleged adjunct, the World Court, or even a temporary congress, is regarded as not only empowering others to do us evil but as surrendering our very sovereignty. Though particular repugnance is aroused by formal obligation to accept a majority decision, the concept of external domination is so broad as to include mere recommendation, regarded as a source of moral obligation, and, indeed, on the logic of nationalist emotion, even membership in a "super-authority" without any authority.

8. *Insulation against entanglement.* This policy, which accounts for the most articulate isolationism of today, is distinctive in that it inter-

dicts, not a definite entanglement, but all action or lack of action creating a serious danger that temptation or necessity will lead to any entanglement. Transgression of this principle of due caution is like sin—something to be recognized in the particular even though one does not know what it is in general. At one time, conformity to the principle dictated chiefly the avoidance in various ways—the Monroe Doctrine, continental expansion, and anti-expansionism in relation to Europe and Asia—of magnetic proximity to areas of world politics. Today the principal concern is an isolation from war (the phrase of President Roosevelt) that consists chiefly in avoiding incident-producing economic relationships with distant belligerents.

America's *Index Actionum Prohibitarum* ends at a point that leaves, believe it or not, at least as much outside as within. Permissible because lacking in commitment or meddlesomeness is all single-handed action, from interposition to war, in behalf of national rights, and, when in accord with comity, in behalf of world interest; moreover, even intervention in behalf of world interest is allowable when there is a coincident national equity. Nor is entanglement seen in free international collaboration such as consultation and coincident action. Those commitments are permissible that do not involve vital political interests demanding flexibility: for example, commitments in respect to economic and humanitarian issues, renunciation of aggression, and consultation. Further, aside from the fact that virtually all of the policies have been subject to exceptions in emergency, more can be tolerated by America's *Index* than appears on its face or on the record. First, certain relations were condemned on bad and reversible judicial logic, such as the assumption that the World Court is not a true judicial body. Second, many of the terms of the policies are vague, and thus play into the hands of a good lawyer able to take advantage of legal ambiguities. Finally, since the concept of substantial alien determination underlying all of the policies is also vague, the continuance of any is subject to the fact that, fundamentally, nothing is entangling or disentangling but thinking makes it so.

Of course, there have been and are extremists, more vocal than numerous, from whom in some mood scarcely any of the traditional liberties is safe. They operate partly by misinterpreting the basic policies, but chiefly by carrying the indefinite preventive policy to what seems to others a morbidity of caution. Some of their phobias—if in a truly terrifying world any fear is a phobia—are the following: extensive commerce, which may lead to political connections; free but parallel action, which, like free love, may lead to marriage or a quarrel; and a French officer's riding in one of our better planes, which may lead to moving America's frontier to France. In their distrust of all other nations—a possible exception is little Finland—some of these super-isolationists verge upon maintaining that international society is a wanton, and that not even if the American marries the wench can he make an honest woman of her. By no means slight, however, is their distrust of at least one of their fellow-Americans, the Chief Executive.

Yet the President has prayed that America may remain "unentangled and free," and in general the many cooperative measures of the Administration, as Secretary Hull emphasizes, lie "strictly within the range of our traditional policies of non-entanglement." Some measures, however, have been cases of squeezing agilely through loopholes in these policies. Thus the ostensible conduct of our own business has been given such form and so timed as to have the effect of economic intervention unneutral toward aggressors. Worse than the acts of this Administration have been its speeches. Nothing in tradition forbidding the speaking of one's mind *en famille,* this safe medium has been used to accomplish the purpose of diplomatic intervention, and even of threatening aggressors with "measures short of war." Worst of all from the viewpoint of isolationism, the advantage and duty of international collaboration have been argued in terms of a Wilsonian ideology that derives them from, of all things, the ideal of self-determination. The new interpretation of this ideal emphasizes the interference with self-determination that is threatened by a now far-flung spirit of aggression, which, in the words of President Roosevelt, places "the deadline of danger" not "within our control" but "in the hands of other nations." In contrast to the old theory that America's peace is distinct from that of others, it is now posited that "when peace has been broken anywhere, peace of all nations everywhere is in danger"—in other words, that America shares with an interdependent world the primary interest of world peace.

The ideal of non-entanglement, dogma though it was, has been but one prolonged phase of a triadic dialectical development: the thesis, continuing ancient political tradition, is self-determination as achieved through the French alliance; the antithesis is self-determination as achieved through non-entanglement; the synthesis, which is now at least in emergence, is self-determination as achieved through both non-entanglement and international relationship. In this synthesis, each element appears in a modification reflecting the influence of the other. International relationship is not special, but collective; freedom of action is not merely nationalistic, but is also designed with regard to international welfare.

The potentiality of America's incipient internationalism can scarcely be weighed at this exceptional moment, when a war in Europe so naturally arouses, not, indeed, our neutrality of feeling, but all the discretion of our inveterate non-interventionism. But a test will be put upon us by the issue of post-war reconstruction that lies ahead if the victors are to be our friends. This issue may not demand America's decision whether or not to abandon any of its traditional policies of reserve—and for the simple reason that the leeway allowed by tradition might well suffice for all moderate ends of international organization. The issue will certainly demand a decision whether to utilize fully this leeway or to yield to further barriers proposed by pseudo-traditionalist extremists. In appraising meliorative collaboration by the standard of national tradition, Americans may do well to consider that the true objective of their historic caution was not isolation, a friendlessness which may subject their destiny to their enemies, but an ideal interpreted to the nation by Washington as "the command of its own fortunes."

6. ISOLATIONISM *vs.* INTERVENTIONISM *

Professor Spykman describes various programs for the protection of the security and interests of the United States, with special reference to the differences in ideological outlook and political sympathy that are implied in isolationism and interventionism.

Almost a quarter of a century has passed since that day in November, 1918, when fighting ceased in the war to end war. It is more than twenty years since President Wilson presented the statesmen of the world with a blueprint for a better international order, one that many people believed would bring peace and security. But the world is again in flames. Advanced technology has created bigger and better engines for mass murder; devastation and destruction is again the ultimate purpose to which the energy of nations is being geared, and human life is again being sacrificed on a large scale for the achievement of national purpose. Another world war is in full swing and the United States is once more an active participant.

We became a full belligerent as the result of Japanese attacks on our island possessions in the Pacific and a declaration of war by Germany and Italy. The form of the attack produced overnight a remarkable national unity and halted for a time the debate over isolation and inter-

* Nicholas J. Spykman, *America's Strategy in World Politics* (New York: Harcourt, Brace & Co., 1942), pp. 3-8. Copyright, 1942, by Harcourt, Brace & Co., Inc. The late Dr. Spykman was Sterling Professor of International Relations and Director of the Institute of International Studies at Yale University.

vention as the most desirable grand strategy for the United States. These two policies represented not only two different programs for the protection of the security and the interests of the United States, they also represented profound differences in ideological outlook and political sympathy. The isolationist position has always had a strong psychological and emotional appeal for broad sections of the population. The American state was created by people who had turned their backs on Europe and most of the immigrants who entered during the nineteenth century wanted to forget the Old World. But the wars and quarrels of that continent, which had disturbed them when they lived across the oceans, continued to disturb them here. European politics still frustrated their desire for freedom and release. A doctrine that tells Americans that they need not bother about Europe is an answer to this deep-seated desire. The most staunch adherents to the policy of intervention have been those who were inspired by idealistic considerations. Some asked participation because they were pro-British; others because they believed that, in a period of ideological warfare, we had a moral obligation to support the people whose social and political structure most closely resembled our own. Many insisted that we should become belligerents in the war because only in that manner could we make good our failure of 1920 and present the post-war world with a system of collective security and durable peace.

Whatever may have been the motives that inspired people to prefer isolation or intervention as policies for the United States, these two programs have different power implications and it is with these implications and with their effect on the position of the United States that this study is concerned. Seen in this light, the two attitudes differed profoundly in their estimate of the relative importance of the balance of power in Europe and Asia for the security of the United States. Paralleling this divergence was a disagreement about the implications of the geographic location of the United States and of the principles that should guide us in our military and political strategy because of this location. The interventionists and the isolationists represented, from this point of view, two distinct geo-political schools of thought.

Those who asked intervention in terms of power considerations took the position that the first line of defense of the United States lies in the preservation of a balance of power in Europe and Asia. Without denying the fact that our geographic location provides certain obvious advantages in the matter of territorial security, they contended that this does not permit us to neglect balance of power considerations. We were not exempt from the necessity of considering policies which all other states in history have been forced to pursue in the interests of survival. In addition to the maintenance of an equilibrium in Europe and Asia, the interventionists saw a second line of defense in the Western Hemisphere. The isolationists, who were aware of the power implications of their program, felt on the other hand, that, because of our unique geographic location between two oceans, we could disinterest ourselves in the power struggle across the water and view with equanimity the possibility of the destruction of the balance of power in Europe and Asia. Our own inherent strength, together with the protection which the oceans afforded, made it not only feasible but wise to adopt a defensive policy on this side of the water and to leave Europe and Asia to their own devices.

The debate on intervention versus isolation, as a debate on the principles of higher strategy that derive from our geographic location, did not begin with the outbreak of the Second World War. It is the oldest issue in American foreign policy, and whenever there has arisen a question of co-operation with a transoceanic power or the need for action in Europe and Asia, it has become a topic for discussion. When, in the early part of the nineteenth century, France contemplated the reconquest of the Spanish colonies with the aid of the Holy Alliance, Great Britain proposed that we join her in common action to oppose this plan. There was a long and bitter debate in which the proponents of independent and unilateral action finally won out. The Monroe Doctrine was an announcement of our intention to defend the hemisphere alone without a European ally.

Later in the century the issue was again debated in connection with our participation in European conferences such as the first and second Moroccan Conferences and the Berlin Conference, all of which dealt with political questions resulting from the struggles of the European powers in Africa. The problem did not present itself at the outset of the Spanish-American War but when, as the result of our victory, the question arose whether we should keep the Philippines, the opponents of retention argued that such a step would be unnatural and against the logic of our geographic position which demands that we should occupy no territories outside this hemisphere. The advocates of surrender lost the debate as far as public policy was concerned and the Philippines have been American territory for more than forty years, but this fact has not stopped the argument. During the whole period there has been objection to our participation in Far Eastern politics.

The First World War made the question once more a burning issue. In April, 1917, we became a full belligerent and the argument was temporarily suspended, but it is to be noted that once again the *fait accompli* by no means ended the debate. Objection to our participation continued during the whole period of the war. With the armistice, the debate entered a new phase and this time the isolationists won: the United States refused to become a member of the League of Nations or to accept political commitments in Europe. But again the issue was not settled. In the post-war period the dispute continued in the form of a controversy over the degree to which the United States should participate in efforts to preserve order in Europe and Asia. The isolationist school remained the dominant influence in the formulation of our foreign policy largely because of its strategic position in the Senate, and our attitude remained one of aloofness and non-participation. Attempts by the interventionists to provide for co-operation with the League system were all voted down and neutrality legislation passed by Congress continued to express the isolationist philosophy right up to the outbreak of the Second World War.

The size of the geographic area in the New World necessary for the creation of an adequate system of defense gradually expanded in the minds of the isolationists. Originally it was the national domain; after the building of the Panama Canal it was extended to include the Caribbean littoral and finally the whole hemisphere. Both interventionists and isolationists made the protection of the New World part of their program, but they disagreed about its relative importance. For the former it represented a second line of defense to which we could withdraw if the policy of intervention in Europe and Asia failed. For the isolationists it represented the first line of defense, a maximum program toward which all energies were to be directed and beyond which no effort need go. Hemisphere defense through hemisphere isolation became the new streamlined version of the old isolationist position.

The United States has again become a participant in war and the old issue therefore takes on a new significance. It presents itself now as a problem, not of peace strategy, but of war strategy and war objectives. Shall we try to direct our war effort primarily at the protection of the Western Hemisphere, focused on the territorial waters of the New World, or shall we strike out and fight offensively across the oceans? Would it be possible for us to live an independent national life within the Western Hemisphere in case the German-Japanese Alliance should be able to crush all resistance in the Old World, or does our freedom and security demand the destruction of the great military empires now being fashioned in Europe and Asia and the re-establishment of a balance of power? Is the world beyond the oceans one from which we can withdraw after victory as we did in 1918, or one whose fate is inescapably interwoven with our own? The Second World War presents the issue of intervention versus isolation in a new phase but it is basically the same question it has always been: shall we protect our interests by defense on this side of the water or by active participation in the lands across the oceans?

There have been numerous attempts to prove the validity of isolation or intervention as sound strategy by reference to precedent and appeal to the authority of the Founding Fathers. Both groups have made generous use of this debating device and our history has been sufficiently rich and varied to provide both parties with excellent arguments. But even if the past should favor one side more than the other, it would not follow that the side thus favored represents the wiser policy. Historical precedent and the voice of the Fathers can be used as a means to gain support for a doctrine but not as proof of its soundness. Not conformity with the past but workability in the present is the criterion of a sound policy. Not specially selected instances in the history of the United States, but the general experience of states should be made the guide for a program of action. . . .

7. A NEO-ISOLATIONIST VIEW *

Isolationists of the period between World Wars I and II tended to assume that our immunity from Europe's wars was permanent (they regarded our involvement in World War I as a temporary aberration and noted that we had gained nothing from the war but the ingratitude of our allies and a huge debt). They opposed alliances and armaments, were cynical about power politics, and pessimistic about internationalism. This form of isolationism may be dead as a political movement, but the American attitudes on which it fed are still alive.

The isolationist neither desired, nor saw any necessity for, the pursuit of an active foreign policy that would bring with it a continuing involvement in international politics. The neo-isolationist will deal with the world, provided it meets his terms. If it will not, he is prepared to "go it alone." Senator Taft's recommendations that we pursue an independent policy in Asia, and his opposition to the commitment of American troops for the defense of Western Europe, are characteristic of the neo-isolationist approach and demonstrate that isolationist longings are still present among our people.

* From the foreign policy section of an address by Robert A. Taft, late United States Senator from Ohio, on May 26, 1953, to a meeting of the National Conference of Christians and Jews.

I cannot tonight discuss all the . . . problems of foreign policy, but as I hear them discussed in the Foreign Relations Committee and at the President's legislative conference, I am impressed with the tremendous difficulty of all of them and the fact that in no case does there seem to be a satisfactory solution.

My discussion of the situation tonight is merely intended to be in the nature of comment and information. I do not intend it as any criticism of what is being done or not done, because I think the problems are so difficult that anyone would have great difficulty in feeling confident that he is right.

During the past three years, the foreign policy of the United States, whether under Democratic or Republican charge, has been based on the general opposition to the spread of communism beyond its present limits, either as an ideology or as an advance by force. Certainly our policy has not been based on any reliance on the United Nations or on any other country.

Unfortunately, the last Administration did not go all out for this policy against communism in Asia until it was too late to make it truly effective. The failure to check communism on the mainland, the unfortunate withdrawal from Korea, has involved us in a war situation and a Communist situation in Asia for which there seems to be no satisfactory solution.

Nevertheless, the last Administration certainly believed in the general policy of opposition to communism, since they backed up Greece and Turkey in 1947, and, of course, in Asia since the Korean war.

Again I point out that this policy is not a policy of working through the United Nations, but is a policy of military alliance. It is an attempt to build up freedom throughout the world and provide arms for all those nations which are sufficiently free so we can be reasonably certain or reasonably hopeful that they will use their arms to fight the Communists if they are attacked.

The difficulty with the United Nations as a means of preventing military aggression was obvious from the beginning. I pointed out in the first speech I made in favor of ratifying the United Nations treaty that it could not possibly prevent aggression because of the veto power which could be used by any one of the five powers to veto united action against themselves and against any one of their satellites.

The United Nations was based on the theory of a five-power control of the world, and whenever one of those powers refused to go along it was hopeless to create any sanctions that would be binding on the other nations to provide troops against aggression.

We made an abortive attempt to rely on the United Nations when the

North Koreans attacked in 1950. It happened that the Russians were boycotting the Security Council, and so we were able to persuade the others to call for troops from all members against the North Koreans.

There is some doubt whether the call was a valid call even then, because the Charter clearly requires the affirmative vote of all of the five controlling nations, and I don't think that absence provides an affirmative vote.

Nevertheless, it was treated as a proper sanction and produced a few troops, in addition to those which we had to send to Korea. But Russia returned at once to the Security Council, and when Communist China attacked, then the United Nations failed to take any action against the real aggressor, and from that time until today has refused in every way to take action or punish the real aggressor.

There has been some attempt to join in defeating an aggressor, but the General Assembly has absolutely no such power under the United Nations Charter. It is very doubtful to me whether we would be wise to try to get up and develop any such power. In an assembly where we have one vote out of seventy, it can be easily turned against us in the future.

I believe we might as well forget the United Nations as far as the Korean war is concerned. I think we should do our best now to negotiate this truce, and if we fail, then let England and our other Allies know that we are withdrawing from all further peace negotiations in Korea.

Even the best truce under present conditions will be extremely unsatisfactory. It will divide Korea along an unnatural line and create an unstable condition likely to bring war again at any moment. It will release a million Chinese soldiers, who no doubt will promptly be moved down to Southern China for use against Chiang Kai-shek or against the French in Indo-China.

It seems to me that from the beginning we should have insisted on a general peace negotiation with China, including a unification of Korea under free Koreans, and a peace against further expansion in Southeast Asia. If we once make this present truce, no matter what we put in the agreement about further negotiations for united Korea, it is no more likely to occur than a united Germany.

In any event, I think we are bound to the policy of preventing Communist aggression where it occurs and where it is within our means to stop it. I have never felt that we should send American soldiers to the continent of Asia, which, of course, includes China proper and Indo-China, simply because we are so outnumbered in fighting a land war on the continent of Asia it would bring about complete exhaustion even if we were able to win. I believe we might as well abandon any idea of working with the United Nations in the East and reserve to ourselves a completely free hand.

This statement is going to shock a good many people who still believe in the United Nations. I believe in the United Nations myself, but not as an effective means to prevent aggression. It does have many methods by which, through peaceful persuasion, it can deter and prevent war.

. . . . .

But no one should be shocked at my suggestion about the United Nations in Korea, because in Europe we have practically abandoned it entirely. When we adopted the North Atlantic Treaty, we did not ask the United Nations' leave, and we did not consult it. We claim that such an organization can be formed under the terms of Section 51 of the Charter and perhaps it can. But to my mind it is the complete antithesis of the Charter itself, and while it may not violate the Charter, it certainly substitutes a military alliance for the United Nations as a means of preventing Soviet aggression.

NATO, following the Greek and Turkish agreements and the contemplated arrangements with Spain, is clearly a military alliance of the old type. We promised to spring to the aid of any nation which is attacked, either by the Russians or by any other nation, including one of the NATO group. Our obligation continues for twenty years.

So today, as since 1947 in Europe and 1950 in Asia, we are really trying to arm the world against Communist Russia, or at least furnish all the assistance which can be of use to them in opposing communism.

Is this policy of uniting the free world against communism in time of peace going to be a practical long-term policy? I have always been a sceptic on the subject of the military practicability of NATO. I am no military expert, but I have never heard an argument that impressed me attempting to show that United States ground forces could effectively defend Europe.

Certainly we seem to have undertaken to defend countries like Norway and Denmark, which it would be almost impossible to defend in case of a sudden Russian attack. I have always felt that we should not attempt to fight Russia on the ground on the Continent of Europe any more than we should attempt to fight China on the Continent of Asia. I have always felt that, this defense must be undertaken by those who occupy Western Europe. After all, there are at least 225,000,000 of them, 50 per cent more people than we have in the United States.

I have always been concerned that once our troops are in Europe, the Russians would be able to bomb all of the factories and communication lines behind them. One atomic bomb would probably destroy a

French port for a year, and eight or ten bombs would cut off most means of supplying our soldiers or withdrawing them in case of retreat.

If we are worried here in this country about the dropping of Russian bombs on American cities and factories, surely it is ten times as easy for them to bomb Western Europe and its ports. Or they could leave Europe alone and devote themselves to a bombing of this country, in which case our European expenses would be of doubtful value.

But there is another difficulty about maintaining the general policy of a unified world-wide opposition to communism by all free nations: we have to have not only the written word but the real sympathetic support of our allies in that job. Recent events in France and England indicate that they are more than anxious to settle with Russia and resume as much trade as possible, which means that as long as Russia talks nicely, the whole military alliance against Russia is weak, even though military preparations behind the lines continue unabated.

Secretary Dulles has tried to reassure the Iron Curtain nations that we are not going to make a deal with Russia, giving the Communists a zone of influence over all the Iron Curtain countries. It seems clear that Mr. Churchill and the French administration would be willing to assign that zone of influence gladly and abandon the Poles, the Czechs, the Hungarians and the Rumanians to the tender mercies of Soviet Russia in return for some cut in armaments, freer trade and promises to behave in the future.

The present Administration has the job of trying to maintain this world-wide alliance against Soviet Russia. We have spent billions for that purpose. I hope that it can be carried through, and only raise here the doubt as to whether it is in fact possible over any long period of years.

It is pretty hard for the United States to claim the right to cut off trade channels which have existed for centuries. I have no doubt about the desirability of the policy if it does not go beyond our economic strength, but I do doubt its possibility.

All that I can urge is two different kinds of tolerance to this tolerant body. The first is that we be tolerant of the situation of every country, that we try to understand their problems and not force upon them a policy they do not approve, either by the pressure of grants of money or grants of soldiers. No doubt they will be glad to get these, but they will be of little use to us unless the policy which they are supposed to enforce is the determined policy of the country concerned.

Second, I urge upon you tolerance of those who are trying their best to conduct our foreign affairs. I think already they know more about the realities of the situation than those who preceded them. I know that they are inspired with the best of good will toward all nations.   They have to meet what seems to me the most difficult problems of foreign policy the United States has ever faced.

Idealism

8. HUMAN RIGHTS AND NATIONAL INTEGRITY *vs.* THE NATIONAL INTEREST *

Idealists, Professor Thompson has said (Selection 2), have offered "moral" nations three alternatives for coping with the world of "archaic power politics."   World government will ultimately do away with power politics.   In the absence of world government, however, the totalitarian states, chief practitioners of power politics, should be "erased from the face of the earth."   "Moral and upright nations," moreover, should forswear relations "with corrupted, power-seeking nations," pursue neutrality policies, and abstain from "all forms of traditional power politics."

There is, then, in idealism, an appeal to universal morality over the heads, so to speak, of the less moral nations.

The specific purpose of President Wilson's address was to clarify the Latin American and more specifically the Mexican policy of the United States.   The address is an outstanding example of the idealist approach to American foreign policy.   In essence, President Wilson asserted that our policy should be defined not in terms of the national interest but in terms of universal moral principles such as human rights and national integrity.

. . . The future, ladies and gentlemen, is going to be very different for this hemisphere from the past.   These States lying to the south of us, which have always been our neighbors, will now be drawn closer to us by innumerable ties, and, I hope, chief of all, by the tie of a common understanding of each other.   Interest does not tie nations together; it sometimes separates them.   But sympathy and understanding does unite them, and I believe that by the new route that is just about to be opened, while we physically cut two continents asunder, we spiritually unite them.   It is a spiritual union which we seek. . . .

There is one peculiarity about the history of the Latin American States which I am sure they are keenly aware of.   You hear of "con-

* From an address by President Woodrow Wilson, delivered in Mobile, Alabama, on October 27, 1913.

cessions" to foreign capitalists in Latin America. You do not hear of concessions to foreign capitalists in the United States. They are not granted concessions. They are invited to make investments. The work is ours, though they are welcome to invest in it. We do not ask them to supply the capital and do the work. It is an invitation, not a privilege; and States that are obliged, because their territory does not lie within the main field of modern enterprise and action, to grant concessions are in this condition, that foreign interests are apt to dominate their domestic affairs, a condition of affairs always dangerous and apt to become intolerable. What these States are going to see, therefore, is an emancipation from the subordination, which has been inevitable, to foreign enterprise and an assertion of the splendid character which, in spite of these difficulties, they have again and again been able to demonstrate. The dignity, the courage, the self-possession, the self-respect of the Latin American States, their achievements in the face of all these adverse circumstances, deserve nothing but the admiration and applause of the world. They have had harder bargains driven with them in the matter of loans than any other peoples in the world. Interest has been exacted of them that was not exacted of anybody else, because the risk was said to be greater; and then securities were taken that destroyed the risk—an admirable arrangement for those who were forcing the terms! I rejoice in nothing so much as in the prospect that they will now be emancipated from these conditions, and we ought to be the first to take part in assisting in that emancipation. I think some of these gentlemen have already had occasion to bear witness that the Department of State in recent months has tried to serve them in that wise. In the future they will draw closer and closer to us because of circumstances of which I wish to speak with moderation and, I hope, without indiscretion.

We must prove ourselves their friends, and champions upon terms of equality and honor. You cannot be friends upon any other terms than upon the terms of equality. You cannot be friends at all except upon the terms of honor. We must show ourselves friends by comprehending their interest whether it squares with our own interest or not. It is a very perilous thing to determine the foreign policy of a nation in the terms of material interest. It not only is unfair to those with whom you are dealing, but it is degrading as regards your own actions.

Comprehension must be the soil in which shall grow all the fruits of friendship, and there is a reason and a compulsion lying behind all this which is dearer than anything else to the thoughtful men of America. I mean the development of constitutional liberty in the world. Human rights, national integrity, and opportunity as against material interests

—that, ladies and gentlemen, is the issue which we now have to face. I want to take this occasion to say that the United States will never again seek one additional foot of territory by conquest. She will devote herself to showing that she knows how to make honorable and fruitful use of the territory she has, and she must regard it as one of the duties of friendship to see that from no quarter are material interests made superior to human liberty and national opportunity. . . .

9. For Democracy and a Universal Dominion of Right *

Another example of the idealist tendency to substitute universal moral principles for the national interest can be found in the concluding paragraphs of the President's message.

President Wilson could have justified American participation in World War I by pointing to the necessity of maintaining the balance of power in Europe which was in danger of being overthrown by Germany and her allies. He could have explained that German hegemony in Europe would imperil the security of the United States. Instead, he chose to describe the war as a struggle between democracy and autocracy. He gave the impression that once the autocrats had been defeated, universal peace and justice would prevail.

We have no quarrel with the German people. We have no feeling towards them but one of sympathy and friendship. It was not upon their impulse that their government acted in entering this war. It was not with their previous knowledge or approval. It was a war determined upon as wars used to be determined upon in the old, unhappy days when peoples were nowhere consulted by their rulers and wars were provoked and waged in the interest of dynasties or of little groups of ambitious men who were accustomed to use their fellow men as pawns and tools. Self-governed nations do not fill their neighbor states with spies or set the course of intrigue to bring about some critical posture of affairs which will give them an opportunity to strike and make conquest. Such designs can be successfully worked out only under cover and where no one has the right to ask questions. Cunningly contrived plans of deception or aggression, carried, it may be, from generation to generation, can be worked out and kept from the light only within the privacy of courts or behind the carefully guarded confidences of a narrow and

* From President Wilson's War Message to Congress, delivered on April 2, 1917.

privileged class. They are happily impossible where public opinion commands and insists upon full information concerning all the nation's affairs. . . .

It is a distressing and oppressive duty, Gentlemen of the Congress, which I have performed in thus addressing you.   There are, it may be, many months of fiery trial and sacrifice ahead of us.   It is a fearful thing to lead this great peaceful people into war, into the most terrible and disastrous of all wars, civilization itself seeming to be in the balance. But the right is more precious than peace, and we shall fight for the things which we have always carried nearest our hearts—for democracy, for the right of those who submit to authority to have a voice in their own Governments, for the rights and liberties of small nations, for a universal dominion of right by such a concert of free peoples as shall bring peace and safety to all nations and make the world itself at last free.   To such a task we can dedicate our lives and our fortunes, everything that we are and everything that we have, with the pride of those who know that the day has come when America is privileged to spend her blood and her might for the principles that gave her birth and happiness and the peace which she has treasured.   God helping her, she can do no other.

10. FOUR FREEDOMS EVERYWHERE IN THE WORLD *

This address is another notable instance of the workings of idealism in American foreign policy.   Mr. Roosevelt spoke of pursuing policies which would strengthen the defense and security of our own nation, and to the degree that he did relate our policy to our security, his views were somewhat more realistic than those of President Wilson.   The general tenor of the address, however, with its juxtaposition of good and evil, the "moral order" and the "order of tyranny," and with its application of the four freedoms "everywhere in the world," illustrates the tendency of the idealist to conceptualize the problems of international politics in terms of abstract principles.

I address you, the Members of the Seventy-seventh Congress, at a moment unprecedented in the history of the Union.   I use the word "unprecedented," because at no previous time has American security been as seriously threatened from without as it is today.

Our national policy is this:

* President Franklin Roosevelt's Message to Congress, delivered on January 6, 1941.

First, by an impressive expression of the public will and without regard to partisanship, we are committed to all-inclusive national defense.

Second, by an impressive expression of the public will and without regard to partisanship, we are committed to full support of all those resolute peoples, everywhere, who are resisting aggression and are thereby keeping war away from our hemisphere. By this support, we express our determination that the democratic cause shall prevail; and we strengthen the defense and security of our own Nation.

Third, by an impressive expression of the public will and without regard to partisanship, we are committed to the proposition that principles of morality and considerations for our own security will never permit us to acquiesce in a peace dictated by aggressors and sponsored by appeasers. We know that enduring peace cannot be bought at the cost of other people's freedom.

In the recent national election there was no substantial difference between the two great parties in respect to that national policy. No issue was fought out on this line before the American electorate. Today, it is abundantly evident that American citizens everywhere are demanding and supporting speedy and complete action in recognition of obvious danger.

Therefore, the immediate need is a swift and driving increase in our armament production.

To change a whole nation from a basis of peacetime production of implements of peace to a basis of wartime production of implements of war is no small task. And the greatest difficulty comes at the beginning of the program, when new tools and plant facilities and new assembly lines and shipways must first be constructed before the actual matériel begins to flow steadily and speedily from them.

The Congress, of course, must rightly keep itself informed at all times of the progress of the program. However, there is certain information, as the Congress itself will readily recognize, which, in the interests of our own security and those of the nations we are supporting, must of needs be kept in confidence.

New circumstances are constantly begetting new needs for our safety. I shall ask this Congress for greatly increased new appropriations and authorizations to carry on what we have begun.

I also ask this Congress for authority and for funds sufficient to manufacture additional munitions and war supplies of many kinds, to be turned over to those nations which are now in actual war with aggressor nations.

Our most useful and immediate role is to act as an arsenal for them as well as for ourselves. They do not need man power. They do need billions of dollars worth of the weapons of defense.

The time is near when they will not be able to pay for them in ready cash. We cannot, and will not, tell them they must surrender, merely because of present inability to pay for the weapons which we know they must have.

I do not recommend that we make them a loan of dollars with which to pay for these weapons—a loan to be repaid in dollars.

I recommend that we make it possible for those nations to continue to obtain war materials in the United States, fitting their orders into our own program. Nearly all of their matériel would, if the time ever came, be useful for our own defense.

Taking counsel of expert military and naval authorities, considering what is best for our own security, we are free to decide how much should be kept here and how much should be sent abroad to our friends who by their determined and heroic resistance are giving us time in which to make ready our own defense.

For what we send abroad, we shall be repaid, within a reasonable time following the close of hostilities, in similar materials, or, at our option, in other goods of many kinds which they can produce and which we need.

Let us say to the democracies: "We Americans are vitally concerned in your defense of freedom. We are putting forth our energies, our resources, and our organizing powers to give you the strength to regain and maintain a free world. We shall send you, in ever-increasing numbers, ships, planes, tanks, guns. This is our purpose and our pledge."

In fulfillment of this purpose we will not be intimidated by the threats of dictators that they will regard as a breach of international law and as an act of war our aid to the democracies which dare to resist their aggression. Such aid is not an act of war, even if a dictator should unilaterally proclaim it so to be.

When the dictators are ready to make war upon us, they will not wait for an act of war on our part. They did not wait for Norway or Belgium or the Netherlands to commit an act of war.

Their only interest is in a new one-way international law, which lacks mutuality in its observance, and, therefore, becomes an instrument of oppression.

The happiness of future generations of Americans may well depend upon how effective and how immediate we can make our aid felt. No one can tell the exact character of the emergency situations that we may be called upon to meet. The Nation's hands must not be tied when the Nation's life is in danger.

We must all prepare to make the sacrifices that the emergency—as serious as war itself—demands. Whatever stands in the way of speed and efficiency in defense preparations must give way to the national need.

A free nation has the right to expect full cooperation from all groups. A free nation has the right to look to the leaders of business, of labor, and of agriculture to take the lead in stimulating effort, not among other groups but within their own groups.

I have called for personal sacrifice. I am assured of the willingness of almost all Americans to respond to that call.

A part of the sacrifice means the payment of more money in taxes. In my Budget Message I recommended that a greater portion of this great defense program be paid for from taxation than we are paying today. No person should try, or be allowed, to get rich out of this program; and the principle of tax payments in accordance with ability to pay should be constantly before our eyes to guide our legislation.

If the Congress maintains these principles, the voters, putting patriotism ahead of pocketbooks, will give you their applause.

In the future days, which we seek to make secure, we look forward to a world founded upon four essential human freedoms.

The first is freedom of speech and expression—everywhere in the world.

The second is freedom of every person to worship God in his own way—everywhere in the world.

The third is freedom from want—which, translated into world terms, means economic understandings which will secure to every nation a healthy peacetime life for its inhabitants—everywhere in the world.

The fourth is freedom from fear—which, translated into world terms, means a world-wide reduction of armaments to such a point and in such a thorough fashion that no nation will be in a position to commit an act of physical aggression against any neighbor—anywhere in the world.

That is no vision of a distant millennium. It is a definite basis for a kind of world attainable in our own time and generation. That kind of world is the very antithesis of the so-called new order of tyranny which the dictators seek to create with the crash of a bomb.

To that new order we oppose the greater conception—the moral order. A good society is able to face schemes of world domination and foreign revolutions alike without fear.

Since the beginning of our American history we have been engaged in change—in a perpetual peaceful revolution—a revolution which goes on steadily, quietly adjusting itself to changing conditions—without the concentration camp or the quick-lime in the ditch. The world order which we seek is the cooperation of free countries, working together in a friendly, civilized society.

This Nation has placed its destiny in the hands and heads and hearts of its millions of free men and women; and its faith in freedom under the guidance of God. Freedom means the supremacy of human rights everywhere. Our support goes to those who struggle to gain those rights or keep them. Our strength is in our unity of purpose.

To that high concept there can be no end save victory.

11. THE MORALISTIC INTERPRETATION OF AMERICAN FOREIGN POLICY *

> Idealist conceptions concerning the nature of international politics have strongly influenced the conduct of our foreign policy throughout our history. Dr. Perkins presents an historical analysis of the influence of moralism on American foreign policy from the early days of our existence as a nation to the American intervention in Korea.

The realistic student of foreign affairs will perforce admit the very large role that is played by sheer physical power in the intercourse of nations. But those who assume that physical power operates apart from all other considerations, and especially apart from what may well be described as moral considerations, display a shallow kind of cynicism that is far removed from the facts. The most absolute and the most unscrupulous dictators are themselves the refutation of this point of view. In international affairs, as in life in general, hypocrisy is the tribute that vice pays to virtue. Adolf Hitler had no public morals whatsoever, so far as his diplomacy was concerned. Yet he constantly branded other people as war-mongers in an effort to make war palatable to his own people; again and again he fabricated stories of atrocities suffered by Germans outside the Reich in order to give some kind of moral validity to his projects of aggrandizement; and he created an ideology around which loyalties could center in an opposition to

* Reprinted by permission of the publishers from Dexter Perkins, *The American Approach to Foreign Policy,* 1952, Cambridge, Mass.: Harvard University Press, copyright, 1952, by the President and Fellows of Harvard College, pp. 63-82. In 1949, Dr. Perkins delivered the Gottesman Lectures at Uppsala University, Uppsala, Sweden. The lecture series was subsequently published by Harvard University Press. Professor Perkins is Professor of History and Chairman of the Department of History, University of Rochester.

Communism. In the same way the present rulers of the Soviet Union, while quite oblivious to any precepts of international morality, constantly talk in terms of such precepts, constantly invoke the Hitlerian device of describing other people as bellicose and sinister in their ambitions, pretend to be interested in disarmament while maintaining the largest armed forces in the world in proportion to their population, and make appeal to an ideology which becomes a kind of faith, with all the moral implications that faith implies, and with the declared end the betterment of the fortunes of the human race. No government in the modern world could treat its people as if moral ideas did not exist, and none would try.

The degree, however, to which moral ideas influence diplomacy, will vary, and the expression of these ideas will vary, with the political constitution and mores of the individual state. In Hitlerian Germany or Soviet Russia, ethical concepts may be a mere device for the advancement of the national interests, a mere support to a largely cynical diplomacy. But we must not imagine that it is only in the dictatorships that this is true. If we contemplate the history of European foreign policy in the nineteenth century we shall find that it often was conducted very largely in secret, and by professional diplomats, who acted independently, to a very large degree, though not absolutely, without regard to public opinion. In such conditions it is not strange that there were many "deals," which were not supposed to see the light of day, and that agreements were often entered into which concerned third parties, and perhaps sacrificed their interests, agreements which might have met with considerable condemnation if they had been made public. In general, putting the matter in another way, a very free hand was left to the professionals by the people themselves, and the professionals naturally made such use as they chose of this freedom, promoting the national interest, as they understood it, no doubt, but referring to public opinion only when they felt compelled to do so, or when they found in it a useful support for their own objectives. Nor have we seen the last of professional diplomacy in our own age. There is still in many countries a long tradition of relative freedom of action for government in the conduct of foreign affairs, and while this tradition is no doubt declining in force, it is still a factor in the actual conduct of foreign relations.

In the United States, on the other hand, to a degree remarkable at least by comparison, a different way of thinking and acting with regard to these matters has developed. American democracy is not by any means precisely like the democracy of European states. There has never been a governing class in America, since the Federalists aspired to that title at the end of the eighteenth century.   The professional diplomat hardly existed in much of the nineteenth century, and he has never occupied the secure position that he once occupied, and to some degree still occupies, in the Old World.   To an extent that is true in no other country, the motivating force in government has come up from the people, rather than down from a political or diplomatic elite.   The average man in America, be he well-informed or ill-informed, is likely to think that he has a right to express an opinion in politics, and to have that opinion considered.   When complex issues are submitted to examination in such a mechanism as the *Fortune* poll, the amazing thing is often the small number of persons who will say that they do not know the answer.   The spirit of American politics suggests that the citizen *does* know the answers, and, in any case, the citizen is likely to think that he knows.   In addition to all this, there has been from the beginning of American politics . . . a dislike of secrecy with regard to foreign affairs, and a habit of public debate on foreign issues.   The great questions of foreign policy have often been submitted to public debate, often discussed with great frankness from more than one point of view, and often decided by the test of public opinion.   No one can understand American diplomacy who does not grasp the importance of the democratic motif in its historic evolution.

Now the mass of men are, of course, not equipped to understand in their infinite ramifications and details the problems that confront the nation in the field of foreign affairs.   If they exercise an influence on policy (and it has just been stated they *do* exercise such an influence in America), they are almost bound, in the nature of the case, to attach themselves to relatively simple concepts, to principles easy to understand, and relevant to their general democratic experience, or to emotional attitudes that spring from the circumstances of the moment. Amongst these considerations, for example, may be the idea that democratic government is the best government on earth (irrespective of the particular situation of a given nation), or the idea that conquest is inherently immoral (without too sharp scrutiny of the American past in this regard), or the idea that it is wrong to negotiate in secret (though it is hard to see how diplomacy could be carried on if there were not at least some secrecy), or the idea that the state is bound by the same moral code as is the individual (though this is a knotty question for philosophers).   And if views such as these are widely diffused throughout the community, and if they are also strongly held, they are bound, of course, to affect the tone of our diplomatic action, and to influence very strongly the actual conduct of our public men. In other words, principles, strongly fused with emotion, will play a very great part in the foreign policy of such a country as the United States. Because this is so, . . . high-sounding declarations and general appeals to international morality will often characterize the utterances of our statesmen, and even their private diplomatic notes. When we say this, we by no means imply that Americans are unique in this regard. But it is, I think, fair to say, that there is a highly moralistic flavor to our diplomacy, as compared with the other nations. To foreigners this lofty moral tone no doubt sometimes seems like cant, or a mere device of the diplomats themselves. But these people do Americans injustice; and the best test of this is to be found in the fact that, on occasion, the government of the United States has put ethical considerations ahead of national interest as it would be defined in the narrow sense of the term.

Before we examine, however, the moralistic overtones in American diplomacy, we must pause to remark that these overtones do not necessarily and inevitably mean that American foreign policy is necessarily "better" than the diplomacy of other nations, even if we maintained, which we do not, that the difference was one in kind and not in degree. For one thing, the over-simplification of the issues which results from an appeal to moral principle may or may not be desirable in practice. The conviction, for example, that democratic government is the best of all governments may lead us to try to impose it on others, without success, and with the result that international irritation ensues. A moral repugnance to imperialism and conquest may blind Americans to the practical difficulties in the way of giving complete independence to nations not yet very well prepared for it. A dislike of secrecy may lead to a degree of publicity in international affairs which makes compromise difficult, and which arouses rather than allays the passions which often play a part in international affairs. The notion that the state must be bound by the same code as the individual may lead to quixotic action and naive judgment in the real world of international affairs. Principles are both useful and dangerous, both inspiring and exacerbating.

Indeed, one of the major difficulties with the moralistic view of foreign policy is that it makes for rigidity. The business of diplomacy is often the business of adjusting rival interests, and rival points of view, of giving a little here and there and of getting a little in return. But if every question is to be invested with the aura of principle, how is adjustment to take place? There is no more difficult problem in the world of individuals than of bringing together contestants who, both from their own point of view, are clad in the armor of unsullied righteousness. The same thing applies to nations.

In the third place, moral judgments, since they rest on a foundation of deep feeling, rather than on exact and precise analysis, may and sometimes do verge on sentimentality. A moral judgment may be very naive in the manner in which it assesses the elements of a complex problem. It has been difficult, for example, for moralists of the Henry Wallace type to accept the fact that the ushering in of an era of good will is not a prime objective of foreign policy for the Soviet Union; the former Vice President up to very recently could not persuade himself that some such ethical objective does not underlie the action of the Kremlin, as it would, no doubt, underlie his own action, if he were where he could act effectively. Or, to take another example, it was easy for most Americans to believe, more deeply than on the basis of the facts they ought to have believed, in the efficacy of the Kellogg Pact, by which nations who signed pledged themselves not to resort to war as an instrument of policy. The promise to be virtuous is not virtue, as the generation which followed before long discovered. In the field of international organization, too, Americans are sometimes deceived by their feelings. World government, for example, is an appealing ideal so long as one feels about it rather than thinks about it. But it is by no means certain that the institutional approach to peace is the best approach, and it is certainly not the only one.

It is not, however, the object of this essay to make a moral judgment on the moralistic approach of the Americans to diplomacy; it is rather my purpose, by reviewing the national story, to make clear how strong this moralistic emphasis has been, and how often it has played a part in foreign policy. Let us look first of all at the strong influence exerted by the democratic ideal upon American action. And here we may begin with the events of the second Washington administration, and with the difficulties of the first President in shaping a course which was to the interest of the nation. There seems to be little doubt what was wise policy for the United States in this initial period. An intellectual or realistic view of the matter would surely have led to an understanding with Great Britain, our principal source of imports, our best customer, and our neighbor in North America, and the holder of our border posts, at a time when we were little equipped to afford the luxury of British hostility. So, of course, Washington viewed the matter; on this basis he acted in the despatch of the Jay mission. Yet such able men as Jefferson and Madison, representing a powerful section of opinion, advocated measures of commercial reprisal against Great Britain, which would probably have been fruitless, and opposed bitterly the treaty of 1794. The basis of their action lay without question, in their sympathy for the French Revolution, in other words, in ideological and moral considerations.

The revolutions in Latin America had a substantial repercussion in the United States. There were certainly many distinctions between the course of the events in that part of the world, and the course of events at home. But the judgment of such an American as Henry Clay took none of these factors into account. In his speeches in the Congress in 1818, he laid great stress on the similarity of the institutions of our southern brethren, and our own, and laid the basis for the structure that was later to become known as Pan-Americanism. The more cautious and intellectual Adams saw a very different picture; he was influenced by motives at once more realistic and more selfish; and the recognition of the colonies, for which Clay clamored, was postponed till 1822, when we had safely acquired the Floridas from Spain. But the ideological note is strong, indeed, in the policy of the Monroe administration itself when we come to the famous declaration of December 2, 1823. In a sense, the famous message is an ideological tract, praising the democratic principle and exalting the democratic forms, in contrast to the monarchies of Europe. And if Monroe had had his way, its ideological character would have been still more complete, for he proposed to add to the message a sympathetic reference to the Greeks and a commentary on the suppression of constitutional government in Spain. Of course it is not to be contended that none but idealistic and moral considerations entered into Monroe's famous pronouncement. In one sense, it was based upon the principle of national security, on the assumption that the restoration of monarchial rule in Latin America was "dangerous to our peace and safety." But this hypothesis would have been difficult to prove, if submitted to the acid test of analysis, especially at the time that the President issued his famous challenge. The prime significance of the message was ideological, and its prime origin lay in a feeling of moral association with our "southern brethren." Europeans clearly recognized this fact; Metternich was by no means alone among European conservatives in bewailing what he foresaw as the separation of the New World from the Old. Indeed, any careful study of the period will make it clear that the young republic of the West was regarded by Continental Europeans as having deliberately and arrogantly laid down a principle which flew in the face of European doctrine, and which was primarily based on very different assumptions from the assumption of legitimacy. The immense enthusiasm which the message aroused in the United States, the press comment of the time, dwelt for the most part very little upon the sense of immediate peril, and very much upon the distinction between the institutions of Europe and the institutions of America.

The moral factors in diplomacy, the sympathy with the democratic ideal, was again expressed in the European revolutions of 1848. The American government acted promptly, almost precipitately, in recognizing the Second French Republic in 1848. The Hungarian revolt was followed with intense enthusiasm by many Americans, and the Taylor administration sent an American representative to Hungary, with instructions to hold out assurances of recognition, if the circumstances warranted. When the Austrian government protested this action, Secretary of State Daniel Webster responded in a despatch whose flowing periods and flamboyant tone make it one of the most remarkable in American diplomatic intercourse. And though, with Russian aid, the independence movement was put down, the patriot Kossuth, when he came to this country, was received with transports of acclaim, and honored by a banquet at which Webster himself was one of the speakers. True, it was not possible for Americans to do anything effective; armed intervention was out of the question, for reasons of geography, if nothing else; but the tension created by this episode was great enough to lead to a temporary interruption of relations between the Austrian minister and the Secretary of State.

The clash of political ideals was again illustrated in the course of events in Mexico in the fifties and the sixties. In the struggle between the liberal and reactionary elements in that country the United States was naturally impelled to take the side of the liberals. It supported the Juarez régime from an early period, and the Buchanan administration even went so far as to negotiate what was virtually a treaty of protectorate with that régime. French intrigues in behalf of monarchy, from the first regarded with suspicion, became the object of pointed reprobation on the part of Seward even in the course of the Civil War, and aroused such widespread indignation during that struggle that in April of 1864, the House of Representatives passed unanimously a resolution condemning the policy of Napoleon III. And, at the end of the war, there was still more emphatic expression of public sentiment, which might conceivably have led to war had it not been for the adroit diplomacy of Seward, and the reaction in France itself against the adventure in Mexico.

The theme of democratic idealism runs through the whole history of Pan-Americanism, which began to find expression in positive form with James G. Blaine. The economic determinist will doubtless discover ulterior motives behind the calling of the Latin-American conference in 1889; and such motives there undoubtedly were. But would it have been possible to weld together the nations of the New World in so close an association on the basis of a trade infinitely less significant than that with Europe? Is it not certain that the belief, whether justified or not, that there existed a similarity of institutions between the states of North and South America had something to do with the success of this important movement? And have not Pan-American conferences again and again asserted the validity of democratic principles, and paid tribute to the democratic ideal?

Nor is it only in this way that the United States has attempted to promote democracy on this side of the Atlantic. Sometimes it has gone further, and has attempted to use its influence more directly. The Central American treaties of 1907 and 1923, with their doctrine that governments arising from revolution ought not to be recognized, was, in a sense, an attempt to impose the American way of orderly election and popular choice upon some of our weaker neighbors. Largely ineffective in practice, it has certainly been; and today not many students of American diplomacy would advocate such policy; but this does not alter the fact that democratic principle affected action. Nor must we forget the still more striking case in which the same idea was applied, that of Woodrow Wilson's attitude towards Mexico. The refusal of the President to recognize the blood-stained régime of Victoriano Huerta was based squarely upon principle, and ironically enough this insistence on principle came very near leading to intervention. No doubt Wilson's policy came in for very sharp criticism from some of those who described themselves as realists, but it was, none the less, resolutely adhered to, and it led, of course, to the fall of the Mexican dictator.

We have already discussed the interventions in the Caribbean. Here the motives, as we have seen, were largely strategic. But, in every case, be it noted, the final act was an election conducted according to democratic principle, and the notion that somehow or other the unruly little peoples of this area could be instructed—and coerced—into accepting American conceptions of popular government was at all times present.

In the evolution of American public opinion with regard to the World War, a sense of democratic morality was certainly one of the factors that shaped the course of policy. Americans, from the beginning, contrasted the political institutions of France and Britain with the institutions of Germany. They were by no means always fair in this regard; to describe Germany as an autocracy in 1914 was stretching things pretty far. They overlooked, also, the fact that the Russian régime was far nearer to political absolutism than either of the governments of the Central Empires. But the fact that the generalization that the war was a struggle of autocracy against democracy had only a partial validity does not in any way diminish the force of the popular sentiment in this regard.   The policy of partiality towards the Allies, and of discrimination against Germany, was in no small degree due to moral considerations.   It explains why the Wilson administration dealt gently with British violations of international law, and held rigidly to principle in dealing with the government in Berlin.   It explains why the President himself, highly trained though he was, could echo the popular generalization in some of the very greatest of his speeches, and why he could proclaim the struggle to be in very truth a struggle involving political forms.

Wilson's war message, indeed, is largely based on this theory.   Democratic governments, he seems to be saying, are peaceful governments; they act on different principles of international morality from those of autocratic governments.   They do not (here Wilson was either misinformed or disingenuous) fill their neighbor state with spies; they do not embark upon ambitious enterprises of conquest.   The peace of the world depends upon the breaking of the force of autocracy and upon the setting-up of democratic régimes.   "The world must be made safe for democracy."   The President goes further.   In a passage more remarkable for its rhetoric than for its prescience he welcomes "the great naive Russian people" to the ranks of the democrats, and actually, in his optimism and exaltation, goes so far as to say that the autocracy which "crowned the summit of Russian political life" was "not in fact Russian in origin, character, or purpose."   Idealism could hardly go further than this.

This same faith in the democratic ideal animated Wilsonian diplomacy in dealing with Germany.   The avowed theory of his speeches was that not the German people, but the rulers of Germany, were to blame for the war, that if the democratic forces in Germany could be liberated, a new nation, to all intents and purposes, would arise.   And insistence on this point of view was certainly a factor, and a very important factor, in bringing about the flight of the Kaiser and the establishment of a republic in the Reich.   It may be that, in this respect, Wilson's policy was not entirely wise; it is possible to argue that a constitutional monarchy would have opposed a more successful resistance to the madness of National Socialism than the republican régime could have done; but, however this may be, the moral conviction that lay behind Wilsonian policy cannot be denied.   To him popular government was something of a religion.   And that he echoed a deep-seated popular sentiment can hardly be doubted.

In another sense, too, the notion of democracy deeply affected the

policy of the war years, and the making of the peace. For the democratic ideal is obviously closely connected with the principle of self-
determination, and to this principle Woodrow Wilson gave pronounced
allegiance. That the peace should rest upon the will of the peoples
concerned was clear to him, clear to him even before the United States
entered the war, set forth in some detail in the famous address of the
22nd of January, 1917. This idea was reenunciated again and again
after America entered the conflict; it is one of the dominating conceptions in the famous Speech of the Fourteen Points. And, of course,
it plays an important part in the negotiation of the treaty of peace. It
was respect for this principle that made Wilson fight tenaciously French
ambitions for the annexation of the Saar, and that led to the setting up
of an international régime in that important region, with provision for
a plebiscite at the end of a fifteen year period; it was on the basis of
this principle that the President contested French designs to detach the
Rhineland from Germany; it was still from the same point of view
that he either actively encouraged, or easily acquiesced in, the various
plebiscites which determined the frontiers of the Reich on the north
in regard to Denmark and on the west with regard to Poland; the
internationalization of Danzig was based on the same conceptions;
and preoccupation with self-determination influenced the arrangements
for the Italian boundary in Istria. Finally, respect for the democratic
ideal led to a wholly new treatment of the problem of the backward
peoples, as we have already seen. It is of course not contended that
Wilson was consistent to the last degree in his attachment to principle.
Few men are. The veto in the treaty on the possible union of Austria
and Germany was hardly defensible; and though the question of the
German population in the Sudetenland was hardly raised while the
President was at Paris he seems never to have been much troubled
by the attitude of the Czechs towards this problem. He wavered, in
other words, in the pressing of his own standards of rectitude, as others
have done before him and will do after him. But that democratic
idealism played an important part in the negotiation of the treaty of
Versailles, and an especially important part in American diplomacy at
Paris, it would be difficult to deny.

The same idealism, whether misguided or not, directed Wilsonian
policy towards Soviet Russia. It was characteristic of the President
that his remedy for the Russian civil war in 1919 was a conference of
all factions, presumably to decide upon a peace based on democratic
principle; and it is understandable that as the autocratic character of
the Russian régime made itself more and more apparent the reaction
of the administration was that of non-recognition. It may perhaps

be questioned whether a sound sense of political realism dictates abstention from diplomatic intercourse with governments whose origins or
whose principles we disapprove. It may be that it is wiser to keep
the channels of communication open, and hope that some breath of
freedom will penetrate from the outside world. But moral reprobation is in some ways a very human form of satisfaction, and no country
has carried it further in the evolution of its policy than the United
States. The policy determined upon by Wilson, and enunciated by
his Secretary of State Bainbridge Colby, was followed by the Harding
and Coolidge administrations, and long after the other great nations
of the world had established relations with the Kremlin, our own government stood aloof. It was not indeed until 1933 that the diplomatic
boycott was ended.

The dislike of the Communist régime did not end with the advent
of the Roosevelt administration. Anti-Communist sentiment influenced
policy to a considerably less degree in the thirties, and was naturally
suppressed, from motives of convenience, in the years of the war.
But it was not slow to revive as soon as the struggle was over. From
the pure point of view of national interest, there was really very little
reason for the United States to concern itself with the character of the
governments that were set up in Bulgaria and Rumania. Yet the
United States made itself from the outset the defender of democracy
in this part of the world, and sought to prevent the transformation of
these two states into satellites of the Kremlin. The case of Poland
was, in many respects, similar, though here the anti-Russian feeling
of American Poles rested on a broader basis than pure ideology. But
a diplomacy less affected by considerations of principle might well
have tried to bargain, and to agree to leave the Soviet government to
pursue its own course in Eastern Europe in exchange for a policy more
considerate of American interests in Western Europe. I do not say,
(let it be clear), that such a policy would have succeeded. It probably
would not have done so. But the fact that it was not even attempted
is surely significant, from the point of view of the student of American
attitudes towards diplomatic problems.

At the present time, moreover, preoccupation with political ideals
has a very large part in our attitude towards China and towards the
new régime which has been established there. It is by no means certain as yet that the new régime at Peking will accept recognition on
terms consistent with the dignity of the recognizing states; but it *is*
clear, on the other hand, that it is going to be extremely difficult for
the government of the United States to recognize the government of
General Mao. Ideological considerations may well affect policy in

this regard for some time to come; and though there were certainly those in the State Department who felt that these considerations were unduly weighted, the force of American public opinion makes extremely difficult any other policy than that of diplomatic boycott. The obstacles to intercourse between the American democracy and states differently organized seem, indeed, to increase rather than diminish with time, and to affect our intercourse, not only with dictatorships of the left, but with dictatorships of the right.

It is impossible to weigh accurately the various elements which entered into the equation in fixing American hostility to Adolf Hitler. It was not only the character of the Nazi régime that influenced Americans. The brutal persecution of the Jews in the domestic sphere, the outrageous international policies of the Fuehrer, and above all, the feeling that the Third Reich was a threat to the physical security of the United States, all played a part in fixing policy. But many of these motives were not present in the attitude assumed towards Franco-Spain. From a purely objective point of view, and on the basis of any careful analysis, Americans might well have reason to judge favorably the policy of the Caudillo. In retrospect, it seems fairly clear that cautious neutrality was the watchword of Spanish policy, that the chances of Spanish intervention on the side of Germany were extremely small. Yet dislike of the government at Madrid led the government of the United States to recall its ambassador in 1946, and to support the resolution in the Assembly of the United Nations which recommended such action. And despite powerful elements in the United States, both military and civil, which urge upon Washington closer relations with Franco, the decision until very recently stood.

There is another instance in which a semi-totalitarian government of the right was treated with obvious distrust by the United States. Our policy towards Argentina since 1943 has been by no means consistent, and one factor in the situation has been the long-maintained neutrality of the government at Buenos Ayres for a substantial part of the war period, and its equivocal attitude even after neutrality was abandoned. But the non-recognition of the Farrell régime, and still more the remarkable intervention of the American ambassador, Spruille Braden, in the electoral campaign of 1946, illustrate once more that ideological considerations play a part in American policy. Since then, it is true, the situation has changed; other elements have entered into the situation; but the facts just cited are significant, none the less.

* * * * *

We spoke of a third manner in which the American moral impulse expressed itself in American diplomacy, that is, in a dislike of secrecy, and especially of secret deals. The general question of secret diplomacy is to be treated later. But the matter of making bargains with one power at the expense of another, a practice of which the history of Europe is full, may well be considered here. And on the whole, the American record is a very good one. There are some exceptions. The not very scrupulous attempt of Thomas Jefferson to bribe the French government into putting pressure on the satellite régime in Spain to cede the Floridas to the United States is a case in point. Yet this attempt met with violent condemnation from John Randolph, until then one of Jefferson's followers, and it came to nothing. We have to come down to relatively recent times to find another episode of doubtful morality of the same general kind. The Taft-Katsura memorandum of 1908, by which the United States bound itself to the recognition of the Japanese position in Korea, in exchange for a pledge to respect the independence of the Philippines, has an extremely "practical" significance. We may cite also the action of Franklin D. Roosevelt at Yalta, in pledging himself in writing, to support the claims of the Soviet Union to their former privileges in Manchuria, at the expense of China, and really behind the back of the government at Peking. It is true that the President was told by his military advisers that it was essential to bring the Russians into the war against Japan. It is also true that the Chinese Nationalists later accepted the arrangement. But it is significant that this "deal" was not even recorded in the archives of the State Department, and that, when discovered, it met with severe reprobation from large sections of American public opinion. Speaking generally, it is fair to say that such oblique transactions have by no means been characteristic of American diplomacy.

But there is a still larger sense in which the moral judgment enters into the formation of American foreign policy. We have spoken of the democratic ideal as influencing American conduct with regard to the First World War. But there was more to the matter than that. The simple judgment of many Americans condemned the Central Empires in 1914 because it was believed that these Empires had started the war. A more refined judgment might point to a long train of causes, and to errors and provocations on both sides. But what was seen in that fateful August was that the Austro-Hungarian government had launched an attack on Serbia, and Germany an attack on Russia. And when these initial acts of aggression (as they were widely regarded) were followed by the violation of Belgian neutrality, in contemptuous disregard of solemn treaty obligations, the partiality of many of our citizens for the cause of the Allies was heightened. It would be foolish to deny the influence of these events on the course of our diplomacy. If Woodrow Wilson did not hold the balance even between the two sets of contestants in the mighty struggle that was unleashed, the reason was that he, like hosts of others, had made a moral judgment with regard to the war from which he could not have freed himself if he would.

Equally striking is the American attitude towards both Japanese and German imperialism in the 30's. The American government, in 1931, could not sit still in the face of the Japanese conquest of Manchuria. The Foreign Offices of Europe were by no means so disposed to a moral judgment, and the British, in particular, hesitated to take any stand against Nippon. But the United States insisted that the question be thoroughly ventilated, and though it was not ready to challenge Tokyo to armed conflict, it put forward the famous Stimson doctrine, and even secured its acceptance by the assembly of the League of Nations. By this doctrine, as is well known, the powers of the world refused to recognize any situation, treaty, or agreement brought about by means contrary to the obligations of the Kellogg Pact, that is by acts of force. Whether such moral pillorying of another government is wise or foolish, a futile gesture or a useful clarification of the record, is beside the point. It represents very clearly the influence of an ethical ideal in the practice of diplomacy.

The same thing can be seen in our later relations with Japan. When it came to the Sino-Japanese war, there was certainly a case for a policy of appeasement from our point of view. Our trade with Japan and our investments in Japan were far greater than our trade with or our investments in China. True, the conquest of the Middle Kingdom by Nippon tended to restrict our commerce, but true, too, we would jeopardize a far more valuable commerce by war. And, in addition, prudential considerations might well have suggested the gentle handling of Tokyo at a time when the situation was increasingly serious in Europe. The British government (of course in a far more critical situation) seemed to be acting on just such calculations when it closed the Burma Road in the spring of 1940. But none of these elements determined American policy. It was impossible for the Roosevelt administration to frame its policy in the Far East without regard to the moral revulsion felt by the American people at the Japanese invasion of China. In the conversations of 1941, the Japanese government made it reasonably clear that it would seek a way to evade its obligations to Germany under the treaty of alliance of September, 1940, if only the United States would grant it a free hand in its ambitious designs on its great neighbor. But it would have been practically and morally impossible for the United States to take any such position, as the polls of public opinion amply attest. Indeed, the attempted *modus vivendi* of November, 1941, broke down just because it was out of the question to tolerate the continued domination of the Tokyo government on the Asian continent. And so the country found itself involved in a two-front war, from the outset, a war that might conceivably (wisely or unwisely, as you will), have been postponed.

The same sense of moral reprobation with regard to aggression showed itself in the American attitude towards Hitler. Not only dislike of totalitarian political forms, but indignation at the aggressions of the National Socialist régime, not only fear of consequences, but moral indignation at the methods of aggrandizement, played a part in the steadily mounting tide of feeling against the Third Reich. By the end of the thirties, too, the American people were coming to a conviction that is more and more influencing policy, the conviction that the use of force for the purposes of domination is inherently immoral and intolerable. Opinion expressed itself decisively with regard to the rape of Austria, and the violent methods that preceded Munich, and rarely have more sincere moral homilies been written by a Secretary of State than those which flowed from the indignant pen of Cordell Hull in this period. It was the same when the Russians attacked Finland. There was, perhaps, something of a case for the Soviet Union, from the point of view of the protection of its own territory. But the war against the Finns was almost universally denounced in the United States. And, in the period since 1945, the steady imposition of Communist power on the satellite states, though not necessarily dangerous to American security, though hardly more, from one angle, than the consolidation of a position already attained by the victories of Russian armies in the war itself, has been met with a steady stream of condemnation in this country.

The last few months, moreover, has seen a more striking assertion than any that preceded of the idea of moral judgment in international affairs. The principle of collective security is an old one, going back in modern times, to the Covenant of the League of Nations. Yet the country backed away from it in the twenties, and hesitated to assert any conclusive leadership either in the Japanese invasion of Manchuria, or with regard to the Italian invasion of Ethiopia, or in the still more obvious case of the German assault on Poland. But the principle itself was reasserted in the Charter of the United Nations, and now it has been put forward with unparalleled vigor in the case of Korea, where American action has brought enthusiastic support from the great majority of the nations of the world. The cold-blooded could have given many reasons why the issue raised by the invasion of South Korea might have been allowed to pass unchallenged. The government of Syngman Rhee, to judge from the elections of May, 1950, had few roots in Korean opinion. The military problem presented by the giving of aid to that government was a difficult one, both because the weather conditions were peculiarly unfavorable to counter operations against the forces of the North, and because the problems of supply were extremely difficult, and finally because the Americans would be fighting with their backs to the sea, in a position where defeat would mean nothing less than evacuation. Finally, there was always the risk that Russia or China would intervene. Yet none of these things affected the issue. The decision taken by President Truman received at this time the almost unanimous support of the nation; it was a decision based in no small degree on fundamental principles of international morality, and on the belief that aggression must, as a matter of principle, be put down. There was, of course, an argument of another kind, and a good one, the argument that appeasement here would only lead to new challenges, until an explosion was inevitable. But this does not invalidate the conclusion that a strong moral impulse influenced American action.

To assert these things, be it said in conclusion, is not to fall into that kind of over-simplification which attributes to a single factor a total influence over events. It is not to say that American foreign policy is always altruistic, that it is not directed by conceptions of national interest, that it is always either in its methods or its objectives to be unqualifiedly commended. It is only to say that *ideas,* and ideas connected wth certain moral preoccupations, are a factor, and a substantially important factor, in the conduct of diplomacy. And there are Americans who would add that some of the strength of the nation flows from just these facts. When men go to war, they are actuated by many motives, by mere conformity, by patriotism, by the fear of danger, by understood self-interest, but also, and not infrequently, by the belief that they are defending right and justice. And whether this belief is justified or not, in the eyes of the sceptical analyst, it is one of the mainsprings of that courageous devotion which brings victory.

Realism

12. AMERICAN FOREIGN POLICY IN THE MODERN WORLD *

> For realists, power is the "single most stubborn social psychological factor by which international behavior is influenced. Only through understanding this phenomenon can man hope to improve the melancholy status of his present situation." Realists attempt to limit concentrations of power and mitigate international tensions which could lead to war. Realists are concerned with the defense of the national interest. They believe that much of our policy has been conducted without reference either to the stubborn fact of power or to the defense of the national interest.
>
> Mr. Kennan, one of the most prominent realist critics of American foreign policy, contends that our approach to international problems during the past fifty years has been "legalistic" and "moralistic." He describes the origins, applications, and results of this approach, and develops the realist doctrine that our policy should be based upon a defense of the national interest.

I see the most serious fault of our past policy formulation to lie in something that I might call the legalistic-moralistic approach to international problems. This approach runs like a red skein through our foreign policy of the last fifty years. It has in it something of the old emphasis on arbitration treaties, something of the more ambitious American concepts of the role of international law, something of the League of Nations and the United Nations, something of the Kellogg Pact, something of the idea of a universal "Article 51" pact, something of the belief in World Law and World Government. But it is none of these, entirely. Let me try to describe it.

It is the belief that it should be possible to suppress the chaotic and dangerous aspirations of governments in the international field by the acceptance of some system of legal rules and restraints. This belief undoubtedly represents in part an attempt to transpose the Anglo-Saxon concept of individual law into the international field and to make it applicable to governments as it is applicable here at home to individuals. It must also stem in part from the memory of the origin of our own political system—from the recollection that we

---

* George F. Kennan, *American Diplomacy 1900-1950* (Chicago: University of Chicago Press, 1951), Mentor Book Edition, pp. 89-101. Used by permission of the publisher. Mr. Kennan has been Director of the Policy Planning Staff of the Department of State and Ambassador to the Soviet Union. At present he is a member of the Institute for Advanced Study, Princeton, N. J.

were able, through acceptance of a common institutional and juridical framework, to reduce to harmless dimensions the conflicts of interest and aspiration among the original thirteen colonies and to bring them all into an ordered and peaceful relationship with one another. Remembering this, people are unable to understand that what might have been possible for the thirteen colonies in a given set of circumstances might not be possible in the wider international field.

It is the essence of this belief that, instead of taking the awkward conflicts of national interest and dealing with them on their merits with a view to finding the solutions least unsettling to the stability of international life, it would be better to find some formal criteria of a juridical nature by which the permissible behavior of states could be defined. There would then be judicial entities competent to measure the actions of governments against these criteria and to decide when their behavior was acceptable and when unacceptable. Behind all this, of course, lies the American assumption that the things for which other peoples in this world are apt to contend are for the most part neither creditable nor important and might justly be expected to take second place behind the desirability of an orderly world, untroubled by international violence. To the American mind, it is implausible that people should have positive aspirations, and ones that they regard as legitimate, more important to them than the peacefulness and orderliness of international life. From this standpoint, it is not apparent why other peoples should not join us in accepting the rules of the game in international politics, just as we accept such rules in the competition of sport in order that the game may not become too cruel and too destructive and may not assume an importance we did not mean it to have.

If they were to do this, the reasoning runs, then the troublesome and chaotic manifestations of the national ego could be contained and rendered either unsubstantial or subject to easy disposal by some method familiar and comprehensible to our American usage. Departing from this background, the mind of American statesmanship, stemming as it does in so large a part from the legal profession in our country, gropes with unfailing persistence for some institutional framework which would be capable of fulfilling this function.

•　　•　　•　　•　　•

In the first place, the idea of the subordination of a large number of states to an international juridical régime, limiting their possibilities for aggression and injury to other states, implies that these are all states like our own, reasonably content with their international borders and status, at least to the extent that they would be willing to refrain from pressing for change without international agreement. Actually, this has generally been true only of a portion of international society. We tend to underestimate the violence of national maladjustments and discontents elsewhere in the world if we think that they would always appear to other people as less important than the preservation of the juridical tidiness of international life.

Second, while this concept is often associated with a revolt against nationalism, it is a curious thing that it actually tends to confer upon the concept of nationality and national sovereignty an absolute value it did not have before. The very principle of "one government, one vote," regardless of physical or political differences between states, glorifies the concept of national sovereignty and makes it the exclusive form of participation in international life. It envisages a world composed exclusively of sovereign national states with a full equality of status. In doing this, it ignores the tremendous variations in the firmness and soundess of national divisions: the fact that the origins of state borders and national personalities were in many instances fortuitous or at least poorly related to realities. It also ignores the law of change. The national state pattern is not, should not be, and cannot be a fixed and static thing. By nature, it is an unstable phenomenon in a constant state of change and flux. History has shown that the will and the capacity of individual peoples to contribute to their world environment is constantly changing. It is only logical that the organizational forms (and what else are such things as borders and governments?) should change with them. The function of a system of international relationships is not to inhibit this process of change by imposing a legal strait jacket upon it but rather to facilitate it: to ease its transitions, to temper the asperities to which it often leads, to isolate and moderate the conflicts to which it gives rise, and to see that these conflicts do not assume forms too unsettling for international life in general. But this is a task for diplomacy, in the most old-fashioned sense of the term. For this, law is too abstract, too inflexible, too hard to adjust to the demands of the unpredictable and the unexpected.

By the same token, the American concept of world law ignores those means of international offense—those means of the projection of power and coercion over other peoples—which by-pass institutional forms entirely or even exploit them against themselves: such things as ideological attack, intimidation, penetration, and disguised seizure of the institutional paraphernalia of national sovereignty. It ignores, in other words, the device of the puppet state and the set of techniques by which states can be converted into puppets with no formal violation of, or challenge to, the outward attributes of their sovereignty and their independence.

This is one of the things that have caused the peoples of the satellite countries of eastern Europe to look with a certain tinge of bitterness on the United Nations. The organization failed so completely to save them from domination by a great neighboring country, a domination no less invidious by virtue of the fact that it came into being by processes we could not call "aggression." And there is indeed some justification for their feeling, because the legalistic approach to international affairs ignores in general the international significance of political problems and the deeper sources of international instability. It assumes that civil wars will remain civil and not grow into international wars. It assumes the ability of each people to solve its own internal political problems in a manner not provocative of its international environment. It assumes that each nation will always be able to construct a government qualified to speak for it and cast its vote in the international arena and that this government will be acceptable to the rest of the international community in this capacity. It assumes, in other words, that domestic issues will not become international issues and that the world community will not be put in the position of having to make choices between rival claimants for power within the confines of the individual state.

Finally, this legalistic approach to international relations is faulty in its assumptions concerning the possibility of sanctions against offenses and violations. In general, it looks to collective action to provide such sanction against the bad behavior of states. In doing so, it forgets the limitations on the effectiveness of military coalition. It forgets that, as a circle of military associates widens in any conceivable political-military venture, the theoretical total of available military strength may increase, but only at the cost of compactness and ease of control. And the wider a coalition becomes, the more difficult it becomes to retain political unity and general agreement on the purposes and effects of what is being done. As we are seeing in the case of Korea, joint military operations against an aggressor have a different meaning for each participant and raise specific political issues for each one which are extraneous to the action in question and affect many other facets of international life. The wider the circle of military associates, the more cumbersome the problem of political control over their actions, and the more circumscribed the least common denominator of agreement. This law of diminishing returns lies so heavily on the possibilities for multilateral military action that it makes it doubtful whether the participation of smaller states can really add very much to the ability of the great powers to assure stability of international life. And this is tremendously important, for it brings us back to the realization that even under a system of world law the sanction against destructive international behavior might continue to rest basically, as it has in the past, on the alliances and relationships among the great powers themselves. There might be a state, or perhaps more than one state, which all the rest of the world community together could not successfully coerce into following a line of action to which it was violently averse. And if this is true, where are we? It seems to me that we are right back in the realm of the forgotten art of diplomacy from which we have spent fifty years trying to escape.

These, then, are some of the theoretical deficiencies that appear to me to be inherent in the legalistic approach to international affairs. But there is a greater deficiency still that I should like to mention before I close. That is the inevitable association of legalistic ideas with moralistic ones: the carrying-over into the affairs of states of the concepts of right and wrong, the assumption that state behavior is a fit subject for moral judgment. Whoever says there is a law must of course be indignant against the lawbreaker and feel a moral superiority to him. And when such indignation spills over into military contest, it knows no bounds short of the reduction of the lawbreaker to the point of complete submissiveness—namely, unconditional surrender. It is a curious thing, but it is true, that the legalistic approach to world affairs, rooted as it unquestionably is in a desire to do away with war and violence, makes violence more enduring, more terrible, and more destructive to political stability than did the older motives of national interest. A war fought in the name of high moral principle finds no early end short of some form of total domination.

In this way, we see that the legalistic approach to international problems is closely identified with the concept of total war and total victory, and the manifestations of the one spill over only too easily into the manifestations of the other. And the concept of total war is something we would all do well to think about a little in these troubled times. This is a relatively new concept, in Western civilization at any rate. It did not really appear on the scene until World War I. It characterized both of these great world wars, and both of them—as I have pointed out—were followed by great instability and disillusionment. But it is not only a question now of the desirability of this concept; it is a question of its feasibility. Actually, I wonder whether even in the past total victory was not really an illusion from the standpoint of the victors. In a sense, there is no total victory short of genocide, unless it be a victory over the minds of men. But the total military victories are rarely victories over the minds of men. And we now face the fact that it is very questionable whether in a new global conflict there could ever be any such thing as total *military* victory. I personally do not believe that there could. There might be a great weakening of the armed forces of one side or another, but I think it out of the question that there should be such a thing as a general and formal submission of the national will on either side. The attempt to achieve this unattainable goal, however, could wreak upon civilization another set of injuries fully as serious as those caused by World War I or World War II, and I leave it to you to answer the question as to how civilization could survive them.

It was asserted not long ago by a prominent American that "war's very object is victory" and that "in war there can be no substitute for victory." Perhaps the confusion here lies in what is meant by the term "victory." Perhaps the term is actually misplaced. Perhaps there can be such a thing as "victory" in a battle, whereas in war there can be only the achievement or nonachievement of your objectives. In the old days, wartime objectives were generally limited and practical ones, and it was common to measure the success of your military operations by the extent to which they brought you closer to your objectives. But where your objectives are moral and ideological ones and run to changing the attitudes and traditions of an entire people or the personality of a regime, then victory is probably something not to be achieved entirely by military means or indeed in any short space of time at all; and perhaps that is the source of our confusion.

In any case, I am frank to say that I think there is no more dangerous delusion, none that has done us a greater disservice in the past or that threatens to do us a greater disservice in the future, than the concept of total victory. And I fear that it springs in large measure from the basic faults in the approach to international affairs which I have been discussing here. If we are to get away from it, this will not mean that we shall have to abandon our respect for international law, or our hopes for its future usefulness as the gentle civilizer of events which I mentioned in one of the earlier lectures. Nor will it mean that we have to go in for anything that can properly be termed "appeasement"—if one may use a word so cheapened and deflated by the abuse to which it has been recently subjected. But it will mean the emergence of a new attitude among us toward many things outside our borders that are irritating and unpleasant today—an attitude more like that of the doctor toward those physical phenomena in the human body that are neither pleasing nor fortunate—an attitude of detachment and soberness and readiness to reserve judgment. It will mean that we will have the modesty to admit that our own national interest is all that we are really capable of knowing and understanding—and the courage to recognize that if our purposes and undertakings here at home are decent ones, unsullied by arrogance or hostility toward other people or delusions of superiority, then the pursuit of our national interest can never fail to be conducive to a better world. This concept is less ambitious and less inviting in its immediate prospects than those to which we have so often inclined, and less pleasing to our image of ourselves. To many it may seem to smack of cynicism and reaction. I cannot share these doubts. Whatever is realistic in concept, and founded in an endeavor to see both ourselves and others as we really are, cannot be illiberal.

13. The Mainsprings of American Foreign Policy: The National Interest vs. Moral Abstractions *

> Dr. Morgenthau describes the American tendency to view international politics in terms of abstract moral principles. He divides the history of American foreign policy into three periods, each of which exhibits a different approach to foreign policy. During the earliest years of our history as a nation, our orientation was realist; we conceived of international politics as a struggle for power, and developed policies based upon the national interest. The ideological period followed; we thought in terms of moral principles but acted in terms of power. The third period began with the war with Spain, and has lasted until our own day; we did and still do think and act in terms of moral abstractions completely divorced from national interests. Dr. Morgenthau documents the consequences of the pursuit of policies based upon moral principles alone, and insists that we return to the wisdom of George Washington and Alexander Hamilton, and defend the national interest.

It is often said that the foreign policy of the United States is in need of maturing and that the American people and their government must grow up if they want to emerge victorious from the trials of our age. It would be truer to say that this generation of Americans must shed the illusions of their fathers and grandfathers and relearn the great principles of statecraft which guided the path of the republic in the

* Hans J. Morgenthau, *American Political Science Review,* December, 1950, pp. 833-854. The author is Professor of Political Science and Director of the Center for the Study of American Foreign Policy, University of Chicago.

first decade and—in moralistic disguise—in the first century of its existence. The United States offers the singular spectacle of a commonwealth whose political wisdom did not grow slowly through the accumulation and articulation of experiences. Quite to the contrary, the full flowering of its political wisdom was coeval with its birth as an independent nation—nay, it owed its existence and survival as an independent nation to those extraordinary qualities of political insight, historic perspective, and common sense which the first generation of Americans applied to the affairs of state.

This classic age of American statecraft comes to an end with the physical disappearance of that generation of American statesmen. The rich and varied landscape in which they had planted all that is worthwhile in the tradition of Western political thought was allowed to go to waste. It became a faint and baffling remembrance, a symbol to be worshipped rather than a source of inspiration and a guide for action. Until very recently the American people seemed to be content to live in a political desert whose intellectual barrenness and aridity were relieved only by some sparse and neglected oases of insight and wisdom. What in that period, stretching over more than a century, went under the name of foreign policy was either improvisation in the face of an urgent problem which had to be dealt with somehow, or—and especially in our century—the invocation of some abstract moral principle in the image of which the world was to be made over. Improvisation as a substitute for foreign policy was largely successful, for in the past the margin of American and allied power to spare generally exceeded the degree to which American improvidence fell short of the demands of the hour. The invocation of abstract moral principles was in part hardly more than an innocuous pastime; for embracing everything it came to grips with nothing. In part, however, it was a magnificent instrument for marshalling public opinion in support of war and warlike policies—and for losing the peace to follow. The intoxication with moral abstractions which as a mass phenomenon started with the Spanish-American War, and which in our time has become the prevailing substitute for political thought, is indeed one of the great sources of weakness and failure in American foreign policy.

It is, however, worthy of note that underneath this political dilettantism, nourished by improvidence and a sense of moral mission, there has remained alive an almost instinctive awareness of the perennial interests of the United States. This has especially been true with regard to Europe and the Western Hemisphere; for in these regions the national interest of the United States has from the beginning been obvious and clearly defined.

In the Western Hemisphere we have always endeavored to preserve the unique position of the United States as a predominant power without rival. We have not been slow in recognizing that this predominance was not likely to be effectively threatened by any one American nation or combination of them, acting without support from outside the Western Hemisphere. It was, then, imperative for the United States to isolate the Western Hemisphere from the political and military policies of non-American nations. The interference of non-American nations in the affairs of the Western Hemisphere, especially through the acquisition of territory, was the only way in which the predominance of the United States could have been challenged from within the Western Hemisphere itself. The Monroe Doctrine and the policies implementing it expressed that permanent national interest of the United States in the Western Hemisphere.

Since a threat to the national interest of the United States in the Western Hemisphere can come only from outside it, that is, historically from Europe, the United States has always striven to prevent the development of conditions in Europe which would be conducive to a European nation's interference in the affairs of the Western Hemisphere or to a direct attack upon the United States. Such conditions would be most likely to arise if a European nation had gained such predominance that it could afford to look across the sea for conquest without fear of being menaced at the center of its power, that is, in Europe itself. It is for this reason that the United States has consistently—the War of 1812 is the sole major exception—pursued policies aiming at the maintenance of the balance of power in Europe. It has opposed whatever European nation—be it Great Britain, France, Germany, or Russia—seemed to be likely to gain that ascendancy over its European competitors which would have jeopardized the hemispheric predominance and eventually the very independence of the United States. Conversely, it has supported whatever European nation seemed to be most likely to restore the balance of power by offering successful resistance to the would-be conqueror. While it is hard to imagine a greater contrast in the way of thinking about matters political than that which separates Alexander Hamilton from Woodrow Wilson, in this concern for the maintenance of the balance of power in Europe—for whatever different reasons— they are one. It is by virtue of this concern that the United States has intervened in both World Wars on the side of the initially weaker coalition and that its European policies have so largely paralleled those of Great Britain; for from Henry VIII to this day Great Britain has invariably pursued one single objective in Europe: the maintenance of the balance of power.

With Asia the United States has been vitally concerned only since the turn of the century, and the relation of Asia to the national interest of the United States has never been obvious or clearly defined. In consequence, the Asiatic policies of the United States have never as unequivocally expressed the permanent national interest as have the hemispheric and European ones; nor have they for that reason commanded the bipartisan support which the latter have largely enjoyed. As a further consequence, they have been subjected to moralistic influences in a measure from which the European and hemispheric policies of the United States have been largely immune. Yet beneath the confusions, reversals of policy, and moralistic generalities, which have made up the surface of our Asiatic policy since McKinley, one can detect an underlying consistency which, however vaguely, reflects the permanent interest of the United States in Asia. And this interest is again the maintenance of the balance of power. The principle that expresses it is the "open door" in China. Originally its meaning was purely commercial. However, in the measure in which other nations, especially Japan, threatened to close the door to China not only commercially, but also militarily and politically, the principle of the "open door" was interpreted to cover the territorial integrity and political independence of China not for commercial but political reasons. However unsure of itself the Asiatic policy of the United States has been, it has always assumed that the domination of China by another nation would create so great an accumulation of power as to threaten the security of the United States.

Not only with regard to Asia, however, but wherever American foreign policy has operated, political thought has been divorced from political action. Even where our long-range policies reflect faithfully, as they do in the Americas and in Europe, the true interests of the United States, we think about them in terms which have at best but a tenuous connection with the actual character of the policies pursued. We have acted on the international scene, as all nations must, in power-political terms; we have tended to conceive of our actions in non-political, moralistic terms. This aversion to seeing problems of international politics as they are and the inclination to viewing them instead in non-political, moralistic terms can be attributed both to certain misunderstood peculiarities of the American experience in foreign affairs and to the general climate of opinion prevailing in the Western world during the better part of the nineteenth and the first decade of the twentieth centuries. Of these peculiarities of the American experience three stand out: the uniqueness of the American experiment, the actual isolation during the nineteenth century of the United States from the centers of world conflict, and the humanitarian pacifism and anti-imperialism of American ideology.

The uniqueness of the American experiment in foreign policy contains two elements: the negative one of distinctiveness from the traditional power-political quarrels of Europe and the positive one of a continental expansion which created the freest and richest nation on earth without conquest or subjugation of others.

That the severance of constitutional ties with the British crown was meant to signify the initiation of an American foreign policy distinct from what went under the name of foreign policy in Europe was a conviction common to the founders of the republic. As Washington's Farewell Address put it: "Europe has a set of primary interests, which to us have none, or a very remote relation. Hence she must be engaged in frequent controversies, the causes of which are essentially foreign to our concerns. Hence, therefore, it must be unwise in us to implicate ourselves, by artificial ties, in the ordinary vicissitudes of her politics, or the ordinary combinations and collisions of her friendships or enmities." In 1796, European politics and power politics were identical; there was no other power politics but the one engaged in by the princes of Europe. "The toils of European ambition, rivalship, interest, humor or caprice" were the only manifestations, on the international scene, of the struggle for power before the American eye. The retreat from European politics, as proclaimed by Washington, could, therefore, be taken to mean retreat from power politics as such.

The expansion of the United States up to the Spanish-American War seemed to provide conclusive proof both for the distinctiveness and moral superiority of American foreign policy. The settlement of the better part of a continent by the thirteen original states seemed to be an act of civilization rather than of conquest and as such essentially different from, and morally superior to, the imperialistic ventures, wars of conquest, and colonial acquisitions with which the history of other nations is replete. Yet it was not so much political virtue as the contiguity of the sparsely settled object of conquest with the original territory of departure, which put the mark of uniqueness upon American expansion. As was the case with Russia's simultaneous eastward expansion toward the Pacific, the United States, in order to expand, did not need to cross the oceans and fight wars of conquest in strange lands, as did the other great colonizing nations. Furthermore, the utter political, military, and numerical inferiority of the Indian opponent tended to obscure the element of power, which was less obtrusive in, but no more absent from, the continental expansion of the United States than the expansionist movements of other nations. Thus it came about that what was in actuality the fortuitous concatenation of two potent historic accidents could take on, in the popular imagination, the aspects of an ineluctable natural development, a "manifest destiny," thus confirming the uniqueness of American foreign policy in its freedom from those power-political blemishes which degrade the foreign policies of other nations.

Yet American isolation from the European tradition of power politics was more than a political program or a moralistic illusion. As concerns involvement in the political conflicts of which Europe was the center, and the commitments and risks which such involvement of necessity implies, American isolation was an established political fact until the end of the nineteenth century. The actuality of this fact was a result of deliberate choice as well as of the objective conditions of geography. Popular writers might see in the uniqueness of America's geographic position the hand of God which had unalterably prescribed the course of American expansion as well as isolation. But more responsible observers, from Washington on, have been careful to emphasize the conjunction of geographic conditions and of a foreign policy which chooses its ends in the light of geography and which uses geographic conditions to attain those ends. Washington referred to "our detached and distant situation" and asked, "Why forego the advantages of so peculiar a situation?"

From the shores of the North American continent, the citizens of the new world watched the strange spectacle of the struggle for power unfolding on the distant scenes of Europe, Africa, and Asia. Since for the better part of the nineteenth century their foreign policy enabled them to retain the role of spectators, what was actually the result of a passing historic constellation appeared to Americans as a permanent condition, self-chosen as well as naturally ordained. At worst they would continue to watch the game of power politics played by others. At best the time was close at hand when, with democracy established everywhere, the final curtain would fall and the game of power politics would no longer be played.

To aid in the achievement of this goal was conceived to be part of America's mission. Throughout the nation's history, the national destiny of the United States has been understood in anti-militaristic, libertarian terms. Where that national mission finds a nonaggressive, abstentionist formulation, as in the political philosophy of John C. Calhoun, it is conceived as the promotion of domestic liberty. Thus we may "do more to extend liberty by our example over this continent and the world generally, than would be done by a thousand victories." When the United States, in the wake of the Spanish-American War, seemed to desert this anti-imperialist and democratic ideal, William Graham Sumner restated its essence: "Expansion and imperialism are a grand onslaught on de-

mocracy . . . expansion and imperialism are at war with the best traditions, principles, and interests of the American people."   Comparing
the tendencies of European power politics with the ideals of the American
tradition, Sumner thought with Washington that they were incompatible.
Yet, as a prophet of things to come, he saw that with the conclusion of
the Spanish-American War America was irrevocably committed to the
same course which was engulfing Europe in revolution and war.

To understand the American mission in such selfless, humanitarian terms was the easier as the United States—in contrast to the
other great powers—was generally not interested, at least outside the
Western Hemisphere, in a particular advantage to be defined in terms
of power or of territorial gain.   Its national interest was exhausted by
the preservation of its predominance in the Western Hemisphere and
of the balance of power in Europe and Asia.   And even this interest in
general stability rather than special advantage was, as we know, not
always recognized for what it was.

Yet while the foreign policy of the United States was forced, by
circumstance if not by choice, to employ the methods, to shoulder
the commitments, to seek the objectives, and to run the risks, from
which it had thought to be permanently exempt, American political
thought continued to uphold that exemption at least as an ideal—an
ideal which was but temporarily beyond the reach of the American
people, because of the wickedness and stupidity either of American or,
preferably, of foreign statesmen.   In one sense, this ideal of a free,
peaceful, and prosperous world, from which popular government had
banished power politics forever, was a natural outgrowth of the
American experience.   In another sense, this ideal expressed in a particularly eloquent and consistent fashion the general philosophy which
during the better part of the nineteenth century dominated the Western
world.   This philosophy contains two basic propositions: that the
struggle for power on the international scene is a mere accident of
history, naturally associated with non-democratic government and,
hence, destined to disappear with the triumph of democracy throughout
the world; and that, in consequence, conflicts between democratic and
non-democratic nations must be conceived not as struggles for mutual
advantage in terms of power but primarily as a contest between good
and evil, which can only end with the complete triumph of good and with
evil being wiped off the face of the earth.

The nineteenth century developed this philosophy of international
relations from its experience of domestic politics.   The distinctive
characteristic of this experience was the domination of the middle
classes by the aristocracy.   By identifying this domination with political

domination of any kind, the political philosophy of the nineteenth century came to identify the opposition to aristocratic politics with hostility to any kind of politics. After the defeat of aristocratic government, the middle classes developed a system of indirect domination. They replaced the traditional division into the governing and governed classes and the military method of open violence, characteristic of aristocratic rule, with the invisible chains of economic dependence. This economic system operated through a network of seemingly equalitarian legal rules which concealed the very existence of power relations. The nineteenth century was unable to see the political nature of these legalized relations. They seemed to be essentially different from what had gone, so far, under the name of politics. Therefore, politics in its aristocratic, that is, open and violent form, was identified with politics as such. The struggle, then, for political power—in domestic as well as in international affairs—appeared to be only an historic accident, coincident with autocratic government and bound to disappear with the disappearance of autocratic government.

It is easy to see how this general climate of opinion, prevailing in the Western world, nourished similar tendencies in the American mind, grown from the specific experiences of American history. Thus it is not an accident that nowhere in the Western world was there such depth of conviction and tenacity in support of the belief that involvement in power politics is not inevitable but only a historic accident, and that nations have a choice between power politics and another kind of foreign policy conforming to moral principles and not tainted by the desire for power. Nor is it by accident that this philosophy of foreign policy found its most dedicated and eloquent spokesman in the American President, Woodrow Wilson.

The illusion that a nation can escape, if it only wants to, from power politics into a realm where action is guided by moral principles rather than by considerations of power, not only is deeply rooted in the American mind; it also took more than a century for this illusion to crowd out the older notion that international politics is an unending struggle for power in which the interests of individual nations must necessarily be defined in terms of power. Out of the struggle between these two opposing conceptions three types of American statesmen emerge: the realist, thinking in terms of power and represented by Alexander Hamilton; the ideological, acting in terms of power, thinking in terms of moral principles, and represented by Thomas Jefferson and John Quincy Adams; the moralist, thinking and acting in terms of moral principles and represented by Woodrow Wilson. To these three types, three periods of American foreign policy roughly correspond: the first covering the first decade of the history of the United States as an independent nation, the second covering the nineteenth century to the Spanish-American War, the third covering the half century after that war.   That this division of the history of American foreign policy refers only to prevailing tendencies and does by no means preclude the operation side by side of different tendencies in the same period, will become obvious in the discussion.

It illustrates both the depth of the moralist illusion and the original strength of the opposition to it that the issue between these two opposing conceptions of foreign policy was joined at the very beginning of the history of the United States, decided in favor of the realist position, and formulated with unsurpassed simplicity and penetration by Alexander Hamilton.   The memorable occasion was Washington's proclamation of neutrality in the War of the First Coalition against revolutionary France.

In 1792, the War of the First Coalition had ranged Austria, Prussia, Sardinia, Great Britain, and the United Netherlands against revolutionary France, which was tied to the United States by a treaty of alliance. On April 22, 1793, Washington issued a proclamation of neutrality, and it was in defense of that proclamation that Hamilton wrote the "Pacificus" and "Americanus" articles.   Among the arguments directed against the proclamation were three derived from moral principles. Faithfulness to treaty obligations, gratitude toward a country which had lent its assistance to the colonies in their struggle for independence, and the affinity of republican institutions were cited to prove that the United States must side with France.   Against these moral principles, Hamilton invoked the national interest of the United States:

> There would be no proportion between the mischiefs and perils to which the United States would expose themselves, by embarking in the war, and the benefit which the nature of their stipulation aims at securing to France, or that which it would be in their power actually to render her by becoming a party.
>
> This disproportion would be a valid reason for not executing the guaranty. All contracts are to receive a reasonable construction. Self-preservation is the first duty of a nation; and though in the performance of stipulations relating to war, good faith requires that its ordinary hazards should be fairly met, because they are directly contemplated by such stipulations, yet it does not require that extraordinary and extreme hazards should be run. . . .
>
> The basis of gratitude is a benefit received or intended, which there was no right to claim, originating in a regard to the interest or advantage of the party on whom the benefit is, or is meant to be, conferred.   If a service is rendered from views relative to the immediate interest of the party who performs it, and is productive of reciprocal advantages, there seems scarcely,

in such a case, to be an adequate basis for a sentiment like that of gratitude. . . . It may be affirmed as a general principle, that the predominant motive of good offices from one nation to another, is the interest or advantage of the nation which performs them.

Indeed, the rule of morality in this respect is not precisely the same between nations as between individuals. The duty of making its own welfare the guide of its actions, is much stronger upon the former than upon the latter; in proportion to the greater magnitude and importance of national compared with individual happiness, and to the greater permanency of the effects of national than of individual conduct. Existing millions, and for the most part future generations, are concerned in the present measures of a government; while the consequences of the private actions of an individual ordinarily terminate with himself, or are circumscribed within a narrow compass.

Whence it follows that an individual may, on numerous occasions, meritoriously indulge the emotions of generosity and benevolence, not only without an eye to, but even at the expense of, his own interest. But a government can rarely, if at all, be justifiable in pursuing a similar course; and, if it does so, ought to confine itself within much stricter bounds. . . . Good offices which are indifferent to the interest of a nation performing them, or which are compensated by the existence or expectation of some reasonable equivalent, or which produce an essential good to the nation to which they are rendered, without real detriment to the affairs of the benefactors, prescribe perhaps the limits of national generosity or benevolence. . . .

But we are sometimes told, by way of answer, that the cause of France is the cause of liberty; and that we are bound to assist the nation on the score of their being engaged in the defence of that cause. . . .

The obligation to assist the cause of liberty must be deduced from the merits of that cause and from the interest we have in its support.

· · · · ·

An examination into the question how far *regard to the cause of Liberty* ought to induce the United States to take part with France in the present war, is rendered necessary by the efforts which are making [*sic*] to establish an opinion that it ought to have that effect. In order to a right judgment on the point, it is requisite to consider the question under two aspects.

I. Whether the cause of France be truly the cause of Liberty, pursued with justice and humanity, and in a manner likely to crown it with honorable success.

II. Whether the degree of service we could render, by participating in the conflict, was likely to compensate, by its utility to the cause, the evils which would probably flow from it to ourselves.

If either of these questions can be answered in the negative, it will result, that the consideration which has been stated ought not to embark us in the war. . . .

The certain evils of our joining France in the war, are sufficient dissuasives from so intemperate a measure. The possible ones are of a nature to call for all our caution, all our prudence.

To defend its own rights, to vindicate its own honor, there are occasions when a nation ought to hazard even its existence. Should such an occasion occur, I trust those who are most averse to commit the peace of the country, will not be the last to face the danger, nor the first to turn their backs upon it.

But let us at least have the consolation of not having rashly courted misfortune. Let us have to act under the animating reflection of being engaged in repelling wrongs, which we neither sought nor merited; in vindicating our rights invaded without provocation; in defending our honor, violated without cause. Let us not have to reproach ourselves with having voluntarily bartered blessings for calamities.

But we are told that our own liberty is at stake upon the event of the war against France—that if she falls, we shall be the next victim. The combined powers, it is said, will never forgive in us the origination of those principles which were the germs of the French Revolution. They will endeavor to eradicate them from the world.

If this suggestion were ever so well founded, it would perhaps be a sufficient answer to it to say, that our interference is not likely to alter the case; that it would only serve prematurely to exhaust our strength.

But other answers more conclusive present themselves.

The war against France requires, on the part of her enemies, efforts unusually violent. They are obliged to strain every nerve, to exert every resource. However it may terminate, they must find themselves spent in an extreme degree; a situation not very favorable to the undertaking anew, and even to Europe combined, an immense enterprise.

To subvert by force republican liberty in this country, nothing short of entire conquest would suffice. This conquest, with our present increased population, greatly distant as we are from Europe, would either be impracticable, or would demand such exertions, as following immediately upon those which will have been requisite to the subversion of the French Revolution, would be absolutely ruinous to the undertakers. . . .

There are two great errors in our reasoning upon this subject. One, that the combined powers will certainly attribute to us the same principles, which they deem so exceptionable in France; the other, that our principles are in fact the same.

If left to themselves, they will all, except one, naturally see in us a people who originally resorted to a revolution in government, as a refuge from encroachments on rights and privileges *antecedently* enjoyed, not as a people who from choice sought a radical and entire change in the established government, in pursuit of new privileges and rights carried to an extreme, irreconcilable perhaps with any form of regular government. They will see in us a people who have a due respect for property and personal security; who, in the midst of our revolution, abstained with exemplary moderation from everything violent or sanguinary, instituting governments adequate to the protection of persons and property; who, since the completion of our revolution, have in a very short period, from mere reasoning and reflection, without tumult or bloodshed, adopted a form of general government calculated, as well as the nature of things would permit, to remedy antecedent defects, to give strength and security to the nation, to rest the foundations of liberty on the basis of justice, order and law; who have at all times been content to govern themselves without intermeddling with the affairs or governments of other nations; in fine, they will see in us sincere republicans, but decided enemies to licentiousness and anarchy; sincere republicans, but decided friends to the freedom of opinion, to the order and tranquillity of all mankind. They will not see in us a people whose best passions have been misled, and whose best qualities have been perverted from their true direction by headlong, fanatical, or designing leaders, to the perpetration of acts from which humanity shrinks, to the commission of outrages over which the eye of reason weeps, to the profession and practice of principles which tend to shake the foundations of morality, to dissolve the social bands, to disturb the peace of mankind, to substitute confusion to order, anarchy to government. . . .

It is therefore matter of real regret, that there should be an effort on our part to level the distinctions which discriminate our case from that of France, to confound the two cases in the view of foreign powers, and to pervert or hazard our own principles by persuading ourselves of a similitude which does not exist. . . .

But let us not corrupt ourselves by false comparisons or glosses, nor shut our eyes to the true nature of transactions which ought to grieve and warn us, nor rashly mingle our destiny in the consequences of the errors and extravagances of another nation.

Must a nation subordinate its security, its happiness, nay, its very existence to the respect for treaty obligations, to the sentiment of gratitude, to sympathy with a kindred political system? This was the question which Hamilton proposed to answer, and his answer was an unequivocal "no." Hamilton unswervingly applied one standard to the issues raised by the opposition to Washington's proclamation of neutrality: the national interest of the United States. He put the legalistic and moralistic arguments of the opposition, represented by Madison under the pseudonym "Helvidius," into the context of the concrete power situation in which the United States found itself on the international scene and asked: If the United States were to join France against virtually all of Europe, what risks would the United States run, what advantages could it expect, what good could it do for its ally?

Considerations such as these, recognized for what they are, have guided American foreign policy but for a short period, that is, as long as the Federalists were in power. *The Federalist* and Washington's

Farewell Address are their classic expression.   Yet these considerations, not recognized for what they are, sometimes even rejected, have determined the great objectives of American foreign policy to this day. During the century following their brief flowering, they have by and large continued to influence policies as well, under the cover, as it were, of those moral principles with which from Jefferson onward American statesmen have liked to justify their moves on the international scene. Thus this second period witnessed a discrepancy between political thought and political action, yet a coincidence in the intended results of both.   What was said of Gladstone could also have been said of Jefferson, John Quincy Adams, Theodore Roosevelt, the war policies of Wilson and Franklin D. Roosevelt: what the moral law demanded was by a felicitous coincidence always identical with what the national interest seemed to require.   Political thought and political action moved on different planes, which, however, were so inclined as to merge in the end.

John Quincy Adams is the classic example of the political moralist in thought and word who cannot help being a political realist in action. Yet even in Jefferson, whose dedication to abstract morality was much stronger and whose realist touch in foreign affairs was much less sure, the moral pretense yielded often, especially in private utterance, to the impact of the national interest upon native good sense.

Thus during the concluding decade of the Napoleonic Wars Jefferson's thought on international affairs was a reflection of the ever-changing distribution of power in the world rather than of immutable moral principles.   In 1806, he favored "an English ascendancy on the ocean" as being "safer for us than that of France."   In 1807, he was by the logic of events forced to admit:

I never expected to be under the necessity of wishing success to Bonaparte. But the English being equally tyrannical at sea as he is on land, & that tyranny bearing on us in every point of either honor or interest, I say, "down with England" and as for what Bonaparte is then to do to us, let us trust to the chapter of accidents, I cannot, with the Anglo-men, prefer a certain present evil to a future hypothetical one.

However, in 1812, when Napoleon was at the pinnacle of his power, Jefferson hoped for the restoration of the balance of power.   Speaking of England, he said that:

It is for the general interest that she should be a sensible and independent weight in the scale of nations, and be able to contribute, when a favorable moment presents itself, to reduce under the same order, her great rival in flagitiousness. We especially ought to pray that the powers of Europe may be so poised and counterpoised among themselves, that their own security may require the presence of all their forces at home, leaving the other quarters of the globe in undisturbed tranquility.

In 1814, again compelled by the logic of events, he came clearly out against Napoleon and in favor of a balance of power which would leave the power of Napoleon and of England limited, but intact:

Surely none of us wish to see Bonaparte conquer Russia, and lay thus at his feet the whole continent of Europe. This done, England would be but a breakfast; and, although I am free from the visionary fears which the votaries of England have effected to entertain, because I believe he cannot effect the conquest of Europe; yet put all Europe into his hands, and he might spare such a force to be sent in British ships, as I would as leave not have to encounter, when I see how much trouble a handful of British soldiers in Canada has given us. No. It cannot be to our interest that all Europe should be reduced to a single monarchy. The true line of interest for us, is, that Bonaparte should be able to effect the complete exclusion of England from the whole continent of Europe, in order, as the same letter said, "by this peaceable engine of constraint, to make her renounce her views of dominion over the ocean, of permitting no other nation to navigate it but with her license, and on tribute to her, and her aggressions on the persons of our citizens who may choose to exercise their right of passing over that element." And this would be effected by Bonaparte's succeeding so far as to close the Baltic against her. This success I wished him the last year, this I wish him this year; but were he again advanced to Moscow, I should again wish him such disasters as would prevent his reaching Petersburg. And were the consequences even to be the longer continuance of our war, I would rather meet them than see the whole force of Europe wielded by a single hand.

Similarly, in 1815, Jefferson wrote:

For my part, I wish that all nations may recover and retain their independence; that those which are overgrown may not advance beyond safe measures of power, that a salutary balance may be ever maintained among nations, and that our peace, commerce, and friendship, may be sought and cultivated by all.

It was only when, after 1815, the danger to the balance of power seemed to have passed that Jefferson allowed himself again to indulge in the cultivation of moral principles divorced from the political exigencies of the hour.

From this tendency to which Jefferson only too readily yielded, John Quincy Adams was well-nigh immune. We are here in the presence of a statesman who had been reared in the realist tradition of the first period of American foreign policy, who had done the better part of his work of statecraft in an atmosphere saturated with Jeffersonian principles, and who had achieved the merger of these two elements of his experience into an harmonious whole.   Between John Quincy Adams' moral principles and the traditional interest of the United States there was hardly ever a conflict.   The moral principles were nothing but the political interests formulated in moral terms, and vice versa.   They fit the interests as a glove fits the hand.   Adams' great contributions to the tradition of American foreign policy, freedom of the seas, the Monroe Doctrine, and Manifest Destiny, are witness to this achievement.

The legal and moral principle of the freedom of the seas was in the hands of Adams a weapon, as it had been two centuries earlier in the hands of Grotius wielded on behalf of the Low Countries, through which an inferior naval power endeavored to safeguard its independence against Great Britain, the mistress of the seas.   The Monroe Doctrine's moral postulates of anti-imperialism and mutual non-intervention were the negative conditions for the safety and enduring greatness of the United States.   Their fulfillment vouchsafed the isolation of the United States from the power struggles of Europe and, through it, the continuing predominance of the United States in the Western Hemisphere.   Manifest Destiny was the moral justification as well as the moral incentive for the westward expansion of the United States, the peculiar American way—foreordained by the objective conditions of American existence— of founding an empire, the "American Empire," as one of the contemporary opponents of Adams' policies put it.

Jefferson and John Quincy Adams stand at the beginning of the second period of American thought on foreign policy, both its most eminent representatives and the heirs of a realist tradition which continued to mould political action, while it had largely ceased to influence political thought.   At the beginning of the third period, McKinley leads the United States, as a great world power, beyond the confines of the Western Hemisphere, ignorant of the bearing of this step upon the national interest and guided by moral principles which are completely divorced from the national interest.   When at the end of the Spanish-American War the status of the Philippines had to be determined, McKinley expected and found no guidance in the traditional national interests of the United States.   According to his own testimony, he knelt beside his bed in prayer, and in the wee hours of the morning he heard the voice of God telling him—as was to be expected—to annex the Philippines.

This period initiated by McKinley, in which moral principles no longer justify the enduring national interest as in the second, but replace it as a guide for action, finds its fulfillment in the political thought of

Woodrow Wilson. Wilson's thought not only disregards the national interest, but is explicitly opposed to it on moral grounds. "It is a very perilous thing," he said in his address at Mobile on October 27, 1913,

to determine the foreign policy of a nation in the terms of material interest. It not only is unfair to those with whom you are dealing, but it is degrading as regards your own actions. . . . We dare not turn from the principle that morality and not expediency is the thing that must guide us, and that we will never condone iniquity because it is most convenient to do so.

Wilson's war-time speeches are but an elaboration of this philosophy. An excerpt from his address of September 27, 1918, opening the campaign for the Fourth Liberty Loan, will suffice to show the continuity of that philosophy:

It is of capital importance that we should also be explicitly agreed that no peace shall be obtained by any kind of compromise or abatement of the principles we have avowed as the principles for which we are fighting. . . .

First, the impartial justice meted out must involve no discrimination between those to whom we wish to be just and those to whom we do not wish to be just. It must be a justice that plays no favorites and knows no standard but the equal rights of the several peoples concerned;

Second, no special or separate interest of any single nation or any group of nations can be made the basis of any part of the settlement which is not consistent with the common interest of all;

Third, there can be no leagues or alliances or special covenants and understandings within the general and common family of the League of Nations;

Fourth, and more specifically, there can be no special, selfish economic combinations within the League and no employment of any form of economic boycott or exclusion except as the power of economic penalty by exclusion from the markets of the world may be vested in the League of Nations itself as a means of discipline and control;

Fifth, all international agreements and treaties of every kind must be made known in their entirety to the rest of the world.

Special alliances and economic rivalries and hostilities have been the prolific source in the modern world of the plans and passions that produce war. It would be an insincere as well as insecure peace that did not exclude them in definite and binding terms. . . .

National purposes have fallen more and more into the background and the common purpose of enlightened mankind has taken their place. The counsels of plain men have become on all hands more simple and straightforward and more unified than the counsels of sophisticated men of affairs, who still retain the impression that they are playing a game of power and playing for high stakes. That is why I have said that this is a peoples' war, not a statesmen's. Statesmen must follow the clarified common thought or be broken.

Yet in his political actions, especially under the pressure of the First World War, Wilson could no more than Jefferson before him discount completely the national interest of the United States. Wilson's case, however, was different from Jefferson's in two respects. For one, Wilson was never able, even when the national interest of the United States was directly menaced, to conceive of the danger in other than moral terms. It was only the objective force of the national interest, which no rational man could escape, that imposed upon him as the object of his moral indignation the source of America's mortal danger. Thus in 1917 Wilson led the United States into war against Germany for the same reasons, only half-known to himself, for which Jefferson had wished and worked alternately for the victory of England and of France. Germany threatened the balance of power in Europe, and it was in order to remove that threat—and not to make the world safe for democracy—that the United States put its weight into the Allies' scale. Wilson pursued the right policy, but he pursued it for the wrong reasons.

Not only did the crusading fervor of moral reformation obliterate the awareness of the United States' traditional interest in the maintenance of the European balance of power, to be accomplished through the defeat of Germany. Wilson's moral fervor also had politically disastrous effects, for which there is no precedent in the history of the United States. Wilson's moral objective required the destruction of the Kaiser's autocracy, and this happened also to be required by the political interests of the United States. The political interests of the United States required, beyond this immediate objective of total victory, the restoration of the European balance of power, traditional guarantor of American security. Yet it was in indignation at the moral deficiencies of that very balance of power, "forever discredited," as he thought, that Wilson had asked the American people to take up arms against the Central Powers! Once military victory had put an end to the immediate threat to American security, the very logic of his moral position—let us remember that consistency is the moralist's supreme virtue—drove him toward substituting for the concrete national interest of the United States the general postulate of a brave new world where the national interest of the United States, as that of all other nations, would disappear in a community of interests comprising mankind.

Consequently, Wilson considered it to be the purpose of victory not to restore a new, viable balance of power, but to make an end to it once and forever. "You know," he told the English people at Manchester on December 30, 1918,

that the United States has always felt from the very beginning of her history that she must keep herself separate from any kind of connection with European politics, and I want to say very frankly to you that she is not now interested in European politics. But she is interested in the partnership of right between America and Europe. If the future had nothing for us but a new attempt to keep the world at a right poise by a balance of power, the United States would take no interest, because she will join no combination of power which is not the combination of all of us. She is not interested merely in the peace of Europe, but in the peace of the world.

Faced with the national interests of the great allied powers, Wilson had nothing to oppose or support them with but his moral principles, with the result that the neglect of the American national interest was not compensated for by the triumph of political morality. In the end Wilson had to consent to a series of uneasy compromises which were a betrayal of his moral principles—for principles can, by their very nature, not be made the object of compromise—and which satisfied nobody's national aspirations. These compromises had no relation at all to the traditional American national interest in a viable European balance of power. Thus Wilson returned from Versailles a compromised idealist, an empty-handed statesman, a discredited ally. In that triple failure lies the tragedy not only of Wilson, a great yet misguided man, but of Wilsonianism as a political doctrine as well.

Yet Wilson returned to the United States, unaware of his failure. He offered the American people what he had offered the allied nations at Paris: moral principles divorced from political reality. "The day we have left behind us," he proclaimed at Los Angeles on September 20, 1919,

was a day of balances of power. It was a day of "every nation take care of itself or make a partnership with some other nation or group of nations to hold the peace of the world steady or to dominate the weaker portions of the world." Those were the days of alliances. This project of the League of Nations is a great process of disentanglement.

While before Paris and Versailles these moral principles rang true with the promise of a new and better world, they now must have sounded to many rather hollow and platitudinous. Yet what is significant for the course which American foreign policy was to take in the interwar years is not so much that the American people rejected Wilsonianism, but that they rejected it by ratifying the denial of the American tradition of foreign policy which was implicit in the political thought of Wilson.

We are here indeed dealing with a tragedy not of one man, but of a political doctrine and, as far as the United States is concerned, of a political tradition.   The isolationism of the interwar period could delude itself into believing that it was but the restorer of the early realist tradition of American foreign policy.   Did it not, like that tradition, proclaim the self-sufficiency of the United States within the Western Hemisphere? Did it not, like that tradition, refuse to become involved in the rivalries of European nations?   The isolationists of the twenties and thirties did not see what was the very essence of the policies of the Founding Fathers—that both the isolated and the preponderant position of the United States in the Western Hemisphere was not a fact of nature, and that the freedom from entanglements in European conflicts was not the result of mere abstention on the part of the United States.   Both benefits were the result of political conditions outside the Western Hemisphere and of policies carefully contrived and purposefully executed in their support.   For the realists of the first period, isolation was an objective of policy, which had to be striven for to be attained.   For the isolationists of the interwar period, isolation was, as it were, a natural state, which only needed to be left undisturbed in order to continue forever.   Conceived in such terms, it was the very negation of foreign policy.

Isolationism, then, is in its way as oblivious to political reality as is Wilsonianism—the internationalist challenge, to which it had thought to have found the American answer.   In consequence, they are both strangers not only to the first, realist phase of American foreign policy, but to its whole tradition.   Both refused to face political reality either in realistic or ideological terms.   They refused to face it at all   Thus isolationism and Wilsonianism have more in common than their historic enmity would lead one to suspect.   In a profound sense they are brothers under the skin.   Both are one in maintaining that the United States has no interest in any particular political and military constellation outside the Western Hemisphere.   While isolationism stops here, Wilsonianism asserts that the American national interest is nowhere in particular but everywhere, being identical with the interests of mankind itself.   The political awareness of both refuses to concern itself with the concrete issues with regard to which the national interest must be asserted.   Isolationism stops short of them, Wilsonianism soars beyond them.   Both have but a negative relation to the national interest of the United States outside the Western Hemisphere.   They are unaware of its very existence.   This being so, both substitute abstract moral principles for the guidance of the national interest, derived from the actual conditions of American existence.   Wilsonianism applies the illusory expectations of liberal reform to the whole world, isolationism empties the realist political principle of isolationism of all concrete political content and transforms it into the unattainable parochial ideal of automatic separation.

In view of this inner affinity between isolationism and Wilsonianism, it is not surprising that the great debate of the twenties and thirties between internationalism and isolationism was carried on primarily in moral terms. Was there a moral obligation for the United States to make its contribution to world peace by joining the League of Nations and the World Court? Was it morally incumbent upon the United States, as a democracy, to oppose Fascism in Europe and to uphold international law in Asia? Such were the questions which were raised in that debate and the answers depended upon the moral position taken. The question which was central to the national interest of the United States, that of the balance of power in Europe and Asia, was hardly ever faced squarely, and when it was, it was dismissed on moral grounds. Mr. Cordell Hull, Secretary of State of the United States from 1933-1944 and one of the most respected spokesmen of internationalism, summarizes in his *Memoirs* his attitude toward this central problem of American foreign policy in these terms:

I was not, and am not, a believer in the idea of balance of power or spheres of influence as a means of keeping the peace. During the First World War I had made an intensive study of the system of spheres of influence and balance of power, and I was grounded to the taproots in their iniquitous consequences. The conclusions I then formed in total opposition to this system stayed with me.

When internationalism triumphed in the late thirties, it did so in the moral terms of Wilsonianism. That in this instance the moral postulates which inspired the administration of Franklin D. Roosevelt happened to coincide with the exigencies of the American national interest was again, as in the case of Jefferson and of the Wilson of 1917, due to the impact of a national emergency upon innate common sense and to the strength of a national tradition which holds in its spell the actions even of those who deny its validity in words. However, as soon as the minds of the American leaders were freed from the inescapable pressures of a primarily military nature and turned toward the political problems of the war and its aftermath, they thought and acted again as Wilson had acted under similar circumstances. That is to say, they thought and acted in moral terms, divorced from the political conditions of America's existence.

The practical results of this philosophy of international affairs, as applied to the political war and post-war problems, were, then, bound to be quite similar to those which had made the allied victory in the First World War politically meaningless. Conceived as it was as a "crusade"—to borrow from the title of General Eisenhower's book—against the evil incarnate in the Axis Powers, the purpose of the Second World War could only be the destruction of that evil, transacted through the instrumentality of "unconditional surrender." Since the threat to the Western world emanating from the Axis was conceived primarily in moral terms, it was easy to imagine that all conceivable danger was concentrated in that historic constellation of hostile powers and that with its destruction political evil itself would disappear from the world. Beyond "unconditional surrender" there was, then, a brave new world after the model of Wilson's, which would liquidate the heritage of the defeated evil, not "peace-loving," nations and would establish an order of things where war, aggressiveness, and the struggle for power itself were to be no more. Thus Mr. Cordell Hull could declare on his return in 1943 from the Moscow Conference that the new international organization would mean the end of power politics and usher in a new era of international collaboration. Three years later, Mr. Philip Noel-Baker, then British Minister of State, echoed Mr. Hull by stating in the House of Commons that the British Government was "determined to use the institutions of the United Nations to kill power politics, in order that by the methods of democracy, the will of the people shall prevail."

With this philosophy dominant in the West—Mr. Churchill provides almost the sole, however ineffective, exception—the strategy of the war and of the peace to follow could not help being oblivious to those considerations of the national interest which the great statesmen of the West, from Hamilton through Castlereagh, Canning and John Quincy Adams to Disraeli and Salisbury, had brought to bear upon the international problems of their day. War was no longer regarded as a means to a political end. The only end the war was to serve was total victory, which is another way of saying that the war became an end in itself. Hence, it became irrelevant how the war was won politically, as long as it was won speedily, cheaply, and totally. The thought that the war might be waged in view of a new balance of power to be established after the war, occurred in the West only to Winston Churchill —and, of course, to Joseph Stalin. The national interest of the Western nations was, then, satisfied insofar as it required the destruction of the threat to the balance of power emanating from Germany and Japan; for insofar, the moral purposes of the war happened to coincide with the national interest. However, the national interest of the Western nations was jeopardized insofar as their security required the creation of a new viable balance of power after the war.

How could statesmen who boasted that they were not "believers in the idea of balance of power"—like a scientist not believing in the law of gravity—and who were out "to kill power politics," understand the very idea of the national interest which demanded above all protection from the power of others? Thus it was with deeply and sincerely felt moral indignation that the Western world, expecting a brave new world without power politics, found itself confronted with a new and more formidable threat to its security as soon as the old one had been subdued. There was good reason for moral indignation, however misdirected this one was. That a new balance of power will rise out of the ruins of an old one and that nations with political sense will avail themselves of the opportunity to improve their position within it, is a law of politics for whose validity nobody is to blame. Yet blameworthy are those who in their moralistic disdain for the laws of politics endanger the interests of the nations which are in their care.

The history of American foreign policy since the end of the Second World War is the story of the encounter of the American mind with a new political world. That mind was weakened in its understanding of foreign policy by half a century of ever more complete intoxication with moral abstractions. Even a mind less weakened would have found it hard to face with adequate understanding and successful action the unprecedented novelty and magnitude of the new political world. American foreign policy in that period presents itself as a slow, painful, and incomplete process of emancipation from deeply ingrained error and of rediscovery of long-forgotten truths.

The fundamental error which has thwarted American foreign policy in thought and action is the antithesis of national interest and moral principles. The equation of political moralism with morality and of political realism with immorality is itself untenable. The choice is not between moral principles and the national interest, devoid of moral dignity, but between one set of moral principles, divorced from political reality, and another set of moral principles, derived from political reality. The basic fact of international politics is the absence of a society able to protect the existence, and to promote the interests, of the individual nations. For the individual nations to take care of their own national interests is, then, a political necessity. There can be no moral duty to neglect them; for as the international society is at present constituted, the consistent neglect of the national interest can only lead to national suicide. Yet it can be shown that there exists even a positive moral duty for the individual nation to take care of its national interests.

Self-preservation for the individual as well as for societies is not only a biological and psychological necessity, but in the absence of an overriding moral obligation a moral duty as well.   In the absence of an integrated international society, in particular, the attainment of a modicum of order and the realization of a minimum of moral values are predicated upon the existence of national communities capable of preserving order and realizing moral values within the limits of their power.   It is obvious that such a state of affairs falls far short of that order and realized morality to which we are accustomed in national societies.   The only relevant question is, however, what the practical alternative is to these imperfections of an international society based upon the national interests of its component parts.   The attainable alternative is not a higher morality realized through the application of universal moral principles, but moral deterioration through either political failure or the fanaticism of political crusades.   The juxtaposition of the morality of political moralism and the immorality of the national interest is mistaken.   It operates with a false concept of morality, developed by national societies but unsuited to the conditions of international society.   In the process of its realization, it is bound to destroy the very moral values which it is its purpose to promote.   Hence, the antithesis between moral principles and the national interest is not only intellectually mistaken but also morally pernicious.   A foreign policy derived from the national interest is in fact morally superior to a foreign policy inspired by universal moral principles.   Albert Sorel, the Anglophobe historian of the French Revolution, well summarized the real antithesis when he said in grudging admiration of Castlereagh:

He piqued himself on principles to which he held with an unshakable constancy, which in actual affairs could not be distinguished from obstinacy; but these principles were in no degree abstract or speculative, but were all embraced in one alone, the supremacy of English interests; they all proceeded from this high reason of state.

May as much be said by a future historian of the American foreign policy of our time!

14. An Attack On Realism — The Balance of Power versus the Coordinate State *

This article is perhaps the most powerful rejoinder to the realistic publications of such men as George F. Kennan and Hans J. Morgenthau. Dr. Tannenbaum describes the realists as "those who would persuade our people to abandon their humanitarian and pacific traditions and frankly adopt the doctrine of power politics and of the balance of power as the basis of their foreign policy." He argues that the realist interpretation is based upon an unscientific analysis of international politics. Statesmen who have played balance-of-power politics, he says, have led their countries into war and eventual ruin. Our policies, on the other hand, were based, and continue to be based, upon our belief in "human freedom, in the equality of men, and in the dignity and independence of nations."

A great debate on the character and purpose of American foreign policy has been precipitated by those who would persuade our people to abandon their humanitarian and pacific traditions and frankly adopt the doctrine of power politics and of the balance of power as the basis of their foreign policy. This doctrine is confessedly, nay gleefully, amoral. It prides itself upon being realistic and takes Machiavelli as its great teacher. It is contemptuous of the simple beliefs of honest men, jeers at the sentimentalism of those who believe that men may strive for peace among nations, and looks upon democracy as a hindrance to skilled diplomacy. It looks with a certain derisive superiority upon the great leaders of this nation from Jefferson and John Quincy Adams to Woodrow Wilson and Franklin Delano Roosevelt and describes them as moralistic and sentimental, and suggests that our models ought to be Richelieu, Clemenceau and Bismarck. Its adherents believe that international wars instead of being made by men and supported by institutions humanly contrived have their origin in the nature of man himself and are inevitable. The best they foresee is an armed balance of power—until the next war—and after that, more skilled diplomacy toward the achievement of the same inevitable end, a new balance of power ending in a new war.

This dreadful doctrine has now won wide acceptance by teachers and scholars in the field of international relations and has, in fact, become the leading theme in such circles in many of the largest uni-

* Frank Tannenbaum, *Political Science Quarterly,* Vol. LXVII, June, 1952, pp. 173-197. The author is Professor of History, Columbia University.

versities. It has become the *science* of international relations—and who would quarrel with science especially when it comes packaged in good clear English and from high sources? But it is not science. It is make-believe. Its scientific basis is false and spurious. It is, in fact, only poor logic based upon false premises, and its claim to be a science is only a bit of unholy conceit. For what we are dealing with is not a tentative hypothesis put forth by humble men as a possible clue for other students to analyze, criticize, modify and reject—or partially accept. No, we are offered a doctrine for national behavior which runs counter to the very essence of the American tradition and are told to accept it in the name of national interest because this science has discovered what that interest is.

This debate is of greater import to the future of the United States than the long running argument between the "interventionists" and the "isolationists." Both of these accepted the basic American belief in international good will, in the doctrine of friendship among nations, in the right of the little nation to abide in security and without fear, in the possibility of finding a way to peace among nations, in the sanctity of international treaties, in the authority of international law, and in the hope that the democratic way, by enhancing human dignity and widening human freedom, would ease the burden of conflict among men and nations. The "interventionists" and "isolationists" differed about how best to translate these ideas into formal policy, but they did not, with strikingly few exceptions, repudiate the doctrine by which this nation has lived from its very inception.

Now the advocates of *Realpolitik* would sweep away all of our old beliefs as foolish, sentimental and moralistic. They would have us build our future upon the concept of the balance of power in international relations, throw all morality and law out of the window as a hindrance and nuisance to skilled diplomacy, divide the world between Russia and ourselves, repudiating our past beliefs, as well as our promises, obligations and treaties that bind us to our many allies, and girdle ourselves by a permanent and huge military establishment—for what?—to carry the happy game of skilled diplomacy from one war to the next. Most of this is explicitly stated in the argument. Some of it, though not stated, is implicit, and constitutes a challenge to the democratic process itself. These doctrines, if adopted and implemented, would convert the United States into a centralized military empire, and in due time destroy the basic democratic institutions by which this government has prospered these many years.

This debate is just beginning. A good deal more will be heard of it in the coming years. A fact that so erudite a scholar as Professor

Hans J. Morgenthau, of the University of Chicago, and so subtle a mind as George F. Kennan are the chief proponents of this dreadful doctrine in the United States will add zest to the debate. The appointment of Mr. Kennan as Ambassador to Russia gives his views immediate significance in American foreign policy. But the American people will not take this advice, for they cannot act upon it without ceasing to be both Christian and a democratic people.

This essay is an attempt to state what has always been the American philosophy of international relations. It brings to the surface the beliefs and the ideals upon which this nation was built as a great federal system, and shows how these same commitments have shaped our foreign policy from the beginning.

We want to be clear on what the debate is about. One side believes that it is necessary, even inevitable, that the relations between nations be built upon the principle of the balance of power. The other believes that it is possible and desirable, if man wishes to save himself from destruction, to organize international relations on the basis of the coördinate state. The first derives its conclusions and its law from the modern national state system of Europe, the other from the experience of the federal system of the United States, from the development of the Organization of American States, from the recent adoption of the principle of the coördinate state on which to frame the Commonwealth of Nations and from the federal history of Switzerland. These two different conceptions of the basis of international organization carry with them underlying assumptions of the nature of man, of the possible role of human institutions as well as implicit attitudes toward the democratic process. The international relations of the United States have unconsciously been dominated by the belief that the relations between states can be made to rest only upon the ideal mutuality, the equal right to abide in freedom and the dignity of all nations—great and small.

An international society, built upon the coördinate state, must of necessity behave differently from one resting upon the concept of centralized power. The first makes coöperation both the means and the ends of its policy. It can, in fact, have no other objectives. Its ends are determined by its means. Its objectives in international as in internal affairs can only be coöperation for the resolution of common difficulties, and its means can again only be coöperation. It accepts the doctrine of live and let live as a matter of course, for its own life is conceived of as a process of continuing accommodation within a world of nonviolent friction.

Friction and differences are taken for granted. They are recognized as a persistent phenomenon. There is no effort at an absolute or perfect solution. The meaning of peace is unwittingly redefined to mean, not the absence of serious difficulties or the disappearance of differences of interest, but the daily haggling over issues toward a workable compromise. An international society composed of "equal" members endowed with unequal resources requires the surrender of the "simplistic" notion of a "solution" of "problems." The very idea of "solution," and the concept of "problem" for which a permanent "solution" is to be had, are both felt to be delusive. There are no "problems" and no "solutions" in the complex of political society or in international relations. There are, in fact, no "social sciences" from which these final ends can be derived. And the beginning of wisdom in these matters is the recognition that man abides in a recalcitrant and imperfect universe.

The world is not fully malleable to the hand of man. All of life, all of society, all of international relations is a developing and changing series of forces upon which no stable form can be imposed by any method. The best that man may contrive are means toward a workable compromise so that change may take place without violence. Friction will go on, differences old and new will continually emerge, and no formula the "scientists," politicians and statesmen can devise will freeze the fleeting moment and permanently balk the hidden and contradictory flux that always moves through the world, and must do so as long as man survives on the face of the earth. These contradictory processes are life itself. If they ceased to be, life—personal, social or international—would also cease. The feasible is not a permanent "solution," but a channel for continuing adjustments among contradictory drives.

A substantial amount of balance between the forces of nature is essential to survival, but the balance is never absolute and is always changing. A stable world is best described as one of relative instability. It is in that sense that there are no solutions and no problems, either within the nation or between the nations. But these compromises can be made only between recognized and existing entities. These entities must not only exist, but be recognized as existing, whether they be men, institutions, societies, corporations or nations. The recognition of their existence implies an acknowledgment of a claim upon all other similar beings because they can only survive mutually, and cannot live in absolute isolation. The condition of mutuality is an equal opportunity to survival, which in turn requires the acceptance of the equal dignity of the existing entities mutually interdependent.

This is the meaning of the "coördinate state" in international relations. It implies a position of equal dignity. It has nothing to do with wealth, power, size, population or culture. It has everything to do with the recognition that compromise is a continuing means of nonviolent friction (peace). It has everything to do with the acknowledgement of the unique sense of "historic personality" which each state has of itself as the only basis of a friendly relationship. It is only if all the states continue to have equal dignity among themselves that changes in power and wealth can be absorbed without undue violence. That is the essence of federalism in international relations. The coördinate state relationship makes it possible to accept the inevitable growth of some and the decline of other states without war and without the loss of "face," because the changes are gradual and absorbed through a process of accommodation by all the members who are equal to each other. Federalism embodies these traits and has been illustrated in many ways by the history of the United States.

The essential character of the American system derives from a federal relationship of coördinate states. Our expectancies and demands upon the world are conditioned by that fact. This does not mean that we have not in our relations to the outside world committed grave errors, and on many occasions denied our own beliefs. The traditional twisting of the "British Lion's tail" is but one example of a species of irresponsibility in international relations. Theodore Roosevelt's interference in the arbitration of the Alaska boundary dispute; his, "I took the Panama Canal"; Wilson's intervention in Haiti and Santo Domingo; the Platt Amendment; the arbitrary senatorial action on Japanese migration; the century-long bullying of Mexico; the numerous landings of American marines in Central America; the indifference to the feelings of foreign nations often expressed in Congressional debates; our constant preachments and moralizations; the subordination of our foreign policies to domestic politics; the support of "big business" and American investors in foreign countries, sometimes without due regard to the legitimacy of their claims; the lack of sensitivity to foreign culture and foreign values and, since the Second World War, the conscious but faltering support of colonialism—these are all part of the story of our failure to abide by our own commitments.

However, these variations from our own professed ideas are the side currents at the edge of the broad stream of our foreign policy. The major drift of our relations with the rest of the world have with more or less consistency responded to the basic tradition of the coördinate state. We have, with the exception of the short but more than memorable episode of the Freedmen's Bureau and Reconstruction, never for long deviated from the idea of equal dignity of the state inside our own federal system, and have therefore never long permitted ourselves to act overtly toward other nations as if we were a centralized state, concerned primarily with the security that rests upon military force and military alliances. We have always sought our security either in isolation or in coöperation with other nations of equal dignity.

This conception of the equal dignity of the state is therefore fundamental to our own thinking about the world. Just what do we mean by the equal dignity of the state? This is a crucial question, for it defines the character of our own federal system. More than that, this concept of the equal dignity of the coöperating state not only represents a basis for our own federal system, but lies at the root of the Organization of American States. What is more, it is a similar concept, not uninfluenced by the American experience, which has come to govern the British Commonwealth of Nations. This same basic definition of the equal dignity of the related members has shaped the long-successful Swiss Confederation. We are therefore dealing with a general principle of organization, of which the American federal system is but a type. And this system of international organization stands in the world as a contrast to the alternative idea of the balance of power between states, and to the doctrines of power politics advanced by the schools of *Realpolitik,* of which Professor Hans Morgenthau and Mr. George Kennan are, at the moment, the most widely recognized proponents in the United States.

Under the American Constitution the states are, in fact, equal in their political authority; and this equality is the condition of the survival of the federal system. It is true, of course, that the powers of the central government have greatly expanded in recent years, due largely to the interpretations of the commerce and welfare clauses of the Constitution. But this increase of the powers of the federal government was by consent of the Congress, and affects all of the states equally. It has set no discrimination between one state and another. Furthermore, the states could by a constitutional amendment, were they so minded, recover whatever part of the powers of the federal government has accrued to it in recent years.

In the American federal system, therefore, there can be no member of lesser dignity or lower status. Legally, they are all endowed with the same kind of independence, possessed of like privileges and subject to similar limitations and duties. The differences between the states are measured by size, population, resources and wealth and not by status and privilege. There are within our federal system no high and no low, no great and no lesser, states.

This description of the place of each separate state in the United States can be applied to the position of each nation within the Pan American system. The differences between the United States and the

Pan American system are very great. The first is a nation with a central government, the other is a loose organization resting upon the consent of its members. But each separate entity of either structure in relation to the other members is very much the same.

In the Pan American system (The Organization of American States as it is now called) each nation is legally equal to any other. Every member nation has one vote. There is no veto. There are no privileged nations grouped in a council possessed of powers denied to the other members. The charter of the organization guarantees each nation its territorial integrity, its sovereignty and independence. No nation or group of nations may intervene in any way in the internal or external affairs of any nation in this hemisphere. All international issues that arise between the member states "shall be settled by peaceful procedures," and attack upon one member is an attack upon all the others. No nations may use economic or political pressure to "force the sovereign will" of any other state for the purpose of gaining some advantage to itself. The territory of each member nation is inviolable, and no territorial acquisitions or other privileges gained by force or other coercion are recognized. All members have an equal place on all of the important committees of the organization, and decisions are, in most instances, made by an absolute majority, in a few by a two-thirds vote.

In commenting on the relationship which exists between the nations in this hemisphere, Dr. Alberto Lleras, formerly president of Colombia and now Secretary General of the Organization of American States had this to say:

Those nations have enjoyed, and will continue to enjoy, the inestimable advantage of being neighbors to one of the greatest empires in all history without suffering the fear of imperialism or the threat of violence, basking in an international order based on law which preserves their independence and guarantees their security and sovereignty more fully with each passing day.

After pointing out that equality of voting power, democratic procedure and majority decisions characterize the working methods of the Organization of American States, Dr. Lleras added, "The same fundamental principle that guides the political life of this country [the United States] prevails in the basic rule of the Organization of American States." Clearly enough, the sixty-year-old organization that includes all of the twenty-one nations of this hemisphere has gradually acquired increasing power and prestige and has developed greater unity and identity. The charter itself speaks of the "spiritual unity" of the continent. This achievement was a matter of slow growth. But that it has grown to its present role and future promise is due to the acceptance of the principle that nations may differ in size, population, resources and power, but that they are alike in dignity and status, possessed of equal privileges and bound by equal duties. The Foreign Minister of Guatemala, Dr. Manuel Salich, expressed the basis upon which the Pan American system has survived—the older ideal of the coördinate state: ". . . here . . . geographic, economic and other differences do not count . . . and . . . our voice, which is that of a small country . . . has, thanks to the generosity of the other twenty Republics, the same moral rank as the rest. . . ."

If the ideals of the coördinate state lie at the base of our own federal system and of the Organization of American States as well, they have also come to play the chief role in the development of the British Commonwealth of Nations. It is interesting to note that, at about the period of the American Revolution when James Wilson, Benjamin Franklin, Thomas Jefferson and James Madison were asserting the doctrine that each colony was coördinate within the Crown and legislatively independent of Parliament, some English publicists were advocating similar ideas as a basis for the reconstruction of the British Empire.

Major John Cartwright, in a series of letters addressed to Parliament in 1774, pleaded for a reform of the British imperial system on substantially the same grounds as those urged by the leaders of the American colonists. He believed that the Empire consisted of a group of states "equal in constitutional status," with coördinate legislatures and a common king. The relations between the American colonies and the mother country he said were similar to those between Hanover and Great Britain or between Scotland and England before 1707. He argued that "I would consider the American governments, like that of Ireland, as sister kingdoms, and I would cement a lasting union with them as between the separate branches of one great family." He wanted the colonies "to be free and independent states" with the King to remain sovereign "in like manner" as he is of Great Britain. He wanted them to be individually and collectively protected against every foreign Power and each guaranteed in its independence with respect to the other colonies. He also urged a treaty to establish a perpetual League of Friendshp for mutual security against all other states. This change would be of great advantage to the Empire for then the King would "receive fifteen independent kingdoms in exchange for as many dependent, and *hardly dependent* provinces, and become the father of three million of free and happy subjects, instead of reigning joint tyrant over so many discontented slaves, or losing by revolt so many of his people."

Similar ideas were advanced by Granville Sharp, the famous abolitionist who in 1774 urged in a pamphlet that the permanent recognition of separate legislative power for each colony ought to be adopted because they would then with the mother country "form *one vast Empire,* which will never be divided" because the maintenance of the British Constitution inviolate in all the colonies would provide "a sufficient band of union" between the imperial Crown of Great Britain and the overseas colonies.

Another proponent of similar views was the widely known radical, Dr. Richard Price, who propounded his ideas in the *Observations of the Nature of Civil Liberty, the Principles of Government, and the Justice and Policy of the War with America* published in 1776. Professor Schuyler summarizes Dr. Price's views in the following words: "His ideal was a voluntary, co-operative alliance of self-governing states, coordinate with each other but united through the crown."

The ideas advocated by Cartwright, Sharp and Price are strikingly similar to those that now provide the theoretical groundwork upon which the Commonwealth is made to rest. Winston Churchill gave eloquent expression to this basis of Commonwealth unity while paying tribute to the late King George VI.

There is no doubt that of all the institutions which have grown up among us over the centuries or sprung into being in our lifetime, the constitutional monarchy is the most deeply founded and dearly cherished by the whole association of our peoples. In the present generation, it has acquired a meaning incomparably more powerful than anyone had dreamed possible in former times. The Crown has become the mysterious link, indeed I may say the magic link, which united our loosely bound but strongly interwoven Commonwealth of nations, states and races. Peoples who would never tolerate the assertions of a written constitution which implied any diminution of their independence are the foremost to be proud of their loyalty to the Crown. We have been greatly blessed amid our many anxieties and in the mighty world that has grown up all around our small island, we have been greatly blessed that this new, intangible, inexpressible, but, for practical purposes, apparently all-powerful element of union, should have leapt into being among us.

It required the American independence, the difficulties in Canada that led up to the Durham Report in 1839, the slow growth of constitutional federalism in Canada, Australia and New Zealand, the tragedies of the First World War, the bloody strife in Ireland and the stubborn, nonresistance movement in India before these ideas could come into their own. The change that has taken place is reflected in the new name for the old British Empire. It came to be called the British Commonwealth of Nations and more recently just the Commonwealth.   The Commonwealth is, therefore, composed of formerly subject peoples. These have now become completely independent nations joined in a voluntary association, each enjoying the fullest sovereignty and complete equality of right.   Great Britain is, in fact, only the older member of the Commonwealth and having greater prestige and moral authority that has come to it from age, experience and a great historical role. It can make no law for, nor veto one made by, its former dominions; the members of the Commonwealth have no compulsory allegiance to Britain.   A member of the Commonwealth can, as Eire did during the Second World War, remain neutral, deny the use of its ports to the Allied navy, continue diplomatic relations with the enemy and still be considered a member of the Commonwealth.   The members of the Commonwealth pay neither tribute nor taxes to Britain.   They control their own foreign affairs, have their own diplomatic representatives, their own armed forces, and make their own immigration policies.   A member nation can secede and break its ties with the Commonwealth, as Burma has done, or remain within the Commonwealth and become a republic as Pakistan and India have done.   The connection between the members does not rest upon a written constitution or a formal body of law.   It would even be difficult to discover a fully documented theory that would describe the association.   It is neither a nation nor a formal federation.

It is not, however, a mere collection of independent units.   It is a flexible association of nations, capable of showing great strength and loyalty in a crisis.

Similarly, Switzerland is a federation composed of members possessed of identical legal status.   The twenty-five cantons of the Swiss Confederation differ greatly in size.   Grisons, for instance, has an area of 2,773 square miles and Zug of 92, while Bern has an estimated population of 790,000 and Uri only 29,000.   These twenty-five cantons have varying forms of government, and the 3,107 communes of which they are comprised retain large degrees of home rule.   The federal government, based on the Constitution of 1848 which was strongly influenced by that of the United States, has only limited powers, and, by more recent constitutional changes, federal legislation is subject to rejection and modification by popular referendum and initiative.   The Swiss cantons have reserved for themselves more of their powers of government than the states of the United States.   Federalism in Switzerland dates back to the Alliance between the three forest districts, Uri, Schwyz and Unterwalden in 1291.   Other districts gradually adhered to the original three and, in spite of a turbulent and warlike history, the principle of federalism survived all vicissitudes. For centuries, general affairs were determined by a Diet composed of ambassadors acting under instructions. For nearly 600 years, the original members of the federation abided by the rule that all disputes between them should be settled by arbitration. Other members gradually joined the original league; Lucerne in 1332, Zurich in 1351, Glarus and Zug in 1352, Bern in 1353. As early as 1481 at the Diet of Stans, the principle of collective security was adopted in the resolution that they would come to the aid of a member attacked by another member. In 1815, the principle of absolute political equality of the cantons was embodied in alloting one vote to each canton, and territorial integrity of each secured by prohibiting the attack of one member by another. Switzerland stands as the oldest and, in some ways, the most successful federation in the Western World.

The history of the four widely different federations we have just discussed merits careful scrutiny by the student of international organization, for they each, in their own way, illustrate the principle of the coördinate state. They also make it clear that the acceptance of that principle is necessary to the growth and survival of a federal system. In the case of the United States, the debate ending in the Missouri Compromise reaffirmed the original proposition that all states stand in relation to each other as equals; that the older states could not sell "a provincial status" to a new state without undermining the foundations of the Union itself. This decision reaffirmed the earlier agreements on an equal vote in the Senate regardless of size of population, on nonintervention by one state in the affairs of another, through the provision for judicial settlement of disputes between states, on territorial integrity established in the rule that no state could be divided or united with another against its own will, and that the states reserve all of their powers not deposited in the federal government by the Constitution. The federal government is thus an indestructible union of indestructible states.

Similarly, in the case of the Organization of American States, it was necessary to reaffirm the coördinate position of each nation before the Pan American system could move forward to become a cohesive international body. That reaffirmation required the surrender of the right to intervention in the internal or external affairs for any reason whatsoever, the guaranteeing of the territorial integrity and the political independence of each member nation, the assertion of the principle of collective security, and the affirmation of political and juridical equality which could be fulfilled only by the outlawing of intervention. And, as in the case of the United States, it required that all disputes between members "shall be settled by peaceful means."

These same conditions have come to define the relations between the members of the Commonwealth of Nations. It is an association of equally independent and sovereign states. There are no great and no lesser members. The Imperial Conference of 1926 agreed that the dominions were "equal in status, in no way subordinate to one another in any aspect of their domestic or external affairs. . . . Equality of status so far as Great Britain and the Dominions are concerned is thus the root principle governing our inter-imperial relations." In February 1948, Ceylon's Independence Act declared that she was "a fully responsible member of the British Commonwealth of Nations, in no way subordinate in any aspect of domestic or external affairs, freely associated and united by a common allegiance to the Crown." But in South Africa "the King for the purpose of reigning in and over the Union is created by our statutes. . . . The King is, therefore, the King of South Africa and not of the Commonwealth. But the Crown has not a 'vestige' of functional reality." In Ireland the symbolic character of the Crown proved unacceptable and the oath was repudiated because it was, according to Mr. de Valera, "an intolerable burden." The Irish preferred to be "externally associated." Mr. de Valera declared that "we are associated with the States of the British Commonwealth of Nations. We are not members of it." To the Burmese, however, the idea of remaining even as an associate of a British Commonwealth proved unacceptable because they considered that the word British implied ownership or subjugation. In 1947, Mr. Thankin Nu, the Burmese Prime Minister, said that they were, however, prepared to consider association with a United Commonwealth. The change of name was made in 1948 in the Amendment of the British Nationality Act, but it was then too late.

The demand for independent sovereignty of the members of the Commonwealth which was first fully manifested by the Irish in 1921 who wanted "external association" has been completely fulfilled. The concepts of dominion status, of a "British" Commonwealth, of the Crown as an essential symbol of unity for all members, have been rejected. The Commonwealth is a free association among completely sovereign states held together by tradition, common historical experience, interest, convenience and a belief that their common history is a bond much stronger than that which rests upon force or upon a symbol which, for reasons of past resentment, is unacceptable to some of the members. Unity here lies in freedom and identity.

It has been a slow process to convert a world-wide Empire into a free association. But the fact that such a change was possible reflects the resiliency of English constitutional traditions. The milieu of the twentieth century made the symbols of dominion over other peoples incompatible with the passionate nationalism that has dominated our time. The insistent claim by every people across the face of the earth of a "historical personality" which must not be denied or impugned has made imperialism, or even the mere trimmings of foreign rule, unacceptable. If the association of many nations, races and cultures which the British Empire represented was not to break up in hatred and strife, then the constitutional design that would hold them together had to be accommodated both to the political realities of the times and to the emotional overtones which they reflect. But once the reconciliation between the older ideas of empire and the more recent belief in the free "historical personality" has been achieved, then the association finds a sounder and more flexible basis of coöperation than it had before. For now all the associates are equal members of the same family. They are all inside the same house. They are strong with a strength that comes from moral identity and voluntary adhesion. In comparison, a military alliance resting on a balance of power is a rope of sand. On a much smaller scale and differently, the Swiss Confederation has found a similar unity based upon a recognition of diversity of race and language, differences of constitutional forms and varying historical traditions.

It will be objected that the use of the United States and Switzerland as examples of international organization distorts the meaning of the word "international." It ought, however, to be clear by now that what saved the American federation, and made it the kind of organization it is, is precisely the acceptance of the principle of identical sovereignty of the several states among themselves. If the Missouri Compromise had gone differently, our federal system would have gone with it, and the Union, if one had survived, would have been a centralized government plagued with the very difficulties of empire we have just been considering. The same is, of course, also true of Switzerland. The long federal history of that remarkable nation illustrates, in a hundred crucial points, the vitality of the principle of equal status. And it was not until that was finally and fully accepted for all cantons that the country settled down to a peaceful political history. It is, therefore, the same principle which operates in all of these four instances of successful international organization based upon the idea of the coördinate states. In the American point of view, the concept of the coördinate state is a general principle of universal applicability. Otherwise how explain our ceaseless penchant for international organization?

The Continental Congress, the United States, the Organization of American States, the League of Nations, the United Nations, the North Atlantic Pact, and the effort to stimulate a European Union are all parts of the same story. In each of these instances, there is visible the common ideal of coöperation among equal states.   How congenial that concept is to the American experience is illustrated at the very beginning of our history not only by the doctrine of equal legislative sovereignty for the colonies advanced by the early leaders as a proper basis for the organization of the British Empire, but in Benjamin Franklin's suggestion after the formation of the American Constitution that Europe follow our example and establish for itself a federal system.   Benjamin Franklin was sagacious and experienced beyond most men and he not only knew the United States but had deep knowledge of England and the Continent. In the ripeness of his years, after helping frame the American Constitution, he felt that it represented a political system that Europe might well adopt for itself.   In the year 1787, Franklin wrote to a European friend:

I send you enclosed the proposed new Federal Constitution for these States.   I was engaged four months of the last summer in the Convention that formed it. . . .   If it succeeds, I do not see why you might not in Europe carry the project of Good Henry the 4th into execution, by forming a Federal Union and One Grand Republic of all its different States and Kingdoms; by means of a like Convention; for we had many interests to reconcile.

The concept of federalism is, with the American people, bred in the bone as part of the idea of political freedom.   We believe that security rests upon coöperation, that coöperation is possible only among equals, that equality eliminates the basic reason for political disruption because equals politically are "coördinate" in dignity and in rank, that this common identity is essential for different states to achieve that unity which makes them members of the same political family.   International coöperation from our point of view requires that all participating members be insiders, and that such a fellowship is in the end an "indestructible union."   That is why the concept of "balance of power" is alien and repugnant to the American people.   We have condemned in others the policies derived from that concept and have rejected them for ourselves. Illustrative of this attitude is President Wilson's statement: ". . . the centre . . . of the old order was that unstable thing which we used to call 'balance of power' . . . a thing determined by the sword . . . thrown in on one side or the other."   And "If the future had nothing for us but a new attempt to keep the world at a right poise by a balance of power, the United States would take no interest, because she will join no combination of power that is not the combination of all of us."

To the advocates of power politics and the balance of power, however, these American convictions and beliefs derived from their own experience are "intoxication with moral abstractions . . . which . . . has become the prevailing substitute for political thought." And Wilson, because he advocated a League of Nations, was driven to "substituting for the concrete national interest of the United States the general postulate of a brave new world where the national interest of the United States, as that of all other nations, would disappear in a community of interest comprising mankind." These same errors were committed by the leaders of the Second World War, Roosevelt and Hull. The reason for their failure is simple and obvious.

How could statesmen who boasted that they were not "believers in the idea of balance of power"—like a scientist not believing in the law of gravity—and who were out "to kill power politics," understand the very idea of the national interest which demanded, above all, protection from the power of others?

The American mind, according to Dr. Hans Morgenthau, has been "weakened in its understanding of foreign policy by half a century of ever more complete intoxication with moral abstractions." The difficulty with American foreign policy is that it is burdened with "utopianism, legalism, sentimentalism [and] . . . neo-isolationism." It does not understand that

Foreign policy, like all politics, is in its essence a struggle for power, waged by sovereign nations for national advantage. . . . By its very nature this struggle is never ended, for the lust for power, and the fear of it, is never stilled. . . . In the life of nations peace is only respite from trouble— or the permanent peace of extinction.

Our great mistake was to assume that the United Nations could be a substitute for the balance of power. We defined it in "Utopian terms of permanent peace and non-competitive, trustful coöperation among the great powers." American policy is wrong because it is interested in the "well-being of all mankind." A nation is under no obligation to keep a treaty. It is, in fact, an "iron law of international politics that legal obligations must yield to the national interest." There is apparently no difference between nations that "have a flair for throwing burdensome obligations overboard in an elegant, unobtrusive fashion, or of chiseling them away with the fine tools of legal misinterpretation" like France has done, and Russia and Germany who "have the disconcerting habit . . . of . . . announcing . . . that a treaty has become a 'scrap of paper.' " These matters are, after all, only "the lawyers' concern" which the statesman can take in his stride in pursuit of the "national interest." Nor need the great Powers be concerned about the interests of third parties; "great powers . . . have by tradition and logic . . .

settled their disputes . . . over the regions where their interest, power and responsibilities were paramount." The business of statesmanship could not be carried on any other way.

It is a legalistic illusion to believe that the United Nations is a substitute for power politics because it is obvious "from the political history of the human race that the balance of power and concomitant spheres of influence are of the very essence of international politics. They may be disregarded at the peril of those who choose to do so but they cannot be abolished."

American policy, therefore, operates with "defective intellectual equipment." Our difficulties derive from our failure to recognize that the "balance of power" is as much a law of politics as gravity is a law of physics and is illustrated by all of human history. This law which apparently is basic to the "science" of international relations has been understood by all the great statesmen, who, each in turn, have successfully ruined their nations and made a shambles out of all those parts of the world where they have been free to work out the "law" and practice the science. Now we too, who have prospered by refusing to apply the science or believe in its basic law, are urged, on grounds of the "national interest," to join the historical procession to national suicide by dividing the world between Russia and ourselves. The fact that it runs counter to every political instinct of the American people merely proves that we are possessed of a "defective intellectual equipment" and, if we consider it immoral and contrary to our experience to trade away the independence and freedom of other nations as part of the bargain, it shows that we are sentimental, moralistic, Utopian and neo-isolationist and we can refuse to take this advice only at our own peril because the balance of power like the law of gravity will work its way regardless of what foolish men may do.

Now we submit that all this has nothing to do with science, and little to do with the infinitely complex influences that have shaped the history of man through time. We suspect that it is a very subjective and private view of the nature of man and of his role on earth. And that view seems to be that man is now and has always been in a sad estate from which he cannot extricate himself. He has no one to help him. He has no law to live by, no morality to support him; he has nothing except the "balance of power"—and if he will not believe in that, then God help him—but in this view of the world even that comfort is denied to man, for it could not abide any concept of a teleological universe. The interesting thing about this point of view is that it should either remain oblivious to or scorn the vast record of coöperative experience among men and nations, and that it should treat the relatively short and exceptional history of the European state system as equivalent to the history of the race across the face of time, and that it should deny the possibility and presumably the desirability of institutional development in the relations between nations.   Institutions are presumably, by some undivulged "law," confined to grow only inside the "sovereign" state.   There must be no extra-national institutions; they would deny the "national interest" and make for "a brave new world" which is the greatest of political sins.

There is another statement of this theme of *Realpolitik* and the balance of power that comes from the influential and highly skilled pen of Mr. George F. Kennan.   In this exposition of the case, there is a kind of urbanity, a kind of sensitivity for the values and shortcomings of the American milieu and a kind of compassion for human frailty that robs it of much of its sting.   It is so gently, so persuasively stated, that the reader finds himself carried along almost to the point of agreement until he realizes that this modest and restrained presentation is, in fact, a repudiation of every value we hold:

I see the most serious fault of our past policy formulation to lie in something that I might call the legalistic-moralistic approach to international problems. This approach runs like a red skein through our foreign policy of the last fifty years. It has in it something of the old emphasis on arbitration treaties, something of the Hague Conferences and schemes for universal disarmament, something of the more ambitious American concepts of the role of international law, something of the League of Nations and the United Nations, something of the Kellogg Pact, something of the idea of a universal "Article 51" pact, something of the belief in World Law and World Government.

This is more than a challenge to our international policies of the last fifty years.   It is a denial of the American beliefs that have sustained American political life from the beginning; for our ideas of foreign policy are part and parcel of our belief in human freedom, in the equality of men, and in the dignity and independence of nations.   The extenuating feature of Mr. Kennan's presentation is its lack of consistency. There is internal evidence that the author has not really made up his mind about these important matters.   He is still ambivalent and groping for the truth, and the "balance of power" has not achieved the status of a "law" like the law of gravity.   This is, in our view, a saving grace —but the damage has been done, for an influential voice has been added to the attempt to persuade the American people that their traditional policy based upon the coördinate state is wrong and has proved a failure.

The proof often presented by those who would force us off our beaten path is the failure of the League of Nations.   A particular instance is made to serve the ends of a universal law.   The League having failed, then all international organizations must fail.   But the reasons for the failure were numerous.   That the League was not based upon the idea of the coördinate state was, in our view, one of its major weaknesses. If all the members of that body had had an equal voice, Italy's attack upon Ethiopia would have been defeated, and sanctions both economic and military would have been effectively applied.   It will be said in reply that the small Powers would have committed the large ones to a possible war in which they would have borne a minor part.   That may or may not be true.   But the way to have avoided the greater tragedy which ultimately destroyed or weakened both the great and the small states was to have acted as the small states would have acted—to enforce the principle that in the modern world there are no separate interests for the small or the large state, that their destinies are collectively involved in each other, and that the violation, by war and oppression, of the independence of even the smallest Power is, in the end, the denial of the possible survival without war even of the largest Power.   For such violation, whatever the grounds on which it is justified, is in effect the building of aggressive power against other nations until they, too, are placed in jeopardy.   In this view of the matter, the structuring of international organization on the coördinate state is the alternative to the balance of power, and to security without permanent militarization. Nor must we permit ourselves to be confused by the argument that the United Nations has failed and that the Atlantic Security Pact is the true substitute in the form of a military alliance.   The Atlantic Security Pact is conceived of as a temporary and instrumental association of a defensive character organized for the purpose of implementing the ideal of the United Nations.   It has nothing to do with the balance of power idea and less to do with dividing the world into spheres of interest between Russia and ourselves.   Its objectives are aimed precisely at an attempt to prevent the permanent militarization which dividing the world into spheres of influence would require, and to escape the destruction of the democratic process which would follow in its wake.

The American people will not accept the program.   They will not consent to the destruction of all that a hundred and fifty years of democratic life has brought them for the sake of being the masters of that part of the world which they could lay hold of.   They will not do it because it runs against their grain, and because they have an alternative which seems more difficult to those hypnotized by the ideal of force and craft but is, in fact, easier and more consistent with our own traditional way with other people, and one we know how to live with because we have always done so.   And that is the organization of as much of the world as we can upon the basis of the coördinate state, not for the sake of achieving a balance of power, but for the sake of building a basis of common defense upon a system of collective security open to all the nations of the world who wish to join it, without losing their independence or their dignity. It may prove impossible under present conditions to build such a system without having to fight a war with Russia, but then at least we will be fighting, as we did before, for the thing we consider worth defending with our lives and treasure. Equally important, our allies and partners will be fighting for things as dear to them as ours are to us. They will find their own values secured in a common defense and a common victory. And our enemy, Russia, will find the peoples of its own satellites striving to enter our common security system just because it is made to rest on the ideal of the coördinate state.

A balance of power settlement would lead our many allies and associates to conclude that they are mere pawns in a game of international politics played at their expense. They would cease to be partners in a great cause; for the division of the world into spheres of influence would automatically destroy the basis of the partnership in the West. That partnership rests upon the assumption that all the members are equal, that their rights cannot be bargained away, that they have to be consulted, that they have to consent freely to changes that affect them. It also rests upon the assumption that there are *no* spheres of influence— that the United States has no rights greater than the least of its members, and that the defense is a joined defense of a common interest, but that the common interest rests upon the particular and unique political personality of each member. It assumes a coördinate relationship, not the position of a great Power with many satellite Powers. The mere acceptance of the idea of a balance of power would undermine the basis of the relationship among free partners formed together and would convert it into an empire with satellites to be ordered about. It would convert the United States from a federal republic to an empire and ultimately destroy the republic. That is what the proposal really means, and that is why it will be resisted by the American people.

Such an arrangement would lead our friends to fall away from us feeling that they had been betrayed, as, in fact, they would have been. They, too, would seek the best bargain—temporarily—and play for higher stakes when the occasion offered. We would find ourselves weaker in the international field, not stronger. We would have voluntarily accepted a great moral defeat, and the power derived from a common cause among nations, all of whom felt identified through interest, belief and outlook, would have been irretrievably lost. The only remaining hope that an association of coördinate states could be gathered together to resist the attempt by Russia to dominate the world would evaporate.   It is difficult to foresee a day more dark and hopeless than the one on which the American people could be persuaded to seek a temporary peace through deliberately sacrificing the principle of voluntary association among nations, and agree to divide the world between Russia and the United States.

No.   With all of our shortcomings and failings, we will not accept the new science and follow the "will-o'-the-wisp" of *Realpolitik*.   We will not abandon the faith we have lived by, nor deny the other nations the right to live in freedom and without fear.   Our commitments are to a world of free men working together in free nations.   The democratic faith that lies at the base of everything we cherish is the overriding law of American policy both at home and abroad.   We cannot surrender our belief in the equal dignity of little nations without, in the end, abandoning our belief in the equal dignity of men.   We will, if we have to, resist to the death the effort to subvert the world to a totalitarian despotism, but we will not bargain with it at the expense of other people and to the destruction of that sense of human integrity and national morality which is part of the substance of our very being.   This may not be "science," but that is the way it is.   We can do no other.   Therein lies our strength.

15. ANOTHER ATTACK ON REALISM —
IN DEFENSE OF INTERNATIONAL LAW AND MORALITY *

Mr. Feller attacks the "neo-realists" on two grounds. Realists, he says, "fall into the obvious error of assuming that preoccupation with international law and moral principles is a peculiarity of American foreign policy." He maintains that all states except those which were openly aggressive have professed a belief in international law and have justified their actions in terms of legal principles. Moreover, the system of international law is not as completely rigid as neo-realists claim. The creation of institutional arrangements, such as those embodied in the United Nations, introduces flexibility into the legal order and allows for peaceful change.

Mr. Feller further asserts that the realist insistence upon a return to "diplomacy" and the necessity to defend "the national interest" offers nothing significant in place of moral principles.

* A. H. Feller, *The Annals of the American Academy of Political and Social Science,* July, 1952, pp. 77-83.   The author was General Counsel and Director of the Legal Department of the United Nations, and Associate Professor of Law, Yale University.

Diplomacy, he says, is merely a procedure without substantive content. The national interest, if applied without reference to some moral standard, "becomes the focus of hostility and fear." Mr. Feller has faith in the United Nations, with all its "shortcomings and mistakes." He believes that the objectives of the United Nations "are the common ground of mankind's will for survival with decency."

Any reader of the now very popular Science Fiction will of course remember that ever recurring scene in which a group of people are riding in a space rocket which is shot out of the gravitational sphere of the earth and is approaching the moon; at one point, always very carefully defined by the science fiction writer, the passengers suddenly find everything turned topsy-turvy.

Anyone who wants to know that feeling can spare himself the expense and discomfort of a rocket trip to the moon. All he needs to do is read or reread the literature and debates on foreign policy of the last few years. This is the sort of thing he will find:

REVERSAL OF VIEWS

Almost from the moment of its birth, the United Nations has been belabored by some critics as a puny, ineffective creature, crippled by the veto, overridden by an antiquated conception of national sovereignty, and incapable of influencing the national policies of its member states. Now suddenly there is a whole new school of thought which pictures the United Nations as a monstrous supergovernment, endowed with mighty powers of interference in the internal affairs of its members, and intent on hamstringing their freedom of action.

For years the debating platforms in the legislative halls in the United States resounded with calls for the elimination or diminution of sovereignty and the immediate establishment of a world federation or world government. Earnest committees drafted detailed constitutions for a new world order to be set up right away. One state legislature after another called for an amendment to the Constitution of this country to enable it to join the new order. Now suddenly there is a movement to do just the opposite—to amend the United States Constitution to limit the normal and traditional treaty powers possessed and exercised since the foundation of this Republic.

Only a little while ago, all our scholars were calling for increasing world community and strengthened collective security. Now we are told that we must look at power realities and must govern our foreign relations by exclusive devotion to the national interest.

This rocket in which we seem to be riding is apparently not just shooting out into space. It is bobbing and weaving in addition. I think we are all getting slightly dizzy, and it is time we took our bearings before sense of direction is lost entirely.

BASIC FACTORS IN INTERNATIONAL POLITICS

There are two basic intractable phenomena of international politics. First, the world consists of separate states, each of them desiring to maintain its national identity and develop its own social and economic order. These states are extraordinarily diverse in size, strength, racial composition, stage of economic development, religious and ideological background, and devotion to the cause of peace. But they are extraordinarily uniform in their adherence to the concept of sovereignty and independence. Every one of them wants just that. The number of these sovereign states has increased in our generation, and it will continue to increase for at least several decades.

The second phenomenon is that the spread of the western technological system—the development of communication and science, and particularly of the destructive capabilities of modern instruments of war—has rendered every one of these states incapable of living in isolation. This is true of the largest states as well as of the smallest. Moreover, as we are coming to learn more and more every month, belief in the possibility of progress through the conscious development of human and material resources—belief which was once limited to western liberal thought—has broken through ancient incrustations to stir up the ambitions and hopes of hundreds of millions in backward areas.

BASIC VALUE OF U.N.

The establishment of the United Nations in 1945 was the most important attempt in history to reconcile these two phenomena of disunity and unity, of sovereignty and community. The Charter was not the product of academic scholarship or visionary idealism; nor was it an opiate brewed by narrow-minded and scheming politicians to deaden the people's desire for true world government. It was drafted and adopted by the responsible representatives of the vast bulk of mankind. Its weaknesses are not due to lack of drafting skill or of devotion or of imagination; they are for the most part inherent in any practicable design for world order in the midst of world tension and conflict.

Whether these weaknesses of detail were inevitable or avoidable, they cannot obscure these two major and enduring accomplishments of the founders: first, a statement of purpose and principles which set forth for the first time a universal creed of aspiration for peace, security, the better-ment of life, and the fostering of human freedom; and, second, the creation of an institution, universal in scope, organized to operate con-tinuously on all problems of international concern.

ENTER THE NEO-REALISTS

These great contributions of the Charter have remained virtually unchallenged throughout the long debates which have been raging on the details of the structure and performance of the United Nations system. I find it a disturbing symptom of our present instability and unease that these principles are now being subjected to at least an indirect attack—and from a source from which I think we might expect something better. A number of scholars are telling us that the real trouble with American foreign policy is its reliance on what they call the "legalistic-moralistic approach"—a rather lengthy name for what we used to call idealism. In their view, foreign policy is essentially a struggle for power, waged by sovereign nations for political advantage, and they believe and tell us with great force that American foreign policy has suffered from the misguided belief that this struggle for power can be suppressed by the acceptance of some system of legal rules and restraints.

The spokesmen for this new school, which we might call the neo-realist school, are among the finest minds, among the most accomplished scholars in political science, in this country. But I think it important to examine the premises on which they have built this doctrine; because I fear that the doctrine, if readily accepted, may have fateful consequences for the future of the conduct of foreign relations.

A WORLD-WIDE CONCEPT

To begin with, it is a mystery to me why these able and sophisticated students of diplomacy have fallen into the obvious error of assuming that preoccupation with international law and moral principles is a peculiarity of American foreign policy. In fact, most governments, certainly very many, have shared a similar, if not as intense or consistent, preoccupation.

Just to take the beginning of this century, the Hague Conferences were not initiated by some American lawyer Secretary of State, but by the Czar of Russia. The relations of Latin American states are replete with treaties and declarations proclaiming general principles of law and morality. It is true that a United States President promoted the League of Nations, but more than forty other states carried it forward for two decades when the United States backed away. And there is no evidence that it took much inducing by the United States to get the other fifty-nine members to join the United Nations, and more than a dozen additional states are trying very hard to become members of that organization. Americans may, I think, be proud of the support and enthusiasm which many of them have been giving to the current efforts to create a wider European community, but it is the farsighted statesmen of Europe that are taking the practical steps toward that end.

As recently as November 1951, Anthony Eden, the Foreign Minister of a state whose foreign policy is not customarily thought to be afflicted with fuzzy-minded naïveté, said this:

> I am more than ever convinced that the nations of the world must submit to the rule of law and abide by it. Confidence can only be created and maintained on a basis of respect for international engagements. It is therefore the duty of all nations, as indeed it is their interest, to respect international authority and uphold it.

And at this moment the people of the Netherlands, with centuries of experience of diplomatic methods and balance-of-power politics, are engaged in amending their constitution to provide for the primacy of international organization and international law.

The point is that historically all states except those which were or are openly predatory have professed belief in an international legal order and have normally justified their actions on the basis of legal principle.

LIMITATIONS OF INTERNATIONAL LAW

This is not to say that nations have always been sincere in their professions, or that the rules of international law have not frequently been broken. We know to our sorrow that they frequently have been broken. The notion that peace could be established forever by the simple proclamation of a world law owes its currency to enthusiastic laymen rather than to international lawyers. These latter have constantly stressed the fragmentary and primitive character of international law and the relatively subordinate role it can play in the conduct of international affairs in a world of sovereign states.

For several centuries there has been an urge to extend the international legal system from the mundane matters dealing with the everyday relations between states to larger political conflicts. Lawyers have frequently cautioned against overambitious attempts to impose such wide-reaching legal restraints without a solution of the underlying economic and social problems and political and psychological tensions. They can only smile wryly when they are now told by one of the outstanding spokesmen of the neo-realists that the incomplete and modest system of international rules which we now have is a "legal strait jacket" impeding the assertion of legitimate national aspirations.

TO FACILITATE PEACEFUL CHANGE

In truth, law is a conservative influence tending toward stability and regularity.   And this has been and will continue to be its major function in the international scene.   At the same time, it has been the constant concern of international lawyers to reconcile this stabilizing influence with the problem of peaceful change, precisely in order to enable the proper expression of legitimate national aspirations.   This is one of the reasons for the creation of institutional arrangements which can introduce the requisite flexibility into the legal order.

There is a perfect case in point in the last few years—the handling of the question of Libia.   Here a colonial people has been enabled to fulfill its national aspiration to independence through the legal and institutional mechanisms of a peace treaty and the action of the General Assembly of the United Nations, and has done this without upheaval and with much less violence than has ever before accompanied the birth of an independent state.   This is an ideal example of the reconciliation of stability and change, of legal principle and national aspiration.

WHENCE THE CONCEPT OF TOTAL WAR?

This neo-realistic thesis, if I may call it that, which I have been describing, possesses a novelty in that it is urged that the extension of the rule of law is a positive danger to international life.   I find this a very startling proposition, and it is supported by imputing to what is called the "legalistic approach" a number of hitherto unsuspected vices.

The most serious charge is that this approach is responsible for the concept of total war and total victory.   It is assumed, without proof, that this concept is a sort of American invention stemming from moral indignation over the failure of other nations to conform their behavior to American standards; in short, that Americans become so incensed at the failure of other nations to be as nice as we are that when we go to war with them we desire to annihilate them.

Surely it cannot be so soon forgotten that the concept of total war was first proclaimed by Imperial Germany in World War I and then by Nazi Germany in World War II.   If the reaction of American and, one must add, Allied public opinion was a mistake, it must be laid to the character of the war initiated by the enemy, and not to a theoretical moral basis which is peculiar to the American character.

There is nothing inherent in legal principle that requires the imposition of the death penalty for all offenses; and there is nothing inherent in justified indignation against an aggressor state that compels war *à outrance* and the total extinction of the aggressor. A sufficient contemporary illustration is the limited character of the United Nations effort to stem aggression in Korea.

CRITERIA OF NATIONAL CONDUCT

Basically, if I understand the neo-realists, they consider it inherently impossible to judge the conduct of states by moral criteria. This is again assumed to be an American idea which, if I may quote one statement, considers it "implausible that people should have positive aspirations and ones that they regard as legitimate, more important to them than the peacefulness and orderliness of international life." And one spokesman finds "a profound and neglected truth," to use his words, in the dictum of Hobbes that "there is neither morality nor law outside the state."

With all due respect, I feel that these remarks do less than justice either to Americans or to other peoples. For many centuries, men have considered political communities subject to moral standards of one sort or another. The notion of the inherent amorality of state conduct introduced by Machiavelli is an aberration, and not an immutable truth. The criteria by which the conduct of states may be judged are not necessarily always the same as those by which we judge the conduct of individuals, and the procedure and organs of judgment must be different.

Moreover, an international order must obviously take account of the relative dispositions of power and the natural limitations of law and sanction. The administration of such an order entails many compromises and much painstaking adjustment of conflicting interests which lie outside the legal realm. In that respect it is different in degree, not in kind, from any domestic order, where law and principle also have their definite limitations.

DIPLOMACY AND INTERNATIONAL ORGANIZATION

There is a tendency in these scholars to lump together in one concept legal-moral principles and the institutional framework for international action; and these two things, when lumped together, are opposed to what are considered to be the tried-and-true methods of old-fashioned diplomacy.

Now, there is no basic incompatibility between the methods of diplomacy and the institutions of an international organization. Conferences and treaties are as much a part of diplomatic technique as are private meetings of diplomats and the carrying of dispatches between capitals by couriers. When the United Nations deals with a political problem, as for instance Palestine or Kashmir or numerous others that I might mention, it seeks solutions which are compatible with power realities, and it operates through a whole range of techniques from private negotiation to full-dress debate before television cameras.

It has been said that the legalistic belief, the idealistic belief as we have previously called it, refuses to take the awkward conflicts of national interest and deal with them on their merits with a view to finding the solutions which are least unsettling to the stability of international life, but that it tries to find some formal criteria of a juridical nature which can define permissible behavior.

I suppose that what is meant by a statement of this kind is some sort of simple, formalistic notion like the Kellogg-Briand Pact, in which in one sentence all governments on earth undertook to outlaw war as an instrument of national policy. Certainly this reproach could not be applied against such an organization as the United Nations, which has devoted its energies to precisely what is recommended—the solution of awkward conflicts on their merits. And anyone who has followed the proceedings of the United Nations knows that that is not easy, and that frequently failure will come where success has been fought for.

It can hardly be discreditable to the United Nations system that, in trying to find solutions to these awkward conflicts, it also operates with some regard for a statement of principles subscribed to by all the nations as their common objective and aspiration.

OBJECTIVE OF DIPLOMACY

To my mind, the basic fault with this neo-realistic approach is that it offers nothing in place of moral principles—nothing, that is, but a return to "diplomacy" and "national interest." What do these mean? "Diplomacy" is merely a procedure. It has no more substantive content than "speaking" or "writing." The techniques of negotiation or persuasion are only a minor part of the problem of the conduct of foreign affairs. I think it is very important for us to train our young men to know these techniques; but the heart of the problem is the question of objective—to what ends are we going to utilize diplomatic resources?

I certainly am not one of those who would decry the pursuit of the national interests as selfish or petty. A sound domestic economy, firmness in the protection of legitimate rights abroad, and the maintenance of strength to ward off attack are essential to national survival. But we cannot advance a concept of national interest abroad without some ideal standard and at the same time convince others that our purposes are beyond reproach.

A majestic procession of great Americans, most of whom have been lawyers, have been the idealists of foreign policy. To mention only some of these names, there are Root, Wilson, Stimson, Hughes, Franklin Roosevelt, Hull, Vandenberg. These men were quite clear that the national interest of their country could be served, and served well, by asserting the influence of the United States for the maintenance and extension of law and justice. They were neither so naïve nor so unrealistic as to ignore the significance of power in world affairs. They realized that the position of a nation in the world cannot be measured only in terms of the size of its armed forces. Without power, a nation may be impotent; without a moral standard respected by other peoples, it becomes the focus of hostility and fear.

TWO POINTS CONCEDED

We certainly need to take to heart two lessons which these recent discussions have very properly read to us. One is that we must dispel a notion unfortunately all too prevalent among us, that a single formula-slogan like "world law," "international organization," or "disarmament" can solve the international puzzle. Our "realistic" scholars will forgive me, I hope, if I suggest that many of their readers will have gained the impression that they also have put forward a formula-slogan under such rubrics as "diplomacy" and "national interest."

The second lesson, and a very proper one, is that the empty mouthing of moral concepts without sincerity or intention to implement them can stultify a national policy. On this point there can be no shadow of disagreement.

A NECESSARY CONCEPT

At the same time I must state my deep conviction that for the long run, the "legalistic-moralistic approach," awkward as those words sound, applied sincerely and with a realistic regard for its short-term limitations, will perforce remain the highroad of a decent and effective foreign policy. And it is only in this way that we shall preserve our balance and our sense of direction.

There are some who would have us believe that by following this road we make ourselves "slaves of the concepts of international law and morality." This is an extraordinary underestimation of the larger aims of foreign policy. The peoples will never believe that true and enduring world peace can be achieved without the eventual creation of a world order based on law and morality.   In my view, they are perfectly right in their belief.   A foreign policy devoted to the careful adjustment of power interests by professional diplomats may work for a time in a limited sphere, but it will never retain the allegiance of the mass of people who yearn for a better world.

U.N. EMBODIES MAN'S BROAD DESIRES

In practical terms, the issue comes down to support of the United Nations idea and of the regional organizations which have recently been created along the same lines.   The nations of the world have committed themselves to the Charter, and the United States is in the forefront. While the preservation and advancement of the national interest must be a cardinal aim of any foreign policy, the upholding of the United Nations and of the regional arrangements consistent with the charter is an integral part of the national interest of every peace-loving state.

The Charter is no mere casual by-product of an American desire for "juridical tidiness."   It is the embodiment of the deeply felt desires and needs of millions of people everywhere for peace, economic well-being and respect for the development of human personality.   These are just as significant as, perhaps more so than, the often ephemeral interests and spheres of influence so beloved by traditional diplomacy.

The United Nations system has its share of shortcomings and mistakes. Those voices which have criticized it have in the main demanded a better instrumentality, a surer and quicker way for attaining the same objectives.   The objectives themselves are the common ground of mankind's will for survival with decency.   It is the task of diplomacy so to conduct the adjustment of affairs between nations as to move toward the accomplishment of these goals.

$\sim\infty$

16. A DEFENSE OF REALISM — ANOTHER "GREAT DEBATE": THE NATIONAL INTEREST OF THE UNITED STATES *

Dr. Morgenthau defends the realist position against "utopian" attacks upon its validity and morality.   Before realism can be pronounced invalid, he says, another theory must be advanced which can bring more order and meaning to international politics than the realist explanation of it in terms of the balance of power.

* Hans J. Morgenthau, *American Political Science Review,* December, 1952 pp. 961-988.   The author is Professor of Political Science, and Director of the Center for the Study of American Foreign Policy, University of Chicago.

He argues that the "key concept" of the realist conception of American foreign policy, the national interest, provides an adequate standard for political action.   He insists that the pursuit of the national interest is most likely to ensure the survival of the United States and simultaneously to contribute to the security of other nations.   On these terms, he concludes, realism does have an important moral content and significance.

The controversy which has arisen on the occasion of Ambassador Kennan's and my recent publications differs from the great historical debates on American foreign policy in two significant respects.   It raises an issue more fundamental to the understanding of American foreign policy and of all politics than those with which the previous "great debates" were concerned, and it deals with the issue largely in terms which are not conducive to understanding.

The great debates of the past, such as the one over intervention *vs.* neutrality in 1793, expansion *vs.* the status quo before the Mexican and after the Spanish-American War, international cooperation *vs.* isolation in the 'twenties, intervention *vs.* abstention in the late 'thirties—all evolved around clear-cut issues of foreign policy.   In 1793 you were in favor of going to war on the side of France or of remaining neutral.   In the 1840's you approved of the annexation of Texas or you did not.   At the turn of the century you supported overseas expansion or you were against it.   In the 'twenties you advocated joining the League of Nations or staying out of it.   In the late 'thirties you wanted to oppose the Axis Powers by all means short of war or you wanted to abstain from intervening.   What separates the "utopian" from the "realist" position cannot be so sharply expressed in terms of alternative foreign policies.   The very same policies can be and are being supported by both schools of thought.   What sets them apart is not necessarily a matter of practical judgment, but of philosophies and standards of thought.

The issue which the present debate raises concerns the nature of all politics and, more particularly, of the American tradition in foreign policy.   The history of modern political thought is the story of a contest between two schools which differ fundamentally in their conception of the nature of man, society, and politics.   One believes that a rational and moral political order, derived from universally valid abstract principles, can be achieved here and now.   It assumes the essential goodness and infinite malleability of human nature and attributes the failure of the social order to measure up to the rational standards to lack of knowledge and understanding, obsolescent social institutions, or the depravity of certain isolated individuals or groups.   It trusts in education, reform, and the sporadic use of force to remedy these deficiencies.

The other school believes that the world, imperfect as it is from the rational point of view, is the result of forces which are inherent in human nature. To improve the world one must work with those forces, not against them. This being inherently a world of opposing interests and of conflict among them, moral principles can never be fully realized, but at best approximated through the ever temporary balancing of interests and the ever precarious settlement of conflicts. This school, then, sees in a system of checks and balances a universal principle for all pluralist societies. It appeals to historic precedent rather than to abstract principles, and aims at achievement of the lesser evil rather than of the absolute good.

This conflict between two basic conceptions of man and politics is at the bottom of the present controversy. It is the same conflict which found its classic expression in the polemic of Burke against the philosophy of the French Revolution. Given the sad state of political thought in our time, it would be vain to expect the spokesmen of political realism to speak with the voice of Burke and the defenders of political utopianism to measure up to the standards of Condorcet and Rousseau. Yet one has a right to expect that scholars discuss the issue without resort to invective and with proper regard for established facts.

In order to refute a theory which pretends to be scientific, it is first necessary to understand what a scientific theory is. A scientific theory is an attempt to bring order and meaning to a mass of phenomena which without it would remain disconnected and unintelligible. Any one who disputes the scientific character of such a theory either must produce a theory superior in these scientific functions to the one attacked or must, at the very least, demonstrate that the facts as they actually are do not lend themselves to the interpretation which the theory has put upon them. When a historian tells us that the balance of power is not a universal principle of politics, domestic and international, that it was practiced in Europe only for a limited period and never by the United States, that it ruined the states that practiced it, it is incumbent upon him to tell us how we can dispose by means of theory of the historic data by which, for instance, David Hume demonstrated the universality of the balance of power and Paul Scott Mowrer and Alfred Vagts its practice by the United States; what Kautilya was writing about in the fourth century B.C. when he summarized the theoretical and practical tradition of Indian statecraft in terms of the balance of power; what the Greek city states, the Roman republic, and the medieval emperors and popes were doing if they did not apply the principles of the balance of power; and how the nations which either neglected these principles or applied them wrongly suffered political and military defeat and even extinction, while the nation which applied these principles most consistently and consciously, that is, Great Britain, enjoyed unrivalled power for an unparalleled length of time.

The historian who wishes to replace the balance of power as the guiding principle of American foreign policy with the "humanitarian and pacific traditions" of the "coördinate state" must first of all explain how it has come about that the thirteen original states expanded into the full breadth and a good deal of the length of a continent, until today the strategic frontiers of the United States run parallel to the coastline of Asia and along the River Elbe.   If such are the results of policies based upon "humanitarian and pacific traditions," never in the history of the world has virtue been more bountifully rewarded!   Yet our historian must explain not only the great sweep of American expansion, but also the specific foreign policies which in their historic succession make up that sweep.   Is it easier to explain the successive shifts of American support from Great Britain to France and back again from the beginning of King George's War in 1744 to the War of 1812 in terms of the "coördinate state" than in terms of the balance of power?   The same question might be asked about the postponement of the recognition of the independence of the Spanish colonies until 1822, when the Floridas had been acquired from Spain and Spain had thereby been deprived of the ability to challenge the United States from within the hemisphere. The same question might be asked about the Monroe Doctrine itself, about Lincoln's policies toward Great Britain and France, and about our successive policies with regard to Mexico and the Caribbean.   One could go on and pick out at random any foreign policy pursued by the United States from the beginning to 1919 and one would hardly find a policy, with the exception perhaps of the War of 1812, which could not be made intelligible by reference to the national interest defined in terms of power—political, military, and economic—rather than by reference to the principle of the "coördinate state."   This inevitable outcome of such an inquiry is well summarized in these words:

Ease and prosperity have made us wish the whole world to be as happy and well to do as ourselves; and we have supposed that institutions and principles like our own were the simple prescription for making them so. And yet, when issues of our own interest arose, we have not been unselfish. We have shown ourselves kin to all the world, when it came to pushing an advantage.   Our action against Spain in the Floridas, and against Mexico on the coasts of the Pacific; our attitude toward first the Spaniards, and then the French, with regard to the control of the Mississippi; the unpitying force with which we thrust the Indians to the wall wherever they stood in our way, have suited our professions of peacefulness and justice and liberality no better than the aggressions of other nations that were strong and not to be gainsaid. Even Mr. Jefferson, philanthropist and champion of peaceable and modest government though he was, exemplified this double temper of the people he ruled. "Peace is our passion," he had declared; but the passion abated when he saw the mouth of the Mississippi about to pass into the hands of France. Though he had loved France and hated England, he did not hesitate then what language to hold. "There is on the globe," he wrote to Mr. Livingston at Paris, "one single spot the possessor of which is our natural and habitual enemy. The day that France takes possession of New Orleans seals the union of two nations, who, in conjunction, can maintain exclusive possession of the sea. From that moment we must marry ourselves to the British fleet and nation." Our interests must march forward, altruists though we are; other nations must see to it that they stand off, and do not seek to stay us.

This realist appraisal of the American tradition in foreign policy was published in 1901 in the *Atlantic Monthly*. Its author was a professor of jurisprudence and political economy at Princeton by the name of Woodrow Wilson.

Nothing more needs to be said to demonstrate that facts do not support a revision of American diplomatic history which tries to substitute "humanitarian and pacifist traditions" and the "coördinate state" for power politics and the balance of power as the guiding principle of American foreign policy. What, then, does support it? Three things: the way American statesmen have spoken about American foreign policy; the legal fiction of the "coördinate state"; finally, and foremost, an emotional urge to justify American foreign policy in humanitarian, pacifist terms.

It is elementary that the character of a foreign policy can be ascertained only through the examination of the political acts performed and of the foreseeable consequences of these acts. Thus we can find out what statesmen have actually done, and from the foreseeable consequences of their acts we can surmise what their objectives might have been. Yet examination of the facts is not enough. To give meaning to the factual raw material of history, we must approach historical reality with a kind of rational outline, a map which suggests to us the possible meanings of history. In other words, we put ourselves in the position of a statesman who must meet a certain problem of foreign policy under certain circumstances and ask ourselves, what are the rational alternatives from which a statesman may choose who must meet this problem under these circumstances, presuming always that he acts in a rational manner, and which of these rational alternatives was this particular statesman, acting under these circumstances, likely to choose?

It is the testing of this rational hypothesis against the actual facts and their consequences which gives meaning to the facts of history and makes the scientific writing of political history possible.

In the process of writing the history of foreign policy the interpretations by statesmen of their own acts, especially if they are made for public consumption, must needs have a strictly subsidiary place. The public self-interpretation by actors on the political scene is itself, of course, a political act which seeks to present a certain policy to its presumed supporters in terms of their moral and political folklore and to those against which it is directed in terms which intend to embarrass and deceive. Such declarations may indeed shed light upon the character and objectives of the policy pursued if they are considered in conjunction with, and in subordination to, rational hypotheses, actions, and likely consequences. Yet it is quite a different matter to interpret the American tradition of foreign policy in the light of a collection of official statements which, like most such statements, present humanitarian and pacifist justifications for the policies pursued. If anybody should be bold enough to write a history of world politics with so uncritical a method he would easily and well-nigh inevitably be driven to the conclusion that from Timur to Hitler and Stalin the foreign policies of all nations were inspired by the ideals of humanitarianism and pacifism. The absurdity of the result is commensurate with the defects of the method.

It is only from a method which accepts the declarations of statesmen as evidence of the character of the policies pursued, that the principle of the "coördinate state" receives a semblance of plausibility. Statesmen and international lawyers have been wont to speak of the "equal dignity" of all states, regardless of "wealth, power, size, population or culture," which I take the principle of the "coördinate state" to mean. It is also referred to as the principle of "federalism in international relations." As its prime examples are cited the relations amongst the states of the Union, the states of the American system, the members of the Commonwealth of Nations, and the members of the Swiss Confederation. If the whole world were organized in accordance with this principle, as are already these four political entities, it is assumed that the freedom, dignity, and peace of all nations would then be assured.

There is no need to examine the theoretical and practical merits of the principle of the "coördinate state," because for none of the four political entities mentioned does the idea of the "coördinate state" provide the principle of political organization. The equality of the states as the political foundation of the United States became obsolescent when Chief Justice Marshall's Supreme Court resolved the ambiguity of the Constitution in favor of the federal government, and it became obsolete when the Civil War proved Chief Justice Marshall's point. The equality of the states survives today only in the shadow and by virtue of the federal government's political supremacy, and without the cohesive force of that supremacy there would be no union of equal states to begin with. That these powers of the federal government are limited and qualified by the principle of federalism, that is, by the constitutionally granted powers of the states, is quite a different matter; it concerns the distribution of powers between federal government and states within a general system of checks and balances, but has nothing to do with the equality of the states as the alleged political foundation of the American system of government. With the exception of the equality of senatorial representation, the principle of the equality of the states is today, as it has been for almost a century, devoid of political content. It serves only as a principle of regional organization, of administrative decentralization, and, above all, of constitutional rhetoric. What it really signifies was pointed out more than fifty years ago by W. A. Dunning when he summarized his answer to the question "Are the states equal under the Constitution?" by saying that "the theory of equal states falls to the ground."

Similarly, the federalism of Switzerland is the result of a long series of civil wars, the last one fought a little more than a century ago, which established the predominance of the German-speaking cantons within the confederation. Here too, it is the existence of predominant power, located in one segment of the federal system, which makes federalism possible in the first place.

By the same token, the unchallengeable supremacy of the United States within the Western Hemisphere has throughout been the backbone of the system of American states. As long as this supremacy is secure, there is, on the one hand, no need for the United States to assert it in the political and military sphere, and, taking it for granted, the United States can well afford to pursue a policy of the Good Neighbor; and there is, on the other hand, no opportunity for the other members of the system to challenge that supremacy effectively. This is what the principle of the "coördinate state" amounts to in the Western Hemisphere. Consequently, whenever there was even a remote possibility that the supremacy of the United States might be challenged, generally through instigation from outside the hemisphere, the United States asserted its superior power within the hemisphere and acted as all states must act under similar conditions.

Whatever possibility for common political action there remains among the members of the Commonwealth of Nations is the result of the interests which these members may have in common.   In other words, the member states may work together or each of them may work with other nations, as their interests dictate.   Their membership in the Commonwealth, as the examples of India, South Africa, Australia, and New Zealand clearly show, has no influence upon this decision; that membership is but a faint remembrance of the times when Great Britain could secure cooperation among the member states on its terms by virtue of its superior power.

What, then, have these four examples of the "coördinate state" in common which would establish them as a distinct type of interstate relationship, and what conclusions can be drawn from them for the organization of the world?   The only thing that these four examples seem to have really in common is the legal stipulation of the equality of the members of the respective systems and this characteristic is not peculiar to them, but a general principle of international law applicable to all sovereign states.   In the political sphere they seem to have nothing in common at all.   What they tend to show, however, is the decisive importance of the distribution of political power for the operation of federal and egalitarian relations among states.   The political cohesion of a federal system is the result of superior power located in some part of it.   It is by virtue of its superior power that the predominant part can afford to grant the other members of the federal system a measure of equality in the non-political sphere.   These observations bring us back to power politics and the balance of power to which the principle of the "coördinate state" was supposed to be the alternative.

In truth, it is not the disinterested consideration of facts which has given birth to the theory of the "coördinate state."   That theory is rather the response to an emotional urge, and since this emotion is not peculiar to a particular author but typical of a popular reaction to the new role which the United States must play in world affairs, it deserves a brief analysis.

One of the great experiences of our time which have impressed themselves upon the American mind is the emergence of the United States as a nation among other nations, exposed to the same opportunities, temptations, risks, and liabilities to which other nations have been traditionally exposed.   This experience becomes the more shocking if it is compared with the expectation with which we fought the Second World War.   We expected from that war a reaffirmation of the secure, detached, and independent position in world affairs which we had inherited from the Founding Fathers and which we had been successful in preserving at least to the First World War.   By avoiding what we thought had been Wilson's mistakes, we expected to emerge from that war if not more independent, certainly more secure than we were when we entered it. In fact, probably not even in the early days of the Republic were we more exposed to danger from abroad than we are today, and never had we less freedom of action in taking care of our interests than we have today.

It is naturally shocking to recognize that a happy chapter in the history of the nation and in one's own way of life has come to an end. There are those who reconcile themselves to the inevitable, albeit with sorrow rather than with glee, and try to apply the lessons of the past to the tasks at hand. There are others who try to escape from a disappointing and threatening reality into the realm of fantasy. Three such escapist fantasies have arisen in our midst in response to the challenge of American world leadership and power: the fantasy of needless American participation in war, the fantasy of American treason, and the fantasy of American innocence.

The first of these fantasies presumes that the present predicament is a result not of necessity but of folly, the folly of American statesmen who needlessly intervened in two world wars. The second of these fantasies attributes the present predicament to treason in high places whereby the fruits of victory were handed to the enemy. The third of these fantasies denies that the predicament is real and prefers to think of it as an intellectual fraud perpetrated upon the American people. To support this fictional denial of the actualities of the present, it draws upon a fictional account of the past. The United States does not need to bear at present the intellectual, moral, and political burdens which go with involvement in power politics and the maintenance of the balance of power; for it has never borne them in the past, never having been thus involved. The golden age of past political innocence sheds its glow upon a but seemingly less innocent present and promises a future in which all the world will follow the example of America, forswear power politics and the balance of power, and accept the principle of the "coördinate state." Our rearmament program, as exemplified in the Atlantic Security Pact, we are told, has nothing to do with the balance of power but aims at the "organization of as much of the world as we can upon the basis of the coördinate state. . . . It may prove impossible under present conditions to build such a system without having to fight a war with Russia, but then at least we will be fighting, as we did before, for the thing we consider worth defending with our lives and treasure." Thus, a fictional account of the American past, begun as an act of uncalled-for patriotic piety, issues in an ideology for a third world war. Escape we must from the unfamiliar, unpleasant, and dangerous present, first into the political innocence of the past and from there into the immediate future of a third world war, beyond which the revived and universalized innocence of the more distant future will surely lie.

We have said that to present the American tradition in foreign policy as having been free from concern with power politics and the balance of power is not warranted by the facts of American history. Yet it might still be argued, and it is actually being argued, that, regardless of the evidence of history, the American people will not be reconciled to power politics and the balance of power and will support only policies based upon abstract moral principles. While in the past the United States might have pursued balance of power policies and while it might be a good thing if it did so again, the American people will not stand for it. Here the emotional appeal to patriotic piety is joined by calculations of political expediency. Yet the case for misrepresenting American history has nothing to gain from either.

There is a strong tendency in all historiography to glorify the national past, and in popular presentations that tendency takes on the aspects of the jingoist whitewash. Even so penetrating a mind as John Stuart Mill's could deliver himself of an essay in which he proved, no doubt to the satisfaction of many of his English readers but certainly of few others, that Great Britain had never interfered in the affairs of European nations and had interfered in those of the Indian states only for their own good. Yet it is the measure of a nation's maturity to be able to recognize its past for what it actually is. Why should we not admit that American foreign policy has been generally hardheaded and practical and at times ruthless? Why should we deny Jefferson's cunning, say, in the Puget Sound affair, the cruelty with which the Indians were treated, and the faithlessness with which the treaties with the Indians were cast aside? We know that this is the way all nations are when their interests are at stake—so cruel, so faithless, so cunning. We know that the United States has refrained from seeking dominions beyond the seas not because it is more virtuous than other nations, but because it had the better part of a continent to colonize.

As has been pointed out elsewhere at greater length, the man in the street, unsophisticated as he is and uninformed as he may be, has a surer grasp of the essentials of foreign policy and a more mature judgment of its basic issues than many of the intellectuals and politicians who pretend to speak for him and cater to what they imagine his prejudices to be. During the recent war the ideologues of the Atlantic Charter, the Four Freedoms, and the United Nations were constantly complaining that the American soldier did not know what he was fighting for. Indeed, if he was fighting for some utopian ideal, divorced from the concrete experiences and interests of the country, then the complaint was well grounded. However, if he was fighting for the territorial integrity of the nation and for its survival as a free country where he could live, think, and act as he pleased, then he had never any doubt about what he was fighting for. Ideological rationalizations and justifications are indeed the indispensable concomitants of all political action. Yet there is something unhealthy in a craving for ideological intoxication and in the inability to act and to see merit in action except under the stimulant of grandiose ideas and far-fetched schemes. Have our intellectuals become, like Hamlet, too much beset by doubt to act and, unlike Hamlet, compelled to still their doubts by renouncing their sense of what is real? The man in the street has no such doubts. It is true that ideologues and demagogues can sway him by appealing to his emotions. But it is also true, as American history shows in abundance and as the popular success of Ambassador Kennan's book demonstrates, that responsible statesmen can guide him by awakening his latent understanding of the national interest.

Yet what is the national interest? How can we define it and give it the content which will make it a guide for action? This is one of the relevant questions to which the current debate has given rise.

It has been frequently argued against the realist conception of foreign policy that its key concept, the national interest, does not provide an acceptable standard for political action. This argument is in the main based upon two grounds: the elusiveness of the concept and its susceptibility to interpretations, such as limitless imperialism and narrow nationalism, which are not in keeping with the American tradition in foreign policy. The argument has substance as far as it goes, but it does not invalidate the usefulness of the concept.

The concept of the national interest is similar in two respects to the "great generalities" of the Constitution, such as the general welfare and due process. It contains a residual meaning which is inherent in the concept itself, but beyond these minimum requirements its content can run the whole gamut of meanings which are logically compatible with it. That content is determined by the political traditions and the total cultural context within which a nation formulates its foreign policy. The concept of the national interest, then, contains two elements, one that is logically required and in that sense necessary, and one that is variable and determined by circumstances.

Any foreign policy which operates under the standard of the national interest must obviously have some reference to the physical, political and cultural entity which we call a nation. In a world where a number of sovereign nations compete with and oppose each other for power, the foreign policies of all nations must necessarily refer to their survival as their minimum requirements.   Thus all nations do what they cannot help but do: protect their physical, political, and cultural identity against encroachments by other nations.

It has been suggested that this reasoning erects the national state into the last word in politics and the national interest into an absolute standard for political action.   This, however, is not quite the case.   The idea of interest is indeed of the essence of politics and, as such, unaffected by the circumstances of time and place.   Thucydides' statement, born of the experiences of ancient Greece, that "identity of interest is the surest of bonds whether between states or individuals" was taken up in the nineteenth century by Lord Salisbury's remark that "the only bond of union that endures" among nations is "the absence of all clashing interests."   The perennial issue between the realist and utopian schools of thought over the nature of politics, to which we have referred before, might well be formulated in terms of concrete interest *vs.* abstract principles.   Yet while the concern of politics with interest is perennial, the connection between interest and the national state is a product of history.

The national state itself is obviously a product of history and as such destined to yield in time to different modes of political organization.   As long as the world is politically organized into nations, the national interest is indeed the last word in world politics.   When the national state will have been replaced by another mode of organization, foreign policy must then protect the interest in survival of that new organization. For the benefit of those who insist upon discarding the national state and constructing supranational organizations by constitutional fiat, it must be pointed out that these new organizational forms will either come into being through conquest or else through consent based upon the mutual recognition of the national interests of the nations concerned; for no nation will forego its freedom of action if it has no reason to expect proportionate benefits in compensation for that loss.   This is true of treaties concerning commerce or fisheries as it is true of the great compacts, such as the European Coal and Steel Community, through which nations try to create supranational forms of organization.   Thus, by an apparent paradox, what is historically relative in the idea of the national interest can be overcome only through the promotion in concert of the national interest of a number of nations.

The survival of a political unit, such as a nation, in its identity is the irreducible minimum, the necessary element of its interests vis-à-vis other units.   Taken in isolation, the determination of its content in a concrete situation is relatively simple; for it encompasses the integrity of the nation's territory, of its political institutions, and of its culture.   Thus bipartisanship in foreign policy, especially in times of war, has been most easily achieved in the promotion of these minimum requirements of the national interest. The situation is different with respect to the variable elements of the national interest. All the cross currents of personalities, public opinion, sectional interests, partisan politics, and political and moral folkways are brought to bear upon their determination. In consequence, the contribution which science can make to this field, as to all fields of policy formation, is limited. It can identify the different agencies of the government which contribute to the determination of the variable elements of the national interest and assess their relative weight. It can separate the long-range objectives of foreign policy from the short-term ones which are the means for the achievement of the former and can tentatively establish their rational relations. Finally, it can analyze the variable elements of the national interest in terms of their legitimacy and their compatibility with other national values and with the national interest of other nations. We shall address ourselves briefly to the typical problems with which this analysis must deal.

The legitimacy of the national interest must be determined in the face of possible usurpation by subnational, other-national, and supranational interests. On the subnational level we find group interests, represented particularly by ethnic and economic groups, who tend to identify themselves with the national interest. Charles A. Beard has emphasized, however one-sidedly, the extent to which the economic interests of certain groups have been presented as those of the United States. Group interests exert, of course, constant pressure upon the conduct of our foreign policy, claiming their identity with the national interest. It is, however, doubtful that, with the exception of a few spectacular cases, they have been successful in determining the course of American foreign policy. It is much more likely, given the nature of American domestic politics, that American foreign policy, insofar as it is the object of pressures by sectional interests, will normally be a compromise between divergent sectional interests. The concept of the national interest, as it emerges from this contest as the actual guide for foreign policy, may well fall short of what would be rationally required by the overall interests of the United States. Yet the concept of the national interest which emerges from this contest of conflicting sectional interests is also more than any particular sectional interest or their sum total. It is, as it were, the lowest common denominator where sectional interests and the national interest meet in an uneasy compromise which may leave much to be desired in view of all the interests concerned.

The national interest can be usurped by other-national interests in two typical ways. The case of treason by individuals, either out of conviction or for pay, needs only to be mentioned here; for insofar as treason is committed on behalf of a foreign government rather than a supra-national principle, it is significant for psychology, sociology, and criminology, but not for the theory of politics. The other case, how-ever, is important not only for the theory of politics but also for its practice, especially in the United States.

National minorities in European countries, ethnic groups in the United States, ideological minorities anywhere may identify themselves, either spontaneously or under the direction of the agents of a foreign govern-ment, with the interests of that foreign government and may promote these interests under the guise of the national interest of the country whose citizens they happen to be. The activities of the German-American Bund in the United States in the 'thirties and of Communists everywhere are cases in point. Yet the issue of the national interest *vs.* other-national interests masquerading as the national interest has arisen constantly in the United States in a less clear-cut fashion.

A country which had been settled by consecutive waves of "foreigners" was bound to find it particularly difficult to identify its own national interest against alleged, seeming, or actual other-national interests represented by certain groups among its own citizens. Since virtually all citizens of the United States are, as it were, "more or less" foreign-born, those who were "less" so have frequently not resisted the tempta-tion to use this distinction as a polemic weapon against late-comers who happened to differ from them in their conception of the national interest of the United States. Frequently, this rationalization has been dispensed with and a conception of foreign policy with which a writer happened to disagree has been attributed outright to foreign sympathy or influence or worse. British influence and interests have served as standard argu-ments in debates on American foreign policy. Madison, in his polemic against Hamilton on the occasion of Washington's Neutrality Proclama-tion of 1793, identified the Federalist position with that of "the foreigners and degenerate citizens among us, who hate our republican government, and the French revolution," and the accusation met with a favorable response in a majority of Congress and of public opinion. However, these traditional attempts to discredit dissenting opinion as being in-fluenced by foreign interests should not obscure the real issue, which is the peculiar vulnerability of the national interest of the United States to usurpation by the interests of other nations.

The usurpation of the national interest by supranational interests can derive in our time from two sources: religious bodies and international organizations. The competition between church and state for determination of certain interests and policies, domestic and international, has been an intermittent issue throughout the history of the national state. Here, too, the legitimate defense of the national interest against usurpation has frequently, especially in the United States, degenerated into the demagogic stigmatization of dissenting views as being inspired by Rome and, hence, being incompatible with the national interest. Yet here, too, the misuse of the issue for demagogic purposes must be considered apart from the legitimacy of the issue itself.

The more acute problem arises at the present time from the importance which the public and government officials, at least in their public utterances, attribute to the values represented and the policies pursued by international organizations either as alternatives or supplements to the values and policies for which the national government stands. It is frequently asserted that the foreign policy of the United States pursues no objectives apart from those of the United Nations, that, in other words, the foreign policy of the United States is actually identical with the policy of the United Nations. This assertion cannot refer to anything real in actual politics to support it. For the constitutional structure of international organizations, such as the United Nations, and their procedural practices make it impossible for them to pursue interests apart from those of the member-states which dominate their policy-forming bodies. The identity between the interests of the United Nations and the United States can only refer to the successful policies of the United States within the United Nations through which the support of the United Nations is being secured for the policies of the United States. The assertion, then, is mere polemic, different from the one discussed previously in that the identification of a certain policy with a supranational interest does not seek to reflect discredit upon the former, but to bestow upon it a dignity which the national interest pure and simple is supposed to lack.

The real issue in view of the problem that concerns us here is not whether the so-called interests of the United Nations, which do not exist apart from the interests of its most influential members, have superseded the national interest of the United States, but for what kind of interests the United States has secured United Nations support. While these interests cannot be United Nations interests, they do not need to be national interests either. Here we are in the presence of that modern phenomenon which has been variously described as "utopianism," "sentimentalism," "moralism," the "legalistic-moralistic approach." The common denominator of all these tendencies in modern political thought is the substitution for the national interest of a supranational standard of action which is generally identified with an international organization, such as the United Nations.   The national interest is here not being usurped by sub- or supranational interests which, however inferior in worth to the national interest, are nevertheless real and worthy of consideration within their proper sphere.   What challenges the national interest here is a mere figment of the imagination, a product of wishful thinking, which is postulated as a valid norm for international conduct, without being valid either there or anywhere else.   At this point we touch the core of the present controversy between utopianism and realism in international affairs; we shall return to it later in this paper.

The national interest as such must be defended against usurpation by non-national interests.   Yet once that task is accomplished, a rational order must be established among the values which make up the national interest and among the resources to be committed to them.   While the interests which a nation may pursue in its relation with other nations are of infinite variety and magnitude, the resources which are available for the pursuit of such interests are necessarily limited in quantity and kind.   No nation has the resources to promote all desirable objectives with equal vigor; all nations must therefore allocate their scarce resources as rationally as possible.   The indispensable precondition of such rational allocation is a clear understanding of the distinction between the necessary and variable elements of the national interest.   Given the contentious manner in which in democracies the variable elements of the national interest are generally determined, the advocates of an extensive conception of the national interest will inevitably present certain variable elements of the national interest as though their attainment were necessary for the nation's survival.   In other words, the necessary elements of the national interest have a tendency to swallow up the variable elements so that in the end all kinds of objectives, actual or potential, are justified in terms of national survival.   Such arguments have been advanced, for instance, in support of the rearmament of Western Germany and of the defense of Formosa.   They must be subjected to rational scrutiny which will determine, however tentatively, their approximate place in the scale of national values.

The same problem presents itself in its extreme form when a nation pursues, or is asked to pursue, objectives which are not only unnecessary for its survival but tend to jeopardize it.   Second-rate nations which dream of playing the role of great powers, such as Italy and Poland in the interwar period, illustrate this point.   So do great powers which dream of remaking the world in their own image and embark upon world-wide crusades, thus straining their resources to exhaustion.   Here scientific analysis has the urgent task of pruning down national objectives to the measure of available resources in order to make their pursuit compatible with national survival.

Finally, the national interest of a nation which is conscious not only of its own interests but also of that of other nations must be defined in terms compatible with the latter. In a multinational world this is a requirement of political morality; in an age of total war it is also one of the conditions for survival.

In connection with this problem two mutually exclusive arguments have been advanced. On the one hand, it has been argued against the theory of international politics here presented that the concept of the national interest revives the eighteenth-century concept of enlightened self-interest, presuming that the uniformly enlightened pursuit of their self-interest by all individuals, as by all nations, will of itself be conducive to a peaceful and harmonious society. On the other hand, the point has been made that the pursuit of their national interest by all nations makes war the permanent arbiter of conflicts among them. Neither argument is well taken.

The concept of the national interest presupposes neither a naturally harmonious, peaceful world nor the inevitability of war as a consequence of the pursuit by all nations of their national interest. Quite to the contrary, it assumes continuous conflict and threat of war, to be minimized through the continuous adjustment of conflicting interests by diplomatic action. No such assumption would be warranted if all nations at all times conceived of their national interest only in terms of their survival and, in turn, defined their interest in survival in restrictive and rational terms. As it is, their conception of the national interest is subject to all the hazards of misinterpretation, usurpation, and misjudgment to which reference has been made above. To minimize these hazards is the first task of a foreign policy which seeks the defense of the national interest by peaceful means. Its second task is the defense of the national interest, restrictively and rationally defined, against the national interests of other nations which may or may not be thus defined. If they are not, it becomes the task of armed diplomacy to convince the nations concerned that their legitimate interests have nothing to fear from a restrictive and rational foreign policy and that their illegitimate interests have nothing to gain in the face of armed might rationally employed.

We have said before that the utopian and realist positions in international affairs do not necessarily differ in the policies they advocate, but that they part company over their general philosophies of politics and their way of thinking about matters political. It does not follow that the present debate is only of academic interest and without practical significance.   Both camps, it is true, may support this same policy for different reasons.   Yet if the reasons are unsound, the soundness of the policies supported by them is a mere coincidence, and these very same reasons may be, and inevitably are, invoked on other occasions in support of unsound policies.   The nefarious consequences of false philosophies and wrong ways of thinking may for the time being be concealed by the apparent success of policies derived from them.   You may go to war, justified by your nation's interests, for a moral purpose and in disregard of considerations of power; and military victory seems to satisfy both your moral aspirations and your nation's interests.   Yet the manner in which you waged the war, achieved victory, and settled the peace cannot help reflecting your philosophy of politics and your way of thinking about political problems.   If these are in error, you may win victory on the field of battle and still assist in the defeat of both your moral principles and the national interest of your country.

Any number of examples could illustrate the real yet subtle practical consequences which follow from the different positions taken.   We have chosen two: collective security in Korea and the liberation of the nations that are captives of Communism.   A case for both policies can be made from both the utopian and realist positions, but with significant differences in the emphasis and substance of the policies pursued.

Collective security as an abstract principle of utopian politics requires that all nations come to the aid of a victim of aggression by resisting the aggressor with all means necessary to frustrate his aims.   Once the case of aggression is established, the duty to act is unequivocal.   Its extent may be affected by concern for the nation's survival; obviously no nation will commit outright suicide in the service of collective security.   But beyond that elemental limitation no consideration of interest or power, either with regard to the aggressor or his victim or the nation acting in the latter's defense, can qualify the obligation to act under the principle of collective security.   Thus high officials of our government have declared that we intervened in Korea not for any narrow interest of ours but in support of the moral principle of collective security.

Collective security as a concrete principle of realist policy is the age-old maxim, "Hang together or hang separately," in modern dress.   It recognizes the need for nation A under certain circumstances to defend nation B against attack by nation C.   That need is determined, first, by the interest which A has in the territorial integrity of B and by the relation of that interest to all the other interests of A as well as to the resources available for the support of all those interests.   Furthermore,

A must take into account the power which is at the disposal of aggressor C for fighting A and B as over against the power available to A and B for fighting C. The same calculation must be carried on concerning the power of the likely allies of C as over against those of A and B. Before going to war for the defense of South Korea in the name of collective security, an American adherent of political realism would have demanded an answer to the following four questions: First, what is our interest in the preservation of the independence of South Korea; second, what is our power to defend that independence against North Korea; third, what is our power to defend that independence against China and the Soviet Union; and fourth, what are the chances for preventing China and the Soviet Union from entering the Korean War?

In view of the principle of collective security, interpreted in utopian terms, our intervention in Korea was a foregone conclusion. The interpretation of this principle in realist terms might or might not, depending upon the concrete circumstances of interest and power, have led us to the same conclusion. In the execution of the policy of collective security the utopian had to be indifferent to the possibility of Chinese and Russian intervention, except for his resolution to apply the principle of collective security to anybody who would intervene on the side of the aggressor. The realist could not help weighing the possibility of the intervention of a great power on the side of the aggressor in terms of the interests engaged and the power available on the other side.

The Truman administration could not bring itself to taking resolutely the utopian or the realist position. It resolved to intervene in good measure on utopian grounds and in spite of military advice to the contrary; it allowed the military commander to advance to the Yalu River in disregard of the risk of the intervention of a great power against which collective security could be carried out only by means of a general war, and then refused to pursue the war with full effectiveness on the realist grounds of the risk of a third world war. Thus Mr. Truman in 1952 is caught in the same dilemma from which Mr. Baldwin could extricate himself in 1936 on the occasion of the League of Nations sanctions against Italy's attack upon Ethiopia only at an enormous loss to British prestige. Collective security as a defense of the *status quo* short of a general war can be effective only against second-rate powers. Applied against a major power, it is a contradiction in terms, for it means necessarily a major war. Of this self-defeating contradiction Mr. Baldwin was as unaware in the 'thirties as Mr. Truman seems to be in 1952. Mr. Churchill put Mr. Baldwin's dilemma in these cogent terms: "First, the Prime Minister had declared that sanctions meant war; secondly, he was resolved that there must be no war; and thirdly, he decided upon sanctions.   It was evidently impossible to comply with these three conditions."   Similarly Mr. Truman had declared that the effective prosecution of the Korean War meant the possibility of a third world war; he resolved that there must be no third world war; and he decided upon intervention in the Korean War.   Here, too, it is impossible to comply with these three conditions.

Similar contradictions are inherent in the proposals which would substitute for the current policy of containment one of the liberation of the nations presently the captives of Russian Communism.   This objective can be compatible with the utopian or realist position, but the policies designed to secure it will be fundamentally different according to whether they are based upon one or the other position.   The clearest case to date for the utopian justification of such policies has been made by Representative Charles J. Kersten of Wisconsin who pointed to these four "basic defects" of the "negative policy of containment and negotiated coexistence":

It would be immoral and unchristian to negotiate a permanent agreement with forces which by every religious creed and moral precept are evil.   It abandons nearly one-half of humanity and the once free nations of Poland, Czechoslovakia, Hungary, Rumania, Bulgaria, Albania, Lithuania, Latvia, Estonia and China to enslavement of the Communist police state.

It is un-American because it violates the principle of the American Declaration of Independence, which proclaims the rights of all people to freedom and their right and duty to throw off tyranny.

It will lead to all-out World War III because it aligns all the forces of the non-Communist world in military opposition to and against all the forces of the Communist world, including the 800,000,000 peoples behind the Iron Curtain.

The policy of mere containment is uneconomic and will lead to national bankruptcy.

This statement is interesting for its straightforwardness and because it combines in a rather typical fashion considerations of abstract morality and of expediency.   The captive nations must be liberated not only because their captivity is immoral, unchristian, and un-American, but also because its continuation will lead to a third world war and to national bankruptcy.   To what extent, however, these considerations of expediency are invalidated by their utopian setting will become obvious from a comparison between the utopian and the realist positions.

From the utopian point of view there can be no difference between the liberation of Estonia or Czechoslovakia, of Poland or China; the captivity of any nation, large or small, close or far away, is a moral outrage which cannot be tolerated.   The realist, too, seeks the liberation of all captive nations because he realizes that the presence of the Russian armies in the heart of Europe and their cooperation with the Chinese armies constitute the two main sources of the imbalance of power which threatens our security.   Yet before he formulates a program of liberation, he will seek answers to a number of questions such as these: While the United States has a general interest in the liberation of all captive nations, what is the hierarchy of interests it has in the liberation, say, of China, Estonia, and Hungary?   And while the Soviet Union has a general interest in keeping all captive nations in that state, what is the hierarchy of its interests in keeping, say, Poland, Eastern Germany, and Bulgaria captive?   If we assume, as we must on the historic evidence of two centuries, that Russia would never give up control over Poland without being compelled by force of arms, would the objective of the liberation of Poland justify the ruin of western civilization, that of Poland included, which would be the certain result of a third world war?   What resources does the United States have at its disposal for the liberation of all captive nations or some of them?   What resources does the Soviet Union have at its disposal to keep in captivity all captive nations or some of them?   Are we more likely to avoid national bankruptcy by embarking upon a policy of indiscriminate liberation with the concomitant certainty of war or by continuing the present policy of containment?

It might be that in a particular instance the policies suggested by the answers to these questions will coincide with Representative Kersten's proposals, but there can be no doubt that in its overall character, substance, emphasis, and likely consequences a utopian policy of liberation differs fundamentally from a realist one.

The issue between liberation as a utopian principle of abstract morality *vs.* the realist evaluation of the consequences which a policy of liberation would have for the survival of the nation has arisen before in American history.   Abraham Lincoln was faced with a dilemma similar to that which confronts us today.   Should he make the liberation of the slaves the ultimate standard of his policy even at the risk of destroying the Union, as many urged him to do, or should he subordinate the moral principle of universal freedom to considerations of the national interest?   The answer Lincoln gave to Horace Greeley, a spokesman for the utopian moralists, is timeless in its eloquent wisdom.   "If there be those," he wrote on August 22, 1862,

who would not save the Union unless they could at the same time save slavery, I do not agree with them. If there be those who would not save the Union unless they could at the same time destroy slavery, I do not agree with them. My paramount object in this struggle *is* to save the Union, and is *not* either to save or to destroy slavery. If I could save the Union without freeing *any* slave I would do it, and if I could save it by freeing *all* the slaves, I would do it; and if I could save it by freeing some and leaving others alone I would also do that. What I do about slavery, and the colored race, I do because I believe it helps to save the Union; and what I forbear, I forbear because I do *not* believe it would help to save the Union. I shall do *less* whenever I shall believe what I am doing hurts the cause, and I shall do *more* whenever I shall believe doing more will help the cause. I shall try to correct errors when shown to be errors; and I shall adopt new views so fast as they appear to be true views.

I have here stated my purpose according to my view of *official* duty; and I intend no modification of my oft-expressed *personal* wish that all men everywhere could be free.

The foregoing discussion ought to shed additional light, if this is still needed, upon the moral merits of the utopian and realist positions. This question, more than any other, seems to have agitated the critics of realism in international affairs. Disregarding the voluminous evidence, some of them have picked a few words out of their context to prove that realism in international affairs is unprincipled and contemptuous of morality. To mention but one example, one eminent critic summarizes my position, which he supposes to deny the possibility of judging the conduct of states by moral criteria, in these words: "And one spokesman finds 'a profound and neglected truth,' to use his words, in the dictum of Hobbes that 'there is neither morality nor law outside the state.'" These are indeed my words, but not all of them. What I actually said was this:

There is a profound and neglected truth hidden in Hobbes's extreme dictum that the state creates morality as well as law and that there is neither morality nor law outside the state. Universal moral principles, such as justice or equality, are capable of guiding political action only to the extent that they have been given concrete content and have been related to political situations by society.

It must be obvious from this passage and from all my other writings on the subject that my position is the exact opposite from what this critic makes it out to be. I have always maintained that the actions of states are subject to universal moral principles and I have been careful to differentiate my position in this respect from that of Hobbes. Five points basic to my position may need to be emphasized again.

The first point is what one might call the requirement of cosmic humility with regard to the moral evaluation of the actions of states. To know that states are subject to the moral law is one thing; to pretend to know what is morally required of states in a particular situation is quite another.   The human mind tends naturally to identify the particular interests of states, as of individuals, with the moral purposes of the universe.   The statesman in the defense of the nation's interests may, and at times even must, yield to that tendency; the scholar must resist it at every turn.   For the light-hearted assumption that what one's own nation aims at and does is morally good and that those who oppose that nation's policies are evil is morally indefensible and intellectually untenable and leads in practice to that distortion of judgment, born of the blindness of crusading frenzy, which has been the curse of nations from the beginning of time.

The second point which obviously needs to be made again concerns the effectiveness of the restraints which morality imposes upon the actions of states:

A discussion of international morality must guard against the two extremes either of overrating the influence of ethics upon international politics or else of denying that statesmen and diplomats are moved by anything else but considerations of material power.

On the one hand, there is the dual error of confounding the moral rules which people actually observe with those they pretend to observe as well as with those which writers declare they ought to observe. . . .

On the other hand, there is the misconception, usually associated with the general depreciation and moral condemnation of power politics, discussed above, that international politics is so thoroughly evil that it is no use looking for ethical limitations of the aspirations for power on the international scene. Yet, if we ask ourselves what statesmen and diplomats are capable of doing to further the power objectives of their respective nations and what they actually do, we realize that they do less than they probably could and less than they actually did in other periods of history. They refuse to consider certain ends and to use certain means, either altogether or under certain conditions, not because in the light of expediency they appear impractical or unwise, but because certain moral rules interpose an absolute barrier. Moral rules do not permit certain policies to be considered at all from the point of view of expediency. Such ethical inhibitions operate in our time on different levels with different effectiveness. Their restraining function is most obvious and most effective in affirming the sacredness of human life in times of peace.

In connection with this passage we have given a number of historic examples showing the influence of moral principles upon the conduct of foreign policy.   An example taken from contemporary history will illustrate the same point.   There can be little doubt that the Soviet Union could have achieved the objectives of its foreign policy at the end of the Second World War without antagonizing the nations of the West into that encircling coalition which has been the nightmare of

Bolshevist foreign policy since 1917.   It could have mitigated cunning for its own sake and the use of force with persuasion, conciliation, and a trust derived from the awareness of a partial community of interests and would thereby have minimized the dangers to itself and the rest of the world which are inherent in the objectives of its policies.   Yet the Soviet Union was precluded from relying upon these traditional methods of diplomacy by its general conception of human nature, politics, and morality.   In the general philosophy of Bolshevism there is no room for honest dissent, the recognition of the intrinsic worth of divergent interests, and genuine conciliation between such interests.   On all levels of social interaction opposition must be destroyed by cunning and violence, since it has no right to exist, rather than be met half way in view of its intrinsic legitimacy.   This being the general conception of the political morality of Bolshevism, the foreign policy of the Soviet Union is limited to a much more narrow choice of means than the foreign policies of other nations.

The United States, for instance, has been able, in its relations with the nations of Latin America, to replace military intervention and dollar diplomacy with the policy of the Good Neighbor.   That drastic change was made possible by the general conception of political morality which has been prevalent in the United States from its very inception.   The United States is a pluralist society which presupposes the continuing existence and legitimacy of divergent interests.   These interests are locked in a continuing struggle for supremacy to be decided by force only as a last resort, but normally through a multitude of institutional agencies which are so devised as to allow one or the other interest a temporary advantage but none a permanent supremacy at the price of the destruction of the others.   This morality of pluralism allows the United States, once it is secure in that minimum of vital interests to which we have referred above, to transfer those principles of political morality to the international scene and to deal with divergent interests there with the same methods of genuine compromise and conciliation which are a permanent element of its domestic political life.

The third point concerns the relations between universal moral principles and political action.   I have always maintained that these universal moral principles cannot be applied to the actions of states in their abstract universal formulation, but that they must be, as it were, filtered through the concrete circumstances of time and place. The individual may say for himself: *"Fiat justitia, pereat mundus";* the state has no right to say so in the name of those who are in its care. Both individual and state must judge political action by universal moral principles, such as that of liberty.   Yet while the individual has a moral

right to sacrifice himself in defense of such a moral principle, the state
has no moral right to let its moral disapprobation of the infringement
of liberty get in the way of successful political action, itself inspired
by the moral principle of national survival.   There can be no political
morality without prudence, that is, without consideration of the political
consequences of seemingly moral action.   Classical and medieval philosophy knew this and so did Lincoln when he said: "I do the very
best I know how, the very best I can, and I mean to keep doing so
until the end.   If the end brings me out all right, what is said against
me won't amount to anything.   If the end brings me out wrong, ten
angels swearing I was right would make no difference."   The issue
between utopianism and realism, as it bears on this point, has been
put most succinctly by Edmund Burke, and what he has to say in the
following passage about revolution, that is, civil war, may well be
applied *mutatis mutandis* to all war.

Nothing universal can be rationally affirmed on any moral or any political
subject.   Pure metaphysical abstraction does not belong to these matters.
The lines of morality are not like the ideal lines of mathematics.   They are
broad and deep as well as long.   They admit of exceptions; they demand
modifications.   These exceptions and modifications are not made by the
process of logic, but by the rules of prudence.   Prudence is not only the first
in rank of the virtues political and moral, but she is the director, the
regulator, the standard of them all.   Metaphysics cannot live without definition; but Prudence is cautious how she defines.   Our courts cannot be more
fearful in suffering fictitious cases to be brought before them for eliciting
their determination on a point of law than prudent moralists are in putting
extreme and hazardous cases of conscience upon emergencies not existing.
Without attempting, therefore, to define, what never can be defined, the case
of a revolution in government, this, I think, may be safely affirmed—that a
sore and pressing evil is to be removed, and that a good, great in its amount
and unequivocal in its nature, must be probable almost to a certainty, before
the inestimable price of our own morals and the well-being of a number of
our fellow-citizens is paid for a revolution.   If ever we ought to be economists
even to parsimony, it is in the voluntary production of evil.   Every revolution
contains in it something of evil.

Fourth, the realist recognizes that a moral decision, especially in the
political sphere, does not imply a simple choice between a moral principle
and a standard of action which is morally irrelevant or even outright
immoral.   A moral decision implies always a choice among different
moral principles, one of which is given precedence over others.   To say
that a political action has no moral purpose is absurd; for political action
can be defined as an attempt to realize moral values through the medium
of politics, that is, power.   The relevant moral question concerns the

choice among different moral values, and it is at this point that the realist and the utopian part company again.   If an American statesman must choose between the promotion of universal liberty, which is a moral good, at the risk of American security and, hence, of liberty in the United States, and the promotion of American security and of liberty in the United States, which is another moral good, to the detriment of the promotion of universal liberty, which choice ought he to make?   The utopian will not face the issue squarely and will deceive himself into believing that he can achieve both goods at the same time.   The realist will choose the national interest on both moral and pragmatic grounds; for if he does not take care of the national interest nobody else will, and if he puts American security and liberty in jeopardy the cause of liberty everywhere will be impaired.

Finally, the political realist distinguishes between his moral sympathies and the political interests which he must defend.   He will distinguish with Lincoln between his *"official* duty" which is to protect the national interest and his *"personal* wish" which is to see universal moral values realized throughout the world.

The issue has been admirably put by Father Wilfred Parsons of Catholic University in defending Ambassador Kennan's position:

Mr. Kennan did not say state behavior is not a fit subject for moral judgment, but only that it should not sway our realization of the realities with which we have to deal. Msgr. Koenig continues: "Should we accept power realities and aspirations without feeling the obligation of moral judgment?" And he appeals to the present writer and other political scientists to say whether this doctrine agrees with Pope Pius XII's messages on peace.

I am sure that most political scientists, and also Mr. Kennan, would agree with the Monsignor that we should not accept those realities "without feeling the obligation of moral judgment." But there is a difference between *feeling* this obligation (and even expressing it) and allowing this feeling to sway our actions in concrete negotiations that deal with the national or world common good. We can still feel and yet deal.

To make my meaning clearer, I understood Mr. Kennan to hold that we went off the beam with Woodrow Wilson, when we began to make our moral disapprobation an *essential part* of our foreign relations, even sometimes at the expense of our own and the world's common good. Logically, such an attitude would inhibit our dealing with Britain, France and a host of countries. Pius XI, speaking of Mussolini after the Lateran Treaty, said he would deal with the devil himself if he must. Here was moral disapprobation, but it was not "carried over into the affairs of states."

This relative position, and not the absolute one of Msgr. Koenig (with which in itself I agree), is, I think, the issue raised by Mr. Kennan, and it is worth debating on that basis.

The contest between utopianism and realism is not tantamount to a contest between principle and expediency, morality and immorality, although some spokesmen for the former would like to have it that way. The contest is rather between one type of political morality and another type of political morality, one taking as its standard universal moral principles abstractly formulated, the other weighing these principles against the moral requirements of concrete political action, their relative merits to be decided by a prudent evaluation of the political consequences to which they are likely to lead.

These points are re-emphasized by the foregoing discussion. Which attitude with regard to collective security and to the liberation of the captive nations, the utopian or the realist, is more likely to safeguard the survival of the United States in its territorial, political, and cultural identity and at the same time to contribute the most to the security and liberty of other nations? This is the ultimate test—political and moral— by which utopianism and realism must be judged.

CHAPTER THREE

Forces That Shape Decisions

THIS CHAPTER IS CONCERNED with the forces that shape American foreign policy decisions. We shall give illustrations of the influence on our policy of the following forces: the policies of other governments; geography; national character and public opinion; pressure groups, political parties, and propaganda; natural resources and the national economy; and science and technology.

In a sense, most of our policies are shaped by the actions of foreign governments. There is some validity in the comparison between international politics and the game of chess. In both, the moves of each player must take into account those of the other. The isolationist notion that one can play the game by ignoring what the other player does will simply not work in chess, nor will it work in international politics. Few people in the United States would maintain that what the Soviet Union does matters little to us. Much of American foreign policy is indeed keyed to completed actions of the Soviet Union or designed to meet actions which that nation might undertake. But to think of American policy as being shaped by Soviet policy *alone* is to omit an important part of the total picture.

It is true that we often speak of American foreign policy as though relations with the Soviet Union were the only factor involved. This indicates the importance of the actions of that nation in the conduct of our affairs. Yet the success of American efforts to combat communism depends upon the actions of other nations as well. Secretary of State Dulles recently declared that the United States might have to change its policies in Europe radically if the French refuse to participate in the European defense effort. Mr. Dulles' remarks not only constituted a warning that the United States might discontinue economic and military assistance to France, but also implied a recognition of the partial dependence of American plans to prevent Communist aggression against Western Europe upon the willingness of specific European nations to participate in the community defense effort. And when the recent declarations and actions of Korean President Syngman Rhee seemed to threaten the hard-won armistice agreement in Korea, Americans had further evidence of the manner in which our policies have been tied to those of other states—in this instance, it even appeared for a time that Mr. Rhee would have his way in spite of anything we could do, and that we would have to go along with him, willy-nilly.

These examples will perhaps suffice to explain the fact that our policy is shaped, in large measure, by the policies of other governments. But there are also other forces that shape decisions. Mr. Louis Johnson, former Secretary of Defense, implied that the maintenance of a strong national economy imposed limits upon our policy when he defended the reduction of expenditures for the armed forces on the grounds that the Soviet Union intended to sit by and placidly watch the United States "spend itself into bankruptcy."

President Eisenhower's State of the Union Message of January 7, 1954, contained one sentence which produced considerable Congressional applause. The President said: "Economic assistance to foreign countries can be reduced." Some members of Congress believe that our huge governmental expenditures strain our economy. Since they are reluctant to reduce appropriations for the military establishment, they seek to effect economies elsewhere. For this and other reasons, economic assistance programs are becoming increasingly unpopular with Congress.

There may or may not be cause for concern that our economy will be unable to bear the burdens of our vast commitments. What is more important than the validity of this position, however, is the fact that strong pressure to reduce expenditures derives in part from this view, and that pressure to economize will probably bring about some changes in policy. We may be able to speak of a "new approach" which will cost less than previous policies and accomplish the same ends. The "new look" may prove to be more successful than the policies of previous administrations, but it seems clear that the innovations of the Eisenhower administration have been and will likely continue to be *shaped,* to a large extent, by a concern for the strength of our national economy.

Probably the most important domestic force that shapes American foreign policy decisions is public opinion. In a democracy we can say *vox populi, vox dei;* but it is also necessary to realize that in the United

States public attitudes are often strongly influenced by what the government says and does. On occasions when no consensus on an issue of international importance exists—as was the case during the period of the Civil War in Spain in the late thirties and the Japanese aggression in Manchuria in 1931—United States policy has been to take no decisive action. More often, however, the relationship between public opinion and the process of decision-making has been more complicated. On some issues of foreign policy, the government must have considerable public support. Mere apathy, or just the absence of significant opposition, would not be sufficient to permit, for example, a change from the present "hard" policy toward the Soviet Union to one of "sweet reasonableness." Drastic departures or innovations must be based upon something more than acquiescence by default. And so, a President or a Secretary of State who is convinced of the wisdom of a policy which lacks popular support may find it necessary to play a kind of duet with public opinion. He may pursue his policy, trusting in his own ability to create a favorable climate of opinion while the policy is in operation.

In any case, our Presidents have rarely been able to lead the nation where consciously or unconsciously it was determined not to go. President Roosevelt's determination prior to Pearl Harbor to abandon the policy of neutrality and President Truman's decision to commit the United States to the defense of South Korea were courageous acts of executive leadership based upon profound insight into the foreign policy *potential* of the American people. If either President had been mistaken about public opinion—as Roosevelt apparently had been earlier, to judge from the reaction to his Chicago Quarantine Address of 1937—he would have had no choice but to backtrack as quickly and as gracefully as possible.

Public opinion, then, actual or potential, exerts a powerful influence on the process of policy formation. President Wilson commented with some bitterness and irony that the American people had permitted him to lead them into war, but had not suffered him to lead them into peace. And during the two decades that followed Wilson's failure to secure American participation in the League of Nations, Congress, presumably with the approval of public opinion, continued to block proposals that the United States join various international organizations. These refusals were only one facet of the isolationist mood of the post-World War I period. Isolationism, as Professor Gabriel Almond has noted, also involved a feeling of cynicism about the war, of intolerance of foreign peoples and ideologies, and of pessimism concerning international politics. The contrast of this climate of opinion with the optimism, tolerance, idealism, and the willingness, even the eagerness to participate in the United Nations Organization which were characteristic of the American mood at the close of World War II is striking; and it is obvious that the policies shaped by one mood will vastly differ from those shaped by the other.

Public opinion shapes policy in several ways. Congress and the President are especially concerned lest their actions arouse intense public disapproval, for although the people's memory is relatively short, they have on occasion remembered their earlier displeasure on election day. The defeat of many isolationist Senators and Representatives during and immediately after World War II was largely due to public dissatisfaction with their pre-Pearl Harbor voting records. Accordingly, letters to the President and members of Congress and public opinion polls are carefully analyzed by our policy makers. (In spite of the pollsters' debacle in the election of 1948, the public opinion poll remains the best instrument we have to determine public sentiment on major issues.) Editorials from leading newspapers all over the country sometimes offer an insight into the way people are thinking about public problems. But perhaps the most effective way the public, or groups of people within the public, can influence the process of policy formation is through the activities of pressure groups.

Some groups, such as the United World Federalists, the Quakers, and advocates of a preventive war on the Soviet Union, pursue their separate enthusiasms. Each is confident that its particular method can solve the international difficulties of the United States—a World Federal Organization would bring peace and order to international relations; the application of Christian principles to the conduct of American foreign policy would alleviate international tension and would eventually eliminate war as an instrument of national policy; the military defeat of the Soviet Union would bring peace and security to the world.

However, although persistence, single-mindedness, and dedication will often win a hearing for a group, only groups with power, especially economic and political power, can hope to influence the process of decision-making in a democratic nation like the United States. Examples of the operation of pressure groups in the field of foreign policy are numerous. The implementation of the Marshall Plan by specific enactment brought a flood of pressure from groups anxious to incorporate some private interest into the legislation: for instance, pressure that the materials be shipped primarily in American vessels; or that a large portion of the Marshall aid be used to purchase surplus agricultural crops in the United States. (This issue seemed to arouse every local agricultural interest in the country.) When powerful group interests are involved, even the simple act of recognizing the government of another nation may become a matter of considerable controversy. Even the deeply rooted pattern of American isolationism has at times been based in part upon the interests of certain groups. Analyses of the election of 1940, for example, have demonstrated that much of the isolationist vote was concentrated in areas with a large population of German or Italian extraction.

Of course, pressure groups are not always successful in their attempts to shape foreign policy. If they are strong enough, however, they may limit the freedom of policy planners. Thus, President Roosevelt may have been certain that the isolationists spoke for a minority of the American people, but he was subject to isolationist pressure, and, therefore, he probably was forced to move more slowly than he deemed wise.

Perhaps these remarks on the role of the policies of foreign governments, of the national economy, and of public opinion and pressure groups will suffice to indicate what is meant by forces that shape decisions. Further comment on the influence of these and other factors upon the process of policy formation will be made as we proceed with the present chapter.

The chapter opens with an illustration of how our policy is shaped by the actual or anticipated actions of foreign governments (Selection 17). An analysis of the influence of geography follows (Selection 18). Next comes a series of selections describing elements of natural character (Selections 19-22), the power and genesis of public opinion (Selections 23 and 24), and the workings of political parties, pressure groups, and propaganda (Selections 25 and 26). The importance of natural resources (Selection 27) and the national economy (Selection 28) are then analyzed. Finally, we examine the influence of science and technology (Selections 29 and 30).

External Pressures

17. Soviet-American Relations since the War *

Probably the most obvious influences shaping American foreign policy are the actions of foreign governments. Mr. Mosely here analyzes the pattern of interaction between the United States and the Soviet Union. He recognizes three major phases in the relationship: the period of partial cooperation and general amity, which

* Philip E. Mosely, *The Annals of the American Academy of Political and Social Science,* May, 1949, pp. 202-211. The author is Professor of International Relations, Columbia University.

lasted until shortly after World War II; the period of American disillusionment with the intentions of the Soviet Union (1945-1947); and the period since 1947, in which specific American policies were adopted to meet the threat which Soviet action had posed. In each period our policies clearly resulted in part either from a reaction to Soviet pressures, or from a belief that little or no pressure existed.

The policy of containment has been criticized because it is a policy of reaction to Soviet action, and, as such, leaves the initiative with the Soviet Union. But even those who insist upon the necessity of maintaining the initiative would hardly deny that, to some extent at least, our policies are bound to be *shaped* by the completed or contemplated actions of other powers.

The problem which now dominates all aspects of postwar politics is that of the antagonism between American and Soviet politics. If there is a ballot on admitting new members to the United Nations, or a decision to be taken on reconstruction in Germany, it cannot be discussed on the merits of the case. Each position is taken with an eye to its effect upon the two contending greatest powers.

The extreme polarization of power is reflected along sensitive frontiers, as in Norway and Iran. It cuts across critical areas of homogeneous nationalities, as in the cases of Germany, Austria, and Korea. It is paralleled in dangerous fissures within many national communities and is reflected in the continuing unrest within Soviet satellites and in the struggles of the Communist parties in France and Italy, in Greece and China. The factors of conflict have been tumultuous and remain dangerous.

The dangers are increased by the fact that both Soviet and American centers of power are largely self-contained; the outlook and purposes of each of these powers are generated internally, are secreted from its own way of life. The intentional or unforeseen repercussions of their acts affect many other peoples in their most sensitive interests and aspirations. In addition, each of these two great powers finds it difficult to arrive at a coherent judgment of the power and intentions of the other.

SOVIET IDEAS OF THE UNITED STATES

When the Soviet leaders look at America, they think primarily of its great economic power. No doubt, they are rather well informed of its strength in specific skills and of its inventiveness. Their insistence upon the validity of a single philosophy prevents them from understanding the political and social experience and outlook which form the underpinning of American society. In applying with extreme rigor the system of piece-rate rewards and penalties to their own workers, they overlook the fact that in America differential incentives to workers rest on a high minimum standard of living. Admitting the technical superiority of American industry, always measuring their own achievements against American statistics, the Soviet leaders also believe unshakably that the American economy is certain to be pounded to pieces from within. And since the United States is now the only other great power, they wait impatiently for the time when that power will disintegrate and American policy will be paralyzed by internal stresses.

The duality in the Soviet evaluation of American strength was clearly shown in the question of a postwar loan. The Soviet representatives were eager to secure a very large loan—figures of six to ten billion dollars were bandied about—and admitted freely that Soviet reconstruction would be immensely facilitated by the inflow of American equipment. On the other hand, they were absolutely convinced that this loan was not something for which they would have to make an effort, even an effort to maintain some degree of diplomatic decorum. They were certain that America would come hat in hand, begging them to accept a large loan, solely for the purpose of staving off a catastrophic depression at home. They felt they would be doing a favor to American manufacturers by giving their rickety economic system a few years of grace. Holding these views, the Soviet leaders assumed that their own offensive against American interests and sentiments was in no way incompatible with the obtaining of a loan.

A similar opaqueness has shaped the Soviet leaders' understanding of American policies in the postwar world. They can recognize that Americans are basically oriented inwards and find it hard to be concerned steadily with world affairs. They know that the United States did not take the initiative in starting either of the world wars in this century. From the full and open discussion of policy which goes on in this country, they can see that most disputes revolve around the question of finding the best way to prevent a new war. Yet the Soviet leaders insist that America is the center of a new and active conspiracy to unleash a new world war.

Believing that the Soviet system alone has solved the inner contradictions of industrial society and that it is bound to expand into ever wider areas and some day to encompass the world, the Soviet leaders conclude that any forces which are outside Soviet control are, potentially or in reality, a menace to their ambition and to their regime. Professing to believe that the non-Soviet world envies the achievements of the Soviet Union and desires to destroy their system, they assume that the forces of the non-Soviet world are bound, sooner or later, to coalesce around the strongest non-Soviet power. Power beyond Soviet control and "anti-Soviet" power tend to become identified in their way of thinking.

In 1941 the Soviet leaders fully expected Britain and the United States to sit idly by while Hitler attempted to destroy the Soviet regime, or even to join with him. The prompt support which the Soviets received in a time of greatest danger, the great contributions of supplies, and the constant efforts to promote closer co-operation did not shake their faith in the dogma of "capitalist encirclement." In February 1946 this basic tenet was reaffirmed by Marshal Stalin as the central point in the postwar Soviet program.

Reasoning from Unsound Premises

The trouble about Soviet reasoning is not that it is illogical—it is usually too strictly logical—but that its premises ignore or distort simple facts which are readily discernible to minds which have not been subjected to the process of "Bolshevist hardening." If "lasting peace" is declared to be possible only under the Soviet system, then, logically, only the Soviet Union and its obedient satellites can be considered truly "peace-loving" countries. Whatever "subjective" horror of war may be expressed by "capitalist" leaders, their governments, "objectively" analyzed, are engaged in "warmongering." Anyone who criticizes or opposes Soviet claims and actions is, of course, "spreading anti-Soviet slander," "undermining peace," "promoting fascism," or "destroying Allied unity." This syllogism rests in turn on an assumption, which cannot be questioned or criticized in areas under Soviet control, that a small group of leaders in command of the régime has, through self-appointed apostolic succession to Lenin, a monopoly of wisdom and virtue.

Of course, the faculty of reasoning logically from unprovable hypotheses to untenable conclusions is not confined to any one group of men, although it seems to appear most often under conditions of absolute power. Such a faculty is dangerous when its pronouncements monopolize access to men's minds, including the minds of those who direct or serve the dictatorship.

There is a continual danger in the Soviet leaders' habit of taking action upon a set of facts which appear as facts to them alone. An even more serious danger lies in the marshaling and interpreting of a commonly perceived body of facts in accordance with a rigidly enforced philosophy, adherence to which is the password to authority and responsibility within the Soviet system.

SOME AMERICAN MISCONCEPTIONS
ABOUT THE SOVIET UNION

Most Americans cannot make up their minds as to whether the Soviet Union is strong or weak. Because the Soviet war effort was greatly assisted through lend-lease, many Americans suppose that the Soviet Union cannot wage a major war on the basis of its own production. This assumption overlooks the fact that up to the turning of the tide at Stalingrad, the Soviet armies had received relatively small quantities of supplies from abroad. Throughout the war, the basic tools of war—artillery, tanks, planes—were almost entirely of Soviet manufacture. It would be short-sighted to suppose that Soviet capacity to wage war is far smaller, or is not actually substantially greater, than it was when the Soviet forces broke the German onslaught.

It is sometimes assumed that a denial of technical equipment and knowledge derived from the West will slow down or even disrupt the development of Soviet industry. It must, however, be assumed that in the production of machine tools the Soviet Union is "over the hump" in the process of industrialization. Failure to obtain abroad certain specialized or more modern types of equipment may delay or hamper but cannot prevent the broad development of Soviet industry on the basis of skills already acquired. Finally, the ratio of total industrial power to war potential varies considerably under diverse systems. The Soviet system gives its leaders great leeway in deciding what proportion of industrial power shall be directed towards military needs.

A contrary assumption is also advanced that the Soviet leaders may lightheartedly engage in a new trial of strength by war, as soon as they feel confident of thereby gaining some immediate and decisive advantage. Their real range of choice seems to lie somewhere between two extremes. It is unrealistic to suppose that they would make concessions from their basic program, either to secure economic aid or to win favor in the eyes of the non-Soviet world. It is also unreasonable to assume that the urge to extend their system to new areas will lead them into war without considering the effect of war upon the low Soviet standard of living or without reflecting on the possibly unpredictable outcome of a war against a powerful, highly ingenious, and relatively impregnable enemy.

If the Soviet leaders have, since 1945, steadily weighted their choice in favor of a relentless political offensive against the non-Soviet world, this may be due to a short-run assumption that the economic advantages which might be gained immediately through a more conciliatory policy are of minor importance to them when compared with the great extension of political power on which they are gambling. It may also be assumed that they have felt sure that a policy of strong pressure offered no risk to their basic security, since the American military machine was being dismantled with great haste and there was no other power to challenge their ambitions.

Because the Soviet Government rules through a centralized dictatorship and severely limits the range of suggestion or criticism allowed to its citizens and to supporters abroad, an American readily assumes that the system is inherently weak, maintained only through the constant stimulation of fear. This impression of political instability has been enhanced by the sensational abandonment of Soviet allegiance by individual citizens and by the much less publicized refusal of several hundreds of thousands of its citizens to return to the Soviet Union. To people accustomed to a régime which periodically submits to the judgment of the voters, these facts suggest weakness, hence, a necessity for such a régime to avoid war at all cost.

This interpretation, natural in American eyes, overlooks many unfamiliar factors: a long tradition of rule by a strong and irresponsible power, the tradition of combining incessant persuasion with coercion, and absence of conscious formulation of alternative programs despite widespread discontent with privations and injustices. It would be shortsighted to disparage the substantial level of disciplined action achieved under the Soviet régime or to assume that internal discontent would be an important factor, especially in a short test of strength. In any major war, of course, a defeated and occupied country may undergo a change of régime, and new currents may come to the surface. In Russia today, or anywhere in Europe, few of these currents would be tender of individual rights.

Popular Appeal of Communism

It is hard for Americans to realize that Communism meets with acceptance and even fanatical support in many segments of the population. Communism remains a powerful force in France and Italy, for American gifts and economic recovery do not reach far into the basic factors making for discontent. Backward countries may be attracted to the Soviet recipe of quick action through dictatorship, rather than to the American method of piecemeal improvement and changes brought about through consent. Where problems of overpopulation, absence of technical skills and capital, and age-old accumulations of social and national resentments set discouragingly high barriers to modernization, the appeal of Communism is bound to remain strong. There it is judged by its promises of "progress"—not by the as yet unknown effects which may follow from the quality and direction of the "progress" it offers. The Soviet leaders choose to regard American democracy as a "conspiracy." It would be equally dangerous for Americans to assume that their own type of democracy is universally admired and desired, and that the strength of Communism resides only in a centralized conspiracy of force.

Since the Soviet leaders accept the duty of spreading their system and rejoice at the appearance of each new "people's democracy," it is easily and widely assumed that this political ambition motivates its leaders at all times with an unvarying emotional intensity. It is difficult to judge the emotional intensities within the Politburo, but it is clear from the record that the outward pressure of Soviet expansionism has fluctuated rather widely over the past thirty-one years. This intensity may vary in the future.

A relative relaxation of the outward thrust may come about in one of several ways. It may arise from a discouraged recognition of solid and impassable barriers erected in its path; or it may develop from the operation of internal factors. In the case of an ideology which offers the only "scientific" basis for prediction, repeated failures to predict accurately may result in the growth of skepticism towards the doctrine of infallibility itself. Or, when a militant ideology has outlived the generation which formulated it in the heat of revolutionary struggle, and becomes the property of a generation which docilely received the tradition ready-made, the fervor of the revolutionary "fathers" may not pass integrally into the postrevolutionary "sons."

The written word of revelation may remain sacrosanct, but if it is believed with, say, 10 per cent less fervor by a new generation, the compulsion to act hazardously on behalf of the doctrine may slacken. As a dogma becomes more rigid, it may not evoke the same desire to act. Since about 1937, Soviet dogma has achieved a remarkable posture of rigidity, unnatural in a people of quick mind and ranging curiosity. Meanwhile, since no confident prediction of a slackening of the Soviet urge to messianic expansion can be made, it has become necessary to act on the assumption that this urge can be restrained only by constructing external barriers and setting clear warning signals.

SOVIET-AMERICAN RELATIONS DURING THE WAR

During the stress of common danger a limited degree of co-operation was established between the Soviet Union and the United States, and a modest amount of combined planning for the postwar period was accomplished. During the war the American Government made many efforts, not always well directed, to win the confidence of a very distrustful group of leaders and to lay the groundwork of a postwar community of interest. It was agreed to establish a new security organization, dominated by the great powers, and specific agreements were reached concerning the postwar occupation and control of Germany and Austria. Some limited successes were achieved, and it could not be said with finality that the Soviet leaders were determined to go their own way in the postwar world and to ignore completely their allies' constant invitations to co-operative action. It can be said that in this phase the Soviet Government insisted on safeguarding its own strength, security, secrecy, and independence of decision, yet was willing, when none of these factors was directly involved, to make limited commitments to joint action. This phase lasted through the Yalta Conference, which marked the high point in the prospects for closer understanding and co-operation.

A fortnight after Yalta there occurred a significant shift in the emphasis of Soviet policy. While the slogan of "Allied unity" continued to be chanted in every key by Soviet propagandists, there took place a rapid ebbing in any signs of Soviet consideration for the interests or hopes of the western Allies. In direct violation of the recently signed Yalta agreements, the Soviet Government proceeded to impose governments of its own choosing upon the smaller countries of eastern Europe. In violation of another part of the Yalta agreement it gave its full support to the minority Lublin regime in Poland, and signed with it a close alliance and a unilateral agreement defining Poland's western boundary, again in disregard of a specific agreement with its allies. At this very time it also backed away, in a significant respect, from implementing the agreement to co-operate with its allies in the postwar control of Germany.

After the signing, in November 1944, of the Allied agreement for establishing joint control over postwar Germany, the three governments of Great Britain, the Soviet Union, and the United States had agreed orally to set up immediately a nucleus of the future control machinery. The three, later four, nucleus control groups could thus, in advance, become accustomed to working together, could adjust their diverse administrative conceptions and establish their twelve working divisions, and would be ready to begin operations within a few days after the German surrender. The Soviet representative on the European Advisory Commission, in London, informed his colleagues that the Soviet nucleus group was being selected, that it was nearly complete, that it was almost ready to join the American and British groups. At Yalta Marshal Stalin agreed to expedite the arrival of the nucleus group, and about ten days later his representative in London informed his American colleague, with obvious satisfaction, that the Soviet group would arrive on a fixed day. Shortly after, the Soviet delegate sent a subordinate to inform the American delegation that the Soviet group was not coming at all. Viewed in retrospect, this reversal was merely one additional sign pointing to a strong trend towards unilateral Soviet policy everywhere in Europe.

Factors in Post-Yalta Shift

There may be several partial explanations of this post-Yalta shift from limited co-operation to an attitude of sharp rivalry. As Soviet troops entered German territory, the dominant voice in Soviet policy may well have passed from the Foreign Ministry, which had until then been responsible for planning the occupation on the agreed basis of joint Allied action, into the hands of the powerful economic ministries, bent on squeezing every bit of economic relief out of Germany, and of the secret police, responsible directly to the Politburo for enforcing Soviet control in occupied areas. Another factor may have been the strong Soviet expectation of a rapid withdrawal of American forces from Europe.

At Yalta, American officials had insisted that the United States Government could not commit its people to any specific and continuing responsibilities in Europe, and that American forces would be withdrawn across the ocean just as rapidly as the availability of shipping would permit. At that stage the Morgenthau "Plan," which dominated official thinking about the German problem, showed no trace of any concern for Germany's longer-range future. Turning Germany into a "pastoral" country would, of course, have left Communism as the sole hope for German survival. Knowing after Yalta that American power would be withdrawn with utmost speed from Europe, the Soviet leaders could also, and did, treat with contempt American protests, even President Roosevelt's personal appeals to Stalin, concerning the open and frequent violations of the Yalta agreements on eastern Europe.

The same factors must have encouraged the Soviet leaders, after digesting the experience of Yalta, to hope that France and Italy, where the native Communist parties were far stronger and better organized than in Poland, Hungary, or Rumania, would also come under Russian Communist domination. In addition, throughout 1944-46 one of the strongest arguments of Communist supporters in western Europe was that America, though it appeared strong and friendly, was an unreliable friend, that its armies were nonexistent in time of peace and its economic assistance would melt away in a postwar economic crisis of its own, while the Soviet Union would remain close at hand and would know how to reward its adherents and punish its opponents.

As the Moscow Politburo wrote to the obstreperous Belgrade Politburo in 1948, the way in which the war ended had, "unfortunately," made it impossible for the Soviet Union to establish "people's democracies" in Italy and France. But if they could not be established in western Germany, France, and Italy by the expeditious means of Soviet military assistance, the same goal might still be achieved through combined pressure from within and without, provided American support were withdrawn and American policy reverted to transoceanic isolationism.

SOVIET-AMERICAN RELATIONS, 1945-47

The new phase of Soviet initiatives and intensive Soviet pressure, which began shortly after Yalta, continued into the spring of 1947. During this period Soviet policy was based on the assumption that France was beyond recovery, that Britain was done as a great power, and that the United States was about to isolate itself from European affairs or fall into economic impotence. At Potsdam there were still some slight traces of willingness on the part of Soviet leaders to give a hearing to the views of their allies and to compromise in minor details. But it was at Potsdam that the Soviet leaders gave frank expression to a program of expansion which, if achieved, would have made their power supreme in Europe and in the eastern Mediterranean.

To list the Soviet demands, flatly presented or delicately adumbrated at Potsdam, is to outline the policy which the Soviet leaders have pursued since 1945 with remarkable persistence. In Germany they wanted to rewrite the Allied agreement on zones of occupation by setting up a separate Ruhr region under three-power control, with a veto assuring them of a high degree of bargaining power. They wanted to slap a ten-billion-dollar reparations mortgage on Germany, regardless of its effects on the survival of the German people or on the American taxpayer. A completely unmanageable mortgage of this kind would have given them unlimited opportunities to promote the Sovietization of all Germany through hunger blackmail. Marshal Stalin tried hard to secure a releas from the Yalta agreements concerning eastern Europe and to secur a *carte blanche* for whatever he might do there. The Soviet delegation pressed for an immediate confirmation of the Polish-German boundary which the Soviet Government had laid down; it reluctantly agreed to consider the boundary as provisional in return for Allied support of Soviet annexation of part of East Prussia.

The Soviet leaders also made it clear that they wanted control of the Turkish Straits, and expressed their "interest" in the Dodecanese Islands. They pressed for the immediate removal of British troops from Greece, and at the same time asked to be relieved of the obligation, signed in

1942, to remove their troops from northern Iran after the end of the war. Stalin did gain a definite advantage in this respect, for he now secured consent to keep his forces in Iran until six months after the end of the war against Japan—not against Germany as had been assumed until then. Stalin's main argument was that "It [Iran] is too near Baku." Marshal Stalin also said he was "definitely interested" in the Italian colonies, but postponed asking for a trusteeship over Tripolitania until six weeks later, at the London Conference of Foreign Ministers. Shortly after Potsdam the Soviet Government also demanded, without success, an equal share in the occupation of Japan.

The Potsdam demands were set forth in a matter-of-fact manner, without the propaganda orchestration which was applied after the going became rough. Nevertheless, they added up to a very substantial program: a strangle hold on the Ruhr and on the entire German economy; an uncontested domination of the one hundred million people of eastern Europe; domination of the eastern Mediterranean through control of Greece, Turkey, and Tripolitania; and domination of Iran.

To the great perplexity and anger of the Soviet leaders, this second phase, outlined at Potsdam, was successful only in those areas where Soviet forces were on the ground at the close of the war. Elsewhere the execution of the program was averted through delaying actions, improvisations, evasion, and by the growth of an awareness in western Europe and America that Soviet ambitions had grown far beyond the "natural" sphere of a concern for security.

In the beginning of the second phase, American opinion was extremely sensitive to any disparagement of Soviet actions or intentions. In the wave of sympathy for Soviet sacrifices in the war, of enthusiasm for Soviet courage, and in the passionate hope that a solid basis of Allied understanding had been found, American sentiment discredited or ignored many facts which, added together, suggested that the Soviet leaders saw no obstacles in the path of their ambition to extend and entrench their power in a world which had been devastated and hollowed out by Nazi brutality and by war. By the end of this phase, which was marked by the Truman Doctrine and the Marshall plan, the pendulum had swung so far, under the hard impact of evidence of the Soviet challenge for power, that anyone who admitted the possibility of ever settling any dispute with the Soviet Government was likely to fall under suspicion of favoring "appeasement."

THE THIRD PHASE

In the third phase, the United States broke with ancient tradition to offer specific assistance and to furnish specific guarantees to countries which lay in the path of Soviet expansionism. Overcoming its scruples concerning the governments in Greece and Turkey, it came to their assistance. The alternative would have been acquiescence in the establishment of a Communist-dominated regime in Greece and the submission of Turkey to Soviet over-lordship, either through Soviet control of the Turkish Straits and of the highlands of eastern Anatolia, or through the installing of a "friendly" regime, according to the Soviet definition. By this decision the United States undertook to deter the Soviet Government from any sudden move to control the eastern Mediterranean.

The United States embarked on a far broader program of strengthening the economic and social structure of western Europe, although the program, announced tentatively in June, 1947, went into effect only in 1948. Instead of joining the Committee of European Economic Co-operation and demanding a large share of American aid for itself and its satellites, the Soviet Government mobilized its supporters in opposition. Its attacks were not fully consistent. It asserted, on one hand, that the program was only a bluff and was bound to fail, and in the same breath denounced it as the spearhead of military aggression directed against the Soviet Union. To offset the attractions of the Marshall plan among its satellites, it established the Cominform in September 1947 and rounded out its control of the Soviet bloc by the Communist seizure of power in Czechoslovakia in February 1948, and by a pact of mutual assistance with Finland in April. The nervous insistence of the Soviet leaders on complete subservience of subsidiary Communist régimes, and their difficulties in securing a reliable picture of the true situation through their overindoctrinated agents, were high-lighted in the falling away, or rather the kicking away, of the Yugoslav member of the Soviet bloc in June. The Soviet correspondence with the Yugoslav Politburo has shown clearly that the only "nationalism" that can be tolerated within the Soviet orbit is Soviet nationalism.

The movement in western Europe for self-protection against Soviet pressure moved steadily forward in 1948 and 1949, from Bevin's speech in January 1948 to the Franco-British agreement for mutual assistance, to the five-power Brussels Pact, and to the signing of the twelve-power North Atlantic Treaty on April 4, 1949. In bolstering western Europe against the massive land power of the Soviet Union, the United States had to choose between two approaches. It could have encouraged the formation of a Western European Union, in the hope that over a period of years this advanced and populous region would become strong enough to be, in itself, a deterrent to a possible Soviet attack or threat of attack, without becoming too closely bound to American policy. Western

Europe might, it was hoped, emerge as a "third force," standing between the Soviet and American centers of power and able to deal effectively with both.

In the short run, however, western Europe has proved too weak to make adequate provision for its own security. It requires American support if it is to constitute even a moderately powerful deterrent. In addition, western Europe is unable to cope with the economic and political rehabilitation of western Germany except with American co-operation. In American policy the consolidation of western Europe and the recovery of Germany have become increasingly closely associated. In order to provide a firm barrier against Soviet domination of western Europe it has become necessary to avert a Soviet domination of all Germany. In order to attract western Germany to the side of the Atlantic powers it is necessary to promote the emergence of an effective economic and political régime in western Germany.

Since 1947 the Soviet Union has lost the momentum of military and ideological expansion in Europe, and political initiative has passed to western Europe and the United States. In China, on the other hand, the American effort to bring together Nationalist and Communist forces, to help in the strengthening of an effective central government, capable of active efforts at reform and of protecting China's national independence, was a failure. Parallel to the effort in Germany, there has been a shift in the occupation of Japan towards more strenuous promotion of economic recovery. The Soviet Government has constantly denounced American policy in Germany and Japan as a plot to acquire additional allies for an attack on the Soviet Union. Since both occupied countries are completely disarmed, these accusations are somewhat wide of the mark. However, the question of how the security of these two countries may be assured poses a serious dilemma. Certainly, there are strong misgivings about permitting any form of rearmament, but it is doubtful if the United Nations, which they can enter only with Soviet approval, can offer sufficient assurance of their continued independence.

RETROSPECT AND PROSPECT

Looking back to Yalta and Potsdam, the Soviet leaders must realize that the successes which they anticipated have, in many instances, eluded their grasp. The hardening of American policy has been due to successive shocks administered by the Politburo. Their relative lack of success they owe, in large part, to their failure to understand the nature of the American polity and the underlying motives of American action abroad. They have underestimated the repugnance with which

Americans view the destruction of the national independence of small but proud peoples. They have overestimated the elements of instability operating within the American economy. The mysterious workings of a democratic public opinion which first praises them to the skies and then turns on them, while they feel they have remained themselves throughout, they explain away by reference to a malevolent "conspiracy." Attributing to others their own habits of thought, they are certain that there is an American "Politburo" which secretly manipulates the press, the economy, and the Government. The fact that the location, the membership, and the operations of this Politburo remain undiscoverable, they attribute to that well-known tradition of American ingenuity.

Beyond the building of adequate deterrents to Soviet expansion, American policy has another duty. It has a difficult path to walk in these next years, strengthening the supports of a tolerable democratic peace and at the same time avoiding provocative actions and gestures. There is no better gift to the Soviet propagandists than speculation in the press by an American officer on how many atomic bombs it would require to "eliminate" the Soviet capacity to make war. American policy makers must likewise be prepared to state the terms on which they would be willing to settle specific problems through negotiation. Such terms have been stated repeatedly with respect to Austria and Korea. When the western German state is a going concern, the United States and its allies must be prepared eventually to negotiate for a reunification of Germany on terms guaranteeing its independence, or else allow the eastern and western German states to work out terms for their own unification.

Even after the American people were pitchforked by Japanese and German aggression into a war for national survival, it was far from clear that they would accept, after the war, any continuing responsibilities beyond their ocean borders. In 1945 they assumed that the United Nations, if firmly supported, would suffice to keep the peace and that they, as a nation, need have no concern for developments abroad beyond some temporary assistance in economic recovery. If the Soviet leaders had curbed their own postwar ambitions, they would have profited by a great fund of good will in America. If, in 1945 and 1946, the Soviet leaders had been less cocksure of the validity of their "scientific" prognosis and had met American interests and sentiments a part of the way, a continuing basis for correct and fairly co-operative relations might have been laid. This did not occur. The philosophy of world-wide expansion, which the Soviet leaders had muted down during the co-operation with Hitler, was turned on full-blast against their recent allies.

In their gamble, the Soviet leaders threw into the discard those human *imponderabilia* which even Bismarck considered as important in the conduct of successful policy as the possession of great power.

Geography

18. GEOGRAPHICAL BOUNDARIES OF AMERICAN POWER *

During the debates on imperialism of the last decades of the nineteenth century, some anti-imperialist spokesmen opposed American expansionist policies in the Pacific and elsewhere on the grounds of the non-contiguity of the territories involved. Puerto Rico, the Philippines, and Hawaii were outside the continental limits of the United States, it was said, and annexation would therefore be dangerous. The reply to this attack was usually an assertion that the United States Navy would make these territories contiguous.

There are some who believe that a large navy and a powerful air arm make all areas of the world equally "contiguous" to America. Mr. Spykman takes a different view. According to his analysis of the geographical position of the United States, the facts of geography do impose limits upon American power.

The Western Hemisphere is an island realm surrounded by the Atlantic, the Pacific, and the Arctic Oceans. It lies between the European and Asiatic ocean fronts of the Eurasian Continent and covers a huge area of about 15 million square miles. This great land mass consists of the two continents of North and South America separated by an American Mediterranean. The continent of North America has the form of an inverted triangle. Its coast lines flare out toward Alaska and Greenland with the result that the most northern outposts are nearest to Asia and Europe. The South American Continent is also shaped like an inverted triangle but placed far to the east of the northern land mass with the bulge of Brazil near the shoulder of Africa. In between these two continental masses lies the American Mediterranean, providing a transit zone between North and South America and between the Atlantic and the Pacific.

The United States occupies a unique position in the world. Her ter-

* Nicholas J. Spykman, *America's Strategy in World Politics* (New York: Harcourt, Brace & Co., 1942), pp. 43-50, 59-62. Copyright, 1942, by Harcourt, Brace & Co., Inc. The author was Sterling Professor of International Relations and Director of the Institute of International Studies, Yale University.

ritory lies in the northern half of the globe, in the area of the great land masses, and is of continental dimensions with all that this implies in terms of economic strength. Fronting on two oceans, the United States has direct access to the most important trading arteries of the world. Her domain is situated between two clusters of dense population in Western Europe and Eastern Asia and, therefore, between the most important economic, political, and military zones.

The continental domain of the United States is an area of about three million square miles between Canada and Mexico, rich in natural resources, with a national economy of great productivity and a population of one hundred thirty-five million. The location and direction of the Rocky Mountains makes the country primarily an area of Atlantic drainage, and variety in topography and climate gives to each section of the country a distinct economic character. The Northeast contains the centers of population and of industrial and commercial activity. The Middle West is essentially agricultural, while the West largely accounts for the stock-raising and non-ferrous metal production of the country.

The section of the hemisphere nearest to Asia is the territory of Alaska. This peninsula, surrounded by the Arctic, the Bering Sea, and the Pacific, has an area of more than half a million square miles, greater than the surface of the Scandinavian countries and Finland. There is probably a hundred thousand square miles of grazing land, and the country is rich in water power and a great variety of minerals. It is a land of great potential possibilities, but its population of sixty thousand is bound to grow only very slowly. Climate, topography, and distance from areas of dense population and commercial activity will inevitably retard its development until resources nearer the industrial centers of the United States are exhausted.

The part of the Western Hemisphere nearest to Europe is the huge ice-covered island of Greenland which approaches Iceland and Spitzbergen. Except for a small area of about one hundred thousand square miles, an ice sheet covers the whole island. The North Atlantic Drift gives the southwest coast a warm climate and a heavy rainfall which permit the growth of a luxuriant vegetation during the summer months. The island produces two important raw materials in great abundance. Cryolite, which accounts for four-fifths of the exports, is mined at Ivigtut, and graphite is found on the west and southwest coasts. The island, except for climatological limitations, would be the natural vestibule for air approaches to this continent.

Between these two continental outposts and the United States lies the Dominion of Canada. It covers an area larger than the forty-eight states but has a population of only about twelve million, a fact largely explained by climate and topography which restrict the economic use of a large part of the area and leave much of it an arctic waste.   The great geographic regions of the country are practically prolongations of those in the United States giving rise to similar economic specialization.   The eastern section extends from the Atlantic to a little beyond Lake Superior, about halfway across the continent.   The central region—the prairie country—rolls for nearly eight hundred miles* to the foothills of the Rocky Mountains.   The western zone, mostly occupied by British Columbia, commences high up in the rugged mountain chains of the Rockies and the Selkirks, which parallel the seacoast, and reaches westward toward the Pacific.   The West represents forestry, grazing and mining; the great prairie provinces, agriculture and particularly wheat growing; and the East, mining, industry, and commerce.   An iron and steel industry has been started with mills in Ontario, operating on ore and coal both imported from the United States, and in Nova Scotia, operating with ore from Newfoundland.   Of the principal energy resources only water power is in abundance in the industrial region.

The Canadian economy shows a great similarity to that of the United States.   It is characterized by a high productivity per capita and a resulting high standard of living.   Although much of the area will forever remain sparsely populated because of climatological and other geographic reasons, the development of natural resources has only begun, and Canada has a future of expansion ahead of her.

By far the greater part of the life of Canada clusters in a narrow belt from one to two hundred miles in width along the Canadian-American border, and of that more than 90 per cent of all that is vital and active is concentrated in the eastern half of the country in the provinces of Ontario, Quebec, New Brunswick, Prince Edward Island, and Nova Scotia.   Here is found the great bulk of Canada's population, her principal industrial, banking, and commercial centers, and her largest cities and chief ocean ports.

Tucked away under the protecting overhang of Labrador, across the Gulf of Saint Lawrence, lies Newfoundland, bare, rocky, exposed to the icy blast of winter, and half-hidden in fog in summer.   It is a land of hardship and poverty on which lumbering, mining, and fishing provide a bare subsistence for a population of three hundred thousand.   Unimportant economically, bankrupt financially, it is of consequence only because of its strategic location at the entrance gate of Canada.

The frontier between the United States and Canada was established long before the acquisition of Alaska, and between the Alaskan and

* Because of the growing importance of aviation, all distances are given in statute miles, even maritime distances which are usually expressed in sea miles.

American borders lies the corridor of British Columbia which provides access to the Pacific for western Canada through the Fraser and Skeena river valleys.   This Canadian territory between the Straits of Juan de Fuca and Dixon Entrance prevents direct overland access from the United States to her northern territory.   The situation seems at first sight to resemble the Polish Corridor without the ethnic question.   A more careful analysis, however, shows a basic difference.   The Polish Corridor is a lowland containing old and well-established roads and railroads which maintain communication between East and West Prussia.   British Columbia is highly mountainous and provides no easy route for north-south communication.   Conquest or purchase cannot change these facts of topography.   The State of Washington and Alaska have always communicated by sea and will undoubtedly continue to do so, at least in peace time.

While Canada is in many ways a northern extension of the type of society found in the United States, the lands below the Rio Grande represent a different world, the world of Latin America.   It is perhaps unfortunate that the English and Latin speaking parts of the continent should both be called America, thereby unconsciously evoking an expectation of similarity which does not exist.   Only if it is realized that the countries to the south are different from the United States in essential geographic features, in racial and ethnic composition, in economic life, and in social customs, ideology, and cultural tradition can we evaluate the significance of this area for our national life and estimate correctly the likelihood of an effective co-operation in a common policy of hemisphere defense.

The Latin American world faces the United States across the Mexican land frontier and from beyond the American Mediterranean of which our country is itself the most important littoral state.   The drainage area of the remaining coastal states and the islands along the eastern rim include a territory of almost two million square miles which contains approximately fifty million people.   It consists of a large part of Mexico, of Central America, Colombia, Venezuela, and of the chain of islands stretching in a great arc from the east of Venezuela to the western end of Cuba which is one hundred fifty miles from Yucatan and seventy-five miles from Key West.   East of Florida and the Greater Antilles lies a second island chain, the Bahamas, which, like a line of closely spaced sentinels, stand guard before the entrance to the Mexican Gulf.   Like its European counterpart, the American Mediterranean is divided into a western Mediterranean—the Gulf of Mexico—and an eastern Mediterranean—the Caribbean Sea.   The distance from New Orleans to Trinidad is roughly comparable to that between Batum and Gibraltar, and the areas of the tributary coastal regions of the two seas are approximately equal.

·   ·   ·   ·   ·

The countries of this Mediterranean world are similar in geological origin, geographic features, and in indigenous plant life and crops. They lie in the northern tropics and the eastern trade winds and at various altitudes show parallel climatic zones. The area is important not only as an exporter of tropical products but also because of great mineral wealth.

Its economic importance lies in the fact that it provides the United States with a tropical raw material zone, practically in her back yard, which, except for an inadequate and badly distributed labor supply, might produce many of the articles now imported from the Asiatic and African tropics. Its chief agricultural products, except sugar, do not compete with the agrarian products of the Middle West, and its minerals provide essential raw materials for our industrial East.

The strategic significance of the American Mediterranean derives not only from the fact that it lies between North and South America, but also from the fact that it lies between the Atlantic and Pacific, a significance enhanced but not created by the construction of the Panama Canal, as the relations between Panama and the Philippines in Spanish times testify. This passageway, completed in 1914, gives the United States the full benefit of her geographic location on two oceans. The canal, although outside the borders, is, none the less, an important link in our coastal navigation and has shortened the sailing distance between Atlantic and Pacific ports by eight thousand miles. Even more important is the fact that it shortened the route from the Pacific states to Europe and from the Atlantic states to Asia, where their respective products are in demand.

·   ·   ·   ·   ·

South America beyond the Equator can be reached only by sea. This applies not only to the United States but also to the republics of Colombia and Venezuela, which lack adequate land communication with their southern neighbors. The main area of the southern continent will continue to function in American foreign policy not in terms of a continental neighbor but in terms of overseas territory. It is true that the original approach of the Spaniards was overland by a road which started in Cartagena and followed the Andean plateau and that a Pan-

American highway is planned to follow the same general route, but under modern conditions this overland approach cannot possibly compete with maritime routes either in commercial or strategic significance.

The other geographic features which determine the relations between North and South America are the position of the great mountain chains and the eastward projection of the southern half of the continent. The meridian of New York is also the meridian of Valparaiso and cuts the southern continent far west of its center. The southern land mass not only has a main axis, the Andes, which runs north and south, but also a secondary axis formed by the Brazilian ranges. The direction of this massif is southwest and northeast which makes the continent broad in the north, that is, in the tropics, and narrow in the south, in the temperate zone. Moreover, its mass juts out far into the Atlantic toward West Africa, with the result that all points below Pernambuco are slightly nearer to Lisbon than to New York.

· · · · ·

History has treated us kindly; geography has endowed us greatly; the opportunities have been well used; and the result is that our country is today the most important political unit in the New World. Geographic and strategic factors, raw materials and population density, economic structure and technological advancement all contribute to give the United States a position of hegemony over a large part of the Western Hemisphere.

The United States is blessed by the happy circumstance that she is a strong power between two weak powers. She need fear no direct assault on her land boundaries, and her security problem is not one of frontier defense. The military equipment of Canada is modest, and her naval power slight. In the technical aspects of the military arm and in strategic position, there is no comparison between the two countries. The advantage is overwhelmingly with the United States. Geology, topography, and climate give the latter the entire continent to draw upon while the same factors sharply restrict what Canada can use of her own domain. The United States excels in man power and resources, has more military aircraft, a greater army and navy, and can seriously cripple both the internal and external communications of her neighbors. In strategic location, as in all other factors of war, the United States dominates Canada.

The defense problem on the southern border resembles in some respects that of the north. The same disparities that give the United

States predominance over Canada also favor her against Mexico.   The total Mexican population is only about one-eighth that of the United States, and natural resources and industrial capacity are even more meager.   There is no navy, an army of approximately fifty thousand men, and a small air force, but neither is well equipped, and the country has had no experience with modern warfare.

It is, therefore, perfectly obvious that the land neighbors of the United States cannot menace her boundaries.   Regional location gives our country a position of unrivaled territorial security.   Canada and Mexico are not in a position to threaten us now and are prevented by geography and lack of resources from ever becoming strong military powers.   They affect the defense problem of the United States, not as primary sources of danger, but only as possible advance bases for enemies from across the oceans.

The American Mediterranean is today a zone in which the United States holds a position of unquestioned naval and air supremacy.   This body of water is now to all intents and purposes a closed sea to which the United States holds the keys, a strategic situation approached only by Great Britain in the Indian Ocean and by Japan in the marginal seas off the coast of northeastern Asia.   No serious threat against the position of the United States can arise in the region itself.   The islands are of limited size, and the topography of Central America, like that of the Balkan peninsula in the European Mediterranean, favors small political units.   Even the countries of large size like Mexico, Colombia, and Venezuela are precluded by topography, climate, and absence of strategic raw materials from becoming great naval powers.   The supremacy of the United States in this area can, therefore, be challenged only by forces from outside the zone, either in South America or in Europe or Asia.

The international trade of the region is at the mercy of the United States, and the littoral states can be blockaded and cut from their access to the world market with the greatest of ease.   For Mexico, Colombia, and Venezuela this means a position of absolute dependence on the United States, of freedom in name only, and, therefore, a situation which the proud citizens of those republics must resent as deeply as the Italians have resented their position on a closed European Mediterranean. Only a very skillful diplomacy and a very thick velvet glove will be able to make the reality of the power relationship tolerable to our good neighbors.

There is no likelihood that the west coast of South America will ever become the seat of great naval strength, although the Chilean navy was strong enough at the time of the Pacific War to discourage the United States from backing up with force her demands for a revision of the peace terms. The political units are small in population, backward industrially, and lack the facilities for building modern armaments. Since the building of the Panama Canal, the comparative naval strength in the region is expressed less in terms of the small local navies than in terms of distance from the bases of the major naval powers. This means a position of relative advantage for the United States. Operating from the Canal Zone she can exert naval pressure far down the coast beyond the southern border of Peru, and only the economic and political center of Chile enjoys the protection which distance and a small air force provide against effective blockade.

In the Atlantic drainage area of South America, beyond the buffer zone of the American Mediterranean and accessible only by sea, lie the two most powerful states of the southern continent. Geographic analysis, however, dispels the illusion of an economic war potential. Brazil is larger than the United States, but much of her territory consists of a tropical forest zone, and the much narrower zone in which her economic life is centered lacks the energy resources and the economic productivity necessary to sustain military power. Argentina, with greater possibilities as an agrarian state because of her location in the temperate zone, is very much smaller than the United States and lacks the basic raw materials for heavy industry without which war strength is unreal. Even combined, these two states could offer no serious threat, and alliance is highly improbable in the light of the inherent conflict that flows from their geographic location.

Relative strength gives the United States an enormous advantage, but relative distance gives these southern states considerable protection. It is true that our navy, operating from bases in the American Mediterranean, could blockade the exit of the Amazon basin and the ports of northern Brazil, but the real political and economic center of that country lies beyond the bulge and outside the radius of simple naval operations. Buenos Aires and the La Plata region are even farther away from Washington, approximately 7,000 miles, or twice as far as Europe. If the United States were willing to go to war and exert herself fully, she could of course defeat both Brazil and the Argentine with comparative ease if the South American opponents found no allies among the naval powers of Europe. But the fact remains that the temperate zone of the southern continent lies too far away from the center of our power to be easily intimidated by measures short of war. The result is that the nations of the extreme south enjoy a sense of relative independence from the United States which the smaller political units of the American Mediterranean can never possess.   The A.B.C. states represent a region in the hemisphere where our hegemony, if challenged, can be asserted only at the cost of war.

National Character — General Aspects

19. MATERIAL OPTIMISM AND SPIRITUAL SELF - CONFIDENCE *

> In this and the two immediately following selections, Mr. Brogan describes a number of facets of American character which have important implications for the development of our foreign policy.
>
> When Mr. Brogan speaks of the American love for the sound of words and the American tendency to accept slogans without analyzing their meaning, is he talking about the taciturn Vermonter or the loquacious Texan, the friendly and take-things-at-face-value Westerner or the cynical resident of New York City?   Perhaps he is talking about a distillation of all common American types, a least common denominator, so to speak, and about a tendency to behave in one way rather than in another.   If the tendency exists, then one may speak of aspects of national character as having the power to shape decisions.

Man does not live by bread alone, even pre-sliced bread, and the material optimism bred by American experience has not been accompanied by an equally incontestable spiritual self-confidence.   Americans are men and women, subject to the strains and ordeals of humanity and they have, besides, inherited from Europe a cultural tradition that fights against mere naive confidence in a world that, every day and in every way, gets better and better.   Nevertheless, the American tradition is tied to the idea of progress.   It has grown during the centuries in which that novel and revolutionary idea took possession of man's mind in the West, and all American experience has seemed to confirm the view that the world is advancing towards something better, to a fuller, richer life for more people, more of the time.   What a great English scholar has written of the Dark Ages, out of which modern Europe and modern America have emerged, is almost comically unlike America.   "If that age was an age of faith, it was not merely on account of its external

* Reprinted from *The American Character* by Denis W. Brogan, by permission of Alfred A. Knopf, Inc., pp. 65-67.   Copyright 1944 by Denis W. Brogan.   The author is Professor of Political Science, Cambridge University.

religious profession; still less does it mean that the men of that age were more moral or more humane or more just in their social and economic relations than the men of today. It is rather because they had no faith in themselves or in the possibilities of human effort, but put their trust in something more than civilization and something outside history."

The American historical experience has been totally different. It has been the product of profound faith in man's possibilities and of repeated historical justification for that faith. It is true that the religious tradition imported from Europe by the earlier settlers, especially in New England, had its ingredient of Christian humility and pessimism. President Eliot of Harvard, in the confident nineteenth century, was proclaiming an old New England attitude when he altered the inscription over the door of the new philosophy building in Harvard from "Man is the measure of all things," chosen by the philosophers, to "What is man that Thou art mindful of him?" chosen by himself. But even President Eliot was full of American optimism, as was made plain when in the person of George Santayana he encountered a representative of genuine Mediterranean pessimistic clarity. Another Eliot, in a later generation, was to take rather the side of Santayana than that of Charles Eliot, but Mr. T. S. Eliot, in choosing to live in England rather than in St. Louis or Boston, passed judgment not only on the American scene but indeed on his own fitness to adorn it.

Even in early New England, as Professor Perry Miller has shown, optimism about the destiny of man and society was always breaking in. The New England Calvinists of the first generation of Massachusetts and Harvard were, by the rigorous standards of sixteenth-century Calvinism, deplorably lax—not quite Arminian, but not really orthodox either. The American experience fought against the orthodox doctrine of Protestant Europe. When Jonathan Edwards in eighteenth-century Massachusetts tried to turn back the tide, he was defeated not merely because of his tactless investigation into the reading habits and the free conversation of the sons and daughters of the best families of Northampton, but because the campaign had already been lost. It was not even a rearguard action that he was fighting; it was a return from Elba for the old orthodoxy, a return that ended with a decisive Waterloo.

American religion was committed, more and more, to an optimistic view of God's purpose in the world and to an identification of that purpose with the purpose of man, especially American man. Religion more and more lost its supernatural and other-world character. God was conceived of as a kind of King of Brobdingnag convinced that "whoever could make two ears of corn, or two blades of grass, to grow upon a spot of ground where only one grew before, would deserve better of mankind, and do more essential service to his country, than the whole race of politicians put together." And not only than politicians but than unproductive saints. The American religious mind was made ready for the acceptance of the optimistic deism of Franklin and Jefferson, and thousands who would have been horrified to admit that they shared the religious views of those great heretics did in fact share more of their views than they suspected and were further removed from the views of old orthodox Christianity than they realized. The evangelical denominations might still insist on faith before works, but faith was expected to show forth its fruits in works, especially in economic works like abstention from extravagant vices like drink and sexual sin; greed or acquisitiveness was not only not condemned but more and more became a virtue.

20. Slogans and Oratory *

America is promises but America is words, too. It is built like a church on a rock of dogmatic affirmations. "We hold these truths to be self-evident, that all men are created equal, that they are endowed by their Creator with certain unalienable Rights, that among these are Life, Liberty and the pursuit of Happiness." "We the People of the United States, in order to form a more perfect Union, establish Justice, insure domestic Tranquillity, provide for the common defense, promote the general Welfare, and secure the Blessings of Liberty to ourselves and our Posterity, do ordain and establish this Constitution." These are only two of the most famous assertions of faith in things unseen, of dogmatic articles denied in good faith by many non-Americans but asserted in good faith by millions of Jefferson's countrymen from July 4th, 1776, to this day. How absurd an ambition for a people to attempt, by a written constitution, to "establish justice"! It is an ambition to make lawyers laugh and philosophers weep. "To promote the general welfare"; what is this entity so confidently labeled? What would a Marxian or a Machiavellian make of it? What an overleaping ambition of the Supreme Court to apply not known statute or case law but "the rule of reason"! What complacent courage in the founders of the Massachusetts Bay Company to identify the decision of John Winthrop, Richard Saltonstall, and the rest to transplant themselves to New England with "the greatness of the work in regard of the consequence,

* Reprinted from *The American Character* by Denis W. Brogan, by permission of Alfred A. Knopf, Inc., pp. 128-131. Copyright 1944 by Denis W. Brogan.

God's glory and the churches good!"   Nevertheless, Massachusetts was founded, and a Saltonstall is governor in this year of grace, 1944, more than three hundred years later.   There have been other consequences, too.   What (possibly non-spontaneous) wisdom was shown by Lord Baltimore and the other Catholics of Maryland who in 1649 noted the evils arising from "the inforcing of the conscience in matters of Religion" and so came out for the toleration of all Christians—this in an age when the Inquisition was still going strong, a year after the Peace of Westphalia, the year of the massacre at Drogheda by Cromwell, a generation before the revocation of the Edict of Nantes? . . .

But these aspirations, these hopes, extravagant or meaningless as they may seem to the critical, have been fighting words, hopes and beliefs leading to action.   So have been the phrases, the slogans, authentic, apocryphal, half-authentic, with which American history and American memory is filled. . . .   These echoes from a heroic if overdramatized past resound still.   "Give me liberty or give me death!" "In the name of the Great Jehovah and the Continental Congress!" "First in war, first in peace, first in the hearts of his countrymen." "Don't give up the ship."   "We have met the enemy and they are ours." "Our federal union, it must be preserved."   "Look at Jackson's men, standing like a stone wall!"   "With malice toward none."   "Public office is a public trust."   "You may fire when ready, Gridley."   "Don't cheer, boys! the poor devils are dying."   "Make the world safe for democracy."   "One third of a nation."   The American man-in-the-street may not attribute all these slogans correctly.   He may think it was Lawrence of U.S.S. *Chesapeake* who said "Don't give up the ship"; almost uniformly he thinks that it was Washington who warned against "entangling alliances," whereas it was Jefferson.   And he *will* mix them up with texts from Scripture.   He may have no more knowledge of the historical context than had the badly frightened citizen who, rescued from a lynching bee, protested: "I didn't say I was against the Monroe Doctrine; I love the Monroe Doctrine, I would die for the Monroe Doctrine.   I merely said I didn't know what it was."   Not all his slogans are reverent.   He may, at times, fall back on "Oh, yeah" or the more adequate "however you slice it, it's still baloney."   But he knows too much to despise the power of speech, to think that Bryan was adequately described when he was compared to the Platte River of his native Nebraska: "Five inches deep and five miles wide at the mouth." The power of even bad oratory is still great.   The power of good oratory is greater.

So the American suspends his irony when a recognized public figure is speaking, or even when he is merely "sounding off."   The American audience listens patiently, even happily, to dogmatic and warm statements in favor of the American constitution, home, woman, business, farmer. An American college president (from the deep South) has been known to impose a severe strain on the discipline of the undergraduates of an Oxford college by addressing them as "clean-limbed, clear-eyed boys." A pastor has been known to describe casting a ballot as a "political sacrament." Senator Vest's panegyric on the dog is only recently condemned as too lush, and a tribute to Southern womanhood is engraved on the pedestal of a statue to a forgotten statesman in Nashville, Tennessee.

21. A Passion for Information *

This national fondness for oratory, for slogans, has another cause or another result. It was an English Puritan leader on trial for his life who said of the execution of Charles I: "This thing was not done in a corner." It was a very American attitude. What Wilson preached—"open covenants openly arrived at"—is what the American people wants and expects to get. Like Wilson, it exaggerates the degree to which this standard of public negotiation is practicable. It is not always possible to negotiate under the klieg lights of congressional or press publicity. There are sometimes good reasons not only for secret negotiations for but confidential commitments. But they have to be very good reasons, advanced by leaders, native or foreign, in whom the American people have trust—and that trust will not be unlimited. No American leader, certainly not Washington or Lincoln, not Jackson or Jefferson at the height of their power, was thought to be above criticism or even above a certain degree of legitimate suspicion. Whitman, when he wrote of "the never-ending audacity of elected persons," voiced a general American belief that all leaders bear watching and that they are in duty bound to make frequent reports on the state of the Union, with or without aid of a fireside. The Americans are all, in this connection, from Missouri; they have got to be shown. They have also got to be told, and so has the world. Again, it is a powerful American tradition at work. Every American child used to learn by heart and many still learn by heart a famous plea for telling the world. For the most sacred of all American political scriptures, the Declaration of Independence, opens with a preamble justifying publicity. "When, in the course of

* Reprinted from *The American Character* by Denis W. Brogan, by permission of Alfred A. Knopf, Inc., pp. 132-134. Copyright 1944 by Denis W. Brogan.

human events, it becomes necessary for one people to dissolve the political bands which have connected them with another, and to assume among the Powers of the earth, the separate and equal station to which the Laws of Nature and of Nature's God entitle them, a decent respect to the opinions of mankind requires that they should declare the causes which impel them to the separation."

The Americans expect from their own leaders—and from the leaders of other countries—a regard for the "Laws of Nature and of Nature's God"; they also expect a "decent respect to the opinions of mankind"— publicly manifested in reasons given and discussed with what may seem excessive freedom and candor of comment. It is a view which gives rise to awkwardness and annoyance, but that can't be helped. The ablest modern publicist, native or foreign, is no match for one of the two greatest writers of political prose who have been Presidents of the United States. And, since I have talked so much of the American passion for oratory, for the spoken word, it is worth recalling that Thomas Jefferson, one of the finest figures in American history, was also easily the worst public speaker of his time, perhaps of any time.

"A decent respect to the opinions of mankind." It is still a phrase to be remembered. It means that the American man-in-the-street expects to get the low-down on all secret conferences, to have international decisions supplied to him before the participants have had time to put their smiles on and pose for the group photograph. If this demand is not forthcoming from official sources, it is provided from unofficial sources. Commentators of varying degrees of knowledge, candor, truthfulness, ingenuity, intelligence, explain and announce. Wildly conflicting guesses are made with equal confidence, and the reader and listener is given a wide range of confidential misinformation—as is his right. The outsider may wonder at the willing suspension of disbelief on which the commentators can count. He may think that Tom Sawyer was a notably representative American in his insistence on romantic possibilities in face of drab and dreary realities. He may wonder whether an eminent law professor has any particular authority for his views on the connection between British policy and Rumanian oil. He may wonder whether anybody wanting to keep a secret would tell it to Walter Winchell or even dare to enter the Stork Club. But these doubts are irrelevant. For the dispensers of secrets are catering to a public that has a village horror of the successful privacy of its neighbors. This public cannot see why Mr. Roosevelt should want to keep his political intentions quiet, any more than Mr. Tommy Manville keeps his matrimonial intentions quiet. Of course, he may *try,* as a football coach keeps his secret plays quiet if the scouts from other colleges let

him.   But it is the duty of columnists and Senators to tell all, as soon as
they have discovered it or even before.   And no agreement that needs
to be kept dark for any length of time has any chance of success in the
United States.   For the American Republic is much more like the
Athenian than like the Venetian Republic.   And Americans, though they
have a great deal to do, have in common with Saint Paul's Athenian
audience a continuous eagerness "to tell or to hear some new thing."

But there is more behind it than this passion for information, for an
elaborate version of corner-grocery gossip.   The American Republic
was founded in the days of the "secret du roi," in the days when Wilkes
was, with some difficulty, made a martyr of for revealing the secret of
Parliament.   A world in which great decisions were made by kings or
oligarchies in secret, and the results communicated to docile subjects,
this was the world against which the founders of the American Republic
revolted.   True, great things have been done in secret even in America.
The Constitution was made in secret—it could not have been made in
public even if the art of eavesdropping had in those days been practiced
as expertly as it is now.   But it was presented, quickly and in its final
form, to the American people, presented to be accepted, or rejected or
amended.   Only so could "We the People of the United States" be
committed.   Only so can they be committed today.

National Character — Specific Attitudes

22. The American People and Foreign Policy *

> Mr. Brogan's comments on general aspects of American
> character may be considered the broad background for Mr.
> Almond's description of specific American attitudes on foreign
> policy. Mr. Almond suggests that American attitudes alternate
> between extreme forms of optimism and pessimism, internationalism
> and isolationism, and cynicism and idealism.

Since Americans tend to exhaust their emotional and intellectual
energies in private pursuits, the typical approach to problems of public
policy is perfunctory.   Where public policy impinges directly on their
interest, as in questions of local improvements, taxation, or social security
policy, they are more likely to develop views and opinions resting on
some kind of intellectual structure.   But on questions of a more remote

* From *The American People and Foreign Policy* by Gabriel A. Almond,
Copyright, 1950, by Harcourt, Brace & Co., pp. 53-65.

nature, such as foreign policy, they tend to react in more undifferentiated ways, with formless and plastic moods which undergo frequent alteration in response to changes in events. The characteristic response to questions of foreign policy is one of indifference. A foreign policy crisis, short of the immediate threat of war, may transform indifference to vague apprehension, to fatalism, to anger; but the reaction is still a mood, a superficial and fluctuating response. To some extent American political apathy is a consequence of the compulsive absorption of energy in private competitiveness. To inform oneself on public issues, to form policies on the basis of careful thought-taking, is hardly a task that is beyond the intellectual competence of a large proportion of the population. The intellectual demands of business life are in some respects as complicated as those of foreign policy. But the American has a powerful cultural incentive to develop policies and strategies relating to his business and professional career, and little incentive, if any, to develop strategies for foreign policy.

The orientation of most Americans toward foreign policy is one of mood, and mood is essentially an unstable phenomenon. But this instability is not arbitrary and unpredictable. American moods are affected by two variables: (1) changes in the domestic and foreign political-economic situation involving the presence or absence of threat in varying degrees; (2) the characterological predispositions of the population. Our knowledge of American character tendencies, meager as it may be, makes it possible to suggest potential movements of opinion and mood which may have significant effects on foreign policy.

1. WITHDRAWAL—INTERVENTION

Given the intense involvement of most Americans with private interests and pursuits, the normal attitude toward a relatively stable world political situation is one of comparative indifference and withdrawal. This was the case throughout the greater part of the nineteenth century, in the period between World War I and II, and . . . in the period immediately following World War II. The existence of this cyclical withdrawal-intervention problem suggests at least two serious dangers for foreign policy decision-making: (1) possible overreactions to threat; (2) possible overreactions to temporary equilibria in world politics. Under ordinary circumstances American emotion and action are directed with considerable pressure in the normal orbits of private competition. However, when threats from abroad become grave and immediate, Americans tend to break out of their private orbits, and tremendous energies become available for foreign policy. Thus, we see the explosions of American energy in World Wars I and II when, after periods of indifference and withdrawal, exceptional feats of swift mobilization were achieved. There is some evidence to suggest that the Russian threat may, if carelessly handled, produce dangerous overreactions. Thus the press conference of Secretary of State Marshall in the spring of 1947, in which he urged the American people to "keep calm," produced what amounted to a war scare. The volatility and potential explosiveness of American opinion must be constantly kept in mind if panic reactions to threat are to be avoided.

The danger of overreaction to threat is only one aspect of this withdrawal-intervention tendency of American opinion. Equally serious is the prospect of overreaction to temporary stabilizations in the world crisis. Because of the superficial character of American attitudes toward world politics, American opinion tends to react to the external aspects of situations. A temporary Russian tactical withdrawal may produce strong tendencies toward demobilization and the reassertion of the primacy of private and domestic values. The pull of "privatism" in America creates a strong inclination to self-deception. And while this is less characteristic of the informed and policy-making levels, it undoubtedly plays an important role here as well. The great American demobilization of 1945, both in the military establishment and in the civilian bureaucracy, and the hasty dismantling of war agencies and controls reflected the overwhelming eagerness to withdraw to private values and normal conditions. This movement was not based on a sober evaluation of the foreign situation and what this might require in military and political terms, but was a response to the overwhelming urge to have done with alarms and external interruptions and get back to the essential and important values.

2. MOOD—SIMPLIFICATION

Closely connected with the withdrawal-intervention pattern is a tendency which has to do with characteristic changes in the internal structure of American foreign policy moods. It has already been pointed out that under conditions of political equilibrium American attitudes toward world politics tend to be formless and lacking in intellectual structure. We define policy, as distinguished from mood, as consisting of a relatively stable intellectual structure including (1) explicit assumptions as to the values involved in domestic or international political conflict, (2) explicit evaluations of the relative costs and efficiency of alternative means of maximizing the value position of one's own country or political group. From the point of view of this criterion, American attitudes tend to range from unstructured moods in periods of equilibrium to simplification in periods of crisis. So long as there is no immediate, sharply defined threat, the attitude is vague and in-definite—e.g., apathetic, mildly apprehensive, euphoric, skeptical. When the crisis becomes sharpened American responses become more specific. Here American distrust of intellectualism and subtlety, the faith in "common sense," and the belief in simple answers lead to over-simplifications of the threat and the methods of coping with it.

While these tendencies are more characteristic of the "uninformed" general run of the population, they affect policy-makers as well. Thus during World War II, the Roosevelt shift from "Dr. New Deal" to "Dr. Win-the-War" reflected this need at the very highest level of policy-making to reduce the issues to simplified proportions. The "uncon-ditional surrender" policy was a similarly oversimplified resolution of the moral and political problems of the war. The journalists and writers who directed American propaganda efforts in World War II solved their complex policy problems by the slogan of "the strategy of truth," which left to the lower-level, competitive policy-making process practically all of the important decisions of propaganda policy during the war. The policy of "non-fraternization" with Germans which was imposed on the American army of occupation similarly was understandable as a gratification of a need for moral simplism, but it bore only a slight rela-tion to the complex and uncomfortable realities on which it was imposed. The entire sequence of American policies toward Germany had this character of mixed moral-expediential improvisations. At first these improvisations were motivated primarily by anti-German reactions; more recently the tendency is toward more pro-German improvisations. At the present time this tendency to oversimplify seems to be taking the form of reducing all the problems of world politics to a simple "East-West" conflict. There is considerable pressure to take as an ally any country or movement which is anti-Communist and anti-Russian.

It would, of course, be an exaggeration to attribute the same degree of "simplism" to policy-makers as might be expected of the "man in the street." But there can be little doubt that the process of foreign policy-making is strongly influenced by this common-sense, improvisation tend-ency. Faith in policy-planning (which means in simple terms, taking the "long view," acquiring sufficient reliable information on which sound policy can be based, weighing and balancing the potential value of military, political, diplomatic, and psychological means in relation to proposed courses of action) has hardly taken root in the American policy-making process.

3.   OPTIMISM—PESSIMISM

The problem of shifts in mood from euphoric to dysphoric expectations is clearly related to those aspects of American opinion already described. The involvement in private concerns, coupled with an optimistic faith in good will, common sense, and simple answers, renders the American public vulnerable to failure.   This reaction tends to result from the frustration of successive improvisations, none of which have been adapted to the complex character of the problem.   Under these circumstances there are two possible dangers: (1) withdrawal reactions; (2) hasty measures motivated by irritation and impatience.   The development of American attitudes toward Russia since the end of the war is an excellent illustration of this problem.   During the war and in the period immediately following its termination there was a widely shared belief among Americans and among American policy-makers that the Russian problem could be readily solved by good will and the "man-to-man" approach.   The continued thwarting of American overtures and con-cessions to the Russians now seems to have produced an attitude of hopeless pessimism.   Pessimism certainly seems to be justifiable on the basis of the facts, but the negativism which has resulted may possibly constitute a danger if negotiation and bargaining with the Russians in principle is interdicted.   The objective problem would seem to be one of choosing the time, the occasion, and the conditions when negotiation might lead to advantage.   There is a similar danger of excessive pes-simism in relation to potential allies.   Perhaps there is a tendency toward a premature "writing off" of peoples whose social and political structures are unstable, countries which don't react with "American speed" to American proposals or which are not ready to commit themselves to the American "side" in as whole-hearted a fashion as we might desire.

4.   TOLERANCE—INTOLERANCE

The point has already been made that the American attitude toward authority, toward moral and ideological norms, contains conflicting elements.   On the one hand, the American is not hemmed in by the mores and morals of "the horse and buggy days," and at the same time he is a conformist, a value-imitator.   He is ready to try new things and new methods, but not if they make him look "different" or "peculiar." The truth of the matter would seem to be that, while he has loosened himself from the bonds of earlier moral standards and beliefs, he has not replaced these guides for conduct with any other set of principles.   The autonomous conscience of Puritanism has been replaced by the "radar-directed" conduct of the "marketer."   He tends to take his judgments as to what is right and wrong, proper and improper, from the changing culture as it impinges on him through the various social institutions and media of communication.   This makes for a certain flexibility in attitudes toward other cultures and ideologies. But the flexibility is negative rather than positive. That is, the American has moved away from older moral and traditional norms without acquiring new bases of judgment. His toleration of difference therefore is unstable, and there is a substratum of ideological fundamentalism which frequently breaks through the surface and has an important impact on foreign policy. Thus in our efforts to stabilize the weakened and chaotic areas of Western Europe we have been prepared to go a long way in aiding "Socialist Great Britain" and the left-inclined powers of Western Europe. But there is a continual sabotage of this tolerance, frequent efforts at ideological imperialism, even occasional interferences at the administrative level, which are motivated by ideological fundamentalism.

In general, this intolerance of difference is more clearly expressed in periods of normalcy. Thus, even though the possibility appears to be remote, the prospect of a recrudescence of isolationism cannot be excluded. A tactical cessation of Russian pressure might produce just this kind of demobilization and withdrawal reaction and the reassertion of older principles of conduct. This is not to say that such a reaction would be decisive so far as policy is concerned; but it is a prospect which sound policy-planning should anticipate.

5. IDEALISM—CYNICISM

In still another respect American moral predispositions may have consequences for foreign policy. The annoyance and irritation of the peoples of foreign countries over American self-righteousness is, on the whole, a relatively minor source of difficulty. Americans would appear to be happiest when they can cloak an action motivated by self-interest with an aura of New Testament selflessness, when an action which is "good business," or "good security" can be made to "look good" too. Similarly there is resistance among Americans over the straightforward expression of conscience-motivated behavior. What is "good" has to be represented as satisfying the criteria of self-interest. They are happiest when they can allay the Christian conscience at the same time that they satisfy self-interested criteria. In this regard the peoples of foreign countries are well protected, perhaps overprotected, by their own cynicism.

But there are a number of respects in which this moral dualism may produce more serious problems for the policy-maker. There would appear to be a certain cyclical trend in American moral attitudes. The great wave of idealism in the first world war gave way to the cynicism about foreign countries of the 1920's. The friendliness for our British and French allies of World War I gave way to bitterness over their defaults on their indebtedness. A little more than a decade ago the little country of Finland had a place at the very center of the American heart because she had kept up her payments on her war debts, while the European powers which had defaulted, and on the fate of which our security rested, were prevented from borrowing money in the American capital market. The chiliastic faith in the reasonableness of the Russians has now been supplanted by deep resentment over their base ingratitude.

American generosity and humanitarianism is a tentative phenomenon. Along with impulses toward good will and generosity, there is a deep-seated suspicion that smart people don't act that way, that "only suckers are a soft touch." In this connection a recent study which appeared in a popular magazine is of considerable interest. This investigation, claiming to have been based on "reliable sampling procedures," reflected a degree of religious piety among Americans considerably greater than had previously been estimated. Of greatest interest was its description of American attitudes toward ethics. It would appear that almost half of the sample was sharply aware of the conflict between what was "right" and the demands of secular life. A somewhat smaller proportion considered that religion influenced their activities in business, political and social life. Considerably more than half felt that their conduct toward neighbors was governed by the golden rule; but more than 80 per cent felt that their neighbors fell considerably short of the golden rule in their conduct toward their fellowmen.

Quite aside from the question of the full reliability of a study asking such "loaded" and personal questions, there seems to be confirmation here for the proposition regarding the moral dualism in the American character. The aspiration to conform to Christian ethical ideals is clearly present among most members of the culture, but there would appear to be a strong apprehension that such standards of conduct are inapplicable because the outside world does not behave that way. Hence any impulse toward ethically motivated generosity is impaired not only by the feeling that it will go unrequited, but that one's neighbors will ridicule it or attribute it to some concealed, self-interested motive.

It would appear to be a reasonable speculation from the foregoing findings that any action involving the giving or loaning of American wealth to foreign peoples, even though it be motivated by calculations of self-interest, activates this fear that "only a sucker is a soft touch." Under conditions of threat, such as those of the present, these doubts and suspicions about "giving things away" have been kept within manageable proportions. But in a period of temporary stabilization when the superficial aspect of the foreign situation encourages withdrawal reactions, these feelings may play a role of some significance.

6.   SUPERIORITY—INFERIORITY

In a sense America is a nation of parvenus.   A historically unique rate of immigration, social, and geographic mobility has produced a people which has not had an opportunity to "set," to acquire the security and stability which come from familiar ties, associations, rights, and obligations.   It is perhaps not accidental that in the vulgarization of psychoanalytic hypotheses in America in the last decades one of the first to acquire popular currency was the "superiority-inferiority" complex.   In more stable stratified societies the individual tends to have a greater sense of "location," a broader and deeper identification with his social surroundings.   He has not *made* his own identity, while in America a large proportion of each generation is *self-made*.   Being self-made produces a certain buoyancy, a sense of mastery, but it leaves the individual somewhat doubtful as to his social legitimacy.   This sense of insecurity and uncertainty may add a strident note to American claims for recognition.   This may explain the stereotype of the American abroad, confronted with complex and ancient cultures, taking alcoholic refuge in assertions of American moral, political, and technical virtue. It may also account for a feeling in the United States that American diplomats are no match for the wiliness and cunning of Old World negotiators.   In other words, Americans typically overreact in their self-evaluations.   They over- and under-estimate their skills and virtues, just as they over- and under-estimate the skills and virtues of other cultures and nations.

It is perhaps this quality among Americans—and among the American elites—which strongly militates against a balanced and emphatic appreciation of cultural and national differences so essential to the development of an effective diplomacy.   One may entertain the hypothesis that Americans tend to judge other nations and cultures according to a strictly American scoreboard, on the basis of which America is bound to win. It is difficult for Americans to accept a humane conception of cultural and national differences.   Somehow, other cultural values must be transmuted into an American currency so that it becomes possible in a competition of national cultures to rate the United States as the "best all-around culture of the year."

There is a noticeable sensitivity among Americans on the score of cultural and intellectual inferiority.   Only recently the American press cited the throngs of visitors to art museums exhibiting the Hapsburg collection of paintings as effectively refuting European claims of

American cultural inferiority. Feelings of crudeness and inferiority are not only expressed in the form of direct refutation by citing such evidence as the above; they also are frequently expressed in the tendency to equate esthetic and intellectual subtlety with lack of manliness— artists and intellectuals are "queers."

This superiority-inferiority ambivalence may manifest itself in policy-making in a number of ways. It may take the direct and perhaps more typical form of cultural arrogance—assertions of the superiority of the American way in politics, in economics, in social relations, in morality, or in the physical amenities of life. In this case the psychological mechanism involved is a reaction-formation; unconscious feelings of inferiority lead to the assertion of superiority. Or it may take the form of an admission of inferiority and an attribution of superiority to other cultures or elite groups. In either case there is an alienation from the real character and potentialities of the self. One either becomes an ideal and non-existent American—a *persona* American—or one rejects one's Americanism entirely and attempts to "pass," for example, into English or French culture. These formulations, of course, state the problem in the extreme for purposes of clarity.

These reactions have a selective appeal among the various elite groups. Thus American artists, writers, and intellectuals have historically tended to manifest inferiority feelings in the form of imitativeness, or in ex-patriation. It has been asserted that members of the American foreign service have tended to assimilate themselves too readily to foreign cultures and aristocratic "sets," perhaps at the expense of their American perspective. The tendency for American families of wealth and prestige to ape the English and Continental aristocracies is too well known to call for detailed comment. All of these groups have in common the quality of having differentiated themselves from the American pattern through extraordinary wealth, through artistic or intellectual deviation, or through long residence abroad. The more "representative" American —the Congressman for example—tends to manifest the simpler form of cultural arrogance.

Either inferiority or superiority feelings in relation to other cultures may have a negative effect on the national interest. Cultural arrogance may alienate other peoples, impair confidence in the United States among actual and potential allies, or aid in some measure in the mobilization of hostile sentiment among neutrals and potential enemies. Cultural subservience, particularly if manifested by American diplomats and negotiators, may result in real and unnecessary sacrifices of the national interest.

The hypothesis may also be advanced that there is a certain periodicity of national moods of confidence and lack of confidence. These have perhaps been associated in the United States with the fluctuations of the business cycle. One may speculate that not least among the catastrophic foreign policy consequences of a serious depression in the United States would be an impairment of national self-confidence, a sudden welling to the surface of underlying doubt, which might result in a weakening of foreign policy resolution, a feeling of being overextended, a need for contraction, for consolidation, for withdrawal.

Public Opinion

23. FOREIGN POLICY AND THE DEMOCRATIC PROCESS *

Public opinion is perhaps the most important of the elements which shape foreign policy decisions. The effect of public opinion is most evident in the formation of short-term policy. Strong and continued public support for President Truman's decision to oppose North Korea's attack upon South Korea eased his task of taking a forceful position in the United Nations against Communist China when China intervened in the war. The force of public opinion may be less spectacular in long-term policy formation, but the influence of general attitudes can be a powerful determinant in this sphere as well. Mr. Truman's decision could hardly have been made without some assurance that there was widespread public agreement on the necessity to oppose aggression.

Mr. Russell reaffirms the importance of public opinion in the formation of American foreign policy. He defines the roles of public opinion as follows: "to fix the limits within which our foreign policy must operate"; to act in a way that will facilitate the execution of our foreign policy; and to "provide the ferment of constructive thinking."

The pattern of life that we know as democracy is the present product of centuries of trials and errors. History has been our cradle. It can be our guide—but it cannot be our limousine. Our way of life will survive in today's bitter ideological controversy only if it continues to provide better answers than any other system. Since democracy is engaged in a life or death competition—life or death, in all probability, not only for our way of life but for us as well—it is mere common

* Francis H. Russell, *Department of State Bulletin,* December 28, 1947, pp. 1253-1255. The author has been Director of the Office of Public Affairs, Department of State.

prudence to check over from time to time the elements that make our system function and see that they are in a healthy state—such things as education, a constant flow of truthful information, widespread discussion, and a maximum development of the intellectual and moral resources of every person.

We shall need an adequate sense of responsibility on the part of those upon whom responsibility rests. In this country, for instance, our newspapers are not only responsible for purveying the news and for editorializing, but they are also responsible for performing, to a large extent, a function that in such a country as England rests in Parliament— the examining of the Executive Branch of the Government both to elicit information and to subject to careful scrutiny the soundness of the Government's policies. Obviously such a function must be carried out with an eye to the national welfare as well as to the headlines.

Another vital function of our democracy is carried on in a way that is not referred to in any constitution. That is the function of public discussion; not mere listening and absorption of facts but the sharp appraisal of views, the give and take of debate, and the arriving at a consensus. In earlier days it was done largely through town meetings that went on in every town and hamlet. Now it takes place to an increasing extent through chamber of commerce groups, labor groups, farm organizations, education and professional societies, women's clubs, foreign-affairs associations—organizations having all kinds of basic interests, all knowing that their interests are related in one degree or another to foreign-affairs developments.

The fact is that a little-noticed revolution in the way in which we do our national thinking is being carried out by the thousands of men and women throughout the country who, by their participation and work in organized groups, constitute a major force in developing and expressing a body of opinion on questions of foreign policy. The interest that gave rise to this movement became noticeably apparent during the First World War. It was stimulated to further growth by the debates over American participation in the League of Nations and by concern over the expansion of totalitarianism during the thirties. The recent war and its aftermath provided another impetus to this grass-roots concern with international affairs. . . .

A public-opinion poll indicates that about one out of every six or seven American adults belongs to an organization where world affairs are discussed. A similar survey indicates that persons having membership in such organizations are 50 percent more likely to be well informed about world affairs than are nonmembers.

At the same time, there has never been a period when the people who have the primary responsibility for formulating and executing our foreign policy have been as conscious as they are today of the need of an informed and understanding public opinion.

All this constitutes a really noteworthy phenomenon of our time. It is the sort of thing that in the long run spells defeat for Communist dictatorship.

·   ·   ·   ·   ·

More and more, I think, we are coming to recognize that as we approach any substantial problem of foreign policy, there is bound to be a period when we must first ascertain what the questions are, a further period when we must make sure that we have all of the available facts, and a further period when we must balance alternatives and make sure that we are adopting the best answer. In a democracy answers cannot come instantaneously. Indeed, if they do, it may be a sign that the democratic process has not been vigorously at work.

Justice Holmes used to remark that there are some statements to which the only answer is, "Well, I'll be damned." There are also, in this world, some situations posing policy problems where any answer that can conceivably be advanced can be conclusively demonstrated to be wrong. There are occasions when it is quite simple to make out a strong case against a particular line of action, and all that can be said in its favor is that an even stronger case can be made against any other course. That is life in this imperfect world. It will do no good to be hysterical or morose about it.

We are also learning the need of sticking with a problem and knowing that the struggle for a better world, like every other struggle, has its thin moments as well as its moments of reward.

For our part, in the State Department, in implementing this democratic process, we are making every effort to find and follow the path of full and frank information that leads between secrecy and public statements consisting only of predigested intellectual pabulum on the one hand and high-pressure propaganda on the other.

In our democracy there are three general ways in which the non-governmental members of our body politic contribute to the strength and success of our foreign policy.

The first role of public opinion is to fix the limits within which our foreign policy must operate: either to support or weaken particular courses of action. Foreign policy in this country can never get very far ahead of or very far behind public opinion. If a particular policy receives public support it is likely to succeed. If it does not, in the long run it will be doomed to failure. In 1937 public opinion was not prepared to support even a quarantine foreign policy. Today it is apparent, from the way in which the Friendship Train has stirred public imagination, from public-opinion polls, from editorial and commentator opinion, that the public is increasingly aware of the kind of world we inhabit and of the implications of that world.

It will be this public opinion that will determine whether we take action for the present emergency arising from the worst drought, flood, and freezing conditions in Europe since the Napoleonic era; whether we take action for the next four-year period of economic recovery from the war; and whether we also go on to take steps to establish a world economic pattern that will promote generally progressive standards of living and stable conditions that are compatible with a peaceful world.

The second function which the public plays with respect to foreign policy is that of executing it. In normal times the day-to-day buying habits of the American people, for instance, have almost as much to do with our economic foreign relations as so-called "policy decisions" in Washington. So does their buying restraint in times like these. Similarly with UNESCO. It is well and good to adopt a charter which says "It is in the minds of men that the defenses of peace must be constructed." But the adoption of the charter accomplishes little if people do not aid in the educational reconstruction of war-devastated countries, make their personal opinion felt in their communities, take an active part in training for peace, join personally in adult education, and promote good will and understanding among the racial and religious groups in their communities.

The third function of the public is to provide the ferment of constructive thinking, to make sure that the fullest possible discussion is given to any particular subject, that all possible alternatives are carefully canvassed so that from this free enterprise of ideas the best will emerge into what we call public opinion. It is not too much to assert that the foreign policy of tomorrow will be the result of the studies and discussion that are going on today all over the country. . . .

24. The President and Public Opinion *

Mr. Reston examines the extraordinary influence on public
opinion which the President of the United States exercises in the

* James Reston, "The Number One Voice." Reprinted from *Public Opinion and Foreign Policy* by Lester Markel, *et al.,* New York, Harper for the Council on

field of foreign policy. He ascribes the President's ability to wield such power to the specific conditions of contemporary international affairs and the greatly increased scope of Presidential access to the people. Mr. Reston then poses the urgent question: Is the President's influence so great as to threaten our democratic institutions?

The President of the United States influences opinion by every public act. The soldiers and the diplomats may or may not command the attention of the people by what they say or do, but the electorate is never indifferent to the slightest activity in the White House. No matter who he is, the President is a symbol of his office and his country. Even the least competent chief executive is the successor of Washington and Lincoln. Consequently, when he speaks, he speaks for America, he influences the lives of Americans, he represents or misrepresents the ideal every man has in his mind of what the President should say or do, and for these reasons, men listen when he speaks.

Moreover, the whole apparatus of the most modern and extensive system of rapid communications ever gathered together in one country is constantly at his disposal. Everything he says or does is news. If he goes to Congress to address the federal legislature, the major radio networks record every word and the television cameras transmit every flicker and expression of his face. If he goes to the country for the week end, he is followed by a battery of reporters and cameramen. If he gets a new dog, or expresses a preference for a picture, or has a daughter who sings, or acquires a new gadget for his desk, the object of his interest is subjected to the same careful scrutiny as a new policy sent to Congress.

The fierce competition of the private agencies gathering and disseminating news provides the President with a ready audience on almost every occasion. He is the "big story." Only a few papers and agencies assign reporters to the State Department and the Defense Department in Washington, but almost all are represented at the White House. Whenever the President holds a press conference, at least 150 reporters attend.

The competition is so sharp that, when the press conference ends, the scramble of reporters for the telephones is a menace to life and limb, and this competition to report what the President says is not restricted to the representatives of press associations, newspapers and the radio. The magazine writers, the newsreel reporters, and even the book publishers are equally eager to have access to material, critical or

Foreign Relations, 1949, pp. 65-77. Mr. Reston is Chief of the Washington Bureau of the *New York Times*.

merely descriptive, about the President and his administration. The President, consequently, more than any member of his administration or any political competitor, because of the preeminence of his office and the competition of the various news agencies, can be assured of getting his views before the people whenever he likes.

He can, for example, appoint committees to study the question at issue and release their findings to the public. On the basis of the study he can have legislation prepared and send it to Congress with a message stating or re-stating his reasons for wishing action. He can go personally to Congress and address both houses in joint session if he believes the matter at issue warrants such dramatic action. He can arrange to make a public speech on the subject whenever he chooses, or simply ask for radio time in order to carry his argument to the people. He can comment on the question at his meetings with the press and radio reporters. He can take it up with his Cabinet, authorizing them to discuss the question openly on Capitol Hill or in public speeches. He can have a message prepared for the newsreel cameras and either deliver the message himself or arrange to have it delivered by some prominent government official.

The President of the United States, in short, is in a unique position to influence the views of his fellow citizens: he is part symbol, part executive, part actor, part "graven image." No man in history ever had such an opportunity to reach so many people so quickly, and so often, with the assurance of an attentive audience as he. That is why, in any study of public opinion in the United States, it is vital to survey the influences that play upon the President and the uses he makes of his great power.

1. THE GROWTH OF THE PRESIDENT'S INFLUENCE

In the early days of the Republic, modern techniques for influencing opinion were not available. The President's influence over the mass of people not only was restricted by space and poor communications, but also by suffrage restrictions which left the business of government in the hands of something approaching a governing class. This situation was not offensive to the aristocratic views of the early Presidents. But Jefferson was an exception; he wrote to Edward Carrington:

. . . the people are the only censors of their governors. . . . The way to prevent these irregular interpositions of the people, is to give them full information of their affairs thro' the channel of the public papers, & to contrive that those papers should penetrate the whole mass of the people. The basis of our governments being the opinion of the people, the very first object should be to keep that right; and were it left to me to decide whether we should have a government without newspapers, or newspapers without a government, I should not hesitate a moment to prefer the latter. But I should mean that every man should receive those papers, and be capable of reading them.

When Lincoln became President, the United States under the influence of the frontier had made long strides in the direction of democratic self-government. More than any of his predecessors in the office, more than many of his successors, Lincoln recognized the power of public opinion. George Fort Milton has written:

None have surpassed Lincoln, and few have equaled him as Chief of Public Opinion, a role as unknown to the Constitution as the equally unofficial headship of the party which nominates him for President. . . .

From inauguration until assassination, he always tried to inform the people of some among the controlling reasons for his policies and acts. While he paid some heed to the sanctity of military secrets, he declined to worship at that shrine. He knew that people had ears, whether the walls had them or not, and took advantage of every appropriate occasion to tell them his innermost thoughts. . . . He seldom made a move without explaining its purpose, and often outlining the whole background of events which had forced the action. He frequently used a particular power right to the limit, but never without letting the people know why circumstances had forced this to be done for the public good.

Presidents coming after Lincoln varied widely in their ability to understand and to guide public opinion. Hayes had "a strong sense of public relations and a good appreciation of the importance of sound public opinion." Cleveland, despite his great abilities as a statesman seemed unable to deal effectively with public opinion. Theodore Roosevelt took full advantage of the publicity value of his colorful personality. His shrewdness in dealing with the press enabled him to put his views effectively before the people. Woodrow Wilson, because he wanted to take the people into his confidence, was the first President to hold press conferences regularly. "Few Presidents before him," writes Pollard, "and only one or two since have been as aware of public opinion and the important relationship of the press thereto as Woodrow Wilson." Until the latter part of his second administration President Wilson, although he did not cultivate a wide variety of contacts, was remarkably sensitive to the trend of popular thinking and feeling:

His general knowledge of the character and thought of the people and their historical tendencies coupled with an almost uncanny ability to sense the aspirations of the people seems to have accounted for his ability to crystallize public opinion and express the common feeling in clear and striking fashion.

Wilson's failure in his fight to bring the United States into the League of

Nations showed that he had lost the close touch with public opinion which was so great a source of strength in earlier years.

The late President Franklin Roosevelt and his press secretary Steve Early, developed these possibilities to a greater degree than any other Washington administration. They were the perfect combination: Roosevelt had the voice for radio, the looks for the camera, the skill of a parliamentarian in answering questions. Early was a good technician, well trained in the needs of correspondents, capable of translating the activities of government into news, shrewd at judging those correspondents who could be trusted and those who couldn't and, with a keen sense of timing, quick to sense when the public wished to hear from the President.

Even Early did not make the most of his own or his boss's possibilities, but he came closer to developing a scientific approach to influencing public opinion than any other employee at the White House since President Wilson inaugurated the regular White House press conference.

Roosevelt introduced the "fireside chat"—the casual informal radio talk to the people in their homes. He chose occasions when they needed guidance on difficult issues, and selected hours when they were most likely to listen in.

All Presidents, however, do not have the "Roosevelt touch" with correspondents. President Truman has adopted the casual Rooseveltian manner in his press conferences, but he has never used the conferences as effectively, and he has seldom attempted the fireside chat technique. The Truman technique, especially during the Presidential campaign of 1948, was in some ways more effective out of Washington than in the capital. When he was formal, he could not duplicate the success of Roosevelt, but as a casual spokesman for himself, speaking directly to the people as his train crossed the country, he was exceptionally provocative and persuasive.

2.　HOW THE PRESIDENT GAUGES OPINION

The occupant of the White House is supposed to have a lonely job, cut off from the pressure of outside opinion, aloof from the freely expressed views of average citizens, and surrounded by yes-men who hesitate to give him a critical analysis of his failings. There is some danger here, but there are ways of minimizing it. The President has unique opportunities to gather information about what the people are thinking. For one thing, the President has access to the studies of public opinion and to the public opinion polls, for such value as they may have. He can, if he likes, have additional surveys made.

Most Presidents have been avid newspaper readers. President Roosevelt had the capacity of scanning half a dozen metropolitan dailies before getting out of bed in the morning and of retaining all the pertinent information they contained. Mr. Truman is not so accomplished a newspaper reader, but he goes through several papers in an average day and in addition keeps abreast of the current flow of events by means of a news ticker installed in the White House press room. The latest news is brought to him throughout the day in short "takes" which he reads whenever he has a free moment. One function of his Press Secretary is to clip and place on his desk particularly significant news items and editorials from papers which the President does not ordinarily see. During much of the New Deal an elaborate central clipping bureau was maintained which studied more than 500 daily and weekly papers, not only for White House consumption but for the benefit of the executive departments as well. Weekly "box scores" of editorial opinion, broken down geographically and by subject matter, were sent regularly to the White House.

On items of particular pertinency, the President may have special studies made by members of his staff or Cabinet. Officials in various federal field offices from one end of the continent to the other may be tapped for public attitudes in their localities on a given policy or proposal, and asked to report the pro's and con's as they find them locally. Or, as has happened on several occasions, the President may send out a scout, perhaps incognito, to take the public pulse on a given issue. The establishment of a system of transient shelters early in the New Deal resulted from a "bumming" trip across the country by George Allen, disguised as a jobless wanderer, at the behest of President Roosevelt.

Before launching his slashing attack against the Eightieth Congress during the recent Presidential campaign, President Truman had his long-time confidant, Leslie Biffle, tour the rural districts of several Midwestern states in the guise of a poultry buyer. With an aged truck and a stack of chicken crates aboard, the usually immaculate Mr. Biffle, dressed in rough work clothes, talked with hundreds of farmers and small-town merchants about chickens and politics, but mostly politics. At the same time, and in somewhat less dramatic fashion, Under-Secretary of the Interior Oscar Chapman toured the Far Western states sounding out local politicos on what sort of campaign the President should wage. David Niles, an executive assistant to both Presidents Roosevelt and Truman, has spent almost as much time outside of Washington as he has in it during the last six years, maintaining contact with the principal minority groups of the country and funneling their sentiments and reactions into the White House.

Most official callers at the White House are regarded skeptically as purveyors of intelligence on public opinion.   There is a tendency among most people to tell so exalted a host as the President of the United States, not the harsh and perhaps unpleasant facts of life, but a glossed-up version designed to please or flatter.   There are exceptions, of course, whom the President and his staff quickly learn to recognize as reliable. Often they are accorded off-the-record conferences with the President, entering through the East Wing where reporters do not keep a vigil, and being permitted to remain considerably beyond the usual 15- or 20-minute visit.   From such visitors as these, a President can often gain fresh and revealing slants on public attitudes not available from official and semi-official sources.

Consultations with members of Congress are a less fruitful means of guidance on public opinion than they would appear to be on the surface. There are a variety of reasons for this.   President Roosevelt, for example, felt there was little that any Congressman could tell him about public opinion that he did not already know.   Sometimes he was right about this, and sometimes wrong, as his ill-fated attempt in 1938 to purge certain Congressmen showed.

On the other hand, President Truman, an alumnus of the Senate, where he served for ten years before becoming Vice President, has frequently consulted Congressmen privately.   The President has friendly relations with many of the leading Senators, who were in the upper chamber when he was there.   On several occasions he has gone from the White House to lunch in the Senate dining room.   Undoubtedly these contacts have been of value to him.

Through all these channels Presidents, therefore, are able to keep abreast of the nation's thinking and to guide their policy by what they learn.   But in the effort to use this knowledge to win support for their policies, other factors make for or against success.   Of these factors the two most important are (a) press relations and (b) coordination within the executive departments.

3. THE PRESIDENT'S RELATIONS WITH THE PRESS

The personal relationship between the President and the working press has an indirect but important bearing on the dissemination of White House news and therefore on public opinion.   No matter how honestly a reporter may strive for accuracy and objectivity in his coverage of news, he is, after all, a human being who responds emotionally to human traits and characteristics in the people on whom he reports. By unconscious nuances and inflections, by unintentional semantic shadings in his copy, he can scarcely avoid sympathetic treatment of a subject he likes, or unsympathetic treatment of one he does not. This varies in great degree among reporters, but it is true to some extent of all of them. In consequence, Herbert Hoover, for example, whose relations with reporters were notably cool, found very few of them in his corner when he needed them during the closing months of his administration. The hostility which his personal aloofness had inspired was intensified by his insistence that press conference questions be presented in advance in writing. Roosevelt went to the opposite extreme, both in his personal relationships with reporters and in the free-style system which he adopted for press conferences. The reaction against the New Deal that began to set in after 1938 would certainly have gone much deeper, it seems reasonable to believe, if FDR had been less personable and persuasive.

President Truman has demonstrated some of the same capacity for attracting the sympathy of the White House correspondents, and he benefits accordingly in their treatment of him. This was most forcefully demonstrated during the 1948 Presidential campaign when, in literally hundreds of dispatches from the candidates' trains, the notion was firmly implanted in the public mind of Truman's warm and human qualities as opposed to the aloofness and impersonal efficiency of his opponent, Governor Dewey.

But good personal relations with the working press are not enough. Much, of course, depends on how the President uses the news-making possibilities of his office, coordinating his actions with important developments elsewhere in the capital. Studies of the news-reading habits of the American people indicate, for example, that they can digest only one big news story at a time. It is, therefore, in the interest of the Executive not to release too many important stories at once, and not to announce new policies at a time when they are likely to be overwhelmed by events on Capitol Hill or elsewhere.

Several examples of failure to observe these principles can be found in the record of the Truman Administration. Certainly one of the most important events of that administration was the formulation of the European Recovery Program, but that great event did not get the newspaper display it deserved. It was announced, after many months of preparation, by Secretary of State George Marshall in a speech at Harvard University, but on the same day President Truman called a press conference and issued two statements, now comparatively unimportant, which blanketed the European recovery announcement.

Similarly the executive branch of the government sometimes fails to recognize that even modern communications can accommodate only so much material in any given day. The last day before Congress rises for a recess is always a busy time when the press associations' wires and the radio news bulletins are occupied with the final rush of legislation. Neglecting this fact the State Department just before the Christmas recess of 1947 released all the material in support of its European Recovery Program—a document running to nearly 150 pages. As a result, this extremely important document was never reported adequately in most of the newspapers of the country.

Some attempts have been made in the past to avoid this kind of conflict. During the war, for example, an effort was made to clear speeches by various agency and department heads so that they did not compete with one another for public attention nor contain conflicting statements, nor disclose information of strategic importance. After the war, Charles Ross, President Truman's press secretary, attempted to time important news releases so as to avoid conflict, and Cabinet officers often cleared their foreign policy speeches with the Department of State, but in peacetime, these procedures have seldom been subject to an orderly routine.

4.   THE TOUGH TASK OF COORDINATION

The President must contrive to coordinate the various departments of the executive branch so that one Cabinet officer is not publicly contradicting another Cabinet officer nor the President himself.   President Truman achieved this cooperation to a large extent during the formulation of the European Recovery Program and Congressional action on it. But in 1948 he did not achieve cooperation on the Palestine question; on this issue the Secretaries of State and Defense were sometimes supporting different policies and at times even differing with the White House itself in public statements.   The President must persuade his Cabinet officers to accept his policies or else force them to resign.   For if he does not, Cabinet officers will be differing privately and before long their private quarrels will get into public discussion, creating a sense of division and disunity in the government.

In recent years there have been many instances of lack of coordination among the executive departments.   For example, when President Truman, after the end of the Second World War, decided on a stern policy of opposition to Soviet expansion, his Secretary of Commerce, Henry Wallace, raised certain objections which were not carefully thrashed out in Cabinet meetings.   As a result, the President and Mr. Wallace gradually drifted further and further apart until the latter was finally forced to resign.

Again, in the late Spring of 1948, the United States decided to grant *de facto* recognition of the state of Israel. This was done in such a way, however, that neither the President nor the State Department had time to inform our ambassadors at the United Nations or in the European capitals. Similarly, about at the same time, the United States sent a long note through General Bedell Smith, its ambassador in Moscow, to the Soviet Government outlining U.S. foreign policy and ending with an indication that the U.S. Government might be willing to enter into diplomatic negotiations on a number of issues that had divided Washington and Moscow. No word of this, however, was passed along to the American ambassadors in Paris and London. Hence, for several days public opinion at home and abroad was confused about the real intentions of U.S. policy.

A third example came during the heat of the 1948 Presidential campaign. President Truman embarrassed his own Secretary of State by proposing to send, under secret and dramatic circumstances, Chief Justice Fred M. Vinson as a special envoy to Moscow to attempt a bilateral settlement of the German question. Coming as a complete surprise to Secretary Marshall and Under-Secretary Lovett, those officials protested so vigorously that the President hastily called off the scheme.

Obviously, incidents such as these create in the minds of Europeans doubt as to the stability of American policy and therefore tend to weaken American prestige. They also confuse and divide American public opinion and make it difficult to mobilize substantial public support for a policy which has been thus badly handled.

5. IS THE PRESIDENT'S POWER DANGEROUS?

In conclusion, there is a tangential consideration growing out of the President's influence over public opinion that is of extreme importance. It is this: The power of the President in the realm of public opinion is now so great that, if it were abused, it might threaten our democratic institutions.

Consider what could happen, for example, if an eloquent and personable President with a well-organized staff really concentrated on the task of swaying public opinion in favor of his policies. Instead of coming into his press conference and saying that he had nothing to announce, he would be prepared to release whatever he liked, and the fact of his announcing it would make it news. Instead of holding his press conferences twice a week, as Franklin Roosevelt did, or once a week as Truman does, he could hold them every day if he chose. Instead of ignoring most of the arguments made against his policies, he could answer these directly or have his Cabinet participate much more than it now does in the debates on measures on Capitol Hill.   Instead of making periodic checks on public opinion when crises arise, he could have much more careful checks made continuously.   He could use the radio much oftener than at present to inform and persuade the voters.

The question, therefore, is no longer whether the President has sufficient power to balance the legislature in the constant battle for the mind of the people.   The past advantage of the Congress has been redressed by modern communications.   The question now is: How will the President use his great, new, extra-constitutional powers?   Will he use them effectively and wisely in order to give the people strong leadership along the paths of democracy and international cooperation, or will he yield to the temptation to abuse them, and his constitutional powers, for his own glorification and to the detriment of our delicately balanced system of government?

The danger of the latter development in the foreseeable future seems remote.   In any case the great safeguard against any such threat is an informed public opinion.

Political Parties, Pressure Groups, and Propaganda

25. POLITICAL PARTIES AND PRESSURE GROUPS *

The assertion is frequently made that American political parties have little influence in the field of foreign policy. Some have cited the lack of party unity, among other factors, to explain this phenomenon.

Mr. Dahl has analyzed the Congressional vote on twenty-six issues of foreign policy and found that "a significant degree of party unity exists on important issues of foreign policy." He contends that unity is attributable, in part, less to a sense of party cohesiveness and regularity, than to the fact that individuals join and seek election as representatives of one party rather than another because they believe the general orientation of the party of their choice roughly corresponds to their own.

Although there are several such forces which tend to hold the parties together, it seems clear that we cannot describe our parties as "responsible" parties. One significant consequence of this fact, in terms of the formation of foreign policy, is that, in the absence of "responsibility," pressure groups which embody "specific and

* From *Congress and Foreign Policy* by Robert A. Dahl, copyright, 1950, by Harcourt, Brace & Co., pp. 45-57.

mobilized opinion" can strongly influence the process of decision-making.

The political party, many American political scientists argue, is potentially the single most important guarantee that the preferences of at least a "majority" of the electorate will be translated into public policy.   In the United States, however, the party is the stepchild of the political system.   It is bullied at every turn by pressure groups.   And the Congressman is not slow to learn who is boss.

THE PARTY

One of the significant aspects of American parties is their lack of discipline and cohesiveness—or, to put it another way, the significant amount of cross-party voting.   Thus, if we take all the recorded votes on questions of foreign policy in the period 1933-48, we find that, with the exception of the Democrats in the House, on only about one-third of the issues were the parties able to muster as many as 90 per cent of their voting members on one side of the issue.

That House Democrats achieved such a large measure of agreement is to be explained partly by the influence of the President on members of his party in the lower house.   Even in the Senate, however, on about two-thirds of the issues of foreign policy, more than eighty per cent of the Democrats voted together, whereas eighty per cent of the Senate Republicans voted together on less than half the issues.

The role of the party in Congressional voting on *foreign policy* nevertheless ought not to be underestimated.   If it is not the "responsible party" of the political scientists' Utopia, neither is it the negligible factor it is sometimes thought to be.

Thus if we examine twenty-six important issues of foreign policy on which record votes were taken in Congress during the years 1933-48, we find that for a nation supposedly lacking in "responsible parties," a significant degree of party unity exists on important issues of foreign policy.   If we define the party stand as that taken by the majority of party members in their voting,* we find that, on the average, between eighty and ninety per cent of the members of each of the two major parties supported the party stand.   Where the parties took stands in opposition to one another, slightly more members voted against the

* This is of course an arbitrary criterion, but given American party organization almost any other criterion is equally so.   If one were to take as the criterion the way in which two-thirds or more of the party members voted, or the position taken in Congressional debates by party leaders, the results on these issues would be almost identical with those given.

party position than on those issues for which national consensus was so great that both parties took the same stand.

In attempting to account for even this degree of party unity, one can find only partial explanation in the formal party machinery in Congress. For the parties rely heavily, particularly in the Senate, on persuasion by discussion and negotiation. Caucuses on foreign policy are infrequent. On the Democratic side, indeed, there have been almost no caucuses at all on foreign policy for several decades. When a caucus is held, an attempt is rarely if ever made these days to take a vote binding on its members; few people now in Congress can recall when a party caucus in either house last took a binding vote. In the Senate Republican conference (as the caucus is called on that side of the Congress) even a *vote* is rare; no conference vote on foreign policy has been taken within recent memory.

The party policy and steering committees likewise depend upon discussion rather than the application of discipline. One important member of the Democratic steering committee in the House has gone so far as to characterize it as "a debating society, in which members decide how they themselves are going to vote but do nothing to carry out the decision for the whole party." In the House, to be sure, the Speaker and the Rules Committee exercise some degree of party control, but their powers today are a pale shadow of those held in the days of Reed and Cannon.

What are potentially perhaps the most effective devices for securing party regularity on an issue are scarcely employed: committee assignments and campaign funds. It is true that committee appointments are usually held up by the leadership until the Speaker is chosen, the rules adopted, the party posts (floor leaders and whips) filled—a ruse that insures party unanimity on the important issues of legislative organization and control. But once these decisions are made, membership itself is a presumptive claim to reappointment. This is not to say that the leadership will refuse to punish a member who consistently flouts the party program; from time to time a member is denied a coveted committee assignment because of his voting record. But such action is highly unlikely once a member has built up a little seniority on the committee; for on the whole, the leadership is timid with its sanctions. As for campaign funds, although each party appears to believe that the other party allots campaign funds in accordance with party regularity, the evidence indicates that such sanctions are used rarely, if at all.

How then can one account for the degree of party regularity that does exist? One obvious reason lies in the consequences of self-selection. Many members are Democrats, or they are Republicans, presumably because they started out with a general mind-set roughly like that of their fellow Democrats or Republicans.   Except for the mavericks in one-party states—both North and South—who join the dominant party only because it is the sole one realistically available to ambitious men, most aspiring legislators no doubt select the one party or the other because its general orientation happens to correspond roughly with their own.

Other legislators select the party first, and only later become aware of the party's orientation.   Representative Sol Bloom, the late chairman of the House Foreign Affairs Committee, described his own evaluation as a Democrat:

> Shortly after the turn of the century, when I moved my principal office to New York, I again found it helpful to establish friendly relations with men who were active in politics.   The fact that they were Democrats, so far as I was concerned nearly fifty years ago, was mostly a coincidence.

> In simplest terms, I became a Democrat in my youth because it was helpful to me to be one.   As I matured I continued to be one largely for the same reason.   I was approaching middle age before I sought, through reading and study, a philosophical justification for the side on which I found myself.

Later identification helps to strengthen party loyalty.   "The party" becomes a symbol of the group to which one belongs; its battles are one's own battles, its victories and defeats a shared experience of the individual Congressman.   A small quantity of group loyalty is perhaps the cheapest of all commodities; few men can get along without some sense of being a fraction of a larger sum.   "Most members just don't like to go against the party," a leader in the lower house has remarked. Thus, Democratic leadership found it unnecessary to caucus on renewal of the Trade Agreements Act in 1948.   "We just knew Democrats would support it," a top-ranking House Democrat explained.

There are also subtle social sanctions not so evident to the outsider but effective for the average member.   The desire to "belong" is not merely a passive but also an active instrument in the hands of the leadership.   One who consistently votes against the party may not suffer expulsion from the party as in England, but he may find himself regarded with hostility by people whose respect and approval he would prefer to have.   "Independence" can be lonely and uncomfortable if one feels that one's colleagues and "natural" allies are increasingly cold.   Disapproval may even be accompanied by the minor political sanctions available to the leaderships; one may be denied a seat on a committee he wants, or, more likely, he will find it difficult to get much accomplished. Both private bills and individually sponsored public bills depend even for consideration, in the lower house at any rate, on a high degree of reciprocity from the leadership.

Members of the President's party may be further motivated by a sense of loyalty to "the Chief," or by a respect for his power, particularly over patronage. Moreover, to break ranks on an administration measure, and thus to endanger the administration, may also threaten one's own seat. On the other side, the minority party has a stimulus to cohere, simply because it is in opposition; victory may cause a letting up of effort, while members of a minority party soberly prepare for the next election.

These are some of the forces that hold the parties together. The resulting organizations are characteristic products of American culture in their combination of undisciplined and erratic individualism with teamwork by discussion and negotiation. To say this is by no means to say that the parties adequately perform the task of providing responsible leadership for an informed citizenry. For as the parties are now organized it is difficult for citizens at election time ever to give their clear consent to a set of party proposals on foreign policy and to receive some substantial assurance that such policies will in fact be carried out when Congress assembles. First, because the parties at the Congressional level are, as we have just seen, loose alliances of individual Congressmen, it is difficult for them to work out a systematic program which they can present to the citizens for endorsement or rejection. And second, even should they leap this hurdle and obtain a more or less clear "national mandate" for their policies, it is by no means certain that the party program will, in practice, be translated into public policy. The serious difficulty in executing a national "mandate" is indicated by the fact that on a number of important foreign policy issues, 20 per cent of the Senate Democrats voted against a majority of their party and voted with a majority of Republicans.

If party machinery provides leadership that is, in this sense, irresponsible, by the same token it creates leaders who are not thrust by necessity into the task of discovering the broad areas of agreement implicit in the community. For it is one thing to arrive at policy by a process that searches out those common purposes on which various and often conflicting minorities may nevertheless agree. But is quite another to make policy by patchwork-compromising that concedes everything to the special claims of an articulate minority, and nothing to the preferences of an unmobilized and inarticulate majority. Yet this is essentially what happens when American political parties encounter the battering ram of pressure groups.

PRESSURE GROUPS

It is a common observation among political scientists that effectiveness of pressure groups in influencing public policy seems to bear an inverse relation to the strength of parties.   The stronger and more cohesive the political parties, the less opportunity for pressure groups to exert direct influence on the legislative process.   In a régime of government by "responsible" parties, pressure groups are more likely to succeed in influencing legislation by action *within the parties* than by direct action upon members of the legislative body.   Conversely, where parties are weak, the pressure groups can act *directly upon the individual legislators,* who have much more to fear from the sanctions of pressure groups than from those of their own parties.

However stylized this picture may be, it correctly expresses a fundamental phenomenon of American politics.   As parties are relatively weak in controlling legislation, so pressure groups are relatively strong. This constitutes a major limitation on political responsibility in the American system.

The strength of pressure groups in the determination of legislative policy is no less evident in foreign than in domestic affairs.   Given the conditions that (1) events frequently permit various interpretations, (2) it is difficult for the Congressman to be sure what his constituents will actively support, and (3) his party has few sanctions with which to punish him if he votes against the party program, the Congressman is a natural victim of organized pressures.

In pressure groups, at least, he finds specific and mobilized opinion. Unless there are equally specific and mobilized counterpressures, the legislator has, it would seem, everything to gain and little to risk by voting with the pressure group.   It may be that if he were to follow the preferences of a large majority of his constituents, he should vote otherwise.   But their preferences are passive, unexpressed, inarticulate, unorganzied, while those of the pressure group are active, specific, articulate, organized.   The decision, to be sure, remains a gamble.   And the Congressman may be wrong in his assessment of pressure group strength.   There is some reason for supposing that his electoral survival is more closely associated with the fate of the party as a whole than with his vote favoring some pressure group on a particular issue.   But to many Congressmen, it still seems the safer course to vote with the pressure group and trust that the preferences of the majority remain passive and unexpressed or happen to coincide with those of the pressure group.

In cases where the size of the pressure group clientele is known and where it is possible to guess at the degree to which the pressure group leadership actually expresses the active preferences of its clientele, the Congressman's choice is less of a gamble. Congressmen live in a milieu where this kind of market calculation must be constantly practiced, and no doubt the experienced Congressman learns to know within broad limits which pressure groups he can politely ignore—or openly oppose— and which he cannot. But plying the market is full of risks. And the odds are still with the pressure groups.

The area in which foreign policy is fought out is noisy with the jangle of pressure groups. The historic role of pressures in shattering party lines on the tariff is too well known to need comment. Nor is it merely the old-fashioned and perennial pressures of economic interest groups that are important today. Issues of foreign policy activate men to organize for the pursuit of values more inclusive than the crasser ends characteristic of most pressure groups. Yet the organized pressures seeking to bend policy to their ends are, for all that, no less the instruments of minorities. International politics and the expectation of violence are so closely related, and insecurities and anxieties are so readily evoked by the threat of war, destruction, and death, that foreign policy must be conducted in an emotion-charged atmosphere where threats, fears, hates, and hopes are quickly mobilized into organized pressures. A large part of the history of American foreign policy since the First World War might be interpreted as a series of successful intimidations by pressure groups, of victories that occurred while the parties cautiously shadowboxed at a safe distance from the real conflict.

In the last days of 1934, to take an example, passage of a resolution of adherence to the World Court during the forthcoming session seemed almost certain. After polling their members, the majority and minority leaders of the Senate estimated that all but seven or eight Democrats and eight or ten Republicans would support the measure. Discussions began in the Senate on January 14, 1935. William Randolph Hearst and other "isolationists" immediately undertook a huge campaign in opposition to the Court proposal. With a staff in the Mayflower Hotel they telephoned influential people throughout the country, and soon telegrams in opposition began to pour into the Senate. On January 29, thirty-six Senators voted against the measure rather than the fifteen to eighteen originally anticipated. This was more than enough to prevent the necessary two-thirds majority, and the measure went down to another of its long series of defeats.

Now there was nothing inherently "undemocratic" about this procedure or the result.   The point is that the parties simply had to stand aside and let the dominant pressures determine the decision.   There was slight possibility that one or the other party would stick by the proposal on the assumption that the views of the pressure group were those of a minority, and that the sensible course even from the narrow view of political advantage was to support the measure and look for party endorsement at the next election.   There was equally slight possibility that one or the other party would, as a party, *oppose* the measure on the assumption that the pressures actually expressed a majority view.   When the pressures run wild, it is every man for himself and the party take the hindmost.

Neutrality, the Spanish Civil War, repeal of cash and carry, lend-lease, United Nations, the British loan, Greek-Turkish aid, European recovery, Palestine—such basic issues of foreign policy as these were automatically at the center of a field of forces of which the private pressure groups were among the most important.

It would be wholly false to assume, however, that the mere strengthening of party responsibility would or should terminate the role of pressure groups in influencing policy.   In a more or less free society composed of people with different and often conflicting interests, outlooks, aims, preferences, and ambitions, pressures will not vanish into thin air simply by the introduction of a more responsible party system.   Minorities will organize to advance their preferences.   If they do not, their preferences will be ignored or flouted; and in a pluralistic society a majority is, after all, largely composed of minorities.   But responsible parties would force such pressures to work within the parties rather than in the legislature.   Disputes now precipitated onto the floor of Congress would be resolved in advance by compromise and negotiation *within the parties.*

The Palestine issue typifies the kind of situation that remains inevitable in a society of complex attitudes.   Some minority groups—historically the most important, perhaps, being the Irish, the Italians, the Poles, the Germans, and among the religious groups, the Catholics—influence American foreign policy out of all proportion to the size of the group because (a) many members of the minority hold their views with *intensity,* i.e., their views significantly determine their political conduct; and (b) the minorities are strategically located.   The rising concern of the Jewish minority with the fate of the Jews in Palestine and in European displaced persons' camps is only the latest of a long series of similar actions by other ethnic or religious groups.   In this case, probably most citizens had no very decided views about the extraordinarily complex problem of Palestine. These citizens who felt intensely about the future of a Jewish state were distinctly a minority; but the intensity of their convictions, that is, their willingness to translate their beliefs into political action, far outweighed their numbers.

As has long been true with the "farm vote," the pro-Israel minority occupied a position of such strategic importance that both parties had to take pro-Israel stands if they did not wish to lose an important bloc of votes.   Political candidates had almost nothing to gain by doing otherwise, and a good deal to lose.   At their national conventions in 1948, both parties adopted pro-Israel planks.   And the one foreign policy issue on which bipartisan exercise of self-restraint completely broke down in the last days of the campaign was American policy toward Israel.   Both presidential candidates were unwilling to neglect the possibility of securing votes on that issue.   Ultimately the American delegation at the United Nations, which was then concerned with the Palestine problem, found it necessary to postpone all discussion of the problem until the election was over.

The significant feature of these events is not only that a minority was able to influence foreign policy in a direction that might not have been taken if the majority had actively stated its preferences—or if, indeed, the majority *had* any preferences, given their understanding of the issues.   For our purposes what is equally significant is the demonstrable inference that even if the parties *were* "responsible," "disciplined," "national" parties (which they are not now) they would have responded to the pressures of the minority.

It is true, nevertheless, that well-organized parties might be in a better position to lay down the terms of the compromise they make with organized minorities.   It would be too much to expect that responsible parties could alter the tendency of politics to maximize the values of the active and to minimize the values of the passive.   But the national political party is, potentially, the means by which the passive and the unorganized are activated and organized.   And it is, potentially, the means by which purposes common to broad numbers of men may be brought to bear on public policy as a force offsetting the narrowly confined values exploited by pressure groups.   As such, the development of responsible national parties is one of the prerequisites to both responsibility and wide agreement on matters of foreign policy.

26. PRESSURE GROUPS AND PROPAGANDA *

Mr. Bailey warns us of the dangers that lie in equating the "mobilized opinion" of pressure groups, or the subtle yet demanding voice of propaganda, with the totality of public opinion. He finds that the distorted claims of pressure groups to represent majority opinion have often been disproved by public opinion polls, and that the false statements of propagandists have been exposed by the revelations of history and scholarship. Sufficient examples can be found in our recent history, however, to demonstrate the effectiveness with which pressure groups and propagandists sometimes operate.

A common error is to confuse public opinion with pressure-group opinion.

One explanation is that the "pressure boys" have perfected techniques for making noise out of all proportion to the numbers of their constituents, and in so doing they provide another example of the "tyranny of the minority." Clever operatives can stir up a tremendous pother, particularly when they assail their congressmen with padded petitions, "parrot" letters, and form telegrams signed with names lifted from the telephone directory.

The nervous legislator, ever anxious for his seat, may easily be misled by the aggressive minority that deluges him with telegrams, while the great and apathetic majority tends to its everyday diversions. He may be unduly impressed when a man whom he has never heard of before appears as the alleged spokesman for 22,000,000 people. The congressman in such circumstances would do well to remember the three London tailors of Tooley Street who, in addressing a petition to the king, began: "We, the people of England . . ." The Townsend old-age plan of the 1930's, backed enthusiastically by superannuates with nothing better to do, had thrown a bad scare into the politicians when a national opinion poll discovered that only a negligible percentage of the voters favored it. The poll takers' pencils pricked the vast bubble.

Pressure groups will not here receive the attention they deserve, because this book is concerned primarily with public opinion, not pressure opinion. Nor will emphasis be placed on individual lobbyists, except in so far as they affected public reactions. The prize case is that of William B. Shearer, whose activities were sensationally exposed in

* Thomas A. Bailey, *The Man in the Street* (New York: The Macmillan Company, 1948), pp. 291-303. The author is Professor of History, Stanford University.

1929. The Big Three Eastern shipbuilding concerns, fearing that naval disarmament would hurt their profits, employed this self-styled "big bass drum" to sabotage the Geneva Disarmament Conference of 1927, at an alleged salary of $25,000 a year for ten years, plus a liberal expense account. The Conference almost certainly would have failed anyhow, but Shearer attributed the result to his "fast and vicious campaign."

The whole sordid story made the headlines three years later, on the eve of the London Disarmament Conference. The American public was aroused, and gave strong support to Hoover's arms-reduction program, thereby defeating the schemes of the armor-plate profiteers. The resulting state of mind contributed powerfully to the dangerous unpreparedness of the 1930's, and played directly into the hands of Senator Nye when he misleadingly spotlighted the machinations of the munitioneers.

The well fed and well groomed lobbyists no doubt have a legitimate role, whether battling reciprocity for the sugar interests, or the St. Lawrence project for the electric power interests, or Argentine beef for the cattle interests, or arms embargoes for the munitions interests. Congressmen need information, and in some respects one-sided information is better than none at all. But the lobbyists in Washington are more numerous than the members of Congress, are often better paid, and are frequently abler men who know more about legislative strategy than the representatives themselves.

It is probably fair to say that most Americans belong to some kind of pressure group, whether as farmers, laborers, veterans, manufacturers, or other special interests. A vast number belong to several such groupings. In a broad sense, the American people are a gigantic pressure group, the most powerful in the world. A partial listing of some of the better known organizations will give some idea of the magnitude of the problem.

The hyphenated Americans, through such organizations as certain Jewish Zionist Groups and the Ancient Order of Hibernians in America, are better organized to promote the interests of a foreign element than the average American is to promote American interests.

The church groups have formed the Federal Council of Churches of Christ in America, the National Catholic Welfare Conference, and other organizations of huge numbers and impressive power. . . .

The farmers, speaking through the National Grange, the Farmers' Union, and the American Farm Bureau Federation have made their voices heard in regard to tariffs and other matters of primary concern to them. The National Grange, with a membership of some 800,000, threw its weight behind the drive to secure the Kellogg-Briand peace pact.

Commercial and manufacturing interests exert tremendous pressure through the National Association of Manufacturers and the Chamber of Commerce of the United States.   They have not distinguished themselves for a liberal and farsighted approach to the tariff, and some of them, in their desire for cheap sweat, have pursued selfish aims with regard to immigration.

The manual laborer, working through the American Federation of Labor and other groups, has been keenly alive to the fate of his highly perishable product.   The only major affiliate of the League of Nations that we ever joined was the International Labor Office in 1934, partly no doubt out of respect for the labor vote.   One should also note that labor organizations have consistently opposed unrestricted immigration, particularly that from the Orient.   In 1900 the humor magazine *Puck* had a missionary explain to a puzzled Chinese that the latter could go to the white man's heaven but not to his country because there was no labor vote in heaven.   At various times labor organizations have favored the World Court; the withdrawal of marines from the Caribbean; the independence of the Philippines with their competing Filipino labor; noninterference by Washington with labor-sympathizing Mexican régimes; the boycotting of Japanese goods (after the attack on China in 1937); and the opposition through boycotts to Communism or Fascism in any form.   Labor unions have not fared too well under the Communists and Fascists.

Veterans' organizations, like the Veterans of Foreign Wars of the United States and the American Legion, have been militantly active. They have generally favored narrow nationalism, patriotic textbooks, suspicion of foreigners (especially Communists), nonrecognition of Russia, the exclusion of aliens, a strong foreign policy, isolation ("Keep Out, Keep Ready" was an American Legion slogan in 1939-1940), a "navy second to none," and a formidable military establishment.   The veterans who in their earlier days were thrust into front lines without proper training or equipment do not have to be converted to the idea of preparedness.

The women, represented by the National League of Women Voters and the American Association of University Women, have also been vocal.   Taking seriously their duties as citizens and mothers, they have generally sponsored a liberal foreign policy, and have campaigned for such objectives as the World Court and international cooperation.   Not wanting their sons to die on foreign fields, they have been unusually ardent advocates of peace.

Anglo-American groups, pooling their strength in such organizations as the English-Speaking Union, have labored for better relations between the Mother Country and the Daughter Country, and in pursuance of their program have published hands-across-the-seas literature.

Preparedness promoters, like the members of the Navy League, have long agitated for bigger and better armed forces.   Herbert Hoover, who was both peace-minded and economy-minded, ran afoul of the Navy League, which allegedly contributed money to defeat him in 1932 and elect Roosevelt, who was regarded as more "ship-minded."

The pacifists have also been energetic in time of peace, although forced to soft-pedal their zeal in time of war.   The best known of these groups is the Carnegie Endowment for International Peace, generously provided with the gold that Andrew Carnegie made from steel.   Much of its activity, especially in published form, may be better classified as educational rather than propagandist.   Dr. Charles A. Beard has rather angrily charged that the various foundations, through fellowships and other subsidies, have induced academicians to scramble onto the peace bandwagon.

The professional patrioteers, such as the Daughters of the American Revolution and the Sons of the American Revolution, have wielded a powerful tomahawk.   They have made their pressure felt for big armies and navies, and against the pollution of the Plymouth Rock stock by foreign immigrants, especially those with dangerous ideologies.

The influence of the super patriots has perhaps been most keenly felt in the writing and adoption of textbooks of history, and to some extent of geography.   These groups have been especially vigilant in demanding that our forefathers be generously gilded, and that our ancient enemies be liberally blackened.   Boards of education and other adopters of textbooks can avoid much tribulation if they favor eulogistic treatment, and particularly if they see to it that foreign ideologies like Communism are mentioned only to be condemned.

All countries do the same thing.   The chief difference between censorship by dictators and censorship by pressure groups is that the former is more ironclad.   In 1927, when naval disarmament was much in the public eye, the Detroit *News* observed: "Disarmament is a help, but what the world needs is a history schoolbook that reads the same in all countries."   Another journal remarked: "Beating swords into plowshares won't help if they keep on beating twisted versions of history into the heads of children."

As the American nation has become more sophisticated and less on the defensive, we have permitted our textbooks to become more critical, although there remains room for improvement.   In 1945, when the country was still under the spell of wartime cooperationist sentiment, a public opinion poll discovered that nearly nine out of ten adults would like to see an international agency set up to examine our textbooks.

More than seven out of ten were willing to change the texts, even as regards Germany, if the accounts were demonstrably unfair.

Certain other nonpatriotic groups are so definitely nonpartisan that they cannot be fairly classified under the heading of pressure or propaganda. Among organizations of this type may be found the Foreign Policy Association, and the Council on Foreign Relations.

Pressure groups, especially those of a hyphenate or ultraliberal complexion, have often hamstrung the work of our diplomats abroad by emitting loud outcries at most inopportune times. In 1945 the State Department, seeking to forestall subsequent criticism, took the unusual step of inviting forty-two of the most important service, educational, and other organizations to send consultants to the San Francisco Conference. The strategy of inviting potential opponents into one's camp undoubtedly contributed to the snowballing of public opinion behind the United Nations Charter.

Propaganda may here be defined as the dissemination of presumed information, frequently with a bias or false twist, for the deliberate purpose of influencing public attitudes and hence action.

In a democracy like ours, propaganda is not necessarily wicked or dangerous. Where there is so much ignorance and apathy, and where the Washington government needs the guidance of an active public opinion, the spreading of information, even though it be one-sided, stimulates debate and perhaps clarifies thinking. Propaganda is vicious if it is false, if it is used for a patently evil purpose, and if it is aimed at people incapable of evaluating it.

The line between a campaign of propaganda and a campaign of education is admittedly a fine and wavering one. If the crusade is led by a non-partisan organization like the Foreign Policy Association, the result may fairly be described as a campaign of education. But unfortunately much of what one may call propaganda is disseminated by partisan groups, with narrowly selfish ends in view, and the truth is badly mishandled. Someone has said that if our side puts on a drive, it is a campaign of education; if the other side does so, it is a campaign of propaganda.

Propaganda in foreign affairs is of peculiar importance to the United States. A similar problem does not exist in a dictatorship, except on a secretive basis, for the state controls the press and radio, and foreign agitators are given short shrift. But in America our virtually unlimited freedom of the press is a boon to the propagandist, whether home grown or imported. The United States as a consequence has been, not only the happy hunting ground of the propagandists, but the battle ground of competing propagandists, as was notably true in 1914 and 1941.

The results were not commensurate with the clamor, partly because these foreign agents cancelled out the labors of one another, and to some extent left the American voter confused and indifferent.

Even where the campaign of education is free from most of the evils of outright propaganda, one grave danger remains. The crusade is apt to deal with slogans and symbols and other mental stereotypes, and thus delude the people into thinking that they are thinking. A healthy democracy cannot exist without thought on the part of a large number of people, and in so far as a "canned" campaign of education discourages such thought, it is doing democracy a dubious service.

An important but dangerous type of propaganda is that disseminated by the Washington government itself. The American taxpayer objects strongly to the use of his own money to propagandize himself, especially in the hands of "bureaucrats" who may be promoting their own ends, as was to some extent true during the days of the New Deal. The congressmen, who do the bidding of the taxpayers, are sensitive, if not violent, on this subject. The administration must proceed with the utmost caution, because Congress holds the purse and may snap it shut if the bureaucrats overstep the line. In time of war, when it is as necessary to mobilize opinion as it is to mobilize men, the government has greater latitude, but, even so, every move must be made with extreme circumspection. The State Department during World War II undertook to explain its work through some innocuous and rather vapid broadcasts, but it was condemned by certain congressmen for putting out propaganda.

Secretary Daniel Webster was forced to sacrifice some territorial claims of both Maine and Massachusetts in the treaty of 1842 with England; and in order to quiet the opposition in these states he resorted to the employment of special propaganda agents. Secretary Seward, after astonishing the entire nation with his treaty for Alaska, spent several hundred dollars of State Department funds in describing for the press the contents of "Seward's Icebox." This was a genuine and much-needed campaign of education, but it would not have fared so well if the public had known that they were being "propagandized" with their own money.

Woodrow Wilson's Fourteen Points address was one of the most potent pieces of propaganda that ever issued from Washington. Wilson deliberately reduced his war aims to these pithy placard paragraphs, so that they could be used to seduce the enemy, unite the Allies, and inspire the home front. He succeeded beyond his fondest expectations when George Creel's Committee on Public Information spread the gospel according to Wilson all over the world in countless millions of pamphlets and leaflets.   In Poland, university men met on the streets, clasped hands, and soulfully uttered one word, "Wilson"; in Italy, candles were burned before his portrait.   But Wilson and Creel on the whole rather overdid things.   Both the American people and outside peoples were led to expect too much, and their subsequent disillusionment more than matched their wartime exaltation.

The Atlantic Charter in World War II was a rather pale imitation of the Fourteen Points, but the Office of War Information carried forward the torch laid down by Creel.   This agency served usefully, both at home and abroad, in disseminating information and building up morale.   It was not a propaganda organization in the strictest sense, and it generally followed the policy of the Creel Committee that the truth about ourselves and what we were doing was propaganda of the most impressive sort.   In the latter stages of the war, the O.W.I. concerned itself with the Negro problem, and the offended Southern congressmen forced the O.W.I. henceforth to direct its propaganda at foreigners.   The organization also aroused anger elsewhere when in a magazine distributed in Russia it described the Middle West and Rocky Mountain areas as drought ridden and undeveloped.   Following an uproar in Congress, prompt apologies were made to the eight maligned states.

In 1945 and 1946 opinion polls found a majority sentiment in favor of a government organization to explain the policies of the United States to the rest of the world.   When the poll takers substituted "our point of view" for "propaganda," the percentage of favorable responses rose sharply, which is a striking commentary on the "sales resistance" that we had developed against "propaganda" following the activities of Senator Nye and others.   In 1947 Washington actually began to beam short-wave radio broadcasts through the Russian Iron Curtain and elsewhere, but this activity was viewed with great suspicion by parsimonious and shortsighted congressmen.   A slash in the annual appropriation subsequently hobbled the educational activities of the State Department in foreign lands.

Foreign agents of various kinds have long been active in the United States.   The present discussion excludes the numerous good-will emissaries, like Mlle. Eve Curie in 1940 and Madame Chiang Kai-shek in 1943.   The latter made an extremely favorable impression on Congress and elsewhere, and contributed to the ignorant agitation for hitting Hirohito first.

An early instance of foreign intermeddling involved Tom Paine, whose persuasive pen was employed by the French government, at a salary of $1,000 a year, to create sentiment favorable to the recently concluded alliance of 1778 with the United States.   During the next twenty or so

years various French propagandists and agents, notably the harebrained
Citizen Genet, sought to poison public opinion against the British so as
to bring about closer cooperation with France.   The British minister in
pre-1812 days, "Copenhagen" Jackson, attempted to unpoison the
public mind regarding Britain when he spent some 700 pounds on the
press and other agencies.   The emissaries of Maximilian likewise sought
to work up sentiment favorable to his puppet régime by a judicious if
inadequate disbursement of money to lobbyists, writers, and newspapers.

In 1879 a French canal company, headed by the dynamic de Lesseps,
was organized to undertake geographical surgery on the isthmus of
Panama, and it spent about $2,000,000 in the United States in an
attempt to quiet American fears regarding an infraction of the Monroe
Doctrine.   Yellow fever and other obstacles ruined the enterprise, and
Philippe Bunau-Varilla, one of the legatees, attempted in 1902 to
salvage something by propagandizing in Washington against the Nicaragua route, alleging dangerous volcanic activities.   He was not making
much headway when Providence came to his rescue with a terrific
eruption on Martinique which killed some 40,000 people.   Eight days
later a Nicaraguan volcano became active, the very mountain engraved
on the postage stamps of the Republic.   Bunau-Varilla descended upon
the Washington stamp dealers, bought ninety stamps, and had one placed
on the desk of each United States senator, with an attached message:
"An official witness of the volcanic activity of Nicaragua."   A volcano-
minded Congress finally voted for the Panama route.

The Hawaiian sugar planters in the 1890's spent considerable money
in the United States to promote annexationist sentiment.   Venezuelan
propagandists in 1895 presented their case against Great Britain with
unusual success.   The ill-starred intervention of the United States in
Cuba during 1898 was urged by Cuban propagandists in America, who
did yeoman work in exaggerating or falsifying conditions so as to play
upon our sympathies.

On the eve of the Russo-Japanese War of 1904-1905, Japanese
propaganda pictured unoffending Japan as being wantonly attacked by
the ungainly Russian bear.   The American public swallowed this version
unquestioningly.   But after Nippon had won a series of astonishing
victories, the Russian propagandists got busy, and by the time of the
Portsmouth Peace Conference they had helped bring about a sharp
reversal in our sympathy for the so-called underdog.

The period of World War I was the heyday of open and unabashed
foreign propaganda in the United States, with the Allies and the Germans
engaged in a competitive courtship of American opinion.   Serious doubts
have been raised as to the effectiveness of this propaganda, but there can

be no doubt that a vast amount of propaganda was issued by both sides.

The German opinion poisoners were at a serious disadvantage from the beginning, despite our large and noisy groups of German-Americans. During the two previous decades we had become increasingly suspicious of the militaristic and imperialistic Germany, with the sabre-rattling Kaiser cast in the role of villain. During the same years we were enjoying unaccustomed deference from the harassed British, and when the chips were down in 1914 we could not fail to see that blood was thicker than the British blockade. Besides, the land of Lafayette was in the Allied camp, and we could never forget our presumed debt.

The Germans were under the additional odium of appearing to be the aggressors, diabolically bent upon wrapping the world in flames. Whatever the responsibility or intentions of the other powers, the gray-clad German hosts broke into Belgium, despite a solemn treaty binding them not to do so. The entire war on the Western Front was fought on Belgian and French soil, and atrocities against the inhabitants, male and female, were as inevitable as they were susceptible of exaggeration. "What gentle souls Attila and Genghis Khan must have been!" exclaimed a South Carolina editor in 1914, after reading the horror tales. One never heard about Allied outrages on German girls because the Allies never got to Germany until after the Reich surrendered, and then one heard a great deal in America about the lust of black French Senegalese.

With reference to Belgium, the Germans felt that they were completely justified in breaking out of an alleged Allied encirclement, but whatever the truth, they appeared to the outside world as wanton aggressors. With reference to the British blockade, the Germans felt that they were completely justified in breaking out of the Allied encirclement by using the submarine in an unrestricted fashion, but whatever the truth, they appeared to the outside world as wanton aggressors when they ruthlessly torpedoed the *Lusitania* and other Allied ships. The Allies did not need to commit atrocities in Germany or on the high seas; their slow starvation of the civilian population of Germany was quiet, unspectacular, and censored.

Aldous Huxley has said that the propagandist merely canalizes an existing stream: "In a land where there is no water he digs in vain." There was little water for the Germans in the United States. The American people were anti-German and pro-Ally before the war ever began, although they wanted to stay out of it. The invasion of Belgium was a fact, not propaganda; the sinking of the *Lusitania* was a fact, not propaganda; the shelling of Paris by "Big Bertha" was a fact, not propaganda; the shooting of Red Cross Nurse Edith Cavell was a fact, not propaganda.

The case of Edith Cavell is most instructive. She not only helped espionage agents but assisted some 250 Allied prisoners through the German lines, and under the laws of war her execution was justified, as was that of several women disposed of by the Allies under similar, if less highly publicized, circumstances. But she was shot, and to the American people there was little or no justification for executing a woman who was also a Red Cross Nurse. It was worse than a crime; it was a blunder.

All these incidents were facts, but the facts were liberally embroidered and embellished by Allied propagandists. Even when some of the distortion and falsehood were torn away, the unlovely basic structure remained, and "Hunnish" excuses got little hearing.

The Germans, moreover, did not understand American psychology. They were too open, too obvious, too lacking in subtlety, and too prone to adopt the technique of the cave man. They never learned to sell themselves before they sold their product—to get themselves accepted, respected, trusted. They tried to stress the facts as they saw them, but the American people were interested not in facts but in fireworks. The Germans failed as propagandists largely because they were dull. They had no heroine like Nurse Edith Cavell, no hero like "Papa" Joffre, no villain like the Kaiser.

The Allies, notably the British propagandists, were smooth and insinuating. Keeping themselves in the background, they permitted pro-Ally Americans of prominence to be their spokesmen, fully realizing that British noblemen with Oxford accents would be less than successful. The burden of the battle was borne by the press and by American leaders —the preachers, the professors, the patrioteers, and others. Some of these professional people, who should have kept their heads better, wrote and said things of which they were not unduly proud in later years.

Disillusionment descended like a heavy fog after the Armistice of 1918. Wilson's ideals were unrealized; the Allies proved to be ingrates and "welshers"; the Germans were found to be not solely guilty in starting the war; and the atrocity stories, with their emphasis on mutilated Belgian babes, were exposed. "Peace is that blessed period," said the Hartford *Times* in 1926, "when it isn't your sacred duty to believe an official lie." In our anger over the exaggeration and falsification, we overlooked the basic facts of aggression and invasion. The American people were pretty thoroughly disillusioned even before the Nye committee began its work.

"Propaganda" spelled "sucker" in the American dictionary, and when war again broke out in 1939, we were determined not to be victimized again. Jay Allen, a well known journalist and lecturer, reported: "In the Midwest one gets the feeling that men are waiting with shotguns to shoot down the first propagandist who mentions Belgian babies." One *Fortune* poll in 1940 showed that the people were definitely on their guard against British and French propaganda.

The story of foreign propaganda in the United States is much clearer for World War II than for World War I. Congress, taking a page from our experiences in the first conflict, passed the Foreign Agents Registration Act in 1938, which required foreign propagandists to register.

British agents were much less active in America during the second conflict than during the first. They were keenly aware of the violent American antipathy to propaganda, and they did not want to hurt their cause by engaging too openly in it. A center of British activity in America was the British Library of Information in New York, which certainly had an innocuous title. A library is a sleepy and harmless place; information is good; publicity is good. The British officials, to an even greater extent than in 1914-1917, were content to let home-grown organizations carry the banner, notably the well organized and active Committee to Defend America by Aiding the Allies. The emphasis was very cleverly on America rather than on the Allies.

In 1939, to a far greater extent than in 1914, the American people were pro-Ally—the polls indicate by as much as 90 per cent. The chief reason why the British did not engage in extensive propaganda activity in this country is that one does not waste ammunition on a fortress already won. As an Iowa farm journal put it after World War I: "If a cause is just it will eventually triumph in spite of all the propaganda issued to support it."

If German propaganda in 1914 was incredibly inept, by 1939, it had become incredibly astute. The master propagandist Dr. Goebbels, having goosestepped the minds of the Germans into line, turned his arts upon the Allies and the Americans. The German Library of Information in New York was quiet and insinuating, and it published an attractive and urbane weekly *Facts in Review,* which kept hatreds pretty well under cover but which sought to counteract the British. This was the first great war in which radio figured as a major weapon, and the ether was made a town hall for competing ideologies. Dr. Goebbels beamed his message of discord to America by short wave, as did the Japanese through "Tokyo Rose" and others.

The Germans were diabolically clever in stressing those things that would arouse distrust against our potential allies. The British had "suckered" us into the last conflict, said Dr. Goebbels, and they would try to do it again. The sly lion was prepared to fight to the last American in a war which England had started. The Germans were jolly good fellows who wanted nothing more than peaceful trade with us, and the Jews were nasty people. The invincible German war machine could not possibly lose; hence support of the British was a complete waste. Much of Dr. Goebbels's effort was directed at dividing class against class, nationality against nationality, and race against race. He praised men like Lindbergh and Wheeler and even Hoover, all of whom were urging America to stay out. Like the British, the Germans were willing to let American organizations bear the brunt of the battle, notably the America First group, which featured Colonel Lindbergh. Many isolationists whose loyalty no one could doubt were embarrassed by the large number of German Bundists and other un-American characters who flocked to their banners. The anti-Hitler complex had become so pronounced by 1941 that the interventionist leaders were regarded as more patriotic than the noninterventionist leaders, who actually were truer to historic American policy.

In 1945 the Attorney General released a report describing activities under the Foreign Agents Registration Act. From June, 1942, to December, 1944, a total of more than 12,000 different propaganda items in twenty-six languages were filed annually with the Department of Justice. Agents of various kinds were associated with thirty-four foreign governments, although only eighteen of them maintained official information centers in the United States. The British spent the most money in 1944, a total of $2,143,000, while three governments-in-exile, Poland, the Netherlands, and Belgium, followed in that order.

The Attorney General noted that most of the propaganda was designed to create good will rather than to influence a specific course of action. Much of the information dealt with the history, culture, and problems of the country in question, with special emphasis on its contributions to the common war effort. Propaganda techniques were becoming more refined, and the Attorney General found it virtually impossible at times to draw a distinct line between political propaganda and good-will informative matter.

The motion picture also serves as a potent instrument of propaganda, for it can reach the tired, the illiterate, and the ignorant, who have only to look and listen. The old silent film was used effectively for pro-Ally purposes during the period of World War I, and popular films were *The Beast of Berlin* and *To Hell with the Kaiser*. The tens of millions of American movie-goers are fortunately not exposed to much foreign propaganda, for there are relatively few foreign films. The Hollywood producers are nervous about their overseas market, and they go to great lengths to avoid offending foreign customers. *For Whom the Bell Tolls* was barred from Spain and Argentina even after it had been heavily muffled, and this sort of thing has resulted in an anemic diet for the American patron.   Hollywood generally steers clear of subjects offensive to foreigners, and one result is an overstressing of the ranch and the boudoir.   Audiences in other countries get a totally false impression of Americans from our movies, which probably constitute the most damaging propaganda against ourselves that has yet been devised.

As the dictators of World War II became near enemies or open enemies, movie producers were less concerned about Axis sensibilities, as evidenced by *The Hitler Gang* and *Confessions of a Nazi Spy*.   The Russian régime was presented in a highly favorable light in *Mission to Moscow*.   *Nurse Edith Cavell* revived pro-Ally sentiment, and *Hitler— Beast of Berlin* recalled memories of the Kaiser.   During the war it was customary to have as villains either sneaking Nipponese or snarling Nazis, thus fixing stereotypes in the malleable mind.

When Confucius wrote: "One picture is worth 10,000 words," he did not have in view the animated picture, and above all the animated picture that talks.   One clever movie may be worth many more than ten thousand soldiers.

Propaganda in time of peace, no matter by whom, is not pretty, but in time of war it becomes downright ugly.   In the midst of World War I, the Boston *Transcript* remarked: "Truth is more of a stranger than fiction."   The rattling of the presses is no less to be feared than the rattling of the machine guns, and the censor's pen is mightier than the sword.

War propaganda is almost invariably warped, for men's imaginations are fevered, and they are easily persuaded to believe the worst about their enemies.   The patriotic propagandist invariably glosses over our shortcomings and magnifies our achievements; he tells only bad about the enemy and good about ourselves.   The enemy always plunders and rapes, while our boys are Little Lord Fauntleroys off on a Sunday-school picnic.   In 1916 the Chicago *Daily News* concluded: "If either of the belligerents in this war knew the depressing facts about themselves that their opponents know, they would surrender at once."

The history of all great conflicts shows that there are always atrocities on both sides, partly because war is the greatest atrocity of all.   From 1914 to 1917 the American people, reading British-censored news stories, got the idea that the Germans were beasts, while the Serbians, Rumanians, Greeks, Italians, Frenchmen, Britishers and Russians never did anything out of line, until of course the Russians turned Bolshevik. The Indianapolis *Star* in 1916 was a bit puzzled to learn that when a

German drops a bomb he could hit only women and children, while an "Allied aviator can throw one into a crowd and never touch a soul except soldiers in uniform."

In 1914 we were too naive and gullible; in 1939 we were too indifferent and blasé. This time the real wolf was on the loose, and we refused to take alarm. We moved with the greatest of reluctance, and then when it was almost too late. The Belgian atrocity stories of 1914, even if they had been wholly true, were but college hazing when compared with the wholesale brutalities of Nazi concentration camps and grisly charnel houses.

Two major safeguards may still be employed in America to combat the wiles of the propagandist. First, education so as to arm the citizen with the facts, with critical attitudes, and with a knowledge of propaganda techniques. Secondly, freedom of speech. Education shades so imperceptibly into propaganda, that if we seek to abolish propaganda we shall imperil legitimate education.

Natural Resources

27. AN INTERNATIONAL MATERIALS POLICY *

The entire issue of *The Annals* in which this selection appeared was devoted to the subject, "The National Interest—Alone or with Others?"

Mr. Fleischmann believes we cannot defend our national interests alone. He opens with the somewhat startling statement that the United States "is a 'have-not' nation with respect to a majority of the metals" required for our military defenses. He asserts that the notion that we were a self-sufficient nation was and continues to be a myth. He makes it abundantly clear that we are dependent upon other nations for many materials absolutely necessary for our security. To the extent that we are dependent, certain restrictions upon our foreign policy become inescapable. For if we can defend our interests only "with others," then we must take into account the wishes of nations with whom we must cooperate.

The general subject under discussion—"The National Interest—Alone or With Others?"—states accurately and succinctly the question to which American policy makers must find the right answer, at the peril of

* Manly Fleischmann, *The Annals of the American Academy of Political and Social Science,* July, 1952, pp. 31-35. The author has been Administrator of the Defense Production Administration and has served with the War Production Board.

national catastrophe.   Our task is made only a little easier because the answer itself is simple, obvious, and indisputable.   What is not so simple is, Can that answer be put into effect in the years to come?

WE ARE NOT SELF-SUFFICIENT

The factual material to answer the question posed is clear, known to every responsible American official, and not subject to much debate. We must start by facing the unpalatable fact that America today is a "have not" nation with respect to a majority of the metals indispensable to the attainment of military strength, and consequently indispensable to national survival.

The world being divided, as it is, into two armed camps, it follows by relentless logic that if we are to defend ourselves we cannot go it alone; we must, in fact, import to survive in a universe where for the moment armed strength is the sole guarantee of existence as an independent nation.   To pursue the syllogism further, since we must import a major portion of our minimum security requirements in many of the key metals, we must also be prepared to export some of the materials which we produce in substantial volume, even when such action may be uncomfortable, inconvenient, and even damaging to American industry in particular cases.

We cannot expect that foreign metal-producing nations will be responsive to our national needs for the things they produce if we turn a deaf ear to their own requirements.   We need a somewhat broader view of this matter of international co-operation than that expressed by one critic of the recent exchange of American steel for British aluminum and tin, when he said that he highly approved of the transaction except for the part where the British were given some of our steel.

How has this very fundamental change in American self-sufficiency come about?   In the first place, it should be noted that the theory of American self-sufficiency has always been to a considerable extent a myth, so the change is not so dramatic as might otherwise be supposed. During World War II we had to import many basic raw materials, even during the height of hostilities, when movement by sea was a hazardous and costly undertaking.   To cite a single example, many American ships were lost by enemy action in the hauling of bauxite from the Caribbean to American shores during that war.

INCREASED REQUIREMENTS

Moreover, in the later years of World War II and ever since, great scientific changes have been afoot which have now culminated in what can be justly described as four major technological revolutions which have drastically altered military science and therefore the conditions of survival, and which certainly will in the next few years alter to a comparable degree the very circumstances of human life. I refer to the epic discoveries in the fields of atomic energy, jet propulsion, electronics, and petro-chemicals. Each of these vast changes is or soon will be intimately related to the basic armament programs upon which our security depends, and their cumulative effect can hardly be overstated.

The impact of these tremendous scientific advances, focused as they were in the field of military science, came at a time when the nation was unwilling to accommodate to them. Unfortunately, each of these industrial revolutions inescapably increases our reliance on imported raw materials.

The end of World War II found the nation impatient of the discipline that would have been required to maintain an adequate munitions program, including the indispensable development of military technology. Military budgets were slashed to the bone and beyond. In the years between 1945 and 1950 the nation engaged in a frenzied demobilization which in retrospect seems to have escaped disaster by the narrowest of margins. Few of the materials most essential to our security were stockpiled in any adequate quantity.

As a result, we are in the main as dependent today as we were in 1945 on the uninterrupted importation of columbium, nickel, cobalt, and tungsten to support our jet aircraft program, to cite but a single example. That example might be multiplied many times. Out of thirty-eight important industrial minerals we are self-sufficient in only nine, and for another twenty domestic production provides less than 60 per cent of our requirements. For seven of these twenty we are dependent on other countries for just about 100 per cent of our requirements.

At the same time, the special material requirements of the mobilization program multiply our needs for particular minerals at a fantastic rate.

Thus, when the facts are known, the question posed for discussion becomes merely rhetorical, since the answer is patent. We may profitably turn to the more complicated problem of what to do about the dangerous situation in which we Americans find ourselves.

GOVERNMENT RESPONSIBILITY

I start with the proposition that the Federal Government has an inescapable responsibility to see to it that our mobilization needs for these imported minerals are met. That responsibility arises from the first and basic duty of any government, namely, the duty of defense and self-preservation. The present administration, or any other administration, would be derelict in its discharge of its constitutional obligations if it did not make every reasonable provision for the solution of these insistent problems.

Let me make it perfectly clear that I am not suggesting for a moment that the government should pre-empt the functions of free enterprise and private trade in any area where such a course is not urgently required. Indeed, it is my conviction that the area of government intervention in this, as in other commercial matters, should and can be held to an absolute minimum. But there is no blinking the fact that when ordinary commercial methods prove inadequate to ensure and protect our supply of these survival necessities, the government must assume the responsibility of making up the deficit. Unfortunately, that is the very situation in which we find ourselves today with respect to many of the materials in question.

The delineation of the proper responsibilities of government and private industry in this condition of international materials shortages is difficult and complicated. Obviously, the United States has the financial resources to set in motion an international auction of materials in which we would be the temporary victors. Such a victory would be a Pyrrhic one at best, however, since it could be won only at the expense of the disruption of the mobilization programs and the economies of our allies whose support we will surely need in the years ahead. Beyond that, such a course would bring in its wake an uncontrollable international inflation whose repercussions would certainly be most severe upon our own domestic economy. In this field, it seems clear to me that the path of wisdom is co-operation, and not cut-throat competition with our friends.

GOVERNMENT METHODS

Let me sketch a few of the methods being used by the government in this emergency period. In the first place, we have encouraged private concerns to expand their production of scarce minerals, here and abroad, by a variety of financial inducements. These have included accelerated amortization with accompanying tax benefits, loans and long-term purchase agreements, sometimes at premium prices designed to bring into production marginal facilities which would otherwise be unworked.

In some cases we have made government-to-government agreements, either for the exchange of materials, as was the case with the British arrangement, or for the unilateral delivery of particular materials by individual countries, as was the case with the agreement made with respect to Chilean copper in 1951 and the recent agreement for the purchase of Indonesian tin.

Finally, we have participated in the International Materials Conference, which is the present-day version of the co-operative arrangements worked out in the comparable emergency of World War II. There has been some criticism of the IMC in the course of recent discussion, on the assumption that there is involved some surrender of national sovereignty to an international agency and some invasion of the prerogatives of free enterprise. I believe that neither criticism is justified.

NATURE OF IMC

In the first place, the International Materials Conference, which consists basically of a meeting of some twenty-six nations of the free world having an interest in the equitable distribution of scarce materials, has no power of any kind, except to make appropriate recommendations to the various participating governments. Our government, and any other government, is free to reject any individual recommended allocation, or all of them, though to pursue the latter course would obviously bring about the speedy demise of the Conference.

The work of the Conference proceeds on the theory that the supply of certain materials is inadequate to meet the needs of all the nations of the free world in a time of international emergency. It is the conviction of those who have studied this problem that the worst way to solve such a situation is by unbridled competitive bidding-up of the short commodity; the best way is by co-operative agreements limiting each nation's consumption of the material until the shortage can be alleviated by restoration of a proper balance between supply and demand.

The IMC is by its very nature an emergency operation, and its existence will surely come to an end when the emergency ends. However, I know of no one who has studied the metals dilemma facing the United States who will predict exactly the date on which all our problems of this kind will be solved.

I should add that the operation of the International Materials Conference is not an allocation system comparable to the Controlled Materials Plan under which domestic distribution of steel, copper, and aluminum is handled during the emergency period. It does not allocate any material from the source, and no nation or individual is required to sell any material to any other nation or individual.

If the arrangements are subject to criticism, it seems to me that the proper criticism is that their effectiveness is limited by the voluntary nature of the international commitments; but perhaps that weakness is inescapable, lacking the urgency of an all-out shooting war.

EFFECTS OF IMC

Based on the results to date, the IMC has unquestionably performed a useful function in bringing about a proper distribution of such key materials as copper, zinc, and sulphur, and the recent softening of international prices for these and other materials is certainly due in large measure to the success that has attended the operation to date.

I want to point out here, too, that had it not been for the collaborative and voluntary arrangements the United States Government has made with the nations of the International Materials Conference, the United States in my judgment would not have got the large share of vitally needed materials which we in fact did get—unless we had been willing to spend an unlimited amount of money, bid up world prices, and injure our own economy and that of our allies.   Through IMC, for example, we have arranged to get a larger share of world supplies of copper than we did formerly, largely in recognition of the needs arising from our tremendous defense effort.

Finally, it should be noted that the IMC has not impaired the normal commercial operations of importers and exporters in the various countries in any manner.   No agreements have been made or are contemplated requiring this nation or any other nation to take over exclusive purchasing functions with respect to the materials allocated pursuant to IMC recommendations.   Normal trade channels are used and will continue to be used as long as they perform effectively.

The exclusive purchasing arrangements with respect to rubber and tin represented exceptions to the United States policy in this respect, and neither material has ever been subject to the operation of the IMC.   As long as private enterprise can do the job, it is my firm conviction that this should be, and I believe will be, this nation's preferred and primary reliance in the field of international trade.

Here, as in many other areas at the very heart of the mobilization effort, cooperative efforts by the government and industry will surely solve our most pressing problems.   I repeat the thought with which I started, however: any government that would ensure the survival of this nation must accept the ultimate responsibility for seeing to it that our imports of these vital commodities remain at a level sufficient to provide for the ever increasing appetite of the military production program, at least as long as the danger of all-out war is a real one.

THE CRISIS WE FACE

The years ahead will be, I think, among the most difficult in our history. We are faced with a crisis as great as any since 1776, and of a character which we are little qualified by experience to meet. This is a crisis of many years of tension, now heightened, now lessened, usually by the volition of our potential enemy. Anyone who follows the foreign dispatches must have been struck in recent months by a new note in the Soviet symphony—by overtones of appeasement and peace talk.

We can hope that this represents a true change of heart, but we must not rely on such assumption even for a moment. It must be apparent now to the Kremlin that the major result of its Korean enterprise has been the revitalization of a tremendous American industrial and military effort which already has favorably altered the balance of power between us.

It seems evident to me that the most strenuous attempts will now be made to rectify that costly blunder and to induce another sleep comparable to that which we enjoyed from 1945 to 1950—a sleep which in retrospect seems more like a nightmare.

A wise national policy will surely disregard such siren songs and will continue resolutely on the path of completing and maintaining an effective military establishment in the years ahead until an international settlement of a permanent nature can be reached.

The demands for imported materials which I have detailed will continue as urgently in 1955 and thereafter as today; as the military program reaches a plateau of preparedness, these demands will in all probability decline in volume, but not in their indispensable nature. We may well hope and expect that at such a time there will be less need for government interference and encouragement of extraordinary arrangements to increase international supply, but it is certain that the ultimate government responsibility in this field will not change.

If we are strong and patient and resolute, we shall certainly surmount this gravest of our continuing security problems. We have been burnt twice in less than ten years by national unpreparedness. It is my hope and belief that the nation has now learned the lesson and that it will not again forget.

TEST OF THE FREE NATIONS

Co-operation in the field of materials has provided one of the real tests to the nations of the free world in jointly achieving the mutual objective of security and the economic well-being necessary to that security. To date, with only minor exceptions, that test has been met successfully by the governments of these nations and by their private citizens whose enterprise and ingenuity in normal commercial operations make this possible.

I say to you that the circumstances of the world in which we live present a clear call to all free nations to continue with the greatest possible speed the development of their material resources and co-operation in their use. We must provide ourselves with the materials necessary to forge our defenses. We must share to survive.

The National Economy

28. BUSINESS AND ARMAMENT *

One of the most troublesome and seemingly permanent problems that face American policy planners is the high cost of preeminence in world affairs. The United States is neither strong enough nor wealthy enough to do all that it might want to do. The maintenance of a national defense establishment at the peak of efficiency is undeniably essential, but one must be mindful of the possibility that huge governmental expenditures may strain the national economy. Any armaments program involves economic risks as well as other risks, and in addition, the necessity to allocate funds for defense and foreign policy must often be balanced against the desirability or necessity to implement various domestic programs. The national economy clearly sets limits to what can be done, and the knowledge that these limits exist influences the kind of domestic and foreign policies we adopt.

In this selection, Mr. Slichter describes the organization of the national economy in the event of war with the Soviet Union or Communist China. His analysis is applicable to the problem with which we are concerned here. During an all-out effort, some or all of the domestic policies he recommends would probably be adopted, but under present conditions there is less disposition to attempt to increase production, with the result that foreign policy must operate within the limits set by a peace-time economy.

The quickening conflict with Russia is not only the most important

* Sumner H. Slichter, *The Atlantic Monthly,* November, 1950, pp. 38-41. Reprinted with permission of the author. Copyright 1950 by the Atlantic Monthly Company, Boston 16, Massachusetts. The author is Lamont Professor, Harvard University.

political fact in the present situation of the United States, but also the most important economic fact. If the fighting in Korea is followed by an open conflict with the Chinese Communists, or through any satellite by a direct engagement with Russia, then we are heading for an all-out war economy. At this writing what we seem to be committed to is a more limited conflict with Russia of indefinite duration, and the necessity of raising the number of men under arms from about 1.4 million to 3 million. With the help of wise diplomacy the additional cost of the contest with Russia may be kept down to about 18 billion dollars a year in terms of the 1950 dollar, or about 7 per cent of the current output of the country. This cost includes 3 billion dollars or more of military aid to other countries, but it does not include all of the extra cost that will have to be met during a period of about one year while original equipment for the enlarged military force is being produced. Bad diplomacy would greatly add to the cost of defense and foreign aid. Hence the figure of 18 billion dollars should be regarded as a minimum one.

How can the goods and services needed for this conflict be provided? Can they be obtained in the main or entirely from increased production, must they be obtained by reducing the proportion of the national output now used to replace and increase industrial plant and equipment, or must they be gained by reducing the current standard of living? How will the increased taxes to pay the annual bill of 18 billion dollars affect the volume of savings and the incentive to produce? Finally, will not the huge increase in the demand for goods start a wage-price spiral, and if so, what should be done about it?

The conflict with Russia is not merely a competition in arms; it is fundamentally a contest in production—and a long-run contest. Consequently, it is of vital importance that the additional goods and services needed for defense and foreign aid come out of an accelerated increase in the output of the country. This would prevent the standard of living of the country from being reduced for longer than several years, and it would mean that American industry would be better prepared to meet a still greater demand for goods in case the conflict with Russia should become even more active than it is now. It is of special importance, moreover, that the outlays on defense and foreign aid shall not retard the replacement and increase of our industrial plant and equipment, as did the Second World War. During the four years of the war (1942 to 1945 inclusive), only 3.8 per cent of the output of the country was used to replace and expand private plant and equipment, in comparison with 8 per cent during the three years (1939, 1940, and 1941) preceding our entry into the war and more than 10 per cent during the four years since

1945. To win the production contest with Russia, the United States should continue to use at least 10 per cent of its output to improve and enlarge its private industrial plant and equipment.

If the war does not spread, it ought to be possible to accelerate the growth of production so that within several years all or most of the goods needed for the conflict with Russia can be provided from increased output. Unfortunately, the government cannot be counted on to go very far in adopting policies designed to stimulate production. Politicians feel little demand from the public that production be encouraged. Consequently, the responsibility for accelerating the increase in output must fall pretty largely upon private enterprise. Industry should be able, however, to raise substantially the rate at which output expands. The pressure of the additional demand caused by the enlarged military services and foreign aid will encourage enterprises to expand capacity; and strange to say, some of the tax policies of the government will have the same effect. There are five principal ways in which industry may be expected to accelerate the growth of output:

1. *The size of the labor force will be increased.* Experience during the Second World War shows that a strong demand for labor will produce a considerable expansion of the labor force. Indeed, it seems clear that the labor force can be expanded sufficiently to prevent the increase in the armed services to 3 million from causing a drop in the number of civilian workers. For example, a rise of only 2 per cent in the proportion of women of 14 years of age or over who are at work would raise the labor force by over a million. Such a rise would leave the proportion of women at work less than it was during the Second World War. Another important opportunity to increase the labor force is by raising the proportion of males over 65 years of age who are at work. This proportion gradually dropped from about 70 per cent in 1890 to about 45 per cent in 1940. Most of this drop was involuntary—that is, men did not quit of their own accord but were retired by management while they were still capable of useful work. The strong demand for labor produced by the Second World War raised to nearly 50 per cent the proportion of males over 65 years of age who were in the labor force.

The increased demand for labor produced by the conflict with Russia will cause many companies to raise the usual retirement age, will encourage unions to oppose premature retirements, and will open employment opportunities for men who have been retired. If the proportion of males above 65 years of age who are at work were raised to the level of 1890, the labor force would be increased by over 1.2 million. Such a large gain in the employment of older workers cannot be looked for within a short time, but the country within two years or less should have the benefit of the output of at least 500,000 more men 65 years of age and over than are now employed.

2. *The rate of technological discovery will be accelerated.* This will happen for several reasons. The shortages of goods created by the conflict with Russia will encourage enterprises to spend more money on developing substitutes for steel, copper, lead, lumber, and other scarce materials. The strong demand for labor will accelerate the increase in the wages of production workers, thus making it more advantageous for employers to spend money on research to keep down labor costs. The conflict with Russia will, of course, accelerate the expansion of research by the government, and many results of this research will be useful to industry. Finally, higher taxes will encourage outlays on research, because these expenditures reduce the tax liability of the spender. To be sure, there are dangers to be guarded against, especially that the urgency of the conflict will cause neglect of fundamental research.

3. *More productive uses of labor will be encouraged.* The conflict with Russia will pull labor out of parts of agriculture which are still over-staffed and where the productivity of labor is relatively low, and will increase employment in manufacturing, transportation, and mining, where the productivity of labor is relatively high. The output of labor in some Southern states, for example, is little more than half the national average, mainly because these workers are producing the wrong things and be-cause the demand for labor in other occupations and other places has not been strong enough to pull more men out of the overstaffed parts of Southern agriculture.

4. *The training of men in crafts, and possibly in professions as well, will be encouraged.* As a result, the United States will have a better trained labor force with a higher proportion of professional men, technicians, and skilled workmen. The labor force of the country has never been as well trained as it should have been—though the ratio of craftsmen and professional workers to all workers has long been in-creasing. The defense program will create the need for thousands of skilled workers to make and maintain armaments. Many of these men will be trained in the armed services themselves and on leaving military service will be available for industry. But the strong demand for labor will encourage employers to train craftsmen, as it usually does. During the thirties, when the demand for labor was weak, the proportion of skilled workers in the labor force dropped, but the strong demand for men in the forties caused the proportion of skilled workers to rise from 11.7 per cent in 1940 to 13.5 per cent in 1949.

Although the need for professional workers as well as craftsmen will be increased, there is danger that universal military training will interfere with the training of professional and technical workers. Yet we must realize that the ability of the country to step up production depends in large measure upon expansion of technological research. In asserting that the contest with Russia would accelerate technological research, I assumed that ways would be found to give military training to the men needed and still not retard an increase in the number of professional workers.

5. *The replacement of equipment will be accelerated.* It is true that the rising cost of equipment and the difficulty of obtaining new equipment will tend to hold down the rate of replacement. On the other hand, higher corporate income taxes will encourage more rapid discarding of old equipment because scrapping old machinery usually reduces tax liability by increasing depreciation allowances. Rising labor costs will cause many companies to review their replacement policies, which, as W. J. Kelly of the Machinery and Allied Products Institute has well said, are often "the product of industrial folklore handed down from one generation to another."

Will these favorable influences upon production be offset in large measure, or even entirely, by the unfavorable effect of higher taxes upon the supply of investment-seeking funds? Part of the 18 billion dollars addition to the output can be obtained without an increase in plant and equipment—by speeding up the replacement of old equipment with new. These replacements are paid for, of course, out of depreciation allowances. But output cannot be raised about 18 billion dollars a year above what it would otherwise be without making the country's plant and stock of equipment larger than they would otherwise be. Part of this additional plant and equipment will be government-owned and will be largely paid for out of taxes. But much of the increase will have to be financed by individual and corporate savings. Can the needed funds be obtained in the face of tax increases on individuals and corporations?

The personal income tax has been raised and may be increased further. The effects of advances in the already stiff income tax rates are a mixture of good and bad. Consumption is limited at a time when expenditures are outrunning the capacity of industry to produce, but, in addition, savings are limited too, and the incentive to invest is weakened. What is needed during the contest with Russia (or at least during the early stages of that contest) is a tax that will principally discourage spending, not saving and investing. A general sales tax on consumer goods would limit spending, but such a tax will not be enacted—though some new excises may be passed. But in spite of increases in the personal income tax, the volume of personal savings available for investment in industry will probably rise to a small extent. The tendency for taxes to reduce personal savings will be offset somewhat by the tendency for shortages of goods, especially durable consumer goods, to increase savings. Furthermore, in the last several years, a high proportion of personal savings has gone into residential building rather than into industry. Shortages of building materials and labor will reduce the proportion of personal savings spent on housing and increase the proportion devoted to industry.

The corporate income tax has been raised from 38 per cent to 45 per cent. In 1948 and 1949, corporations had available about 11 billion dollars of undistributed profits to spend on increasing productive capacity, and in 1947 they had about 7 billion. Will not the increase in the corporate income tax prevent the much needed growth of industry by limiting the funds available for reinvestment?

There is danger that this will happen. Fortunately, however, most of the increase in the corporate income tax will soon be passed on in the form of higher prices—as has happened during the last ten years. Since corporations even in 1943 and 1944 under price control were able to make a profit after taxes of 4.2 cents to 4.3 cents per dollar of sales, it is reasonable to expect that profits after taxes may equal 4.5 cents per dollar of sales. With corporate sales of 400 billion dollars a year or more, total corporate profits would be 18 billion or more—enough to permit sufficient increases in dividends to offset the rise in the cost of living and to leave about 9 billion dollars of earnings for reinvestment. This is less than corporations have recently been reinvesting. Nevertheless, it is probably more than they would have continued to reinvest had the Korean war not occurred. They would undoubtedly have made substantial increases in dividends and cut the amount of profits that they reinvested.

Particularly harmful to the much needed expansion of industry would be a badly designed excess-profits tax. As a general rule, the industries where profits are exceptionally large need to increase their capacity. Expansion of capacity in the industries where profits are largest would help to adjust supply to demand and to bring profits down. A poorly designed excess-profits tax, by taking most of the profits that might be used for expansion, would retard the increase of capacity at many points where expansion is badly needed. If an excess-profits tax is enacted, its tendency to retard the growth of industry should be mitigated by a provision that only part of the regular rates apply to profits spent on new plant and equipment.

My conclusion is that the total volume of personal savings and corporate savings is likely to be somewhat smaller than it has been, but that the funds available for investment in industry will be larger than would have been available in the absence of the Korean war. The explanation of this seeming contradiction is that the drop in residential construction will make a larger proportion of personal savings available for industry, and that the quickening conflict with Russia, by discouraging increases in dividends, will cause cuts in corporate saving to be less than they otherwise would have been. This conclusion indicates, however, that the funds available for expanding industry will be only about as large as they recently have been—perhaps somewhat more from personal savings and less from corporate savings. This prospect indicates the need for public policies designed to encourage investment in industry.

One of the most certain consequences of conflict with Russia will be a rising price level. People are likely to spend such a large proportion of their incomes after taxes for consumer goods that the output will not meet the demand. The bargaining position of unions will be strong and they will get substantial wage increases which will reinforce the upward spiral.

The rise in prices is bound to be uneven and to create many serious injustices. Nevertheless, the people evidently regard a moderately rising price level (say nearly 10 per cent a year) as a lesser evil than the steps necessary to prevent it—such as stiffer indirect controls (strict controls on credit, substantial taxes on spending, a budget deficit financed by real savings rather than by bank credit) or direct controls (wage and price ceilings and rationing). At any rate, the politicians seem to feel no strong demand from the people that rising prices be prevented, and government policies (as distinguished from the talk of officials) are probably more inflationary than anti-inflationary.

If the country is going to have a moderately rising price level, with all the inequities that go with it, steps should be promptly taken to see that all parts of the community share as fairly as possible in the inflation. Especially must all unorganized workers—such as government employees, white-collar workers, clergymen, college professors, and others —have their compensation linked automatically to the cost of living. Rents, pensions, and such payments as tuitions in colleges and schools also will need to increase automatically as prices rise. Savers will need to avoid putting their money into savings banks or into bonds, where the purchasing power of their savings will drop. Adjusting wages, pensions, and rents to increases in prices would strengthen inflationary influences but would make inflation less unfair.

Even more important than how to reduce the inequities of inflation is the question of how rising prices will affect the volume of output and hence the ability of the United States to win the production contest with

Russia. A very rapid rise in prices, more rapid than is likely, would cause much hasty, ill-considered, and wasteful spending on plant and equipment as well as on consumer goods, and thus would retard the rise in output. A moderate rise in prices, say about 10 per cent or a little less a year, would not cause much wasteful spending. But such a rise might eventually lead the people to change their minds about wage and price controls and rationing. This would be unfortunate because wage and price ceilings and rationing would be bad for the standard of living. They would prevent industry from producing goods in the proportions that consumers most desire, and therefore would reduce the return that consumers get for their dollars. Price ceilings would also cause a drop in the quality of goods. Consequently, it is important that the rise in prices be kept slow enough and that the inflation be kept fair enough so that the community will not reduce the productivity of industry by insisting on comprehensive direct controls.

Retarding the rise in prices is not easily accomplished when trade-unions are in an exceptionally strong bargaining position and are rapidly pushing up wages. Nevertheless, stiffer indirect controls, by making it harder for employers to pass on wage increases, would probably cause them to do a better job of bargaining with unions. The main features of a program of stiffer indirect controls would be substantial reductions in government civilian spending, stricter control of bank credit, cuts in the prices at which farm products are supported, and a real attempt to induce people to save by offering them a government savings bond payable in a fixed amount of purchasing power rather than a fixed number of dollars.

This analysis indicates that the best way to limit the disrupting effect of the conflict with Russia upon the domestic economy is to accelerate the expansion of production. If the conflict with Russia were to cause production to increase at 4 per cent instead of 3 per cent a year and if the additional outlays on defense and foreign aid were about 18 billion dollars a year (in 1950 dollars), the gain in production, after about six years, would entirely offset the increased military expenditures. As a matter of fact, since the expanded defense program is likely to produce an early and substantial increase in the labor force and a corresponding jump in production, the reduction in the standard of living by defense expenditures may last considerably less than six years.

Stepping up the expansion of production can be achieved. Success depends particularly upon avoiding two great dangers: the government must not handicap industry by unduly taxing away supplies of invest-ment-seeking funds, and military policy must not prevent the increase in professional and technical workers badly needed for expanding technological research. If these two dangers can be avoided, the United States will win the production contest with Russia. Furthermore, if Russia causes the United States to step up the increase in output, the contest between the two countries will, within several years, give America a higher rather than a lower standard of living. If the rise in money incomes can be kept broad and not confined to a few groups, such as trade-union members and farmers, the advance in the standard of living will extend to most parts of the community.

Science and Technology

29. SCIENCE AND AMERICAN POWER *

Americans are known throughout the world for their "know-how." This term probably refers to the ability to get things done in the scientific and technical realm rather than in other fields of endeavor. The "Seabees," construction battalions which did so much useful work in the Pacific Theater during the last war, boasted about their "know-how." "The difficult we do immediately," they said, "the impossible takes a little longer." They were expert users of machines, well versed in the technological aspects of twentieth century civilization.

American foreign policy is greatly strengthened by the fact that the Americans are a technical people. With the aid of machines, a relatively small American fighting force becomes a powerful instrument of destruction. Science and technology contribute greatly to American power. In this article, Mr. Lerner analyzes the development of American attitudes and skills in the scientific and technical fields.

The big paradox about science in America is that with all its vaunted use it is not given full sway; that while it is worshipped it is also feared; that while its strength is linked with the atmosphere of freedom in which it has developed, it has not released the social imagination nor fortified the social will; that the finest flowering of scientific genius in the realm of technology somehow manages to exist side by side with primitive and animistic taboos in the realm of social thought and action.

We live today in the shadow of a scientific triumph whose immensity will give its name to an entire world epoch to come—the release of

* Max Lerner, *The American Scholar,* Autumn, 1946, pp. 439-448. The author is a political columnist for the *New York Post,* and Dean of the Division of the Social Sciences, Brandeis University.

atomic energy. The discovery was the result of world knowledge, levying upon contributions from scientists of many nations. But it was America that took over the knowledge, organized it, fitted it together, underwrote the engineering work required, and got out in front with every indication that it means to stay in front. How have the Americans achieved this position? Why should it have been exactly they who were destined to wield to the fullest the power of science and wear most jauntily the greenest bays of its glory?

For the beginning of an answer we must look to the growth of American civilization. America was born at the beginning of the great age of science. When we think of the major inventions of the modern world we think naturally of the 19th and 20th centuries, and the full flowering of technology. But back of this flowering were the long centuries when the seed grew in the earth. The *saeculum mirabile* of European science was, by the common suffrage of its historians, the seventeenth. The same expansive forces that produced the scientific discoveries of that century produced the American settlements as well. Europe was pent-up. It reached out intellectually, as it reached out physically, for new frontiers. In England the history of the Royal Society paralleled that of the plantation companies, and men were tinkering with test-tubes in laboratories throughout the 17th and 18th centuries while other men were fighting out the battles of dogma and religious freedom, mercantilism and economic freedom. When we remember that the whole atmosphere surrounding the settlement and peopling of America was an atmosphere of scientific beginnings, it becomes more congruous to think of America itself as an experiment on the vast laboratory of a continent. Except in a climate of innovation America would have been impossible, and in the innovating social climate of America, inventions were bound to flourish.

They did not, of course, until the primary needs of physical and political survival had been met. Until after the Revolutionary War, Benjamin Franklin and Benjamin Rush were the only American scientists of account. Science, the heir of centuries of intellectual development, could not flourish in a wilderness. It needed universities, laboratories, leisure. Nor could the Americans move into the realm of scientific experiment with all their lusty strength until they first had a sense of that strength, which did not come until the Revolution had been fought and the Constitution consolidated. But once launched on its career American science had everything in its favor for a rapid sweep across the world horizons.

For one thing, it was close enough to the European intellectual heritage to be able to tap its accumulated knowledge; yet it had also the freedom of distance—the extra margin of freedom from the accustomed grooves of thinking which often hemmed a European scientist in. One of the clearest examples of this double-truth may be found in Benjamin Franklin's career as a scientist. . . .

Franklin is one of the great names in electricity, with his "single fluid theory" of electricity, his coining of new terms for the science, his theory of the Leyden jar, and his conclusions about the relation of lightning and electricity. He started his puttering about with the theory of electricity when an English friend sent him some rudimentary equipment with a few hints on how to use it. Without the European scientific tradition he would have been helpless: but from that point on, being far from Europe, he was on his own, with a joyous sense of excitement in his discoveries, and working in an atmosphere of intense popular interest. So much was he on his own that often when he wrote his friends in Europe about his experiments, he didn't know whether what he had discovered was old or new. Nor did he know whether terms already existed for what he observed, or whether his own newly-coined terms were the first. With the growth of his fame as a scientist, his European friends sent him the literature containing the orthodox vocabulary and the traditional ideas on electricity. As Cohen observes in his introduction, "As he learned from books, rather than his own investigations, he ceased to have a free unfettered mind. As he became more and more familiar with the literature of electricity, he made fewer and fewer discoveries until finally he made no more."

Franklin's career had some other things in it that Cohen recounts and that are symbolic of the career of American science. He was the subject of a grotesque incident in England: his lightning-rod was discussed in the Royal Society, which when asked to protect a powder magazine from the effects of lightning, recommended the Franklin lightning-rod, with pointed conductors below the surface of moist earth. An English member of the committee, Benjamin Wilson, dissented on the matter of "points" and insisted on blunt conductors or "knobs" instead. He continued to attack Franklin and split the Society on the matter, without success—until the Revolutionary War. Here George III intervened, ordered "blunt" conductors for the royal palace, and when the President of the Royal Society refused to reverse the committee's recommendation on the Franklin rod, the King forced his resignation.

One may take this delightful story as a symbol of the European institutional hindrances from which American science was free. It could pursue the laws of Nature without troubling about the laws of monarchies; it could work in an atmosphere in which (except for the period of the New England theocracy) it did not have to cope with a codified body of religious taboos nor with a church rooted in state power; it did not have to reckon with either priestly or aristocratic castes. It was free to open and develop the resources of a Continent.

But these were negative freedoms. The positive strengths that American science had lay in the fact that the resources of the Continent were there to develop, and that the whole impulse of America was to do exactly that. In that impulse were tied together the main threads of the American mind—its Puritan emphasis on work and works, its drive to capitalist exploitation, its sense of newness and curiosity, its confidence in itself, its feeling of illimitable horizons and a staggering destiny. Even the economic ruling class, which emerged in the Industrial Revolution after Franklin's death, was anything but hostile to the science which underlay the technological changes that had created it. In Europe the class of economic rulers had to give primacy and prestige to the political rulers and the social aristocracy; in America its sway was undisputed. Its great hope lay exactly in science. For only science could conquer the needed domain for these rulers, strip the forests, open the land, build the railroads, pick the cotton, thresh the wheat, harness the energy. The rich prize of the Continent lay open and inviting; the best skilled labor and technical brains had been drawn to it; the floodgates were down.

But let me state clearly in what sense America has excelled in science. Not so much in "pure" science or scientific theory. It was partly that America came too late to take part in the greatest scientific discoveries: mathematics came to birth in Egypt and Babylonia, geometry in Greece, astronomy in the Renaissance; chemistry rose to importance in the 18th century. America has developed no Pythagoras, no Aristotle, no Euclid or Archimedes, no Copernicus or Galileo, no Newton, no Lavoisier, no Darwin or Mendel, no Planck or Mach or Einstein. There was still room for American pure scientists of the stature of Willard Gibbs or Simon Newcomb; and in the present generation so much of the talent of European science that was not killed off by fascism has sought refuge in America, and so much research money has been made available for "pure" research by the corporations and the armed services who have had proof in the past that pure science pays off in the end, that from now on the American record in scientific theory may come to occupy the place that Greece, England and Germany have had in the past.

But up to now the great American achievement has been less in theory than in its application, less in the discovery of laws than in the fashioning of "inventions," less in "science" itself than in technology and engineering. To be sure, Americans have taken their share of the burden of lonely scientific thinking; they have assumed more than their share of the organization of scientific research; their laboratories are the greatest and best-equipped in the world, and the experimental scientific habit of thought has entered the American consciousness as deeply as the consciousness of any people in history. But where America has gone farthest ahead has been in applied science. Wherever in the world and whenever in history men have made strides in the understanding of how nature works, it is almost invariably the Americans who have carried farthest the application of that understanding.

One of the flaming symbols of this fact is the atom bomb. Atomic theory was hot on the trail of nuclear fission in every great country in the world, but it remained for the Americans to carry to completion the task of releasing the atom's explosive and destructive force. To the theory itself scientists from every great country in the world contributed, including the enemy countries of Germany and Austria and Italy. The achievement of the Americans was an engineering achievement; the division of the necessary research into thousands of parts and its distribution among all the research centers of the country; the fitting of the findings together into an intricate pattern; the construction of plants, machinery, machine-tools; the combination of wealth and economic power with inexhaustible research and precision.

The Russians may someday be capable of similar feats, perhaps even of greater. But for the present the Americans rule the field in the application of science to technology. Again we must ask: why?

The Greek civilization made greater individual contributions to scientific theory than the American has. It moved from myth to science. But somehow the Greeks never crossed the threshold from science to technology. Centuries before the Christian era, three men of Miletus on the coast of Asia Minor—Thales, Anaximander and Anaximenes—pierced to the beginnings of science; in Sicily three others —Pythagoras, Parmenides and Empedocles—laid the foundations for theories on which men have been building for centuries; in the little town of Abdera in Thrace, two men—Leucippus and Democritus—first evolved the atomic theory of the constitution of matter. At the height of Greek achievement, a Macedonian called Aristotle synthesized systems more staggeringly comprehensive than any man before or after him was capable of. Yet Greek science stopped with these world-views. It did not run machines, relieve labor of its burdens, pile up wealth and power. Why?

The effort to account for the failure of Greek technology may in turn shed light on my query about the success of American technology. Democritus, who first formulated the atomic theory, will no doubt re--

main a greater name in the history of science than Oppenheimer, who supervised the scientific work on nuclear fission and the atom bomb. But Oppenheimer lives in a social atmosphere wholly different from that of Democritus, or even of Aristotle centuries later.

As Max Beer, J. L. Hammond and Benjamin Farrington have pointed out, what kept the Greeks from using their science was their institution of slavery at the base of their social system. The thinking was done by free men and citizens; the work was done by slaves. Where there is a contempt for labor there is a separation from the sources of experience with nature, an incapacity for induction and verification, a blindness as to the practical imperatives that shape innovation. The American scientist, no matter how rich or famous, has never cut himself off thus from these sources of experience. While he has been less a creator of world-views than the Greek scientists or even the modern European, he has been persistently the discoverer of new ways of getting old and new things done. Greek science developed greatly in the context of Greek political and moral individualism, but in the context of slavery and the aristocratic attitude toward work it could go no further than science, and was truncated before it could reach technology. American technology developed also in the context of individualism, but there were no taboos of the ruling class to truncate it.

If the South had triumphed in the Civil War and had gone on to spread over the whole American civilization the social implications of the "peculiar institution," the same fate might have befallen American science as befell Greek. The Civil War was thus more than a moral or a constitutional struggle. Exactly because it was fought over moral and constitutional issues it was also a crisis in technology. Calhoun dreamt of a Greek Republic in the South, and the ruling class in a South-dominated system of slavery might, like the Greek, have lived more graciously than the capitalist class that emerged the victor from the Civil War. It might even have produced a finer flowering of literature and philosophy. But the ruling class that did emerge created a social psychology and an ethos in which, whatever else might be said of it, science was at a premium and technology was cherished.

It was a ruling class which, having triumphed over a rival system of economic organization, went on to the even greater triumphs of the conquest of a Continent and the economic empire of the world. It lavished its gifts on science because science in turn opened a cornucopia of profits. It whipped technology on because, with every new discovery, new areas of investment were opened and new heights of productivity were reached. If it be said that in the process of overcoming the Southern system of feudal slavery the capitalist ruling class created a new industrial helotry, in which men are tied not to the land but to the machine, the answer is yes. But where the Greek ruling class used its helots to keep the technological *status quo,* the American rulers use theirs to increase their profits, and to do that they need always to raise the level of technology and productivity. The level of American technology will cease to rise just as soon as the American economic rulers grow so blind in their pursuit of particular profits and power that they allow the economy as a whole to collapse; and just as soon as the "pathos of distance" between the corporate rulers and the industrial helots becomes too great to be bridged by the dignity of work and the passion for technology.

I turn now to another facet of the inquiry. If we say that American strength is the result of American science and technology, it would be equally true to say the character of American science and technology sheds some light on the inner nature of that strength. The question about a civilization is not whether it uses science, but what sciences it uses, and what use it makes of them.

The characteristic Greek sciences were botany, zoology, biology and mathematics, as befitted a people who were interested in the individual and the category and their relations. The characteristic sciences of American technology turned out to be chemistry and physics, electronics and radiation, as benefits a people who are interested in energy and speed, communication and power. Thus the American sciences are a key to the crucial traits of the American civilization. They are the sciences of power.

Spengler had at least a half-truth by the tail when he wrote (in his famous chapter on *Faustian and Apollinian Nature-knowledge*): "Force is the mechanical Nature-picture of western man. . . . The primary ideas of this physics stood firm long before the first physicist was born." While this theory that the science-type in any civilization exists long before the science does is mainly pretty good poetry, it is provocative enough not to be ignored. Veblen came perhaps closer to the same problem when he linked the American "technology of physics and chemistry" (a quarter-century ago radiation and electronics had not yet emerged) with the "absentee ownership" by and of corporations. And if you push absentee ownership and corporate powers still farther back, you get the "natural rights" of property.

Here I think we reach a significant relationship. The American conceptions of science were hand in hand with the American conceptions of nature: the Declaration of Independence, with its theory of the natural rights of the individual, necessarily was the forerunner of the great inventions of the nineteenth century. The *Federalist Papers* are in themselves a microcosm of the forces in the American mind that were to shape the uses of science: on the one hand, an equilibrium-politics, and on the other hand, a deep drive to establish the principle of a central authority with the power to govern. The two may seem inconsistent to the critical student of today, and their inconsistency has been shown in the creaking of the American governmental machine: yet the important fact is that they were both part of the 18th century American mind, and the sense of natural law in the equilibrium principle coexisted with the power-sense in the principle of central authority.

These two—the sense of natural law and the power-sense—have been the formative forces in American science and technology, as they have been in American political science and economics. The "reception" that the Americans gave the principles of John Locke, as Walton Hamilton has analyzed it and Merle Curti has traced it, is another instance of the transforming drive in the American civilization: for the Locke that came out of American thought was very different from the Locke that came into it from the English. It is in the nature of a civilization's "genius" that whatever material it devours it transforms in the image of its own stereotype. When John Locke came out of the American transforming machine his name was Andrew Carnegie or Henry Ford. The Declaration of Independence became the "due process" decisions of the Supreme Court. Tom Paine's flaming pamphlet on natural law became the comfortable doctrines that bolstered property-exploitation. The American's conception of Nature became corporate absentee ownership, and its servant and handmaiden was the technology of chemistry and physics.

The congruity between American science and the driving spirit of American political and economic development was the congruity of élan and force. The geography and resources of America invited a physics of force, and the role of Nature in American political thinking reflected it and prepared the ground for it. Out of the sciences of force came American technology and the machine-process; and they in turn cast their spell upon science.

30. The American Way in War *

Mr. Brogan discusses another aspect of the fact that American
scientific and technological achievement contribute to American

* Reprinted from *The American Character* by Denis W. Brogan, by permission of Alfred A. Knopf, Inc., pp. 162-165. Copyright 1944 by Denis W. Brogan. The author is Professor of Political Science, Cambridge University.

power.   His observations on the manner in which Americans wage
war   follow   quite   logically   from   Mr.   Lerner's   analysis.   Mr.
Brogan, however, does not speak of science and technology alone.
"A   country,"   he   says,   "has   the   kind   of   army   its   total   ethos,   its
institutions, resources, habits of peaceful life, make possible to it."
Yet Mr. Brogan does not underestimate the importance of science
and   technology.   He   calls   it   "the   height   of   imprudence"   for
Germany and Japan to have provoked "the great makers and users
of machines" to a "war of machines."

A   country   has   the   kind   of   army   its   total   ethos,   its   institutions,   resources, habits of peaceful life, make possible to it.   The American
army   is   the   army   of   a   country   which   is   law-respecting   without   being
law-abiding.   It is the army of a country which, having lavish natural
wealth   provided   for   it   and   lavish   artificial   wealth   created   by   its   own
efforts, is extravagant and wasteful.   It is the army of a country in which
melodramatic   pessimism   is   often   on   the   surface   but   below   it   is   the
permanent   optimism   of   a   people   that   has   licked   a   more   formidable
enemy than Germany or Japan, primitive North America.   It is the
army of a country whose national motto has been "root, hog, or die."
When convinced that death *is* the alternative, the hog roots.   It is the
army of an untidy country which has neither the time, the temperament,
nor   the   need   for   economy.   It is the army of a country in which great
economic   power   is   often   piled   up   for   sudden   use;   a   final   decisive
military blow is merely a special variety of "corner."   It is the army
of a country of gamblers who are more or less phlegmatic in taking and
calculating   their   losses,   but   who   feel   with   all   their   instincts   that   they
can never go wrong over a reasonable period of time in refusing to sell
America short.

So the American way of war is bound to be like the American way of
life.   It is bound to be mechanized like the American farm and kitchen
(the farms and kitchens of a lazy people who want washing machines
and   bulldozers   to   do   the   job   for   them).   It is the army of a nation
of colossal business enterprises, often wastefully run in detail, but winning by their mere scale and by their ability to wait until that scale tells.
It is the army of a country where less attention is paid than in any
other   society   to   formal   dignity,   either   of   persons   or   of   occupations,
where   results   count,   where   being   a   good   loser   is   not   thought   nearly
so important as being a winner, good or bad.   It is the country where
you try anything once, *especially* if it has not been tried before.   It is a
country that naturally infuriates the Germans with their pedantry and
their pathological conception of "honor."   It is a country that irritates
the English with their passion for surface fidelity to tradition and good

form.   It is the country of such gadget-minded originals as Franklin and Ford.   It is a country whose navy, fighting its first great battles a century and a half after it could boast of Paul Jones, recovered from a great initial disaster and taught the heirs of Togo with what speed the heirs of Decatur and Farragut could back out of their corners, fighting. The Coral Sea, Midway, these are dates for the world to remember along with the new Thermopylae of the Marines at Wake Island or the new Bloody Angle of Tarawa.   It is a country—and so an army—used to long periods of incubation of great railroads and great victories.   It is the army of a people that took a long time to get from the Atlantic to the Pacific and that found the French and the Spaniards and the Russians before them.   But they got there and stayed.   The two hundred and fifty years from Virginia to California, like the four years from Washington to Richmond, must be remembered by us—and the Germans.   That General Washington, after six years of barely holding his own, combined with the French fleet to capture a British army as easily as taking a rabbit in a snare—that is to be remembered too, for it was a matter not of fighting but of careful timing, of logistics.

That typical western soldier and adventurer, Sam Houston, waiting patiently until the Mexicans had rushed on to deliver themselves into his hands at San Jacinto—that is to be remembered.   It is not Custer, foolhardy and dramatic with his long hair and his beard, who is the typical Indian fighter, but great soldiers like Sherman and Sheridan planning from St. Louis or Chicago the supplying of frontier posts, the concentration of adequate force.   The Indian chiefs Joseph and Rain-in-the-Face were often artists in war at least on a level with Rommel. But to the Americans war is a business, not an art; they are not interested in moral victories, but in victory.   No great corporation ever successfully excused itself on moral grounds to its stockholders for being in the red; the United States is a great, a very great, corporation whose stockholders expect (with all their history to justify the expectation) that it will be in the black.   Other countries, less fortunate in position and resources, more burdened with feudal and gentlemanly traditions, richer in national reverence and discipline, can and must wage war in a very different spirit.   But look again at the cast-iron soldier of the Civil War memorial.   A few years before, he was a civilian in an overwhelmingly civil society; a few years later he was a civilian again in a society as civilian as ever, a society in which it was possible to live for many years without ever seeing a professional soldier at all, in which 25,000 soldiers, mainly in the Indian country, were invisible among fifty million people minding their own business.   Such a nation cannot "get there fustest with mostest."   It must wait and plan till it can get there with mostest.

This recipe has never yet failed, and Berlin and Tokyo realize, belatedly, that it is not going to fail this time—that in a war of machines it is the height of imprudence to have provoked the great makers and users of machines and, in a war of passions, to have awakened, slowly but more and more effectively, the passions of a people who hitherto have fought only one war with all their strength (and that, a civil war), but who can be induced by their enemies, not by their friends, to devote to the task of making the world tolerable for the United States that tenacity, ingenuity, and power of rational calculation which decided between 1861 and 1865 that there should be a United States which would twice crush the hopes of a nation of military professionals, to whom war is an art and a science, to be lovingly cultivated in peace and practised in war. For Americans, war is almost all of the time a nuisance, and military skill a luxury like Mah-Jongg. But when the issue is brought home to them, war becomes as important, for the necessary period, as business or sport. And it is hard to decide which is likely to be the more ominous for the Axis—an American decision that this war is sport, or that it is business.

CHAPTER FOUR

The Formation of
American Foreign Policy

WE HAVE NOTED some of the forces that shape foreign policy decisions. A complete description of the process of policy formation, however, must also include an analysis of the constitutional and institutional framework within which decisions are made and carried out. Our decisions are based in part upon the theoretical conception we have of the nature of international politics; our policy is shaped by certain forces; but we also have a constitutional system which establishes the right of some to make policy; and finally, there are institutions within which decisions are made and translated into action.

In a democracy, there is usually no more unanimity of opinion on the subject of foreign policy than there is on domestic policy. If the aims of foreign policy are stated in very general terms, a powerful consensus can as a rule be summoned to support them. All of our citizens, or nearly all of them, are presumably in favor of national security, the establishment of a just and lasting peace, and the eventual liberation of captive peoples from Soviet domination. Difficulties arise, however, when those charged with the responsibility for implementing these aims attempt to pursue policies which they believe are directed toward the realization of our objectives. On such specific policies, a considerable difference of opinion exists among the officials of our government, the press, and the public at large. This difference is perhaps most apparent in the development of policy on the following subjects: military and economic assistance programs; the desirability of making the secrets of our atomic energy program available to our Western European allies; and the means which should be employed to overthrow the Communist governments of Eastern Europe, to set up democratic governments in their places, and, at the same time, to forestall the outbreak of World War III.

The difficulties of securing support for specific policies are compounded by the fact that sometimes the American people demand that mutually contradictory policies be pursued. President Wilson was faced with this dilemma. In an address which he delivered in Pittsburgh early in 1916, he noted: "There are two things which practically everybody who comes to the Executive Office in Washington tells me. They tell me, 'The people are counting upon you to keep us out of this war.' And in the next breath what do they tell, 'The people are equally counting upon you to maintain the honor of the United States.' Have you reflected that a time might come when I could not do both?" Mr. Wilson owed his re-election in 1916, in large measure, to the prevailing belief that "he kept us out of war" and to widespread confidence that he would be able to continue to do so. Yet how could American prestige and honor be maintained without the danger of becoming involved? Finally, as we know, the President asked Congress for a declaration of war. A few years later, however, disillusionment with the results of the war to make the world safe for democracy spread throughout the country; and there were many who questioned whether the United States had ever had any interest in joining the Allies, and wondered whether we had expended so much blood and treasure merely because of Wilson's idealism, because of the machinations of sinister munitions makers, or because of the marvelous efficiency of British propaganda.

The overriding reason—if any—for our decision in 1917 is not important here. Certain suggestions concerning our involvement in the war have been made elsewhere in this volume (see pages 86-89). What is significant is the manner in which Mr. Wilson's decisions were made, and the manner in which other decisions are made by our government.

And when this part of the process of policy formation is understood, there are yet other questions which must be answered: Who speaks for the United States? How can the people of France or China or Canada determine which of the many voices they hear expresses the policy of the American Government? Other nations find it difficult to understand why the policy of the United States often does not take the form of a clear pronouncement of a responsible government with a unified point of view, but rather appears to consist of a seemingly contradictory, or at least confusing, series of statements by individuals claiming to speak for the American people or its government. The President's voice may blend or clash with those of Senators, Representatives, important diplomats, and famous generals and admirals. President

Wilson may have believed that adherence to the League of Nations was a cardinal principle of American foreign policy; the Senate ultimately decreed otherwise.   Since 1947, serious controversies have arisen over the problems of American policy toward China.   Among the voices heard on this issue were those of the President and various officials of the State Department in Washington, foreign service officers on duty in China, American Ambassadors to China, the Chinese Nationalist "bloc" in the Senate, and General Douglas MacArthur.

Obviously, some of these voices did not merely express impotent dissent; many were voices of power.   The United States did not join the League of Nations.   More than one student of international affairs has suggested that President Truman's Far Eastern policy was often indecisive and inconsistent because, in large measure, he became the captive of his own opposition.   It is easy to predict that President Eisenhower's attempt to continue the European policies of his predecessor will be hampered by members of his own party who have long opposed an internationalist "Europe first" orientation.

These remarks will serve to indicate the kind of problem with which this chapter is concerned.   The following three specific questions will probably cover the entire range of problems here under consideration: What are the limits of authority of the President and Congress in the process of policy formation?   How are these limits determined?   What are the procedures by which the President and the Congress make and implement their decisions?

In the United States, each of the institutions of government has a rather clearly defined role in the process of policy formation.   In other countries, as in Great Britain, this role may be determined primarily by custom and tradition; but here, it is determined by definition and delimitation in a formal constitution, and by the continuous interpretation, by the courts and on all policy-making levels, of the limits of authority and responsibility of the executive and legislature.

In the United States (as in Great Britain) the exigencies of an emergency tend to concentrate more power in the executive.   In times of extreme urgency, someone must act, and the President is the logical official to make decisions affecting the entire nation, without immediate reference to legislative bodies.   It may be difficult to establish the exact year when the United States entered the era of extended crisis, but whether our continuing involvement began in 1931 with the Japanese invasion of Manchuria, or later, when the aggressive designs of Hitler's Germany became clear, it is certain that we are well into the second decade of a period during which crisis has been and still is the rule.   Moreover, it is impossible to foresee when international tensions will abate.   Since crisis, tension, and emergency are the rule, it is not surprising to find that the President has assumed overwhelming power in the field of foreign affairs. This has not taken place without any attempt on the part of Congress to limit his power; the Bricker Amendment is merely the most recent effort in that direction. The times we live in, however, tend to work against any permanent success on the part of Congress—or of the Courts for that matter—in redefining the roles of American governmental institutions in such a manner that the President's power would be reduced. One need only to cite three important aspects of American foreign policy in the mid-Twentieth Century, its complexity, its fluidity, and its high cost, to make clear that logic alone calls for executive leadership.

The development and implementation of American foreign policy in our troubled era calls for knowledge, skill, and sophistication. Moreover, since changes occur on the diplomatic scene with alarming frequency, it is especially important that our information concerning events in foreign lands be correct and timely. As chief executive and commander-in-chief of the armed forces, the President has access not only to the wide experience of the personnel of the State Department, but also to all other information-gathering agencies of the government. Congress, of course, is kept informed by the executive branch, but while the President can make quick decisions based upon his own estimate of the situation, there are, in Congress, quorums, majorities, and influential party leaders that must be convinced—a slow procedure at best.

In the matter of appropriations, Congress has a decisive voice. But here, too, the President plays an important role. Programs that require the expenditure of funds must be referred to Congress. Presidential recommendations for appropriations may be amended upwards or downwards, or even ignored, but the starting point for Congressional debate is most often the President's program. It must also be remembered that, to secure Congressional support, the President has at this disposal the immense prestige of his office, his position as party leader, his control over patronage, and his ability, in extreme cases, to appeal directly to the people.

To summarize briefly, then: since the President's power tends to increase in emergency situations, the period of crisis through which the United States has been passing has brought with it a tremendous increase in the authority and responsibility of the chief executive in the field of foreign affairs.

But we must also look elsewhere for the sources of his power. Foreign policy in the United States is formulated and implemented within a constitutional and institutional framework. The Constitution of the

United States initially established the distribution of powers among the President, the Senate, and the House of Representatives. The Constitution, however, does not say very much about the roles of the executive and the legislature, and what it does say is stated in very general terms. Indeed, it is perhaps indicative of the isolationist temper of the times that the framers of the Constitution merely adumbrated the distribution of powers to conduct foreign affairs. Checks and balances are correlated, functions are separated, and powers are enumerated, but the vast reservoir of powers necessary to attain the objectives of our foreign policy are nowhere explicitly analyzed and apportioned. Certain specific powers are delegated to the President, to Congress, or to the Senate alone, but the sum of these only amounts to a partial definition; the allocation of many important powers remains unmentioned.

This chapter deals with the constitutional and institutional framework within which decisions in American foreign policy are made and implemented. The first selection contains extracts from the Constitution of the United States (Selection 31). The second is the United States Supreme Court decision which established the preeminence of the President in the field of foreign affairs (Selection 32). These are followed by a description of the treaty-making process (Selection 33), an advisory opinion of a United States Attorney-General concerning the applicability of treaties and executive agreements in specific situations (Selection 34), the Supreme Court decision which redefined the doctrine that a treaty, along with the Constitution and the laws of the United States, ranks as the "supreme law of the land" (Selection 35), an explanation and defense of the Bricker Amendment (Selection 36), and an attack on the Bricker proposals by Senator Fulbright (Selection 37).

After this exposition of the constitutional framework, several selections analyze the organizational structure for foreign policy formation (Selection 38), and the roles of the President (Selection 39), the Congress (Selection 40), and the Senate (Selection 41).

Constitutional Framework: Distribution of Powers

31. THE SOURCE OF THE POWERS — THE CONSTITUTION OF THE UNITED STATES

The following extracts from the Constitution of the United States are the source of the distribution of powers in the field of foreign policy among the executive, legislative, and judicial branches of the Government.   Most of the provisions of the Constitution do not refer to foreign policy, an indication that the framers of the Constitution did not anticipate that foreign policy would play a major role in the life of the new Republic.   As with other provisions of the Constitution, the simple and general statements regarding the distribution of these powers have had to be interpreted by the United States Supreme Court.   Two important Supreme Court decisions have therefore been included in this section, United States *v.* Curtiss-Wright Export Corporation (Selection 32), and Missouri *v.* Holland (Selection 35).

ARTICLE I.

Section 1.   All legislative powers herein granted shall be vested in a Congress of the United States, which shall consist of a Senate and House of Representatives.

· · · · ·

Section 8.   (1).   The Congress shall have power to lay and collect taxes, . . . to pay the debts and provide for the common defense and general welfare of the United States; . . . .

· · · · ·

(10).   To define and punish piracies and felonies committed on the high seas, and offenses against the law of nations;

(11).   To declare war, grant letters of marque and reprisal, and make rules concerning captures on land and water;

(12).   To raise and support armies, but no appropriation of money to that use shall be for a longer term than two years;

(13).   To provide and maintain a navy; . . . .

· · · · ·

Section 10.   . . .

· · · · ·

(3).   No State shall, without the consent of Congress, . . . keep troops, or ships of war in time of peace, enter into any agreement or compact with another State, or with a foreign power, or engage in war, unless actually invaded, or in such imminent danger as will not admit of delay.

ARTICLE II

Section 1. (1). The executive power shall be vested in a President of the United States of America. . . .

•   •   •   •   •

Section 2. (1). The President shall be commander in chief of the army and navy of the United States, ...

(2). He shall have power, by and with the advice and consent of the Senate, to make treaties, provided two thirds of the Senators present concur; and he shall nominate, and by and with the advice and consent of the Senate, shall appoint ambassadors, other public ministers and consuls, ...

•   •   •   •   •

Section 3. He shall from time to time give to the Congress information of the state of the Union, and recommend to their consideration such measures as he shall judge necessary and expedient; . . . he shall receive ambassadors and other public ministers; . . .

•   •   •   •   •

ARTICLE III

Section 1. The judicial power of the United States shall be vested in one Supreme Court, and in such inferior courts as the Congress may from time to time ordain and establish. . . .

Section 2. (1). The judicial power shall extend to all cases, in law and equity, arising under this Constitution, the laws of the United States, and treaties made, or which shall be made, under their authority; —to all cases affecting ambassadors, other public ministers and consuls; —to all cases of admiralty and maritime jurisdiction; . . . .

(2). In all cases affecting ambassadors, other public ministers and consuls, and those in which a State shall be party, the Supreme Court shall have original jurisdiction. . . .

•   •   •   •   •

ARTICLE VI

•   •   •   •   •

Section 2. This Constitution, and the laws of the United States which shall be made in pursuance thereof; and all treaties made, or which shall be made, under the authority of the United States, shall be the supreme law of the land; and the judges in every State shall be bound thereby, anything in the constitution or laws of any State to the contrary notwithstanding. . . .

32. THE POWERS OF THE PRESIDENT — UNITED STATES *vs.* CURTISS-WRIGHT EXPORT CORPORATION *

In this case, the United States Supreme Court defined the powers of the President in the field of foreign policy.

In 1934, following the outbreak of war between Paraguay and Bolivia, Congress, by joint resolution, authorized the President to embargo the movement of arms and munitions to the warring countries. After the President had proclaimed the embargo, however, the Curtiss-Wright Export Corporation shipped war goods to Bolivia. Curtiss-Wright argued that Congress had unconstitutionally delegated its powers to the President, that the President had exceeded his powers, and that the Corporation could not, therefore, be held to have committed any crime.

The Court ruled that the scope of legislative and executive power was broader in the field of foreign affairs than in domestic affairs. Mr. Justice Sutherland derived the powers of the federal government to conduct foreign relations not only from the Constitution, but also from the fact that the United States was a sovereign nation and a member of the family of nations. Moreover, in the conduct of foreign affairs, he said, the President is vested with "delicate, plenary and exclusive power. . . ."

Mr. Justice Sutherland delivered the opinion of the Court, saying in part:

. . . *First.*   It is contended that by the joint resolution, the going into effect and continued operation of the resolution was conditioned (a) upon the President's judgment as to its beneficial˙effect upon the reestablishment of peace between the countries engaged in armed conflict in the Chaco; (b) upon the making of a proclamation, which was left to his unfettered discretion, thus constituting an attempted substitution of the President's will for that of Congress; (c) upon the making of a proclamation putting an end to the operation of the resolution, which again was left to the President's unfettered discretion; and (d) further, that the

---

* 299 U.S. 304; 81 L. Ed. 255; 57 Sup. Ct. 216 (1936).

extent of its operation in particular cases was subject to limitation and exception by the President, controlled by no standard. In each of these particulars, appellees urged that Congress abdicated its essential functions and delegated them to the Executive.

Whether, if the joint resolution had related solely to internal affairs it would be open to the challenge that it constituted an unlawful delegation of legislative power to the Executive, we find it unnecessary to determine. The whole aim of the resolution is to affect a situation entirely external to the United States, and falling within the category of foreign affairs. The determination which we are called to make, therefore, is whether the joint resolution, as applied to that situation, is vulnerable to attack under the rule that forbids a delegation of the law-making power. In other words, assuming (but not deciding) that the challenged delegation, if it were confined to internal affairs, would be invalid, may it nevertheless be sustained on the ground that its exclusive aim is to afford a remedy for a hurtful condition within foreign territory?

It will contribute to the elucidation of the question if we first consider the differences between the powers of the federal government in respect of foreign or external affairs and those in respect of domestic or internal affairs. That there are differences between them, and that these differences are fundamental, may not be doubted.

The two classes of powers are different, both in respect of their origin and their nature. The broad statement that the federal government can exercise no powers except those specifically enumerated in the Constitution, and such implied powers as are necessary and proper to carry into effect the enumerated powers, is categorically true only in respect of our internal affairs. In that field, the primary purpose of the Constitution was to carve from the general mass of legislative powers *then possessed by the states* such portions as it was thought desirable to vest in the federal government, leaving those not included in the enumeration still in the states. . . . That this doctrine applies only to powers which the states had, is self evident. And since the states severally never possessed international powers, such powers could not have been carved from the mass of state powers but obviously were transmitted to the United States from some other source. . . .

It results that the investment of the federal government with the powers of external sovereignty did not depend upon the affirmative grants of the Constitution. The powers to declare and wage war, to conclude peace, to make treaties, to maintain diplomatic relations with other sovereignties, if they had never been mentioned in the Constitution, would have vested in the federal government as necessary concomitants of nationality. . . . As a member of the family of nations, the right and power of the United States in that field are equal to the right and power of the other members of the international family. Otherwise, the United States is not completely sovereign. The power to acquire territory by discovery and occupation (Jones v. United States, 137 U.S. 202), the power to expel undesirable aliens (Fong Yue Ting v. United States, 149 U.S. 698), the power to make such international agreements as do not constitute treaties in the constitutional sense (B. Altman & Co. v. United States, 224 U.S. 583), none of which is expressly affirmed by the Constitution, nevertheless exists as inherently inseparable from the conception of nationality. This the Court recognized, and in each of the cases cited found the warrant for its conclusions not in the provisions of the Constitution, but in the law of nations. . . .

Not only, as we have shown, is the federal power over external affairs in origin and essential character different from that over internal affairs, but participation in the exercise of the power is significantly limited. In this vast external realm, with its important, complicated, delicate and manifold problems, the President alone has the power to speak or listen as a representative of the nation. He *makes* treaties with the advice and consent of the Senate; but he alone negotiates. Into the field of negotiation the Senate cannot intrude; and Congress itself is powerless to invade it. As Marshall said in his great argument of March 7, 1800, in the House of Representatives, "The President is the sole organ of the nation in its external relations, and its sole representative with foreign nations." *Annals,* 6th Cong., col. 613. . . .

It is important to bear in mind that we are here dealing not alone with an authority vested in the President by an exertion of legislative power, but with such an authority plus the very delicate, plenary and exclusive power of the President as the sole organ of the federal government in the field of international relations—a power which does not require as a basis for its exercise an act of Congress, but which, of course, like every other governmental power, must be exercised in subordination to the applicable provisions of the Constitution. It is quite apparent that if, in the maintenance of our international relations, embarrassment—perhaps serious embarrassment—is to be avoided and success for our aims achieved, congressional legislation which is to be made effective through negotiation and inquiry within the international field must often accord to the President a degree of discretion and freedom from statutory restriction which would not be admissible were domestic affairs alone involved. Moreover, he, not Congress, has the better opportunity of knowing the conditions which prevail in foreign countries, and especially is this true in time of war. He has his confidential sources of information. He has his agents in the form of diplomatic, consular and other officials.   Secrecy in respect of information gathered by them may be highly necessary, and the premature disclosure of it productive of harmful results.   Indeed, so clearly is this true that the first President refused to accede to a request to lay before the House of Representatives the instructions, correspondence and documents relating to the negotiation of the Jay Treaty—a refusal the wisdom of which was recognized by the House itself and has never since been doubted. . . .

In the light of the foregoing observations, it is evident that this Court should not be in haste to apply a general rule which will have the effect of condemning legislation like that under review as constituting an unlawful delegation of legislative power.   The principles which justify such legislation find overwhelming support in the unbroken legislative practice which has prevailed almost from the inception of the national government to the present day. . . .

The result of holding that the joint resolution here under attack is void and unenforceable as constituting an unlawful delegation of legislative power would be to stamp this multitude of comparable acts and resolutions as likewise invalid.   And while this Court may not, and should not, hesitate to declare acts of Congress, however many times repeated, to be unconstitutional if beyond all rational doubt it finds them to be so, an impressive array of legislation such as we have just set forth, enacted by nearly every Congress from the beginning of our national existence to the present day, must be given unusual weight in the process of reaching a correct determination of the problem.   A legislative practice such as we have here, evidenced not by only occasional instances, but marked by the movement of a steady stream for a century and a half of time, goes a long way in the direction of proving the presence of unassailable ground for the constitutionality of the practice, to be found in the origin and history of the power involved, or in its nature, or in both combined. . . .

The uniform, long-continued and undisputed legislative practice just disclosed rests upon an admissible view of the Constitution which, even if the practice found far less support in principle than we think it does, we should not feel at liberty at this late day to disturb.

We deem it unnecessary to consider, seriatim, the several clauses which are said to evidence the unconstitutionality of the joint resolution as involving an unlawful delegation of legislative power.   It is enough to summarize by saying that, both upon principle and in accordance with precedent, we conclude there is sufficient warrant for the broad discretion vested in the President to determine whether the enforcement of the statute will have a beneficial effect upon the reestablishment of peace in the affected countries; whether he shall make proclamation to bring the resolution into operation; whether and when the resolution shall cease to operate and to make proclamation accordingly; and to prescribe limitations and exceptions to which the enforcement of the resolution shall be subject. . . .

33. THE TREATY-MAKING PROCESS *

Mr. Whittington describes the procedures by which the United States enters into treaties with other nations. He begins with the negotiation of the treaty by the President and ends with the exchange of ratifications and the proclamation by the President that a treaty has been signed and is in effect.

．　　．　　．　　．　　．

In the field of treaty making, the President is the sole authority for entering into negotiations and for concluding agreements with foreign countries. The one limitation upon his authority is that set forth in paragraph 2 of section 2 of Article II of the Constitution, reading:

He shall have power, by and with the advice and consent of the Senate, to make treaties, provided two-thirds of the Senate present concur.

It is necessary that we take the time to comment briefly upon the relative functions of the President and of the Senate in regard to the making of treaties.

It is sometimes incorrectly stated that the Senate ratifies a treaty. It is true that the Constitution provides that two-thirds of the Senators present shall give their advice and consent to the making of treaties, and failure of the Senate to give such advice and consent has prevented in a few instances the ratification of treaties. Nevertheless, the approval of a treaty by the required number of Senators does not ratify a treaty and is not mandatory upon the Executive.

Perhaps the principal factor to be borne in mind with respect to the Executive authority in the making of treaties is this: At every point until an international agreement becomes effective the authority of the

* William V. Whittington, "How the United States Enters into Treaties with Other Nations," *Congressional Digest,* August-September, 1938, pp. 195-197. *Congressional Digest* is *not* a government publication but an independent monthly featuring controversies in Congress, pro and con, and not controlled by any party, interest, class, or sect. The author has been Legal Assistant of the Treaty Division, Department of State.

President is sole and exclusive, with the one exception provided in the Constitution.   The President's control, therefore, may be either positive or negative.   With reference to the negative control, I quote a portion of an address delivered recently by Hunter Miller, Historical Adviser and Editor of Treaties of the Department of State:

. . . He may refuse to permit a proposed treaty to be signed on behalf of the United States; if signed he may refuse to send it to the Senate; if sent to the Senate he may withdraw it at his pleasure; if acted on favorably by the Senate he may refuse to ratify it; and he may even ratify it and refuse to exchange the ratifications.   At any stage in the making of a treaty, until it is internationally complete, the President may, in the exercise of his own discretion, bring the proceedings to an end.

Before proceeding to a study of the various types of agreements and the procedure for their negotiation, we should have a definition of terms.

As to the distinction between a bilateral and multilateral treaty, I believe there is no confusion.   A bilateral treaty is, in its simplest terms, an agreement or contract between two governments with respect to certain matters of mutual interest.   A multilateral treaty is one that has been signed and effected as between three or more governments and dealing with matters of more or less common interest to all of them.

In using the term "treaty" we do so with the language of the Constitution in mind.   That is to say, those international agreements which are submitted to the Senate of the United States for its advice and consent to the ratification thereof are deemed to be treaties in the Constitutional sense.   They may be called many other things by the nations interested. For instance, they may be referred to as treaties, or as conventions, or as protocols, acts, articles, contracts, or agreements; but it is convenient and proper to refer to them collectively as treaties.

The procedure in the making of bilateral treaties may be considered in two parts, the first being that up to and including signature, and the second being that which follows signature.

Probably the first question requiring attention is this: How do the two countries get together?   There are, of course, many ways in which this may be done, but perhaps the most usual method is for one or the other of the governments to communicate to the other, through diplomatic channels, its desire to negotiate an agreement covering certain matters.   In such case, it is customary for the government proposing the agreement to submit to the other a complete draft or text of the proposed arrangement.

Thereafter, the actual negotiations may take place in the capital city of either of the interested nations, or at any other place, as the competent authorities may consider most expedient.   Let us say that the negotiations are carried on in Washington, D. C.   In such case, the ambassador or minister or other qualified plenipotentiary of the foreign country will represent his government in the negotiations, and for that purpose will consult directly with the Secretary of State or other qualified officers within the Department of State.   Throughout the negotiations, the representative of the foreign country may keep in touch with his government and will pursue the negotiations in accordance with instructions from his government.

It may be that the negotiations—that is to say, the discussions and consultations with a view to reaching an agreement with respect to subject matter and terminology—will be completed within a comparatively short time.   On the other hand, these negotiations may and often do require months or even years, depending upon the complexity or controversial nature of the matters to be dealt with in the proposed treaty.

Eventually, we shall assume, an agreement is reached on all points. It is probable that the text of the agreement has been prepared in the languages of both countries, carefully compared and found to be identical so far as the substance of the provisions is concerned.   The treaty then may be drawn up for signature, duplicate originals thereof being prepared in what is referred to as the *alternat*—that is, with parallel columns containing the two languages side by side, the language of one of the countries being the left-hand column of one of the originals while in the other original that language will appear in the right-hand column. We shall refer to this again.

A time and a place are fixed for the signing of the treaty.   Let us say the place is an office in the Department of State.   Shortly before the time fixed for signature, the qualified plenipotentiary of the foreign nation and the Secretary of State of the United States will appear, and the documents will be placed in readiness for signature.   Other interested officers of both governments may be present to assist in or to observe the procedure of signing.   When all is in readiness, there having been a formal presentation of full powers, the treaty will be signed, and the respective seals of the plenipotentiaries will be affixed.

The treaty having been duly signed and sealed, the plenipotentiary of the foreign nation will retain one of the duplicate originals for transmission to the foreign office of his government, and the other duplicate original will be retained in the archives of the Department of State, subject to the further procedure required in regard to senatorial approval, and ratification.

The negotiations having been completed and the treaty having been concluded (that is, signed and sealed), we are prepared to consider the method by which the treaty is brought into force. For this purpose, it is believed that it would simplify matters greatly if we follow step by step the actual procedure in effecting a comparatively recent treaty— the treaty between the United States of America and Mexico terminating Article VIII of the treaty of December 30, 1853 (the Gadsden Treaty).

This treaty was signed April 13, 1937. On April 19, 1937, the Secretary of State sent to the President a letter (or report), enclosing one of the signed and sealed originals of the treaty, for submission to the Senate of the United States. On April 22, 1937, the President sent to the Senate a message, together with the letter from the Secretary of State and the treaty. On that same date, the treaty was read the first time in the Senate and was referred to the Committee on Foreign Rela- ions, and it was ordered that the treaty, together with the President's message and the accompanying letter of the Secretary of State, be printed in confidence for the use of the Senate. Accordingly, there was printed a confidential Executive document for the use of the Senate, copies thereof being furnished to the Treaty Division of the Department of State for confidential use.

It was on June 10, 1937, almost two months after the treaty was signed, that the Committee on Foreign Relations of the Senate submitted its Executive Report, recommending that the Senate "do advise and consent to the same." As of this date, the injunction of secrecy imposed by the Senate was removed and the treaty was made public. That did not mean that the treaty was approved by the Senate, but merely that copies thereof would be available for general distribution.

On June 29, 1937, about three weeks after the Committee on Foreign Relations had submitted its favorable report, the Senate of the United States gave its advice and consent to the ratification of the treaty, without amendment or reservation. Needless to say, in some cases the Senate has given its advice and consent only with certain reservations, which it has been necessary to communicate to the other government in order to ascertain whether the latter would accept them.

At this point, the function of the Senate ends. The remaining action is for the Executive. An instrument of ratification is prepared in the Treaty Division for the Signature of the President of the United States. This instrument recites the steps that already have been taken, then usually it sets forth the text of the treaty exactly, and concludes with a statement to the effect that the treaty is thereupon confirmed and ratified. In the case of the treaty with Mexico which we are considering, this instrument was signed and sealed by the President of the United States on July 15, 1937, a little more than two weeks after the Senate had given its advice and consent.

Meanwhile, the treaty was under consideration by the Government of Mexico in accordance with its own procedure. It was not until November 9, 1937, that the instrument of ratification of that Government was signed and sealed. It sometimes happens that the foreign government will ratify a treaty before its ratification by this Government.

Under the terms of the treaty, as is now customary with bilateral treaties, the ratifications were to be exchanged at a specified place and the treaty was to go into effect when such ratifications had been exchanged. The instruments of ratification of the treaty were exchanged formally in the Department of State at Washington, December 21, 1937. The treaty thereupon entered into effect internationally, despite the fact that under our national procedure the President had yet to proclaim it.

It is the practice of the Department of State at the present time to prepare instruments of ratification in duplicate, both being signed and sealed by the President. One of these is delivered to the foreign government; the other is placed in the archives with the original signed treaty. This has not always been the case, but as we have indicated already it would not be feasible to attempt an explanation of all the variations in procedure.

There is but one other step in our national procedure, namely, the promulgation of the treaty by the President. There is prepared in the Treaty Division, for the President's signature, a proclamation commencing with the statement that a treaty of a certain kind with a certain country has been signed at a certain place and date, and then setting forth word for word the treaty as signed, and concluding that the treaty has been made public, "to the end that the same and every article and clause thereof may be observed and fulfilled with good faith by the United States of America and the citizens thereof." The President of the United States issued his proclamation of the treaty with Mexico on December 27, 1937, less than a week following the exchange of ratifications.

Thus terminates the procedure, as far as the effectiveness of the treaty is concerned, but that is by no means the end of the work that must be done. There remains the matter of publication, of recording, of distribution, and of various other labors, which are done by the Treaty Division of the Department of State.

34. TREATY OR EXECUTIVE AGREEMENT?

AN ADVISORY OPINION

In the late summer of 1940, negotiations were in progress concerning the delivery of American naval units to Great Britain in exchange for the acquisition by the United States of certain naval and air bases controlled by Britain. President Roosevelt asked Attorney General Robert Jackson for his advice with regard to the President's authority to conclude an Executive Agreement covering the proposed arrangements. Mr. Jackson's reply follows.

My Dear Mr. President: In accordance with your request, I have considered your constitutional and statutory authority to proceed by Executive agreement with the British Government immediately to acquire for the United States certain offshore naval and air bases in the Atlantic Ocean without awaiting the inevitable delays which would accompany the conclusion of a formal treaty.

The essential characteristics of the proposal are:

(a) The United States to acquire rights for immediate establishment and use of naval and air bases in Newfoundland, Bermuda, the Bahamas, Jamaica, Santa Lucia, Trinidad, and British Guiana, such rights to endure for a period of 99 years and to include adequate provisions for access to and defense of such bases and appropriate provisions for their control.

(b) In consideration it is proposed to transfer to Great Britain the title and possession of certain over-age ships and obsolescent military materials now the property of the United States and certain other small patrol boats which, though nearly completed are already obsolescent.

(c) Upon such transfer all obligation of the United States is discharged. The acquisition consists only of rights, which the United States may exercise or not at its option; and if exercised, may abandon without consent. The privilege of maintaining such bases is subject only to limitations necessary to reconcile United States use with the sovereignty retained by Great Britain. Our Government assumes no responsibility for civil administration of any territory. It makes no promise to erect structures, or maintain forces at any point. It undertakes no defense of the possessions of any country. In short, it acquires optional bases which may be developed as Congress appropriates funds therefor, but the United States does not assume any continuing or future obligation, commitment, or alliance.

The questions of constitutional and statutory authority, with which alone I am concerned, seem to be these:

First: May such an acquisition be concluded by the President under an Executive agreement, or must it be negotiated as a treaty, subject to ratification by the Senate?

Second: Does authority exist in the President to alienate the title to such ships and obsolescent materials; and if so, on what conditions?

Third: Do the statutes of the United States limit the right to deliver the so-called mosquito boats now under construction or the over-age destroyers by reason of the belligerent status of Great Britain?

There is, of course, no doubt concerning the authority of the President to negotiate with the British Government for the proposed exchange. The only questions that might be raised in connection therewith are (1) whether the arrangement must be put in the form of a treaty and await ratification by the Senate or (2) whether there must be additional legislation by the Congress.

Ordinarily, and assuming the absence of enabling legislation, the question whether such an agreement can be concluded under Presidential authority or whether it must await ratification by a two-thirds vote of the United States Senate involves consideration of two powers which the Constitution vests in the President.

One of these is the power of the Commander-in-Chief of the Army and Navy of the United States, which is conferred upon the President by the Constitution but is not defined or limited. Happily, there has been little occasion in our history for the interpretation of the powers of the President as Commander-in-Chief of the Army and Navy. I do not find it necessary to rest upon that power alone to sustain the present proposal. But it will hardly be open to controversy that the vesting of such a function in the President also places upon him a responsibility to use all constitutional authority which he may possess to provide adequate bases and stations for the utilization of the naval and air weapons of the United States at their highest efficiency in our defense. It seems equally beyond doubt that present world conditions forbid him to risk any delay that is constitutionally avoidable.

The second power to be considered is that control of foreign relations which the Constitution vests in the President as a part of the executive function. The nature and extent of this power has recently been explicitly and authoritatively defined by Mr. Justice Sutherland, writing for the Supreme Court. . . .

* * * * *

The President's power over foreign relations while "delicate, plenary, and exclusive" is unlimited. Some negotiations involve commitments as to the future which would carry an obligation to exercise powers vested in the Congress. Such Presidential arrangements are customarily submitted for ratification by a two-thirds vote of the Senate before the future legislative power of the country is committed. However, the acquisitions which you are proposing to accept are without express or implied promises on the part of the United States to be performed in the future. The consideration, which we later discuss, is completed upon transfer of the specified items. The Executive agreement obtains an opportunity to establish naval and air bases for the protection of our coastline but it imposes no obligation upon the Congress to appropriate money to improve the opportunity. It is not necessary for the Senate to ratify an opportunity that entails no obligation.

There are precedents which might be cited, but not all strictly pertinent. The proposition falls far short in magnitude of the acquisition by President Jefferson of the Louisiana Territory from a belligerent during a European war, the Congress later appropriating the consideration and the Senate later ratifying a treaty embodying the agreement.

I am also reminded that in 1850, Secretary of State Daniel Webster acquired Horse Shoe Reef, at the entrance of Buffalo Harbor, upon condition that the United States would engage to erect a lighthouse and maintain a light but would erect no fortification thereon. This was done without awaiting legislative authority. Subsequently the Congress made appropriations for the lighthouse, which was erected in 1856. (*Malloy, Treaties and Conventions,* Vol. 1, p. 663.)

It is not believed, however, that it is necessary here to rely exclusively upon your constitutional power. . . . I think there is also ample statutory authority to support the acquisition of these bases, and the precedents perhaps most nearly in point are the numerous acquisitions of rights in foreign countries for sites of diplomatic and consular establishments —perhaps also the trade agreements recently negotiated under statutory authority and the acquisition in 1903 of the coaling and naval stations and rights in Cuba under the act of March 2, 1901 (ch. 803, 31 Stat. 895, 898). In the last-mentioned case the agreement was subsequently embodied in a treaty but it was only one of a number of undertakings, some clearly of a nature to be dealt with ordinarily by treaty, and the statute had required "that by way of further assurance the Government of Cuba will embody the foregoing provisions in a permanent treaty with the United States."

The transaction now proposed represents only an exchange with no statutory requirement for the embodiment thereof in any treaty and involving no promises or undertakings by the United States that might raise the question of the propriety of incorporation in a treaty.   I therefore advise that acquisition by Executive agreement of the rights proposed to be conveyed to the United States by Great Britain will not require ratification by the Senate.

35. "THE SUPREME LAW OF THE LAND" — MISSOURI vs. HOLLAND *

In this case, the United States Supreme Court clarified the effect of the provisions of a treaty upon the constitutionality of laws of the United States.

The Court ruled that the exercise of the powers of the Federal government, in a sphere hitherto closed to it as an area of exclusive State prerogatives, could be justified on the basis of the provision of the Constitution that treaties become "the supreme law of the land," along with the Constitution and the laws of the United States. Thus, whereas the Courts had denied to Congress the power to regulate the killing of migratory birds on the ground that such action constituted an invasion of the powers reserved to the States, the subsequent conclusion of a treaty with Great Britain established a constitutional basis for legislative enactment on the same subject. A recent attempt to solve the problem of "legislation by treaty" —to use the term adopted by critics of the Missouri-Holland doctrine—has been made by Senator Bricker of Ohio, with the support of many of his colleagues in the Senate, and of significant legal and editorial opinion.

Mr. Justice Holmes delivered the opinion of the Court, saying in part: . . . as we have said, the question raised is the general one whether the treaty and statute are void as an interference with the rights reserved to the states.

To answer this question it is not enough to refer to the Tenth Amendment, reserving the powers not delegated to the United States, because by Article II, section 2, the power to make treaties is delegated expressly, and by Article VI, treaties made under the authority of the United States, along with the Constitution and laws of the United States, made in pursuance thereof, are declared the supreme law of the land.   If the treaty is valid, there can be no dispute about the validity of the statute under Article I, section 8, as a necessary and proper means to execute the powers of the government.   The language of the Constitu-

* 252 U.S. 416; 64 L. Ed. 641; 40 Sup. Ct. 382 (1920).

tion as to the supremacy of treaties being general, the question before us is narrowed to an inquiry into the ground upon which the present supposed exception is placed.

It is said that a treaty cannot be valid if it infringes the Constitution, that there are limits, therefore, to the treaty-making power, and that one such limit is that what an act of Congress could not do unaided, in derogation of the powers reserved to the states, a treaty cannot do.   An earlier act of Congress that attempted by itself and not in pursuance of a treaty to regulate the killing of migratory birds within the states had been held bad in the district court.   United States v. Shauver, 214 Fed. 154; United States v. McCullagh, 221 Fed. 288.   Those decisions were supported by arguments that migratory birds were owned by the states in their sovereign capacity for the benefit of their people, and that under cases like Geer v. Connecticut, 161 U.S. 519, this control was one that Congress had no power to displace.   The same argument is supposed to apply now with equal force.

Whether the two cases cited were decided rightly or not, they cannot be accepted as a test of the treaty power.   Acts of Congress are the supreme law of the land only when made in pursuance of the Constitution, while treaties are declared to be so when made under the authority of the United States.   It is open to question whether the authority of the United States means more than the formal acts prescribed to make the convention.   We do not mean to imply that there are no qualifications to the treaty-making power; but they must be ascertained in a different way.   It is obvious that there may be matters of the sharpest exigency for the national well-being that an act of Congress could not deal with, but that a treaty followed by such an act could, and it is not lightly to be assumed that, in matters requiring national action, "a power which must belong to and somewhere reside in every civilized government" is not to be found. . . .   We are not yet discussing the particular case before us, but only are considering the validity of the test proposed. With regard to that, we may add that when we are dealing with words that also are a constituent act, like the Constitution of the United States, we must realize that they have called into life a being the development of which could not have been foreseen completely by the most gifted of its begetters.   It was enough for them to realize or to hope that they had created an organism; it has taken a century and has cost their successors much sweat and blood to prove that they created a nation. The case before us must be considered in the light of our whole experience, and not merely in that of what was said a hundred years ago.   The treaty in question does not contravene any prohibitory words to be found in the Constitution.   The only question is whether it is forbidden by some invisible radiation from the general terms of the Tenth Amendment. We must consider what this country has become in deciding what that amendment has reserved.

The state, as we have intimated, founds its claim of exclusive authority upon an assertion of title to migratory birds—an assertion that is embodied in statute. No doubt it is true that, as between a state and its inhabitants, the state may regulate the killing and sale of such birds, but it does not follow that its authority is exclusive of paramount powers. To put the claim of the state upon title is to lean upon a slender reed. Wild birds are not in the possession of anyone; and possession is the beginning of ownership. The whole foundation of the state's rights is the presence within their jurisdiction of birds that yesterday had not arrived, to-morrow may be in another state, and in a week a thousand miles away. If we are to be accurate, we cannot put the case of the state upon higher ground than that the treaty deals with creatures that for the moment are within the state borders, that it must be carried out by officers of the United States within the same territory, and that, but for the treaty, the state would be free to regulate this subject itself.

As most of the laws of the United States are carried out within the states, and as many of them deal with matters which, in the silence of such laws, the state might regulate, such general grounds are not enough to support Missouri's claim. Valid treaties, of course, "are as binding within the territorial limits of the states as they are elsewhere throughout the dominion of the United States." . . . No doubt the great body of private relations usually fall within the control of the state, but a treaty may override its power. . . .

Here a national interest of very nearly the first magnitude is involved. It can be protected only by national action in concert with that of another power. The subject-matter is only transitorily within the state, and has no permanent habitat therein. But for the treaty and the statute, there soon might be no birds for any powers to deal with. We see nothing in the Constitution that compels the government to sit by while a food supply is cut off and the protectors of our forests and our crops are destroyed. It is not sufficient to rely upon the states. The reliance is vain, and were it otherwise, the question is whether the United States is forbidden to act. We are of the opinion that the treaty and statute must be upheld. . . .

36. A DEFENSE OF THE BRICKER AMENDMENT *

Much of the discussion regarding the Bricker Amendment, the arguments pro and con, the analyses of the political pressures and divisions within the Republican Party, the charges that the Amendment's enactment presages a return to isolationism, and the counter-assertions that the Amendment merely seeks to protect the people against the possibility of a presidential usurpation of power, have largely neglected one important aspect of the proposal: the wide support which it seemingly enjoys.   On several occasions during the period of intense discussion on the merits of the Amendment, students of the political scene were certain that a vote in the Senate and House of Representatives would yield the necessary two-thirds vote required to amend the Constitution.   The next step in the amending process, that of securing the ratification of the legislatures of three-fourths of the States, seemed likewise assured.   That this attempt to strengthen the hand of Congress against the President in the field of foreign policy is based upon something more than an inter-party squabble is clear.   Mr. Eisenhower has proved to be as reluctant to accept the restrictions of the Amendment as was Mr. Truman before him.

Perhaps the Amendment's popularity derives from a belief that many of President Roosevelt's "blunders" would have been avoided if he had had to secure Congressional approval to make certain agreements—Yalta, for example.   Perhaps some of Senator Bricker's supporters are concerned with the possibility that the United States might, at some time in the future, enter into a treaty, or make an executive agreement, which would be the basis for subsequent legislation in fields denied to Congress as unconstitutional in the absence of the treaty (See Selection 35, Missouri v. Holland).   Whatever the reasons for its popularity, however, it seems clear that the Bricker Amendment is an attempt to redistribute the power between the executive and the legislature on terms more favorable to the legislature than the Constitution now provides.

SENATE JOINT RESOLUTION 1

S. J. Res. 1, as amended by the Senate Judiciary Committee, contains the following three substantive sections:

Sec. 1.   A provision of a treaty which conflicts with this Constitution shall not be of any force or effect.

* John W. Bricker, "Making Treaties and Other International Agreements," *The Annals of the American Academy of Political and Social Science,* September, 1953, pp. 134-144.   The author is United States Senator from Ohio.

Sec. 2.   A treaty shall become effective as internal law in the United States only through legislation which would be valid in the absence of treaty.

Sec. 3.   Congress shall have power to regulate all executive and other agreements with any foreign power or international organization.   All such agreements shall be subject to the limitations imposed on treaties by this article.

Section 1 subjects the President and the Senate to constitutional restraints in the exercise of the treaty-making power comparable to those which limit their action as participants in the enactment of ordinary legislation.   This was, of course, the original intent of the framers of the Constitution and was reflected in early judicial dicta.

Section 2 prevents the President and the Senate from using treaties as an instrument of domestic legislation without the participation of the House of Representatives.   In addition, section 2 protects the reserved powers of the states by preventing Congress from acquiring by treaty legislative power which it does not possess in the absence of treaty. This, too, is in accord with the original purpose of the Bill of Rights and the contemporaneous constitutional construction of learned men.

Section 3 removes any doubt as to the power of Congress to regulate the making of executive and other agreements.   In addition, section 3 places the same limitations on executive agreements as are placed on treaties by sections 1 and 2.

Objection Answered

Though opponents of the amendment contend that it would revive treaty procedures embodied in the Articles of Confederation, the amendment actually brings the Constitution up to date in the light of an international environment dimly foreseen, if at all, in 1787.   Of course the Constitution is flexible enough to meet a variety of new military, economic, and technological developments.   To amend it with the rise of each new problem would result in a document having the specificity of the Internal Revenue Code.   The problems dealt with by Congress under the foreign commerce clause did not change basically when transportation by steam and air supplanted the sailing vessel.   On the other hand, the problems of international intercourse in an atomic age are for the most part novel and unprecedented.

In my judgment, adoption of the constitutional amendment proposed in S. J. Res. 1 would facilitate the making of treaties and other international agreements; clarify legislative, executive, and judicial responsibilities in the field of foreign policy; reduce friction between the Congress and the President; and, most important, firmly establish in the Constitution the principle that extensive participation in world affairs need not, and should not, result in any diminution of liberty at home.

UNDOUBTED CONSTITUTIONAL SUPREMACY AN AID
TO TREATY-MAKING

At the present time neither the President nor the Senate can be certain that any treaty provision in conflict with the Constitution would be set aside by the Supreme Court.   Senators may not be quite so sure as Mr. Dulles was when he said that treaties "can override the Constitution," but almost all Senators recognize that there is at least a reasonable doubt concerning the supremacy of the Constitution over treaty law.   As a result, some treaties, highly desirable in many respects, may not be signed by the President or approved by the Senate because of fear of undermining the constitutional rights of the American people.   A prime example of the resulting dilemma is the Genocide Convention still awaiting action four years after its submission to the Senate.

The Genocide Convention had tremendous popular support from the lay public.   Recent knowledge of Nazi and Communist barbarities created unanimous support for the avowed purpose of the treaty. Leaders of the American Bar Association stood virtually alone in opposing the treaty as written.   Their analysis of the Genocide Convention disclosed a grave threat to freedom of speech and press, and the rights of persons accused of crimes.   Proponents of the treaty denied that such dangers existed.   Neither interpretation is unreasonable.

Accordingly, the Senate does not dare consider the merits of the Genocide Convention until it is convinced that no interpretation of the treaty can be effective to prejudice any constitutional right.   Article III of the Constitution limits the judicial power of the Supreme Court to "cases" and "controversies."   The Court cannot render an advisory opinion to guide the President and the Senate in the exercise of their treaty power.

No doubt all ambiguities and defects in the Genocide Convention could be cured by a series of reservations.   However, this road to ratification was blocked by the International Court of Justice.   In an opinion dated May 28, 1951, the Court held that substantial reservations to the Genocide Convention would nullify the act of ratification.   In conformity with this opinion many proposed multilateral treaties expressly restrict the right to attach reservations, or prohibit them completely.

At the time the Constitution was adopted, almost all treaties were bilateral or limited to signature by relatively few nations.   Consequently, the subject matter could be confined to problems of immediate concern to the parties, and the contractual obligation stated in precise language. Reservations to the treaty amounting to a counteroffer created no particular difficulty. Today, the multilateral treaty is the rule rather than the exception. With scores of nations involved, the use of precise language and an unrestricted right of reservation become virtually impossible.

Testifying in opposition to S. J. Res. 1, Secretary Dulles said he "would not press at the moment" for ratification of the Genocide Convention. Unless the Constitution is amended as proposed in S. J. Res. 1, the Genocide Convention is probably only the first of many multilateral treaties that will fail to be ratified by the United States because of uncertainty concerning the nature and extent of constitutional protection. S. J. Res. 1 would eliminate this embarrassing dilemma and facilitate ratification of many worth-while treaties.

CONGRESSIONAL OMNIPOTENCE A DETERRENT TO TREATY-MAKING

Section 2 of S. J. Res. 1 reverses the doctrine of *Missouri v. Holland* which holds that a treaty may empower Congress to legislate in areas prohibited by the Tenth Amendment in the absence of treaty.

Reversal of *Missouri v. Holland,* according to Secretary Dulles, would cripple the treaty-making power by creating "a no man's land in foreign affairs," and by requiring "the concurrence of all 48 states" to make effective many types of treaties. The calamitous results predicted will not come to pass upon the adoption of S. J. Res. 1.

Other federal states have participated effectively in world affairs without placing their constituent units at the mercy of an unlimited treaty-making power. Canada is perhaps the best example. It was held in *Canada v. Ontario and Other Provinces* that labor legislation passed by Parliament to implement a treaty could not supersede conflicting legislation enacted under the powers reserved to the provinces.

In addition, the United States got along very well for many years without benefit of the *Missouri v. Holland* doctrine. In fact, the case cited most frequently to prove that no amendment is necessary because no treaty can "authorize what the Constitution forbids" involved a treaty entered into in 1853 with France on a reciprocal internal state basis. As late as 1948 the United States and China entered into a treaty on the same basis. Section 2 of S. J. Res. 1 merely holds the State Department to this reassuring policy pronouncement made only last year:

Furthermore, where the subject matter covers fields in which the States have a paramount interest, such as the formation and regulation of corporations and the ownership of property, the treaty provisions have been worked out with the same careful regard for the States' prerogatives and policies that has traditionally characterized agreements of this type.

The argument was made in opposition to S. J. Res. 1, however, that unless the federal government can acquire power by treaty which it would not possess in the absence of treaty, the United States could not make the conventional commercial treaties, extradition treaties, treaties regulating traffic in narcotics, and treaties for the control of the military uses of atomic energy. These arguments completely ignore the fact that Congress at one time or another has found ample power, entirely apart from any treaty on the subject, to regulate the subject matter in treaties claimed to be outlawed by S. J. Res. 1. . . .

The Federal-State Clause

There can be little doubt that *Missouri v. Holland* represents a potentially serious roadblock to Senate approval of many treaties favored by the President. The Senate will necessarily be more sensitive to the impact of treaties on state powers than the President. The difference in the constituencies represented sets up a source of friction in legislative-executive relationships with respect to treaty policy. In the past, the full implications of *Missouri v. Holland* have been somewhat obscured by incorporating in treaties a so-called federal-state clause. A fairly typical federal-state clause is that found in Article 19 (7) (b) of the Constitution of the International Labor Organization, reading in part as follows:

> In the case of a federal State, the following provisions shall apply:
> (b) In respect to Conventions and Recommendations which the federal Government regards as appropriate under its constitutional system, in whole or in part, for action by the constituent States, provinces, or cantons rather than for federal action, the federal Government shall—
> > (i) make, in accordance with its Constitution and the Constitutions of the States, provinces or cantons concerned, effective arrangements for the reference of such Conventions and Recommendations . . .

The language quoted above is applicable to some hundred ILO treaties. A similar clause may be found in scores of other proposed treaties. Prior to the debate on any treaty-control amendment, it was generally assumed that a so-called federal-state clause adequately protected the reserved powers of the states against invasion by treaty. It is now abundantly clear that such a clause, if effective at all, merely lifts from Congress any international obligation to exercise its full legislative power.   The supremacy clause of Article VI as interpreted in *Missouri v. Holland* empowers Congress, acting pursuant to a treaty, to strip the states of their reserved powers under the Constitution.   No federal-state clause can prevent that result.

Unless section 2 of the amendment becomes a part of the Constitution, the Senate, now realizing the ineffectiveness of a federal-state clause, may refuse to approve many treaties to which it might give its consent if states' rights were adequately protected.   Or, by approving treaties containing an ineffective federal-state clause, the Senate would empower future Congresses to ride roughshod over the constitutionally reserved powers of the several states.   Only by reversing the doctrine of *Missouri v. Holland* can the Senate be spared this Hobson's choice.

THE CLAIM OF EXECUTIVE OMNIPOTENCE IN FOREIGN AFFAIRS

Legislative-executive relations on foreign policy matters will, except for temporary periods, continue to be marred by friction and discord until such time as the constitutional responsibilities of the President, the Senate, and the whole Congress are more clearly delineated.   The framers of the Constitution made no effort to fix responsibility with respect to international agreements other than treaties.   To complicate the problem further, "treaty" was not defined.   No doubt the framers of the Constitution expected their omission to be corrected in the light of experience.   That has not been done.   In the meantime, what should have been a harmonious sharing of foreign policy responsibilities has too often been a contest of strength marked by mutual recrimination between the President and the Congress.   A fully effective foreign policy cannot be formulated or carried out in such an atmosphere.   The solution provided in S. J. Res. 1 is to confirm the power claimed by Congress to regulate the making of executive and other agreements, subject to the veto power of the President, but leave the President as the sole agent of the United States in the initiation and conduct of negotiations with foreign governments.

Though not specifically mentioned in the Constitution, the making of international agreements other than treaties is recognized by implication. The Constitution, though denying any treaty power to the states, provides that they may, with the consent of Congress, "enter into any Agreement or Compact . . . with a foreign Power."   It would be most anomalous if the states had a power to make international agreements other than treaties which the national government lacked.   This fact was recognized by Congress during President Washington's first term, when it authorized the Postmaster General to conclude postal conventions with the postmasters of foreign countries.

It was never intended, of course, that executive and other agreements should make resort to the treaty procedure optional at the discretion of the President. The alleged superfluity of the treaty-making clauses of the Constitution ignores the careful consideration given to those clauses in the Constitutional Convention and in the state ratifying conventions. The argument amounts to nothing less than a plea for executive omnipotence in violation of constitutional processes. Moreover, if executive omnipotence is conceded to exist with respect to the making of all international agreements, exclusive executive direction of domestic policy will be the inevitable aftermath.

DISTINCTION BETWEEN TREATIES AND OTHER INTERNATIONAL AGREEMENTS

What, then, did the Founding Fathers have in mind when they used the word "treaty" and took such pains to see that this vast power was not centered in one man? In the first place, as Hamilton said in *The Federalist,* No. 75, the treaty power "relates neither to the execution of the subsisting laws, nor to the enaction of new ones," the objects of the power being "contracts with foreign nations," and not "rules prescribed by the sovereign to the subject." In addition, all available evidence as to the framers' intent shows that they intended the word "treaty" to encompass all international agreements known to them as treaties and all agreements thereafter made possessing comparable characteristics and importance. For example, the Founding Fathers relied heavily on *Le Droit des Gens* published in 1758 by Emmerich von Vattel, the famous Swiss jurist and international lawyer. Vattel's book drew this distinction between treaties and international agreements other than treaties:

Section 152.   Treaties of Alliance and other public treaties. . . .   A treaty, in Latin *foedus,* is a pact entered into by sovereigns for the welfare of the State, either in perpetuity or for a considerable length of time.

Section 153.   Compacts, agreements or conventions.   Pacts which have for their object matters of temporary interest are called agreements, conventions, compacts. They are fulfilled by a single act and not by a continuous performance of acts.

From Washington's day to this, Presidents have vigorously challenged the idea that the exclusive procedure for consummating international agreements of great importance or durability is the treaty method. Nevertheless, Vattel's distinction has shown an amazing vitality.   As late as 1939, Assistant Secretary of State Francis B. Sayre said:

International agreements involving political issues or changes of national policy and those involving international arrangements of a permanent character usually take the form of treaties.   But international agreements embodying adjustments of detail carrying out well-established national policies and traditions and those involving arrangements of a more or less temporary nature usually take the form of executive agreements.

The Distinction Blurred

In the past ten years the effort to use treaties and executive agreements interchangeably has been intensified.   Dr. Wallace McClure, one-time chief of the Treaty Division, Department of State, wrote in 1941:

The President, acting with Congress, where simple majorities prevail, can, in the matter of international acts, legally accomplish under the Constitution anything that can be legally accomplished by the treaty-making power as specifically defined in the Constitution. . . .

The result is that for controversial international acts the Senate method may well be quietly abandoned, and the instruments handled as executive agreements. But for large numbers of purely routine acts, about which no public opinion exists and no question as to their acceptability arises, the present [treaty] method is desirable as saving the time of the House of Representatives.

Senators know only too well that the McClure theory received at least partial acceptance in the Department.   Many international agreements have been made by the President alone or approved by the Congress which were many times more important than treaties submitted to the Senate during the same period.   Before reviewing the present administration's opposition to congressional regulation of executive and other agreements, it should be clearly understood that neither President Eisenhower nor Secretary of State Dulles subscribes to the McDougal-Lans-McClure theory that treaties and executive agreements are wholly interchangeable.

Speaking in opposition to congressional regulation of executive agreements, Secretary Dulles said:

It has long been recognized that there is an undefined, and probably undefinable, borderline between Executive agreements which may be made by the President alone and those that require validation by the Senate as treaties, or the Congress as laws.

EXECUTIVE SUPREMACY DECLARED

Mr. Dulles conceded that this "undefined" borderline had caused controversy between the executive and legislative branches of government. He did not explain his reason for believing that the President was better able than the Congress to respect the "undefinable borderline." However, in an obviously sincere effort to promote friendly co-operation, the Secretary of State was authorized by the President to announce the following policy:

> Differences of opinion resulting from these difficulties have given rise in the past to disputes between the executive branch and the Congress concerning the handling of international agreements. It must be recognized that it would be extremely difficult, if not impossible, to fit all agreements into set categories. At times there may be disagreement as to the manner in which agreements are to be dealt with. While recognizing this, the Executive cannot surrender the freedom of action which is necessary for its operations in the foreign-affairs field. In the interest of orderly procedure, however, I feel that the Congress is entitled to know the considerations that enter into the determinations as to which procedures are sought to be followed. To that end, when there is any serious question of this nature and the circumstances permit, the executive branch will consult with appropriate congressional leaders and committees in determining the most suitable way of handling international agreements as they arise.

The policy outlined above cannot assure friendly co-operation. It is as though one of three partners whose duties and responsibilities were not well-defined in the partnership agreement should announce that he, after consulting with the other two, would make all the final decisions on a vitally important phase of the business. The courts will resolve disputes stemming from an ambiguous partnership agreement; they have consistently refused to pass on the merits of "political questions," particularly those involving foreign relations.

OPPOSITION UNSOUNDLY BASED

The State Department's opposition to the executive agreements section of S. J. Res. 1 is based on a number of misconceptions. First, it was argued that S. J. Res. 1 as introduced would prevent the President from making any agreement for which Congress had not given prior authorization. Although rather farfetched, this objection has been overcome in the revised text recommended by the Senate Judiciary Committee.

A second misconception is Mr. Dulles' belief that the danger attached to agreements not ratified by either House of Congress "cannot be great" because such agreements "cannot constitutionally become law of the land." The Secretary of State apparently overlooks the decision in *United States v. Pink* holding that the unratified Roosevelt-Litvinov Assignment superseded the law of the State of New York. The Supreme Court said:

> A treaty is a "law of the land" under the supremacy clause . . . of the Constitution. Such international compacts and agreements as the Litvinov Assignment have a similar dignity.

A third misconception is that Congress cannot be trusted to legislate wisely with respect to the making of international agreements other than treaties. The fact is that Congress in recent years has authorized in advance or subsequently approved approximately 85 per cent of all major executive agreements.

Basically, the administration's objection to congressional regulation of executive agreements as a matter of right stems from an unsound view of the constitutional separation-of-powers doctrine. For example, Mr. Dulles asserted that the President had "exclusive jurisdiction in relation to the current conduct of foreign affairs." A memorandum prepared by the Legal Adviser of the State Department reveals this basis for that conclusion:

> Perhaps the unique feature of our Constitution is the provision for the separation of powers between the legislative, executive, and judicial, each supreme in its field, the whole constituting a system of checks and balances. The proposed amendment would destroy this separation insofar as it relates to the President's constitutional authority in the realm of foreign affairs.

Almost all students of government know that executive, legislative, and judicial powers are not contained in hermetically sealed compartments. Each branch, though primarily responsible in its own field, participates to a considerable degree in the work of the other two branches. The President, for example, is a partner in the legislative process and a very significant factor in the judicial process. The constitutional system of checks and balances was designed to ensure co-operation between three branches of federal government. It was not intended to inspire competition for power among three branches of government, each exercising a supreme and exclusive authority in its own field. This co-operative concept of governmental separation of powers is particularly important in foreign relations. All Americans recognize today that foreign-policy decisions represent life-and-death issues. They insist that the determination of foreign policy, insofar as practicable, be made the responsibility of the President and all 531 members of Congress.

CONCLUSION

Insofar as treaties are involved, S. J. Res. 1 does not limit the powers of the President in foreign affairs. By clear and unmistakable language, the amendment applies only to the domestic consequences of a treaty. The amendment is, in effect, a bill of rights against the treaty-making power.

With respect to executive agreements, the proposed amendment does have some international consequences. It would place other nations on notice that the power of the President to bind the United States without the co-operation of the Senate or of the Congress is not unlimited. It repudiates the claim that survival in an atomic age requires executive omnipotence in the field of foreign affairs.

Adoption of the proposed constitutional amendment would eliminate perennial sources of friction and discord in legislative-executive relations. Nothing is more important to the formulation and execution of a successful American foreign policy.

37. The Bricker Amendment,
An Attempt to Escape the World *

This address was delivered several weeks before the Senate voted its opposition to the Bricker Amendment. Senator Fulbright emphasizes the political effects of the amendment, particularly the changes it would bring about in the constitutional framework of the American government. He believes that Senator Bricker's proposal is an expression of an isolationist longing to "escape the world" and to "turn our backs" on unpleasant facts—in effect, to escape from reality by undercutting vital constitutional powers of leadership.

Mr. President, the American Constitution is one of the miracles of man's history. It was hammered out initially by great men in a series of great debates. Then it was subjected to the most searching examination in another series of debates carried on throughout the Thirteen States before it was finally adopted.

Generation after generation of Americans has turned to the Federalist debates for enlightenment, not only as to the foundations of the Constitution but also for enlightenment upon the philosophy of democratic

* J. W. Fulbright, *Congressional Record*, February 2, 1954, pp. 1065-1067. The author is United States Senator from Arkansas.

government in the United States.   The Constitution is our most brilliant, as it is our most enduring, political success.   It has been a preeminently workable document adaptable to the incalculable social and political changes that have occurred upon this continent and in the world since it was written nearly two centuries ago.   Under it this Nation has successively weathered the mightiest civil war of all time and three world wars stretching from the days of Napoleon to those of Kaiser Wilhelm II, Hitler, and Mussolini.   Nor is this all.   Under it also the American people have achieved more happiness and prosperity for a longer time and over a wider area than any other system ever erected by men.

The reader of the constitutional debates feels, again, a solemn pride in his country.   The debaters were gifted men.   They constituted, indeed, such a brilliant company as has rarely been found anywhere, and whose like we have not had since their passing.   Widely and deeply educated, they drew upon all the legal-philosophical sources of the ancient and contemporary world.   Themselves learned, they respected both learning and the learned.   They were free of that swinish blight so common in our time—the blights of anti-intellectualism.   I should like to remind you, if I may, that this blight, hitherto alien to our democracy, was endemic in Fascist Italy and Germany as it is endemic today in Soviet Russia.

The Founding Fathers were children of the age of enlightenment. They believed in reason.   They sought to convince other men by persuasion rather than to try to bludgeon them into submission by force. They were serene in the belief that reason, applied to human affairs could bring men to a better way of life and living.   They had an immense contempt for the debater who descended to the low level of personalities.   They detested the use of slogans and epithets, for their use is the last refuge of the mentally insecure and the intellectually bankrupt.   They appealed to men's minds; not to their passions.   In short, they were reasonable men seeking to establish a new state upon a rational foundation so firm that it could withstand the stress of change in decades to follow.

And here, if I may divert for a moment, I should like to say that I am tired of name calling directed at anyone who does not agree with the other fellow.   I am prepared to debate the principles in which I believe.   I am not, however, prepared to indulge in any contest of name calling, for not only is this repulsive but it is also, as I see it, an offense to manners that govern the conduct of decent men, and it is anti-democratic in the operation of a democratic society.

The Founding Fathers pursued rationality in their acts and in their debates for another reason.   They believed that our democratic society presupposes the code of the gentleman.   It does not expect saintly conduct of men.   It does, however, expect that they should conduct themselves with a decent respect for the opinions of mankind.   But when they do not do so, when public men indulge themselves in abuse, when they deny others a fair trial, when they resort to innuendo and insinuation, to libel, scandal, and suspicion, then our democratic society is outraged, and democracy is baffled.   It has no apparatus to deal with the boor, the liar, the lout, and the antidemocrat in general.

Under the Constitution, the United States has gone from weakness to strength, from strength to greater strength, from isolation to world leadership, until now we are a people having an unparalleled prosperity at home and an unprecedented power abroad.

The Founding Fathers were, I repeat, eminently successful in their efforts.   Only once was their work violently challenged.   And we paid a stupendous price for that challenge in blood, treasure, and heartbreak.   At that time, as you know, there were fanatics in Boston and there were other fanatics in Charleston.   Men hurled epithets at one another, they refused to listen to reason, faith gave way to fanaticism, and, as Americans venomously distrusted one another, we came to a bloody civil war.

It is then no small thing to drastically alter the Constitution by an amendment that in effect throttles the President of the United States in his conduct of foreign relations.   It is indeed bewildering to see the Constitution, which for so long has been the bulwark of our liberties and the primary source of our political strength, come under such violent attack as we have not witnessed since the 1850's.   It is even more bewildering when one considers that, so far from being a "loophole" in our Constitution as is now claimed, the treaty-making power was perhaps the most urgent reason for calling the Constitutional Convention.   Treaties made under the Articles of Confederation were not enforceable as internal law.   The debates of the Convention and the Federalist papers show the extreme care taken in the formulation of this power, and the system of checks and balances applicable to it.

But today I am less concerned with the Bricker amendment in its direct constitutional sense than I am with it as evidence of a disturbing phase of present day thinking common to many men.

The essence of their malady, as I see it, is this: It is an attempt to escape the world.   As troubles and problems, many of them apparently insoluble, pile one upon the other, an irresistible desire to escape it all wells up in their consciousness.   Political scientists call this tendency to withdraw from the struggle and to pretend it does not concern us isolationism.   The psychologists tells us that it is a very natural yearning of a deeply troubled adult to return to the peace and quiet of prenatal security.

Whatever the instinct or the motive we know that such retreat from the world is impossible.   Our salvation, if we are to be saved, will come from looking the facts in the face and following wise policies based upon those facts.

We often talk about adopting a tough policy in foreign affairs.   I suggest that loose talk about being tough is evidence more of weakness than strength, for a strong man who really believes in himself does not try to impress the other fellow by being tough.   We need, not toughness, but toughmindedness; that is, the willingness and ability to look facts in the face, however bitter they may be, to appraise them at their true worth and then to act calmly, judiciously, and determinedly.

I shall not attempt here even to state, much less appraise, the facts of the perilous, troubled world in which we live; a world perhaps teetering to destruction even as we sit here.

Senators are well acquainted with the events of recent years.   Suffice it to say that the world order of the last 300 years, under which we developed great wealth and power, has been destroyed.   Europe, the predominant influence in that period, is stricken and unable to direct the course of events.

The spread of modern technology into hitherto backward lands has created opportunities and possibilities for peaceful or warlike developments heretofore unimagined.

In a word the destruction of the old established pattern of world power has left us in a period of inevitable and unpredictable change.   These are the facts of life, and not idle speculation.   We will not be able to go back to the halcyon days of 1900, but must, on the contrary, continually face unforeseeable perils.   This being true we shall not triumph by any device, whether isolation, neutrality, or the Bricker amendment, whose underlying objective is a retreat from the world.

One reason of course that we should like to retreat from the world is that struggle—constant, unremitting, blood-and-sweat struggle—is the primitive law of all life on this planet.   Struggle successfully, and you survive.   Fail to struggle enough, and you perish.   The record of mankind is replete with illustrations of tribes and nations long vanished from the face of the earth because they were unable to meet the conditions of struggle imposed upon them either by their environment or by human enemies.   History records their passing but nature does not weep for them.

Nature—pitiless in a pitiless universe—is certainly not concerned with the survival of Americans or, for that matter, of any of the two billion people now inhabiting this earth.   Hence, our destiny, with the aid of God, remains in our own hands.

Mr. President, we have been given at times to adopting methods that seem strange to a civilized and enlightened people.   For these methods, in essence, are those of the witch doctor in a primitive African village. He attempts to drive away the evil spirit by beating drums or by chanting cabalistic incantations.   We who are brought up in the tradition of science are saddened by this spectacle, knowing how fruitless it is.   But incantations can be chanted in more ways than one, and when we do it by assuming that we can banish the evil spirits of an evil world by turning our backs upon our knowledge, retreating from the facts of life, and placing our faith in methods that all history and all experience have demonstrated to be futile.

Our enemy is not the President of the United States, whether the incumbent, his successor to come, or his predecessors.   Indeed, so far as President Eisenhower is concerned it is an unbelievable spectacle to see Members of the Senate—particularly members of his own party— trying to hamstring him in the exercise of perhaps the most solemn and far-reaching obligations of his office—namely, the conduct of our foreign relations—when not long ago this Nation gave its life into his hands by making him the supreme commander of our military forces.   And one's amazement becomes greater in the face of this spectacle seeing that recently the American people, believing not only in his high qualities as a man but also in his high abilities as a diplomat trained in the hard school of experience, elected him President of the United States at a period when the successful or unsuccessful conduct of our foreign relations may mean the life or death of this Nation.

Mr. President, the Constitution charges the President with the duty of conducting our foreign relations by and with the advice of the Senate. It makes him the leading actor; not a spectator and a mere witness. And this role has been discharged by successive Presidents of the United States throughout the nearly two centuries' duration of the Constitution. It was never intended by the Founding Fathers that the President of the United States should be a ventriloquist dummy sitting on the lap of the Congress.

I do not share the fears of an ignorant or willful President or Senate, and this faith on my part is not merely an innocent trust in individuals, present and future.   It is a faith in the form of government which we have known for 165 years; in the traditions and history of the institutions of the Presidency, the Senate, and the Supreme Court; and in the ability of our people, present and future, to regulate those institutions through the processes of government, as they have in the past.

Yet we have come to this constitutional crisis—not, I believe, because Members of this Senate, whether Democrat or Republican, have little faith in President Eisenhower's wisdom and patriotism. We have come to it, I think, because in our desperation to escape the world that we can never escape, we are seeking some device of magic that would enable us to accomplish an impossible end.

Many years ago I read an old-fashioned oration on George Washington by Edward Everett. Everett said that, "Commonsense was eminently a characteristic of George Washington." I could not have been more disappointed and disillusioned than by this appraisal of one of my heroes. For as a boy I naturally thought of Washington as a dashing figure on a horse leading his troops into battle, or crossing the ice-caked Delaware to strike the Hessians at night. It was years later that I realized the significance of Edward Everett's words and understood that without George Washington's commonsense it might have been impossible to establish this democracy. Washington has been dead now some one-hundred-and-fifty-odd years. But commonsense is as valuable now as it was in his day, even if it is apparently becoming rarer. I suggest that we could return to it with the greatest benefit to us all.

Presidents come and go. Some are wise; some are less wise. Some are strong; some are less strong. Some are gifted; some are less gifted. This is true, too, of all the men who have sat in Congress since the founding of this Nation. But all our Presidents, our Congresses, and the members of our Supreme Court proceeding with such wisdom as was given them, and operating under the checks and balances of our constitutional system, erected here a system of government without parallel among civilized men.

In so doing they were aware of the wisdom of George Washington when he said in his Farewell Address:

Toward the preservation of your Government and the permanency of your present happy state, it is requisite, not only that you steadily discountenance irregular opposition to its acknowledged authority, but also that you resist with care the spirit of innovation upon its principles, however specious the pretext. One method of assault may be to effect, in the forms of the Constitution, alterations which will impair the energy of the system; and thus to undermine what cannot be directly overthrown. In all the changes to which you may be involved, remember that time and habit are at least as necessary to fix the true character of governments, as of other human institutions—that experience is the surest standard by which to test the real tendency of the existing constitution of a country—that facility in changes, upon the credit of mere hypothesis and opinion, exposes to perpetual change from the endless variety of hypothesis and and opinion; and remember, especially, that for the efficient management of your common interests in a country so extensive as ours, a government of as much vigor as is consistent with the perfect security of liberty is indispensable. Liberty itself will find in such a government, with powers properly distributed and adjusted, its surest guardian.

Mr. President, I am opposed to the Bricker amendment and urge the Senate to reject it.

Institutional Framework: Executive, Legislative, Administrative

38. THE ORGANIZATIONAL STRUCTURE *

> This selection describes and analyzes the major components of the institutional framework within which foreign policy is formulated and executed. Selections dealing with the President, the Congress, and the Senate follow. They are, of course, primarily devoted to the understanding of the role of the component under discussion, and references to other components remain incidental. This introductory selection by Messrs. Cheever and Haviland is an attempt to interrelate all of the major components of the mechanism for the formulation and execution of foreign policy.

. . . the conduct of United States foreign policy depends upon close teamwork between the President and Congress. Yet in comparison with the parliamentary system there is little to compel coordination of policy at the top of the political hierarchy, since the President and Congress are separately responsible to the electorate and are frequently elected to office at different times and in different climates of opinion. The President has no power to dissolve Congress in the event that Administration policy is not supported by the necessary funds or legislation. A stalemate must await resolution by elections fixed by the calendar and

---

* Reprinted by permission of the publishers from Daniel S. Cheever and H. Field Haviland, Jr., *American Foreign Policy and the Separation of Powers,* Cambridge, Mass.: Harvard University Press, copyright 1952, by the President and Fellows of Harvard College, pp. 23-26, 28-38. Mr. Cheever has served in the Department of State and is Assistant Professor of Government and Associate Chairman of the International Affairs Program, Harvard University. Mr. Haviland has been a member of the Foreign Economic Administration.

not by political exigencies. While the very necessity for action in times of crisis may prevent stalemate, as in the European crisis of 1947-48, when a Democratic President was faced with a Republican Congress, there is no guarantee that this will happen.

It is important to recall, moreover, that the Cabinet is not a Cabinet in the sense of British or Canadian practice. Its members are administrative heads of the great departments responsible only to the President, and they do not have seats in Congress. In this sense, the Cabinet is of little value as a corporate body in obtaining support for Administration programs on Capitol Hill. Nor do the departments have parliamentary undersecretaries to present a "government" or "cabinet" position on the floor of Congress in a "question hour." In an effort to achieve unity and consistency of action a conscious effort is often made in times of crisis to place certain Cabinet members, particularly the Secretaries of State and Defense, above the level of partisan politics. Furthermore, the Cabinet functions very largely as a meeting place for the heads of departments and plays a relatively minor role in assisting the President to coordinate the many facets of foreign policy. This is amply demonstrated by recent war memories of public officials which indicate that such important decisions as that requiring unconditional surrender by the Axis powers were taken by the President in the absence of agreement even among those department heads most closely involved in foreign affairs.

Under the pressure of circumstances, however, through the device of recently created cabinet-level interdepartmental committees, the President now may seek the collective views of his chief advisers on matters of high policy. This is an inevitable consequence of the fact that foreign policy is bigger than the Department of State. Many other departments and agencies have considerable control over the basic instruments of foreign policy. The Departments of Commerce and of Labor and the Tariff Commission, for example, originally established by act of Congress with domestic concerns in mind, have come to exert an unanticipated influence in foreign affairs since a policy of isolation has been abandoned.

Since there are political implications even in the activities of the United Nations specialized agencies dealing with such matters as world health and agriculture, technical matters have increasingly been subordinated to politics, and steps have to be taken to promote the coordination of all aspects of foreign policy. The expanded scope of foreign affairs also bears on the problem of legislative-executive relations. The State Department has a lively interest in many matters over which it has no direct control. These include legislation arising in Congressional committees other than the Foreign Affairs or the Foreign Relations Committees. They include proposals originating in many departments and agencies other than State. The task of building a consistent foreign policy involves a gigantic job of integration. Good working relations with Capitol Hill depend in large measure upon the extent to which the foreign activities of the United States are coordinated. Congress is quick to protest when executive agencies seem to be working at cross purposes.

Most noteworthy of the Cabinet committees to coordinate policy is the National Security Council, established by act of Congress in 1947 and amended in 1949, which now includes the President, the Vice-President, the Secretaries of State, Defense, and the Treasury, the Chairman of the National Security Resources Board, and, with the passage of the Mutual Security Act of 1951, the Director of the Mutual Security Administration. There is some flexibility in the Council's membership, for the President may invite other officials to attend the meetings of the Council. These have included the officials in charge of the old Economic Cooperation Administration, the Office of Defense Mobilization, and the Central Intelligence Agency. The Council is chaired by the President and in his absence reportedly by the Secretary of State. Here machinery exists to bring foreign policy into line with military commitments and domestic capabilities. In some respects this development resembles the coordination of foreign and military policy in British practice. For this purpose a Cabinet committee was created as early as 1904, called originally the Committee of Imperial Defense and now simply the Defense Committee. While the Secretary of State for Foreign Affairs is a member, the Prime Minister or a deputy is chairman. The issue raised for both systems is the relation of the Foreign Office or State Department to this high-level policy committee. In both cases a large measure of the coordinating task falls on the respective foreign-affairs departments.

The National Security Council is purely advisory, although its conclusions are usually accepted by the President. It is serviced by an executive secretary and a small staff of individuals whose responsibility is strictly procedural. It is by no means a full-blown "cabinet secretariat," such as was developed under Lord Hankey as Secretary to the British Cabinet and the Committee on Imperial Defense.

•   •   •   •   •

Interdepartmental committees other than the National Security Council also play important roles in coordinating the diverse elements of foreign policy. The National Security Resources Board is charged with the long-range aspects of providing economic resources sufficient to support national policy. Its chairman is ex officio a member of the National Security Council and advises the President on the coordination of foreign policy with military, industrial, and civilian mobilization. . . . While the Office of Defense Mobilization has responsibility for mobilization in the short range, the National Security Resources Board is responsible for the long-range effects and problems of mobilization as these affect foreign and domestic policy.

The National Advisory Council on International Monetary and Financial Problems, chaired by the Secretary of the Treasury and including in its membership the Secretaries of State and Commerce, the chairman of the Federal Reserve Board and the Export-Import Bank, and the Director for Mutual Security, is primarily responsible for furnishing the President integrated advice on the foreign economic policy of the United States. Below the cabinet level over thirty interdepartmental committees serve to integrate policy in the executive branch on such matters as international aviation, trade agreements, shipping, and international social and cultural affairs. Those committees in which foreign policy is the dominant concern are usually chaired by representatives of the Department of State.

Another important presidential aide that helps to coordinate the foreign-policy-making process, as part of its over-all task of holding the executive financial reins, is the Bureau of the Budget. Its Legislative Reference Division has the responsibility of clearing all executive-agency reports to Congress, including requests for legislation, to be certain that they are in harmony with the total executive program. The Fiscal Division takes external problems into account as it advises the President on the broad long-range implications of the executive budget. The Division of Administrative Management is concerned with the operating efficiency of the executive apparatus. Thus, because substantive programs are constantly being shaped by the power of the purse, the Bureau of the Budget wields tremendous influence in foreign as in domestic affairs.

THE STATE DEPARTMENT

In spite of the growing complexity of foreign affairs, the consequent mushrooming of interdepartmental committees, and the establishment of the Mutual Security Agency, the Department of State remains the principal source of advice to the President on foreign-policy formulation. As noted, however, it now must seek government-wide integration of advice.   Consequently it participates heavily in interdepartmental activity.

Problems are placed for action in one of six major operating bureaus, each headed by an Assistant Secretary of State as "operating vice-president" with considerable latitude to make day-to-day decisions in this area of responsibility according to the general policy directives laid down by the Secretary and his staff.   Five of the operating bureaus deal with the principal geographic areas of the world, and one deals principally with the United Nations and the specialized agencies.   Within each bureau there are functional experts to advise the political officers on such matters as intelligence, public information programs, and foreign economic policies.   Thus in the Bureau of European Affairs there are officials working on the Schuman Plan, the build-up of armed forces in Western Europe, and the politics of French labor movements.   Diplomatic missions and consular offices report, generally speaking, to the Assistant Secretary of the appropriate geographic bureau, while the missions to the United Nations report to the Bureau of United Nations Affairs.

At the "staff" level the Secretary of State is assisted by the five above-mentioned Assistant Secretaries and other officials, including the Under Secretary, and by two Deputy Under Secretaries, one in charge of departmental administration, including the loyalty and security of personnel, and the other in charge of the coordination of policy matters. To accomplish this latter task, the Deputy Under Secretary for substantive affairs supervises staff meetings of important officials and the State Department's Executive Secretariat.

Also at the staff level are an Assistant Secretary for Public Affairs and an Assistant Secretary for Economic Affairs.   The former, on the one hand, assists the Secretary in the all-important problem of cultural and public-opinion aspects of foreign policy and, on the other hand, is responsible for such operations under the immediate supervision of a general manager as the "Voice of America" and the Student Exchange Program.   The Assistant Secretary of State for Economic Affairs provides advice on economic and social matters from a global standpoint and serves as a point of communication and coordination with other departments and agencies engaged in such matters.   In fact, the Department of State was urged by the Hoover Commission to avoid encroaching on the work of such departments as Treasury, Commerce, and Labor, but to advise these agencies so that their operations might be conducted in a manner consistent with the foreign policy of the United States.   For example, it maintains close working relations with the Office of International Finance in the Treasury Department, the

Office of International Trade in the Commerce Department, and the Office of International Labor Affairs in the Labor Department.

Other elements at the staff level in the State Department include the Legal Adviser, the Counselor, a Special Assistant for Intelligence, and the Policy Planning Staff, which is theoretically free of day-to-day decisions so as to provide a look ahead in world affairs. Finally, there is an Assistant Secretary for Congressional Relations, responsible for the important task of maintaining close working relations with "the Hill." He cannot, however, replace the Secretary or other high officials in this respect. His task is to keep in touch with events in Congress for the Department's information and to perform a host of tasks beneficial both to the State Department and to Congress. Crucial policy matters are generally laid before the committees of Congress by the Secretary himself. Yet the Assistant Secretary and his staff of roughly twenty-five people have much to do. During the 81st Congress they took the lead in planning and coordinating the presentation of over fifty drafts of legislation in addition to nearly forty treaties and executive agreements. State Department letters to members of Congress for one year number many thousand. Finally, the State Department's contacts with "the Hill," including periodic briefing seminars, are regularized and scheduled by this staff. Foreign-service personnel are also encouraged to keep in close touch with their Congressmen.

Foreign policy cannot be compartmentalized into either a regional or a functional scheme of organization, however, and great pains are taken in the Department to ensure that the interrelation of all questions of policy is carefully considered. Since the work load cannot be carried without specialization, the object of departmental organization is to provide both the requisite specialization and the integration that are implicit in the phrase "total diplomacy." Recently the Foreign Affairs and Foreign Relations Committees of the House and Senate, respectively, have established "consultative subcommittees" which conform to the organization of the Department of State. This step is designed to increase consultation between the Department and the committees on programs and problems of common concern.

The Department is staffed by two separate personnel organizations— the Foreign Service of the United States, a career group obligated to serve at home or abroad, and the Civil Service, working primarily in the home department and in special capacities overseas for generally limited and infrequent tours of duty that include international conferences. This division of personnel has tended in the past to increase the problems of coordination in the State Department and in the executive branch. The Foreign Service Act of 1946 was enacted as the result of close teamwork between a subcommittee of the House Foreign Affairs Committee and the administrative officials of the Foreign Service itself, without the full benefit of the normal process of legislative clearance by the Bureau of the Budget.   The President, it appeared, was not to be permitted to organize his foreign affairs officials as his staff advisers thought best.

The basic act of 1946 has been amended, however, so as to transfer to the Secretary of State the authority formerly exercised by the Director General of the Foreign Service.   The Secretary of State is now in effective control of all his subordinates, and the administration of both services is the immediate responsibility of the Deputy Under Secretary for Administration.   Recommendations have been made by the Hoover Commission and others for a single Foreign Affairs Service in the Department of State, combining the Foreign Service and Civil Service personnel in the State Department.   A departmental announcement of April 1951 indicates that this may be accomplished in the course of time by greatly increasing the size of the present Service to include individuals trained in the many specialties now required for the conduct of foreign policy.

Not all overseas operations are managed by the Department of State. The Economic Cooperation Agency and now the Mutual Security Agency have controlled to a very considerable degree the instrument of economic aid in foreign affairs.   In the field, working relations between the foreign-aid mission and the diplomatic mission, though generally good, have at times proved difficult.   In the case of Western Germany, however, the United States High Commissioner was also the principal ECA representative.

In sum, the Department of State takes the lead in the formulation of foreign policy.   While its coordinating role has been somewhat reduced, it also has important responsibilities in this respect.   More than any other department it is primarily a Presidential staff agency and, with the exception of specific matters such as the amount of United States contributions to international organizations, is not required to furnish yearly reports to Congress.   Increasing care is being taken to ensure that all overseas operations, such as foreign aid and technical-assistance programs, are administered so as to implement the policies laid down principally by the Department of State.

THE LEGISLATIVE BRANCH

Congress, it has been noted, has an effective veto over many aspects of foreign policy, particularly in its exercise of the appropriations power.

Its crucial role was demonstrated in the years prior to the Second World War by the Neutrality Acts, during the war by the Lend Lease and UNRRA resolutions, and in the postwar period by the Marshall Plan and the rearmament program. Since the initiative for the formulation of foreign policy rests generally with the executive branch, however, the role of Congress, particularly the House, is rather like that of a jury before which the State Department must prove its case.

There are occasional modifications of this relation, however. In the case of the North Atlantic Treaty, the Senate Foreign Relations Committee and particularly its Minority Leader, Senator Vandenberg, joined hands with the State Department in the initiation of policy. To a considerable extent Congress can also initiate foreign policy through the appropriation of funds for specific purposes. A China Aid Program was included in the ECA program by the 80th Congress in spite of the obvious reluctance of the Administration. Such legislation may be vetoed by the President, but often at the risk of losing a total program that seems indispensable or cannot afford delay. Similarly, Congress attempted to make mandatory the granting of a $62,500,000 loan to Spain through ECA by its inclusion in a $36,000,000,000 appropriation bill. The President, in approving the total bill, insisted that the provision in question was unconstitutional and that the most he would agree to was a loan by the Export-Import Bank.

Congress has also sought to direct foreign policy by attaching legislative riders to appropriation acts. The Third Deficiency Appropriation Act of 1951 contained an anticommunist rider to restrict trade between the free world and the Soviet Union. The President, in signing the Act, declared that he did so because the appropriations it carried were "so urgently needed" and because the rider permitted some latitude in its execution. It was, he noted, a piece of legislation "quite unrelated to the major purpose of the Act, which is to appropriate funds." Although it affected foreign policy directly, "it was never considered by the House Foreign Affairs Committee or the Senate Foreign Relations Committee."

Short of impeachment, there seems to be no way that Congress can compel the President to accept its view on the way in which foreign relations should be conducted. On the basis of court precedents . . . , the power of the President to direct foreign affairs as he thinks best within broad limits would probably be sustained.

Congress, what is more, influences the conduct of foreign policy by means of legislation affecting the structure of the executive branch, including both agencies, such as the State Department, and the Mutual Security Agency, and committees, such as the National Security Council. Indeed Congress, despite the recommendations of the Hoover Commission, has been reluctant to grant the President a free hand in executive "housekeeping." This puts a premium on effective collaboration between the branches. For example, Congress had one view regarding the administration of the Foreign Service in 1946 and the President, on the advice of the Bureau of the Budget, had another.

The primary problem posed by the organization and procedure of Congress is that there is no one central point of coordination and control over foreign policy in the legislative branch. The division of control over important instruments of foreign policy among the departments of the executive branch has its counterpart in the lack of coordination among the standing committees of both the House and the Senate. The executive branch, however, has achieved far greater centralization through the work of the Executive Office of the President, the State Department, and interdepartmental committees than has been forthcoming on Capitol Hill. For example, telecommunications, transportation and shipping fall under the jurisdiction of the Interstate and Foreign Commerce Committees of House and Senate. The Ways and Means Committee of the House has dealt with trade agreements and the extension of the Reciprocal Trade Agreement Program. The authorization of funds for the Export-Import Bank and jurisdiction over matters affecting the International Monetary Fund and the International Bank for Reconstruction and Development rest with the Banking and Currency Committees. Congressional committees, moreover, have a degree of power that is, generally speaking, unique among legislative bodies. A committee's attitude on policy very largely determines the attitude of the entire House or Senate. Committees may alter administration measures at will or may even pigeonhole them.

It is evident, then, that the Foreign Relations and Foreign Affairs Committees are at present unable to draw together the many elements of foreign-policy activity on Capitol Hill. The jurisdiction of these committees is no longer of sufficient scope to perform the task. Other committees jealously guard their prerogatives regarding matters that increasingly are involved in foreign policy, and the Department of State can neglect them only at its peril.

A recent development stemming from the investigatory power of Congress is the creation of "watchdog committees." These are joint Congressional committees established to supervise the execution of policies that have been laid down by act of Congress. Examples are the Joint Committees on Foreign Economic Cooperation and on Atomic Energy.

Committee structure introduces another important factor in legislative-executive relations, the role of the committee chairman. He attains his powerful position by seniority, a method irreverently described as the "senility" rule. Thus a man with little background or ability in the field of foreign policy may emerge as chairman of a crucial committee. The President therefore has little or no choice in the selection of these Congressional figures with whom he must collaborate. Yet it is fair to say that the rule of seniority probably eliminates a mad scramble for power and places in the chair someone who is at least experienced in the committee's work.

This decentralization of authority in Congress over important instruments of foreign policy raises severe problems. First, it strains legislative-executive relations, since a carefully integrated executive program may be torn apart as the result of uncoordinated activity on Capitol Hill. Second, the Department of State and other agencies must deal with many congressional committees if the United States is to behave with consistency of purpose in world affairs. This places a well-nigh intolerable burden on these agencies if all legislation dealing with foreign affairs is to be consistent with the objectives of our foreign policy. Finally, policies in support of the general interest are difficult to frame since Congress, lacking effective party discipline, is highly susceptible to the particular interests advanced by sectional and other pressure groups which focus on the highly autonomous committees.

Representatives, faced with the necessity of running for office every two years, are susceptible to the pressures of well-organized lobbies, some of which now appear to be supported in part by foreign interests and many of which have a special ax to grind in world affairs. While Senators are more secure with their six-year terms of office, the Senate is also responsive to special interests, sectional and otherwise. The greater the specialization of legislative activity through the authority of the standing committees, the more effective become the pressures of lobbyists. Congress often fails to place particular interests sufficiently in the perspective of the general or national interest. When issues affecting the safety and welfare of the entire country and its allies are at stake, this deficiency becomes dangerous.

How then are the various components of foreign policy drawn together on Capitol Hill? Within each house the Appropriations Committee becomes, in fact, a significant point of control. For the House, the Rules Committee, through its important power to regulate the flow of legislation to the floor, may also influence the character of foreign policy. At one time, for example, this Committee shaped foreign policy by refusing to clear a bill reported favorably by the House Foreign Affairs Committee on the matter of grain shipments to India. It was hoped that the professional staffs of Congressional committees, enlarged by the

Reorganization Act of 1946, would assist in coordinating committee action by communication with each other and with executive officials. While there may be some improvement in this respect, jealousy regarding committee prerogatives has tended to extend also to the staffs.   Indeed, Congress has no adequate over-all staff work to assist in drawing together the work of the various committees.   In the Senate, the Armed Services and Foreign Relations Committees have held joint hearings on matters of common interest such as the dispatch of troops to Europe and the dismissal of General of the Army Douglas MacArthur from his Far East commands, an inquiry that included many aspects of Asiatic policy since 1944.   Joint hearings of House and Senate standing committees, however, have not proved acceptable, principally from the Senate point of view.

Conference committees, of course, iron out differences emerging from the bills reported out by the standing committees of each chamber. They also eliminate unfortunate features in many instances which have often resulted from the pressures that Congressmen and Senators are reluctant to challenge on the record.   Many an item has been included in a bill in the genuine hope and expectation first, that it will disappear in conference, or second, that it will not be implemented by the President.   Yet they can also be dangerous since they assume such great power or add or omit items with little control by the parent bodies.

In some instances coordination is sought by the creation of special committees of members drawn from the standing committees that are concerned with a given problem.   Thus the Select Committee on Foreign Aid in the House (the Herter Committee) was composed of representatives from the Committees on Rules, Interstate and Foreign Commerce, Appropriations, and Foreign Affairs.   The support the Marshall Plan enjoyed on the floor of the House was enhanced by the fact that both political parties were represented in the membership of this committee.   Bipartisanship helps to coordinate policy in Congress and with the White House, but is inevitably limited to matters of major concern on which there is a wide area of agreement.   It is difficult to have politics stop at the water's edge when foreign and domestic policy are so closely interrelated and when issues of foreign policy may figure in a presidential campaign.

Party policy committees in the House and Senate are further aids in developing an integrated party program in matters of foreign policy. Party leadership helps to bridge the gap between the President and Congress and between the two houses of Congress, but party discipline is usually conspicuous by its weakness in the United States.

It seems fair to say that Congress remains without any very dependable method of integrating the control of foreign policy. It is evident that United States foreign policy depends very heavily on there being men of good will in both Congress and the White House. Success or failure in foreign affairs is also contingent on the degree of confidence that the executive elicits on Capitol Hill and in the electorate. Given effective leadership, government under the separation of powers presents difficulties but not insuperable obstacles to the proper conduct of foreign affairs. Yet the institutional setting influences Congressional attitudes toward foreign policy. Publicity is the very stuff of a Congressional career, and it can be secured if the Representatives or Senators appear vigilant in defending "American" principles against the subversive wiles of the executive in general and the Department of State in particular. Attacks on executive officials, whether principled or not, have, in some instances, paid off in terms of partisan advantage. Since publicity is Circe to the legislator, secret intelligence rests uneasily in his bosom, and cooperation with foreign and military policy officials is awkward at best.

Friction between the President and Congress, however, can be explained only in part by the mechanical structure of government and the perversity of character. It rests in part on the heterogeneous nature of American society, made up of diverse sectional and economic interests that over the years have shaped our governmental practices. The responsibilities and problems that face the United States are frustrating and require the wisdom of experience and broad public consensus on fundamental issues. As these develop, governmental machinery will prove more equal to the task.

39. The American President and Foreign Relations *

Professor Laski analyzes the role of the executive branch of the government in the field of foreign affairs. He touches upon a wide range of perplexing problems in the organization and control of foreign policy, and in the interrelation of foreign and domestic policy. He confines his observations to the administration of President Truman, but the principal difficulties involved in the President's role in foreign relations which Mr. Laski describes have been characteristic of many other administrations as well. Some

* Harold J. Laski, *The Journal of Politics*, February, 1949, pp. 171-205. Copyright the Southern Political Science Association. *The Journal of Politics* is published by the Southern Political Science Association in cooperation with the University of Florida. The late Mr. Laski was Professor of Political Science at the London School of Economics and Political Science and Chairman of the British Labor Party Executive Committee.

problems which Mr. Laski explores have assumed importance even
in the first years of the Eisenhower administration—e.g., conflicts
with Congress, bipartisanship, the effect of domestic policy upon
foreign policy and vice versa.

The makers of the American Constitution seem, broadly speaking, to
have divided the conduct of relations between the United States and
foreign countries into two parts.   On the one hand, there was the actual
conduct of discussion with the governments of foreign countries.   This,
in their judgment, was what Thomas Jefferson called "executive altogether," save that most of the persons appointed by the President to
represent the United States abroad were subject to confirmation by the
Senate.   On the other hand, the approval of treaties required their
submission to the Senate which could not only amend them, but was
taken to reject them unless a two-thirds majority voted in their favor.
The making of war was placed in a special position; only the two Houses
of Congress could declare war.   Since, moreover, most presidential
action required the expenditure of money, and since all financial initiative
rests with the House of Representatives, that body may fairly be said
to have been given an indirect relationship to the presidential control
of foreign affairs.   It looks as though the men of Philadelphia were
determined that, whatever use the President might make of his powers
in this realm, both the results he achieved, and the persons through
whom he formally achieved them, should be subject to the scrutiny and
control of Congress.

It is hardly necessary nowadays to point out how infinitely more
complex the control of American foreign relations has become than
anything which could have been imagined by the men at Philadelphia.
On the executive side, there is no validity in the assumption that the
President will any longer put his chief reliance upon the men he has
nominated to the Senate upon the assumption that they will be his chief
instruments, if confirmed, in the conduct of foreign affairs; on this aspect
of presidential action, Colonel House, under Woodrow Wilson, and Mr.
Harry Hopkins, under Franklin Roosevelt, are only the most striking
examples of influential advisers with more influence than those officially
appointed for the purpose of assisting him; and both House and Hopkins
were part of a tradition which now has the sanction of more than a
century's experience behind it.   On the executive side, also, is the so
far undetermined area of presidential action which derives from his
authority as Commander-in-Chief of the Armed Forces of the United
States.   In this aspect, presidential action may not only authorize the
waging of war (no doubt disguised under one or another of a growing

number of euphemisms) and the secret connivance, as with Theodore Roosevelt, in the organisation of revolution in a foreign country; it may also mean the ability to take action the consequences of which will make it almost inescapable for Congress to declare war, if requested by the President to do so.

On the legislative side, the gap between the formal authority conferred, and the actual authority exercised, is only less striking. Since the Senate rejected the Treaty of Versailles in 1920, no one is ever likely to assume that its power is not, where it chooses to exert it, both living and impressive in this realm. But no one, either, can seriously doubt that the growth, alongside the treaty-making power, of a presidential ability to make "agreements," and to build "understandings," which lead to action substantially equivalent to treaties, has very greatly enhanced the status of the President in comparison with that of the Senate. To this must be added an increase in his influence which comes from the discretionary authority he exercises. This may be an implied discretion, as when he decides to recognise, or not to recognise the new government of some territorial Power seeking sovereign status, or decides that, for reasons he deems satisfactory, arms or other commodities of vital import, like oil or steel scrap, shall not be exported to a *de jure* government; when Franklin Roosevelt decided that Republican Spain should not be permitted to import arms from the United States, he was, in fact, deciding that, given the actual circumstances, General Franco should overthrow the *de jure* government, and reign in its stead as a Fascist dictator over Spain. Or there may be conferred upon the President specialised explicit discretion, as when he is authorised, under certain conditions, to make tariff adjustments with other countries. Or there may be the extension of his authority which comes from the fact that an immense instrument, like the European Relief Programme, is, under ultimate congressional approval, administered both in Washington, and in Europe, by men who, at least in the large outlines of their policy, must be able to command his confidence.

No doubt this growth of presidential power was, in large degree, inevitable as the United States assumed an ever-greater role in international affairs. No doubt, also, both the speed of the growth, and its size, have increased because, since the outbreak of the First World War in 1914, there has been no period in which crisis, actual or looming, has not set the perspective of presidential action. No doubt, further, the impact of presidential power has varied with the character and habits of the men in the White House; the contrast between the impact of President Roosevelt and that of President Truman has been striking, not least in the difference in their ability to mobilise public opinion on their

side in face of a critical, or, still more, a hostile Congress.   It is, moreover, probably true that the scale upon which its power has compelled
the abandonment of isolationism in the United States, has also made it
necessary for the President to give to American foreign policy an
institutional basis which transcends the boundaries of the party he temporarily leads.   Once there is an interventionist America, there must be,
broadly speaking, a unified America.   That means that no President can
afford to repeat the mistake Woodrow Wilson made over the Treaty of
Versailles; he cannot make his foreign policy a party issue merely.
That is why Franklin Roosevelt invited two eminent Republicans, Mr.
Henry L. Stimson and Colonel Frank Knox, to take office in his Cabinet
as Secretary of War, and of the Navy, respectively; why, also, from the
San Francisco Conference onwards, American foreign policy has been
made by the President in conjunction with a small body of advisers,
chosen in part from Senators of the rival party, whose influence upon the
President's mind has, obviously, been very great.   It is, indeed, possible
that when Mr. Truman lost control of Congress in the mid-term elections
of 1946, he leaned more upon the advice of Senator Vandenberg, the
Republican Chairman of the Senate Committee on Foreign Relations,
than upon that of any of the three men who have held office under him as
Secretary of State.

It is here that the growth of presidential power is subject to a limitation
of primary importance.   To be the master of foreign policy, he must,
first of all, be in unquestionable control of his party.   His party must,
in the second place, have a majority in Congress, and especially in the
Senate.   He must be sure, in the third place, that the policy he seeks
to apply, is, in fact, carried out by the officials of the State Department,
in particular, and any other Departments which may be involved.   Under
these circumstances, where the President is in control of Congress, it
would be difficult not to agree that his is by far the major role in the
making of foreign policy.   He has the initiative; and he has the majority
necessary to implement the results of his initiative.   When he is not in
control of Congress, however, his position is a different one.   He has
the choice between taking his own line, without consultation with the
relevant leaders of the Opposition, in the hope that the policy he proposes
may be accepted by them, especially if, like Woodrow Wilson in 1919-
1920, he believes himself capable of securing such popular support
that the majority in the Senate will not dare to resist his policy; or,
alternatively, like President Truman, he may associate the leader of
the Opposition with the executive process of negotiation and decision,
on the presumption that this association in fact binds the Opposition
to support any policy it co-operates in making.

What, clearly, is fundamental if the President follows the second line is the fact that in accepting a co-operator who, at least formally, is confined to an advisory function, he is, in fact, accepting a potential master. There is, for example, no point, after the congressional elections of 1946, at which President Truman could have afforded to break with Senator Vandenberg. Had he done so, Senator Vandenberg's position as chairman of the Foreign Relations Committee of the Senate would have secured the rejection of any proposals the President might have made to the Senate. For all effective purposes, upon those matters which Senator Vandenberg held strong views and upon which he was prepared to take his stand, he held, in fact, what amounted to a veto power over the presidential initiative. Indeed, there is an important sense in which the Senator was bound to feel that he could compel agreement from the President. For, first of all, he knew that he had the backing of the Republican majority in the Senate. He knew, second, that the President must face re-election in 1948 and would need all the aid he could invoke from his ability to maintain congressional unity on foreign affairs. He knew, third, that the conjuncture of these two factors would make both the President and the State Department eager to think of how they could win his agreement to each move they proposed even in their private discussion, before they reached the point of joint consultation. He would thus be sure that he was the decisive figure in the shaping of policy, unless the President were willing to risk a defeat not only as humiliating as that suffered by Woodrow Wilson, but one, also, fraught with far graver consequences to the United States. For, in 1920, Russia was so weak that American withdrawal into isolationism did not affect the pattern of European power until the advent of Adolph Hitler to the leadership of Nazi Germany. After 1945, the withdrawal of the United States from Europe would have left it in a position where the strength and prestige of Russia could not have been challenged by any European state. An American withdrawal, under these conditions, would have meant the rapid acceptance of socialism over all of Europe or the forcible imposition of communism, perhaps, even, the development of a United States of Europe built upon socialist or communist foundations. In these circumstances, disagreement between the President and Congress on foreign affairs, with Congress in a position very largely to defeat any presidential initiative, would obviously have gravely impaired American influence. A bipartisan foreign policy thus became imperative unless the United States were to return to isolationism. Since this had become a political and economic impossibility, the real character of American foreign policy was bound to be shaped by the will of the Republican party. A situation of this character, in short, means that the President who seeks to maintain an American influence abroad which is proportionate to its power must accept the terms upon which his opponents are willing to lend him their authority in the Senate.

If this analysis is accurate, it seems logically to follow that, where the President and Congress are of the same party, the mainspring of authority in foreign affairs lies with him if, like the two Roosevelts, and Woodrow Wilson from 1913 until the congressional election of 1918, he chooses to exert it. Where the President is in the minority in Congress, the separation of powers is likely to involve either the paralysis of American influence in all matters where there are strong differences of opinion among the American people, or a bi-partisan policy in which the President is bound to be at a heavy disadvantage in negotiations with a man in the powerful position of Senator Vandenberg.

The pursuit of a bi-partisan policy raises considerations of the highest interest and importance. Can American foreign policy be so separated from American domestic policy that there can be unity in the one field, while there is conflict in the other? Is this unity, in fact, anything more than a temporary expedient which is likely to disappear whenever there is the normal position of a President with Congress behind him? Are there forces at work in the making of American foreign policy which permit the assumption that a bi-partisan policy will continue independently of the President's relation to Congress? Does this assumption depend upon the decision by America to play an active role in world-affairs? Does it depend on the continuance of a crisis-situation, the "cold-war," for example, that has been waged between the United States and Soviet Russia since 1946? How far does it depend upon the personality of the President? Could he, for example, be in a minority in Congress, and yet secure such popular support for his policy as to compel the majority to accept his views? All of these questions arise out of the experience of three years and a half of President Truman's administration. If none of them is wholly new, all of them are set in a new and significant perspective by the overwhelming power of the United States in the world today, and its obvious will to exercise that power.

A word is necessary, first, upon American power and the will to exercise it. This is not, of course, a conscious determination by the United States to dominate the world. It might, indeed, be argued that the fear and insecurity of the American people are almost proportionate to the immense productive power at their command. They have rather been driven into the exercise of leadership by the impersonal forces of the world-situation than sought for it by the kind of *Machtpolitik* we associate with Bismarck or with Hitler. They could not retreat into isolation without producing an economic catastrophe in Europe—perhaps one in Asia as well—which would be followed sooner rather than later by an economic catastrophe in the United States. The American decision to assist European recovery upon so large a scale is therefore, not merely magnanimity—though there is a large element of magnanimity in the popular support for it—but also profound self-interest as well. For without the European Recovery Programme there would be important areas of American industry and agriculture in which depression would quickly develop, and, with depression, large-scale unemployment. The desire to prevent the degeneration of Europe into chaos is undoubtedly an important motive in the Marshall Plan. A poverty-stricken Europe, driven to desperation, quite obviously could have no hope of standing on its own feet. There is a serious probability that it would accept communism as the only programme out of which some gleam of hope might emerge. The Marshall Aid offers it a period of assistance that it may find its way back to health. At the end of this period, it is assumed that Europe—or, at least, the Western nations which have accepted the European Recovery Programme—will not only have recovered from the disastrous effects of the War, but will be able to treat with America in something like normal market conditions.

But the European Recovery Programme is only one arm of American foreign policy. The other, to which the name of the "Truman Doctrine" has been applied, argues that the critical condition of civilisation is overwhelmingly the fault of Russia. The communist leaders of Russia, it is said, do not want to see the emergence of a stable and prosperous Europe under American patronage. They therefore refuse to assist in making a just and reasonable peace. They pursue a determined policy of imperialist expansion either to reduce European states on their borders to the position of helpless satellites, or, beyond the border states, as in France and Italy, to use the local communist parties to prevent any return there to order and stability, by persuading them to organize the dislocation of production by mass-strikes and the obvious danger of internal revolution. The "Truman Doctrine"—which both the Democratic and Republican parties accept—therefore pledges the aid of arms and finance to any state which is threatened, like Greece or Turkey, by the expansionism of Communist Russia. If these do not suffice to stem the Russian advances, the "Truman Doctrine" accepts the obligation to protect the "sovereign" independence of any threatened state by the actual intervention of American armed forces. Granted this further obligation, it then becomes necessary for the government of the United States to embark upon a great rearmament programme to fulfill it.

Roughly speaking, the government of the United States is spending about five billion dollars annually on E.R.P. in this, its first year, and about three times as much on military and naval preparedness in case a satisfactory peace cannot be imposed upon Soviet Russia through organizing the recovery of Western Europe as a bulwark against the advance of communism. This is the famous policy of "containing" Russia which Mr. George Kennan of the State Department was able to persuade the President and his advisers, Democratic and Republican alike, to accept as an insurance against the spread of communism.

The bi-partisan approach in foreign policy does not, on this view, enable a President who has lost control of Congress to be the effective source of initiative in this field. But it must be noted that the unity achieved on foreign policy has not been achieved on domestic. Here there are wide differences between the announced policies of President Truman and the Republican party in fields like price-control, low-cost housing, the place of trade unions in industry, and fair employment practices; and these are mainly differences which affect the mass of what Franklin Roosevelt called "underprivileged" Americans. On all of these, no possibility of a bi-partisan approach has emerged. It can hardly, indeed, emerge since, obviously, the agreement to "contain" Russia means large-scale rearmament, and the cost of this is, even with so wealthy a country as the United States, unlikely to be too long compatible with the heavy expenditure on the European Relief Programme. and the possibility of war with the Soviet Union and its allies. That possibility not only involves immense American military expenditures, including subsidies for armament purposes to Russia's non-Communist neighbors, like Greece and Turkey, and Kuomintang China; it also compels Western Europe, despite its economic difficulties, to rearm lest, as the flank of the United States in its present role as an active world-power, it should be attacked by Soviet Russia before American assistance can help it to resist communist invasion. The result, this is to say. of the present bi-partisan policy in foreign affairs is to make domestic policy in the United States, and a good deal of West European defense policy subject to the implications of the fact that unity on the international plane has been maintained between the President and Congress.

The problem then arises of whether this domestic subordination to the claims of foreign policy is merely temporary, and likely to disappear following the results of the election of 1948 in which the victor was given a party majority in both houses of Congress. It is difficult to see why this should be the case except under one or both of two conditions. The first is a change in the foreign policy of the United States from one which looks upon war as possible, and prepares for it, to one which looks on peace as probable and organizes for it; the second is the willingness of the taxpaying classes in the United States to bear a much heavier burden in income tax and duties upon inheritance. The first condition would set the President free to urge domestic policies devised to relieve the position of the underprivileged without an increase in the general level of taxes. The second would enable the "cold war" to continue, while affording the fiscal possibility of a progressive domestic policy. It ought, however, to be added that, given the character of the two major American parties, it is not easy to see how the level of taxes could be increased unless there arose conditions in the United States more or less comparable with those with which Franklin Roosevelt had to deal in the grave situation of the Great Depression and its aftermath. The emergence of those is at least postponed because the effect of large-scale rearmament is that it acts, for a period at least, as a public works programme. The men whom it employs, the volume of commodities for which it calls, create, almost like war itself, boom conditions in which there is a low rate of unemployment and a high rate of profit. Sooner or later, indeed, large-scale rearmament is seriously likely to lead to inflation, and thence to measures of which the outcome is either war itself or a depression which, as the history of Fascist Italy and Nazi Germany makes evident, can only be overcome by war, or a drastic reconstruction of the internal social order.

On the view here urged, the President with this majority in Congress is free to change the foreign policy based upon a lack of a majority upon certain conditions. He must be able to dissipate the atmosphere in which it has become widely assumed that large-scale preparations for war are necessary. That is, let it be emphasized, a task which demands high qualities of leadership. It means not only the ability to overcome the tense psychology he is bound to meet at home by reason of the fact that large-scale rearmament is possible only when citizens have been persuaded that they have solid grounds for fear. It also means that the President must have a peace plan acceptable to the forces supposedly hostile to the United States and, at the same time, unlikely to turn his own public against him by leaving it, as Mr. Neville Chamberlain left Great Britain in the aftermath of Munich in 1938, with a deep sense of national humiliation. There is necessarily involved in it the suspension of large-scale rearmament, and, therefore, a plan to prevent that suspension resulting in serious unemployment. Given the economic capacity of the United States, a foreign policy which looks to peace requires a domestic policy which ensures the continuance of high employment. That domestic policy, in a word, involves a programme of large-scale expenditure on public works, like housing, and an increase in the standard of life of the underprivileged in the United States.

For the alternative which would confront a peace-making President would be the replacement of external tension by internal tension. Instead of a relatively high internal solidarity based on a common front against a supposed foreign enemy, the American people would be deeply divided between those who approved of a domestic policy looking towards a higher standard of common welfare, and those who disapproved of it, on a variety of grounds varying from resentment against high taxation to the philosophic conviction that it is an evil thing for the government of the United States to interfere with the free working of the market economy. The position is well illustrated by the experience of Franklin Roosevelt. Entering the White House at a moment when the whole nation was in the grip of the fear caused by the Great Depression, he encountered no opposition until he had liberated the nation from the grip of fear. Thenceforward, until at least his election to a third term, it is scarcely an exaggeration to say that his domestic policies divided the nation more deeply than at any time—excepting possibly 1896 with the issues raised by Bryan—since the Civil War. The division began to close as the shadows of war began to loom over the United States itself. The need for large-scale armaments increasingly pushed the New Deal programme to one side, and the need for common solidarity against external danger provided a means of healing, at least temporarily, the conflict between Mr. Roosevelt and his opponents. It is hardly excessive to say that, after the election of 1940, the need to prepare for war was too great to permit a programme of legislation which might have hindered a full alliance between the President and the business community, for that alliance was essential to arm the United States and its allies against the Axis Powers.

But it must be noted that the alliance was a domestic programme as well. It broadly satisfied labour because it provided full employment at a satisfactory level of wages. The solidarity of the war-time effort was, therefore, not only the outcome of a common appreciation that victory was urgent, but, also, of the fact that the economic consequences of waging it enabled the President to avoid the immense issues of social principle by which he had been previously divided from his opponents. It left his supporters, including the trade unions, generally content to acquiesce in this avoidance. This was the case partly on national grounds, and partly because, for the war period, at least, the position of full employment at a satisfactory wage-level left labour leaders disinclined to push forward questions of social principle. In this attitude, they were supported by the great mass of workers for whom questions of this kind were obscured by the vast spectacle of a struggle between life and death of global proportions.

Generally speaking, this is to say, the fact of war enhanced, as always, the presidential authority by making the executive character of international action so obviously more important than the legislative. Congress could not afford to deny the broad character of presidential demand for the quite simple and obvious reason that it would then have to bear the responsibility of any American set-back in the conflict. This is, moreover, a situation that is bound to recur if ever the United States should be involved in a future struggle of serious proportions. War on any important scale, once it has begun, is bound to make the President overwhelmingly the predominant element in the Constitution. It is not only that he is Commander-in-Chief; it is not only, either, that the speed required by action in the field gives to his view of policy an authority that Congress is not in a position to challenge; it is, above all, that, given a large-scale war, he alone can effectively mobilise public opinion on his side. For the President alone has, of necessity, the continuous possession of the material which affects public opinion. All the agencies of direct war-action are responsible, in the first place, to him. He only can organise American relations with foreign states. The very fact that so supreme an undertaking as the manufacture of the atomic bomb can take place without even the knowledge of Congress, and in despite of the immense expenditure involved, is sufficient proof of the primacy he is likely to enjoy until hostilities are virtually at a close.

But it is in the nature of the American system that the temporary exaltation of one element in the Constitution will be followed, sooner or later, by its depression. Just as war exalts the presidential power, so does peace exalt congressional, and, above all, senatorial power. That was the case after the Mexican War in 1846; it was the case after the Civil and Spanish-American Wars; it was the case after the First World War. The renovation of congressional authority is bound, especially if the President loses control in the mid-term election, to deprive him of the largely unchallengeable supremacy he has enjoyed. He is left, in the main, with three choices. He can challenge Congress; here, in the main, he is likely to be defeated unless he acts under the shadow of looming crisis. He can woo Congress; if he does so with the skill of McKinley he is likely to arrive at a *modus vivendi,* though, as Grant's experience over San Domingo, and Franklin Pierce's over Cuba, make plain, his persuasion is only likely to be successful if his proposals express a generally accepted policy which the congressional leaders were already prepared to approve. The same point emerges in the history of successive presidential efforts, after 1920, to link the United States to membership in the Permanent International Court, under the auspices of the League of Nations.   But where the President faces a Congress in which he has no majority, the balance of power, outside a period of war, passes generally to the Senate, and, in detail, to its Foreign Relations Committee —above all, it passes to the Chairman of that Committee.   The President has then the choice between his own foreign policy which, without the kind of relations Mr. Truman has had with Senator Vanderberg, will be hampered and stayed at every turn, and a foreign policy acceptable to the Foreign Relations Committee and, especially, to its Chairman.   In either case the real consequence is bound to be that, through its Chairman, the Foreign Relations Committee of the Senate has a contingent veto over the presidential control of foreign affairs.

It is, moreover, obvious that, crisis apart, the President's authority is likely, in the normal way, to be in danger under two sets of circumstances, quite apart from the situation when he is in a minority in Congress.   He is likely to have less influence towards the close of his administration than he had at the beginning.   He has exhausted the authority which the patronage gives him.   Members of Congress are more concerned with their own re-election than with his, and they are bound to consider the issue of whether he is likely to be re-elected at all. This emerges unmistakably, even under a determined President like James K. Polk, as soon as it is clear that he is not a candidate for re-election; it was obvious in the second term of James Madison, when the real leadership in foreign affairs was taken out of his hands by Henry Clay.   It is here that the second circumstance becomes important.   It is unlikely that, crisis apart, any President will be the directive force in foreign affairs unless he is determined upon leadership in this sphere. Once he is uncertain of his direction, like Madison before the War of 1812, or Franklin Pierce in his handling of the Caribbean question, the constitutional centre of gravity will shift over to the Senate.   In all normal circumstances, a President who wants to lead in foreign affairs must know how to take the lead.   Perhaps the classic example of this attitude in action is the famous speech of Franklin D. Roosevelt, on "quarantining the aggressors" at Chicago in 1937.   That was the beginning of an educational campaign which, despite opposition in Congress and out of it, enabled him not merely to take a united people into the war after Pearl Harbour, but, from September 3, 1939, both to make it clear where the sympathies of the United States government lay, and to secure from Congress (as in the remarkable exchange with Great Britain of the fifty destroyers for the bases in the Caribbean) effective assistance for it against Nazi Germany which had overrun most of Western Europe.

There is no need to prove in detail that the initiative taken by President Roosevelt—an initiative, indeed, which he began to exercise even before he took office—was on a level far above anything that his successor attempted. It is, of course, only just to point out that, as Vice-President, Mr. Truman had known little, if anything, more of his predecessor's purposes than it was open to any well-informed citizen to know. He did not sit in the Cabinet nor have the circulation of its papers; he was not a confidential intimate of the President; his position debarred him from membership of the relevant Senate Committees. When he was suddenly thrust into Mr. Roosevelt's place, he was bound, at least for a period, to accept his predecessor's officials, as well as his predecessor's policies. He had to acquaint himself with a complex web of facts, of which he was seriously unaware, before he could begin to follow a line of his own. He lacked any real acquaintance with the foreign statesmen involved, as well as with the foreign officials, both on the civilian and on the defence side. He followed a President of world-wide prestige; and he had none of the authority that an elected President normally possesses as of his own right. Necessarily, therefore, President Truman was hardly in a position to give a lead for the first few months he was in office, and at the points where, had he wished, he might have begun to do so, the victory of the Republicans in the election of 1946 took any chance of effective power out of his hands. It cannot often have been the case that, as from 1946, his announcements on Middle Eastern questions should have been flanked by messages from subordinate officials in the State Department to the Arab governments there, assuring them that they need not take the President of the United States as meaning what he said.

One may assume that, under any circumstances, there would have been a swing away from overwhelming authority in foreign affairs that President Roosevelt exercised during the War; as it may be assumed that, in each of the two parts of Mr. Truman's Presidency, he suffered under a grave handicap which assured a swifter and stronger swing than would have been the case if President Roosevelt had lived to the end of his fourth term. The central problem now is how far any of the precedents of the past are applicable to the position of President Truman after January, 1949. For he will be the first American President of a country which has turned its back on isolationism; the United States cannot now avoid a positive foreign policy for the decisive reason that there must necessarily be a new parallelogram of international forces in the shaping of which the United States is bound to play, perhaps for many years, a part second to that of no other government. Not only is it a member of the United Nations; quite apart from its commitments under the Charter of that body, it has now "entangling alliances" all over the world. And it has these "entangling alliances" at a period when, though hostilities have ceased, not only has the peace not been made either with Germany or with Japan, but the "cold war" between the United States and Russia, as well as the grave economic situation, all put before the President a position it has not been necessary to confront in any previous period.

The difficulties involved in this position exist at two different levels, though each is connected with the other. The first is whether it is proposed to continue a bi-partisan foreign policy; the second is the general relation between the President and Congress in foreign affairs. It is reasonable to assume that a President with a majority in Congress, especially in the Senate, would not be likely to secure the continuous collaboration of the minority party. For were it so to collaborate, it would necessarily occupy a position in which, though it might have influence, it would certainly not have power, and would be bound to seem responsible for policies over which it exercised no authority. Since the foreign policy of the United States will now deeply involve its domestic policies also, an attempt to continue bi-partisan relations when the President's party is in control of Congress would tie the hands of the Opposition to a degree that might easily be fatal not only to its right to criticism, but also to its ability to pull over to its side an effective public opinion in cases where it was hostile to decisions actually taken. It could do little to affect the persons chosen by the President either for public posts or as confidential advisers. It would be unable to see any diplomatic papers save those which the President chose to place before it, and it could only use such of these as the President might choose to permit. It is permissible to suggest that, even if an effort were made to continue the bi-partisan relationship, under these circumstances, it would break down.

In light of the 1948 election results, the problem becomes that of seeking to probe the relationship of the President and Congress in the present circumstances in which his party possesses a majority in both House and Senate. Both the executive and legislative powers will then be acting in a situation which corresponds to no past American tradition. The United States will be committed to continuous and positive action in which, to maintain the pattern of politics it has approved, it must maintain its leadership. It must stay in Europe both in a military and in an economic sense. It must make sure of its access to the Middle East. It must be certain that it remains the dominating power in the Pacific. It either must come to an accommodation with Russia, or it must continue to wage the "cold war" against its government. Upon the assumption that it avoids actual war, it must continue not only itself to re-arm, but also to see that the governments with which it is in close collaboration continue to arm also. In broad outline, this policy, in the international field, is the basis upon which Mr. Truman is bound to act. Are the historic relationships between the President and Congress capable of bearing the burden implied in a policy of this character?

.　　.　　.　　.　　.

The American constitutional system makes rivalry for power and credit an inherent principle of its operation. This is especially the case in the realm of foreign affairs since the President has the doubly exceptional authority derived, first, from the fact that he is the Commander-in-Chief of the Armed Forces of the United States, and, second, that all executive power in the diplomatic field is ultimately vested in him. On the other hand, the treaty-making power of the Senate, and its right to pass upon the acceptability of many minor appointments, give it a commanding position in this realm that it has never been willing to yield. Despite a good deal of anger and frustration on both sides over particular incidents, which began in George Washington's first term of office, the system worked well enough until the entry of the United States into the First World War. The rejection by the Senate of the treaty negotiated at Versailles by President Wilson brought into the foreground the supreme question of whether a constitutional system, which had been established when the United States was not only a relatively small and weak Power but also one which was anxious to mingle as little as possible in international relations, would work in a United States which, by 1945, was at once incapable, even if it desired, of isolationist policies, and had become one of the two major Powers in the world. Short of a third global war, moreover, it is the clear destiny of the United States to hold that outstanding position for many years to come.

Where the major emphasis of authority in America is likely to lie in foreign affairs for the future it is impossible to predict; there are far too many unknowns in the equation to make the outcome one about which there is the right to confidence. A series of bad mistakes by strong-minded Presidents might easily lead to an insistence by both Houses, the Senate in particular, on the rigorous and detailed supervision of policy-making they have the constitutional right to impose. A blind and angry opposition by Congress to a great President, who was able to mobilise a strong public opinion behind him would, above all if that public opinion expressed itself in electoral terms, endow the presidential office with a capacity for initiative it would not prove easy to diminish. Much, obviously, will depend upon the wisdom with which the President chooses his cabinet officers, above all, of course, in the Department of State, of Defense, and of the Treasury; and a good deal will turn on the attention that is given to the quality of the officials, both temporary and permanent, in those Departments which have a real share in the making of policy.   Moreover, apart from the degree to which the President can make foreign affairs interesting the psychology of crisis will matter; so, too, will the wisdom with which he, and some half dozen of his chief advisers, handle the important members of Congress, and learn how to secure for themselves the good will of the journalists and the radio commentators.   Their significance in this contest will be apparent to anyone who examines with care the public relations of the White House generally, and catches, even from the coldness of the printed page, the skill and dexterity with which Franklin Roosevelt handled his press conferences through just over twelve years of passionate controversy.

The one prophecy I venture to make is that, in the coming years, a great deal more of American foreign policy will be made informally rather than upon the plane which calls at once for legislative approval and action.   There will be an increase in the number of those who act as the confidential advisers of the President, men like Colonel House and Mr. Harry Hopkins; the *eminence grise,* once he has shown his talent for the art, will play a greater role over a wider area of policy. More will be done by executive agreement, of which the exchange of letters between Secretary Lansing and Viscount Ishii is perhaps the classic example, than by formal treaty-making.   This is because, in the next years, the pace of events is likely to be swift, the decisions to be made so numerous, the risk of conflict too great, for any President, save the type who passively submits to every gust of opinion that blows from the Capitol, to deal more than he must inevitably do with foreign policy in terms that involve the obligation constantly to resort to Congress, and to spend time and energy already overwhelmingly occupied in trying to overcome a natural disposition to differences of approach.

The task of overcoming the disposition to differences of approach will not be easily fulfilled by a tired man, by an angry or irritable man, or by one who holds himself aloof from the opinion he has to conquer. That is why, in the next generation, events are likely to prove that the merely "available" President will no longer be adequate to the supreme office in the Government of the United States.   A world has emerged in which, if American leadership is to be proportionate to American power, that leadership can come from the President alone. The test of the American system will depend upon its power to produce great Presidents. Without them, the people of the United States will be like passengers in an aeroplane the pilot of which can neither utilise the full power of its engines nor be certain of the field upon which it is wise to land.

40. CONGRESS AND FOREIGN POLICY *

Mr. Griffith notes that the present role of Congress in the field of foreign policy "extends far beyond mere treaty ratification." He attributes these increased responsibilities to our involvement in "total diplomacy."

At first glance, a contradiction appears to exist between what has been said earlier in this volume regarding the President's pre-eminence in foreign policy matters during a period of crisis, and Mr. Griffith's remarks concerning the role of Congress. There is no contradiction, however. Considerations of foreign policy loom so large at the present time as compared with past decades, that the activities of all agencies concerned with foreign affairs have greatly increased in scope. Congress has indeed assumed tremendous new powers in this field. But the increment has derived from the expanded nature of American foreign policy itself; there has been no corresponding decrease in the influence of the President.

The traditional story of American foreign policy has been a story of treaties and diplomatic negotiations, interspersed with accounts of wars. Such treatment inevitably led to an emphasis on the roles of the President and his Secretary of State. Congress was regarded as either subordinate or obstructionist, or both. For example, in reflecting upon the events following World War I, in which the role of the United States Senate was to a large extent decisive, the emphasis even in the scholarly writings has been directed toward altering the two-thirds rule or circumventing the treaty-making procedure.

It is only recently that the co-ordinate and even affirmative role of Congress has been recognized in this tremendously important field. With this recognition has grown a realization that tactics directed toward

* Ernest S. Griffith, "The Place of Congress in Foreign Relations," *The Annals of the American Academy of Political and Social Science,* September, 1953, pp. 11-21. The author is Director of the Legislative Reference Service, Library of Congress.

promoting a given policy must be shifted from bypassing or handling Congress to convincing Congress.   Over and above this, ways and means must often be found whereby the responsibility for policy formulation may itself be shared with the legislative branch.

In other words, the congressional role in foreign policy today extends far beyond mere treaty ratification.   For example, the traditional role of a congressional committee in investigation and criticism is applied to foreign affairs as never before.   The advice function, technically confined to the Senate, has come to include the House also, especially in the formulation of programs and in the implementing of these programs in the appropriation process.   Over and above even this relatively new role, Congress performs a further function by playing its part in the leadership necessary to enlighten public opinion as well as to reflect it. More and more in fact, as well as under the Constitution, Congress is a co-ordinate member of a foreign policy team; and this co-ordinate membership extends to the House as well as to the Senate.

CONSTITUTIONAL PROVISIONS

It was Corwin who bluntly stated that the constitutional status accorded the Executive and Congress was a standing invitation to struggle for control over foreign relations.   These provisions are familiar to the readers.   Treaties are to be concluded by the President with the advice of the Senate, and ratified by two-thirds vote.   Powers over foreign commerce are among those on which Congress is eligible to legislate; but such powers may also be exercised in treaties.

In recent years the role of the Executive has been enormously extended through the wide scope left for administrative action and through the delegated power to conclude reciprocal trade agreements.   While Congress has retained the power to declare war, the President commands the armed services and controls many of the preliminary steps the taking of which may make the difference between war and peace. In his exercise of this command, the dispute as to whether the President may permanently station troops abroad has been left for some future consensus of legislature, executive, and judiciary.   The Great Debate of 1951 left this issue essentially unresolved, though it did secure an agreement by the President to consult, as well as a resolution by Congress requesting him to consult.

COMMITTEES

One must realize that the Foreign Relations and Foreign Affairs Committees are by no means the only committees importantly concerned with foreign policy. The Ways and Means and Finance Committees deal with the tariff, and Armed Services shares the responsibility with Foreign Relations for the use of our forces overseas—a use which makes foreign policy as well as executes it. The role of the Appropriations Committee is frequently decisive in programs. A degree less important but still important are committees such as Agriculture, Labor, and Commerce. The handling of the problem of internal security by the Judiciary Committees has foreign repercussions. The Committees on Government Operations to a major extent determine the structure and to some extent the interrelations of the organization of foreign affairs.

The Joint Committee on the Economic Report, with its over-all view of the domestic economy, inevitably finds itself involved in international considerations. The Public Works Committee of the House has before it the proposals for the St. Lawrence Seaway. Merchant Marine and Fisheries is constantly considering international issues. International finance is the prerogative of the Banking and Currency Committees, at least in its institutional expression. The Interior and Insular Affairs Committees have responsibility for the future of the islands of the Pacific insofar as we are involved in them. Even the committees on the District of Columbia find international considerations urged upon them in dealing with problems such as segregation, which interest other peoples.

It is hard to find a committee that is not in some fashion concerned with foreign policy. The interrelations of contemporary society have no more striking manifestation.

CONGRESSIONAL RESOLUTIONS

The formal provisions of the Constitution have been supplemented by usages no less far-reaching in their aggregate effect. First of these to note is the congressional resolution. I am not referring here to the joint resolution, which in its legal effect is equivalent to an Act of Congress, but rather to the simple and concurrent resolutions through which Congress frequently expresses its views on a particular matter. These resolutions naturally form certain clearly defined categories.

Best known in recent years have been the ones which have sought to give the Executive advance assurance as to the attitude which it may expect in Congress. Thus, Congress pledged itself in advance to support an international organization at the close of World War II.

More usual are the resolutions which attempt to give directives to the Executive or guidance as to congressional attitudes on problems facing the nation. These have no binding effect, but they may and frequently do have very great influence. They include such subjects as a United States of Europe, support for Franco Spain or Chiang Kai-shek, or a United Ireland.   Where they deal with the foreign policy of another nation, it is assumed that the State Department will so inform this other nation and possibly work toward the end in question.

Such resolutions may be embarrassing or they may be found helpful to the State Department, according to whether they coincide with the Department's own views and at the same time do not impair the public relations thereof.

Other resolutions may be of a negative or warning nature, indicating an absence of support in connection with some policy which it is supposed is under consideration in the executive branch.   Still others may deal with the congressional ideas as to the correct procedural relationship between Congress and the Executive.

In any event, the effect of these resolutions is by no means completely dependent upon whether or not they actually pass one or both Houses. The mere fact of their introduction itself is some indication of congressional attitudes, and usually results in State Department activity in congressional consultations and in exploration of ways and means of meeting congressional desires, or at least of ascertaining the extent to which such desires are in fact shared by others than those sponsoring the original move.   They are also likely to influence in one fashion or another the other nation or nations involved in their substance.

There are many times in which Congress can make its views known somewhat irresponsibly without creating the type of severe reaction which would be created if the executive branch through ordinary diplomatic channels or through public pronouncements seemed to be resorting to pressure.   The congressional resolution is just what it purports to be, an indication of opinion and attitude, and is not in itself overt in its results or effect.   It is, however, often an interesting and significant counterweight or response to the increasing tendency on the part of the President to use the executive agreement as an instrument of international action.

CONGRESSIONAL INVESTIGATIONS

The weapon of congressional investigation is much in the public eye, in domestic as well as in international affairs.   It is the popular opinion that its principal use is found in forcing accountability of the executive branch.   While this is doubtless true, the investigations fulfill a number of other functions of co-ordinate importance.   These include the education of the public and the exploration of the feasibility of a new or changed government policy.   The investigations of the dismissal of

General MacArthur set out to be a calling to account of the Executive. They became much more an instrument in the education of the public; and in the end they resulted in a very considerable crystallization of congressional opinion as regards our whole policy in the Far East.

Moreover, accountability itself has many facets. It may involve conformity to the law; it may involve efficiency of performance; it may also involve loyalty matters. In any event, the investigative process is a major congressional instrument, and as the investigations of overseas information and of the China policy have shown, it can affect matters for good or evil in a fashion which has no real parallel in most other large nations. These investigations are part and parcel of our constitutional system. The reward of a successful investigation in service to the nation is very considerable, entirely apart from any effect on the political fortunes of the investigators.

In the publicity given to congressional investigations, it is sometimes lost sight of that most of the hearings of the standing committees of Congress are on concrete measures which have been introduced by individual members, often at the instigation of the executive branch. This holds true in foreign affairs no less than in domestic legislation.

At what point the hearing on a specific measure ends and an investigation of the problem begins is by no means clear, nor need it be. In either instance the congressional hearing provides an excellent forum for bringing out into the open the views of the various groups which make up the warp and woof of American political, economic, and social life. To the Congressman, who more often than not is a lawyer, the hearing is the counterpart, in the legislative process, of the courtroom in the judicial process. By means of a battle of protagonists, much truth may emerge. Cross-questioning of witnesses may bring out hidden meanings and lay bare motives.

With the presence of the press and even of television, popular education on the issues involved can be furthered. It is often the subject of comment that a Cabinet Minister in the British Government finds his reputation strengthened or impaired by the question hour in the House of Commons. Hearings before an American congressional committee are far more grueling and exacting, and the caliber of the man is more thoroughly tested. Likewise, the issues involved receive a much more thorough public airing, although, it must be admitted, at the expense of a great deal of irrelevance and repetition.

These public hearings are not necessarily very important in the formation of the Members' own opinions. Equal weight must be assigned to the give-and-take of discussion in executive sessions, the research of the committee staffs, the informal contacts, and the still fairly pervasive influence of political party. Nonetheless, the committee hearing has a major place among those institutions of the American Constitution which are the products of usage rather than of formal language. Even foreign governments must be prepared for exhaustive examination of their policies, even though the witnesses are American citizens.

These congressional hearings do not conform to the dignity and secrecy of traditional diplomacy, nor on the other hand do they reveal the ambiguity, the double talk, the dodging of issues which likewise characterize its traditional methods.

FLOOR DEBATE AND SPEECHES

No account of congressional influence dares omit the very important role played by speeches both within and outside of Congress. These, too, are part of the processes of opinion formation, popular education, and congressional influence in foreign nations as well as in our own. To the totalitarian countries, unaccustomed to freedom of speech or to irresponsible pronouncements, it seems incredible that a speech by a Member of Congress in his home district does not in some fashion represent government policy as a whole. Protests occasionally arise from such talks, and resentment or appreciation is accorded them abroad, as well as here, according to the point of view. Even a single speech by an ordinary Member of Congress may threaten to produce an international incident and influence the policy of a foreign nation.

Those foreign nations who know us better will and do pay attention to these speeches, but they do not attach to them undue importance. They recognize such speeches as useful to themselves as well as to the American people in this fascinating, sometimes embarrassing, but always vitally important process of a democratic people making up its mind.

APPROPRIATIONS PROCESS

No account of the role of Congress in foreign policy could possibly be complete without indicating the tremendous importance of actions by the Appropriations Committees, and of the appropriations process in general. In foreign as well as in domestic affairs, the Appropriations Committees and their recommendations and the bills as finally passed may more nearly represent the real purpose of Congress than do the authorizing acts. It is not an uncommon occurrence for a pressure group to have its way in the latter case, and for the real will of Congress to express itself at the time of appropriations.

Perhaps a more correct statement would be to the effect that an affirmative authorizing measure expresses the judgment of Congress on the issue involved, more or less devoid of its relationship to certain other issues. The appropriation bill, however, filters the views of the Members on the substantive measure through their modifying or sobering attitudes toward economy in general.

It is not that the appropriations process goes counter to the wishes of Congress; it is rather that it brings to bear another modifying or overriding point of view applicable to any measure involving the expenditure of money. When a given sum has been authorized at the time of passing the original act, it does not indicate by any means that Congress has decided that this authorization is the sum which is or should be appropriated. Congress is fully aware of the role of its Appropriations Committees, and expects these committees to go further into the problem of whether the sum in question is in fact necessary or whether the objectives of the act itself can be carried out more economically than the sum authorized would indicate.

Congress claims to be reluctant to legislate in appropriation bills, and such legislation is ordinarily subject to a point of order. However, by more or less general consent, most major appropriation bills are now reported to the floor of the House under a closed rule which prohibits the raising of points of order concerning them. Such restriction does not apply in the Senate, and consequently points of order are more likely to prevail in the upper house.

Nevertheless, by one means or another, provisos or instructions are often inserted in appropriation bills which in effect determine or modify policy. Such determination or modification is over and above the necessary modifications implicit in ample or restricted funds. As more and more of our foreign policy is determined by programs of foreign aid, by the size of the armed services, and by the extent of the appropriations for the various branches of the State Department itself, so more and more the Appropriations Committees will, in fact if not in name, constitute themselves a kind of third house of Congress which will play its own role in policy formulation and adoption.

CHANGED NATURE OF FOREIGN POLICY

We have already had occasion to mention that this is an age of total war and of totalitarian governments. Perhaps we have not yet realized the inner nature of the response which democracies seem almost compelled to make to the threats thus involved. It is not that we are engaged at the present time in a total war in the ordinary military sense of the word. The situation is much more subtle and the nature of the struggle is much more sophisticated. Nonetheless, we do seem to be engaged in a total war, in the sense that our enemies are ready and willing to take whatever steps may seem to them to be necessary within the margin of their own safety to bring about our weakening and our destruction as a free people. In other words, we are engaged in a struggle for survival.

This introduces a new type of diplomacy and a new type of national conduct and national obligation. In the early days the objective of diplomacy and foreign policy was certainly to enhance the interests of the particular nation concerned. In relatively few instances did a *delenda est Carthago* motivate the peacetime conduct of a people or of a people's government. At the most, there was a desire to weaken a potential enemy, but not to destroy him, unless he had given overt evidence of the intention to destroy one's own state.

An exception may perhaps be found in the religious wars. The present struggle between the Soviet Union and world communism on the one side and the cluster of nations to which we are giving leadership on the other is more akin to a religious war than to the political or strategic war to which our textbooks are accustomed. If we use the hackneyed phrase of a war between ways of life or a war between civilizations or a war between philosophies, we can see the all-embracing nature of the struggle. It is a "total diplomacy" in which we are now engaged.

This involves much more than a realization that a nation's economic potential is itself a major safeguard of its military potential. Beyond economics lie the social and spiritual realms in which a nation's morale stands or falls. From their point of view, the Communists are completely right in realizing that they can best weaken others by spreading discord, suspicion, and internal conflict within the ranks of their enemies. Here is a weapon no less powerful than the atomic bomb.

In such a setting, foreign policy requires a degree of popular support in all its major sectors which was not necessary when considerations were predominantly military and when the issues were largely confined to foreign trade or colonial territory or border disputes or dynasties. The initiative of the Executive in diplomacy must be accompanied by more than a mere ratification of a treaty. This is pre-eminently so today, when the "program" has emerged as the major instrument in foreign affairs. Such programs run the gamut from economic strength and aid to cultural interchange. They include psychological warfare and extension of trade and a number of other objectives only a degree less important.

CONGRESS AND POPULAR INTEREST

It is in this setting that the new role of Congress in foreign policy can best be understood. It is not merely the fact that these programs call for substantive legislation and substantial appropriations, tremendously important though both of these factors are in a congressional agenda. It is rather that popular interest has grown to a point never before reached in ostensible peacetime, and popular support is absolutely essential if these programs are to operate successfully.

This has its impact on Congress. Moreover, Congress rightly dramatizes these issues in its hearings and in its floor debates. Congressmen rightly stress such issues in their visits to their constituencies and states. The electorate, on its part, loses few opportunities either individually or collectively to manifest its interest in these matters. Editorial and news columns of newspapers, the script of commentators, the courses in colleges and universities, the sermons in churches, alike contain a far higher percentage of content regarding, and interest in, international affairs than ever before during our peacetime history.

Here is also the basic explanation of the enhanced role of the House of Representatives, a role becoming almost co-ordinate with that of the Senate. Here is the explanation of the tremendously important role played by party leadership in Congress and by the Appropriations Committees.

Minority groups of special national origin have always been with us since the days in which immigration was a very considerable factor in our national life, and have figured in the subsequent political complexion of our national elections. A certain amount of this type of interest has always spilled over into our legislative body. What is different today is that to these special interests has now been added a more general literacy and sophistication on the part of millions of our people, which has rendered interest in foreign policy a much more balanced thing than in the days when the troubles of Ireland and the woes of Poland were the issues most felt emotionally.

THE EXPERIENCE OF CONGRESSMEN

The traditional picture of a Congressman has been long outmoded by the facts. We are dealing today, not only in the committees immediately responsible for foreign policy but in Congress in general, with a far more qualified group of men than is generally realized. For a dozen years foreign affairs have been at the very center of a large part of congressional deliberation and experience. Measures of foreign policy have been before one or more committees almost daily. Debates on the floor, even on issues presumably primarily domestic, have been filled with references to foreign affairs, and the number of debates on foreign policy itself has grown enormously. So also has a Member's correspondence in this field, and so also has the number of visits from constituents concerned with foreign matters.

In other words, through the sheer experience of discussions, debates, and conferences, a Member, however illiterate in this field he may have been prior to his coming to Congress, finds himself precipitated into the very center of our international concern.

A world war and a world reconstruction and a world communism have been jointly responsible for this. However much an individual may long for the day when the United States can go its own way, the decision that it should not go its own way, the decision that it is inextricably involved with other nations, has been made, not so much by ourselves as by them. Paramount in this is the virtual declaration of war by world communism, whose world horizon requires a corresponding world horizon on our part.

Official trips abroad to study one problem or another are increasingly frequent, not only by members of the Foreign Relations and Foreign Affairs Committees, but by those from the Appropriations and Government Operations Committees as well. Nor are such trips confined to these three clusters of committees. Within the past year or two, a dozen others have sent one or more of their members overseas to study some problem within the jurisdiction of the committee. In connection with the original consideration of the Marshall Plan, well over two hundred Members of both Houses made such overseas investigations prior to the final decision of Congress in the autumn of 1947.

The experience of members of the Foreign Relations and Foreign Affairs Committees is intensive in the extreme. It is not merely the constant consideration of problems in hearings and in executive sessions. Briefings by the State Department, the Mutual Security Agency ,and representatives of other federal agencies are increasingly frequent. So also is the growing practice of informal luncheons and dinners and informal conferences either on Capitol Hill or in the precincts of the agency itself. Increasing use has been made of Members of Congress in connection with international conferences, as delegates as well as observers.

Entirely apart from staff aids or other *ad hoc* facilities to be brought to bear upon specific problems, there are today in Congress highly qualified specialists on almost any major problem facing the nation. It must further be borne in mind that these specialists have commanded the respect and confidence of their own membership frequently to a degree exceeding that of the representatives of the executive branch. Whether these rival generators or experts in foreign policy are good or bad in the aggregate is not the point. It is the *fact* that we are registering. This specialized competence arising out of experience, even more than out of study, must be taken into account in policy formulation and in identifying centers of leadership in our government in general.

FORMAL EDUCATION OF CONGRESSMEN

Over and above the rich education which comes from experience is the fact that the Members of Congress today have a higher level and quality of formal education than before. College graduates have been increasing, and so also have those who hold graduate degrees. The percentage of lawyers remains very high, and the level of prelegal and legal education has been steadily rising.

It is important in calling attention to this increase in formal education that one does not overestimate its value. It by no means follows that persons with such an education are better legislators or better informed than those who have gained their knowledge through experience without the benefit of the more systematic but probably more esoteric training in university halls. All these considerations are under the heading "other things being equal." Congress, as well as the electorate as a whole, unmistakably reflects the higher and higher level of education in the United States that has been such a marked phenomenon in recent years.

NONPARTISANSHIP

The role of partisanship in foreign policy must be considered along with the changing role of partisanship in Congress in general. Few people realize today how little there is of partisanship at the point of actual congressional decision. A considerable majority of the committees of both Houses are nonpartisan in their executive sessions. This does not mean that there are not differences of opinion, but the differences are not along party lines. Party does assume the responsibility for organization of Congress, and certainly the party which is not that of the President is constantly searching for points of vulnerability and criticism in the conduct of administration. This usually does not constitute opposition to policies as such, but rather to minor aspects or emphases.

In the field of foreign affairs, both this tendency to nonpartisanship and this tendency to criticize details are unusually prominent. There is in Congress a general feeling that our nation should present a united front to the rest of the world. This takes the form with many Members of a sense of high obligation not to make foreign policy, as such, a partisan matter. There is also a feeling that the partisan element in the opposition to the League of Nations following World War I and to the Versailles Treaty was a mistake not to be repeated. The Senate in particular has been extremely sensitive to the numerous proposals to alter the two-thirds rule required for treaty ratification, and also to the tendency to advocate executive agreements in place of treaties, so as to by-pass this particular constitutional provision. One reaction has certainly been a determination on the part of large numbers of Senators to make the two-thirds rule workable in terms of international needs.

On the other hand, interest in foreign policy is widespread, and the scope of foreign policy is world-wide. This means that it involves a multiplicity of detail as regards particular areas, which necessarily offers vulnerable targets for detailed criticism. It was this tendency to detailed criticism on the part of the opposition which presented no special incongruity along with its general support of the administration's foreign policy. Chiefly, there was sharp criticism of certain aspects of its Far Eastern conduct. When this criticism more and more seemed to be warranted by what was felt to be the failure involved in the loss of China to the Communists, the criticism reached a rising tide, and bipartisanship broke down at this point.

Perhaps even this is not the correct way of stating this situation. There were Democratic critics and Republican supporters of the President as regards his Far Eastern policies. Especially following the hearings on the removal of MacArthur, a considerable consolidation of opinion as between parties and as between Congress and the President took place for the time being.

Actually, issues in foreign policy do not readily lend themselves to partisan orientation. Emphasis on Europe or on Asia as an alternative has nothing to do with being a Republican or a Democrat, insofar as these latter represent any regional or economic groupings. Even the tariff finds Republicans of the seaboard ranged against their own fellows in the interior.

All in all, partisanship has recently proved a relatively minor obstacle to any successful collaboration between the two branches of government. There have been obstacles in congressional activity, but they have for the most part not been of a partisan nature.

•   •   •   •   •

CONCLUSION

In conclusion, our Constitution is not likely to be amended in the near future in any substantial fashion. Change will come, if at all, in the field of judicial interpretation and usage. As I wrote elsewhere:

We are a world power. Our cultural leadership, our military strength, our political influence, to some extent even our economic power—these have not been of our own seeking. There probably never was a more reluctant world leader in all history than the United States. Yet this very reluctance makes us less feared and more readily followed. Other peoples have tended to personify us in the shape of the individual who happened to be our President at a given time. They have assumed that the voice of the President was necessarily the total voice of America. Yet these other peoples that make up the world, free and regimented alike, need more than an understanding of our President: they need to understand the influence of our representative body, the Congress. They need to see Congress as a living symbol, to see that our Republic has Congress too among its institutions of leadership—incorporating not only the hesitations and cross purposes of its people but also their sense of responsibility and the agreement on objectives and instruments which these people's assembled representatives have produced following hard study and discussion.

41. THE ROLE OF THE SENATE *

Like Mr. Griffith, Senator Gillette writes of the increase in the "foreign affairs work load" in recent years. The Senator relates the increase to the growing participation of the United States in world affairs, which has brought with it not only expanded responsibilities but also tremendous opportunities for the Senate to serve the nation.

. . . . .

EVOLUTION THROUGH THE YEARS

The struggle between the President and the Senate over control of foreign policy is inevitable in the structure of the Constitution. The conflict between them is a "built-in" feature of our basic charter. The conflict has persisted with varying degrees of intensity since the first years of the new Republic, and it will persist as many years more, or longer, unless and until there is a fundamental revision of the Constitution itself.

Treaty Making

The conflicts of the period from 1789 to 1805 established the prece-

* Guy M. Gillette, "The Senate in Foreign Relations," *The Annals of the American Academy of Political and Social Science,* September, 1953, pp. 49-57. The author is United States Senator from Iowa.

dents for the battle that has continued ever since. In the early period only thirteen treaties as such were submitted to the Senate. Not a single treaty was submitted between 1805 and 1815. From the latter date until 1841 there was a period of relative quiet in the struggle, and the real period of senatorial domination came in the years between 1869 and 1898. Treaty after treaty submitted by the Executive in that period was rejected or withdrawn. A second period of Senate dominance followed World War I, and there are certain signs that another such period may be dawning at the present time.

The framers of the Constitution had expected that the Senate would be consulted in advance of treaty formulation, as the Congress of the Confederation had been. President Washington at first attempted to carry out this practice, but the unavoidable conflict between the Senate and the Executive obliged him to abandon this procedure almost at the start.

Senators feared their constitutional prerogatives were being invaded, while the Executive Department feared its hands would be tied in international negotiation if the Senate tried to participate in every stage of treaty-making.

Using its power of amendment, the Senate up to the year 1901 had so altered between 80 and 90 treaties placed before it that almost one third of them failed entirely or were abandoned. In the following 25 years, 58 proposed treaties were changed by the Senate, and of this number, almost 40 per cent were definitely abandoned or discarded because of these changes.

The Senate has also made frequent use of its power to confirm Presidential nominations to diplomatic posts. In the early years the Senate used this auxiliary power not merely to determine the qualifications of a person named to a foreign post but also to determine whether a particular mission was necessary or not. When Presidents were about to undertake negotiation of a treaty they used to submit to the Senate the names of the persons who were to conduct the negotiations. The Senate could and did reject such nominations because it did not want the treaty to be negotiated. Even when the Senate did not reject a nomination outright, as in the case of the Jay Treaty of 1795, it could exert enough pressure to require the negotiator's name to be withdrawn in favor of another.

After 1815 the Presidential practice of submitting the names of treaty negotiators to the Senate was stopped, and the Senate thereby found its power to control or influence foreign policy through confirmation of appointments somewhat diminished.

In the twentieth century the Senate has used its power of confirmation to influence policy but has approached the matter in a different manner:

by insisting that its consent is required for appointment of American representatives to any international organization. This approach was first used with respect to the League of Nations, and it has been followed in connection with the United Nations and its affiliates. It is also used in the case of the Economic Co-operation Administration and its successor, the Mutual Security Agency.

To sum up the conflict between the Senate and the President over control of foreign policy, it seems clear that the cycle of senatorial or Presidential predominance corresponds with the cycle of weak and strong Executives in the White House.

The moment Senators sense that the hand of the President is weakening in foreign policy, there is an immediate rush to occupy the space vacated by the executive power. Like nature, politics abhors a vacuum. Sometimes the President's power is weak because of his own character and actions or failure to act, in which case the Senate's power simply flows into the area and pre-empts it. Sometimes the weakening of the Presidential power is the result of a conscious drive for control over foreign policy or particular areas of foreign policy by certain Senators, in which case the Executive is forced into retreat and his power is almost literally snatched from his hands by the advancing members of the Senate.

The best situation, of course, is one in which both the Executive and the Senate recognize each other's respective powers and responsibilities and work together in a co-operative spirit toward the achievement of the common goal. Rarely if ever in our history has this situation obtained to the degree it did in the years following World War II, but recent signs suggest that the era of Executive-Senate harmony in foreign affairs may be coming to an end.

SENATE'S FOREIGN AFFAIRS WORK LOAD

The tremendous increase in the foreign affairs work load of the Senate in recent years is, of course, a direct consequence and reflection of the growing participation of the United States in world affairs and the rise of this country to its present pre-eminent position as leader among the nations striving to establish a peaceful world community and to prevent totalitarian domination, whether by German and Japanese totalitarians before 1945 or by Russian and Chinese since.

Both Houses of Congress have been heavily burdened with questions relating to foreign policy: foreign relief, rehabilitation grants and loans, and foreign economic, technical, and military assistance. But the Senate's burden has been even greater because of its role in the treaty process. The United Nations Charter, the "satellite" treaties, the Rio Treaty, the North Atlantic Treaty and its several protocols, the Japanese Peace Treaty and the security treaties with the Pacific nations, and the German Contractual Agreement have all required tremendous work in the Senate that the House was spared.

In addition there have been the great foreign policy debates in which Senators have participated in greater number and with greater intensity than ever before, both in the struggle between isolationism and intervention in the years before Pearl Harbor, and in the other debates that have arisen in recent years as the bipartisan accord on foreign policy has partially broken down. The raging storm that followed the dismissal of General MacArthur for months engaged the full attention of more than a score of Senators in the Armed Services and Foreign Relations Committees as well as the time of many other Senators participating in the verbal struggle in the Senate and elsewhere. The Korean War and the political strife accompanying it in Congress have occupied an enormous amount of time of Senators.

Foreign policy has become a prime, if not the prime, issue in the political contests of the nation, and it is hence not surprising that the time of individual Senators and of the Senate as a body should be increasingly taken up with matters relating to foreign affairs.

While I have been unable to find a statistical analysis of the proportion of time occupied by foreign policy on the Senate floor in recent years, it is beyond doubt that never before in history have Senators been so preoccupied with such questions and never before has foreign policy taken so great a portion of the time in floor debate and action.

One measure of the new importance of foreign affairs is the care which Senators seeking greater public recognition and advancement take to become expert in foreign policy.

Another token of the importance which Senators attach to foreign policy is the long and growing list of applications for seats on the Foreign Relations Committee. In the present session of Congress this committee has serving on it the chairmen of three committees (Interstate Commerce, Judiciary, and Labor) and the ranking majority or minority members of four committees, a record unmatched by any other committee of the Senate except Appropriations.

Wider Scope of Senatorial Participation

Whereas for the first century and a half of the nation's history, the only matters of foreign policy to come before the Senate were treaties and nominations of ambassadors, today the Senate, as well as the

House, is almost continually at work on some phase of the manifold problems of our new role in world affairs.

Military problems are so intertwined with foreign policy, and economic policy is so involved in both of them, it is no exaggeration to say that in the mid-twentieth century the Congress as a whole is concerned more with matters affecting, or affected by, the world at large than by all other problems together. Reciprocal trade, tariffs, imports and exports, foreign loans, economic, technical, and military assistance, exchange of students and other persons, foreign relief, displaced persons and refugees overseas information and propaganda, espionage, atomic energy, the United Nations, the North Atlantic Treaty Organization, military strategy and appropriations, international agreements of a hundred varieties, the organization and administration of vast and complicated programs—all these and many other subjects closely linked with foreign relations are constantly before the Congress. And I see no prospect that the load will diminish for years to come.

PROCEDURES AND METHODS OF OPERATION

With the exception of treaties, the procedures of the Senate in dealing with foreign policy matters are no different from those employed for any other legislation. Bills or resolutions are introduced by Senators, either on their own initiative or at the request of the administration, and are referred to the Committee on Foreign Relations.

If the measure is one of sufficient importance, the whole Committee gives it its consideration; if not, it is referred to a subcommittee for preliminary study. Public or closed hearings, or both, are held to obtain testimony from administration witnesses and private citizens. The Committee in executive session marks up the bill for referral to the Senate. A report is prepared by the staff on the basis of the testimony, the expressed views of Committee members, and the language of the bill as amended by the Committee, and finally the measure is reported to the full Senate and placed oñ the calendar to be called up as part of the normal legislative process. Sometimes the bill or resolution never sees the light of day after it reaches the Committee. Sometimes, though rarely, it may be reported unfavorably.

Debate on the floor precedes votes on amendments and on the bill. Amendments may be reported out by the Committee itself, or be proposed by any Senator on the floor during the period prior to its consideration or adoption. If it is a bill originating in the Senate, after its passage it is sent to the House. If it originated in the House, and the Senate has amended it, it must return to the House for further action.

In either case, differences are accepted or the bill is sent to conference between the two Houses to compromise the differences. When both Houses have approved the conference report, the measure goes to the President for signature.

In the case of treaties, the House, of course, has no function. The Executive Department files the document with the Senate under the seal of secrecy. It is referred to the Foreign Relations Committee, where the same procedure of consideration, study, and hearings is followed. If approved by the Committee, the treaty is placed on the executive calendar. If the Committee or any Senator wishes to change the treaty, a reservation is offered. If the reservation is adopted by the Senate, the treaty cannot become effective until the Executive has secured the agreement of the other signatories to the change. When debate on a treaty is ended, a two-thirds majority of the Senators present is needed to ratify the treaty, which, if ratified, is returned to the President.

In the case of confirmation of nominations to high diplomatic or foreign policy posts, the procedures do not differ from those used for any confirmation by the Senate of nominations to other government offices. A simple majority vote is needed in the Senate to complete the confirmation.

PROMINENT FIGURES IN THE SENATE

Limiting ourselves to the past 30 years or so, and omitting any present members of the Senate, a list of figures whose service in the Senate had a powerful, if not always decisive impact on foreign policy, would have to include Senators Henry Cabot Lodge, Sr., James Reed, Hiram Johnson, William Borah, Arthur Vandenberg, Robert LaFollette, Jr. and Tom Connally.

Most of these Senators, it will be noted, were isolationists. Senators Lodge and Reed led the fight against the League of Nations. From the end of World War I until the dramatic change from isolationism by Senator Vandenberg in the last years of the Second World War, the Foreign Relations Committee was predominantly isolationist in character. The majority of the members opposed the foreign policies of both Presidents Wilson and Roosevelt, mostly because of their traditional isolationism and partly because of political motives. Senators Johnson, Borah, LaFollette, and, until his great change, Vandenberg, were uncompromising adherents and advocates of an isolationist and neutralist America. By his change Vandenberg made possible the development of the bipartisan accord on foreign policy that was of such momentous significance in the years following the drafting of the United Nations

Charter and the end of World War II. Under Senator Connally, who, except for the 80th Congress, was chairman of the Foreign Relations Committee throughout this period until the present Congress, and with the leadership of Senator Vandenberg in the Republican party, the Committee altered its former outlook completely and became one of the stanchest supporters of the policies aimed at checking Soviet expansion. But in doing so, the Committee fully retained its independence of the Executive and upheld the power of the Senate in foreign relations.

THE SENATE'S SHARE IN FORMULATING FOREIGN POLICY

As I have remarked earlier, there has been a cyclical movement in the struggle between the Senate and the President over control of foreign policy, with Senate predominance coinciding with weak or indecisive Presidents, and Presidential predominance coinciding with strong and determined Chief Executives.

Regardless of the fluctuations in relative party strength in recent years, by and large the two groups have worked together remarkably well, and the country as well as the free world has benefited thereby.

The preliminary studies leading to drafting the United Nations Charter brought the first close collaboration among leading Senators and the administration. The Senate's share in formulating our UN policy at that time was very great. It was the argument that the Senate would never ratify the Charter without the veto provision that determined American insistence on unanimous agreement among the permanent members of the Security Council. It is a source of irony to those of us who from the start opposed the veto provision to find that while the Soviet Union has abused the veto power nearly to the point of paralyzing the UN, the United States has never once had recourse to it.

Throughout the first five years of President Truman's tenure in the White House, the presence of a bipartisan majority on foreign policy in the Senate not only made it possible to carry out the major policies and programs required to organize the free world and check the Communist expansion, but also assured the Senate a large share of influence and responsibility in formulating the broad policy and programs. Many of the most important legislative enactments in foreign aid bills, for example, were amendments proposed by Senators.

Since the untimely death of Senator Vandenberg, the bipartisan accord has weakened considerably, but that has not necessarily prevented many Senators from determining foreign policy to a greater degree, in some instances, than the Executive.

Largely because of the Far East disaster, foreign policy has frequently in recent years been a football of partisan politics. It is perhaps going too far to say that Senators who chose to make Far Eastern policy a domestic political issue were thereby able to share in formulating new policy, but in a number of cases they have been able to prevent carrying out of existing policy of which they did not approve.

Because the Senate is one of the greatest sounding boards in the world, with no restrictions on debate to prevent full development of a question, it is a natural platform for individual or group efforts to modify existing policy or institute new policies. Senate agitation was largely responsible for the gradual termination of the dismantling program in Germany, for tightening control over East-West trade, for changing the emphasis in the Far East and bringing about a drastic revision of policy regarding Formosa, for bringing Greece and Turkey into NATO, and for many other alterations and innovations in policy.

By amendments to the ECA and MSA legislation the Senate has taken the lead in urging the unification and integration of the Western community, particularly the European portion of that community. It was a Senate proposal that broke the deadlock on how ECA was to be administered. It was a Senate proposal that brought about reorganization of the Mutual Security Agency last year.

The Senate has continued to exercise influence over foreign policy through its power of confirmation. Perhaps the outstanding case was that involving Mr. Paul Hoffman. Senate pressure was instrumental in securing the nomination of Mr. Hoffman, a Republican, as ECA Administrator in a Democratic administration, and thereby instrumental in keeping Congressional support of this major bipartisan project.

On the whole, the record of the Senate in recent years has been a commendable one. There have been a few misguided efforts to force the Executive to take certain steps which may well have not been in the long-term national interest, but when one looks at the lengthy list of major treaties and agreements that have gone through the Senate, and one notes by what a large majority most of them have been approved, it can be seen that there has been a very considerable measure of bi-partisan co-operation and also a very sizable measure of senatorial agreement with the general policies. This could have come about only because of the great care that was taken in securing the advice and consent of the Senate in the process of developing and maturing the policies and programs. The increasing use of Senators as delegates to international conferences is a highly encouraging tendency that promises even closer co-operation and understanding.

CHAPTER FIVE

The Expression of
American Foreign Policy

AMERICAN FOREIGN POLICY, like the foreign policy of other nations, is expressed in actions and words; and of the two, actions usually speak louder. We can be certain that our policy toward the nations of Western Europe is one of support, because we have assisted them by economic and military means. We know that our policy toward South Korea is to defend it from North Korean and Chinese Communist aggression but not to assist President Rhee to unify Korea by force. We are aware that our policy toward Spain has recently changed, because we have begun to build military bases there. Our actions have indicated what our policies are. Of course, we signed an agreement with Spain which established the terms for the new phase of relations with that country, and we are a signatory of the North Atlantic Treaty, which makes it clear that we are committed to defend the countries of the North Atlantic community. Before the outbreak of war in Korea, however, the defense perimeter of the United States did not include Korea. One might have concluded from the statements of the Secretary of State that the United States did not intend to defend that nation. Indeed, it has been suggested that the Soviet Union relied upon our words—only to find that our actions belied them.

This reliance upon words alone seems to lead to other ambiguities. Britain and France, for example, assumed certain obligations in their treaties with the Soviet Union which appear to conflict with their obligations as signatories of the North Atlantic Treaty. To determine which of the two sets of treaties takes precedence in British and French policy, one would have to look elsewhere than to the texts of their treaties. One must obviously take careful note of the changes which have occurred in British and French attitudes toward the Soviet Union since the conclusion of their agreements with that country. And one must also recognize that very close and friendly relations exist between the United States on the one hand, and Britain and France on the other. Legally, therefore, the Soviet Union might expect that Britain and France would abide by their treaties with her; realistically, however, she cannot.

There have been numerous instances in history of treaties that were "scraps of paper" and agreements which were broken, so to speak, before the signatures on the documents had had the time to dry. In fact, it can be said with some justification that powerful nations sometimes break agreements for the same basic reason as they make them— because they believe their interests demand certain actions rather than others. Yet, in spite of the evidence that nations occasionally behave in this manner, it would be incorrect to say that the texts of treaties and other agreements, the speeches of important officials, and the published memoranda of international conferences offer no significant clues to the policy which a state, and even a powerful state, will pursue.

In this chapter, we are concerned with the expression of American foreign policy. By presenting the texts of pronouncements, the protocols of international conferences, and the texts of treaties and executive agreements, we will attempt to show the various methods apart from action itself which are used to make our policies known to the world.

A very common method of informing the world of new developments in American foreign policy is by pronouncements of the most important officials of the government. The President and the Secretary of State most often make the formal policy announcements. Presidents Monroe and Truman personally proclaimed the doctrines that bear their names, and Secretary of State Marshall outlined the plan for the reconstruction of Europe's war-ravaged economies.

By the end of 1946, it was apparent that relations between the Soviet Union and the Western powers were deteriorating. Anglo-Americans viewed Soviet policy in China, Iran, Poland, and elsewhere, as evidence of a growing imperialism. The Russians, believing the West to be hostile to her Communist regime, contended that her national interest demanded friendly neighboring states in Europe, the Middle East, and Asia. When General George C. Marshall took office as Secretary of State in January, 1947, one problem had to be met immediately. The Greek Government was attempting to deal with chaotic economic conditions and a Communist rebellion. The situation in Greece became even more critical when Great Britain gave notice of her inability to continue to bear the financial burdens she had assumed there. It seemed clear that the contemplated British withdrawal would further weaken the position of the Greek Government.

On March 12, 1947, President Truman addressed a Joint Session of Congress. Specifically, he outlined a program of economic and military aid to Greece and Turkey. In more general terms, he pictured the problem of Greece as part of a world problem which would have to be dealt with on a world-wide basis. The Truman Doctrine (as the policy enunciated in the speech has since become known) implied that world Communism would have to be met wherever it threatened independent nations, and that it would be the policy of the United States to assist those nations to maintain their independence.

During March and April of 1947, the Administration was studying the problem of European reconstruction. The Truman Doctrine had been criticized because of its unilateral approach, its military aspects, and its presentation as an anti-Soviet measure. Administration leaders feared that public reaction to extending the Doctrine to Western Europe without modification could prove to be unsympathetic. A new approach seemed imperative. On May 8, Under-Secretary of State Dean Acheson made an important but little noticed speech at Cleveland, Mississippi. He defended past American expenditures for foreign relief and reconstruction. He asserted that it was in our own interest to assist foreign nations to become self-supporting, since there could be neither prosperity nor peace for the United States unless there was stability in the world. He argued that the immediate problem arose from the eight billion dollar difference between our exports of sixteen and our imports of eight billion. We must import more, he said, and arrange for the financing of foreign purchases. Since we could not extend a helping hand to all countries, our assistance would have to be concentrated in areas where it would be most effective in building political and economic stability and in promoting democratic institutions.

Mr. Acheson's address (which may have been the first trial balloon) was followed on June 5, 1947, by an address by Secretary of State George C. Marshall at Harvard University. The Secretary was the commencement speaker, but he did not deliver the usual "go out and conquer the world" speech. Instead, he chose this occasion to announce the fundamental principles of the Marshall Plan.

Why did Mr. Marshall choose to announce his plan in this manner? He could have called a press conference. He could have initiated action through normal diplomatic channels. He could have requested the President formally to notify Congress. It is probable the Secretary believed that the setting—dignified, solemn, impressive, and entirely lacking in partisan connotations—was particularly suitable for the announcement of a program directed against "hunger, poverty, desperation, and chaos." Perhaps, and this is probably the most important reason for the choice of the Harvard platform, he wanted to know the reaction of American and foreign public opinion to his proposals. The press conference might have accomplished the same ends, but not without appearing to lend an air of formality which he may have deemed premature.

Exaggerated attention is sometimes paid to the remarks of important officials, but if the government has determined to pursue a certain course of action, verbalization of the new policy will have to take place sooner or later. Moreover, since the implementation of policy frequently depends upon Congressional cooperation, the President must be careful to cultivate the necessary support in Congress and among the people in advance of his formal declarations. The situation in Greece, however, may have been so critical and the specific remedy proposed so urgently needed, that there was no time for this type of careful preparation— hence, the direct and formal approach to Congress. The Marshall Plan would obviously require considerable study and a huge outlay of funds. The request for legislative enactment, therefore, had to be withheld until support for the Plan had reached the proportions required to assure Congressional approval. Moreover, there was the risk that public reaction to the Marshall address would be the same as that which greeted President Roosevelt's suggestion to quarantine the aggressor nations. In that case, the Plan could have been withdrawn without too much loss of face for the Administration. But the immediacy of the situation in Greece called for a bold, direct, and formal approach to Congress by the President himself; and the dangers for American security inherent in the chaos and civil war in Greece and in the exposed position of Turkey may have led the President to decide to throw the enormous weight of his office into play and risk the tremendous loss of prestige for himself and his Administration that would have resulted from Congressional refusal to provide funds for the new policy.

These examples indicate that the mode of official pronouncement chosen may depend upon the nature of the policy which is contemplated. Similarly, the expression of American foreign policy in treaties, executive agreements, and international conferences usually derives from the circumstances in which the policy was conceived and the purpose for which it was intended. The dependence of the choice of the mode of expression upon the circumstances in which the policy is developed is perhaps most evident in the protocols of international conferences. But the use of treaties and executive agreements can also be related to circumstance and purpose.

The only manner in which the United States can be legally obligated to pursue a certain policy over a long period is by treaty (the North Atlantic Treaty is binding for twenty years). It is generally supposed that any important obligations, even if short term, should also be embodied in treaties, presumably because the United States ought not to be committed to anything of a significant nature by action of the President alone. In some instances, the President may conclude an executive agreement with the government of another nation. Since he can make such agreements without reference to Congress, except if implementation of the agreement necessitates legislative enactment, it is usually assumed that he can commit only his administration and not that of his successor, and that the subject matter of the agreement will be of relatively minor importance. Because of the constitutional provision that ratification of a treaty requires the approval of two thirds of the Senators present and voting, however, Presidents have increasingly resorted to executive agreements. President Franklin Roosevelt probably would not have succeeded in getting Senate approval of a treaty embodying the destroyer-bases agreement with Britain, and so he concluded an executive agreement which accomplished the same end. And President Theodore Roosevelt's customs house agreement with Santo Domingo was negotiated *after* the Senate had refused to approve a treaty covering the same subject matter.

To summarize briefly, there are four significant means of expression, apart from action, by which our policies are made known to the world. This chapter presents examples of official pronouncements made in different modes, according to the circumstances of the times and the intent of the policy (Selections 42-44), the protocols of international conferences (Selection 45), executive agreements (Selection 46), and treaties (Selection 47).

Official Pronouncements

42. QUARANTINE THE AGGRESSORS *

Sometimes an official pronouncement is made to determine whether a policy should be put into effect. The President and

* An address by President Franklin D. Roosevelt, delivered at Chicago, Illinois, on October 5, 1937.

other policy-making officials may not always know the temper of the people. Of course, they have at their disposal the resources of the information-gathering agencies of the government. But they cannot be quite sure of their information. This lack of certainty is particularly vexing when a change of policy is contemplated. The people may have been supporting a policy which moved in a certain direction. Will they support a change?

President Roosevelt's Quarantine Speech was a pronouncement by the highest official of the government. Yet it led to no immediate specific action, because it failed to elicit any measure of public support. The address was a "trial balloon." In October, 1937, the Japanese were waging war against China. Civil war was raging in Spain. The world seemed headed for "a breakdown of all international order and law." President Roosevelt evidently tried to do two things in this speech: to acquaint foreign governments with the views of the administration in control of the American Government, and to ascertain the willingness of the American people to support a more forceful line of action by their government.

. . . The political situation in the world, which of late has been growing progressively worse, is such as to cause grave concern and anxiety to all the peoples and nations who wish to live in peace and amity with their neighbors.

Some 15 years ago the hopes of mankind for a continuing era of international peace were raised to great heights when more than 60 nations solemnly pledged themselves not to resort to arms in furtherance of their national aims and policies. The high aspirations expressed in the Briand-Kellogg Peace Pact and the hopes for peace thus raised have of late given way to a haunting fear of calamity. The present reign of terror and international lawlessness began a few years ago.

It began through unjustified interference in the internal affairs of other nations or the invasion of alien territory in violation of treaties and has now reached a stage where the very foundations of civilization are seriously threatened. The landmarks and traditions which have marked the progress of civilization toward a condition of law, order, and justice are being wiped away.

Without a declaration of war and without warning or justification of any kind, civilians, including women and children, are being ruthlessly murdered with bombs from the air. In times of so-called peace, ships are being attacked and sunk by submarines without cause or notice. Nations are fomenting and taking sides in civil warfare in nations that have never done them any harm. Nations claiming freedom for themselves deny it to others.

Innocent peoples and nations are being cruelly sacrificed to a greed for power and supremacy which is devoid of all sense of justice and humane consideration.

To paraphrase a recent author, "perhaps we foresee a time when men, exultant in the technique of homicide, will rage so hotly over the world that every precious thing will be in danger, every book and picture and harmony, every treasure garnered through two millenniums, the small, the delicate, the defenseless—all will be lost or wrecked or utterly destroyed."

If those things come to pass in other parts of the world let no one imagine that America will escape, that it may expect mercy, that this Western Hemisphere will not be attacked, and that it will continue tranquilly and peacefully to carry on the ethics and the arts of civilization.

If those days come "there will be no safety by arms, no help from authority, no answer in science. The storm will rage till every flower of culture is trampled and all human beings are leveled in a vast chaos."

If those days are not to come to pass—if we are to have a world in which we can breathe freely and live in amity without fear—the peace-loving nations must make a concerted effort to uphold laws and principles on which alone peace can rest secure.

The peace-loving nations must make a concerted effort in opposition to those violations of treaties and those ignorings of humane instincts which today are creating a state of international anarchy and instability from which there is no escape through mere isolation or neutrality.

Those who cherish their freedom and recognize and respect the equal right of their neighbors to be free and live in peace, must work together for the triumph of law and moral principles in order that peace, justice, and confidence may prevail in the world. There must be a return to a belief in the pledged word, in the value of a signed treaty. There must be recognition of the fact that national morality is as vital as private morality. . . .

There is a solidarity and interdependence about the modern world, both technically and morally, which makes it impossible for any nation completely to isolate itself from economic and political upheavals in the rest of the world, especially when such upheavals appear to be spreading and not declining. There can be no stability or peace either within nations or between nations except under laws and moral standards adhered to by all. International anarchy destroys every foundation for peace. It jeopardizes either the immediate or the future security of every nation, large or small. It is, therefore, a matter of vital interest and concern to the people of the United States that the sanctity of international treaties and the maintenance of international morality be restored.

The overwhelming majority of the peoples and nations of the world today want to live in peace.   They seek the removal of barriers against trade.   They want to exert themselves in industry, in agriculture, and in business, that they may increase their wealth through the production of wealth-producing goods rather than striving to produce military planes and bombs and machine guns and cannon for the destruction of human lives and useful property.

In those nations of the world which seem to be piling armament on armament for purposes of aggression, and those other nations which fear acts of aggression against them and their security, a very high proportion of their national income is being spent directly for armaments.   It runs from 30 to as high as 50 per cent. . . .

The situation is definitely of universal concern.   The questions involved relate not merely to violations of specific provisions of particular treaties; they are questions of war and of peace, of international law, and especially of principles of humanity.   It is true that they involve definite violations of agreements, and especially of the Covenant of the League of Nations, the Briand-Kellogg Pact, and the Nine-Power Treaty.   But they also involve problems of world economy, world security, and world humanity.

It is true that the moral consciousness of the world must recognize the importance of removing injustices and well-founded grievances; but at the same time it must be aroused to the cardinal necessity of honoring sanctity of treaties, of respecting the rights and liberties of others, and of putting an end to acts of international aggression.

It seems to be unfortunately true that the epidemic of world lawlessness is spreading.

When an epidemic of physical disease starts to spread, the community approves and joins in a quarantine of the patients in order to protect the health of the community against the spread of the disease.

It is my determination to pursue a policy of peace and to adopt every practicable measure to avoid involvement in war.   It ought to be inconceivable that in this modern era, and in the face of experience, any nation could be so foolish and ruthless as to run the risk of plunging the whole world into war by invading and violating in contravention of solemn treaties the territory of other nations that have done them no real harm and which are too weak to protect themselves adequately. Yet the peace of the world and the welfare and security of every nation is today being threatened by that very thing.

No nation which refuses to exercise forbearance and to respect the freedom and rights of others can long remain strong and retain the confidence and respect of other nations. No nation ever loses its dignity or good standing by conciliating its differences and by exercising great patience with and consideration for the rights of other nations.

War is a contagion, whether it be declared or undeclared. It can engulf states and peoples remote from the original scene of hostilities. We are determined to keep out of war, yet we cannot insure ourselves against the disastrous effects of war and the dangers of involvement. We are adopting such measures as will minimize our risk of involvement, but we cannot have complete protection in a world of disorder in which confidence and security have broken down.

If civilization is to survive the principles of the Prince of Peace must be restored. Shattered trust between nations must be revived.

Most important of all, the will for peace on the part of peace-loving nations must express itself to the end that nations that may be tempted to violate their agreements and the rights of others will desist from such a course. There must be positive endeavors to preserve peace.

America hates war. America hopes for peace. Therefore, America actively engages in the search for peace.

43. The Truman Doctrine *

Mr. Truman may have chosen the dramatic device of a message to Congress for several reasons: the immediacy of the problems, in Turkey and especially in Greece, appeared to call for a direct and personal approach; there was the obvious necessity to mobilize public opinion quickly and effectively behind his new policy proposals; and, finally, his program required the appropriations of large sums, and he had to have Congressional concurrence.

The gravity of the situation which confronts the world today necessitates my appearance before a joint session of the Congress.

The foreign policy and the national security of this country are involved.

One aspect of the present situation, which I wish to present to you at this time for your consideration and decision, concerns Greece and Turkey.

The United States has received from the Greek Government an urgent appeal for financial and economic assistance. Preliminary reports from

* A message to Congress by President Harry S. Truman, March 12, 1947.

the American Economic Mission now in Greece and reports from the American Ambassador in Greece corroborate the statement of the Greek Government that assistance is imperative if Greece is to survive as a free nation.

I do not believe that the American people and the Congress wish to turn a deaf ear to the appeal of the Greek Government.

Greece is not a rich country. Lack of sufficient natural resources has always forced the Greek people to work hard to make both ends meet. Since 1940 this industrious and peace-loving country has suffered invasion, four years of cruel enemy occupation, and bitter internal strife.

When forces of liberation entered Greece they found that the retreating Germans had destroyed virtually all the railways, roads, port facilities, communications, and merchant marine. More than a thousand villages had been burned. Eighty-five per cent of the children were tubercular. Livestock, poultry, and draft animals had almost disappeared. Inflation had wiped out practically all savings.

As a result of these tragic conditions, a militant minority, exploiting human want and misery, was able to create political chaos which, until now, has made economic recovery impossible.

Greece is today without funds to finance the importation of those goods which are essential to bare subsistence. Under these circumstances the people of Greece cannot make progress in solving their problems of reconstruction. Greece is in desperate need of financial and economic assistance to enable it to resume purchases of food, clothing, fuel, and seeds. These are indispensable for the subsistence of its people and are obtainable only from abroad. Greece must have help to import the goods necessary to restore internal order and security so essential for economic and political recovery.

The Greek Government has also asked for the assistance of experienced American administrators, economists, and technicians to insure that the financial and other aid given to Greece shall be used effectively in creating a stable and self-sustaining economy and in improving its public administration.

The very existence of the Greek state is today threatened by the terrorist activities of several thousand armed men, led by Communists, who defy the Government's authority at a number of points, particularly along the northern boundaries. A commission appointed by the United Nations Security Council is at present investigating disturbed conditions in northern Greece and alleged border violations along the frontier between Greece on the one hand and Albania, Bulgaria, and Yugoslavia on the other.

Meanwhile, the Greek Government is unable to cope with the situation. The Greek Army is small and poorly equipped. It needs supplies and equipment if it is to restore authority to the Government throughout Greek territory.

Greece must have assistance if it is to become a self-supporting and self-respecting democracy.

The United States must supply that assistance. We have already extended to Greece certain types of relief and economic aid, but these are inadequate.

There is no other country to which democratic Greece can turn.

No other nation is willing and able to provide the necessary support for a democratic Greek Government.

The British Government, which has been helping Greece, can give no further financial or economic aid after March 31. Great Britain finds itself under the necessity of reducing or liquidating its commitments in several parts of the world, including Greece.

We have considered how the United Nations might assist in this crisis. But the situation is an urgent one requiring immediate action, and the United Nations and its related organizations are not in a position to extend help of the kind that is required.

It is important to note that the Greek Government has asked for our aid in utilizing effectively the financial and other assistance we may give to Greece, and in improving its public administration. It is of the utmost importance that we supervise the use of any funds made available to Greece, in such a manner that each dollar spent will count toward making Greece self-supporting, and will help to build an economy in which a healthy democracy can flourish.

No government is perfect. One of the chief virtues of a democracy, however, is that its defects are always visible and under democratic processes can be pointed out and corrected. The Government of Greece is not perfect. Nevertheless it represents 85 per cent of the members of the Greek Parliament who were chosen in an election last year. Foreign observers, including 692 Americans, considered this election to be a fair expression of the views of the Greek people.

The Greek Government has been operating in an atmosphere of chaos and extremism. It has made mistakes. The extension of aid by this country does not mean that the United States condones everything that the Greek Government has done or will do. We have condemned in the past, and we condemn now, extremist measures of the right or the left. We have in the past advised tolerance, and we advise tolerance now.

Greece's neighbor, Turkey, also deserves our attention.

The future of Turkey as an independent and economically sound state is clearly no less important to the freedom-loving peoples of the world than the future of Greece. The circumstances in which Turkey finds itself today are considerably different from those of Greece. Turkey has been spared the disasters that have beset Greece. And during the war the United States and Great Britain furnished Turkey with material aid.

Nevertheless, Turkey now needs our support.

Since the war Turkey has sought additional financial assistance from Great Britain and the United States for the purpose of effecting that modernization necessary for the maintenance of its national integrity.

That integrity is essential to the preservation of order in the Middle East.

The British Government has informed us that, owing to its own difficulties, it can no longer extend financial or economic aid to Turkey.

As in the case of Greece, if Turkey is to have the assistance it needs, the United States must supply it. We are the only country able to provide that help.

I am fully aware of the broad implications involved if the United States extends assistance to Greece and Turkey, and I shall discuss these implications with you at this time.

One of the primary objectives of the foreign policy of the United States is the creation of conditions in which we and other nations will be able to work out a way of life free from coercion. This was a fundamental issue in the war with Germany and Japan. Our victory was won over countries which sought to impose their will, and their way of life, upon other nations.

To insure the peaceful development of nations, free from coercion, the United States has taken a leading part in establishing the United Nations. The United Nations is designed to make possible lasting freedom and independence for all its members. We shall not realize our objectives, however, unless we are willing to help free peoples to maintain their free institutions and their national integrity against aggressive movements that seek to impose upon them totalitarian regimes. This is no more than a frank recognition that totalitarian regimes imposed upon free peoples, by direct or indirect aggression, undermine the foundations of international peace and hence the security of the United States.

The peoples of a number of countries of the world have recently had totalitarian regimes forced upon them against their will. The Government of the United States has made frequent protests against coercion and intimidation, in violation of the Yalta Agreement, in Poland, Rumania, and Bulgaria. I must also state that in a number of other countries there have been similar developments.

At the present moment in world history nearly every nation must choose between alternative ways of life. The choice is too often not a free one.

One way of life is based upon the will of the majority, and is distinguished by free institutions, representative government, free elections, guaranties of individual liberty, freedom of speech and religion, and freedom from political oppression.

The second way of life is based upon the will of a minority forcibly imposed upon the majority. It relies upon terror and oppression, a controlled press and radio, fixed elections, and the suppression of personal freedoms.

I believe that it must be the policy of the United States to support free peoples who are resisting attempted subjugation by armed minorities or by outside pressures.

I believe that we must assist free peoples to work out their own destinies in their own way.

I believe that our help should be primarily through economic and financial aid which is essential to economic stability and orderly political processes.

The world is not static, and the *status quo* is not sacred. But we cannot allow changes in the *status quo* in violation of the Charter of the United Nations by such methods as coercion, or by such subterfuge as political infiltration. In helping free and independent nations to maintain their freedom, the United States will be giving effect to the principles of the Charter of the United Nations.

It is necessary only to glance at a map to realize that the survival and integrity of the Greek nation are of grave importance in a much wider situation. If Greece should fall under the control of an armed minority, the effect upon its neighbor, Turkey, would be immediate and serious. Confusion and disorder might well spread throughout the entire Middle East.

Moreover, the disappearance of Greece as an independent state would have a profound effect upon those countries in Europe whose peoples are struggling against great difficulties to maintain their freedoms and their independence while they repair the damages of war.

It would be an unspeakable tragedy if these countries, which have struggled so long against overwhelming odds, should lose that victory for which they sacrificed so much. Collapse of free institutions and loss of independence would be disastrous not only for them but for the world. Discouragement and possibly failure would quickly be the lot of neighboring peoples striving to maintain their freedom and independence.

Should we fail to aid Greece and Turkey in this fateful hour, the effect will be far-reaching to the West as well as to the East.

We must take immediate and resolute action.

I therefore ask the Congress to provide authority for assistance to Greece and Turkey in the amount of $400,000,000 for the period ending June 30, 1948. In requesting these funds, I have taken into consideration the maximum amount of relief assistance which would be furnished to Greece out of the $350,000,000 which I recently requested that the Congress authorize for the prevention of starvation and suffering in countries devastated by the war.

In addition to funds, I ask the Congress to authorize the detail of American civilian and military personnel to Greece and Turkey, at the request of those countries, to assist in the tasks of reconstruction, and for the purpose of supervising the use of such financial and material assistance as may be furnished. I recommend that authority also be provided for the instruction and training of selected Greek and Turkish personnel.

Finally, I ask that the Congress provide authority which will permit the speediest and most effective use, in terms of needed commodities, supplies, and equipment, of such funds as may be authorized.

If further funds, or further authority, should be needed for purposes indicated in this message, I shall not hesitate to bring the situation before the Congress. On this subject the Executive and Legislative branches of the Government must work together.

This is a serious course upon which we embark.

I would not recommend it except that the alternative is much more serious.

The United States contributed $341,000,000,000 toward winning World War II. This is an investment in world freedom and world peace.

The assistance that I am recommending for Greece and Turkey amounts to little more than one tenth of one per cent of this investment. It is only common sense that we should safeguard this investment and make sure that it was not in vain.

The seeds of totalitarian regimes are nurtured by misery and want. They spread and grow in the evil soil of poverty and strife. They reach their full growth when the hope of a people for a better life has died.

We must keep that hope alive.

The free peoples of the world look to us for support in maintaining their freedoms.

If we falter in our leadership, we may endanger the peace of the world—and we shall surely endanger the welfare of our own Nation.

Great responsibilities have been placed upon us by the swift movement of events.

I am confident that the Congress will face these responsibilities squarely.

44. THE MARSHALL PLAN *

Secretary Marshall's address is analogous to the "Quarantine the Aggressors" speech of President Roosevelt (Selection 41). To some extent it also constituted a "trial balloon," but the difference between the two speeches is immediately apparent. Mr. Roosevelt's speech aroused widespread disapproval. Mr. Marshall's speech elicited instantaneous praise. The policy suggested in his address became formalized in the Marshall Plan legislation. The analogy with Mr. Roosevelt's address will perhaps be more apparent if one imagines a situation in which the sentiments expressed by Mr. Marshall found no appreciable support in Congressional, press, or public opinion. In that case, the Marshall Plan would very likely have suffered the same fate as Mr. Roosevelt's plan to quarantine the aggressors.

I need not tell you gentlemen that the world situation is very serious. That must be apparent to all intelligent people. I think one difficulty is that the problem is one of such enormous complexity that the very mass of facts presented to the public by press and radio make it exceedingly difficult for the man in the street to reach a clear appraisement of the situation. Furthermore, the people of this country are distant from the troubled areas of the earth and it is hard for them to comprehend the plight and consequent reactions of the long-suffering peoples, and the effect of those reactions on their governments in connection with our efforts to promote peace in the world.

In considering the requirements for the rehabilitation of Europe, the physical loss of life, the visible destruction of cities, factories, mines, and railroads was correctly estimated, but it has become obvious during recent months that this visible destruction was probably less serious than the dislocation of the entire fabric of European economy. For the past 10 years conditions have been highly abnormal. The feverish preparation for war and the more feverish maintenance of the war effort engulfed all aspects of national economies. Machinery has fallen into disrepair

* An address by Secretary of State George C. Marshall, delivered at Harvard University, June 5, 1947.

or is entirely obsolete. Under the arbitrary and destructive Nazi rule, virtually every possible enterprise was geared into the German war machine. Long-standing commercial ties, private institutions, banks, insurance companies, and shipping companies disappeared, through loss of capital, absorption through nationalization, or by simple destruction. In many countries, confidence in the local currency has been severely shaken. The breakdown of the business structure of Europe during the war was complete. Recovery has been seriously retarded by the fact that two years after the close of hostilities a peace settlement with Germany and Austria has not been agreed upon. But even given a more prompt solution of these difficult problems, the rehabilitation of the economic structure of Europe quite evidently will require a much longer time and greater effort than had been foreseen.

There is a phase of this matter which is both interesting and serious. The farmer has always produced the foodstuffs to exchange with the city dweller for the other necessities of life. This division of labor is the basis of modern civilization. At the present time it is threatened with breakdown. The town and city industries are not producing adequate goods to exchange with the food-producing farmer. Raw materials and fuel are in short supply. Machinery is lacking or worn out. The farmer or the peasant cannot find the goods for sale which he desires to purchase. So the sale of his farm produce for money which he cannot use seems to him an unprofitable transaction. He, therefore, has withdrawn many fields from crop cultivation and is using them for grazing. He feeds more grain to stock and finds for himself and his family an ample supply of food, however short he may be on clothing and the other ordinary gadgets of civilization. Meanwhile people in the cities are short of food and fuel. So the governments are forced to use their foreign money and credits to procure these necessities abroad. This process exhausts funds which are urgently needed for reconstruction. Thus a very serious situation is rapidly developing which bodes no good for the world. The modern system of the division of labor upon which the exchange of products is based is in danger of breaking down.

The truth of the matter is that Europe's requirements for the next three or four years of foreign food and other essential products—principally from America—are so much greater than her present ability to pay that she must have substantial additional help or face economic, social, and political deterioration of a very grave character.

The remedy lies in breaking the vicious circle and restoring the confidence of the European people in the economic future of their own countries and of Europe as a whole. The manufacturer and the farmer throughout wide areas must be able and willing to exchange their products for currencies, the continuing value of which is not open to question.

Aside from the demoralizing effect on the world at large and the possibilities of disturbances arising as a result of the desperation of the people concerned, the consequences to the economy of the United States should be apparent to all. It is logical that the United States should do whatever it is able to do to assist in the return of normal economic health in the world, without which there can be no political stability and no assured peace. Our policy is directed not against any country or doctrine but against hunger, poverty, desperation, and chaos. Its purpose should be the revival of a working economy in the world so as to permit the emergence of political and social conditions in which free institutions can exist. Such assistance, I am convinced, must not be on a piecemeal basis as various crises develop. Any assistance that this Government may render in the future should provide a cure rather than a mere palliative. Any government that is willing to assist in the task of recovery will find full cooperation, I am sure, on the part of the United States Government. Any government which maneuvers to block the recovery of other countries cannot expect help from us. Furthermore, governments, political parties, or groups which seek to perpetuate human misery in order to profit therefrom politically or otherwise will encounter the opposition of the United States.

It is already evident that, before the United States Government can proceed much further in its efforts to alleviate the situation and help start the European world on its way to recovery, there must be some agreement among the countries of Europe as to the requirements of the situation and the part those countries themselves will take in order to give proper effect to whatever action might be undertaken by this Government. It would be neither fitting nor efficacious for this Government to undertake to draw up unilaterally a program designed to place Europe on its feet economically. This is the business of the Europeans. The initiative, I think, must come from Europe. The role of this country should consist of friendly aid in the drafting of a European program and of later support of such a program so far as it may be practical for us to do so. The program should be a joint one, agreed to by a number, if not all, European nations.

An essential part of any successful action on the part of the United States is an understanding on the part of the people of America of the character of the problem and the remedies to be applied. Political passion and prejudice should have no part. With foresight, and a willingness on the part of our people to face up to the vast responsibility which history has clearly placed upon our country, the difficulties I have outlined can and will be overcome.

International Conferences

45. THE YALTA AGREEMENTS *

Among the means of making known the policies of the United States are the published agreements of international conferences to which the United States has been a party.

During World War II, unilateral action could generally not be taken because of the necessity to maintain close collaboration with other powers. This made the use of the unilateral official pronouncement impractical. There was no time for consultation with the other powers in advance of the pronouncement. The treaty process would have been too time-consuming and would have involved public discussion and official debate at a time when secrecy and speed were of the essence. A series of executive agreements with each of the powers involved would have been cumbersome.

The international conference, conducted in secret with the least number of persons present, remained as the only alternative. The participating powers become aware of our policy during the course of the conference; others by observing our subsequent actions, and eventually by consulting the published protocols.

PROTOCOL OF PROCEEDINGS, FEBRUARY 11, 1945

The Crimea Conference of the Heads of the Governments of the United States of America, the United Kingdom, and the Union of Soviet Socialist Republics which took place from February 4th to 11th came to the following conclusions:

I. *World Organization*

It was decided:

(1) that a United Nations Conference on the proposed world organization should be summoned for Wednesday, 25th April, 1945, and should be held in the United States of America.

(2) the Nations to be invited to this Conference should be:

* From The Protocols of Proceedings at the Crimea Conference, February, 4-11, 1945.

(*a*)   the United Nations as they existed on the 8th February, 1945; and

(*b*)   such of the Associated Nations as have declared war on the common enemy by 1st March, 1945.   (For this purpose by the term "Associated Nation" was meant the eight Associated Nations and Turkey.)   When the Conference on World Organization is held, the delegates of the United Kingdom and United States of America will support a proposal to admit to original membership two Soviet Socialist Republics, i.e., the Ukraine and White Russia.

(3)   that the United States Government on behalf of the Three Powers should consult the Government of China and the French Provisional Government in regard to decisions taken at the present Conference concerning the proposed World Organization.

(4)   that the text of the invitation to be issued to all the nations which would take part in the United Nations Conference should be as follows:

Invitation

"The Government of the United States of America, on behalf of itself and of the Governments of the United Kingdom, the Union of Soviet Socialist Republics, and the Republic of China and the Provisional Government of the French Republic, invite the Government of———— to send representatives to a Conference of the United Nations to be held on 25th April, 1945, or soon thereafter, at San Francisco in the United States of America to prepare a Charter for a General International Organization for the maintenance of international peace and security.

"The above named governments suggest that the Conference consider as affording a basis for such a Charter the Proposals for the Establishment of a General International Organization, which were made public last October as a result of the Dumbarton Oaks Conference, and which have now been supplemented by the following provisions for Section C of Chapter VI:

"C.   VOTING

"1.   Each member of the Security Council should have one vote.

"2.   Decisions of the Security Council on procedural matters should be made by an affirmative vote of seven members.

"3.   Decisions of the Security Council on all other matters should be made by an affirmative vote of seven members including the concurring votes of the permanent members; provided that, in decisions under Chapter VIII, Section A and under the second sentence of paragraph 1 of Chapter VIII, Section C, a party to a dispute should abstain from voting.

"Further information as to arrangements will be transmitted subsequently.

"In the event that the Government of ——— desires in advance of the Conference to present views or comments concerning the proposals, the Government of the United States of America will be pleased to transmit such views and comments to the other participating Governments."

Territorial Trusteeship.

It was agreed that the five Nations which will have permanent seats on the Security Council should consult each other prior to the United Nations Conference on the question of territorial trusteeship.

The acceptance of this recommendation is subject to its being made clear that territorial trusteeship will only apply to (a) existing mandates of the League of Nations; (b) territories detached from the enemy as a result of the present war; (c) any other territory which might voluntarily be placed under trusteeship; and (d) no discussion of actual territories is contemplated at the forthcoming United Nations Conference or in the preliminary consultations, and it will be a matter for subsequent agreement which territories within the above categories will be placed under trusteeship.

II. *Declaration on Liberated Europe*

The following declaration has been approved:

"The Premier of the Union of Soviet Socialist Republics, the Prime Minister of the United Kingdom and the President of the United States of America have consulted with each other in the common interests of the peoples of their countries and those of liberated Europe. They jointly declare their mutual agreement to concert during the temporary period of instability in liberated Europe the policies of their three governments in assisting the peoples of the former Axis satellite states of Europe to solve by democratic means their pressing political and economic problems.

"The establishment of order in Europe and the re-building of national economic life must be achieved by processes which will enable the liberated peoples to destroy the last vestiges of Nazism and Fascism and to create democratic institutions of their own choice. This is a principle of the Atlantic Charter—the right of all peoples to choose the form of government under which they will live—the restoration of sovereign rights and self-government to those peoples who have been forcibly deprived of them by the aggressor nations.

"To foster the conditions in which the liberated peoples may exercise these rights, the three governments will jointly assist the people in any European liberated state or former Axis satellite state in Europe where in their judgment conditions require (*a*) to establish conditions of internal peace; (*b*) to carry out emergency measures for the relief of distressed peoples; (*c*) to form interim governmental authorities broadly representative of all democratic elements in the population and pledged to the earliest possible establishment through free elections of governments responsive to the will of the people; and (*d*) to facilitate where necessary the holding of such elections.

"The three governments will consult the other United Nations and provisional authorities or other governments in Europe when matters of direct interest to them are under consideration.

"When, in the opinion of the three governments, conditions in any European liberated state or any former Axis satellite state in Europe make such action necessary, they will immediately consult together on the measures necessary to discharge the joint responsibilities set forth in this declaration.

"By this declaration we reaffirm our faith in the principles of the Atlantic Charter, our pledge in the Declaration by the United Nations, and our determination to build in cooperation with other peace-loving nations world order under law, dedicated to peace, security, freedom and general well-being of all mankind.

"In issuing this declaration, the Three Powers express the hope that the Provisional Government of the French Republic may be associated with them in the procedure suggested."

III. *Dismemberment of Germany*

It was agreed that Article 12 (*a*) of the Surrender Terms for Germany should be amended to read as follows:

"The United Kingdom, the United States of America and the Union of Soviet Socialist Republics shall possess supreme authority with respect to Germany. In the exercise of such authority they will take such steps, including the complete disarmament, demilitarisation and dismemberment of Germany as they deem requisite for future peace and security."

The study of the procedure for the dismemberment of Germany was referred to a Committee, consisting of Mr. Eden (Chairman), Mr. Winant and Mr. Gousev. This body would consider the desirability of associating with it a French representative.

IV. *Zone of Occupation for the French and Control Council for Germany*

It was agreed that a zone in Germany, to be occupied by the French

Forces, should be allocated to France.   This zone would be formed out of the British and American zones and its extent would be settled by the British and Americans in consultation with the French Provisional Government.

It was also agreed that the French Provisional Government should be invited to become a member of the Allied Control Council for Germany.

V. *Reparation*

·   ·   ·   ·   ·

[Approved protocol printed following paragraph XIV.]

VI. *Major War Criminals*

The Conference agreed that the question of the major war criminals should be the subject of enquiry by the three Foreign Secretaries for report in due course after the close of the Conference.

VII. *Poland*

The following Declaration on Poland was agreed by the Conference:

"A new situation has been created in Poland as a result of her complete liberation by the Red Army.   This calls for the establishment of a Polish Provisional Government which can be more broadly based than was possible before the recent liberation of Western part of Poland. The Provisional Government which is now functioning in Poland should therefore be reorganized on a broader democratic basis with the inclusion of democratic leaders from Poland itself and from Poles abroad.   This new Government should then be called the Polish Provisional Government of National Unity.

"M. Molotov, Mr. Harriman and Sir A. Clark Kerr are authorized as a commission to consult in the first instance in Moscow with members of the present Provisional Government and with other Polish democratic leaders from within Poland and from abroad, with a view to the reorganization of the present Government along the above lines.   This Polish Provisional Government of National Unity shall be pledged to the holding of free and unfettered elections as soon as possible on the basis of universal suffrage and secret ballot.   In these elections all democratic and anti-Nazi parties shall have the right to take part and to put forward candidates.

"When a Polish Provisional Government of National Unity has been properly formed in conformity with the above, the Government of the U.S.S.R., which now maintains diplomatic relations with the present Provisional Government of Poland, and the Government of the United

Kingdom and the Government of the United States of America will establish diplomatic relations with the new Polish Government of National Unity, and will exchange Ambassadors by whose reports the respective Governments will be kept informed about the situation in Poland.

"The three Heads of Government consider that the Eastern frontier of Poland should follow the Curzon Line with digressions from it in some regions of five to eight kilometres in favour of Poland. They recognize that Poland must receive substantial accessions of territory on the North and West. They feel that the opinion of the new Polish Provisional Government of National Unity should be sought in due course on the extent of these accessions and that the final delimitation of the Western frontier of Poland should thereafter await the Peace Conference."

VIII. *Yugoslavia*

It was agreed to recommend to Marshal Tito and to Dr. Subasic:

(*a*) that the Tito-Subasic Agreement should immediately be put into effect and a new Government formed on the basis of the Agreement

(*b*) that as soon as the new Government has been formed it should declare:

(i) that the Anti-Fascist Assembly of National Liberation (AUNOJ) will be extended to include members of the last Yugoslav Skupstina who have not compromised themselves by collaboration with the enemy, thus forming a body to be known as a temporary Parliament and

(ii) that legislative acts passed by the Anti-Fascist Assembly of National Liberation (AUNOJ) will be subject to subsequent ratification by a Constituent Assembly; and that this statement should be published in the Communique of the Conference.

IX. *Italo-Yugoslav Frontier; Italo-Austria Frontier*

Notes on these subjects were put in by the British delegation and the American and Soviet delegations agreed to consider them and give their views later.

X. *Yugoslav-Bulgarian Relations*

There was an exchange of views between the Foreign Secretaries on the question of the desirability of a Yugoslav-Bulgarian pact of alliance. The question at issue was whether a state still under an armistice regime could be allowed to enter into a treaty with another state. Mr. Eden suggested that the Bulgarian and Yugoslav Governments should be informed that this could not be approved.   Mr. Stettinius suggested that the British and American Ambassadors should discuss the matter further with M. Molotov in Moscow.   M. Molotov agreed with the proposal of Mr. Stettinius.

XI. *Southeastern Europe*

The British Delegation put in notes for the consideration of their colleagues on the following subjects:

(*a*) the Control Commission in Bulgaria

(*b*) Greek claims upon Bulgaria, more particularly with reference to reparations

(*c*) Oil equipment in Rumania.

XII. *Iran*

Mr. Eden, Mr. Stettinius and M. Molotov exchanged views on the situation in Iran.   It was agreed that this matter should be pursued through the diplomatic channel.

XIII. *Meetings of the Three Foreign Secretaries*

The Conference agreed that permanent machinery should be set up for consultation between the three Foreign Secretaries; they should meet as often as necessary, probably about every three or four months.

These meetings will be held in rotation in the three capitals, the first meeting being held in London.

XIV. *The Montreux Convention and the Straits*

It was agreed that at the next meeting of the three Foreign Secretaries to be held in London, they should consider proposals which it was understood the Soviet Government would put forward in relation to the Montreux Convention and report to their Governments.   The Turkish Government should be informed at the appropriate moment.

The foregoing Protocol was approved and signed by the three Foreign Secretaries at the Crimean Conference, February 11, 1945.

E. R. STETTINIUS, Jr.

M. MOLOTOV

ANTHONY EDEN

PROTOCOL ON GERMAN REPARATION, FEBRUARY 11, 1945

The Heads of the three governments agreed as follows:

1. Germany must pay in kind for the losses caused by her to the Allied nations in the course of the war.   Reparations are to be received in the first instance by those countries which have borne the main

burden of the war, have suffered the heaviest losses and have organised victory over the enemy.

2. Reparations in kind are to be exacted from Germany in three following forms:

(*a*) Removals within 2 years from the surrender of Germany or the cessation of organised resistance from the national wealth of Germany located on the territory of Germany herself as well as outside her territory (equipment, machine-tools, ships, rolling stock, German investments abroad, shares of industrial, transport and other enterprises in Germany, etc.), these removals to be carried out chiefly for purpose of destroying the war potential of Germany.

(*b*) Annual deliveries of goods from current production for a period to be fixed.

(*c*) Use of German labour.

3. For the working out on the above principles of a detailed plan for exaction of reparation from Germany an Allied Reparation Commission will be set up in Moscow.   It will consist of three representatives —one from the Union of Soviet Socialist Republics, one from the United Kingdom and one from the United States of America.

4. With regard to the fixing of the total sum of the reparation as well as the distribution of it among the countries which suffered from the German aggression the Soviet and American delegations agreed as follows:

"The Moscow Reparation Commission should take in its initial studies as a basis for discussion the suggestion of the Soviet Government that the total sum of the reparation in accordance with the points (*a*) and (*b*) of the paragraph 2 should be 20 billion dollars and that 50% of it should go to the Union of Soviet Socialist Republics."

The British delegation was of the opinion that pending consideration of the reparation question by the Moscow Reparation Commission no figures of reparation should be mentioned.

The above Soviet-American proposal has been passed to the Moscow Reparation Commission as one of the proposals to be considered by the Commission.

WINSTON S. CHURCHILL
FRANKLIN D. ROOSEVELT
JOSEPH V. STALIN

February 11, 1945.

AGREEMENT REGARDING JAPAN, FEBRUARY 11, 1945

The leaders of the three Great Powers—the Soviet Union, the United

States of America and Great Britain—have agreed that in two or three months after Germany has surrendered and the war in Europe has terminated the Soviet Union shall enter into the war against Japan on the side of the Allies on condition that:

1. The status quo in Outer-Mongolia (The Mongolian People's Republic) shall be preserved;

2. The former rights of Russia violated by the treacherous attack of Japan in 1904 shall be restored, viz:

(*a*) the southern part of Sakhalin as well as all the islands adjacent to it shall be returned to the Soviet Union,

(*b*) the commercial port of Dairen shall be internationalized, the preeminent interests of the Soviet Union in this port being safeguarded and the lease of Port Arthur as a naval base of the U.S.S.R. restored,

(*c*) The Chinese-Eastern Railroad and the South-Manchurian Railroad which provides an outlet to Dairen shall be jointly operated by the establishment of a joint Soviet-Chinese Company it being understood that the preeminent interests of the Soviet Union shall be safeguarded and that China shall retain full sovereignty in Manchuria;

3. The Kuril Islands shall be handed over to the Soviet Union.

It is understood, that the agreement concerning Outer-Mongolia and the ports and railroads referred to above will require concurrence of Generalissimo Chiang Kai-shek. The President will take measures in order to obtain this concurrence on advice from Marshal Stalin.

The Heads of the three Great Powers have agreed that these claims of the Soviet Union shall be unquestionably fulfilled after Japan has been defeated.

For its part the Soviet Union expresses its readiness to conclude with the National Government of China a pact of friendship and alliance between the U.S.S.R. and China in order to render assistance to China with its armed forces for the purpose of liberating China from the Japanese yoke.

JOSEPH V. STALIN
FRANKLIN D. ROOSEVELT
WINSTON S. CHURCHILL

February 11, 1945

Executive Agreements

46. THE DESTROYERS - FOR - BASES AGREEMENT *

At the end of 1940, it was extremely doubtful whether President Roosevelt could have secured the necessary two-thirds vote in the Senate in favor of this agreement. Even if he had been successful, the delays involved in obtaining Senate approval might have proved costly for the British effort against Germany. The President believed it was in our interest to assist Britain, and he wanted to help her as quickly as possible.

The opinion of Attorney-General Jackson concerning the constitutionality of concluding an executive agreement to exchange destroyers for bases has already been cited (Selection 34). But other considerations besides the question of legality prompt Presidents to employ executive agreements instead of treaties. Treaties require a two-thirds affirmative vote by the Senate, and the process of confirmation is often a time-consuming one. Executive agreements of this type come under the purview of Congress only if appropriations are necessary to implement them, and even then, a majority vote is all that is required for Congressional action.

Although recent criticism of the use of these agreements has focused upon the President's authority to make binding arrangements without Congressional approval (it is said that the blunders committed at Yalta would have been avoided if Congress had been consulted), many executive agreements are in fact made under the authority of Congressional enactment, and others are submitted to Congress during the negotiations.

AMBASSADOR LOTHIAN TO SECRETARY OF STATE HULL

I have the honor to inform you that in view of the friendly and sympathetic interest of His Majesty's Government in the United Kingdom in the national security of the United States and their desire to strengthen the ability of the United States to cooperate effectively with the other nations of the Americas in the defense of the Western Hemisphere, His Majesty's Government will secure the grant to the Government of the United States, freely and without consideration, of the lease for immediate establishment and use of naval and air bases and facilities for entrance thereto and the operation and protection thereof, on the Avalon Pen-

* From an exchange of notes between the Ambassador of Great Britain to the United States, Lord Lothian, and Secretary of State Cordell Hull, September 2, 1940.

insula and on the southern coast of Newfoundland, and on the east coast and on the Great Bay of Bermuda.

Furthermore, in view of the above and in view of the desire of the United States to acquire additional air and naval bases in the Caribbean and in British Guiana, and without endeavoring to place a monetary or commercial value upon the many tangible and intangible rights and properties involved, His Majesty's Government will make available to the United States for immediate establishment and use naval and air bases and facilities for entrance thereto and the operation and protection thereof, on the eastern side of the Bahamas, the southern coast of Jamaica, the western coast of St. Lucia, the west coast of Trinidad in the Gulf of Paria, in the island of Antigua and in British Guiana within fifty miles of Georgetown, in exchange for naval and military equipment and material which the United States Government will transfer to His Majesty's Government.

All the bases and facilities referred to in the preceding paragraphs will be leased to the United States for a period of ninety-nine years, free from all rent and charges other than such compensation to be mutually agreed on to be paid by the United States in order to compensate the owners of private property for loss by expropriation or damage arising out of the establishment of the bases and facilities in question.

His Majesty's Government, in the leases to be agreed upon, will grant to the United States for the period of the leases all the rights, power, and authority within the bases leased, and within the limits of the territorial waters and air spaces adjacent to or in the vicinity of such bases, necessary to provide access to and defense of such bases, and appropriate provisions for their control.

Without prejudice to the above-mentioned rights of the United States authorities and their jurisdiction within the leased areas, the adjustment and reconciliation between the jurisdiction of the authorities of the territories in which these areas are situated, shall be determined by common agreement.

The exact location and bounds of the aforesaid bases, the necessary seaward, coast and anti-aircraft defenses, the location of sufficient military garrisons, stores and other necessary auxiliary facilities shall be determined by common agreement.

His Majesty's Government are prepared to designate immediately experts to meet with experts of the United States for these purposes. Should these experts be unable to agree in any particular situation, except in the case of Newfoundland and Bermuda, the matter shall be settled by the Secretary of State of the United States and His Majesty's Secretary of State for Foreign Affairs.

SECRETARY OF STATE HULL TO AMBASSADOR LOTHIAN

I have received your note of September 2, 1940. . . .

I am directed by the President to reply to your note as follows:

The Government of the United States appreciates the declarations and the generous action of His Majesty's Government as contained in your communication which are destined to enhance the national security of the United States and greatly to strengthen its ability to cooperate effectively with the other nations of the Americas in the defense of the Western Hemisphere.   It therefore gladly accepts the proposals.

The Government of the United States will immediately designate experts to meet with experts designated by His Majesty's Government to determine upon the exact location of the naval and air bases mentioned in your communication under acknowledgment.

In consideration of the declarations above quoted, the Government of the United States will immediately transfer to His Majesty's Government fifty United States Navy destroyers generally referred to as the twelve-hundred-ton type.

Treaties

47. THE NORTH ATLANTIC TREATY

The Treaty was signed on April 4, 1949, and American ratification followed on July 25.   The short and relatively simple text makes it clear that the policy of the United States will be to consider an attack upon any of the other signatories as an attack upon the United States itself.

PREAMBLE

The Parties to this Treaty* reaffirm their faith in the purposes and principles of the Charter of the United Nations and their desire to live in peace with all peoples and all governments.

They are determined to safeguard the freedom, common heritage and civilization of their peoples, founded on the principles of democracy, individual liberty and the rule of law.

They seek to promote stability and well-being in the North Atlantic area.

* Belgium, Canada, Denmark, France, Iceland, Italy, Luxembourg, Netherlands, Norway, Portugal, United Kingdom and United States.

They are resolved to unite their efforts for collective defense and for the preservation of peace and security.

They therefore agree to this North Atlantic Treaty:

ARTICLE 1

The Parties undertake, as set forth in the Charter of the United Nations, to settle any international disputes in which they may be involved by peaceful means in such a manner that international peace and security, and justice, are not endangered, and to refrain in their international relations from the threat or use of force in any manner inconsistent with the purposes of the United Nations.

ARTICLE 2

The Parties will contribute toward the further development of peaceful and friendly international relations by strengthening their free institutions, by bringing about a better understanding of the principles upon which these institutions are founded, and by promoting conditions of stability and well-being. They will seek to eliminate conflict in their international economic policies and will encourage economic collaboration between any or all of them.

ARTICLE 3

In order more effectively to achieve the objectives of this Treaty, the Parties, separately and jointly, by means of continuous and effective self-help and mutual aid, will maintain and develop their individual and collective capacity to resist armed attack.

ARTICLE 4

The Parties will consult together whenever, in the opinion of any of them, the territorial integrity, political independence or security of any of the Parties is threatened.

ARTICLE 5

The Parties agree that an armed attack against one or more of them in Europe or North America shall be considered an attack against them all; and consequently they agree that, if such an armed attack occurs, each of them, in exercise of the right of individual or collective self-defense recognized by Article 51 of the Charter of the United Nations, will assist the Party or Parties so attacked by taking forthwith, individually and in concert with the other Parties, such action as it deems necessary, including the use of armed force, to restore and maintain the security of the North Atlantic area.

Any such armed attack and all measures taken as a result thereof shall immediately be reported to the Security Council. Such measures shall be terminated when the Security Council has taken the measures necessary to restore and maintain international peace and security.

ARTICLE 6

For the purpose of Article 5 an armed attack on one or more of the Parties is deemed to include an armed attack on the territory of any of the Parties in Europe or North America, on the Algerian departments of France, on the occupation forces of any Party in Europe, on the islands under the jurisdiction of any Party in the North Atlantic area north of the Tropic of Cancer or on the vessels or aircraft in this area of any of the Parties.

ARTICLE 7

This Treaty does not affect, and shall not be interpreted as affecting, in any way the rights and obligations under the Charter of the Parties which are members of the United Nations, or the primary responsibility of the Security Council for the maintenance of international peace and security.

ARTICLE 8

Each Party declares that none of the international engagements now in force between it and any other of the Parties or any third state is in conflict with the provisions of this Treaty, and undertakes not to enter into any international engagement in conflict with this Treaty.

ARTICLE 9

The Parties hereby establish a council, on which each of them shall be represented, to consider matters concerning the implementation of this Treaty. The council shall be so organized as to be able to meet promptly at any time. The council shall set up such subsidiary bodies as may be necessary; in particular it shall establish immediately a defense committee which shall recommend measures for the implementation of Articles 3 and 5.

ARTICLE 10

The Parties may, by unanimous agreement, invite any other European state in a position to further the principles of this Treaty and to contribute to the security of the North Atlantic area to accede to this Treaty. Any state so invited may become a party to the Treaty by depositing its instrument of accession with the Government of the United States of

America.   The Government of the United States of America will inform each of the Parties of the deposit of each such instrument of accession.

ARTICLE 11

This Treaty shall be ratified and its provisions carried out by the Parties in accordance with their respective constitutional processes. The instruments of ratification shall be deposited as soon as possible with the Government of the United States of America, which will notify all the other signatories of each deposit.   The Treaty shall enter into force between the states which have ratified it as soon as the ratifications of the majority of the signatories, including the ratifications of Belgium, Canada, France, Luxembourg, the Netherlands, the United Kingdom and the United States, have been deposited and shall come into effect with respect to other states on the date of the deposit of their ratifications.

ARTICLE 12

After the Treaty has been in force for ten years, or at any time thereafter, the Parties shall, if any of them so requests, consult together for the purpose of reviewing the Treaty, having regard for the factors then affecting peace and security in the North Atlantic area, including the development of universal as well as regional arrangements under the Charter of the United Nations for the maintenance of international peace and security.

ARTICLE 13

After the Treaty has been in force for twenty years, any Party may cease to be a party one year after its notice of denunciation has been given to the Government of the United States of America, which will inform the Governments of the other Parties of the deposit of each notice of denunciation.

ARTICLE 14

This Treaty, of which the English and French texts are equally authentic, shall be deposited in the archives of the Government of the United States of America.   Duly certified copies thereof will be transmitted by that Government to the Governments of the other signatories.

In witness whereof, the undersigned plenipotentiaries have signed this Treaty.

Done at Washington, the fourth day of April, 1949.

CHAPTER SIX

The Contemporary Design of American Foreign Policy

So FAR, our attention has been focused upon theoretical approaches to foreign policy, and upon the process of policy formation. We have noted that our government is limited in what it can do, not alone by the thought of how a friendly foreign government or potential adversary might respond, or the desirability or necessity to reply to some action of another government, but also by forces within the United States which shape decisions. We have seen, moreover, that there is a constitutional framework within which the power to formulate and execute foreign policy is distributed, and an institutional framework within which the formulation and execution of policy is carried on. Finally, we have reviewed the principal means used to make our policy known to the world.

Nowhere in this volume, however, have we been, or shall we be, primarily concerned with the specific content of our policy. A reader who wanted to know what our policy is in Iran, or toward the Philippines, or concerning the international control of atomic energy, could not here find the information he sought. For specific policies sometimes change very rapidly, and it is doubtful whether there would be much value in a recital of the details of American foreign policy as of this writing. In addition, the broader and more enduring aspects of our policy would tend to be obscured by such details.

In this chapter, we shall deal with the "grand design" of our foreign policy. Thus, rather than answer the question: What is American policy toward Belgium?, we would describe the position Western Europe occupies in the general scheme of American foreign policy. The maintenance of the independence of Western Europe from Soviet control will continue to be one of the most important principles of our policy for the foreseeable future at least.   We think the security of every part of this area is intimately bound up with our own security.   It should, accordingly, be clear that our policy in Belgium is to support her—economically, so that communist strength there will wane, and militarily, so that the threat of Red Army aggression will recede.

Much has been said about the fact that the world in which we live is very different from that of our fathers.   One basic new fact of contemporary international affairs is the division of the world into two competing power blocs, one led by the United States, the other by the Soviet Union.   It is too early to speak of any third bloc of nations uncommitted to either side and sufficiently powerful to influence significantly the outcome of the struggle between East and West.   India and Indonesia are sometimes spoken of as the nucleus of a "third force" which one day will be able to assume a role approximately equal in power and influence to that of the American or the Soviet bloc.   At the present time, however, this "third force" lacks the power and organization to play a major role.

Many Americans understand that they are living in a bi-polar world. Few, however, are aware of the complicated nature of the conflict between East and West.   For the United States and its allies are not merely engaged in a cold war with a state called the Soviet Union and its allies. If this were all there is to the conflict, there would be little confusion in the counsels of American foreign policy concerning the formulation of policy to counteract the aggressive tendencies of the Soviet Union. In past years, alliances have been met by counter alliances, improvements in armaments have been met by further improvements, budgetary allotments for new and better and bigger armies and navies have been met by still larger budgetary allotments.   Something new has been added to the old-fashioned struggle for power among states; and the new thing is the communist ideology.

When American leaders speak of the necessity to oppose Soviet totalitarianism, are they speaking primarily about Soviet power within the arsenal of which the communist ideology is one weapon among many? Or, are they referring to communism, the influence of which can be attributed only partly to the military might of the Soviet Union?

When the Soviet Union attempts to subjugate Iran, this is perhaps understandable power politics.   Powerful nations have been notorious throughout history for the eagerness with which they have overrun weak neighboring countries.   The tasks of Soviet communist agents may be greatly facilitated by the activities of local communist groups and by deteriorating economic and social conditions in Iran, and particularly in the Iranian province which borders upon Soviet territory; but the main weapon of the Soviet Union in this area is probably Soviet military power, not the power of attraction of communism. Soviet policy toward Iran, may, therefore, be understood in power-political terms. Soviet support of Communist parties in other parts of the world, however, may stem primarily from the desire to assist ideological comrades to win success in their own countries, and only incidentally from power-political motives.

One of the most striking features of current American foreign policy is the number and variety of policies that have been adopted to attain our objectives of peace and security. The development of several parallel and complementary American policies indicates not only the world-wide scope of the East-West conflict and the dual nature of the threat of Soviet totalitarianism, but also the presence of other problems as well. Some of these may be only distantly related to the major struggle; they may, nevertheless, contain imminent or potential dangers for American security. It is true that we sometimes act as if we believed all our difficulties could be traced to a single source—the aggressive inclinations and actions of the Soviet Union. Few people who have seriously thought about international affairs, however, accept the notion of one single moving force determining the course of events. It seems clear that even if the Soviet Union and communism were suddenly to vanish from the earth, American policy planners would still be faced with many problems—nationalism in Asia and Africa, the decline of Western European power and prestige, and population pressures in certain areas, to mention only a few.

American policy planners have concentrated, of course, upon the main problem, the threat of Soviet aggression. But they have generally been under no compulsion to seek a simple "once and for all" solution, and they have not adopted any single-cause theory of international conflict. They evidently believe that the problems of international affairs are complex; consequently, they have pursued one policy here, another there; sometimes they have pursued these policies alternately, at other times simultaneously. The pattern of American response to the Soviet threat is one of attacking the problems created by the threat from a variety of angles. Thus, the policy of containment implies the use of force to oppose aggression; the emphasis on information programs indicates an attempt to block the spread of communism through a modification of public opinion abroad; the Point Four Program is based upon a belief that the attraction of communism for people in underdeveloped areas can be reduced by economic development through technical assistance;

our participation in collective security pacts with the Pan-American and North Atlantic nations rests upon the hope that the threat of collective action will deter aggression.

These policies may or may not contradict each other, but each policy embodies a somewhat different diagnosis of the nature of the threat. The use of force, the improvement of economic conditions, the presentation of a united front against aggression, the influence of world public opinion—all these are factors which, the United States believes, are involved in the problem and its solution.

This chapter is divided into four sections. In the first, we consider the dual nature of the threat of Soviet totalitarianism. This duality creates very real problems for American policy planners. If they assume that the communist ideology presents the greater danger, and if it is true that communism feeds upon misery and poverty, then the major task of our policy would appear to be social and economic reform in countries threatened with communist subversion from within. If, on the other hand, Soviet power is more to be feared than communism, then we must look primarily to our military defenses. The assumption that the enemy is a shifting combination of military power and ideological subversion leads to the difficult task of formulating both military and economic policy, in the hope that our efforts will not strain our economy, and yet aware that we must do enough to cope with both power political and ideological threats. This latter position is the one usually adopted by those charged with the responsibility to formulate and execute foreign policy.

In this section, we shall present an analysis based upon the view that the communist ideology is the primary cause of East-West conflict (Selection 48), and another analysis based upon the view that the major source of danger to American and Western security is Soviet power (Selection 49). In later portions of this chapter, illustrations will be found of the fact that American leaders have recognized the existence of both dangers, and have not accepted the belief that one is all-important, the other merely incidental.

In some areas of the world our stake is greater than in others. Policies which have proved successful in one part of the world may be futile or worse in another setting. Broadly stated, Europe—especially Western Europe—and Asia are the most important areas of the world for us—important in terms of the relations between their interests and security, and our own. Moreover, American policies toward the democratic, literate, and industrial nations of Western Europe cannot generally be applied without change to the poor, overpopulated, illiterate, and agricultural countries of Asia. For these reasons, the second section of this chapter is devoted to a consideration of the two major theaters of East-West conflict, Europe (Selection 50), and Asia (Selection 51).

In the last two sections, our objectives and the basic policies adopted to achieve them will be subjected to a critique of both the definition of our objectives and the methods by which we seek to attain them.   One shortcoming of many analyses of contemporary and ephemeral political phenomena is the fact that new factors continually arise, new Presidents take office, dictators die and others take their places; and much of what is said today may be outdated or partially lose its specific meaning by tomorrow.   By concentrating on *principles* of American foreign policy, we shall perhaps be able to avoid most shortcomings of this type.

Since President Eisenhower took office, there has been some movement away from the policy of containment and toward a policy of liberation.   Mr. Kennan, author of the policy of containment, has left the State Department.   Leading figures in the Government have indicated that they believe containment is a passive policy which leaves the initiative in the hands of the Soviet Union, and that the world situation calls for new and positive steps.   But evidence of this new approach is lacking at the moment.   Specifically, we have made it clear that any attempt on the part of Communist China to interfere in the war in Indo-China would meet with immediate American retaliation.   In this instance at least, the policy of containment appears to be still in force. Perhaps the basic difficulty with the position of supporters of the policy of liberation is that although containing the Soviet Union has been, and might continue to be, possible by engaging in a number of limited "police actions," no one seems to know how to liberate the captive nations behind the Iron Curtain without provoking World War III.

In a like manner, most of the other fundamental approaches and policies of the United States—the principle of "negotiation from strength," the Point Four Program, our policy in the United Nations, our economic policy—have presumably been reevaluated by the new Administration.   In none of these matters, however, has there yet been any evidence of significant change.   Only in the new approach of President Eisenhower to the international control of atomic energy has there been a qualitative departure from the policy of his predecessor.

Some question could be raised about the inclusion of Point Four and the exclusion of the policies of economic aid and military assistance. The latter two, however, can be classified under the principle of "negotiation from strength."   The Point Four Program is primarily long-range policy representing a fundamental approach on the level of others listed above.

Section three, then, opens with an analysis of the policy of containment (Selection 52). Next come a description of the process of creating situations of strength (Selection 53), two selections devoted to the principles and problems of the Point Four Program (Selections 54 and 55), and a description of American policy in the U.N. (Selection 56). One of President Eisenhower's major foreign policy declarations (Selection 57) is followed by an expression of the foreign economic policy of his administration (Selection 58). The section closes with the President's new proposals regarding the international control of atomic energy (Selection 59), and Secretary of State Dulles' statement on the policy of "Massive Retaliation" (Selection 60).

The fourth and last section consists of a critique of American foreign policy: Ex-President Herbert Hoover's restricted view of the national interest (Selection 61), an attack on the policy of containment (Selection 62), an analysis of the dangers inherent in the principle of negotiation from strength (Selection 63), a dissenting opinion on the merits of the Point Four Program (Selection 64), and a description and criticism of our specific policies in the United Nations (Selection 65).

The Nature of the East-West Conflict

48. THE IDEOLOGICAL CONFLICT*

Mr. Malik's statement offers an account of the conflict between East and West in ideological terms. The author sees some good in the Soviet system and points to some bad aspects of the Western system, but he is not neutral. He is intensely pro-Western. The thesis he develops has widespread support in Western circles.

Considerable difference of opinion exists between those who see the East-West conflict primarily in military-political terms and those, like Mr. Malik, who see it as a war of ideas and competing ways of life. Is the Soviet Union engaged in an "old-fashioned" struggle for power in which the communist ideology is merely one weapon among many? Or is the conflict one of competing ideologies in which the Communists rely upon military force as one weapon in their arsenal?

Which point of view dominates the thinking of American policy-

---

* Charles Malik, "War and Peace," a statement made before the Political Committee of the General Assembly of the United Nations, November 23, 1949. The author is Minister of Lebanon in the United States, and Chairman of the United Nations Commission on Human Rights.

makers at a given moment is of crucial importance. Those who accept an analysis of the conflict in ideological terms tend to adopt policies which stress ideological antidotes to communism—Marshall Plans for Western Europe, Point Four Programs to improve living standards in underdeveloped countries, and defensive alliances with only those nations which meet the test of ideological purity (not with Franco or Tito, for example). And those who adopt the other view tend to rely upon the concentration of adequate military counterforce to meet the Soviet threat, to stress military aid to Western Europe and elsewhere rather than economic assistance, and to support alliances with any power prepared to stand against the Soviet Union.

Since the East-West conflict is probably neither wholly ideological nor wholly military-political but a confusing mixture of the two, there are comparatively few "pure" types of analyses like Mr. Malik's. That is why his statement is especially valuable. By concentrating on one aspect of the problem, he gives us a clear view, free of the confusions which may enter when one tries to present the complete picture.

. . . . .

Peace presupposes mutual trust. Without the confidence, the sincere and convinced confidence, of one party in the peaceful nature of the ultimate motives and objectives of the other, there can be no sense of security, and therefore no peace.

Rightly or wrongly, the non-Communist world is convinced that Communism in general and the Soviet Union in particular do not really want peace; that every peace offensive on the part of the Soviet Union is but a strategic or tactical war-device determined by the particular situation of international relations and by the particular stage of the development of Communism: in reality just a phase of an over-all war plan.

It is this that we must examine. We must determine whether this deep-seated conviction of the non-Communist world, of the common man as well as the leaders of Western democracies, is justified or not. The question is not: Is the Western world really thus convinced? The question is: Is the Western world justified in being thus convinced?

To answer this crucial question, we have to turn to the Soviet Union itself and not to the Western world—to the record and practice of the Communist State in the past, and primarily to the teachings of Communism about the past, the present and the future.

Fortunately, the answer to this question is not far to seek. For there is an essential relationship between Communist philosophy and practice. The leaders of the Communist movement have also been its teachers and masters. Every decisive action undertaken by the Communist parties or the Communist States has been the direct result of a certain aspect of Communist philosophy; and the Communist teachers have invariably devoted considerable time and energy to the clarification of that aspect of the Communist ideology which sheds particular light upon, and determines the course of the action in question. Communism is an ideology formulated for, and unfolding itself in, and conditioning the course of a movement. It is to this ideology that we must turn to answer our question. What is then the Communist philosophy of revolution?

An examination of classical Marxism and its orthodox Soviet interpretation reveals four fundamental theses of Marxism with respect to revolution. These are: *first,* Marxism is essentially a revolutionary doctrine; *secondly,* the revolutionary change of the structure of society from the so-called bourgeois to the so-called proletarian pattern, which is the objective of the Communist movement, can be achieved only through the forcible overthrow of the existing regimes and the violent seizure of power; *thirdly,* even though the Communist revolution may succeed, and the dictatorship of the proletariat may be established securely in one country or a few countries, such success cannot be complete or secure unless it contributes effectively to the victory of the revolution in all countries; and, *fourthly,* even though the rise and the victory of the Communist revolution, in one country and eventually in all countries, is an inevitable result of the nature of capitalism and its final stage, imperialism, yet this inevitable result can and should be accelerated and actualized by human effort, namely by the action of Communist parties and States. Upon the truth of these four theses all the orthodox teachers of Communism agree.

The first thesis is that Communism is essentially a revolutionary doctrine and movement. For in accordance with its vision of reality, its conception of action is determined. The Marxist vision of reality is dialectical through and through. Hence, the Communist movement arising out of this dialectical metaphysics is necessarily dynamic and militant.

Nothing perhaps conveys this revolutionary spirit, which is essentially characteristic of Marxism, better than the opening and the closing words of the *Manifesto.* "A spectre is haunting Europe—the spectre of Communism," write Marx and Engels at the beginning of that celebrated document. They conclude it with the battle-cry:

The Communists disdain to conceal their views and aims. They openly declare that their ends can be attained only by the forcible overthrow of all existing social conditions. Let the ruling classes tremble at a Communist revolution. The proletarians have nothing to lose but their chains. They have a world to win.

Working men of all countries, unite!

We have it on the authority of Lenin that the essential and the distinctive characteristic of the Marxist ideology is its revolutionary aspect. And we have it on the authority of Stalin that the peculiar merit of Lenin is precisely his understanding of Marxism as essentially revolutionary, and his rescuing of Marxist revolutionism from the pacifist interpretation, or rather misinterpretation, of Marxism, made by the "opportunist" leaders of the Second International. Certainly Marx himself was not wrong when he described his own teachings as "in essence critical and revolutionary."

We come now to the second thesis. A teaching or movement may be revolutionary in one of two senses; either by merely advocating the total change of the ruling class of society and the radical transformation of existing civilization in all its patterns, structures and presuppositions; or by conceiving this radical transformation as possible only through the forcible seizure of power and the violent overthrow of the ruling classes and shattering of the established regimes. Apart from the question of political domination, the teachings of Jesus Christ were certainly revolutionary but only in the first sense. Communism is revolutionary in both senses. It has taken into its proud hands the course of events.

In 1871 Marx wrote to Kugelmann that "the precondition of any real people's revolution" is "not, as in the past, to transfer the bureaucratic and military machinery from one hand to the other, but to *break it up.*" Hence Lenin declares that "the replacement of the bourgeois by the proletarian state is impossible without a violent revolution."

Several corollaries follow from this thesis. (1) The revolutionary Communist is antagonistic to reform. "To a revolutionary," writes Stalin, "the main thing is revolutionary work and not reforms; to him reforms are by-products of the revolution. . . . The revolutionary will accept a reform in order to use it as an aid in combining legal work with illegal work, to intensify, under its cover, the illegal work for the revolutionary preparation of the masses for the overthrow of the bourgeoisie." (2) The revolutionary Communist is dissatisfied with parliamentary "opposition" and "legal measures" for the transformation of bourgeois society into proletarian society. "Does not the history of the revolutionary movement," asks Stalin, "show that the parliamentary struggle is only a school for and an aid in organizing the extra-parliamentary struggle of the proletariat, that under capitalism the fundamental problems of the working-class movement are solved by force, by the direct struggle of the proletarian masses, their general strike, their insurrection?" (3) The proletarian revolution must not wait until the proletariat constitute a majority in a country, but should take advantage, as Stalin says, paraphrasing the words of Lenin, "of any favourable international and internal situation to pierce the front of capitalism and hasten the general issue." (4) The proletariat must ally itself with any other revolutionary element in order to hasten the overthrow of the bourgeoisie: it must ally to itself the peasantry, the semi-proletarian elements of the population, and the revolutionary elements in colonies fighting for liberation from so-called imperialism.

The third thesis is that the Communist revolution,—which initially aims at being world-wide in its scope; and which, at its various stages, requires different and appropriate strategies; and which is at present in its third stage, after the victory of the proletariat in Russia,—the Communist revolution, I say, must, in the words of the *Manifesto,* "everywhere support every revolutionary movement against the existing social and political order of things" (p. 38); and, in the words of Lenin, must do "the utmost possible in one country *for* the development, support and awakening of the revolution *in all countries*"; and, in the words of Stalin, "must regard itself not as a self-sufficient entity but as an aid, as a means of hastening the victory of the proletariat in other countries."

The conception of strategy is very essential to Communist doctrine. It means, as Stalin defines it, "the determination of the direction of the main blow of the proletariat at a given stage of the revolution, the elaboration of a corresponding plan for the disposal of the revolutionary forces (the main and secondary reserves), the fight to carry out this plan throughout the given stage of the revolution." As the Communist revolution has already passed through two stages and is at present in its third stage, Communist strategy has changed accordingly, Stalin assures us. He defines the strategy of this third stage as follows:

Objective: to consolidate the dictatorship of the proletariat in one country, using it as a base for the overthrow of imperialism in all countries. The revolution is spreading beyond the confines of one country; the period of world revolution has commenced.

The main forces of the revolution: the dictatorship of the proletariat in one country, the revolutionary movement of the proletariat in all countries.

Main reserves: the semi-proletarian and small-peasant masses in the developed countries, the liberation movement in the colonies and dependent countries.

The reserves of the revolution Stalin divides into two classes, direct and indirect. Of the first he cites "the proletariat of the neighbouring countries"; of the second, the "contradictions, conflicts and wars . . .

among the bourgeois states hostile to the proletarian state, which can be utilized by the proletariat in its offensive or in manoeuvering in the event of a forced retreat."

It is the task of Communist leadership, which has in mind at every stage the ultimate victory of the revolution in all countries, "to make proper use," at the present stage, "of all these reserves for the achievement of the main object of the revolution."

Among the "principal conditions which ensure strategic leadership," Stalin emphasizes the following two:

First: the concentration of the main forces of the revolution at the enemy's most vulnerable spot at the decisive moment, when the revolution has already become ripe. . . .

Second: the selection of the moment for the decisive blow, of the moment for starting the insurrection.

Hence, also, one of the main tasks of the dictatorship of the proletariat, "on the morrow" of victory, is "to arm the revolution, to organize the army of the revolution for the struggle against foreign enemies, for the struggle against imperialism."

The fourth fundamental thesis of the Communist theory of revolution is that the rise and victory of the proletarian revolution is not merely inevitable, being dialectically determined by the nature of capitalism and imperialism, but also can be accelerated by human effort, and must be participated in by the class-conscious workers, provoked by the Communist Parties, and awakened and supported by the established Communist regimes. For Marxism is not merely a "scientific" theory which predicts what will happen, but also a call for what should happen; and Communism is not merely a spectatorial prediction of the inevitable, but also an exhortation for effective and fruitful struggle to make the inevitable actual. "Marx said that the materialist theory could not confine itself to explaining the world, that it must also change it," writes Stalin. The *Manifesto* emphasizes that Communists should "never cease, for a single instant, to instil into the working class the clearest possible recognition of the hostile antagonism between bourgeoisie and proletariat." (p. 38.) Referring to "the teaching of Marx and Engels regarding the inevitability of a violent revolution," Lenin says: "The necessity of systematically fostering among the masses *this* and just this point of view about violent revolution lies at the root of the *whole* of Marx's and Engels' teaching." Stalin says: "The Party cannot be a real party if it limits itself to registering what the masses of the working class feel and think. . . . The Party must stand at the head of the working class; it must see farther than the working class; it must lead the proletariat, and not follow in the tail of the spontaneous movement." In short, the masters and leaders of Communism are unanimous in their view of Communism as a mission, a call for revolution to which man must respond in action, and not merely a "scientific" prediction of the inevitability of the revolution.

There is a naïve doctrine of war preached by Communism, namely that the cause of war is to be sought in the capitalist system itself, in the imperialistic rivalries between nation-states for the division of the world between them. But we must assert that Communism's own doctrines of revolution are no less, perhaps even more, disturbing than imperialist rivalries and wars. Those who perpetually point to, emphasize, and seek to acerbate the flames of civil strife, who elevate revolution into a creed, and seek to make it a science, cannot claim to be the exclusive lovers of peace. No one today preaches that nations *ought* to go to war with each other: the Communists *do* preach that revolution and civil war are inherent in all but Communist societies, and *do* seek to push the revolution to its bitter end.

The war of class against class is no less savage and fierce than the war of nation against nation: the strife of brother against brother, of neighbour against neighbour, is no less horrible than strife between states: peace and harmony, once they are disturbed *within* a community, are no easier, and are possibly more difficult to restore than a disturbed peace and harmony between nations.

While our presence here in this organization is the proof that we have abandoned the idea of settling disputes between ourselves by force and the resort to war, the Communists have not abandoned the idea of revolution, the idea of civil war and class struggle.

In view of this Communist doctrine of revolution, is it any wonder that the non-Communist world sincerely and clearly believes that Communism and the Communist State *mean* world-wide revolution, the wholesale overthrow of existing regimes in all countries? Is it any wonder that the non-Communist world must look after its own defenses? So long as the Communist ideology is the foundation and determinant of Soviet policy, is it not absolutely stupid and naïve to suppose that the Soviet Union can really have a genuine desire for the security and stability of the rest of the world? Is it not obvious, except to the blind or frightened, that the only "peace" allowable by Communism is the peace of a forcibly communized and totalitarianly regimented world? Faced with the olive branches which Soviet spokesmen offer, we can only conclude that they are cynical if temporary tactics imposed by the present situation of international relations and valid only so long as this situation continues to prevail. They carry no assurance whatsoever that Communism has given up its own form of aggression. For, corresponding to the Communist outlook on historical development and international relations, there is a Communist form of threat to the peace *sui generis;* and international peace, as well as the security, stability, and sovereignty of non-Communist states, may be threatened not merely by the open attack of a Communist state against their borders, but also by its provocation and support of Communist revolutions within their borders. And therefore the non-Communist world will be perfectly stupid, and indeed about to dissolve, if it does not look feverishly to its own defenses against possible Communist aggression, whether external or internal, and if it does not seek adequately to meet the challenge of the Soviet Union.

These are harsh conclusions, but so are the premises from which they are drawn. I assure you it has not been a pleasure to draw these conclusions, for my little country is on good terms with the Soviet Union and obviously desires nothing but peace with that great Republic. It has been a source of infinite anguish to me that I had to face these facts. For truth is above politics, and so long as logic is logic the proposition that Communism, by damning the non-Communist world, *means* war and revolution, is as true as the multiplication table. I shall rejoice as a child if Mr. Vyshinsky can refute me, not indeed by vituperation and rhetoric, but by cold and honest reasoning. For the whole issue of war and peace in our generation hinges on whether Communism is or is not militant and revolutionary.

How can war be prevented? What can the United Nations do to prevent war? Is a Third World War inevitable? All these questions are misleading and utterly superficial. They pose the wrong question. They blind themselves to the real situation. It isn't as though we had a real state of peace dangerously shivering on the brink of war, concerning which therefore the supreme question would be how to prevent ourselves from going over the precipice. It is rather that we have a real state of fundamental conflict and unrest, and have had it on our hands for decades, and the supreme question is therefore how to resolve it, how to bring about a settlement, how to end the present time of troubles. It isn't as though there were already agreement and concord, and the supreme question therefore was how to prevent disagreement and discord. It is rather that there is already the most radical basic disagreement, and the supreme question therefore is how to achieve real, fundamental understanding. For there can be no greater disagreement than when one wants to eliminate your existence altogether. The Communist doctrine of war and revolution postulates the inevitability of war and conflict; it ascribes war to the every essence of history and existence; it cannot conceive truth without dialectical opposition; and therefore, according to it, everything must sooner or later issue into conflict. Dialectical material-ism is the primordial doctrine of eternal conflict. War is always there potentially. The original state is not rest and peace; the original state is struggle and change. Hence when rest and peace and understanding supervene, dialectical materialism at once suspects them: they are not natural! Dialectical materialism can rest its sight only on the vision of unrest and revolution. It cannot be happy except in the belief that we are already on our way to the abyss. This is what we are ultimately dealing with. I submit it is not an ordinary form of government, a common type of philosophy. It is a radical challenge which cannot be left unanswered. Therefore the question is not whether war can be prevented, for we are in a sense in the midst of it; the question is whether and how war can be ended. The question is not whether a Third World War is inevitable; the question is whether peace, with dialectical ma-terialism's absolute negation of peace, is really possible.

. . . . . .

There is a point-to-point antithesis between the outlook of Com-munism and the outlook of the highest traditions of the West with respect to the fundamental categories of existence.

The outlook of Communism on everything is determined by its fundamental materialist ontology. The nature of things, values and processes of history is accordingly simplified. In this oversimplification of the complex ultimate elements of existence lies the fundamental inadequacy of the Communist outlook in general.

Man, you and I in person, is conceived as a purely material being, whose spiritual and inward experiences and achievements are nothing more than modifications attendant upon and reducible to the movement of the matter which he is. The dignity of man—which the Classical tradition saw as consisting of man's rational and creative powers, and the Christian tradition as emanating from man's status as the Image of God destined for eternal life—is replaced, in the Communist philosophy, by the status of man as a unit in a multitude, a part of a greater whole, determined in his worth, like that whole itself, by his contribution to the production of material goods. So engrossed are the Communists in the materialistic phenomena of capital and labor and sheer economic goods that man is conceived, to use the famous phrase of Stalin, as at best "the most precious capital."

Religion, which the West has invariably conceived as the response of man to the Divine Presence, Communism conceives as a product of the economic structure of society, conditioned and determined in its rise as well as in its value by this structure. The deepest stirrings of the human soul in the presence of Divine Glory and in response to Divine Love—which have characterized saintliness and produced the best in philosophy and art in the West—are thus envisioned by Communism as nothing more than superstitions propagated by exploiters for the doping of the exploited, and are to be combated systematically, albeit tactfully. Religion is "the opium of the people."

The representative thinkers of the West regarded ethics as rooted essentially in the nature of man and in the absolute order of values, both of which are grounded in the transcendent order of the Divine. Communism rejects the very conception of absolute standards of ethics or unconditional moral judgments or obligations. "We say that our morality is wholly subordinated to the interests of the class-struggle of the proletariat," declares Lenin; "We deduce our morality from the facts and needs of the class-struggle of the proletariat." Mr. Vyshinsky writes:

Communist morality, of which Lenin spoke in 1920, penetrates into ever broadening strata of our society. The actions, the entire conduct, of the honorable Soviet citizen to social and personal life is dictated by the interests of our socialist revolution, the interests of the people, and by the task of the triumphant consummation of communism. For this reason implacable hatred for enemies of the revolution, struggling against foes of the people, against Trotsky-Bukharin spies and diversionists who acted for the bourgeoisie in striving to overthrow the existing socialist order in the USSR and to reestablish capitalism, is one of the most important principles of communist morality.

According to the genuine traditions of the West, the human person has a complex relation to society, which is such that, on the one hand and in one sense, the individual is a part of society, and, on the other hand and in another sense, the human person is a whole which cannot be reduced to the quantitative dimension of a mere part, and is of a certain ultimacy which cannot be suspended or relegated in favour of the interests of society; for man is a being to whom the order of the Divine and the Absolute is accessible, and in whose encounter with, and response to, this order, lies his worth and axiological ultimacy. It is on the grounds of this dual-status of the human person that his rights and obligations can be harmonized, and the rights of the person and those of society can be conceived as concordant and not discordant. To Communism, man's worth is conditional, not absolute; derivative, not ultimate. Man, every man, exists *for* society; society exists *for* the production of material goods. Man is a part of a greater whole, which, in turn, is instrumental to an impersonal and material end.

The deepest traditions of the West conceived of man as the subject of basic and inalienable and universal rights, rights which are based upon his very nature and which are embodied in natural law. From Sophocles to the Stoics and Cicero, and from St. Paul and the Church Fathers to St. Thomas, to Suarez and to Grotius, and even to the philosophers of the eighteenth century and the thinkers of the American and French Revolutions, natural law has been looked upon as the immediate basis of human rights. Communism rejects the very idea of intrinsic and inalienable human rights. Rights are not acknowledged and recognized —literally, re-cognized—and discovered by the Collective in the very nature of man, but are rather conferred upon the person by the collective, granted to the individual by society. They are conditionally given, and may be withdrawn. Rights that are absolute and unconditional, rights that are natural and inalienable, rights that inhere in the very nature and dignity of man as a person, are rejected by Communism in theory, and trampled by Communist states in practice.

Freedom of thought, freedom of conscience, freedom of expression, freedom of artistic creativity, freedom of association—and all the fundamental freedoms of man which pertain to the very dignity of personality—are tolerated to the extent, and only to the extent, to which they conform to the strict requirements of the interests of Communism as interpreted by Communist leadership. Mr. Vyshinsky writes:

Having given the toilers freedom of speech, assemblies, street parades, press, and so on, the Soviet government explicitly excluded the nonlabor classes from enjoyment of this freedom. . . . Having assured genuine freedom of press to the toilers, the Soviet government did not extend this freedom to the nonlaboring strata.

In our state, naturally, there is and can be no place for freedom of speech, press, and so on for the foes of socialism. . . . Freedom of speech, of the press, of assembly, of meetings, of street parades, and of demonstrations are the property of all the citizens in the USSR, fully guaranteed by the State upon the single condition that they be utilized in accord with the interest of the toilers and to the end of strengthening the socialistic social order.

The tragic fate of intellectuals, scientists, poets and musicians under Communist rule—whether of those who heroically remain loyal to their best lights at the risk of liquidation, or those who disgracefully retrace their steps and make public retractions—is not surprising. The Communist state—or, at least, the dictatorship of the proletariat—like any other form of totalitarianisn, necessarily suffocates spontaneity, inner dynamism, freedom and diversity. The spirit of man, which can be itself and its best self only in freedom and love and genuine communion, is choked and annihilated by totalitarianism. The loftiest heroism summoned in the human heart by an ideology of materialism is at best formal and one-sided, pathetically narrow in scope and tragically impoverished in content. The noblest achievements of the human spirit are initially unauthenticated by indoctrination, censorship and spiritual enslavement. Man is not respected by being declared "the most precious capital"; for man *is* only when he is viewed as a destiny-bearing and a destiny-burdened being, and when his relation to himself and to others and to God springs freely and responsibly from the inner depths of his soul.

The totalitarian control by the state of every source of independence and freedom is absolutely contrary to nature and man. That the state, the mere organ of government and order, is the source of every law, every truth, every norm of conduct, every social and economic relationship; that no science, no music, no economic activity, no philosophy, no art, no theology, is to be permitted except if it is state-licensed and state-controlled: all this is so false, so arrogant, so autocratic and tyrannical that no man who has drunk deep from the living waters of the Western Platonic-Christian tradition can possibly accept it. The State does not come in the first place; it comes in the tenth or fifteenth place. The University is higher than the State; the tradition of free inquiry is higher than the State; the Church is higher than the State; the family is higher than the State; natural law is higher than the State; the intimate circle of love and friendship is higher than the State; God is higher than the State; within limits, free economic activity is higher than the State. Far from the State determining the proper nature and limits of autonomy of these other things, they set proper limits to the activity of the State, so that if the State trespasses these limits, it ceases to be the State: it becomes a tyrant. By the word "higher" I mean that the University, the Church, the family, etc., contain sources of truth and being that are not only utterly independent of the State and belong to a separate realm altogether, but that this truth and being is qualitatively superior to any truth and being belonging to the State as such, so that a ruler, or king, or dictator, passing a scientist, or mother, or priest, or saint, or lover, or philosopher, should take off his hat and bow to him or her in all respect; and should in addition sit at his or her feet and learn truths which his State could never teach him. The destruction of all this intermediate plenum of freedom is the most grievous sin committed by totalitarianism, of whatever stripe.

.   .   .   .   .

It is fairly easy to work out a critique of Communism. The doctrine is only a hundred years old, and its effective entrenchment in the great Eurasian heartland is barely thirty years old.   Besides, its basic literature is fairly compact: you have the writings of Marx, Engels, Lenin and Stalin, which are fully accessible to any student.

It is far more difficult to elaborate a fundamental critique of the West. You do not have here a handful of masters as in the Communist world; you do not have a well-marked-out body of official literature.   Governmental policy and action is not informed by rigid theory as in the Communist world.   There is endless variety and difference, considerable looseness of connection, and a great deal of fumbling and muddling-through and empiricism.

Yet a general critique is necessary, because war and peace are not only a function of Communism: they depend also on the state of health and illness in Western culture.

There are many phases of Western life which are repulsively materialistic.   The spirit of business and gain, the maddening variety of things exciting your concupiscence, the utter selfishness of uncoördinated activity, all this is not something to attract and inspire.   To the superficial observer who is unable to penetrate to the core of love and truth which is still at the heart of the West, there is little to choose between the soulless materialism of the West and the militant materialism of the East.

There is a general weakening of moral fibre.   One gains the impression that the great fund of moral strength which has been handed down from the tears and labours of the ages is not being creatively replenished. There is thus unregeneration, a terrifying wastage of substance.

Quality is in eclipse.   Quantity and size dominate.   Not the better and truer, but the larger and physically stronger: these call forth moral approbation.

I must say in all humility that the leadership of the West in general does not seem to be adequate to the unprecedented challenges of the age.   There is a tragic dearth of men, men who are so genuinely in touch with the truth and with the hearts of their fellow men as to have only to open their mouths to be loved and believed and followed.   The world desperately cries for masters; for it is only the voice of conviction and truth that is going to save us.

There is a corresponding bankruptcy of fundamental ideas.   There is thus in this realm an unequal struggle for the hearts of men between Communism and the West.   Communism displays a set of generic ideas —I believe for the most part false—in which it passionately believes, for which Communists are willing—I believe misguidedly—to die.   There is no comparable ideological passion in the West.   The talk about democracy, freedom, representative government, is woefully inadequate: it deals for the most part with pure form, sheer external machinery. It does not satisfy man's deepest cravings for friendship and understanding and truth and love.

Politically the West will not serve the cause of peace by allying itself with dark regimes just because it is more expedient not to disturb them. Such regimes are running sores on the body politic of humanity. The West must be honest enough to rebuke and challenge them. It must firmly lead them into the broad ways of responsible change. Their peoples are poised to see whether the West acts from principle or from expediency. And the subversive whispers of world revolution become more and more potent the more these peoples despair of their rulers and the West.

Nor does it do merely to reject Communism. A positive alternative must be suggested. The only effective answer to Communism is a genuine spiritualized materialism which seeks to remove every trace of social injustice without loss of the higher values which constitute the very soul of the West. Communism cannot be met by a mere *nay;* it requires a mighty *yea* which will do full justice to man's material needs but will at the same time place them in their subordinate position in the scale of values.

The complaint is often made that our debates in the United Nations degenerate into "propaganda." But propaganda can be overcome only by lifting the quality of debate to a higher plane. If profound ideological themes were introduced, then all attempts at propaganda would appear silly and crude. If there is propaganda, it is only because there is on the other hand ideological impotence. The tragedy of the world today is that the traditions which embody the deepest truth are not bothering clearly, sufficiently, responsibly, boldly to articulate themselves.

Nor is it sufficient in this cruel century to be happy and self-sufficient. You must step forth and lead, and not only in material things. It is not enough to realize good institutions and to leave it to others to copy them. For man isn't only an ape: he does not only mimic the good example of others. Man thirsts after ideas. If the habits and institutions of the West are not adapted for the production of a ringing message, full of content and truth, satisfying the mind, appealing to the heart, firing the will, a message on which one can stake his whole life, then in the present world, in which there is, perhaps as never before, a universal hunger for truth and justice and rest, the West cannot lead. Leadership must pass on to others, no matter how perverted and false these others might be. For the *Logos* prefers and can finally utilize a false prophet far better than no prophet at all.

If your only export in these realms is the silent example of flourishing political institutions and happy human relations, you cannot lead.   If your only export is a distant reputation for wealth and prosperity and order, you cannot lead.   Nor can you really lead if you send forth to others only expert advice and technical assistance.   To be able to lead and save yourself and others, you must above everything else address their mind and soul.   Your tradition, rooted in the glorious Græco-Roman-Hebrew-Christian-Western-European-humane outlook, supplies you with all the necessary presuppositions for leadership.   All you have to do is to be the deepest you already are.   The challenge of this epoch is not Communism, but is whether Western society, conceived in the joyous liberties of the Greek city-states and nurtured on Christian charity, can still recover from the worship of false and alien gods and return to its authentic sources.   The challenge of the moment is whether modern man, distracted and overwhelmed by himself and by the world, can still regain the original integrity of his soul.

Whatever be the weakness and decadence of the West, it still has one saving glory: the University is free, the Church is free.   It is a great thing to preserve unbroken the tradition of free inquiry started by Plato and Aristotle, and the tradition of love started by God.   Truth can still be sought and God can still be loved and proclaimed in joy and freedom.   And this fact alone is going to save us.   It will not be by pacts, or by atomic bombs, or by economic arrangements, or by the United Nations, that peace will be established, but by the freedom of the Church and the University each to be itself.   Communism does not know what it has done when it subjected the Church and the University to its own dictates.

·   ·   ·   ·   ·

The two worlds, then, face each other across a terrible chasm.   The Communist world, believing in the rottenness of the non-Communist world, in the inevitability of its downfall, in the danger to itself from any too protracted a delay in that downfall, must needs, by the compulsion of its own doctrine, do everything in its power to promote and hasten that catastrophic event.   It is therefore necessarily goaded to intervene.   The method it advocates is violent revolution; the promise it holds out is material security, social justice and the abolition of discrimination and exploitation.   This, then, is the great challenge facing us from the other side of the chasm.   The history of the present generation will consist mainly in the response we shall make to this challenge.

If the Western world adopts Communist methods, it will betray its dearest traditions.   It will then rebel against itself.   Communism will have won.   For nothing pleases Communism more than to see the West forsake its holy tradition of love and persuasion.   If, on the other hand, the West holds out the Communist promise alone, again it will betray itself.   For the West lives under, and has been blessed by the sway of the teaching that it is not by bread and security alone that man liveth. The greatest expression of this dialectic between security and freedom, and of the genuine Western position in this regard, was made precisely by a Russian; namely, by Dostoyevsky in the Grand Inquisitor in *The Brothers Karamazov*.   The only adequate response to the Communist challenge is the rediscovery and the reaffirmation by the West of the highest spiritual values by which it has lived and prospered and moved the ages.

It ought to be very bluntly stated that a world that is relatively imperfect from the economic and material point of view, but that retains at its heart the core of love and truth and freedom which has for three thousand years characterized Western civilization at its best, is vastly to be preferred to any world, no matter how absolutely perfect materially and economically, which rejects this creative core of love and truth and freedom.   The perfect soul can always correct the imperfect body, but where there is no soul, even the most perfect body is soon but dust and ashes.

The challenge then is twofold.   Are the benefits promised by Communism unattainable except by Communist means, namely by subversion, violence and revolution?   Whatever the means, are Communist values and benefits unattainable except at the cost of the more traditional values which make up in reality the soul of the West?

And this twofold challenge imposes on the Western world the following task: how to attain all the positive and good ends which Communism boasts of *without* resorting to Communist means, and *without* destroying the higher tested values of Western civilization at its best, namely freedom, responsibility of the individual, the primacy of the personal and spiritual and intellectual, the trust in reason and the belief in God.

In order to be able to meet this formidable challenge in its own way, the non-Communist world must first of all, and as a purely negative condition, look after its own defenses.   The non-Communist world cannot afford to assume that where militant Communism could strike and could get away with it, it would not strike.

Accepting the challenge, keeping possible Communist intervention at bay, utilizing to the full its own infinite positive resources, sharing its life and goods in larger justice and freedom, the Western world ought to develop a strong and healthy civilization.   All the Communist gains will be there, without the Communist losses. In the fullness of time the Communist world will find itself at a tremendous disadvantage. It will behold across the chasm, even if dimly, an image of real beauty and strength. And it might then deign to meet and discuss and come to terms. Then perhaps the Russian soul, with her deep spirituality and her genuine urge at universalism, will reaffirm itself, and the offshoot, which is Communism, will come back to its origin, chastened and penitent.

49. THE STRUGGLE FOR POWER *

The views of the Research and Policy Committee are dramatically opposed to those of Mr. Malik. The Committee understands the East-West conflict as exclusively a power conflict. Mr. Malik only suggested that there was a struggle between rival powers and concentrated his attention upon the ideological conflict; the Committee speaks about ideology as merely another weapon in the military-political conflict.

The threat to our security exists because of the expansion of Soviet power in the wake of the war and because of unsettled conditions in many parts of the non-communist world which provide temptation and opportunity for further expansion of communist power. The power of the Soviet bloc has thus come into conflict with our interests or those of our allies at many points around the world.

To assess the nature and extent of the threat, therefore, two questions may be asked: What are the intentions of the Soviet Union and what are its capabilities, its strengths and weaknesses, for carrying them out? What is the willingness and the ability of the non-communist countries, their strengths and weaknesses, to resist political, military and other action by the Soviets and their satellites, allies and supporters?

We must also ask to what extent the threat to our security is a military threat—that is, a threat of all-out war with the Soviet Union. And we must ask to what extent it is a threat whose present nature is political and economic. For example, how great is the threat that, as a result of

* "The Threat to Our National Security," a statement on national policy by the Research and Policy Committee of the Committee for Economic Development, New York, September, 1952, pp. 3-11. The Committee for Economic Development is a "non-profit organization of 145 leading businessmen and educators." It is concerned with "objective economic research and education." It is supported by "voluntary contributions from business and industry and is non-partisan and non-political."

political and economic deterioration in Europe and Asia and of local communist subversion or successful aggression, the morale of the non-communist world may gradually decline, and the United States might be forced into general war at some later time?   How great is the threat that, as a result of such developments, the United States might be diplomatically isolated to the extent that we would eventually be in danger of losing a war with the Soviet Union?

SOVIET INTENTIONS

The aims and methods of Soviet foreign policy can be estimated from two principal sources.   One is the teachings and writings which make up the official Marxist-Leninist-Stalinist doctrine and are accepted as authoritative by the Communist Party of the Soviet Union and by other national communist parties.   The other is the foreign policy which the U.S.S.R. has actually followed, and particularly its policy during and since World War II.

Communist doctrine holds that real international peace and security are impossible on this side of a successful world communist revolution. It holds that the communist and "capitalist" (i.e., all non-communist) economic and political systems are, by necessity, hostile to each other. It holds that the two systems must inevitably come into violent collision and that, in the final struggle, communism will triumph.   So much is reasonably clear.   But communist doctrine gives no clear-cut answer to the question: How does the Soviet Government believe that this final showdown will or should occur?   Evidence may be found in communist writings and speeches of the belief that the non-communist world will in time be weakened by its own internal conflicts, to the point where it can be fairly easily pushed over by a combination of military and other means.   Evidence can also be found of a belief that the final showdown will result from a serious economic crisis in the capitalist world which will lead to an "imperialist war" against the Soviet Union.

Nor does communist doctrine alone provide a basis for predicting Soviet foreign policy.   The evidence suggests no ideological or moral reluctance on their part to use war, local or general, as an instrument of foreign policy.   On the other hand, the men of the Kremlin do not seem to think in terms of a fixed timetable or date by which their objective, world communism (that is, a world empire under Soviet domination) must be achieved.   Unlike Hitler, they do not seem to be under a compulsion to reach their goal quickly, within the lifetime of their present leaders.   Thus, while communist doctrine makes clear the final aim of Soviet policy, helps to explain the implacable hostility which the Soviet

Government shows toward other countries, and reveals something of their principles of strategy and tactics, it does not by itself make clear the more immediate intentions of Soviet foreign policy. These must therefore be estimated primarily on the evidence of past Soviet policy, particularly since World War II.

That evidence suggests that Soviet policy is aggressive and expansionist but that, so far at least, it has been careful to avoid precipitating a general war with the United States. It suggests that the U.S.S.R. will do everything in its power short of general war to weaken, confuse, divide, demoralize and subvert free countries. It suggests that this, rather than all-out war, will be the preferred Soviet strategy at least for the next few years.

In the present situation of the world, there are nevertheless major risks of all-out war. Our estimate of Soviet intentions may be mistaken; the Soviets may in fact be planning total war or steps which would lead to it. General war could break out accidentally as the result of a major miscalculation by one side of the other's reactions to its moves. It is therefore necessary also to prepare against the contingency that there may be an all-out war within the next few years.

Finally, there is no evidence that the shorter-run intentions of Soviet foreign policy are fixed and rigid. Communist doctrine makes much of realism and of flexibility and opportunism in strategy and tactics. The Soviets will take advantage of opportunities presented by other countries for Soviet expansion and communist subversion. At the same time, it seems probable that Soviet foreign policy will be highly flexible and responsive to American actions, adapting to changes in our foreign and military policy.

SOVIET STRENGTHS AND WEAKNESSES

The output of Soviet industry and the capacity of the Soviet economy to produce the industrial materials essential for war are far below those of the American economy. For example, in 1950, Soviet coal production is estimated at 52%, crude oil at 14%, steel at 29%, copper at 31%, electric power at 23% and automotive vehicles at 5% of our own. Moreover, food production and the low productivity of agricultural labor are weak points in the Soviet economy. Their transportation system is inadequate and chronically overburdened. But these figures and facts do not tell the whole story. Since 1945, Soviet policy has placed a very much heavier emphasis on military output and on strengthening the "mobilization base" of its economy than has American policy. As a result, the Soviet economy, despite its much smaller overall industrial capacity and the need to repair war damage, has been able to maintain very large military forces and a high level of munitions output, as well as to produce atomic weapons.

The Soviets' military effort, with its emphasis on ground forces and tactical air power, appears to have given them a considerable military superiority on most of the continent of Europe and Asia. But the local superiority of Soviet military power in most of Eurasia, though it would doubtless permit the Soviet armies to win battles and gain territory, would not necessarily determine the outcome of a third world war. In all-out war, we would rely on our greatly superior economic potential and our ability to damage their industry and disrupt their weak and vulnerable transport system by strategic bombardment from bases within reach of their industrial centers to determine the final outcome.

Yet this reliance is safe only if we have prepared sufficiently to protect our essential industry and our strategic striking power from a surprise knockout; and if we and our allies have developed a sufficient force in being and a broad enough "mobilization base" to be able to retain necessary bases in Europe, Asia and Africa and to make a rapid come-back on the ground as well as in the air.

From a political point of view, the Soviet Union's ability to maintain large forces in peacetime and to persuade or coerce its satellites and its Chinese allies to do likewise, gives Moscow an important political weapon with which to intimidate neighboring non-communist countries. Another major asset of the Soviet Government, is, of course, its ability to organize, direct and maintain the loyalty of communist fifth columns abroad. Though these local communist organizations are typically quite small, they are, in a number of non-communist countries, the most tightly disciplined and effective political group, able to exploit local trouble in furtherance of Soviet strategy.

It is, however, easy to exaggerate both the military and the political strength of the Soviet Union and the communist bloc. In the longer run, perhaps, the political weaknesses of the Soviet Union and its foreign empire may be the most significant. Potential disaffection within the Soviet Union, for example in the Ukraine, is a persistent factor of weakness. In the Eastern European satellites, the powerful force of national loyalty works against the Soviet imperial regime and cannot be used to reinforce it as in Russia. The corrosive effects of Titoism on the reliability of satellite military forces and on economic support appear to be emerging. The continuous movement of refugees past the iron curtain in Europe, despite the extreme hazards of escape and the present inadequate provision in Western countries for their care, and the never-ending succession of purges and campaigns of intimidation, show how little success the communists have had in arousing mass loyalty to the satellite regimes.

Potentially, a serious political weakness of the communist bloc lies in the uncertain relationship between the Kremlin and its new Chinese allies. If the Peiping regime consolidates its position and grows in self-confidence, will the totalitarian aims of Soviet imperialism collide with Chinese national communism? Looking further ahead, the masters of the Kremlin should have grave cause for concern over the longest land frontier in the world which separates the vast and comparatively empty spaces of Siberia from China, with its very rapid population growth and its age-old tradition of expansion.

In sum, provided our military preparations are adequate to protect our industry from a surprise knockout, to build a broad mobilization base and to retain necessary bases in Europe, Asia and Africa, three conclusions may be drawn about the military threat to our security during the next few years:

(1) It does not appear likely that the Soviet Union will deliberately choose general war during the next few years in preference to a more gradual strategy for achieving its aim: a world Soviet empire.

(2) There are, nevertheless, inherent in the present situation of the world, major risks of all-out war.

(3) If total war occurs during the next few years, we should be able to win it.

What, then, of the political and economic aspects of the threat to our security from Soviet communism—in the next few years and at a later time? To answer this question it is first necessary to review present political and economic conditions in the non-communist world.

THE DANGER TO OUR SECURITY ARISING FROM POLITICAL AND ECONOMIC DETERIORATION IN THE NON-COMMUNIST WORLD

American foreign policy since World War II has been centrally concerned with an effort to restore the economic health and political stability of that part of the Eurasian continent which is not under Soviet or communist control. This American effort has been a response to a growing recognition of the serious character of the economic and political problems of Europe, the Middle East, Southeast Asia and Japan.

Nearly everywhere the masses of the people are demanding better living standards. In the United States, blessed with a very large and dynamic economy, a united people and a strong democratic tradition, our economic and political systems have risen to this need; the same is true of a few other countries. But in much of Western Europe, the economic expansion necessary to satisfy desires for a higher standard of living is not taking place. In much of Asia, internal order, stable government, economic and social reform and other basic conditions of economic progress and political stability are yet to be achieved. Throughout much of the world there has been a weakening of faith in existing institutions, a decline of traditional loyalties and a corresponding lack of effective non-communist leadership.

It is these conditions and the discontent and disaffection they create which make Soviet communism really dangerous to Europe and Asia. For communism offers to these people a way of expressing resentment or despair and, however falsely, an apparent escape from a seemingly hopeless present.

What is the connection between this and American security? In the case of Western continental Europe, the connection is clear. If we should permit this region or a major part of it to fall into communist hands, the result would be a very large shift in the present balance of economic power and military potential between East and West. For this reason, the United States has, by the North Atlantic Treaty and the NATO rearmament effort, in effect informed the U.S.S.R. that we consider the freedom of Western Europe vital to our security and that the invasion of this region by major communist forces would be the beginning of general war. Had we not made this perfectly clear, the Soviets might have been tempted to seize a part or all of Western Europe, with the hope that we would not intervene.

The situation of Japan is somewhat similar: the loss of Japan to the communists would make a major difference in the balance of power in Asia and the Pacific. For that reason, we have made a mutual security agreement with the Japanese Government, presumably with the immediate aim of decreasing the danger that the Soviets or their allies might be tempted to take aggressive actions against Japan.

When we consider the other areas now immediately vulnerable to communist aggression or subversion—the Middle East and parts of Southeast Asia—the considerations are less clear cut. If it is assumed that the Soviet Union does not want general war now or in the next few years, may it not also be assumed that the Soviets are unlikely to launch large scale invasions by Soviet or satellite troops against Western Europe and Japan, which are protected by clear-cut American security guarantees and mutual security arrangements? In these circumstances, would we not expect the Soviets to reserve their more openly aggressive and military tactics for areas like Southern Korea and Indo-China, which are not strategically vital to the United States and where, therefore, the communists may hope to make dramatic gains without resistance or, at the worst, to be engaged in a conflict which will remain localized? This was, from all appearances, the Soviet reasoning about the Korean aggression.

Such communist actions present us with a difficult problem. The country attacked may not be vital to our security from a strictly military point of view. The Soviets can therefore hope that we and our allies will not resist or, having resisted initially, will tire of an indecisive contest and make a settlement favorable to the communists—giving them, perhaps, a position from which they can later renew the attack with greater chances of success. But, if we should fail to resist such communist tactics or, better, to deter them, the effects on political strength and morale in other parts of the non-communist world would be serious.

This conclusion is most important for an understanding of the American security problem. What we may have most to fear over the next few years is the effect of further piecemeal Soviet or communist political or military gains on the morale and the cohesion of the free nations, and particularly on their willingness to cooperate with each other and with us for their own security and ours. The danger is that a series of such gains would give rise in the more vulnerable areas, including Western Europe, to a wave of defeatism and neutralism and a conviction of the futility or the danger of further resistance of communism.

Moreover, serious political and economic deterioration in some non-communist countries, even if it involves no immediate threat of communist subversion, could have a similar effect. The state of political and economic health in Europe and Asia makes further crises and deterioration possible.

If, by failure of the United States and other countries to counter it effectively, the communists were allowed to succeed in a strategy of attrition, and if the non-communist world allows the demoralizing effects of future communist successes to be compounded by serious political and economic crises, the United States could be faced in a few years time with an extremely serious situation, and a grave danger of general war. One possibility is that the Soviets might be so emboldened by increasing disunity in the free world that they might take actions which would force the United States into a general war. Another possibility which cannot be lightly dismissed is that a series of further communist successes and the weakening or collapse of Western alliances might cause the United States to take actions—such as full mobilization—which would lead the Soviets to conclude that war was imminent and that they had better strike first. A third possibility is that Americans might become so disheartened by communist gains and by the growth of neutralist sentiment in Europe and Asia that the United States might retreat into isolationism—making it possible for the Soviets over a period of several years to take control of Western Europe and Japan and to prepare a direct assault on the Western Hemisphere.

We mention these possibilities, not because we consider them in any sense inevitable, but because we believe Americans should face realistically what might happen if American policy is inadequate.

To summarize: Provided the American and allied military build-up is adequate in the sense indicated above, the principal threat to our security over the next few years does not appear to be a danger of defeat in general war with the Soviet Union. Nor is it the most likely assumption that the Soviets will in the next few years deliberately choose general war, in preference to a more gradual strategy, to achieve their goal of world-wide empire. We must, nevertheless, recognize the dangers of general war inherent in the present world situation. The principal threat to American security appears to us to be that, in the absence of adequate action by the United States and its allies, the economic weakness and political instability of many non-communist countries will lead to piecemeal communist gains and periodic crises within the free world, which will undermine its morale and political solidarity and isolate the United States. Unless prevented by successful policies, positive as well as defensive, this deterioration could lead, after a few years, to a most serious danger of general war, and even to a situation in which the Soviets' relative power had been so augmented by territorial gains or alliances in Europe and Asia that they could successfully attack the Western Hemisphere.

⌒ ୨ୣ⌒

Major Theatres of U.S.—Soviet Conflict

50. Our Stake In Europe *

Mr. Earle examines the nature of America's stake in Europe. He believes that the Truman Doctrine, the Marshall Plan, and American collaboration in European defense plans offer conclusive evidence that the United States realizes the extent of its interests in Europe and is willing to translate these interests into specific assistance, both military and economic.

*Edward Mead Earle, "A Half-Century of American Foreign Policy: Our Stake in Europe, 1898-1948," *Political Science Quarterly,* Vol. LXIV, June, 1949, pp. 168-188. The author is a member of the Institute for Advanced ·Study, Princeton, New Jersey.

•   •   •   •   •

. . . Our stake in Europe is and always has been greater, infinitely greater, than our stake in the Far East.   Indeed it is part of our stake in the Far East, for, as Tyler Dennett has pointed out, the Far East is only the backdoor of Europe.   For three centuries or more the destinies of the world, including those of the Far East, have been settled on the battlefields or at the council tables of Europe.   The sea lanes of the Atlantic, in peace and war, historically have been a more critical national interest to us than the broad reaches of the Pacific.   Judged by the experience of two world wars—to go no further back in our history—we have no strategic interest anywhere comparable to our stake in the coastal states of Western Europe and their insular and continental possessions in the Atlantic basin.

We gave emphatic recognition to these truths when, at the very outset of World War II, we decided to treat Germany as the heart, brain and fighting edge of the entire Axis coalition; accordingly we gave top priority in men and weapons to the European theatre.   And the defeat of Japan, it should be remembered, was achieved on the beaches of Normandy and in the skies over Berlin as well as in the savage fighting at Iwo and in the relentless bombing of the Japanese homeland by the B-29's. (Curiously enough, the Japanese themselves—much more remote from Europe than we, and with no cultural ties with European peoples—have always understood that the "strife of Europe" was an essential element, or a conditioning factor, in their plans for imperial aggrandizement. They have never deluded themselves into believing that the politics of Europe were of no concern to them.)

However, not even the most enthusiastic proponent of world power for the United States would have been so prescient or so temerarious fifty years ago as to prophesy that the United States would become as deeply involved in Europe as it is today.   The earliest and most determined critics of our "traditional policy of non-interference in European affairs" would concede that we had come far and fast since 1914.   The "Truman Doctrine," the Marshall Plan, and the prospective military alliance with the Western European nations are a recognition of the fact—so often and so heatedly denied, officially and otherwise, during the past half-century—that as a nation we have a large stake in the economic stability and political equilibrium of Europe.   Our present policies presume, if you like, that we have a vital interest—as some have long insisted—in the balance of power in Europe.   But they go even further and assert that we intend to play a conscious and, presumably, a decisive part in the maintenance of that balance.   They proclaim, as we have so frequently proclaimed in the past, that we have a sympathetic concern with the cause of freedom in the European world; but here again they go further and . . . make it clear that we intend to translate that concern into political and economic support.

One may quote in this connection the report of 25 February 1948, of the Senate Committee on Foreign Relations on S. 2202, "a bill to promote the general welfare, national interest, and foreign policy of the United States through necessary economic and financial assistance to foreign countries which undertake to co-operate with each other in the establishment and maintenance of economic conditions essential to a peaceful and prosperous world":

The American people, victorious in battle, look out upon a world disrupted by war and shaken by its aftermath. Our efforts to win back to peace have included unswerving support of the United Nations, as well as generous assistance to foreign countries in need of aid. The decision which must now be made is whether we shall continue the effort to achieve our goal: The establishment of a stable world with free political institutions and the rule of law. Events of the next few years may well decide the issue. World stability and European stability are inseparable; free institutions and genuine independence cannot perish in Europe and be secure in the rest of the world. We must therefore shape our course upon the basis of our determination whether the countries of Europe can preserve their liberties and independence if they do not achieve economic recovery. The committee is convinced they cannot.

The Committee here places its primary emphasis upon economic assistance by the United States to the nations of Europe; but the collateral evidence, including the Economic Recovery Act itself, makes it plain that our motives and interests are political as well. "It is declared to be the policy of the people of the United States [reads the Act] to sustain and strengthen principles of individual liberty, free institutions, and genuine independence in Europe" by participation in a joint recovery program. It would be a mistake to underestimate our deep-rooted and heartfelt concern for the welfare of our fellow men in Europe; no decent American would leave unheard or unanswered the call for help which comes from those who are hungry, cold, unclothed, or who otherwise have been victimized by the war and its resultant devastation. In addition, however, the Economic Recovery Program is an intelligent recognition on our part that wealth is a form of power, that economic means can be used to promote the political interests of the United States, broadly conceived—what Washington called our "interest guided by justice." E.R.P., therefore, is intelligent statecraft founded upon an enlightened self-interest. It is concerned, among other things, with helping the Western European states to resist Soviet subversion or aggression, which we cannot regard as other than "dangerous to our peace and safety."

In this sense it must be admitted that we are participants in an undeclared civil war in Europe. If we are thereby involved in an ideological struggle with the Soviet Union it is because we are an integral part of Western European civilization and have a vital interest in its survival. Once more, as in 1917 and in 1940, we face the disheartening prospect that the problems of Europe will be resolved either by the hegemony of a single Power or by the restoration of some sort of balance of power. The former alternative would be as inacceptable to Europe and to us as it was in the days of Louis XIV, Napoleon, William II, and Hitler. The latter—the restoration of a balance of power—requires continuous and large-scale participation of the United States in European affairs. To the latter course we have committed ourselves.

. . . . .

When the struggle with Germany was over in 1945, Europe was cold and hungry, bleeding from a thousand wounds, living 'midst rubble and devastation. Her industry was shattered, the delicate arteries of her transportation system severed at innumerable places, the fertility of her soil sadly depleted. She was suffering, too, from the trauma of war and occupation. Her political and social fabric was rent by dissension and treason. According to all pat formulas Europe, in such dire straits, should have gone Communist. To be sure, communism took great strides forward, as it is almost certain to do where there is widespread misery and confusion; but communism was not embraced by Europe, and communism did not conquer Europe. With the single exception of Czechoslovakia—a very special case—it was only behind the lines of the Red Army that Communist governments were installed; and even there they were brought into being, in most instances, by a carefully trained Fifth Column aided by the persuasive powers of bayonet, truncheon and noose. Communism has not cashed in, as its high priests believed it would, on "imperialist war."

We cannot believe, therefore, that the peoples of Western Europe, "if left to themselves, would embrace it of their own accord"; but they are not being left to themselves. They are being bullied and subverted. Because we have so great a stake in the recovery, the independence and the security of the nations of the Atlantic World we cannot regard other "than as a manifestation of an unfriendly disposition toward the United

States" the effort of any Power to menace their freedom or to intervene in their affairs "for the purpose of oppressing them, or in controlling in any other manner their destiny."

A specter is haunting Europe, and it is not the specter of communism. It is the specter of Soviet imperialism, Soviet subversive methods, and Soviet military power. Were Europe's problems exclusively or even primarily those of recovery from an appallingly destructive war, they would be solved, however slowly and arduously; Europe always has shown extraordinary resilience to war. But the problem of Western Europe is, rather, that of assuring survival of the institutions under which it has lived, with change and variation, since the great British and French revolutions. These institutions are threatened by Soviet power, resourcefully and pitilessly exerted to its own ends. To this power only equal or greater power can be interposed. At the moment the chief, perhaps the only, hope of those who still cherish the Western European heritage—from which America itself was born—is American power. Without power even the righteous perish; hence the day is come when the New World indeed is called upon to redress the balance of the Old.

It is a new, distasteful experience for Americans to realize that the recovery and stability of the world cannot be achieved or maintained without active participation by them in European affairs. It is likewise a new, and even more distasteful, experience to know that such participation will require, for an indefinite future, that we be a formidable military power. For we do not like power; we distrust it and detest it. It was also a new, and distasteful, experience for the American nation to find itself the object of a hostile Axis coalition in 1940 and the victim of a sneak attack on American soil in 1941. However, power is not necessarily coarse, brutal and sordid; it can be used with a "decent respect to the opinions of mankind." It can be the guardian of right and freedom as well as of national interest. Even in the service of the best cause, it must be remembered, power must be used with dignity, restraint, wisdom, and what a colleague of mine calls "style." If it is so used, the ultimate verdict upon our time need not be, what Gibbon called all history, "a record of the crimes, follies, and misfortunes of mankind."

51. THE PROBLEM OF ASIA *

Europe-first and Asia-first policies have contended for primacy among American policy makers from the Japanese attack on Pearl Harbor to the present day. The basic argument of the "Europe-Firsters" can be described as follows: The United States does not have the power to be equally effective in all parts of the world at the same time. The defense of Europe is much more closely linked to the security of the United States than the defense of Asia. In the short run, therefore, we have no choice but to apply the preponderant part of our military and economic assistance to Europe. This orientation was essentially the basis for General Omar Bradley's remark that an extension of the Korean War to the Chinese mainland would involve us in "the wrong war, at the wrong place, at the wrong time, and with the wrong enemy." The basic argument of the "Asia-Firsters" can be described as follows: It is futile to talk of saving Europe while Asia, the most populous part of the world, is in imminent peril of falling to the communists. The loss of China to communism and the war in Korea are just some of the fruits of a policy of neglect. In the long run, if we save Europe and lose Asia, we shall have lost the contest with communism. In essence, these are the arguments upon which the position of General Douglas MacArthur is based.

Perhaps the basic differences in the two approaches stem from the fact that the problems of the two areas are different. In Europe we must maintain an existing system of states, and ensure their continued independence and territorial integrity. In Asia, the problem is not to maintain but to improve—not merely to return living standards up to a pre-World War II level, but to alleviate long-established conditions of appalling misery and poverty.

Mr. Douglas here describes the problem of Asia. He is not an "Asia-Firster," but he believes that conditions are dangerous, and he suggests an American policy which will prevent Asia's turning to communism for an answer to its problems.

One who loses himself in the villages of Asia for weeks on end returns to America profoundly disturbed. The America he loves is not the America the people of Asia see. The attitudes we express, the words we use, the policies we pursue too often injure rather than help the cause of freedom-loving people. The reason is that we live in one world, the

---

* William O. Douglas, *Strange Lands and Friendly People* (New York: Harper and Brothers, 1951), pp. 315-327. Copyright, 1951, by William O. Douglas. The author is Associate Justice of the United States Supreme Court.

people of Asia in a different world. They do not understand us nor we them. To most Americans Asia is a continent of strange lands and strange people. The attitudes and viewpoints of Arabs, Persians, and Indians often puzzle us. They react in ways that frequently fill us with doubt and alarm. At times they seem to be mere instruments of Russian policy, venting their spleen on us. They seem remote and aloof, even unwilling to understand us. Our doubts and suspicions grow until we wonder if they are not in truth aligned with Russia for our ultimate destruction. Being filled with confusion we lose our power and strength. As the Bhagavad Gita says, "Confusion is not the nature of a leader."

The world is different than we in America have thought. Asia is in revolution. There are rumblings in every village from the Mediterranean to the Pacific. A force is gathering for mighty effort. We think of that force as communistic. Communists exploit the situation, stirring every discontent and making the pot boil. The revolutions which are brewing are not, however, Communist in origin nor will they end even if Soviet Russia is crushed through war. *The revolutionaries are hungry men who have been exploited from time out of mind. This is the century of their awakening and mobilization.*

What I saw and heard as I traveled this vast territory that lies under the southern rim of Russia reminded me very much of what I had read about other revolutions. The spirit that motivates these people is pretty much the same as the spirit that inspired the French and the American Revolutions. The abuses against which our American forebears protested in 1776 were piled high. They are listed in our Declaration of Independence: dissolution of legislative bodies by the King; corruption of judges; maintenance of a standing army and quartering of troops among the people; imposition of taxes without the consent of the colonies; transporting citizens beyond the seas for trial of offenses committed here. These and other practices of the King brought our people to a boiling point; and we declared ourselves free.

The complaints of the peasants of Asia are just as specific as those in our own Declaration of Independence; and to them they are just as important. The absence of medical care always comes first. The absence of schools is always second. Then comes land reform. These people have a passion for land ownership that we Americans can understand. We expressed it in our homestead laws and in the great westward movement that built a nation out of a wilderness. Next comes the desire to learn how to farm the modern way. The right to vote, the right to elect a representative government, the power to expel and punish corrupt officials—these too are important claims. Finally, the people of this area have a new sense of nationalism. It reflects itself in many ways—the growing tendency in underdeveloped and exploited countries to nationalize their natural resources and keep the profits for themselves; the desire to have local capital a partner with foreign capital in developing the nation; an exultant feeling of independence and resentment against intermeddling by outside powers. . . .

For centuries Asia has been under the domination of the foreigner. The Arab world has been dominated by the Turks for the last four hundred years; Persia by the Russians and British for the last one hundred fifty; India by the British for three hundred years; the Philippines by Spaniards and by Americans; Indonesia by the Dutch; China by the Boxer powers; and so on. Those were mostly forms of imperialism that exploited the nations and left nothing for the peasants. That day is over and done with. Asia is united in one cause—to be rid of the foreigners' domination. In southeast Asia that unity receives powerful impetus from a race and color consciousness that is a dominant and often overriding factor in basic policy issues.

There are professional agitators who stir this brew of discontent; but the rebellious drive comes from the masses. I have not seen a village between the Mediterranean and the Pacific that was not stirring uneasily.

The faces of these people and their words keep coming back to me. Some of their words sting.

A peasant of India pointing to dead bodies of those who had died of starvation and asking me, "Is America the good nation we were told when it destroys its surplus potatoes and lets people die?"

The peasant at a thrashing floor in Bashan, south of Damascus, shaking a pitchfork as he asked me, "Why should a few men own all the land and make us work for nothing?"

The searching eyes and the imploring voice of an Iraqi villager near Basra who said, "I would be glad to live like a dog if only there was hope for my children."

A peasant in a dusty village in Persia on the road between Tehran and Tabriz presented the complaints of his people with the vigor of a Thomas Paine, "When Russian influence was strong in Persia and the Tudeh party flourished, our rent dropped to one third of the crop. Now American influence runs Persia and our rents are up to 50 per cent and more."

American foreign policy has never been addressed to the conditions under which these revolutions flourish. Democracy, peace, aggression are important words to us; but to those in the hinterland they are apt to be hollow and meaningless. America's voice when heard in this poverty and disease-ridden belt often sounds coarse and cheap—not because we intend it but because we do not know the world in which we live.

We tell about our high standard of living, how well our workers eat, the fine houses they live in.   And it sounds like boasting and bragging.

We finance agrarian projects for the benefit of the landlords instead of requiring, as we do in our domestic projects, that the beneficiaries be the men who work the land.

We send technical experts abroad to help in seed selection, soil conservation, malaria control and the like.   But we never raise our voice for reform of the vicious tenancy system of Asia under which increased production inures to the benefit of a few.   We seem to forget that health programs unrelated to land distribution projects, minimum wages, maximum hours of work and the like merely increase the number of people among whom the existing poverty must be rationed.

We talk about democracy and justice; and at the same time we support regimes merely because they are anti-Communist—regimes whose object is to keep democracy and justice out of reach of the peasants for all time, so as to protect their own vested interest.

We put billions of dollars behind corrupt and reactionary governments which exempt the rich from income taxes and fasten the hold of an oligarchy tighter and tighter on the nation.   At the same time we fail to support to the hilt men who back reforms that would stem the tide of Communism.

The matter was best summed up by Musa Bey Alami of Jericho.   He came up to Jerusalem to see me; and a small group of us sat under a pepper tree in an ancient and lovely garden talking about this problem. Across the Valley of Judgment to the east was the Mount of Olives —crowned with dark-green conifers and somber in the afternoon sun. Below was Gethsemane where giant olive trees—perhaps the very ones that sheltered Christ in His sorrow—spread their light-green leaves. Across from it were the walls of Jerusalem and the Golden Gate sealed tight against the Day of Judgment.   A breeze swept across the mountains of Judea and touched the Old City with a cool breath.   Talk turned to the Western powers.   The group expressed the view that the United States, Great Britain, and France were following policies that were certain to be destructive of democratic standards and would lead to the seizure of control over the area by the Communists.   Musa Bey Alami spoke with intensity of feeling.   His words tumbled in a torrent as if they had been pent up too long:

"America talks about individual freedom and preaches it to the Arab people.   That is idle talk, for we Arabs well know that in the countries of the Middle East the rights of free press, freedom of assembly, and other individual rights exist to no greater extent than they do in the Soviet satellites of Europe. Those rights are denied to all in the Middle East except supporters of the regimes in power. And yet the Western powers support and control these regimes."

These Arabs discussed how it was that no government in the Middle East would long endure if the weight of the Western powers was against it. Neither these governments nor the people want to join the Soviet axis; it is to the West that they look for leadership and guidance; it is with the West that they want to keep their partnerships in oil, in irrigation, and in industry. The West therefore has leverage which it should use.

Musa Bey Alami made a special plea, "Please tell the people of America not to lecture us about democracy. Don't tell our people that they must choose between democracy and communism. The people of this region are not free to make the choice. They are slaves. They are illiterate. They have no present escape from their misery. There is for them no such thing as liberty."

A young Arab turned to Musa Bey Alami and said: "Say what we think America should do."

"America should help us get rid in a peaceful way of the feudal system that holds us in its grip. America should throw its weight on the side of the honest, liberal elements which can be found in every country. If, for example, America had done that in China—if America had demanded a real liberal program as a condition of financial help—China would not be Communist today."

"Would not that be intervention?" someone asked.

"Call it intervention if you like," said Musa Bey Alami. "But when American influence is used to prop up or to strengthen a corrupt or reactionary political regime, that is also intervention."

I learned on my journeys that what Musa Bey Alami said expressed the views of the young, liberal, idealistic leaders who are to be found in every country across this vast stretch of land.

There are liberal forces in practically all of the Asian countries. At times they are either in a minority position in the cabinet or outside the government completely. But each of these nations has men who have the dream of a new freedom for their people, who have the character and ability to rid the nation of the feudal system that is as old as Asia. In other words, there is both the leadership and the energy within these countries to accomplish the necessary programs of social reconstruction. Yet to date our weight has been with the opposing forces.

Our great weakness has been our negative attitude. We have been anti-Communist. We have been pledged to root it out and expose it for all its ugliness.   We have taken up the hunt inside our country for every human being who was, is, or may be a Communist.   Yet no matter how feverish our efforts, the red tide of communism seems to spread abroad.   We are seized with panic as the waters lap at feeble dikes.   So we rush to the support of every group that opposes Soviet communism. That puts us in partnership with the corrupt and reactionary groups whose policies breed the discontent on which Soviet communism feeds and prospers.

The second basic reason for our default is that we have relied more and more on our military to do our thinking and planning for us. Beginning in 1945 with the fall of Japan and continuing until the removal of General Douglas MacArthur by President Truman on April 10, 1951, we entrusted the management of our policy toward Asia largely to the Army.   The military, rather than the diplomats, in fact made policy for us.   It is no reflection on the military to deplore that fact.   The situation in Asia is delicate and complex.   It requires astute handling at the political level—the best that we can muster in skill and understanding.   As a consequence of our negative attitude and military approach to problems, the tide of Soviet communism has picked up momentum.

Our third grave mistake has been our subservience to British policy in the Middle East.   Britain has long treated Persia, as it has other countries in this area, as a colony.   We have largely back-stopped the British throughout this region.   The British oil concession in Persia is a good example.   It is a concession obtained years ago by the British in a corrupt and unconscionable way.   Millions of pounds were spent in bribing officials.   The concession was extremely favorable to the British, extremely unfair to the Persians.   We were silent when England during recent years tried to force the concession on rebellious Persian governments.   The British are thoroughly hated in the Middle East; and we, by supporting British policy there, have had some of that hate directed to us.

Our fourth major error has been our belief that we could save the world from communism by dollars.   We have wasted billions in that way and have little to show for it.   Our vast expenditures in Asia have ended up largely in the hands of corrupt people.   We have financed the causes of those who want to hold the people in serfdom.   In doing so we have alienated the support of the masses.   The depreciation of our prestige abroad has about kept pace with the depreciation of the dollar at home.

It is ideas that will win, not dollars.   Dollars are secondary.   We have planned things pretty much in reverse.   Our reports and projects call for vast industrial undertakings—the installation of factories and plants in Asia and the development of its natural resources. We seem bent on trying to remake the East in our own image, to transform it from an agricultural to an industrial economy. That will eventually happen; but the process must be slow. Many other things must be done too. While industrialization should move ahead, it must be done cautiously and on a small, selective scale. There will be tragedy in the other course. For example, Asia has the cheapest labor market in the world. Trade unionism there is in its infancy. Skilled labor will not receive more than ninety cents or a dollar a day. The labor supply is almost unlimited. Factories built in these cheap labor markets, where no real trade unions are known, could easily be the greatest sweatshops in the world. They would tend to drag down the free workers of the world by cheap competition. Resulting tariff barriers would only increase the friction between East and West. The vast industrial projects for Asia which one hears discussed in Washington, D. C., would merely quicken the tempo of exploitation of the masses and hasten the day when the Communists take over.

It is frequently said that even if industrialization cannot be hurried, modernization of farms can be. And so great efforts are made to introduce mechanized farming in Asia. Even that is not so simple as it sounds. The introduction of modern methods of agriculture to Asia has been too fast. It already has become a project wasteful both of American dollars and of the expectation of the peasants.

In August, 1950, I found in Kurdistan (northwest Persia) $500,000 worth of farm machinery owned by one large operator that was idle for lack of spare parts; and even if the spare parts had been available there were no mechanics to do the repair work. No spare parts could be obtained, because there was no foreign exchange to buy them. Near Kermanshah, Persia, I saw dozens of water pumps, used for irrigating sugar beets, that were out of commission because some simple part had worn out. Since no parts were available, the crops were jeopardized. At Bareilly in Uttar Pradesh, India, . . . I saw 500 tractors, 375 of which were laid up for repairs and spare parts. When farm machinery is sold in this part of the world, trade schools for mechanics to service the machines must also be established; and plants to manufacture parts must often be built.

The place to start reform in Asia is with the land. The basic illness there is the vicious tenancy system. All other ills stem from that. No other project will be worthy of American aid unless it is tied to that. Land reform above all else is the starting point for launching the counter-revolution against communism. No program of reform can long succeed unless land reform is first carried through. That is the philosophy of the present Shah of Persia who recently distributed Royal Lands to the peasants in 4,000 villages. As the Shah told me, "The pride of land ownership inculcated and the incentive given to increased production will raise the standard of life of the people and prove a bulwark against any political infiltration."

American dollars can help on a small scale in some phases of the land reform problem. American capital obviously cannot finance the redistribution of the land. That must be done by each country, either on the installment basis as India is doing it, or as Ireland did it. The plight of Ireland's tenants was perhaps as severe as anything one sees in Asia. At least Jonathan Swift over two hundred years ago painted a dismal picture in *A Modest Proposal*. I stopped in Ireland in 1949 to see what had been done, and learned that the Irish had solved the heart of the problem without the use of much cash. Under the Land Act of 1923 the tenant got the land through the agency of a Land Commission and the landlords got Land Bonds (later guaranteed as to principal and interest by the British government). They turned out to be one of the best investments in Ireland, the bonds going to a premium.

There is one clear way in which our dollars can be put to a constructive use in Asia. We would, for example, revolutionize much of the Middle East if we threw our weight behind the right kind of TVA along the Tigris and Euphrates. If we insisted, as a condition of our financial help, that every farm that is watered by the project be owned by the man who works it and that no man own more than say, thirty acres, there would be the start of a peaceful but powerful revolution in the Middle East. A basis would have been laid for public health projects, modern villages, good schools, and all the other things that raise the standard of living of people. Iraq, which has a population of three and a half million, could on this principle support forty million; Persia, which has sixteen million people, could support one hundred million.

It is ideas and projects such as the TVA that will start Asia on the road to freedom. A TVA that is the instrument for making every farmer a landowner will be remembered throughout all time and identify America with the force that would influence Asia in the democratic way of life.

America is fitted by tradition for directing and guiding revolutions. We won our freedom by revolution and set the example which today inspires the peasants of Asia. We cannot remake the world in our image; but we can help those who are seeking an escape from squalor to find alternatives to communism. We cannot do it by talking democracy and peace. We can do it only by making our foreign policy understandable in terms of the aspirations of these people. Our foreign policy must be specifically related to the land problem. We should be behind those who sincerely have as their motto—"the man who works the land should own it." If that were our announced policy, if that were the word that went out from all our embassies and legations, the masses of Asia would soon be on a basis of understanding with us.

This would not be a new form of imperialism. America would not be dictating policies to governments. But every government would know where the weight of America's influence would be and the kind of projects that would enlist American support. They would know that if American dollars were to be obtained for the financing of any projects, those projects would have to serve the interests of the masses. The implementation of that kind of political program would be relatively easy. . . .

This kind of foreign policy would have far-reaching consequences. It would mean that in every capital of Asia American sympathy and understanding would be behind the liberal, progressive groups, whose mission it is to break the hold of the feudal system. Groups who enjoyed the prestige of that kind of American support would be in a strong political position. Asians do not want any foreign domination—American, British, or Russian. They do not want any form of imperialism. They are passionately opposed to becoming colonies either of the West or of Russia. But by and large they do want friendship and cooperation with the western world. They want the West as a partner in many of their undertakings. They want the help of the West as an ally. They have a fear of any dependency on Soviet Russia, whose imperialistic designs on Asia are more ominous than those of any foreign power in history.

A foreign policy of a positive political character for Asia would have tremendous military value. We cannot possibly defend with our armies the wide perimeter stretching from Japan to Morocco. We have not the men to do it. Anyone who has seen the jungles of Malaya and the swamps of Indo-China knows we could easily lose our armies in them. Soviet Russia's military strategy takes this into account. She does not plan to dissipate her own strength in that way. Behind her military strategy is a program of political action. Her aim is to get native Communists in control of every country. Then these countries will become neutral in a pro-Soviet sense or raise local armies (Korean style) to fight her battles for her. We cannot defeat those tactics by military action, for we are too small and the military theaters are too scattered. We can counter that military strategy only by a program of political action of our own.

An Asian foreign policy of the character I have described will require faith and courage—courage born of reason, not of hysteria, not of fear.

1. It means that we must give up the idea that the world can or ought to be standardized to American specification. Bullets will not kill communism. The world will for a long time have great numbers of Communists in it. Moreover, the new world that the Asians desire to create and which fits them best is not of the architectural design that we would choose for ourselves. The new world of Asia will be different from ours; it will have a large element of socialism which we would not want for ourselves. We must learn tolerance of new ideas. We must remember that a distinctive characteristic of the universe is diversity. The world will not be remade in the image of the West. All the legions of the empires failed and their failure is today's problem.

2. There are tremendous tensions inside Asia—tensions of religion, traditions, political ambitions, nationalism. Those tensions will survive even if communism sweeps nation after nation into its orbit. Many of the tensions are in fact created by the perilous propinquity of Russia —by the nearness of Russian armies and planes, by the appetite of the Soviets for power. Soviet expansion does not necessarily mean Soviet supremacy. The Asian imperialism which the Soviets are building can be made the source of Soviet weakness, rather than Soviet strength. Asia needs the West if she is to escape the tyranny of the Soviets and a complete dependency on the Soviet economy. The conflicts between what Asians want and what the Soviets are trying to get from them are so great that statesmanlike management can make Soviet expansion in Asia Russia's greatest menace.

3. America, the nation of surplus food, must find ways and means of sharing her surplus with the world. Gandhi said, "It is the fundamental law of nature, without exception, that nature produces enough for our wants from day to day; and if only everybody took enough for himself and nothing more there would be no pauperism in this world; there would be no man dying of starvation." That idea will not be denied. It presses for acceptance in Asia where millions have died from starvation since World War II ended. We must enter the Asian markets (particularly India) with our food and expend our surplus there, obtaining in return where possible raw materials which we need. But the important thing is to send our surplus food into these deficit areas, expecting primary payment in the good will which we sorely need in that part of the world.

Our aim should be the development of partners for world peace rather than customers for our surplus goods. If we take the contrary course we will deny the American ideal and harm ourselves far more than Soviet propaganda can ever do.

4. The greatest heritage that America has in the East comes from our teachers and missionaries. Through our educational emissaries the people of Asia came to know the warm and understanding heart of America. We have had no more important ambassadors of good will in the Arab world than Dr. Bayard Dodge and Dr. S. B. L. Penrose of American University in Beirut. None did America higher service in Persia than Dr. Samuel M. Jordan, who taught for about forty years in Tehran. The primary political task of Soviet Russia in China after the fall of the Nationalist government was to liquidate one hundred years of American friendship and good will, built largely through our cultural ties, including our missions.

If we are to save Asia from communism, we must by deed as well as by word show her people our true Christian attitude. We must emulate the teacher and missionary, identify ourselves with the aspirations of the peasants, and help them by kindness and understanding achieve a fuller life. We must go to the East with humility not condescension, mindful of our debt for the great cultures which the East has given us.

5. We Americans have been used to quick, clean-up jobs of critical situations. By temperament we want things acomplished in a hurry and to have a project over and done with. The political program of which I speak is long term; it cannot be done quickly. We need patience to see it through; the wisdom to nurture it in our time and to make another generation the stewards of it.

6. Security for the United States and the other democracies will be found not in the balance of armed might but in the balance of political power. We will be secure only when the bulk of the world is aligned on the democratic front. That is the reason for the tremendous urgency of a *political* rather than a *military* program in Asia.

Such a program to be successful must be geared to the hopes and aspirations of the masses of the people. Dollars and guns cannot build these alliances. Only faith and understanding and ideas that are liberal in their reach will create the conditions under which democratic influence will flourish. Neither wealth nor might will determine the outcome of the struggles in Asia. They will turn on emotional factors too subtle to measure. *Political alliances of an enduring nature will be built not on the power of guns or dollars, but on affection.* The ties that will hold the people of Asia close to each other and close to us will be of that character.   We must work at that level, if we want to be partners in the exciting Asian history that is about to be written.   We must, in other words, go to the East with warmth and understanding. The rewards will be bitter if we continue to go the other way.   It is clear to one who travels the villages of Asia that if we continue to play the role we have played in the last five years, these people will become united in one great crusade—a crusade against America.   Nothing would be more needless, nothing more tragic.   Yet the anti-American attitude in Asia continues to mount—*for to Asians America is too powerful to cooperate with them and too rich to understand them.*

7.   We Americans tend to judge people by their *standard of living* and to consider "backward" all who do not know our conveniences, such as plumbing, refrigerators, window screens, and electricity.   Those are false yardsticks.   The important criterion is not the rate of progress of a people but the *standard of life* which its leaders espouse and to which they aspire.   Yet even then it is easy to judge harshly.   Democracy as we know it will take generations to develop in Asia.   After all, we ourselves are not yet perfect.   Democracy cannot be imposed from without or from above; it comes from within a people as a result of education and experience.   We must learn tolerance of crude beginnings and not be harsh in our judgments.

The people of Asia want the good things of life; but they also want freedom and justice.   The desire for freedom and justice is indeed the powerful motive force behind the revolutions that sweep Asia.   Communism does not offer that *standard of life.*   We of the West have it for ourselves and can help Asia attain it.   Freedom and justice are indeed our missions in life.   If we forget that, we will never receive the verdict for civilization.

General Objectives and Attempts at Realization

52. The Policy of Containment *

When Mr. Kennan's article first appeared, it was signed simply "X."   The disclosure that the article had been written by an important official of the State Department led to speculation that the

* George F. Kennan, "The Sources of Soviet Conduct," *Foreign Affairs,* July, 1947, pp. 566-582.   Reprinted by permission of *Foreign Affairs* (New York). The author has been Director of the Policy Planning Staff, Department of State, and Ambassador to the Soviet Union.   He is at present a member of the Institute for Advanced Study, Princeton, New Jersey.

Government had adopted the policy which he recommended, and the subsequent pronouncement of the Truman Doctrine made it clear that this conjecture had been correct.

Mr. Kennan believes that containment of the Soviet Union by the United States is both necessary and feasible. Specifically, he recommends the "adroit and vigilant application of counter-forces at a series of constantly shifting geographical and political points, corresponding to the shifts and maneuvers of Soviet policy." His argument is based upon an analysis of the political personality of the Soviet Union. The frustration of this personality by successful containment, he says, will "promote tendencies which must eventually find their outlet in either the break-up or the gradual mellowing of Soviet power."

The policy of containment has been one of the most important of recent American foreign policies. Spokesmen for the Eisenhower administration, however, have expressed dissatisfaction with it and have professed a preference for a policy of "liberation." Nevertheless, the new administration's refusal to support President Rhee's desire to liberate North Korea, and the Government's inability to exploit the feelings of unrest among the peoples of the Soviet satellites of Eastern Europe—in both cases, "liberation" might have touched off World War III—suggests that the policy of containment, or a slightly altered version of it, will probably continue to be one of our fundamental policies for some time to come.

The political personality of Soviet power as we know it today is the product of ideology and circumstances: ideology inherited by the present Soviet leaders from the movement in which they had their political origin, and circumstances of the power which they now have exercised for nearly three decades in Russia. There can be few tasks of psychological analysis more difficult than to try to trace the interaction of these two forces and the relative role of each in the determination of official Soviet conduct. Yet the attempt must be made if that conduct is to be understood and effectively countered.

It is difficult to summarize the set of ideological concepts with which the Soviet leaders came into power. Marxian ideology, in its Russian-Communist projection, has always been in process of subtle evolution. The materials on which it bases itself are extensive and complex. But the outstanding features of Communist thought as it existed in 1916 may perhaps be summarized as follows: (a) that the central factor in the life of man, the factor which determines the character of public life and the "physiognomy of society," is the system by which material goods are produced and exchanged; (b) that the capitalist system of production is a nefarious one which inevitably leads to the exploitation of the working class by the capital-owning class and is incapable of developing adequately the economic resources of society or of distributing fairly the material goods produced by human labor; (c) that capitalism contains the seeds of its own destruction and must, in view of the inability of the capital-owning class to adjust itself to economic change, result eventually and inescapably in a revolutionary transfer of power to the working class; and (d) that imperialism, the final phase of capitalism, leads directly to war and revolution.

The rest may be outlined in Lenin's own words: "Unevenness of economic and political development is the inflexible law of capitalism. It follows from this that the victory of Socialism may come originally in a few capitalist countries or even in a single capitalist country. The victorious proletariat of that country, having expropriated the capitalists and having organized Socialist production at home, would rise against the remaining capitalist world, drawing to itself in the process the oppressed classes of other countries." It must be noted that there was no assumption that capitalism would perish without proletarian revolution. A final push was needed from a revolutionary proletariat movement in order to tip over the tottering structure. But it was regarded as inevitable that sooner or later that push be given.

For 50 years prior to the outbreak of the Revolution, this pattern of thought had exercised great fascination for the members of the Russian revolutionary movement. Frustrated, discontented, hopeless of finding self-expression—or too impatient to seek it—in the confining limits of the Tsarist political system, yet lacking wide popular support for their choice of bloody revolution as a means of social betterment, these revolutionists found in Marxist theory a highly convenient rationalization for their own instinctive desires. It afforded pseudo-scientific justification for their impatience, for their categoric denial of all value in the Tsarist system, for their yearning for power and revenge and for their inclination to cut corners in the pursuit of it. It is therefore no wonder that they had come to believe implicitly in the truth and soundness of the Marxian-Leninist teachings, so congenial to their own impulses and emotions. Their sincerity need not be impugned. This is a phenomenon as old as human nature itself. It has never been more aptly described than by Edward Gibbon, who wrote in *The Decline and Fall of the Roman Empire*: "From enthusiasm to imposture the step is perilous and slippery; the demon of Socrates affords a memorable instance how a wise man may deceive himself, how a good man may deceive others, how the conscience may slumber in a mixed and middle state between self-illusion and voluntary fraud." And it was with this set of conceptions that the members of the Bolshevik Party entered into power.

Now it must be noted that through all the years of preparation for revolution, the attention of these men, as indeed of Marx himself, had been centered less on the future form which Socialism* would take than on the necessary overthrow of rival power which, in their view, had to precede the introduction of Socialism. Their views, therefore, on the positive program to be put into effect, once power was attained, were for the most part nebulous, visionary and impractical. Beyond the nationalization of industry and the expropriation of large private capital holdings there was no agreed program. The treatment of the peasantry, which according to the Marxist formulation was not of the proletariat, had always been a vague spot in the pattern of Communist thought; and it remained an object of controversy and vacillation for the first ten years of Communist power.

The circumstances of the immediate post-revolution period—the existence in Russia of civil war and foreign intervention, together with the obvious fact that the Communists represented only a tiny minority of the Russian people—made the establishment of dictatorial power a necessity. The experiment with "war Communism" and the abrupt attempt to eliminate private production and trade had unfortunate economic consequences and caused further bitterness against the new revolutionary régime. While the temporary relaxation of the effort to communize Russia, represented by the New Economic Policy, alleviated some of this economic distress and thereby served its purpose, it also made it evident that the "capitalistic sector of society" was still prepared to profit at once from any relaxation of governmental pressure, and would, if permitted to continue to exist, always constitute a powerful opposing element to the Soviet régime and a serious rival for influence in the country. Somewhat the same situation prevailed with respect to the individual peasant who, in his own small way, was also a private producer.

Lenin, had he lived, might have proved a great enough man to reconcile these conflicting forces to the ultimate benefit of Russian society, though this is questionable. But be that as it may, Stalin, and those whom he led in the struggle for succession to Lenin's position of leadership, were not the men to tolerate rival political forces in the sphere of power which they coveted. Their sense of insecurity was too great. Their

---

* Here and elsewhere in this paper "Socialism" refers to Marxist or Leninist Communism, not to liberal Socialism of the Second International variety.

particular brand of fanaticism, unmodified by any of the Anglo-Saxon traditions of compromise, was too fierce and too jealous to envisage any permanent sharing of power.   From the Russian-Asiatic world out of which they had emerged they carried with them a skepticism as to the possibilities of permanent and peaceful coexistence of rival forces. Easily persuaded of their own doctrinaire "rightness," they insisted on the submission or destruction of all competing power.   Outside of the Communist Party, Russian society was to have no rigidity.   There were to be no forms of collective human activity or association which would not be dominated by the Party.   No other force in Russian society was to be permitted to achieve vitality or integrity.   Only the Party was to have structure.   All else was to be an amorphous mass.

And within the Party the same principle was to apply.   The mass of Party members might go through the motions of election, deliberation, decision and action; but in these motions they were to be animated not by their own individual wills but by the awesome breath of the Party leadership and the overbrooding presence of "the word."

Let it be stressed again that subjectively these men probably did not seek absolutism for its own sake.   They doubtless believed—and found it easy to believe—that they alone knew what was good for society and that they would accomplish that good once their power was secure and unchallengeable.   But in seeking that security of their own rule they were prepared to recognize no restrictions, either of God or man, on the character of their methods.   And until such time as that security might be achieved, they placed far down on their scale of operational priorities the comforts and happiness of the peoples entrusted to their care.

Now the outstanding circumstance concerning the Soviet régime is that down to the present day this process of political consolidation has never been completed and the men in the Kremlin have continued to be predominantly absorbed with the struggle to secure and make absolute the power which they seized in November 1917.   They have endeavored to secure it primarily against forces at home, within Soviet society itself. But they have also endeavored to secure it against the outside world.   For ideology, as we have seen, taught them that the outside world was hostile and that it was their duty eventually to overthrow the political forces beyond their borders.   The powerful hands of Russian history and tradition reached up to sustain them in this feeling.   Finally, their own aggressive intransigence with respect to the outside world began to find its own reaction; and they were soon forced, to use another Gibbonesque phrase, "to chastise the contumacy" which they themselves had provoked. It is an undeniable privilege of every man to prove himself right in the thesis that the world is his enemy; for if he reiterates it frequently enough and makes it the background of his conduct he is bound eventually to be right.

Now it lies in the nature of the mental world of the Soviet leaders, as well as in the character of their ideology, that no opposition to them can be officially recognized as having any merit or justification whatsoever. Such opposition can flow, in theory, only from the hostile and incorrigible forces of dying capitalism. As long as remnants of capitalism were officially recognized as existing in Russia, it was possible to place on them, as an internal element, part of the blame for the maintenance of a dictatorial form of society. But as these remnants were liquidated, little by little, this justification fell away; and when it was indicated officially that they had been finally destroyed, it disappeared altogether. And this fact created one of the most basic of the compulsions which came to act upon the Soviet régime: since capitalism no longer existed in Russia and since it could not be admitted that there could be serious or widespread opposition to the Kremlin springing spontaneously from the liberated masses under its authority, it became necessary to justify the retention of the dictatorship by stressing the menace of capitalism abroad.

This began at an early date. In 1924 Stalin specifically defended the retention of the "organs of suppression," meaning, among others, the army and the secret police, on the ground that "as long as there is a capitalist encirclement there will be danger of intervention with all the consequences that flow from that danger." In accordance with that theory, and from that time on, all internal opposition forces in Russia have consistently been portrayed as the agents of foreign forces of reaction antagonistic to Soviet power.

By the same token, tremendous emphasis has been placed on the original Communist thesis of a basic antagonism between the capitalist and Socialist worlds. It is clear, from many indications, that this emphasis is not founded in reality. The real facts concerning it have been confused by the existence abroad of genuine resentment provoked by Soviet philosophy and tactics and occasionally by the existence of great centers of military power, notably the Nazi régime in Germany and the Japanese Government of the late 1930's, which did indeed have aggressive designs against the Soviet Union. But there is ample evidence that the stress laid in Moscow on the menace confronting Soviet society from the world outside its borders is founded not in the realities of foreign antagonism but in the necessity of explaining away the maintenance of dictatorial authority at home.

Now the maintenance of this pattern of Soviet power, namely, the pursuit of unlimited authority domestically, accompanied by the cultivation of the semi-myth of implacable foreign hostility, has gone far to shape the actual machinery of Soviet power as we know it today. Internal organs of administration which did not serve this purpose withered on the vine. Organs which did serve this purpose became vastly swollen. The security of Soviet power came to rest on the iron discipline of the Party, on the severity and ubiquity of the secret police, and on the uncompromising economic monopolism of the state. The "organs of suppression," in which the Soviet leaders had sought security from rival forces, became in large measure the masters of those whom they were designed to serve. Today the major part of the structure of Soviet power is committed to the perfection of the dictatorship and to the maintenance of the concept of Russia as in a state of seige, with the enemy lowering beyond the walls. And the millions of human beings who form that part of the structure of power must defend at all costs this concept of Russia's position, for without it they are themselves superfluous.

As things stand today, the rulers can no longer dream of parting with these organs of suppression. The quest for absolute power, pursued now for nearly three decades with a ruthlessness unparalleled (in scope at least) in modern times, has again produced internally, as it did externally, its own reaction. The excesses of the police apparatus have fanned the potential opposition to the régime into something far greater and more dangerous than it could have been before these excesses began.

But least of all can the rulers dispense with the fiction by which the maintenance of dictatorial power has been defended. For this fiction has been canonized in Soviet philosophy by the excesses already committed in its name; and it is now anchored in the Soviet structure of thought by bonds far greater than those of mere ideology.

So much for the historical background. What does it spell in terms of the political personality of Soviet power as we know it today?

Of the original ideology, nothing has been officially junked. Belief is maintained in the basic badness of capitalism, in the inevitability of its destruction, in the obligation of the proletariat to assist in that destruction and to take power into its own hands. But stress has come to be laid primarily on those concepts which relate most specifically to the Soviet régime itself: to its position as the sole truly Socialist régime in a dark and misguided world, and to the relationships of power within it.

The first of these concepts is that of the innate antagonism between capitalism and Socialism. We have seen how deeply that concept has become imbedded in foundations of Soviet power. It has profound implications for Russia's conduct as a member of international society.

It means that there can never be on Moscow's side any sincere assumption of a community of aims between the Soviet Union and powers which are regarded as capitalist. It must invariably be assumed in Moscow that the aims of the capitalist world are antagonistic to the Soviet régime, and therefore to the interests of the peoples it controls. If the Soviet Government occasionally sets its signature to documents which would indicate the contrary, this is to be regarded as a tactical maneuver permissible in dealing with the enemy (who is without honor) and should be taken in the spirit of *caveat emptor*. Basically, the antagonism remains. It is postulated. And from it flow many of the phenomena which we find disturbing in the Kremlin's conduct of foreign policy: the secretiveness, the lack of frankness, the duplicity, the wary suspiciousness, and the basic unfriendliness of purpose. These phenomena are there to stay, for the foreseeable future. There can be variations of degree and of emphasis. When there is something the Russians want from us, one or the other of these features of their policy may be thrust temporarily into the background; and when that happens there will always be Americans who will leap forward with gleeful announcements that "the Russians have changed," and some who will even try to take credit for having brought about such "changes." But we should not be misled by tactical maneuvers. These characteristics of Soviet policy, like the postulate from which they flow, are basic to the internal nature of Soviet power, and will be with us, whether in the foreground or the background, until the internal nature of Soviet power is changed.

This means that we are going to continue for a long time to find the Russians difficult to deal with. It does not mean that they should be considered as embarked upon a do-or-die program to overthrow our society by a given date. The theory of the inevitability of the eventual fall of capitalism has the fortunate connotation that there is no hurry about it. For forces of progress can take their time in preparing the final *coup de grâce*. Meanwhile, what is vital is that the "Socialist fatherland"—that oasis of power which has been already won for Socialism in the person of the Soviet Union—should be cherished and defended by all good Communists at home and abroad, its fortunes promoted, its enemies badgered and confounded. The promotion of premature, "adventuristic" revolutionary projects abroad which might embarrass Soviet power in any way would be an inexcusable, even a counter-revolutionary act. The cause of Socialism is the support and promotion of Soviet power, as defined in Moscow.

This brings us to the second of the concepts important to contemporary Soviet outlook. That is the infallibility of the Kremlin. The Soviet concept of power, which permits no focal points of organization outside the Party itself, requires that the Party leadership remain in theory the sole repository of truth. For if truth were to be found elsewhere, there would be justification for its expression in organized activity. But it is precisely that which the Kremlin cannot and will not permit.

The leadership of the Communist Party is therefore always right, and has been always right ever since in 1929 Stalin formalized his personal power by announcing that decisions of the Politburo were being taken unanimously.

On the principle of infallibility there rests the iron discipline of the Communist Party. In fact, the two concepts are mutually self-supporting. Perfect discipline requires recognition of infallibility. Infallibility requires the observance of discipline. And the two together go far to determine the behaviorism of the entire Soviet apparatus of power. But their effect cannot be understood unless a third factor be taken into account: namely, the fact that the leadership is at liberty to put forward for tactical purposes any particular thesis which it finds useful to the cause at any particular moment and to require the faithful and unquestioning acceptance of that thesis by the members of the movement as a whole. This means that truth is not a constant but is actually created, for all intents and purposes, by the Soviet leaders themselves. It may vary from week to week, from month to month. It is nothing absolute and immutable—nothing which flows from objective reality. It is only the most recent manifestation of the wisdom of those in whom the ultimate wisdom is supposed to reside, because they represent the logic of history.

The accumulative effect of these factors is to give to the whole subordinate apparatus of Soviet power an unshakeable stubbornness and steadfastness in its orientation. This orientation can be changed at will by the Kremlin but by no other power. Once a given party line has been laid down on a given issue of current policy, the whole Soviet governmental machine, including the mechanism of diplomacy, moves inexorably along the prescribed path, like a persistent toy automobile wound up and headed in a given direction, stopping only when it meets with some unanswerable force. The individuals who are the components of this machine are unamenable to argument or reason which comes to them from outside sources. Their whole training has taught them to mistrust and discount the glib persuasiveness of the outside world. Like the white dog before the phonograph, they hear only the "master's voice." And if they are to be called off from the purposes last dictated to them, it is the master who must call them off. Thus the foreign representative cannot hope that his words will make any impression on them. The most that he can hope is that they will be transmitted to those at the top, who are capable of changing the party line. But even those are not likely to be swayed by any normal logic in the words of the bourgeois representative. Since there can be no appeal to common purposes, there can be no appeal to common mental approaches. For this reason, facts speak louder than words to the ears of the Kremlin; and words carry the greatest weight when they have the ring of reflecting, or being backed up by, facts of unchallengeable validity.

But we have seen that the Kremlin is under no ideological compulsion to accomplish its purposes in a hurry. Like the Church, it is dealing in ideological concepts which are of long-term validity, and it can afford to be patient. It has no right to risk the existing achievements of the revolution for the sake of vain baubles of the future. The very teachings of Lenin himself require great caution and flexibility in the pursuit of Communist purposes. Again, these precepts are fortified by the lessons of Russian history: of centuries of obscure battles between nomadic forces over the stretches of a vast unfortified plain. Here caution, circumspection, flexibility and deception are the valuable qualities; and their value finds natural appreciation in the Russian or the Oriental mind. Thus the Kremlin has no compunction about retreating in the face of superior force. And being under the compulsion of no timetable, it does not get panicky under the necessity for such retreat. Its political action is a fluid stream which moves constantly, wherever it is permitted to move, toward a given goal. Its main concern is to make sure that it has filled every nook and cranny available to it in the basin of world power. But if it finds unassailable barriers in its path, it accepts these philosophically and accommodates itself to them. The main thing is that there should always be pressure, unceasing constant pressure, toward the desired goal. There is no trace of any feeling in Soviet psychology that that goal must be reached at any given time.

These considerations make Soviet diplomacy at once easier and more difficult to deal with than the diplomacy of individual aggressive leaders like Napoleon and Hitler. On the one hand it is more sensitive to contrary force, more ready to yield on individual sectors of the diplomatic front when that force is felt to be too strong, and thus more rational in the logic and rhetoric of power. On the other hand it cannot be easily defeated or discouraged by a single victory on the part of its opponents. And the patient persistence by which it is animated means that it can be effectively countered not by sporadic acts which represent the momentary whims of democratic opinion but only by intelligent long-range policies on the part of Russia's adversaries—policies no less steady in their purpose, and no less variegated and resourceful in their application, than those of the Soviet Union itself.

In these circumstances it is clear that the main element of any United States policy toward the Soviet Union must be that of a long-term, patient but firm and vigilant containment of Russian expansive tendencies. It is important to note, however, that such a policy has nothing to do with outward histrionics: with threats or blustering or superfluous gestures of outward "toughness."   While the Kremlin is basically flexible in its reaction to political realities, it is by no means unamenable to considerations of prestige.   Like almost any other government, it can be placed by tactless and threatening gestures in a position where it cannot afford to yield even though this might be dictated by its sense of realism.   The Russian leaders are keen judges of human psychology, and as such they are highly conscious that loss of temper and of self-control is never a source of strength in political affairs.   They are quick to exploit such evidences of weakness.   For these reasons, it is a *sine qua non* of successful dealing with Russia that the foreign government in question should remain at all times cool and collected and that its demands on Russian policy should be put forward in such a manner as to leave the way open for a compliance not too detrimental to Russian prestige.

In the light of the above, it will be clearly seen that the Soviet pressure against the free institutions of the western world is something that can be contained by the adroit and vigilant application of counter-force at a series of constantly shifting geographical and political points, corresponding to the shifts and maneuvers of Soviet policy, but which cannot be charmed or talked out of existence.   The Russians look forward to a duel of infinite duration, and they see that already they have scored great successes.   It must be borne in mind that there was a time when the Communist Party represented far more of a minority in the sphere of Russian national life than Soviet power today represents in the world community.

But if ideology convinces the rulers of Russia that truth is on their side and that they can therefore afford to wait, those of us on whom that ideology has no claim are free to examine objectively the validity of that premise.   The Soviet thesis not only implies complete lack of control by the West over its own economic destiny, it likewise assumes Russian unity, discipline and patience over an infinite period.   Let us bring this apocalyptic vision down to earth, and suppose that the western world finds the strength and resourcefulness to contain Soviet power over a period of ten to fifteen years. What does that spell for Russia itself?

The Soviet leaders, taking advantage of the contributions of modern technique to the arts of despotism, have solved the question of obedience within the confines of their power. Few challenge their authority; and even those who do are unable to make that challenge valid as against the organs of suppression of the state.

The Kremlin has also proved able to accomplish its purpose of building up in Russia, regardless of the interests of the inhabitants, an industrial foundation of heavy metallurgy, which is, to be sure, not yet complete but which is nevertheless continuing to grow and is approaching those of the other major industrial countries. All of this, however, both the maintenance of internal political security and the building of heavy industry, has been carried out at a terrible cost in human life and in human hopes and energies. It has necessitated the use of forced labor on a scale unprecedented in modern times under conditions of peace. It has involved the neglect or abuse of other phases of Soviet economic life, particularly agriculture, consumers' goods production, housing and transportation.

To all that, the war has added its tremendous toll of destruction, death and human exhaustion. In consequence of this, we have in Russia today a population which is physically and spiritually tired. The mass of the people are disillusioned, skeptical and no longer as accessible as they once were to the magical attraction which Soviet power still radiates to its followers abroad. The avidity with which people seized upon the slight respite accorded to the Church for tactical reasons during the war was eloquent testimony to the fact that their capacity for faith and devotion found little expression in the purposes of the régime.

In these circumstances, there are limits to the physical and nervous strength of people themselves. These limits are absolute ones, and are binding even for the cruelest dictatorship, because beyond them people cannot be driven. The forced labor camps and the other agencies of constraint provide temporary means of compelling people to work longer hours than their own volition or mere economic pressure would dictate; but if people survive them at all they become old before their time and must be considered as human casualties to the demands of dictatorship. In either case their best powers are no longer available to society and can no longer be enlisted in the service of the state.

Here only the younger generation can help. The younger generation, despite all vicissitudes and sufferings, is numerous and vigorous; and the Russians are a talented people.   But it still remains to be seen what will be the effects on mature performance of the abnormal emotional strains of childhood which Soviet dictatorship created and which were enormously increased by the war.   Such things as normal security and placidity of home environment have practically ceased to exist in the Soviet Union outside of the most remote farms and villages.   And observers are not yet sure whether that is not going to leave its mark on the over-all capacity of the generation now coming into maturity.

In addition to this, we have the fact that Soviet economic development, while it can list certain formidable achievements, has been precariously spotty and uneven.   Russian Communists who speak of the "uneven development of capitalism" should blush at the contemplation of their own national economy.   Here certain branches of economic life, such as the metallurgical and machine industries, have been pushed out of all proportion to other sectors of economy.   Here is a nation striving to become in a short period one of the great industrial nations of the world while it still has no highway network worthy of the name and only a relatively primitive network of railways.   Much has been done to increase efficiency of labor and to teach primitive peasants something about the operation of machines.   But maintenance is still a crying deficiency of all Soviet economy.   Construction is hasty and poor in quality. Depreciation must be enormous.   And in vast sectors of economic life it has not yet been possible to instill into labor anything like that general culture of production and technical self-respect which characterizes the skilled worker of the West.

It is difficult to see how these deficiencies can be corrected at an early date by a tired and dispirited population working largely under the shadow of fear and compulsion.   And as long as they are not overcome, Russia will remain economically a vulnerable, and in a certain sense an impotent, nation, capable of exporting its enthusiasms and of radiating the strange charm of its primitive political vitality but unable to back up those articles of export by the real evidences of material power and prosperity.

Meanwhile, a great uncertainty hangs over the political life of the Soviet Union.   That is the uncertainty involved in the transfer of power from one individual or group of individuals to others.

This is, of course, outstandingly the problem of the personal position of Stalin.   We must remember that his succession to Lenin's pinnacle of preeminence in the Communist movement was the only such transfer of individual authority which the Soviet Union has experienced.   That transfer took 12 years to consolidate.   It cost the lives of millions of people and shook the state to its foundations. The attendant tremors were felt all through the international revolutionary movement, to the disadvantage of the Kremlin itself.

It is always possible that another transfer of preeminent power may take place quietly and inconspicuously, with no repercussions anywhere. But again, it is possible that the questions involved may unleash, to use some of Lenin's words, one of those "incredibly swift transitions" from "delicate deceit" to "wild violence" which characterize Russian history, and may shake Soviet power to its foundations.

But this is not only a question of Stalin himself. There has been, since 1938, a dangerous congealment of political life in the higher circles of Soviet power. The All-Union Congress of Soviets, in theory the supreme body of the Party, is supposed to meet not less often than once in three years. It will soon be eight full years since its last meeting. During this period membership in the Party has numerically doubled. Party mortality during the war was enormous; and today well over half of the Party members are persons who have entered since the last Party congress was held. Meanwhile, the same small group of men has carried on at the top through an amazing series of national vicissitudes. Surely there is some reason why the experiences of the war brought basic political changes to every one of the great governments of the West. Surely the causes of that phenomenon are basic enough to be present somewhere in the obscurity of Soviet political life, as well. And yet no recognition has been given to these causes in Russia.

It must be surmised from this that even within so highly disciplined an organization as the Communist Party there must be a growing divergence in age, outlook and interest between the great mass of Party members, only so recently recruited into the movement, and the little self-perpetuating clique of men at the top, whom most of these Party members have never met, with whom they have never conversed, and with whom they can have no political intimacy.

Who can say whether, in these circumstances, the eventual rejuvenation of the higher spheres of authority (which can only be a matter of time) can take place smoothly and peacefully, or whether rivals in the quest for higher power will not eventually reach down into these politically immature and inexperienced masses in order to find support for their respective claims? If this were ever to happen, strange consequences could flow for the Community Party: for the membership at large has been exercised only in the practices of iron discipline and obedience and not in the arts of compromise and accommodation. And if disunity were ever to seize and paralyze the Party, the chaos and weakness of Russian society would be revealed in forms beyond description.

For we have seen that Soviet power is only a crust concealing an amorphous mass of human beings among whom no independent organizational structure is tolerated. In Russia there is not even such a thing as local government. The present generation of Russians have never known spontaneity of collective action. If, consequently, anything were ever to occur to disrupt the unity and efficiency of the Party as a political instrument, Soviet Russia might be changed overnight from one of the strongest to one of the weakest and most pitiable of national societies.

Thus the future of Soviet power may not be by any means as secure as Russian capacity for self-delusion would make it appear to the men in the Kremlin. That they can keep power themselves, they have demonstrated. That they can quietly and easily turn it over to others remains to be proved. Meanwhile, the hardships of their rule and the vicissitudes of international life have taken a heavy toll of the strength and hopes of the great people on whom their power rests. It is curious to note that the ideological power of Soviet authority is strongest today in areas beyond the frontiers of Russia, beyond the reach of its police power. This phenomenon brings to mind a comparison used by Thomas Mann in his great novel *Buddenbrooks*. Observing that human institutions often show the greatest outward brilliance at a moment when inner decay is in reality farthest advanced, he compared the Buddenbrook family, in the days of its greatest glamour, to one of those stars whose light shines most brightly on this world when in reality it has long since ceased to exist. And who can say with assurance that the strong light still cast by the Kremlin on the dissatisfied peoples of the western world is not the powerful afterglow of a constellation which is in actuality on the wane? This cannot be proved. And it cannot be disproved. But the possibility remains (and in the opinion of this writer it is a strong one) that Soviet power, like the capitalist world of its conception, bears within it the seeds of its own decay, and that the sprouting of these seeds is well advanced.

It is clear that the United States cannot expect in the foreseeable future to enjoy political intimacy with the Soviet régime. It must continue to regard the Soviet Union as a rival, not a partner, in the political arena. It must continue to expect that Soviet policies will reflect no abstract love of peace and stability, no real faith in the possibility of a permanent happy coexistence of the Socialist and capitalist worlds, but rather a cautious, persistent pressure toward the disruption and weakening of all rival influence and rival power.

Balanced against this are the facts that Russia, as opposed to the western world in general, is still by far the weaker party, that Soviet policy is highly flexible, and that Soviet society may well contain deficiencies which will eventually weaken its own total potential. This would of itself warrant the United States entering with reasonable confidence upon a policy of firm containment, designed to confront the Russians with unalterable counter-force at every point where they show signs of encroaching upon the interests of a peaceful and stable world.

But in actuality the possibilities for American policy are by no means limited to holding the line and hoping for the best. It is entirely possible for the United States to influence by its actions the internal developments, both within Russia and throughout the international Communist movement, by which Russian policy is largely determined. This is not only a question of the modest measure of informational activity which this government can conduct in the Soviet Union and elsewhere, although that, too, is important. It is rather a question of the degree to which the United States can create among the peoples of the world generally the impression of a country which knows what it wants, which is coping successfully with the problems of its internal life and with the responsibilities of a World Power, and which has a spiritual vitality capable of holding its own among the major ideological currents of the time. To the extent that such an impression can be created and maintained, the aims of Russian Communism must appear sterile and quixotic, the hopes and enthusiasm of Moscow's supporters must wane, and added strain must be imposed on the Kremlin's foreign policies. For the palsied decrepitude of the capitalist world is the keystone of Communist philosophy. Even the failure of the United States to experience the early economic depression which the ravens of the Red Square have been predicting with such complacent confidence since hostilities ceased would have deep and important repercussions throughout the Communist world.

By the same token, exhibitions of indecision, disunity and internal disintegration within this country have an exhilarating effect on the whole Communist movement. At each evidence of these tendencies, a thrill of hope and excitement goes through the Communist world; a new jauntiness can be noted in the Moscow trend; new groups of foreign supporters climb on to what they can only view as the band wagon of international politics; and Russian pressure increases all along the line in international affairs.

It would be an exaggeration to say that American behavior unassisted and alone could exercise a power of life and death over the Communist movement and bring about the early fall of Soviet power in Russia. But the United States has it in its power to increase enormously the strains under which Soviet policy must operate, to force upon the Kremlin a far greater degree of moderation and circumspection than it has had to observe in recent years, and in this way to promote tendencies which must eventually find their outlet in either the break-up or the gradual mellowing of Soviet power. For no mystical, Messianic movement— and particularly not that of the Kremlin—can face frustration indefinitely without eventually adjusting itself in one way or another to the logic of that state of affairs.

Thus the decision will really fall in large measure in this country itself. The issue of Soviet-American relations is in essence a test of the over-all worth of the United States as a nation among nations. To avoid destruction the United States need only measure up to its own best traditions and prove itself worthy of preservation as a great nation.

Surely, there was never a fairer test of national quality than this. In the light of these circumstances, the thoughtful observer of Russian-American relations will find no cause for complaint in the Kremlin's challenge to American society. He will rather experience a certain gratitude to a Providence which, by providing the American people with this implacable challenge, has made their entire security as a nation dependent on their pulling themselves together and accepting the responsibilities of moral and political leadership that history plainly intended them to bear.

53. NEGOTIATION FROM STRENGTH *

The policy of negotiation with the Soviet Union "from strength" rests upon the belief that the Soviet leaders despise weakness and admire strength. Any attempt to reach a settlement with the Soviet Union would be foredoomed to failure, therefore, unless the United States could sit at the council table backed by the certain knowledge of her strength—military, political, and economic. The Soviet Union would also be aware of the "fact" of American power, and somewhat more favorably disposed toward the compromises necessary to achieve settlement of differences.

Mr. Bohlen describes the process of creating situations of strength, a process which involves the adoption of policies designed not as ends in themselves, but as the base from which to negotiate. Here again, it is clear from the recent efforts to create new situations of strength around the periphery of Soviet power (in Japan and Paki-

---

* Charles E. Bohlen, "Creating Situations of Strength," *Department of State Bulletin*, August 4, 1952, pp. 167-171. The author has been Counselor of the State Department, and in 1953 became Ambassador to the Soviet Union.

stan, for example) that the principle of negotiation from strength continues to be basic in the thinking of American policy planners, notwithstanding the change of administration.

Exactly what do we mean when we say "situations of strength"? How and why was the concept developed? How has U.S. foreign policy operated to create situations of strength on behalf of the free world?

These are vital questions. They demand pointed answers. But they can be adequately answered only if we understand the qualities of U.S. foreign policy which have made it possible to think in terms of global strategy. So I should like to begin by briefly examining some of these qualities.

The first point I would make here is that our foreign policy must be one of enlightened self-interest. A nation that does not constantly look to its self-security toys with its very existence. That, I think, is perfectly obvious.

But there are different roads to security even as there are different concepts as to what security involves. Security has been used as a disguise for conquest and imperialism.

Our concept of self-security is quite different. Our concept is firmly rooted in the belief that we can best preserve our way of life in a world of peace and decency. It is dedicated to the conviction that our best hope for such peace and decency lies in the full-time cooperation of sovereign nations, all of them seeking the common progress of humanity. It is based upon the understanding that the free nations—the United States among them—cannot be unconcerned so long as poverty, disease, and illiteracy remain the constant companions of two thirds of the human race.

This concern is not only humanitarianism, although this element must be present in the foreign policy of a democracy. But that does not mean that it is a policy of simple charity. Emphatically not! We are willing to help others to help themselves because, in doing so, we are helping ourselves.

And that brings me to a second quality of U.S. foreign policy. It is a cooperative policy. It accepts the principle that we cannot stand alone in this kind of world—that we dare not stand alone.

The days when the Atlantic and Pacific served us as protective moats —as "insulation" to use the phrase of the late Senator Vandenberg— are behind us. Great oceans have become mere puddles. The miracle of modern technology has given us immediate neighbors in London, Paris, Canberra, and Bangkok. Horse and buggy isolationism is outmoded in an atomic age.   What happens anywhere in the world is of concern everywhere.

When you couple this smaller, more closely knit, technologically advanced world with the rise of a new great power, the Soviet Union, you can easily see why we Americans cannot stand alone.   The emergence of the Soviet Union as a great power at the close of World War II was bound to have a global impact.   Soviet policies and actions since the close of the war have made that impact a dangerous one.

There is no need to belabor the Soviet menace before this audience. You know the Soviet postwar record.   You understand the nature of the threat posed for all free men.   And you understand—I am sure— that the United States must work closely with other free nations if freedom and peace are to weather the onslaughts of this new imperialism.

REALISTIC POLICY NEEDED

A third and necessary element of U.S. foreign policy is realism. Our foreign policy must reflect the ideals and principles so deeply rooted in our tradition.   It must concern itself with things as they really are—not only with things as we would like them to be.   It seeks to meet specific situations as they arise as well as to anticipate such situations.

It would be wonderful if this were indeed the best of all possible worlds.   It would be fine if we could immediately realize our fondest ideals.

But this is not that kind of world.   There are many influences and many ambitions at work on the international scene.   And these influences and ambitions are not readily subject to control by a push button in Washington.

Foreign policy cannot be made in a vacuum.   Foreign-policy objectives cannot be accomplished in keeping with a strict timetable. There are just too many intangibles.

There are those who would apply the rigid rules of abstract physical science to international politics.   It would be very helpful if it were possible to reduce foreign policy to an exact science.   But it is not possible to do so.

A sound foreign policy must deal in possibilities and probabilities as well as in certainties.   Only then can it be realistic.   Only then can it operate with reasonable flexibility.

A fourth quality of U.S. foreign policy which I should like to mention is its genuine democracy.   It is not made in an ivory tower.

U.S. foreign policy is fully representative of domestic public opinion. It is an expression of our way of life.

Secretary of State Dean Acheson made that clear in a nation-wide address back in 1949. He said:

In the long run, and very often in the short run, it is you citizens of this Republic, acting directly through public opinion and through the Congress, who decide the contours of our policies and whether those policies shall go forward or waver and stop.

Current events clearly support Mr. Acheson's statement. The 1952 political conventions at Chicago are cases in point. Foreign policy has been a fundamental issue before both conventions. Foreign policy is a basic plank in both platforms.

Are not political parties the vehicles through which the people grant governmental power to those of their choice? Of course they are.

In the last analysis, the makers of foreign policy in any democracy must—as a matter of right and necessity—be responsive to the voice of the people.

These, then, are some of the basic qualities which should be in U.S. foreign policy. Enlightened self-interest, realism, democratic inspiration, and the cooperative spirit—these are the qualities necessary to bring into being the "situations of strength" concept we are here to discuss.

These are the qualities which have made it possible for the United States to assume its responsibilities of free-world leadership in meeting the No. 1 problem posed by World War II. What was that No. 1 problem?

It was a problem of power relationships made acute by the approach taken by Soviet Russia.

USING POWER TO CURB POWER

There is an old Chinese proverb which says: "Use power to curb power."

In a sense, that is what the free nations have had to do in the postwar period.

Now, I do not mean to imply by this that power is an end in itself or that we have gone power-mad. Power, insofar as free men are concerned, is a means to an end. It is a means through which the United States is seeking to preserve its security and to work with others in building a world of peace and progress. It is a means through which the free nations can work together to deter totalitarian aggression.

This, I might say, is a highly significant point. In international politics, power does not necessarily have to be used to be effective. The very fact that it exists is often enough to get results.

Now, I have said that the No. 1 problem of the postwar period—from our point of view—was one of power relationships.   And I have already noted that the rise of a new and special form of state power—Soviet Russia—was of crucial importance.

The fact is that the power situation in the postwar world is very different from anything we have had at any other time since the rise of the modern nation-state system.   For the first time in modern history, we have a world in which there are only two major centers of power. Power—to use the technical phrase—is bipolarized.

On the one hand, we have the Soviet Union and its satellites.   On the other, we have what amounts to a coalition of free nations with the United States playing a leading role.

This role is not one we have sought.   It has been thrust upon us by the very nature of our position in world affairs.   It has been thrust upon us and we have been obligated to accept it.

When I say that the United States is central to the free-world coalition, I say it with humility and understanding of the grave responsibilities imposed upon us.   I say it in the urgent hope that we shall not fail to help preserve in the world that freedom and liberty to which our entire foreign policy is dedicated.   I say it with the conviction that our own well-being is dependent upon our free-world partners even as theirs is dependent upon us.

This is true—to a great extent—because existing power relationships leave a good deal less room for maneuver in foreign affairs than was once the case.   Balance of power politics no longer means what it meant before the first global war was fought.   The day of the buffer state and the zone of influence is rapidly passing.   Any major strategic move in today's world is of immediate concern to all nations and all peoples.

At the turn of the century, there were half a dozen or more nations who could lay claim to being powers of the first rank.   If one of these nations became unduly threatening, or aggressive, there were always several other nations who—by uniting with the weaker of the two—could offset the power of the stronger.   This was the classical conception of balance-of-power politics in operation.

At the turn of the century, it was possible for a war to be fought in the Balkans, the Near East, or the Far East without involving or even directly affecting the major powers.

But today's world is different.   There is a Cold War on between freedom and calculated tyranny.   And that war is global in scope. There is friction at virtually every point where the free and slave worlds meet.

The fight against aggression in Korea is all too tangible proof of this. Every major power has had a hand in the Korean situation in one way or another.

Korea, I might add, will appear in the history books of the future as one of the most significant events of this or any other era. For here, genuine collective security operated to halt a deliberate, naked aggression for the first time in modern history. The United Nations has truly won its spurs in Korea. It has upheld, in full, the principles upon which it was founded.

Think of what the United Nations has accomplished in Korea. It has driven the Communists back along most of the battle line beyond the point from which they started their unprovoked, brutal assault in June of 1950. It has preserved the independence of the Republic of South Korea. It has served notice on all potential aggressors that aggression cannot be launched anywhere with impunity.

Had the United Nations allowed the Communists to get away with their aggression, the existing power situation would have developed to the extreme disadvantage of the free world. To have allowed Korea to go by default would have been a tremendous blow to the free peoples of Asia. It would have encouraged the Kremlin and its cohorts to move against the periphery of the free world again at their convenience. It would have strengthened the possibilities of an all-out global war and weakened considerably the containment policy which is so basic to U.S. foreign policy and the defense of the free world as a whole.

EMERGENCE OF THE CONTAINMENT POLICY

I should like now to talk a little about the containment policy and about the creation of situations of strength which that policy demands.

The first thing that we must bear in mind in this connection is that the conditions which gave rise to the idea of containment did not spring up overnight. They were in the process of development for many months.

World War II did see the Soviet Union emerge as a great power. But it was not until the free nations had exhausted every possibility at the conference table and the Soviets had clearly indicated by their actions their unwillingness to cooperate that the containment policy emerged.

In short, the containment policy was a reaction to Soviet actions. It was a reaction to an aggressive imperialism which became more and more evident in the months immediately following the war. It was a reaction to Soviet moves which represented an utter departure from pledges taken at the conference table.

The Soviet Union refused to honor its agreement to sponsor free elections in Eastern Europe. The Soviets shook their fist at Turkey and at Iran. They encouraged Communist subversion of the legitimate Greek Government. They allowed huge stocks of Japanese military equipment to fall into the hands of the Chinese Communists in Manchuria and thus —in effect—went back on the promise they had made at Yalta to throw their full support to the Chinese Nationalist Government.

Speaking of Yalta, the charge has been made that our failure to "get tough" at the conference table allowed Moscow to help itself to Eastern Europe, China, and North Korea. I want to state categorically that this charge is absolutely without foundation.

The fact is that the Soviets received nothing by negotiation that they did not already or were not about to control by the presence of the Red Army. Soviet territorial gains have not been made by words exchanged at the conference table.

The containment policy—being a realistic policy—has thus had to concern itself more with Soviet actions than with Soviet words. In fact, it was a specific concrete action which can be said to have brought the containment policy into operation.

The scene was Iran. In early 1946, Soviet troops were still stationed in northern Iran. Further, they were interfering with the Iranian Government's attempts to govern in Azerbaijan, a key province in northern Iran. The Soviets refused to withdraw their troops from Iran despite a clear treaty obligation to do so.

The situation was brought to the attention of the United Nations. It was thoroughly aired in open debate. The peoples of the world were given a chance to learn—in great detail—what was going on in Iran. The result: Pressures exerted by an aroused world opinion—an opinion educated by U.N. debate—forced the Soviets to withdraw their troops.

The United Nations had proved itself an effective forum for the settlement of a dispute which was threatening the peace. The containment process operated for the first time because the free nations—working through the United Nations—contained an obvious Soviet effort to extend its influence into neighboring Iran.

You will note that I have referred to the "containment process." The Truman Doctrine of March 1947 was the first application of the containment policy in its more definitive form. The President's decision to aid the Greeks and the Turks, and congressional support of that decision, brought the containment policy to fruition as a total plan of action.

We helped the legitimate Greek Government to defeat the Communist-led revolt and thus created a situation of strength in Greece.

Today, a stable Greece is a full-fledged partner in the North Atlantic Treaty Organization.

In helping the Turks to modernize and equip their army, we helped to support a strong determination to withstand Soviet demands for control of the vital Dardanelles. We helped to create a situation of strength which has been vitally important in keeping Soviet imperialism from driving to the Persian Gulf and the Mediterranean.

Now it has been said that the containment policy is a purely negative affair. Words such as "negative" and "positive" are very misleading unless we understand clearly what we mean.

Containment is negative only in the sense that it does not envisage the use of armed force in aggressive action. It is no more negative than the doctrine of individual and collective defense is negative. It has meant and it means that the free nations of the world will do all in their power—including armed resistance—in the event of aggression, to prevent the free areas of the world from falling under Communist tyranny. In every other sense our present policy, of which containment is only one element, is positive.

The programs of mutual assistance among the nations of the free world are anything but negative. They are not only designed to contain and deter the aggressor; they are designed to maintain and strengthen the stability of free nations everywhere. They are designed to give us a strong boost on the road toward universal peace and humanitarian cooperation. They are designed to supplement, in full, the work of the United Nations.

Let us look briefly at some of these programs. Take the Marshall Plan, for example. The end of World War II saw the nations of Western Europe in economic chaos. Poverty was rampant. Destruction in most countries was terrible to behold. Countries which have served as battlefields look like battlefields long after the cannon have stopped roaring. Morale was at a dangerous low. Communist parties were at the height of their power. The possibility that Soviet power might move into much of Western Europe without firing a shot was a grim one.

OBJECTIVES OF THE MARSHALL PLAN

In the face of this situation, Secretary of State George C. Marshall arose to make a public address which was to initiate the great plan which bears his name. In that address, he said:

> Our policy is directed not against any country or doctrine but against hunger, poverty, desperation, and chaos.

The Marshall Plan was designed to help the Europeans help themselves get back on their economic feet. It was designed to help them develop internal stability. It was designed to help them preserve their freedom and their liberties through an economic rebirth capable of coping with subversion from within and expansionism from without.

Self-help and mutual cooperation—these were the terms upon which the United States offered the Western Europeans the means of helping themselves. And the nations and peoples of Western Europe accomplished a near miracle in the process.

The situation in Western Europe today speaks for itself. And to the extent that stability has been restored and communism forced into retreat—to that extent have we Americans helped to build a bastion of strength on behalf of our own security and free men everywhere.

Let us look at another of our positive programs: The Point Four Program.

Here is a program which first saw the light of day some 3 years after the containment policy became effective. But it is a logical outgrowth of the latter.

Point Four is a happy combination of genuine idealism and a means of strengthening the free world as a whole. Its purpose is to help the free peoples of the world, through their own efforts, to produce more food, more clothing, more materials for housing, and more mechanical power to lighten their burdens.

In helping underdeveloped areas to help themselves, we are working for a better standard of living among the less fortunate peoples. We are helping to eliminate the discontent of the poverty-stricken. We are helping to build their fortitude and strengthen their desire to withstand the impact of communism.

Are we not—through Point Four—building situations of strength? Of course, we are.

Consider, if you will, the various regional defense pacts to which we are party. All of these have been developed in conformity with the U.N. Charter. They are designed to strengthen the security of the nations immediately involved. But they are also designed to help the United Nations move more efficiently to meet a breach of the peace should it occur in an area covered by a regional agreement.

The North Atlantic Treaty Organization (NATO) is the most far-reaching of these regional agreements. But our mutual defense arrangements in the Pacific and with our Latin American neighbors are certainly of equal importance to our security and the peace of the world.

Through NATO, the free nations have erected an expanding defense force—a deterrent power designed to preserve the security of Western

Europe and that of the entire North Atlantic area. Equally impressive is the fact that we have managed to work out the organization and the techniques for making this defensive mechanism operate effectively.

This, I might say, was no simple task. Extreme nationalism has always been a difficult problem for those who would build unity. The distrust of ages is not easily dispelled in months or even years.

NATO—like the Schuman Plan, the Marshall Plan, and the European Payments Union—is a tribute to the masterful statesmanship of the Western Europeans themselves. They have overcome much of the pride and prejudice of centuries in their common interest. In doing so, they have added much to our own well-being and to the cause of peace as a whole.

Western Europe—for all the problems that continue to plague it today —is indeed a bulwark of strength for the United States as well as for the entire free world.

I have tried to give you a brief account of a few of the positive measures designed to create situations of strength in which the United States has had a crucial hand. I have sought to present an honest, realistic picture of how these measures are related to our drive for genuine security and our urge for a decent peace.

These measures certainly do not represent perfection in any sense of the word. They have not solved the great power dilemma of our time. They have not made one world out of two.

But I believe that they are real milestones of accomplishment. They have set us well on the road we are seeking to travel. There are important lessons to be learned through what these programs have accomplished if we are but willing to learn.

The free peoples are demonstrating that power—material power— is on their side.

If we can but preserve our unity of spirit as well as our unity of action, we shall certainly better our chance of developing the sort of world climate in which all men can breathe freely.

This may not happen for years. It may not happen for generations. But it is the challenge of our time.

An eighteenth century philosopher once said:

Power is not happiness. Security and peace are more to be desired than a name at which nations tremble.

If we but heed that advice and use our power wisely and with moderation, I believe that we will achieve the genuine security and peace we seek.

54. POINT FOUR, THE PRESIDENTIAL DIRECTIVE*

The Point Four Program is based upon the belief that, since "more than half of the people of the world are living in conditions approaching misery," it is part of a policy of enlightened self-interest to help these people to achieve a better life. Communism, it is argued, appeals very strongly to peoples living in poverty. If the United States, through the Point Four Program, can assist them to alleviate their poverty, a great blow will be struck at the assertion that only communism can solve the problems of underdeveloped areas. The nations so assisted by the United States, moreover, will then adhere to the coalition of the free world.

· · · · ·

Fourth, we must embark on a bold new program for making the benefits of our scientific advances and industrial progress available for the improvement and growth of underdeveloped areas.

More than half the people of the world are living in conditions approaching misery. Their food is inadequate. They are victims of disease. Their economic life is primitive and stagnant. Their poverty is a handicap and a threat both to them and to more prosperous areas.

For the first time in history, humanity possesses the knowledge and the skill to relieve the suffering of these people.

The United States is preeminent among nations in the development of industrial and scientific techniques. The material resources which we can afford to use for the assistance of other peoples are limited. But our imponderable resources in technical knowledge are constantly growing and are inexhaustible.

I believe that we should make available to peace-loving peoples the benefits of our store of technical knowledge in order to help them realize their aspirations for a better life. And, in cooperation with other nations, we should foster capital investment in areas needing development.

Our aim should be to help the free peoples of the world, through their own efforts, to produce more food, more clothing, more materials for housing, and more mechanical power to lighten their burdens.

We invite other countries to pool their technological resources in this undertaking. Their contributions will be warmly welcomed. This should be a cooperative enterprise in which all nations work together

* From President Harry S. Truman's Inaugural Address, January 20, 1949.

through the United Nations and its specialized agencies wherever practicable. It must be a world-wide effort for the achievement of peace, plenty, and freedom.

With the cooperation of business, private capital, agriculture, and labor in this country, this program can greatly increase the industrial activity in other nations and can raise substantially their standards of living.

Such new economic developments must be devised and controlled to benefit the peoples of the areas in which they are established. Guarantees to the investor must be balanced by guarantees in the interest of the people whose resources and whose labor go into these developments.

The old imperialism—exploitation for foreign profit—has no place in our plans. What we envisage is a program of development based on the concepts of democratic fair-dealing.

All countries, including our own, will greatly benefit from a constructive program for the better use of the world's human and natural resources. Experience shows that our commerce with other countries expands as they progress industrially and economically.

Greater production is the key to prosperity and peace. And the key to greater production is a wider and more vigorous application of modern scientific and technical knowledge.

Only by helping the least fortunate of its members to help themselves can the human family achieve the decent, satisfying life that is the right of all people.

Democracy alone can supply the vitalizing force to stir the peoples of the world into triumphant action, not only against their human oppressors, but also against their ancient enemies—hunger, misery, and despair.

55. PROBLEMS OF POINT FOUR

From an address by former Secretary of State Dean Acheson, delivered at the National Conference on Economic and Social Development in Washington, D.C., April 9, 1951—an analysis of the development and problems of the Point Four Program.

Very often before the committees of Congress and in other audiences to which I have spoken I have been asked the question, "Do you think it right that in our requests from the Congress we should have so large a proportion of our funds requested for military purposes as against the smaller portion which goes into the constructive work of the world?" And I always say: "I think it's very sad, it is nothing that we want; we would much prefer to have it otherwise."

We are taking the leadership in the world in trying to make it otherwise. We have proposals now which are being discussed in the United Nations which would lead to disarmament, lead to the world being relieved of this dreadful burden. But until that can be accomplished we must, whether we like it or not, spend a large part of our time and effort, just as the early settlers of this country had to do, in protecting ourselves, in building up our defenses so that behind that shield the peaceful work can go on.

And this, in passing, leads me to refer to a matter which is perhaps connected with it, and that is the matter of organization. So often in talking about programs of this sort we get distracted into the matter of organization. I'd like to say only one word about that, and that is that it's a characteristic of the human mind that if it fixes itself very intently upon a purpose, and in order to accomplish any purpose you have to fix yourself intently upon it, but if you do that then that purpose begins to expand until after a time in your mind it encompasses the whole world. I see this happening in all the departments of government all the time.

People can start saying, "Well, this is a matter of foreign policy and since it's a matter of foreign policy the State Department must do it and foreign policy affects everything in the world," so that people who take that view want to tend to expand the jurisdiction of the State Department. Or if you start from the point of view of the Treasury Department or the Department of Agriculture or the Department of Commerce you can say this leads to that and that leads to the next thing, and so this department should control all. And so you find people who say, "All you have to do is to find two characteristics in a program that means that it should be organized and managed by one organization" and those two characteristics are (1) if it's overseas, and (2) if it's economic.

Now, everything that is not in the United States, Canada, or Mexico, in a sense is overseas. And everything that is not purely military is economic and even most of the military program is economic. So that this conception, in which you must have an overseas organization which will run everything outside the United States, is, I think, to lose sight of the real purpose of some of these programs. I will not go on with this at length but merely say that the economic work which is being done in Europe itself in connection with the military program is far more closely associated with the military program than it is with the sort of thing that we are doing here in Point Four. So I urge you not to waste your time on these matters of organization at present but to concentrate on the main point.

So we not only have to build our shield here, our military shield, but we have to give great effort and great thought to the economic environment as well as the security environment.   And here I'm sorry to say that there is much to discourage the person who is interested in helping to get international developments in the economic field.   It isn't enough to have programs which will develop undeveloped areas, if you have a completely stagnant situation in the exchange of goods throughout the world.   We all know that in the early stages of development of under-developed areas we must concentrate on the agricultural side of affairs. And that means that there must be considerable trade in other goods. And if one has a situation where trade is stagnant because of barriers, because of lack of foreign exchange, because of all the impediments to it which exist, there will be a very great break and great drag upon the development of underdeveloped areas, no matter how enthusiastic we are about Point Four and no matter how much effort we put into it.

I have been working for 12 years on the effort to free international trade from some of its barriers and I regret to say that there are as many now as there were when we began and the outlook is discouraging.   But we must continue to fight for it and you must continue to help us because this matter of freeing trade throughout the world and bringing about a greater exchange of goods is essential for the purpose that you are meeting here today to consider.

COOPERATION FROM PRIVATE INVESTORS AND ORGANIZATIONS URGED

Similarly, in the economic field, there is the matter of investment. Unless there is a climate to encourage investment abroad you will not get the developments in underdeveloped areas which we are seeking. And unhappily the climate does not seem to be getting better but in many parts of the world to be getting worse.   There seems to be an idea that there is something bad about foreign investment in some parts of the world.   Companies, people who have put a great deal of money, a great deal of effort into developments in underdeveloped areas are treated as though they were enemies of the country in which they are working. If that goes on it just means that there will not be foreign investment and there will not be, as you all know, governmental capital sufficient to do this job.   And, after all, it doesn't make much difference whether the investment is the property of all the citizens of the country or some of the citizens.   If the whole climate for the reception of foreign invest-ment in a country is bad, then the capital will not go there, whether it's private or governmental.

And, again, there must be an environment which is congenial to the exchange of persons and ideas.   If, in parts of the world, foreigners are regarded as suspicious and as enemies, then again you have a lack of the necessary environment to carry on the purposes which we want here. In other words, this must be a two-way street, there must be friendliness on the side of those whom we are trying to help as well as the desire on our part to be of help. And all through everything that we do we must keep in mind that what we are after here is to preserve and safeguard the underlying human values.

It's very helpful to me to have this opportunity to come and talk with you. A conference of this sort, this conference is of tremendous importance to the carrying out of this program because this program is fundamentally not something which a government as a government carries out. Now, I don't mean by that merely that private organizations are very important in actually carrying out programs abroad. That is true, but even more than that the entire effort that the government agency carries out here is really carried out through private organization.

We do not have in the Government sufficient people to staff these operations, sufficient people to give us all the ideas, to give us all the working groups which are necessary. We turn to you. We turn to the colleges, to the groups, and to the organizations in the United States. And it is only if we are successful all together in doing this work, as one great undertaking in which we are all concerned, that it will be successful. It takes the unending labor of organizations such as yours to make young men and women want to go into this sort of work and want to go into it with a sense of dedication, with a sense of believing, as the early missionaries to this country believed, that there is something worth any degree of sacrifice in the task.

I know, in speaking with you, that I do not have to convince you that the Point Four Program is a good program. I don't have to stress its importance. What you would like me to do is to talk, in the first place, about the subject of the morning, the Program in Action. And in doing that, again I shall do it not with the purpose of trying to build up your enthusiasm—because that is built up and you understand this program —but from the point of view of pointing out some of the underlying factors which we have to have in mind when we operate here.

UNDERSTANDING NECESSARY TO ALLAY SUSPICIONS

And, again, if I may go back to a hackneyed subject, in order to understand the limitations which are necessary in the Program in Action and the methods which are necessary, we have to remind ourselves once more what it is that we are trying to do and what is the background out of which our present efforts emerge. Now, that background, . . .

is that two ideas of greatest importance are striking millions of people in the underdeveloped parts of the world at the same time, striking them with great suddenness and with great power. And these two ideas are, first of all, that a life of misery is not foreordained, that something can be done about it, that much can be done about it. And the second idea is that independence, freedom from foreign domination and foreign direction, is within their grasp and nothing is going to be allowed to interfere with that.

Now these two ideas are ideas which have moved peoples profoundly over the centuries and they are hitting people, millions of people, in the underdeveloped areas for the first time with great power since the war.

And that leads to tremendous ferment. It leads to tremendous comings and goings in the population and the thoughts of the population. The purpose of the Point Four Program is to help direct this energy, this ferment, into peaceful channels of development, rather than into mere chaos. We know perfectly well that there is a tendency to look for panaceas. Indeed in many parts of the world these two thoughts which I have been describing to you are often confused. Many people in many parts of the world are led to believe that the mere attainment of national independence will bring automatically the fuller life, the freedom from poverty and misery and disease. We know of course that that is not the case. Therefore, these people, once being disappointed—because being free they are not immediately in good shape—turn to another panacea, which is that of communism, which promises them that if they will embrace this doctrine then all these things will happen.

But what the Point Four Program is intended to do is to say we have knowledge, we have skills which you have seen and which are in part the cause of this great ferment which is going on in your minds. We are ready to share them with you. And we wish to work out with you methods by which you can know what we know and we can help you develop your own resources for your own purposes.

LIMITATIONS IN THE PROGRAM

Now, this being so, if we look at the nature of the people and the nature of the situation with which we are dealing we begin to see some necessary limitations in the Program in Action. One necessary limitation comes from the fact that many, if not most, of the peoples with whom we are dealing are suspicious of foreigners. Foreigners have come to them very often in the past and not always, or perhaps not often, with the best results. Therefore, they are suspicious. Why are these people coming to us? Why are they offering to do this for us?

Is there some hidden purpose?   Is there some desire on their part to get control of our country?   These are the questions they ask themselves.

Then there is the limitation of the absorptive capacity of the peoples we are trying to help.   Absorptive in several ways.   First of all, they must take it in through their mind and through the training of their hands.   And this cannot be done overnight.   This is a long process.

Then there is the confusion in their minds as to what they want. Some want one thing and some another.   Very often they haven't the real knowledge to understand what it is that they really need at the moment.   There is a great desire in every part of the world for industrialization and there is very little understanding of how dangerous that is until there is in sight a strong agricultural base.

I think in all the times that I have talked with visitors from foreign countries since the war and, indeed, during the war, everyone who has come into my office starts out with, "We would like a steel mill."   Well, they want a steel mill in every single country in the world.   It makes no difference whether they have ore or coal or anything else.   The steel mill is the mark of civilization, and that is what they want.

Now, it's not a question of pouring vast sums of money and vast numbers of technicians into these areas.   It couldn't be done if we wanted to do it.   Sometimes I have been in meetings where people talk about billions of dollars or hundreds of thousands of technicians being poured all over the world.   Those people never stop to think of where the technicians are going to sleep and what they are going to do.   The mere question of housing of the missions which are already being sent out is a serious one in parts of the world where there aren't many houses. This thing has got to be done sensibly.

ADJUSTING TO INTERNAL SITUATIONS
IN FOREIGN COUNTRIES

Now, without going on further into a theoretical discussion, let me speak of one or two actual situations to show what can be done and what should not be done.

The first real necessity for success is that what you offer to do or what you're doing is something which the country wants.   Now, often it's very hard to bring that about because the country doesn't know what it wants and if what it wants is the right thing for it, then what you should do is to get in behind that and help with all your power and not say, "Oh well, I wouldn't do it just this way, I would do it that way." If they have a good idea and one that is an effective one, get behind it and help them.

That is the situation in India. There the program is one which the Indians have worked out themselves. True, they have worked it out with the help of American technicians, but they sought the technicians. We didn't force the technicians on them. They came out themselves with their own money. They employed these technicians. And they went to India and they developed an Indian governmental program which was started. So that when we came into the picture we could throw our help into something which had been developed by India with our people merely training the Indians who are training their comrades how to carry on this program. Immediately the thing caught hold like a prairie fire and the Government has now organized with us the Indo-American Fund, a joint undertaking, something which they started, something which they believe in. And we put all our effort and funds into that.

Starting with a small group where boys from these villages were taught the fundamentals of what they should do to increase food production and have better public health. Starting with that training school, boys, young men go back to their villages and persuade the elders of the village to adopt this rather revolutionary idea. This spreads on from there to other villages which have heard about this. They in turn come in to look at it and find everybody with two or three times as much food as they had before. The newcomers say, "We want that." Thus you finally get a program where the propulsive force comes from the country itself, and we are going along to help it.

Now, you find other situations where the country not only doesn't know what it wants but isn't equipped to play any part in getting it. And there a great mistake would be made if we went in and said, "This is what you want, here are a lot of Americans, we will do this. We will undertake to train your people." What you have got to do is to start at the very beginning.

There was a situation such as that in one country which we are helping. There, as in almost all these places, the great need was for an increase in the food supply. When we got to the country we found that the only people dealing with agriculture was the thing called a "Bureau," which was made up of six people with a budget of $6,000 a year. Six people in the entire country dealing with agriculture! Well, you couldn't get anywhere until the country itself was better organized to be a partner in this effort. And therefore, the first job was to show them how to develop the proper bureaus to carry on agricultural extension work in their country. That was done. Then programs were developed in conjunction with this new governmental outfit.

The other day I had a visit from some people in a very small country and they had come up to say, "Go easy. Take it easy. We are being overwhelmed by good will." They had at the same time six international organizations—the United States organization and four private ones—descend on them. And they said there were almost more "good-willers" in the country than there were citizens in the country. The country was simply bewildered. It didn't know what to do. People were starting projects and deciding they weren't any good and, the happy phrase, "cutting their losses," didn't carry much conviction to the population.

So finally we said, "Now, let's all get together here and let's all sit down and work out some coordinated plan, get the people and the government of the country in agreement with this and then go ahead a little more slowly."

You must adjust what you're doing to the absorptive capacity of the country and the willingness of the country to have you carry on the program. Money isn't the right way to go at it. Money is essential, money is necessary. Sometimes a lot of money is necessary, as in the Indian program where in order to carry out and reach the goals within the time which is allotted we must move much faster than the pure theory of technical assistance would permit.

EXPORTATION OF THE AMERICAN IDEA

Those are some of the ideas which can be developed much more fully with others in your panel discussions this morning. But what I should like to leave with you are the points which I have just made.

First of all, that Point Four is one among many points. It is not the whole foreign policy. It cannot succeed unless the whole foreign policy succeeds.

Second, it must be adjusted. The work that we do must be adjusted to the condition, the situation in the country. It must be infinitely flexible.

Third, and it follows from the second, do not be doctrinaire about Point Four. Do not be like the Socialist Party where you have the pure doctrine and then 50 splinter doctrines coming off it. Do not say, "This is with Point Four and this is without Point Four." That sort of rigid thinking, I believe, gets us nowhere. Point Four must mean that we are primarily engaged in helping to teach these people how to help themselves.

Now, what is necessary to bring that about in a particular country depends on that country. And, therefore, do not be rigid. Do not have purely doctrinaire ideas.

And, finally, one last thought. We have said over and over again that this is exporting the American idea, the American Revolution, or the American dream. It is very true, but if that is true let us be sure, and be terribly sure, that we are preserving the American dream, the American idea, in America.

Do not let us be smug and believe that merely because you can read in the books that America was like this, or that Abraham Lincoln said it was like this, it will be like that without our constant effort and our constant fighting to make our country what we want it to be and what we believe it has been and will be in the future.

56. THE COLD WAR AND THE UNITED NATIONS *

One of our most important means of attaining peace and security is to support the United Nations. It has been said that any American policy which appeals to our sense of realism, and which at the same time can be understood and defended in idealist terms, is bound to find widespread public support. Elements of what might be called enlightened self-interest are strong in our approach to the United Nations.

Mr. Gross lists four reasons for our support of the U.N. It is interesting to note that each reason contains elements of both the idealist and realist approach to international politics. Mr. Gross is opposed to the ejection of the Soviet Union from the United Nations. Since he is an official of our government, we may presume that the reasons he offers represent the official view on this oft-repeated proposal.

Most of us have at one time or another wondered why the Soviet Government thought it useful or necessary to sign the U.N. Charter. For surely the Charter is not only the antithesis of everything international communism stands for, but it has been proved over and over again that the Kremlin leaders never had the slightest intention of complying with the Charter in the first place.

Soviet adherence to a system of international cooperation was, of course, rooted in a cynical interpretation of Soviet self-interest. For this reason, there are a few who argue that the mere fact that the Soviet Government joined is clear evidence that we were foolish to have done so, and for that matter, that we should "pull out" precisely because the Soviets have stayed in. There may be a certain allure in forming policy

* Ernest A. Gross, *Department of State Bulletin,* February 23, 1953, pp. 316-322. The author is Deputy United States Representative to the United Nations.

on the basis of doing everything contrariwise to the Soviets.   However, most people hesitate to let the Kremlin navigate our ship, which they could thus do, merely by pointing our compass south if they wanted to send us north.

My reason for mentioning Soviet adherence to the Charter is not to speculate concerning their motives for doing so.   The stark fact is that the Soviet system is in open revolt against the Charter.   The question arises whether, under that circumstance, the United Nations has a survival value, either from the point of view of our national interest in particular or that of the free world in general.

It is necessary to appraise the United Nations in the light of its original purposes, its method of operation, and our own stake in it. But, more particularly, we must consider where the United Nations is left—and where we are left—by reason of what I have called the Soviet revolt against the Charter.

These are the questions with which I now propose to deal.

NATURE AND PURPOSES OF THE U.N.

Like all determined efforts to achieve collective security, the United Nations was born of the greatest of all "collective insecurities"; that is, a world war.   One frequently hears the question asked whether it is possible to develop a workable system for collective security in the presentday world.   The question is a fair one, but I suspect it means different things to different people because of the many variables of the definition of the term "collective security."   I must confess that, as I define the term, the question does not arise at all.   To me, collective security is merely a way of describing the objective of sharing the burdens and responsibilities of common defense.   To the extent that common interests are identified and common exertions made to carry them out, there is a growing, constantly changing, dynamic creation of collective security.

The United Nations represents the high point, up to this moment of recorded history, of world-wide efforts to identify common interests and to develop procedures for sharing the burdens of common defense of those interests.

The U.N. Charter does not commit the error of interpreting too narrowly the interests which men share merely by reason of being members of the human society.   It recognizes the diverse and widespread enemies to these common human interests.   Nor does the Charter err by giving short weight or measure to the means by which these enemies can be cooperatively faced.

To put it more plainly, the Charter counts among the enemies of decent human society not only aggression and imperialisms great and small, but also those equally ancient enemies of man: disease, poverty, illiteracy, and slavery. Therefore, when I define collective security as the means of sharing the burdens of common defense, I include these among the enemies and perils against which we erect our defenses.

The primary specific purposes of the U.N. Charter are (1) the maintenance of international peace and security, and (2) the promotion of conditions in the world which, in the language of the Charter, are "necessary for peaceful and friendly relations among nations" (article 55). It is obvious these two primary purposes are interrelated. For example, we find that international disputes frequently involve differences of view regarding the method and timing for giving effect to the Charter principle of equal rights and self-determination of peoples.

Generally, with regard to the maintenance of international peace and security, the functions of the United Nations are conceived to be to assist in the settlement of disputes and to take action to prevent breach of the peace or to repel aggression.

The framers of the Charter draw a distinction between procedures for settling international disputes (as to which no organ of the United Nations was given power to make enforceable decisions) and action in the case of breach of the peace. The United Nations is a voluntary association of sovereign states. Few, if any of them, were willing to vest in an organization that degree of sovereignty which would be involved in dictating the terms of the settlement of a dispute. Would the people of the United States be willing to delegate to the United Nations, or any other body, the right, let us say, to award the Panama Canal to another state in the unlikely event that we found ourselves involved in a dispute with another state which laid claim to the Canal?

Nevertheless, the General Assembly and the Security Council may *recommend* terms of settlement of a dispute. Hence, the distinction drawn in the Charter between disputes and breaches of the peace is more theoretical than real.

With regard to action to prevent breaches of the peace (as distinguished from the settlements of disputes) or to restore international peace or security if it has been broken, the decision and enforcement powers of the United Nations were deliberately limited by the veto. I think it is important to evaluate correctly the problem created by the Soviet abuse of the veto. There is no doubt the Soviet Government has abused its reserved power, but this, along with the Soviet boycott and walkout, is merely a symptom of its general attitude of defiance and revolt against the Charter.

I think it is illusory to blame the voting procedure as the cause of difficulty, rather than as a symptom of the disease. Nor do I believe that the major powers, including the U.S. Government or people, would favor a change in the Charter leaving to majority vote decisions involving the use of force or matters closely connected therewith. That is my personal view.

It is also the view of such an expert on the Charter as Dr. Pasvolsky, who, incidentally, has pointed out the fact that the possible effect of the voting arrangements agreed upon at San Francisco was foreseen. He says:

> There were no illusions as to the limitations that such an arrangement would impose upon the effectiveness of the proposed organization, nor as to the possibility that the great privilege which the major nations thus claimed for themselves might be abused. . . . The underlying theory, however, was that if one of the major nations were to prove recalcitrant, or were to refuse to abide by the rules of international behavior that were being inscribed in the Charter, a situation would be created in which the recalcitrant nation might have to be coerced; and it was apparent that no major nation could be coerced except by the combined forces of the other major nations. This would be the equivalent of a world war, and a decision to embark upon such a war would necessarily have to be made by each of the other major nations for itself and not by any international organization.

I think this analysis is borne out by the disposition of a similar question arising under the North Atlantic Treaty. It will be recalled that article 5, the heart of the treaty, provides that in the event of an armed attack against any party to the treaty, each other party will take, and I quote, "such action as it deems necessary" to restore and maintain the security of the area. This language was, of course, carefully considered, and, although it is a commitment of the highest moral value, I believe that its explicit reservation of the right of unilateral decision is relevant to an appraisal of the question whether the U.S. Government would be prepared completely to forego its veto power.

This is not to say that we, the U.S. Government, have not sought consistently to limit the area in which the veto is used. I, myself, voiced the attitude of our Government on this matter during a meeting of the Security Council in 1950 in which I said: "It is the policy of the United States to restrict the use of the veto by extending whenever possible, by example, by precedent or by agreement, the area of Security Council action in which the veto is not applicable." The fact remains that each of the major powers, without any illusions on the subject, kept in its own pocket a key with which it could lock the door to substantive decisions by the Security Council.

However, it is true nevertheless that this fact has proved to be of little significance principally for two reasons. In the first place, as has already been pointed out, the same Soviet intransigence which accounts for its abuse of the veto power would also have led the Kremlin to do what it could to obstruct the carrying out of decisions of which it disapproved. And the facts of power being what they are, an attempt to coerce Soviet compliance would involve the highest policy for each state in determining its own course of action.

Second, a U. N. *recommendation,* as distinguished from a Security Council decision, has a political and moral compulsive quality which I do not believe was fully appreciated at San Francisco. One has to observe the vehemence, not to say violence of arguments for or against a resolution, proposed for adoption by the General Assembly relating to, let us say, human rights, self-determination, Palestine, disarmament—to give but a few illustrations—to realize how much importance is attached to recommendations by the General Assembly. And it should be remembered that the General Assembly, under the Charter, has no power to make decisions, but is limited entirely to recommendations. Moreover, it is revealing that from the very start of the aggression in Korea, both the Security Council and the General Assembly have limited themselves to making recommendations to member states. Nor was it the threat of the veto that produced this result in the Security Council in June and July of 1950, inasmuch as the Soviet representative was not present in the chamber for these meetings.

These considerations, I think, have a direct bearing upon an appraisal of the value of the United Nations in the painful and patient efforts to develop a collective-security system. The veto-free General Assembly, where the organized community of nations passes moral and political judgments, assumes more and more importance as Soviet intransigence becomes more and more obvious. It has been possible by procedural means wholly within the Charter to make the General Assembly a more workable mechanism for the purpose of dealing with disputes and threats to the peace. This was, of course, done through the Uniting for Peace Resolution adopted by the General Assembly in 1950.

I turn now to the second major purpose of the United Nations; that is, the promotion of world conditions necessary for peaceful and friendly relations among nations. The work of the specialized agencies, such as the World Health Organization, Food and Agriculture Organization, and the like, as well as the work of the Technical Assistance program, the activities of the Economic and Social Council in the field of human rights, and the supervision by the Trusteeship Council of areas of the world which do not govern themselves—all these activities I shall not do more than mention. Their basic importance is too well understood to require argument.

The point I wish to stress here, however, is that the framers of the Charter were aware that such matters as higher standards of living, full employment, health, cultural and educational problems, and respect for human rights and fundamental freedoms—that all these matters are basic to conditions of stability and well being which, and I again quote the words of the Charter, are "necessary for peaceful and friendly relations among nations." It is in this way that the Charter identifies that common interest which must underlie common effort.

The fact that the Soviet Government fails to cooperate or to contribute toward efforts to deal with common problems does not diminish the necessity for facing them. I do not suppose anyone would argue that the World Health Organization should be disbanded because the Russians are not members. Yet, this is precisely what would happen if the advice were heeded of those who advocate disbanding the United Nations on the ground that the Soviet Government is not carrying out its Charter obligations.

OUR STAKE IN THE U.N. FUTURE

This leads me to consideration of the future of the United Nations and our stake in it, keeping in mind the nature and purposes of the organization as I have attempted to outline them above.

It has become somewhat fashionable to say that part of the difficulty faced by the United Nations at home arises from the fact that it was "oversold" to the American people. Perhaps this is the right word—I do not wish to quibble about the word—but I wonder whether it would not be more accurate to say its nature and purposes were *misunderstood*, rather than *overvalued*.

It is true that certain assumptions, or I should say hopes, were in the air at San Francisco. These included the hope that the peace treaties would be speedily settled, that those who suffered so grievously, including the Soviets, would be willing to cooperate to restore their economies and rebuild their cities, and that the horrors of the war would have taught even the Communists the values of collective measures against aggression. The frustration of these hopes, however, has not, in my judgment, invalidated the premises upon which the United Nations was founded. To the contrary, I believe the very frustration of these hopes has underscored the necessity for carrying on the effort. I say this because the United Nations was not born of these hopes, but as a response to a perceived need, created by what I have referred to as the "collective insecurity" of two world wars.   The hopes I have mentioned generated a degree of enthusiasm in support of these efforts.   And it is natural that the frustration of the hopes has diminished the enthusiasm.

However, it is a dangerous *non sequitur* to argue from this that the abandonment of the hopes justifies the abandonment of the organization.   I think we would all agree that if Soviet obstruction in the United Nations outweighed the advantages we derive from carrying on the organization as now constituted, we should indeed withdraw.   The answer depends, among other things, upon an analysis of what are the objectives of our leadership, and what is our national self-interest in this matter.

Starting from the definition of collective security, which strikes me as a realistic one—the objective of sharing the burdens and responsibilities of common defense—it follows that it is in our enlightened self-interest to develop this community of interest and effort to the maximum practicable extent.

I do not believe it is a digression to consider at this point the nature of our system, particularly as contrasted to that of the international Communist conspiracy.   Our society is, of course, based upon a moral and legal structure.   This is exemplified by the Constitution with its Bill of Rights, the device of the truly secret ballot to select our leaders and the tradition of accountability of those leaders.   Ours is a society which reflects the optimistic assumption that human beings by nature desire to cooperate with each other to their mutual benefit, and that the creation of conditions in which such cooperation can be carried on is the first duty of a society.   Free exchange of ideas and information, the maintenance of conditions of health and welfare, and loyalty to a code of ethics and morality form the sinews of our social structure.

The totalitarian system, classically illustrated by Soviet communism, is, on the contrary, founded on pessimism.   The urge to unrestrained power, to aggression, and to dictatorship may be explained as an expression of a philosophy which I would call the "expectation of evil."   It is not enough to explain Soviet imperialism as being based on a fear of encirclement.   The question is why do totalitarian systems characteristically fear encirclement?   Why, in particular, does the Soviet ideology base its system not only upon a preconceived hostility to our way of life, but also upon an inner compulsion as well as an avowed commitment to destroy it?

Dictatorships can only be maintained by suspicious and fearful men who expect evil from their fellow men.   Success in the competition for power goes to him who most ruthlessly acts on the basis of fear and suspicion, who most cleverly rationalizes his ruthlessness, and who never for a moment relaxes his expectation of evil from his colleagues. These he regards as fellow-conspirators rather than as friendly associates.

A contrast between the assumptions on which their system and ours is based goes to the root of the problem as how best to organize the international society to deal with the menace with which our own way of life is confronted.

There is an important principle to be deduced from the fact that both their system and ours, contrasting as they may be, have one attribute in common; that is, that they as well as we are driven by a law of human conduct to apply the same standards in their dealings abroad which they apply in their relationships at home. We have all observed the practice of Soviet representatives in the United Nations of putting forward positions which are, in themselves, extreme. We have seen that they put forward these extreme positions with an air of finality which discourages negotiation and often with attacks on motive as well as with a violence of expression which offends the listener.

Visitors to the U.N. debates often wonder why the Kremlin leaders ordain the use of these techniques and whether they hope or expect to convince anyone by them. However, if one follows, even casually, the methods of expression used by the ruling group within the Soviet Union itself—in speeches by party leaders, in periodicals, and radio broadcasts—one finds exactly the same manner as is employed by Soviet representatives in international forums such as the United Nations.

The objective both at home and abroad is not to convince, but to coerce. Coercion and fear are woven into the police-state fabric as part of its very nature.

Soviet representatives to the United Nations are themselves driven by fear with a close checkrein.

Now, with respect to our own system, there is a healthy and inevitable demand that our spokesmen well and truly reflect the American tradition and way of life. The public opinion which guides and restrains the government of a democracy forbids governmental spokesmen in international forums, even for short periods or on specific issues, from putting up a false front.

Accordingly, for quite different reasons, we find that both in the case of a democratic society and of a police state, there is an apparently inexorable "law of consistency" which can be simply stated: It is impossible for a society to reserve one set of standards to be used at home and apply another set of standards in its dealings abroad.

The identity between the principles of the U.N. Charter and the Constitution of the United States is often overlooked or forgotten. The principles of the Charter are not only a direct reflection of our own culture and traditions, but they are at the same time principles to which men of all races, places, and religions respond and lay claim. It is to our clear advantage that governments throughout the world be committed to them.

WHY WE SHOULD SUPPORT AND STRENGTHEN THE U.N.

I would list the following four principal reasons why it is in our national interest to support the United Nations and seek to strengthen it.

1. *It is probably the most potent and certainly the most convenient method of identifying interests common to the free world and of stimulating common effort to meet dangers confronting those interests.*

The United States, richly endowed as it is, has acquired a position of leadership in the world by reason of forces beyond its control—forces which shape the destinies of nations as well as of man. The power, which is ours by nature, and which we constantly generate by reason of the excellence of our system and our attributes, is one of the important facts of international life. However, as President Roosevelt said in his last message on the state of the Union (January 1945):

. . . in a democratic world, as in a democratic nation, power must be linked with responsibility, and obliged to defend and justify itself within the framework of the general good.

Our whole system is based upon the proposition that power is not an end in itself and that force, like fire, is a friend of man only when it is managed and controlled. As the historian, Bagehot, said: "It is the function of force to give moral ideas time to take root."

The United Nations is therefore the link between power and responsibility.

For a democracy, world leadership can be maintained only by following the rules of behavior—the code of responsibility—which shapes its own society at home. The essential bond is moral unity, and this can only be based upon a knowledge of common objectives and confidence in our integrity. The U.N. Charter defines the common objectives of a free society. Our commitment to carry them out builds confidence in our sense of responsibility. Moreover, the United Nations is one of a set of mechanisms, however imperfect, designed to carry out these common objectives.

I stress the fact that the United Nations is but one mechanism. It was never intended to supplant other forms of diplomatic, political, and economic intercourse.

2. *The second important consideration, which flows from what I have just said, is that the United Nations provides the framework and the foundation for regional organizations and other collective activities to keep the peace.*

As one looks back, for example, to the debates in the Senate which attended the formation of the North Atlantic Treaty Organization (NATO), and as one reads the report of the Foreign Relations Committee of the Senate, one is struck by the close relationships which were perceived between the North Atlantic Treaty Organization and the United Nations.

Thus, the Foreign Relations Committee was at pains to emphasize that the North Atlantic Treaty Organization was not what it called "an old-fashioned military alliance," but that, if it could be called an alliance at all, it is, in the words of the Committee, "an alliance against war itself." Truly this is a concept which is justified, but which I submit can be justified *only* on the basis that NATO is designed as a fortress to defend the Charter.

The United Nations is the rock upon which this and other regional fortresses are built. It is, moreover, important that we should not become confused as to which is the rock and which the fortress.

The foundation supplied by the United Nations for collective action is, of course, most dramatically illustrated by Korea. The United Nations, during the current session of the General Assembly, achieved its greatest moral unity with regard to the Korean aggression when 54 nations voted for a resolution sponsored by the Government of India. In supporting this resolution, the entire free world rallied around the moral principle that the prisoners of war should not be forced against their will to return to slavery or death.

The Communist aggressors in Korea, together with their Soviet sponsors and supporters, have been morally isolated by this unanimity. The consequences are bound to be far reaching, particularly in those areas of Asia, Africa, and the Middle East which have now declared their allegiance to the standards of morality in which they have such a deep and common interest. For, in the last analysis, it must be clear that the Communist aggression in Korea, if it had been permitted to go unchecked, would have extinguished one of the oldest and proudest nationalist movements in the world—that of the Koreans. The preservation of this nationalism is therefore symbolic of the principle of self-determination, which is both the goal and the aspiration of populations in many areas of the world. Korea is an example of how a common interest can be identified and supported. For here we have seen the growth of a realization among 54 nations of the world that they have a common interest not only in resisting aggression, but also in supporting a nationalist movement which has survived a history of oppression and subjugation.

3. *A third consideration justifying our support of the United Nations is the importance of developing methods to aid in settling international disputes.*

I do not believe this point requires an extended justification. However, it is an objective which takes on a particular urgency in the face of Soviet attempts to exploit all disagreements and disputes arising in the free world. This is, of course, particularly true with respect to disputes involving national aspirations for self-government and independence. The relative ease with which these moves can be subverted has always been recognized in Communist dogma. In 1924, for example, Marshal Stalin said: "The national movements for the freeing of the oppressed countries from the imperialist yoke contain unexhausted revolutionary possibilities."

Similarly, with respect also to disputes not involving so-called "colonialism," the Soviet Government passes up few opportunities to fish in troubled waters. A year ago, the Soviet representative in the Security Council suddenly intervened in a debate concerning the dispute between India and Pakistan over the disposition of the State of Kashmir. The burden of the Soviet intervention was to attack the honored and respected U.N. representative as a "tool and spy of Wall Street imperialism." He also assailed the motives of the United States and the United Kingdom, professing the absurd belief that it was our objective to gain control of the State of Kashmir for some sordid purposes of our own.

We are preoccupied quite understandably with problems caused by the tensions between the Soviet system and the free world. However, we should not permit ourselves to disregard the fact that the problems which divide and separate the free world, within itself, are serious and that some of the greatest successes of the United Nations in its short history have been the settlement of these conflicts or the bringing about of the end of armed warfare. Illustrations may be found in Indonesia, Palestine, and Kashmir.

4. *Finally, it is essential for us to support the constructive work of the United Nations in the economic and social fields. These are the problems which form the highest common denominators of interest in binding together the peoples of the world—those who are free and those who wish to be free.*

"KICKING THE RUSSIANS OUT"

I concede that one may accept everything I have said up to this point as justifying our continued participation in and support of the United Nations, and yet ask whether it would not be better from our point of view if the Soviet Government and its satellites were not in the organization. This is more popularly referred to as "kicking the Russians out." It is a legitimate question, and I should like to deal with it, expressing purely personal views.

I have already said that if we should conclude that Soviet participation in the United Nations is disadvantageous to our enlightened self-interest, it would be foolish for us to continue to support the organization as presently constituted. It is my contention that the interests of the free world and the principles of the Charter, which reflect those interests, are better served by our not disbanding and destroying the organization. That would, of course, be the result of our withdrawal. There is no way of expelling the Soviet Government, even if this should be desired, inasmuch as the Soviet Government could veto an attempt to deprive it of U.N. membership. But I assume that when people talk about "kicking the Russians out," they realize this, and what they really mean is that we should withdraw and, so to speak, "take the United Nations Charter with us." Incidentally I am not certain whether, under such circumstances, our copyright would be universally recognized!

Now, as I see it, there are a number of advantages which accrue to the free world from Soviet membership in the organization. And this, despite the fact that the Soviet Government and its satellites have failed to participate in the constructive work of the organization, have abused their veto power, and have in other ways carried on their revolt against the Charter system. Indeed, I think it may be said fairly that in any real sense of the word the Soviet Government has never really "joined" the United Nations. But they are members and, except for a relatively brief period of general walk-out on the Chinese representation issue, they attend meetings of the Security Council, of the General Assembly, and of other principal organs of the United Nations.

I think one may list the following advantages to us in their continuing to do so, if it is in fact their intention to do so.

In the first place, their commitment to the Charter is a convenient and I should say important method of holding them accountable. It is important to realize that the Charter is a code of conduct which is inconsistent with, and excludes the ideology of, international communism. Although, of course, they only pay lip service to the Charter, nevertheless, whatever the reason they may have had in signing the

Charter, they did sign a covenant at San Francisco which is an anti-Marxist "manifesto." They find themselves now either in open revolt against the Charter, or forced to resort to fraud and distortion in their pretenses at carrying it out.

It is of some significance that they have never, so far as I am aware, admitted to departing from the requirements of the Charter. They have always, on the contrary, gone to extreme lengths to profess adherence to it and pay lip service to it.

It would serve no useful purpose that I can see to release them from their pledges, however much they may violate them in practice.

Second, they are subject to psychological, moral, and political pressures in the U. N. forum. The United Nations is inherently what might be called an "open system." There is no room within the United Nations for secret conspiracies, plots, or hiding places. The pressures of the forum are intangible but nevertheless real. And I believe that the proof of this may be found in the extreme lengths to which Soviet spokesmen often go in attempting to rationalize or justify courses of action, however false their explanation may be.

Third, and I would in many ways regard this as the most important consideration of all—they are constantly forced to reveal the true nature and purposes of the Soviet system. The debate on the Korean question which took place in the first part of the seventh session of the General Assembly illuminates this point.

Mr. Vyshinsky, at one point while arguing against the principle that prisoners of war should be free to decide whether they wished repatriation, startled the Political Committee by baldly proclaiming that the prisoner had no will other than the will of the state.

It is difficult to dissemble in an open forum, and Soviet lies are easily unmasked. The United Nations is the supreme forum of self-revelation and I do not believe the Soviet system comes out of this market place for trading ideas with better bargains than we do.

Fourth, their presence in the organization and the processes of the organization itself enable weak or wavering states to cooperate with us without the appearance of choosing sides. It is perhaps unfortunate that neutralism or tendencies toward "third force" positions exist, but they do constitute facts of international life.

I have no doubt that it was considerably easier for the small states represented on the Security Council to vote in 1946 to call upon the Soviet Government to withdraw troops from Iran than it would have been for those states to have made separate diplomatic representations to the Soviet Foreign Office on this issue.

Finally, I think it is of value that the Soviet representatives are available for discussion. The example which leaps to mind is of course the informal discussions which led to the lifting of the Berlin blockade. I think it is unlikely that we shall, at least for a long time, be able to conclude so-called "general settlements" with the Soviet leaders. It is much more likely that the discussion and exploration of specific issues may perhaps over a long period produce a certain measure of agreement. Accordingly, it is of value to have a forum in which constant contact of individuals representing the respective governments may facilitate the exploration of these matters in a routine fashion.

The question is sometimes asked why, since the Soviet Government has unquestionably sponsored and supported the Korean aggression, they should be permitted to retain membership in the United Nations. I have already pointed out there is no way of expelling them, since they can veto a decision of that sort.

Even if this were not so, I think it does not take full account of the realities of the situation to regard membership in the United Nations as a sort of badge of merit. There are advantages in universal membership, even including recalcitrants, for reasons which I have just attempted to explain. However, one must distinguish here between the problem presented by the application of certain states for membership in the United Nations, since here the standards for admission are prescribed in article 4 of the Charter. So long as article 4 provides, as it does, that membership in the United Nations is open to peace-loving states which accept the Charter obligations and in the judgment of the organization are able and willing to carry out these obligations, such a judgment must be made in good faith. It is indeed difficult to say that states such as Rumania, Bulgaria, and Albania are "peace-loving" or "are able and willing to carry out the obligations of the U. N. Charter."

It may be that it would have been wiser to omit these qualifications for new membership. Personally, I find it a cause of some regret that the Charter was written in this way. However, so long as these conditions for membership are imposed, I see no alternative but to honor them. Subject to this, I believe that the wider the membership of the United Nations, the more advantageous to the interests of the free world.

I should like to conclude by quoting remarks which I set down in print about 2 years ago, which I believe were timely then and, if anything, more timely now:

The United Nations is not a mere Charter of Containment. It is, potentially, a Charter of Liberation. It pledges liberation from the age-old enemies of poverty, disease, and fear of conquest.

The Charter is a magnet drawing vast populations who see in the Charter the expression of their hope and determination to live their own lives in well-being and freedom.

Our purpose is to make the magnet irresistible, strongly charging it with our own support and our own strength.

Even within the slave world of the Soviet Union and its satellites, there is now unrest and ferment. When national aspirations are subverted, when human aspirations are suppressed, an explosive force is built up. What that force can do when it generates sufficient pressure, we have already seen, and seen with encouragement, in the successful effort of Yugoslavia to free itself from Soviet domination. These same forces are at work in Eastern Europe and we may expect that in the course of time they will assert themselves in China, too. The free world will expand because men everywhere want to be free.

Every advance we make in the struggle for liberation is a step toward a world in which the Soviet leaders will be compelled to practice as well as to preach the doctrine of peaceful co-existence. When this has been achieved, peaceful co-existence may develop into mutual cooperation. Then the people of Russia as well as those in the satellite states, will once again take their rightful place in the family of mankind.

~⊙~

57. THE CHANCE FOR PEACE *

This selection is the first significant official expression of foreign policy by the new President. It is difficult, at least from this address, to determine the precise differences of approach between the President and Mr. Truman. A recital of broad attitudes is basic to an understanding of general foreign policy objectives, but an analysis of "dynamic" and "new" policies can be made more easily in terms of changes in the intensity and direction of specific policies. During the first year of his administration, Mr. Eisenhower was carried along, to a great extent, by the momentum created by his predecessor. The time when this momentum continued to be important is past, and we can already see from his new proposals in the field of atomic energy (Selection 59), that he has begun to strike out on his own.

In this selection, Mr. Eisenhower indicates what the American people and their government are willing to do for the cause of peace, and asks "What is the Soviet Union ready to do?"

In this spring of 1953 the free world weighs one question above all others: the chance for a just peace for all peoples.

* An address by President Dwight D. Eisenhower, delivered before the American Society of Newspaper Editors and broadcast to the nation over combined radio and television networks on April 16, 1953.

To weigh this chance is to summon instantly to mind another recent moment of great decision. It came with that yet more hopeful spring of 1945, bright with the promise of victory and of freedom. The hope of all just men in that moment too was a just and lasting peace.

The 8 years that have passed have seen that hope waver, grow dim, and almost die. And the shadow of fear again has darkly lengthened across the world.

Today the hope of free men remains stubborn and brave, but it is sternly disciplined by experience. It shuns not only all crude counsel of despair but also the self-deceit of easy illusion. It weighs the chance for peace with sure, clear knowledge of what happened to the vain hope of 1945.

In that spring of victory the soldiers of the Western Allies met the soldiers of Russia in the center of Europe. They were triumphant comrades in arms. Their peoples shared the joyous prospect of building, in honor of their dead, the only fitting monument—an age of just peace. All these war-weary peoples shared too this concrete, decent purpose: to guard vigilantly against the domination ever again of any part of the world by a single, unbridled aggressive power.

This common purpose lasted an instant and perished. The nations of the world divided to follow two distinct roads.

The United States and our valued friends, the other free nations, chose one road.

The leaders of the Soviet Union chose another.

THE ROAD FOLLOWED BY THE UNITED STATES

The way chosen by the United States was plainly marked by a few clear precepts, which govern its conduct in world affairs.

First: No people on earth can be held, as a people, to be an enemy, for all humanity shares the common hunger for peace and fellowship and justice.

Second: No nation's security and well-being can be lastingly achieved in isolation but only in effective cooperation with fellow nations.

Third: Any nation's right to a form of government and an economic system of its own choosing is *inalienable.*

Fourth: Any nation's attempt to dictate to other nations their form of government is *indefensible.*

And fifth: A nation's hope of lasting peace cannot be firmly based upon any race in armaments but rather upon just relations and honest understanding with all other nations.

In the light of these principles the citizens of the United States defined the way they proposed to follow, through the aftermath of war, toward true peace.

This way was faithful to the spirit that inspired the United Nations: to prohibit strife, to relieve tensions, to banish fears. This way was to control and to reduce armaments. This way was to allow all nations to devote their energies and resources to the great and good tasks of healing the war's wounds, of clothing and feeding and housing the needy, of perfecting a just political life, of enjoying the fruits of their own free toil.

THE ROAD FOLLOWED BY THE SOVIET UNION

The Soviet government held a vastly different vision of the future.

In the world of its design, security was to be found, not in mutual trust and mutual aid but in *force:* huge armies, subversion, rule of neighbor nations. The goal was power superiority at all cost. Security was to be sought by denying it to all others.

The result has been tragic for the world and, for the Soviet Union, it has also been ironic.

The amassing of Soviet power alerted free nations to a new danger of aggression. It compelled them in self-defense to spend unprecedented money and energy for armaments. It forced them to develop weapons of war now capable of inflicting instant and terrible punishment upon any aggressor.

It instilled in the free nations—and let none doubt this—the unshakable conviction that, as long as there persists a threat to freedom, they must, at any cost, remain armed, strong, and ready for any risk of war.

It inspired them—and let none doubt this—to attain a unity of purpose and will beyond the power of propaganda or pressure to break, now or ever.

There remained, however, one thing essentially unchanged and unaffected by Soviet conduct: the readiness of the free nations to welcome sincerely any genuine evidence of peaceful purpose enabling all peoples again to resume their common quest of just peace.

The free nations, most solemnly and repeatedly, have assured the Soviet Union that their firm association has never had any aggressive purpose whatsoever. Soviet leaders, however, have seemed to persuade themselves, or tried to persuade their people, otherwise.

And so it has come to pass that the Soviet Union itself has shared and suffered the very fears it has fostered in the rest of the world.

This has been the way of life forged by 8 years of fear and force.

What can the world, or any nation in it, hope for if no turning is found on this dread road?

A LIFE OF FEAR

The worst to be feared and the best to be expected can be simply stated.

The *worst* is atomic war.

The *best* would be this: a life of perpetual fear and tension; a burden of arms draining the wealth and the labor of all peoples; a wasting of strength that defies the American system or the Soviet system or any system to achieve true abundance and happiness for the peoples of this earth.

Every gun that is made, every warship launched, every rocket fired signifies, in the final sense, a theft from those who hunger and are not fed, those who are cold and are not clothed.

THE COSTS OF A WORLD IN ARMS

This world in arms is not spending money alone.

It is spending the sweat of its laborers, the genius of its scientists, the hopes of its children.

The cost of one modern heavy bomber is this: a modern brick school in more than 30 cities.

It is two electric power plants, each serving a town of 60,000 population.

It is two fine, fully equipped hospitals.

It is some 50 miles of concrete highway.

We pay for a single fighter plane with a half million bushels of wheat.

We pay for a single destroyer with new homes that could have housed more than 8,000 people.

This, I repeat, is the best way of life to be found on the road the world has been taking.

This is not a way of life at all, in any true sense.   Under the cloud of threatening war, it is humanity hanging from a cross of iron.

These plain and cruel truths define the peril and point the hope that come with this spring of 1953.

This is one of those times in the affairs of nations when the gravest choices must be made, if there is to be a turning toward a just and lasting peace.

It is a moment that calls upon the governments of the world to speak their intentions with simplicity and with honesty.

It calls upon them to answer the question that stirs the hearts of all sane men: *is there no other way the world may live?*

BEGINNING OF A NEW ERA

The world knows that an era ended with the death of Joseph Stalin. The extraordinary 30-year span of his rule saw the Soviet Empire expand to reach from the Baltic Sea to the Sea of Japan, finally to dominate 800 million souls.

The Soviet system shaped by Stalin and his predecessors was born of one World War. It survived with stubborn and often amazing courage a second World War. It has lived to threaten a third.

Now a new leadership has assumed power in the Soviet Union. Its links to the past, however strong, cannot bind it completely. Its future is, in great part, its own to make.

This new leadership confronts a free world aroused, as rarely in its history, by the will to stay free.

This free world knows, out of the bitter wisdom of experience, that vigilance and sacrifice are the price of liberty.

It knows that the defense of Western Europe imperatively demands the unity of purpose and action made possible by the North Atlantic Treaty Organization, embracing a European Defense Community.

It knows that Western Germany deserves to be a free and equal partner in this community and that this, for Germany, is the only safe way to full, final unity.

It knows that aggression in Korea and in southeast Asia are threats to the whole free community to be met by united action.

This is the kind of free world which the new Soviet leadership confronts. It is a world that demands and expects the fullest respect of its rights and interests. It is a world that will always accord the same respect to all others.

So the new Soviet leadership now has a precious opportunity to awaken, with the rest of the world, to the point of peril reached and to help turn the tide of history.

Will it do this?

We do not yet know. Recent statements and gestures of Soviet leaders give some evidence that they may recognize this critical moment.

We welcome every honest act of peace.

We care nothing for mere rhetoric.

We care only for sincerity of peaceful purpose attested by deeds. The opportunities for such deeds are many. The performance of a great number of them waits upon no complex protocol but upon the simple will to do them. Even a few such clear and specific acts, such as the Soviet Union's signature upon an Austrian treaty or its release of thousands of prisoners still held from World War II, would be impressive signs of sincere intent.   They would carry a power of persuasion not to be matched by any amount of oratory.

WORKING FOR PEACE

This we do know: a world that begins to witness the rebirth of trust among nations *can* find its way to a peace that is neither partial nor punitive.

With all who will work in good faith toward such a peace, we are ready, with renewed resolve, to strive to redeem the near-lost hopes of our day.

The first great step along this way must be the conclusion of an honorable armistice in Korea.

This means the immediate cessation of hostilities and the prompt initiation of political discussions leading to the holding of free elections in a united Korea.

It should mean, no less importantly, an end to the direct and indirect attacks upon the security of Indochina and Malaya.   For any armistice in Korea that merely released aggressive armies to attack elsewhere would be a fraud.

We seek, throughout Asia as throughout the world, a peace that is true and total.

Out of this can grow a still wider task—the achieving of just political settlements for the other serious and specific issues between the free world and the Soviet Union.

None of these issues, great or small, is insoluble—given only the will to respect the rights of all nations.

Again we say: the United States is ready to assume its just part.

We have already done all within our power to speed conclusion of a treaty with Austria, which will free that country from economic exploitation and from occupation by foreign troops.

We are ready not only to press forward with the present plans for closer unity of the nations of Western Europe but also, upon that foundation, to strive to foster a broader European community, conductive to the free movement of persons, of trade, and of ideas.

This community would include a free and united Germany, with a government based upon free and secret elections.

This free community and the full independence of the East European nations could mean the end of the present unnatural division of Europe.

REDUCTION OF ARMAMENTS

As progress in all these areas strengthens world trust, we could proceed concurrently with the next great work—the reduction of the burden of armaments now weighing upon the world. To this end we would welcome and enter into the most solemn agreements. These could properly include:

1. The limitation, by absolute numbers or by an agreed international ratio, of the sizes of the military and security forces of all nations.

2. A commitment by all nations to set an agreed limit upon that proportion of total production of certain strategic materials to be devoted to military purposes.

3. International control of atomic energy to promote its use for peaceful purposes only and to insure the prohibition of atomic weapons.

4. A limitation or prohibition of other categories of weapons of great destructiveness.

5. The enforcement of all these agreed limitations and prohibitions by adequate safeguards, including a practical system of inspection under the United Nations.

The details of such disarmament programs are manifestly critical and complex. Neither the United States nor any other nation can properly claim to possess a perfect, immutable formula. But the formula matters less than the faith—the good faith without which no formula can work justly and effectively.

A NEW KIND OF WAR

The fruit of success in all these tasks would present the world with the greatest task, and the greatest opportunity, of all. It is this: the dedication of the energies, the resources, and the imaginations of all peaceful nations to a new kind of war. This would be a declared total war, not upon any human enemy but upon the brute forces of poverty and need.

The peace we seek, founded upon decent trust and cooperative effort among nations, can be fortified, not by weapons of war but by wheat and by cotton, by milk and by wool, by meat and by timber and by rice. These are words that translate into every language on earth. These are needs that challenge this world in arms.

This idea of a just and peaceful world is not new or strange to us. It inspired the people of the United States to initiate the European Recovery Program in 1947. That program was prepared to treat, with like and equal concern, the needs of Eastern and Western Europe.

We are prepared to reaffirm, with the most concrete evidence, our readiness to help build a world in which all peoples can be productive and prosperous.

This Government is ready to ask its people to join with all nations in devoting a substantial percentage of the savings achieved by disarmament to a fund for world aid and reconstruction. The purposes of this great work would be to help other peoples to develop the undeveloped areas of the world, to stimulate profitable and fair world trade, to assist all peoples to know the blessings of productive freedom.

The monuments to this new kind of war would be these: roads and schools, hospitals and homes, food and health.

We are ready, in short, to dedicate our strength to serving the *needs,* rather than the *fears,* of the world.

We are ready, by these and all such actions, to make of the United Nations an institution that can effectively guard the peace and security of all peoples.

I know of nothing I can add to make plainer the sincere purpose of the United States.

I know of no course, other than that marked by these and similar actions, that can be called the highway of peace.

I know of only one question upon which progress waits. It is this: *What is the Soviet Union Ready To Do?*

Whatever the answer be, let it be plainly spoken.

Again we say: the hunger for peace is too great, the hour in history too late, for any government to mock man's hopes with mere words and promises and gestures.

The test of truth is simple. There can be no persuasion but by deeds.

Is the new leadership of the Soviet Union prepared to use its decisive influence in the Communist world, including control of the flow of arms, to bring not merely an expedient truce in Korea but genuine peace in Asia?

Is it prepared to allow other nations, including those of Eastern Europe, the free choice of their own forms of government?

Is it prepared to act in concert with others upon serious disarmament proposals to be made firmly effective by stringent U.N. control and inspection?

If not, where then is the concrete evidence of the Soviet Union's concern for peace?

The test is clear.

There is, before all peoples, a precious chance to turn the black tide of events. If we failed to strive to seize this chance, the judgment of future ages would be harsh and just.

If we strive but fail and the world remains armed against itself, it at least need be divided no longer in its clear knowledge of who has condemned humankind to this fate.

The purpose of the United States, in stating these proposals, is simple and clear.

These proposals spring, without ulterior purpose or political passion, from our calm conviction that the hunger for just peace is in the hearts of all peoples—those of Russia and of China no less than of our own country.

They conform to our firm faith that God created men to enjoy, not destroy, the fruits of the earth and of their own toil.

They aspire to this: the lifting, from the backs and from the hearts of men, of their burden of arms and of fears, so that they may find before them a golden age of freedom and of peace.

58. U.S. ECONOMIC FOREIGN POLICY *

> Mr. Asher lists five "broad objectives of the economic side of U.S. foreign policy." He points out, as many others concerned with economic policy have done before him, that if we wish to maintain our present high level of exports, we must either increase our imports, or be prepared to continue foreign aid programs on a large scale.
>
> Mr. Asher's article closes with a description of the principal activities of the American Government in the economic field.

The broad objectives of the economic side of U.S. foreign policy can be stated rather simply:

1.   We want economic conditions in the free world which will attract peoples and governments toward the democratic system of political freedom, as opposed to totalitarian systems like Soviet communism.

2.   We have a special interest in the economic strength of our partners in the North Atlantic Treaty Organization, and of the countries on the periphery of Soviet power.   In the North Atlantic Treaty area we want economic conditions which will enable the NATO countries to devote a substantial part of their resources to the common military effort for as long as is necessary, without preventing improvements in their

* Robert E. Asher, *Department of State Bulletin,* July 6, 1953, pp. 3-8.   The author is a special assistant to the Assistant Secretary for Economic Affairs, Department of State.

standards of living.   In countries on the periphery of Soviet power we want to eliminate economic weaknesses that threaten political stability and invite Communist subversion.

3.   We want economic conditions in the free world which will promote material well-being and which will allow employment, production, trade, and investment to develop in ways that enrich human life.

4.   A free-world economy which would meet these objectives ought to be one of healthy, stable expansion.   It ought to afford all countries increasing opportunities for economic growth and improving standards of living.   It ought to operate so that economic gains are distributed equitably within countries.   It ought to be free of prolonged or severe depressions and to be capable of weathering temporary economic crises without serious strain.

5.   The way in which these goals are pursued is also, in a sense, a part of the objectives themselves.   We should try to create an international community of effort for common purposes, a process to which each member would make an equitable contribution.   We should try to avoid the extremes of either forcing unwanted programs and policies on others as a condition of our help, or of undertaking actions ourselves which are unmatched by appropriate actions in the countries which benefit from them.

Let me add promptly that I know of no corresponding 5-point program for achieving the strong, prosperous, democratic world we would like to see.   Americans tend to believe that everything that is desirable is possible, that America can do anything it sets out to do.   Denis Brogan has referred to this as "the illusion of American omnipotence."   Not only do we cling to this inspiring illusion but after allowing it to over-simplify our problems, we try to shortcut our way to a solution.   One year it's the Bretton Woods agreement that will solve our postwar economic problems; another year it's the Marshall Plan; then it's technical assistance; today, it's "trade, not aid."   We tend to overwork these slogans and, in doing so, to blind ourselves to the complexity and the long-range character of our foreign-economic problems.   To avoid this pitfall, the new administration is extremely anxious to obtain a careful, impartial re-examination of our whole foreign-economic policy.   The job in all probability will be done by a 17-member commission that will include bipartisan representation from both Houses of Congress, as well as public members appointed by the President.

The administration wants to make sure that we have a well-rounded, consistent foreign policy whose economic aspects properly reinforce and compliment its political and military aspects.   Today, 8 years after the end of World War II, the economic situation of the free world is still shaky and still in need of shoring up. Canada and the United States remain islands in a troubled sea.

INTEREST ABROAD IN U.S. ECONOMY

The importance of our foreign-economic policy has been driven home to me again and again at international meetings during the past few years. At these conferences the U.S. delegation has to listen attentively to what other delegates say because most of them aim their remarks at the United States. We have to be even more careful about what we say. A slight error in emphasis, a minor bit of carelessness, on the part of one of our delegates would have the room buzzing and the press representa-tives phoning their offices in no time flat. This is because relatively minor policy changes on our part—the prospect of a new tariff rate on garlic, an embargo on imports of peanuts, little ups and downs in our requirements for coffee, copper, bananas, or tin—can have major re-percussions in other parts of the world.

Coffee, which I just mentioned, is our leading imported commodity. We spend more dollars for coffee than for anything else we buy abroad. But because our shopping list is big, coffee accounts for only 11 or 12 percent of the dollar value of our total imports. A $100 million increase or decrease would have no significant effect on the U.S. economy.

From the point of view of relations with our neighbors, the matter is much more serious. There are at least 6 countries—Brazil, Colombia, El Salvador, Guatemala, Costa Rica, and Haiti—that earn from 50 to 90 percent of all their dollars from coffee exports. Whether they can maintain or improve the living standards of their people depends very largely on the U.S. coffee market which, in turn, depends primarily on the general level of U.S. prosperity.

This example may help to explain why other countries are so deeply concerned about the health of the U. S. economy. Will we maintain an expanding economy at home? Will we avoid depression or recession? Will we make it harder or easier for other countries to sell us their goods?

Our foreign policy is thus not something apart from domestic policy. What we do here at home to control inflation and avoid deflation, to maintain full employment, to protect minorities, to encourage freedom of speech and thought has profound effects throughout the world. Foreign policy is not something that can be left to experts in the State Department, the Defense Department, and the Mutual Security Agency.

It's a job for everyone. An effective foreign policy requires an alert and informed citizenry in the United States, sensitive to the foreign implications of what sometimes seem to be purely domestic issues.

As Secretary Dulles reminded the House Ways and Means Committee recently, the United States accounts for "50 percent of the total production of non-Communist countries. We are the world's largest exporter and the world's largest importer. We are the greatest creditor nation in the world and the most important single source of the free world's capital needs. We lead in the development of new inventions and new skills."

In spite of the fact that, in absolute terms, we export and import in such huge quantities, our economy as a whole is less dependent on foreign trade than that of almost any other country except the Soviet Union. Nevertheless, important segments of the American economy have a large stake in export markets. During the last few years we have exported nearly one half of our wheat, two fifths of our cotton and rice production, and one fourth of our production of tobacco. We also export more than one fifth of our output of tractors. On the import side, the United States is heavily dependent on imports for a number of essentials, including 100 percent of our supplies of tin and natural rubber, 92 percent of our manganese requirements, and 50 percent of our tungsten.

TRADE PATTERN UNBALANCED

The pattern, however, is extremely unbalanced.

The U.S. exports far more than it imports; most other countries are unable to export enough to pay for the imports that they desperately need. This continues to be true despite the tremendous assistance rendered under the Marshall Plan and the fact that, by the end of 1952, industrial production in Western Europe was 40 percent above prewar levels. It continues to be true despite technical assistance, development loans, and other measures which have helped some of the underdeveloped countries make notable advances in recent years.

The imbalance is more persistent and deeper rooted than any of us realized a few short years ago. It is attributable only in small part to the fact that rearmament has required resources which might otherwise have been used to increase European exports or civilian consumption in Europe. Western Europe has had difficulty in obtaining dependable markets in the United States for its exports, and in competing with American exporters in Latin America and Asia. Theoretically, Western Europe could restrict its imports still further to correspond with its relatively lower earning power in world markets. In practice, this policy would threaten European living standards to the point where political stability would be imperiled, and it might jeopardize the economic health of non-European nations. For Western Europe, increased production and productivity within Europe, the further development of Asia and Africa as sources of supply and as markets for European products, as well as increased European exports to the United States and the dollar area, are essential.

Similarly, the economic future of Japan hinges on her ability to develop expanding trade with the rest of the free world. On the one hand, Japan is cut off almost completely from traditional markets and sources of supply on the mainland of China. At the same time, she faces substantial barriers to the export of goods to free-world countries. In the United States the tariff rates on Japanese goods are still at the high levels imposed by the Tariff Act of 1930. Japan is able to sustain her economy today only because of the very large purchases being made there by the United States for the support of U.N. forces in Korea. Sooner or later such purchases are sure to be cut drastically.

The reduction of barriers to world trade has been and continues to be a major economic objective of the United States. The Reciprocal Trade Agreements Act adopted in 1934 authorizes reductions of tariffs and other barriers to trade in return for comparable concessions from other countries. It has been renewed every 2 or 3 years. In 1951 it was extended until June 12, 1953, and at the same time it was substantially amended.

There are vocal groups in the United States who want greater protection against foreign competition. They may extoll "competition" among American industries; preface the word "competition" with the word "foreign," however, and it immediately becomes something sinister. People who would reject out-of-hand the notion that the Government should tax the television industry for the purpose of protecting the motion-picture industry, or tax nylon producers to protect wool-growers, or put a quota on cigarette production to avoid injury to cigarmakers and pipemakers, see nothing inconsistent in demanding protection for some of these same industries from the lesser threat of foreign competition.

Can highly paid American workers compete with lower-paid foreign workers? The thing to compare is not the daily or weekly wage of the American and the foreign worker, but the wage cost per unit of output. If a gadget taking 25 man-hours to produce in some other country can be produced here in 10 man-hours, the wage cost will be lower here than abroad, even though the hourly earnings here are twice as high as in the foreign country. If the American wage is $2 an hour, the labor cost of the gadget will be $20.   If the wage in the foreign country is half the American level, or $1 an hour, the labor cost of the imported gadget would be $25, and the chances are that the American product could undersell the foreign one.

Our high wage levels are possible because such factors as up-to-date machinery, good organization, mass markets, and eagerness to adopt improved methods have resulted in a phenomenally high output per worker.   One of our major problems is to restore international balance by encouraging a stepping up of productivity in other parts of the free world so that their output per man or per acre will be less lopsided in relation to ours.   They must get themselves into a better position both to satisfy their own needs and to market their products throughout the world, including the rich North American market.

ALTERNATIVES TO INCREASING IMPORTS

The plain fact is that unless we are prepared to import more, or to continue foreign aid indefinitely on a massive scale, we will not be able to maintain anything like our present level of exports.   Other countries have to be able to sell to us in order to buy from us.   They are now selling to us at a rate of less than $11 billion per year.   They are receiving more than $15 billion worth of American goods.   The gap between what they earn and what they get is being closed by military and economic assistance programs that create a donor-recipient relationship as irksome to our allies as it is to us.   The slogan "trade not aid" was imported from Great Britain, not made in America.

Within the last year or so, more and more Americans have been facing up to the only alternatives the trade front offers, i.e., larger imports, lower exports, or continued free grants of U.S. resources to make up the difference.   Not all of them come out with the same answer, of course.   Some feel that our postwar exports have been freakishly high and should be reduced.   Others believe that more turmoil would be created if wheat, cotton, and tobacco growers were deprived of their export markets and forced to turn to poultry raising, truck farming, and other forms of production for the domestic market.

Many leaders of U.S. opinion in recent months have spoken in favor of a more liberal import policy.   The National Association of Manufacturers, the U.S. Chamber of Commerce, the American Farm Bureau Federation, the National Cotton Council, the United States Tobacco Associates, the Committee for Economic Development, the Congress of Industrial Organizations, the American Federation of Labor, and the Detroit Board of Commerce have gone on record to this effect.

Other countries, particularly Japan and the industrialized countries of Western Europe, tend to regard U.S. import policy as the key to whether or not we can be depended upon to behave as the world's largest creditor nation and most important supplier of essential commodities. They tell us in the U.N. Economic and Social Council, the Economic Commission for Europe, and elsewhere, how vitally they will be affected by our decisions next year on the future of the Trade Agreements Act. On a lesser scale they regard simplification of our complicated customs procedures as another important index of the way in which America is moving. Almost every foreign official one talks to can give hair-raising examples of businessmen in his country whose products get hopelessly tangled in the jungle of American tariff and customs procedures. Some learned to their sorrow that tariff rates for plate glass differ according to the thickness and area of the glass, that dolls and toys are subject to 11 different rates, that cotton shirts ordinarily charged a 25 percent duty must pay a 50 percent duty if initials are embroidered on them. Some grew old and gray and cynical in the months or years that elapsed before their final liability was decided.

Other European manufacturers have from time to time bumped their heads against the "Buy American" laws under which our Government procurement agencies give preference to domestic suppliers unless the price of the foreign commodity, after payment of the tariff, is at least 25 percent below the comparable American product. They would like to see this extra road block removed.

Soviet delegates attend the plenary sessions of the Economic Commission for Europe. They're not the least bit bashful. Recently, they have said, in effect, to the European nations: "Look, fellows, it's a pipe dream to expect the United States to adopt more liberal trade policies and make it easier for you to compete with American producers. Americans want to dump their surplus production abroad, but they don't want to buy from you and they don't want you to sell to us. Don't let the Americans push you around. We'd love to buy your machinery, we'd love to increase our trade with you."

We, the United States, have pointed to the progress toward trade liberalization that we and other free countries have made since 1934, and particularly to our magnificent record of international assistance during the postwar period. As for machinery exports to the U.S.S.R., as long as millions of people live in fear of Soviet aggression it has seemed elementary commonsense for us to urge our friends to withhold from the Soviet bloc any goods that might increase its war potential. Moreover, we believe, the Soviets eventually want to become self-sufficient anyhow, and therefore don't desire a permanent strengthening of trade ties with the free world.

Nevertheless, the East-West trade issue remains a thorny one. Unlike the United States, a number of other countries have traditionally secured a substantial portion of essential imports—grain, coal, and timber, in particular—from Eastern Europe and have sold both producer's and consumer's goods to that area in return. In the present situation, they are more than willing to withhold items of obvious strategic importance. But they are responsible sovereign states, not satellites. They do not recognize any U.S. right to decide unilaterally what course of action they should follow. As for Japan, trade with mainland China was even more important to her in prewar days than trade with Eastern Europe was to Western Europe. Until Burma, Thailand, Formosa, and the rest of Southeast Asia became more important markets, it is hard to see where Japan should turn to compensate adequately for the loss of her China trade.

PURPOSE OF REGIONAL ECONOMIC COMMISSIONS

The United States is a member not only of the U.N. Economic Commission for Europe (ECE), but also of the Economic Commissions for Latin America and for Asia and the Far East. All three commissions have the same general purpose: to expedite economic reconstruction, to expand the level of economic activity, to strengthen the ties between the countries of the region and between the region and the rest of the world. They have no laws to administer, no funds to distribute, no sanctions to impose. Their function is largely the educational one of discussing common problems and persuading officials of the member governments to adopt measures that are recognized as desirable in the common interest. Each commission has a competent professional secretariat which prepares an annual economic survey of the region and other basic information.

The Economic Commission for Europe has been seriously handicapped by the East-West split. Its members are politically and economically more sophisticated than the members of the Asian and Latin American commissions. Whereas the Europeans are more interested in trade problems, the members of the other commissions, coming from so-called underdeveloped areas, are concerned primarily with economic development problems.

The Economic Commission for Asia and the Far East is by all odds the most picturesque. It offers more variety in delegates' costumes, with turbaned Indians, Burmese men in colorful skirts, Philippine delegates in beautifully embroidered shirts, and all in the exotic but poverty-ridden surroundings of the Far East. Its problems are the most overwhelming.

The Latin American Commission falls somewhere between the other two. Impressive economic headway has been made in Central and South America in the last 5 or 6 years. The governments, by and large, are determined to maintain and, if possible, increase the pace. The average per capita income in the area is still under $250 per year. In Asia it is less than half of that. In the United States it is about $2,000.

A number of the underdeveloped countries are one-crop countries, nations whose welfare depends almost entirely on the American and European markets for their tin, or rubber, or sugar. Small shifts in demand can cause great misery. Continued economic progress on their part requires, in their view, greater stability in the world market for their raw material exports. They are consequently groping for arrangements that would reduce the violent and often uneconomic fluctuations in the prices of primary commodities.

International commodity agreements have been suggested as a means of stabilizing the market. Such agreements are hard to negotiate. When surpluses are in the offing, consumers hope for price declines and shy away from premature commitments. When shortages occur, producers are anxious to make up for lean times and charge what the market will bear. The result is that whether we and other governments feel kindly or unkindly toward commodity agreements in principle, not very many are concluded in practice. The International Wheat Agreement stands almost alone.

A second area of concern to the underdeveloped areas is the need for increased food production. In the early postwar years, every country wanted a steel mill, every country was going to be self-sufficient in textiles and export to other countries; none was going to import. Gradually the overriding importance of increased food production has come to be understood, thanks in part to the educational work of U.S. representatives. The tremendous possibilities of enriching the poorer areas of the world through better seeds, fertilizers, and farm implements, fairer distribution of the available land, cheaper credit, and agricultural extension work, are being realized. A comprehensive land-reform program has been undertaken in Formosa. The same is true in India. A dramatic effort is being made in Iran. Important reforms were introduced in Japan during the period of American miiltary occupation. The new Government in Egypt seems determined to move forward in the field of land reform. A program has been initiated in Southern Italy, an area which can properly be classed with the underdeveloped areas of the world. The results of such programs in terms of increased human dignity are even more important than the immediate economic results.

Despite the importance of increased food production and agrarian reforms in the underdeveloped areas, industrial undertakings still have the greatest allure. Politically, they symbolize development in the eyes of the have-nots. Economically, they draw surplus population from the countryside and, by diversifying the economy, make it less vulnerable to shocks from abroad. Through loans and technical assistance the United States is helping in the construction of steel plants, cement plants, power plants, and other basic facilities in various parts of the world. We will have to continue to help transform ancient, static, agrarian economies into more dynamic, more diversified, better-balanced mixtures of industry and agriculture.

BENEFITS OF TECHNICAL ASSISTANCE

Technical assistance remains one of the most important weapons in our foreign economic policy arsenal. The underdeveloped countries tend to stress their need for grants and loans, but grants and loans without adequate preparation to use them effectively will do little to speed the actual development process. One of the reasons for the feeling of greater hopefulness one gets in India and Pakistan, is the presence there of a corps of responsible trained public officials and businessmen who know how to prepare and organize projects, how to teach and supervise others, how to put paper plans into operation. With their cooperation, the fruits of some of the U.S. and U.N. technical-assistance projects are becoming apparent. In Latin America, where technical assistance has had a longer history, progress is even more notable.

The touchiness regarding outside aid which exists among peoples of the underdeveloped countries is not always appreciated by Americans. It is even more acute in nations that have just won their independence than in those that have had it for a long time. Nothing could be more erroneous than the notion that Asia, the Middle East and Africa are eager to get U.S. aid and reluctant to stand on their own feet. Their people are extremely sensitive about outside aid, though less sensitive when it comes via the politically irreproachable United Nations than when it comes directly from the United States. They need foreign technicians, foreign capital, and foreign equipment, but the conditions under which they obtain them can make or break their governments. At the U.N. meetings the Soviets have repeatedly pointed out the risks which other countries run when they increase their dependence upon foreign technicians and foreign capital, or strengthen their ties with the United States.

Our own security is too intimately bound up with the security of other free-world nations to allow us the luxury of washing our hands of countries that exasperate us. Neither can we impose alien programs and policies upon other peoples. Yet we have to reconcile these hard facts with the commonsense policy of avoiding a bigger burden than we can carry. Our assistance should be matched by reasonable efforts on the part of other countries. After all, their future depends primarily on their own domestic decisions; what we do, at best, is to provide the extra push that can get them started or help them over the hump.

Other countries have erected trade barriers that ought to be eliminated. Many of their financial and exchange and credit policies could stand revamping. So could their tax programs. Underdeveloped countries in need of capital can do much to improve the climate for foreign and domestic investment. Their development plans will have to be flexible enough to encourage more initiative and experimentation. We have a right to ask for action along these lines from them. We exercise that right both in our international discussions and in our direct dealings with foreign governments.

In this process of mutual education, frictions and misunderstandings are bound to arise. The development process, like the course of true love, is seldom smooth; it creates lots of stresses and strains. The lure of higher wages may bring people off the land and into the cities, where a change in the economic situation may leave them temporarily jobless and stranded. Selfish groups now occupying a privileged status may lose their privileges, resent that fact, and stir up trouble. The Communists will fish where the waters are troubled. Progress and stability are hard to reconcile.

We will be quite unrealistic if we expect 100 percent success in the sense that all nations aided directly or indirectly by the United States will adopt our brand of politics or economics, or will agree with us in the United Nations or elsewhere. Failure on our part to act in ways that will expand trade and help fulfill the pent-up aspirations of the underdeveloped areas can assure the loss of large regions important to the security of the United States. Unfortunately, though, even the most skillful actions cannot guarantee that those areas will stay on our side.

59. A New Approach to Atomic Energy *

Delivered immediately after the Bermuda Conference, Mr. Eisenhower's address to the General Assembly of the United Nations dramatically emphasizes the role of atomic weapons in the East-West conflict. Although much of the address deals with old frustrations on the matter of atomic control and a summary of recent atomic developments, notable is the new proposal for a pooling of atomic materials for international atomic research. Mr. Eisenhower's proposal is important as a fresh approach to the continuing problem of atomic weapons and their uses.

When Secretary General Hammarskjold's invitation to address this General Assembly reached me in Bermuda, I was just beginning a series of conferences with the Prime Ministers and Foreign Ministers of Great Britain and of France. Our subject was some of the problems that beset our world.

During the remainder of the Bermuda Conference, I had constantly in mind that ahead of me lay a great honor. That honor is mine today as I stand here, privileged to address the General Assembly of the United Nations.

At the same time that I appreciate the distinction of addressing you, I have a sense of exhilaration as I look upon this assembly.

Never before in history has so much hope for so many people been gathered together in a single organization. Your deliberations and decisions during these somber years have already realized part of those hopes.

But the great tests and the great accomplishments still lie ahead. And in the confident expectations of those accomplishments, I would use the office which, for the time being, I hold, to assure you that the Government of the United States will remain steadfast in its support of this body. This we shall do in the conviction that you will provide a great share of the wisdom, of the courage and the faith which can bring to this world lasting peace for all nations and happiness and well-being for all men.

Clearly, it would not be fitting for me to take this occasion to present to you a unilateral American report on Bermuda. Nevertheless, I assure you that in our deliberations on that lovely island we sought to invoke those same great concepts of universal peace and human dignity which are so clearly etched in your Charter.

* An address by President Dwight D. Eisenhower, delivered to the General Assembly of the United Nations, December 8, 1953.

Neither would it be a measure of this great opportunity merely to recite, however hopefully, pious platitudes.

I therefore decided that this occasion warranted my saying to you some of the things that have been on the minds and hearts of my legislative and executive associates and on mine for a great many months —thoughts I had originally planned to say primarily to the American people.

I know that the American people share my deep belief that if a danger exists in the world, it is a danger shared by all—and equally, that if hope exists in the mind of one nation, that hope should be shared by all.

Finally, if there is to be advanced any proposal designed to ease, even by the smallest measure the tensions of today's world, what more appropriate audience could there be than the members of the General Assembly of the United Nations.

I feel impelled to speak today in a language that, in a sense, is new— one, which I, who have spent so much of my life in the military profession, would have preferred never to use.

That new language is the language of atomic warfare.

The atomic age has moved forward at such a pace that every citizen of the world should have some comprehension, at least in comparative terms, of the extent of this development, of the utmost significance to every one of us. Clearly, if the peoples of the world are to conduct an intelligent search for peace, they must be armed with the significant facts of today's existence.

My recital of atomic danger and power is necessarily stated in United States terms, for these are the only incontrovertible facts that I know. I need hardly point out to this assembly, however, that this subject is global, not merely national in character.

On July 16, 1945, the United States set off the world's first atomic test explosion. Since that date in 1945, the United States of America has conducted forty-two test explosions.

Atomic bombs today are more than twenty-five times as powerful as the weapons with which the atomic age dawned, while hydrogen weapons are in the ranges of millions of tons of TNT equivalent.

Today, the United States stockpile of atomic weapons, which, of course, increases daily, exceeds by many times the explosive equivalent of the total of all bombs and all shells that came from every plane and every gun in every theatre of war through all the years of World War II.

In size and variety the development of atomic weapons has been no less remarkable. This development has been such that atomic weapons have virtually achieved conventional status within our armed services.

In the United States services, the Army, the Navy, the Air Force and the Marine Corps are all capable of putting this weapon to military use.

But the dread secret and the fearful engines of atomic might are not ours alone.

In the first place, the secret is possessed by our friends and allies, Great Britain and Canada, whose scientific genius made a tremendous contribution to our original discoveries and the designs of atomic bombs.

The secret is also known by the Soviet Union.

The Soviet Union has informed us that, over recent years, it has devoted extensive resources to atomic weapons. During this period, the Soviet Union has exploded a series of atomic devices, including at least one involving thermonuclear reactions.

If at one time the United States possessed what might have been called a monopoly of atomic power, that monopoly ceased to exist several years ago. Therefore, although our earlier start has permitted us to accumulate what is today a great quantitative advantage, the atomic realities of today comprehend two facts of even greater significance.

First, the knowledge now possessed by several nations will eventually be shared by others, possibly all others.

Second, even a vast superiority in numbers of weapons, and a consequent capability of devastating retaliation, is no preventive, of itself, against the fearful material damage and toll of human lives that would be inflicted by surprise aggression.

The free world, at least dimly aware of these facts, has naturally embarked on a large program of warning and defense systems. That program will be accelerated and expanded.

But let no one think that the expenditure of vast sums for weapons and systems of defense can guarantee absolute safety for the cities and the citizens of any nation. The awful arithmetic of the atomic bomb does not permit of such an easy solution. Even against the most powerful defense, an aggressor in possession of the effective minimum number of atomic bombs for a surprise attack could probably place a sufficient number of his bombs on the chosen targets to cause hideous damage.

Should such an atomic attack be launched against the United States, our reactions would be swift and resolute. But for me to say that the defense capabilities of the United States are such that they could inflict terrible losses upon an aggressor—for me to say that the retaliation capabilities of the United States are so great that such an aggressor's land would be laid waste—all this, while fact, is not the true expression of the purpose and hope of the United States.

To pause there would be to confirm the hopeless finality of a belief that two atomic collossi are doomed malevolently to eye each other indefinitely across a trembling world. To stop there would be to accept helplessly the probability of civilization destroyed—the annihilation of the irreplaceable heritage of mankind handed down to us generation from generation—and the condemnation of mankind to begin all over again the age-old struggle upward from savagery toward decency and right and justice.

Surely no sane member of the human race could discover victory in such desolation. Could anyone wish his name to be coupled by history with such human degradation and destruction?

Occasional pages of history do record the faces of the "Great Destroyers," but the whole book of history reveals mankind's never-ending quest for peace and mankind's God-given capacity to build.

It is with the book of history, and not with isolated pages, that the United States will ever wish to be identified. My country wants to be constructive, not destructive. It wants agreements, not wars, among nations. It wants itself to live in freedom and in the confidence that the people of every other nation enjoy equally the right of choosing their own way of life.

So my country's purpose is to help us move out of the dark chamber of horrors into the light, to find a way by which the minds of men, the hopes of men, the souls of men everywhere, can move forward toward peace and happiness and well being.

In this quest, I know that we must not lack patience.

I know that in a world divided, such as ours today, salvation cannot be attained by one dramatic act.

I know that many steps will have to be taken over many months before the world can look at itself one day and truly realize that a new climate of mutually peaceful confidence is abroad in the world.

But I know, above all else, that we must start to take these steps—now.

The United States and its allies, Great Britain and France, have, over the past months, tried to take some of these steps. Let no one say that we shun the conference table.

On the record has long stood the request of the United States, Great Britain and France, to negotiate with the Soviet Union the problems of a divided Germany.

On that record has long stood the request of the same three nations to negotiate an Austrian peace treaty.

On the same record still stands the request of the United Nations to negotiate the problems of Korea.

Most recently, we have received from the Soviet Union what is in effect an expression of willingness to hold a four-power meeting. Along with our allies, Great Britain and France, we were pleased to see that this note did not contain the unacceptable preconditions previously put forward.

As you already know from our joint Bermuda communiqué, the United States, Great Britain and France have agreed promptly to meet with the Soviet Union.

The Government of the United States approaches this conference with hopeful sincerity. We will bend every effort of our minds to the single purpose of emerging from that conference with tangible results toward peace—the only true way of lessening international tension.

We never have, we never will, propose or suggest that the Soviet Union surrender what is rightfully theirs.

We will never say that the peoples of Russia are an enemy with whom we have no desire ever to deal or mingle in friendly and fruitful relationship.

On the contrary, we hope that this coming conference may initiate a relationship with the Soviet Union which will eventually bring about a free intermingling of the peoples of the East and of the West—the one sure, human way of developing the understanding required for confident and peaceful relations.

Instead of the discontent which is now settling upon Eastern Germany, occupied Austria and the countries of Eastern Europe, we seek a harmonious family of free European nations, with none a threat to the other, and least of all a threat to the peoples of Russia.

Beyond the turmoil and strife and misery of Asia, we seek peaceful opportunity for these peoples to develop their natural resources and to elevate their lot.

These are not idle words of shallow vision. Behind them lies a story of nations lately come to independence, not as a result of war but through free grant of peaceful negotiation. There is a record already written of assistance gladly given by nations of the West to needy peoples and to those suffering the temporary effects of famine, drought and natural disaster.

These are deeds of peace. They speak more loudly than promises or protestations of peaceful intent.

But I do not wish to rest either upon the reiteration of past proposals or the restatement of past deeds. The gravity of the time is such that every new avenue of peace, no matter how dimly discernible, should be explored.

There is at least one new avenue of peace which has not yet been well explored—an avenue now laid out by the General Assembly of the United Nations.

In its resolution of November 18, 1953, this General Assembly suggested—and I quote—"that the Disarmament Commission study the desirability of establishing a subcommittee consisting of representatives of the powers principally involved, which should seek, in private, an acceptable solution—and report such a solution to the General Assembly and to the Security Council not later than 1 September, 1954."

The United States, heeding the suggestion of the General Assembly of the United Nations, is instantly prepared to meet privately with such other countries as may be "principally involved," to seek "an acceptable solution" to the atomic armaments race which overshadows not only the peace but the very life of the world.

We shall carry into these private or diplomatic talks a new conception.

The United States would seek more than the mere reduction or elimination of atomic materials for military purposes.

It is not enough to take this weapon out of the hands of the soldiers. It must be put into the hands of those who will know how to strip its military casing and adapt it to the arts of peace.

The United States knows that if the fearful trend of atomic military build-up can be reversed, this greatest of destructive forces can be developed into a great boon for the benefit of all mankind.

The United States knows that peaceful power from atomic energy is no dream of the future.   That capability, already proved, is here now—today.   Who can doubt, if the entire body of the world's scientists and engineers had adequate amounts of fissionable material with which to test and develop their ideas, that this capability would rapidly be transformed into universal, efficient and economic usage?

To hasten the day when fear of the atom will begin to disappear from the minds of people and the governments of the East and West there are certain steps that can be taken now.

I therefore make the following proposals:

The governments principally involved, to the extent permitted by elementary prudence, to begin now and continue to make joint contributions from their stockpiles of normal uranium and fissionable materials to an international atomic energy agency.   We would expect that such an agency would be set up under the aegis of the United Nations.

The ratios of contributions, the procedures and other details would properly be within the scope of the "private conversations" I have referred to earlier.

The United States is prepared to undertake these explorations in good faith.   Any partner of the United States acting in the same good faith will find the United States a not unreasonable or ungenerous associate.

Undoubtedly initial and early contributions to this plan would be small in quantity. However, the proposal has the great virtue that it can be undertaken without irritations and mutual suspicions incident to any attempt to set up a completely acceptable system of world-wide inspection and control.

The atomic energy agency could be made responsible for the impounding, storage and protection of the contributed fissionable and other materials. The ingenuity of our scientists will provide special, safe conditions under which such a bank of fissionable material can be made essentially immune to surprise seizure.

The more important responsibility of this atomic energy agency would be to devise methods whereby this fissionable material would be allocated to serve the peaceful pursuits of mankind. Experts would be mobilized to apply atomic energy to the needs of agriculture, medicine and other peaceful activities. A special purpose would be to provide abundant electrical energy in the power-starved areas of the world. Thus the contributing powers would be dedicating some of their strength to serve the needs rather than the fears of mankind.

The United States would be more than willing—it would be proud— to take up with others "principally involved" the development of plans whereby such peaceful use of atomic energy would be expedited.

Of those "principally involved" the Soviet Union must, of course, be one.

I would be prepared to submit to the Congress of the United States, and with every expectation of approval, any such plan that would:

First, encourage world-wide investigation into the most effective peacetime uses of fissionable material;

Second, begin to diminish the potential destructive power of the world's atomic stockpiles;

Third, allow all peoples of all nations to see that, in this enlightened age, the great powers of the earth, both of the East and of the West, are interested in human aspirations first rather than in building up the armaments of war.

Fourth, open up a new channel for peaceful discussion and initiate at least a new approach to the many difficult problems that must be solved in both private and public conversations if the world is to shake off the inertia imposed by fear and is to make positive progress toward peace.

Against the dark background of the atomic bomb, the United States does not wish merely to present strength, but also the desire and the hope for peace.

The coming months will be fraught with fateful decisions. In this Assembly, in the capitals and military headquarters of the world; in the hearts of men everywhere, be they governed or governors, may they be the decisions which will lead this world out of fear and into peace.

To the making of these fateful decisions, the United States pledges before you—and therefore before the world—its determination to help solve the fearful atomic dilemma—to devote its entire heart and mind to find the way by which the miraculous inventiveness of man shall not be dedicated to his death, but consecrated to his life.

I again thank the delegates for the great honor they have done me in inviting me to appear before them and in listening to me so courteously. Thank you.

60. A POLICY OF "MASSIVE RETALIATION" *

> Mr. Dulles recognizes that many of the foreign policies pursued by previous administrations were "good." He criticizes these policies, however, as "insufficient" and "emergency" policies, and calls for "long-range policies" to serve our "long-time interests."
>
> The Secretary's major specific departure from the policy of the Truman Administration is his proposal that the defense of the free world be based upon "local defenses reinforced by the further deterrent of massive retaliatory power."

It is now nearly a year since the Eisenhower Administration took office. During that year I have often spoken of various parts of our foreign policies. Tonight I should like to present an over-all view of those policies which relate to our security.

THE GOOD IN PAST POLICIES

First of all, let us recognize that many of the preceding foreign policies were good. Aid to Greece and Turkey had checked the Communist drive to the Mediterranean. The European Recovery Program had helped the peoples of Western Europe to pull out of the post-war morass. The Western powers were steadfast in Berlin and overcame the blockade with their airlift. As a loyal member of the United Nations, we had reacted with force to repel the Communist attack in Korea. When that effort exposed our military weakness, we rebuilt rapidly our military establishment. We also sought a quick buildup of armed strength in Western Europe.

* An address delivered by Secretary of State John Foster Dulles before the Council on Foreign Relations, New York City, January 12, 1954.

These were the acts of a nation which saw the danger of Soviet Communism; which realized that its own safety was tied up with that of others; which was capable of responding boldly and promptly to emergencies. These are precious values to be acclaimed. Also, we can pay tribute to Congressional bipartisanship which puts the nation above politics.

THE INSUFFICIENCY OF PAST POLICIES

But we need to recall that what we did was in the main emergency action, imposed on us by our enemies. Let me illustrate.

1. We did not send our Army into Korea because we judged, in advance, that it was sound military strategy to commit our Army to fight land battles in Asia. Our decision had been to pull out of Korea. It was Soviet-inspired action that pulled us back.

2. We did not decide in advance that it was wise to grant billions annually as foreign economic aid. We adopted that policy in response to the Communist efforts to sabotage the free economies of Western Europe.

3. We did not build up our military establishment at a rate which involved huge budget deficits, a depreciating currency and a feverish economy, because this seemed, in advance, a good policy. Indeed, we decided otherwise until the Soviet military threat was clearly revealed.

We live in a world where emergencies are always possible and our survival may depend upon our capacity to meet emergencies. Let us pray that we shall always have that capacity. But, having said that, it is necessary also to say that emergency measures—however good for emergency—do not necessarily make good permanent policies. Emergency measures are costly, they are superficial and they imply that the enemy has the initiative. They cannot be depended on to serve our long-time interests.

THE NEED FOR LONG-RANGE POLICIES

This "long-time" factor is of critical importance. The Soviet Communists are planning for what they call "an entire historical era," and we should do the same. They seek, through many types of maneuvers, gradually to divide and weaken the free nations by over-extending them in efforts which, as Lenin put it, are "beyond their strength, so that they come to practical bankruptcy." Then, said Lenin, "our victory is assured." Then, said Stalin, will be "the moment for the decisive blow."

In the face of this strategy, measures cannot be judged adequate merely because they ward off an immediate danger. It is essential to do this, but it is also essential to do so without exhausting ourselves.

When the Eisenhower Administration applied this test, we felt that some transformations were needed.

It is not sound military strategy permanently to commit U.S. land forces to Asia to a degree that leaves us no strategic reserves.

It is not sound economics, or good foreign policy, to support permanently other countries; for in the long run, that creates as much ill will as good will.

Also, it is not sound to become permanently committed to military expenditures so vast that they lead to "practical bankruptcy."

Change was imperative to assure the stamina needed for permanent security. But it was equally imperative that change should be accompanied by understanding of our true purposes. Sudden and spectacular change had to be avoided. Otherwise, there might have been a panic among our friends, and miscalculated aggression by our enemies.

We can, I believe, make a good report in these respects.

COLLECTIVE SECURITY

We need allies and collective security. Our purpose is to make these relations more effective, less costly. This can be done by placing more reliance on deterrent power, and less dependence on local defensive power.

This is accepted practice so far as local communities are concerned. We keep locks on our doors; but we do not have an armed guard in every home. We rely principally on a community security system so well equipped to punish any who break in and steal that, in fact, would-be aggressors are generally deterred. That is the modern way of getting maximum protection at a bearable cost.

What the Eisenhower Administration seeks is a similar international security system. We want, for ourselves and the other free nations, a maximum deterrent at a bearable cost.

Local defense will always be important. But there is no local defense which alone will contain the mighty land power of the Communist world. Local defenses must be reinforced by the further deterrent of massive retaliatory power. A potential aggressor must know that he cannot always prescribe battle conditions that suit him. Otherwise, for example, a potential aggressor, who is glutted with manpower, might be tempted to attack in confidence that resistance would be confined to manpower. He might be tempted to attack in places where his superiority was decisive.

The way to deter aggression is for the free community to be willing and able to respond vigorously at places and with means of its own choosing.

So long as our basic policy concepts were unclear, our military leaders could not be selective in building our military power. If an enemy could pick his time and place and method of warfare—and if our policy was to remain the traditional one of meeting aggression by direct and local opposition—then we needed to be ready to fight in the arctic and in the tropics; in Asia, the Near East and in Europe; by sea, by land and by air; with old weapons and with new weapons.

The total cost of our security efforts, at home and abroad, was over $50,000,000,000 per annum, and involved, for 1953, a projected budgetary deficit of $9,000,000,000; and $11,000,000,000 for 1954. This was on top of taxes comparable to war-time taxes; and the dollar was depreciating in effective value. Our allies were similarly weighted down. This could not be continued for long without grave budgetary, economic and social consequences.

But before military planning could be changed, the President and his advisers, as represented by the National Security Council, had to take some basic policy decisions. This has been done. The basic decision was to depend primarily upon a great capacity to retaliate, instantly, by means and at places of our choosing. Now the Department of Defense and the Joint Chiefs of Staff can shape our military establishment to fit what is *our* policy, instead of having to try to be ready to meet the enemy's many choices. That permits of a selection of military means instead of a multiplication of means. As a result, it is now possible to get, and share, more basic security at less cost.

THE FAR EAST

Let us now see how this concept has been applied to foreign policy, taking first the Far East.

In Korea this Administration effected a major transformation. The fighting has been stopped on honorable terms. That was possible because the aggressor, already thrown back to and behind his place of beginning, was faced with the possibility that the fighting might, to his own great peril, soon spread beyond the limits and methods which he had selected.

The cruel toll of American youth, and the non-productive expenditure of many billions has been stopped. Also our armed forces are no longer largely committed to the Asian mainland. We can begin to create a strategic reserve which greatly improves our defensive posture.

This change gives added authority to the warning of the members of the United Nations which fought in Korea that if the Communists renewed the aggression, the United Nations' response would not necessarily be confined to Korea.

I have said, in relation to Indochina, that if there were open Red Chinese Army aggression there, that would have "grave consequences which might not be confined to Indochina."

I expressed last month the intention of the United States to maintain its position in Okinawa. This is needed to ensure adequate striking power to implement the collective security concept which I describe.

All of this is summed up in President Eisenhower's important statement of December 26. He announced the progressive reduction of the United States ground forces in Korea. He pointed out that United States military forces in the Far East will now feature "highly mobile naval, air and amphibious units"; and he said in this way, despite some withdrawal of land forces, the United States will have a capacity to oppose aggression "with even greater effect than heretofore."

The bringing home of some of our land forces also provides a most eloquent rebuttal to the Communist charge of "imperialism."

NATO

If we turn to Europe, we see readjustments in the NATO collective security effort. Senator Vandenberg called the North Atlantic Treaty pledges "the most practical deterrent and discouragement to war which the wit of man has yet devised." But he said also that "if the concept and objective are to build sufficient forces in being to hold the Russian line . . . it presents ruinous corollaries both at home and abroad."

In the first years of the North Atlantic Treaty Organization, after the aggression in Korea, its members made an emergency buildup of military strength. I do not question the judgment of that time. The strength thus built has served well the cause of peace. But the pace originally set could not be maintained indefinitely.

At the April meeting of the NATO Council, the United States put forward a new concept, now known as that of the "long haul." That meant a steady development of defensive strength at a rate which will preserve and not exhaust the economic strength of our allies and ourselves. This would be reinforced by the striking power of a strategic air force based on internationally agreed positions.

We found, at the Council of last December, that there was general acceptance of the "long haul" concept, and recognition that it better served the probable needs than an effort to create full defensive land strength at a ruinous price.

EDC

One of the emergency aspects of NATO is that it was begun before there was a solid foundation.

For example, Western Europe cannot be successfully defended without a defense of West Germany. West Germany cannot be defended without help from the Germans. German participation is excluded by the armistice arrangements still in force.

The West German Republic needs to be freed from the armistice; and new political arrangements should be made to assure that rearmed Germans will serve the common cause and never serve German militarism.

The French produced a plan to take care of this matter. It was to create a European Defense Community, composed of France, Italy, Belgium, the Netherlands, Luxembourg, and West Germany. They would have a European Army, including Germans, but there would be no national armies in West Europe.

A treaty to create this Defense Community was signed in May 1952. But when the Eisenhower Administration took office last January, no Government had sought parliamentary ratification, and the project was nigh unto death.

President Eisenhower is deeply convinced that there can be no long-term assurance of security and vitality for Europe, and therefore for the Western world including the United States, unless there is a unity which will include France and Germany and end the disunity which has led to recurrent wars, and in our generation to two World Wars. As NATO's Chief Commander, and now as President, he continues to make clear the importance which the United States attached to the consummation of the European Defense Community and, we would hope thereafter, a Political Community.

Until the goals of EDC are achieved, NATO, and indeed future peace, are in jeopardy. Distrust between France and Germany is inflammable and already Communist agents are looking to it as a means for international arson.

There are of course immense difficulties in the way of the final consummation of Franco-German unity. But we have confidence that peace will soon have the indispensable foundation of the EDC.

ECONOMIC AID

New collective security concepts reduce non-productive military expenses of our allies to a point where it is desirable and practicable also to reduce economic aid. There was need of a more self-respecting relationship, and that, indeed, is what our allies wanted. Trade, broader markets and a flow of investments are far more healthy than intergovernmental grants-in-aid.

There are still some strategic spots where the local governments cannot maintain adequate armed forces without some financial support from us. In these cases, we take the judgment of our military advisers as to how to proceed in the common interest. For example, we have contributed largely, ungrudgingly, and I hope constructively, to end aggression and advance freedom in Indochina.

The Technical Assistance Program is being continued, and we stand ready to meet non-recurrent needs due to crop failures or like disasters.

But, broadly speaking, foreign budgetary aid is being limited to situations where it clearly contributes to military strength.

THE HOPE

In the ways I outlined we gather strength for the long-term defense of freedom. We do not, of course, claim to have found some magic formula that ensures against all forms of Communist successes. It is normal that at some times and at some places there may be setbacks to the cause of freedom. What we do expect to ensure is that any setbacks will have only temporary and local significance because they will leave unimpaired those free world assets which in the long run will prevail.

If we can deter such aggression as would mean general war, and that is our confident resolve, then we can let time and fundamentals work for us. We do not need self-imposed policies which sap our strength.

The fundamental, on our side, is the richness—spiritual, intellectual and material—that freedom can produce and the irresistible attraction it then sets up. That is why we do not plan ourselves to shackle freedom to preserve freedom. We intend that our conduct and example shall continue, as in the past, to show all men how good can be the fruits of freedom.

If we rely on freedom, then it follows that we must abstain from diplomatic moves which would seem to endorse captivity. That would, in effect, be a conspiracy against freedom. I can assure you that we shall never seek illusory security for ourselves by such a "deal."

We do negotiate about specific matters but only to advance the cause of human welfare.

President Eisenhower electrified the world with his proposal to lift a great weight of fear by turning atomic energy from a means of death into a source of life.   Yesterday, I started procedural talks with the Soviet Government on that topic.

We have persisted, with our Allies, in seeking the unification of Germany and the liberation of Austria.   Now the Soviet rulers have agreed to discuss these questions.   We expect to meet them soon in Berlin.   I hope they will come with a sincerity which will equal our own.

We have sought a conference to unify Korea and relieve it of foreign troops.   So far, our persistence is unrewarded; but we have not given up.

These efforts at negotiation are normal initiatives that breathe the spirit of freedom.   They involve no plan for a partnership division of world power with those who suppress freedom.

If we persist in the courses I outline we shall confront dictatorship with a task that is, in the long run, beyond its strength.   For unless it changes, it must suppress the human desires that freedom satisfies—as we shall be demonstrating.

If the dictators persist in their present course then it is they who will be limited to superficial successes, while their foundation crumbles under the tread of their iron boots.

Human beings, for the most part, want simple things.   They want to worship God in accordance with the dictates of their conscience.   But that is not easily granted by those who promote an atheistic creed.

They want to think in accordance with the dictates of their reason. But that is not easily granted by those who represent an authoritarian system.

They want to exchange views with others and to persuade and to be persuaded by what appeals to their reason and their conscience.   But that is not easily granted by those who believe in a society of conformity.

They want to live in their homes without fear.   But that is not easily granted by those who believe in a police state system.

They want to be able to work productively and creatively and to enjoy the fruits of their labor.   But that is not easily granted by those who look upon human beings as a means to create a powerhouse to dominate the world.

We can be sure that there is going on, even within Russia, a silent test of strength between the powerful rulers and the multitudes of human beings.   Each individual no doubt seems by himself to be helpless in this struggle.   But their aspirations in the aggregate make up a mighty force.

There are signs that the rulers are bending to some of the human desires of their people.   There are promises of more food, more household goods, more economic freedom.

That does not prove that the Soviet rulers have themselves been converted. It is rather that they may be dimly perceiving a basic fact, that is that there are limits to the power of any rulers indefinitely to suppress the human spirit.

In that God-given fact lies our greatest hope. It is a hope that can sustain us. For even if the path ahead be long and hard, it need not be a warlike path; and we can know that at the end may be found the blessedness of peace.

Critique

61. A RESTRICTED VIEW OF THE NATIONAL INTEREST *

The way in which one defines the national interest of the United States strongly influences and perhaps determines the policies which one will deem necessary to defend that interest.

Mr. Hoover defines the national interest primarily in terms of the security of the Western Hemisphere and the necessity to maintain a sound national economy. He is prepared to go "all-out" to defend the Americas against attack, and the economy against the strains of inflation, high taxation, and creeping socialism. He is willing to defend Western Europe, not, however, by an "all-out" effort, but by American air and sea power backed by Western European ground forces. Mr. Hoover appears to imply that our interests in the Western Hemisphere and the national economy are greater than our interests in Western Europe.

The Sabbath Day is an appropriate day to discuss our problems of peace. Unfortunately on this Sabbath Day, despite our full goodwill to mankind, peace rests upon defense from Communist aggression. And that is also defense of our religious faiths.

One year ago we engaged in a great debate on our foreign and military policies.

At that time we were repeatedly told that United States policies were based upon what was called "a calculated risk," which meant risk of war or economic degeneration. With that as a basis of national policies, a changing world demands constant recalculation of the risk and reconsideration of alternative action.

The risks are so great that, with our experience over the past year, the Congress should now again recalculate these risks.

* An address by Ex-President Herbert Hoover, delivered to a nation-wide radio and television audience on January 7, 1952. Reprinted from *The New York Times*, January 8, 1952, p. 6.

I do not propose on this occasion to review how we got into these dangerous cold and hot wars, but to start from where we are now.

To indicate the necessity for recalculation of risks, I will make a little appraisal of the situations in the world in general.

A year ago, when I addressed the American people, the North Atlantic Pact had been in operation for over a year. Up to that time, despite huge subsidies and sacrifices by the American people, the nations of Europe, except Britain, had done little in mutual defense. And in this address today, unless otherwise stated, I do not include Britain in the term "Continental Western Europe."

During the course of the debate a year ago we were told that a European defense army of upward of forty ground divisions would be created under General Eisenhower by the end of 1952, with twenty more divisions by the end of 1954.

We were told four more American divisions were to be shipped to Europe in addition to the two we already had there.

But what has happened?

The rearming of Western Europe is mainly dependent upon the French and the Germans. A year ago, in urging that we send our divisions, General Eisenhower stated to the Congress that the French promised fifteen battle-worthy divisions by the end of 1952 and presumably more by the end of 1953. A few days ago, the French Defense Minister indicated that they contemplated only ten divisions for the European army, of which none was complete and half of them were only 50 per cent recruited.

The settlement by which Western Germany is to be given a certain degree of independence and is to contribute twelve divisions has not yet gone beyond the paper stage. No battle-worthy German divisions are in sight—certainly not before 1953.

The British have announced that their four divisions on the continent will not be a part of the European army, but that they "will cooperate." Britain would be a friend, but would not marry Mr. Europe. That is a form of independence.

In sum, the only substantial additions to West Europe ground armies during the two years past have been the American divisions we have sent over.

Aside from American and British divisions it would be difficult to find ten battle-worthy divisions in the Western European army today. And it would appear that even the sixty-division army is two or three years away.

This proposed sixty-division army compares with over 200 equipped divisions which these same Western European nations placed in the field within sixty days after the outbreak of each of the World Wars.   And their manpower and productivity are greater today.

In that debate a year ago, we were told that the Communist armies comprised 300 divisions, 20,000 planes and 30,000 tanks.   No one contended that sixty European divisions, even if created, could do more than temporarily halt an invasion.   Our side in that debate replied that this was not a calculated risk but that it was a calculated Dunquerque.

I may say at once that all the American people are interested in the growth of unity in continental Europe and their preparation of adequate ground armies for their defense.   We earnestly hope that General Eisenhower will succeed in his difficult task.

There has been some progress during the past year in allaying age-old discords and dissensions.   But they are obviously not yet cured.

Among the forces which obstruct progressive Western European statesmen are the potent Socialist and Communist parties.   These parties also have widely spread the belief that American subsidies and our urging are for the purpose of using Europe for American cannon fodder.   Yet the Western European nations are contributing less than 10 per cent of the total military expenditures of the North Atlantic Pact nations.

Another cause of Western European inertia is its attitude as to the risk of Communist invasion.   That attitude is profoundly different from the attitude of Washington.

There is in Europe today no such public alarm as has been fanned up in the United States.   None of those nations has declared emergencies or taken measures comparable with ours.   They do not propagandize war fears or war psychoses such as we get out of Washington.   Not one European country conducts such exercises in protection from bombs as we have had in New York.

I recently made an inquiry from European sources as to why they calculate this risk of invasion as so much less than does Washington.

The sum of this inquiry was that there was little public belief that there was risk of a Russian invasion in the near future.   Their reasons for this belief were:

First: They said that the Russian ground armies could have overrun Europe in a two-months' campaign any time in the past five years and can no doubt do it during several years to come.   That they have not done so seems proof to these observers that the Kremlin realizes several difficulties in making a Red world out of the West.

Second: They said that the Communists hesitate to stir up a war in the West because they can see no final military victory.   That the Russians know they cannot invade the United States with armies, however much they might trouble us with bombs. Therefore, they said the Russians have no taste for a war where they cannot effectively destroy their enemy.

Third: They said that the Kremlin realizes that invasion of Western Europe would add a dozen nationalities to the centrifugal forces and oppositions which already trouble them from the thirty-odd races they dominate. They said the proof of these oppositions was the fact that the Communists have sent 15,000,000 politically objectionable persons to slave camps. In addition, nationalism is not dead in those nations, as witness Yugoslavia.

Fourth: They said the Kremlin knows that the industrial potential they would secure by invading Western Europe is mostly an illusion. The reason they gave is that if Europe were blockaded by the Americans or British, and Russian transport into Europe were paralyzed by bombing, Europe would be 30 per cent short in fuel, 25 per cent short in food, and without non-ferrous and hardening metals. They stated that under such a blockade, Western European industrial production would diminish rapidly and ultimately stop.

Fifth: They said the Kremlin had at last learned that its conspiracies of boring from within have failed to secure more than a minor percentage of men's minds in the western world. Its left-arm activities have there raised implacable walls to such ideological victories.

Sixth: They said the opportunities for the Kremlin are in Asia and that its face is turned east, not west.

Seventh: They said Stalin has every reason to be satisfied with the progress of economic confusion in the United States and in Western Europe.

Eighth: Finally, they said the Communists know that, if they invade Western Europe, their own war potential will be destroyed by an atomic war from the air and a blockade from the sea, even if they succeed on land.

I cannot say whether these eight assumptions are correct or not. But they do contribute to Western Europe's lack of hysterics and their calculation of low risk and therefore, their lack of hurry to arm.

In any event, this whole European situation requires that the United States recalculate our own risks and reconsider the possible alternatives.

In South Asia and the Middle East we are witnessing vast readjustments of political power. Behind the slogan, "Asia for the Asiatics," lie two centuries of the white man's exploitation. These forces have lighted a prairie fire of revolution against the West. They are removing the "white man's burden."

America had no part in the exploitation. Yet too often we find that many of these nations vote against the United States in the United Nations.

During the past year in Korea, the United Nations vetoed General MacArthur's policies of destroying the Chinese air sanctuary in Manchuria and the employment of Chiang Kai-shek's armies to save American lives. Accordingly, we denied ourselves victory.

A negotiation was begun six months ago for a cease-fire. The American people welcomed its promise to stop the loss of blood and lives of their sons. But three things have come of it. Far from cease-fire, over 20,000 Americans have been wounded and nearly 5,000 have been killed there since the negotiations began.

Yet in this negotiation we have retreated from the original purpose of unity and independence for Korea to an appeasement idea of a division of Korea about where it was before. Finally, during these negotiations the Chinese have built up a great air force. What the outcome may be, we do not know. But I will presently suggest some lessons we now ought to learn from this experience.

The outstanding phenomenon in the United States is the dangerous overstraining of our economy by our gigantic expenditures.

The American people have not yet felt the full impact of the gigantic increase in Government spending and taxes. Yet we already suffer from the blight of inflation and confiscatory taxes.

We are actually in a war economy except for world-wide shooting. We are diverting more and more civilian production to war materials. We are placing a greater portion of our man-power under arms. All this creates scarcity in civilian goods and increased spending power; both of which fan the flames of inflation.

We are constantly told that measures are being taken by the Government to "prevent" inflation. This ignores the fact that we are in the middle of inflationary operations at this very minute. Ever since the end of the Second World War the purchasing power of our money, measured in wholesale price indexes, has decreased 40 per cent.

Controls of the type we have imposed on wages and prices cannot in the long run prevent inflation. The experience of six great commercial nations in two wars has proved that they are, at best, a retarding device.

Under the demands of Washington we are confronted with a probable Federal deficit of $30,000,000,000 to $40,000,000,000 for immediate rearmament. We already have Government obligations and currency of $280,000,000,000. And private credit is dangerously over-expanded. In the brief period since the war, private credit has swelled by $130,000,000,000.

The Government will need to cover part of its deficit by selling its bonds or notes, some part of which must be sold to the banks. That is direct inflation of credit and results in an addition to the currency in the form of bank check money.

The two pressures—scarcities and expanding credit, or paper money—are the irresistible forces of inflation. They are already being expressed in gray markets and a sporadic spiral of high wages and then higher prices.

Our standard of living will be reduced in millions of families. Rising prices are coming through the kitchen while taxes are invading our homes through the front door.

These huge taxes are also overstraining our economy. Moreover, they have probably reached the point of diminishing return. That is indicated by the fact that the various taxes on the top bracket incomes if all put together can possibly exceed 100 per cent. If all remaining untaxed income above that level of the salary and expense allowance of a United States Senator were confiscated, it would bring only about $2,000,000,000 annually to the Federal Treasury, which would last about ten days, and that assumes that these taxpayers would continue to work for nothing, which they will not do.

It is the average family who pays the bulk of taxes both income and hidden. Among them are corporation taxes. These are ultimately passed on to their customers or the corporation would quickly go bankrupt.

Families with incomes of from $3,000 to $4,000 a year will pay in total taxes an average of over $900 a year. The double effect of inflation and taxes is indicated by the fact that a family with $3,000 net annual income ten years ago must now earn $6,000 to maintain the same standard of living.

And this spending and taxes is not a quickie program. When our great military forces are assembled, they must continue to be paid for. Due to constant new inventions in weapons, the new devices must continuously replace the old. That will cost more billions.

A man may carry a load of 300 pounds across the room, but he will break his back if he carries it around the block.

Communism is an evil thing. It is contrary to the spiritual, moral and material aspirations of man. These very reasons give rise to my conviction that it will decay and die of its own poisons. But that may be many years away and, in the meantime, we must be prepared for a long journey.

There are men who welcome these inflation and tax pressures because these forces drive to socialize the income of our people. That is the inevitable end, even if it were not the avowed purpose. If this form of creeping socialism continues, we may be permitted to hold the paper title to property, while bureaucracy spends our income. Along this road the erosion of our productive capital and the destruction of incentives to economic progress are inevitable.

In view of this past year's experience, and these rising pressures, the Congress should again re-examine our situation.

I believe there are methods more effective to check the Communist menace in the long run and at the same time to lessen our domestic dangers.

As a basis for test I may repeat the essentials of the proposals some of us made a year ago which were supported by many military and economic authorities:

First: That the first national purpose of this republic must be the defense of this final Gibraltar of freedom—and that is the Western Hemisphere.

Second: That the only way to save Europe from destruction is to avoid the Third World War. The real and effective deterrent which we can, within our resources, contribute to that end is in cooperation with the British to expand our already strong air and navies up to a striking force. The Communists know that such a striking force could destroy their military potential if they started an invasion and it could punish any such aggression. And this applies to aggression against other non-Communist countries as well as Western Europe.

In Korea, however correct the original decisions to use ground armies may have been, our experience during the past year has certainly demonstrated that we should have relied upon air and sea forces to punish that aggression. We should have avoided most of the sacrifice of 20,000 American boys and the injury of 80,000 others. The long-run injury to the South Koreans would have been less devastating.

Third: That the only way we can hold the initiative in this "cold war" is not to scatter our ground armies all around the 25,000 miles of Communist borders but to concentrate on such a highly mobile striking force by air and sea.

Three weeks ago General Wedemeyer, one of our greatest military strategists, stated we should not dissipate our ground armies over the world and should put our emphasis upon a striking force of air and sea power.

Fourth: That we should furnish such munitions as we can afford to other nations who show a determined will to defend themselves.

Fifth: That to maintain the economic strength of the United States and to prevent its socialization does not permit our building up great ground armies in addition to overwhelming air and sea forces and supply of munitions to other nations. If our economy should collapse, Stalin's victory over the world would be complete. We cannot take that risk.

Sixth: That true friendship with Western European nations requires they be told certain things in no uncertain terms. They should realize the limit of our economic aid in this deterrent air and sea power and munitions. That, protected by this shield, we expect them on the basis of their performance in previous wars, and now with the aid of munitions from us, to realize that ground armies are Europe's own sole problem. We should state that we expect them to provide ground protection for our airfields within their boundaries. We should state that not only will we send no more ground troops, but that we expect they will rapidly relieve us of that burden except to protect our airfields outside the NATO countries.

And they should be told that their delays leave our 250,000 American garrison in Europe in a most exposed position.

Seventh: Our relations to the United Nations charter should be revised. It must not be allowed to dominate the internal sovereignty of our Government. Our courts have already made decisions that the charter overrides our domestic laws.

Recalculation of our policies along these lines would greatly reduce our economic risks. By restricting our ground armies and ultimately reducing them to the force necessary to protect our homeland and our essential air bases outside of European NATO countries, together with a reduction or postponement of 30 per cent in our Federal civil expenditures, we could assure our economic strength. We could return thousands of young men to their shops, their farms and their colleges. We could apply real brakes upon this drift to inflation; we might stop the plunge into socialism; we could avoid increase in taxes. But above all, we could better halt the spread of communism over the world.

It has been said that in these evil times peace can be preserved only through strength. That is true. But the center and final reserve of strength of the free world lies in the North American continent. Nothing must be permitted to weaken this bastion. We should recalculate our risks.

I pray that we shall have peace and preservation of our American way of life. I hold firmly to the belief that a third World War is neither necessary nor inevitable.

And in this summary of our position and our prospects I have used only facts and the terms of sober reason. But because I have avoided words appropriate to a deep emotion, this statement may not convey the extent of my anxiety for the future of my country and for the world. I must admit that on this Sabbath Day that my anxiety is even greater than it was one year ago.

I have no despair; I am firm in my confidence and my belief that an informed American people can and will solve their menacing problems. They have met every challenge over 170 years of national life.

∽ଓଏ∾

62. AN EVALUATION OF THE POLICY OF CONTAINMENT *

This selection is a critique of the policy of containment as embodied in the article "The Sources of Soviet Conduct" by George F. Kennan (Selection 52). Mr. Harold J. Laski has described Mr. Lippmann's analysis as "devastating." From the vantage point of several years' experience with the policy, we can see that some of Mr. Lippmann's predictions have come to pass, others have not.

An anonymous article on "The Sources of Soviet Conduct" appeared in the quarterly journal *Foreign Affairs* for July 1947 and shortly afterwards it was republished in *Life* magazine. By its quality alone it would have commanded wide attention. For it was manifestly the work of a man who had observed the Soviet regime closely with a trained eye and an educated mind, and had arrived at a theory as to why the conduct of the Soviet government reflects "no abstract love of peace and stability, no real faith in the possibility of a permanent happy coexistence of the socialist and capitalist worlds, but rather a continuous, persistent pressure towards the disruption and weakening of all rival influence and rival power." . . .

We must begin with the disturbing fact, which anyone who will reread the article can verify for himself, that Mr. X's conclusions depend upon the optimistic prediction that the "Soviet power . . . bears within itself the seeds of its own decay, and that the sprouting of these seeds is well advanced"; that if "anything were ever to occur to disrupt the unity and the efficacy of the Party as a political instrument, Soviet Russia might be changed overnight (*sic*) from one of the strongest to one of the weakest and most pitiable of national societies"; and "that Soviet society may well (*sic*) contain deficiencies which will eventually weaken its own total potential."

Of this optimistic prediction Mr. X himself says that it "cannot be proved. And it cannot be disproved." Nevertheless, he concludes that

* Walter Lippmann, *The Cold War* (New York: Harper and Bros., 1947), pp. 9, 11-16, 18-27, 60. Copyright, 1947, by Walter Lippmann. The author is a columnist and political analyst for the *New York Herald Tribune*.

the United States should construct its policy on the assumption that the Soviet power is inherently weak and impermanent, and that this unproved assumption warrants our entering "with reasonable confidence upon a policy of firm containment, designed to confront the Russians with unalterable counterforce at every point where they show signs of encroaching upon the interests of a peaceful and a stable world."

I do not find much ground for reasonable confidence in a policy which can be successful only if the most optimistic prediction should prove to be true. Surely a sound policy must be addressed to the worst and hardest that may be judged to be probable, and not to the best and easiest that may be possible. . . .

In Mr. X's estimates there are no reserves for a rainy day. There is no margin for safety for bad luck, bad management, error and the unforeseen. He asks us to assume that the Soviet power is already decaying. He exhorts us to believe that our own highest hopes for ourselves will soon have been realized. Yet the policy he recommends is designed to deal effectively with the Soviet Union "as a rival, not a partner, in the political arena." Do we dare to assume, as we enter the arena and get set to run the race, that the Soviet Union will break its leg while the United States grows a pair of wings to speed it on its way? . .

Surely it is by no means proved that the way to lead mankind is to spend the next ten or fifteen years, as Mr. X proposes we should, in reacting at "a series of constantly shifting geographical and political points, corresponding to the shifts and maneuvers of Soviet policy." For if history has indeed intended us to bear the responsibility of leadership, then it is not leadership to adapt ourselves to the shifts and maneuvers of Soviet policy at a series of constantly shifting geographical and political points. For that would mean for ten or fifteen years Moscow, not Washington, would define the issues, would make the challenges, would select the ground where the conflict was to be waged, and would choose the weapons. And the best that Mr. X can say for his own proposal is that if for a long period of time we can prevent the Soviet power from winning, the Soviet power will eventually perish or "mellow" because it has been "frustrated." . . .

Now the strength of the western world is great, and we may assume that its resourcefulness is considerable. Nevertheless, there are weighty reasons for thinking that the kind of strength we have and the kind of resourcefulness we are capable of showing are peculiarly unsuited to operating a policy of containment.

How, for example, under the Constitution of the United States is Mr. X going to work out an arrangement by which the Department of

State has the money and the military power always available in sufficient amounts to apply "counterforce" at constantly shifting points all over the world? Is he going to ask Congress for a blank check on the Treasury and a blank authorization to use the armed forces? Not if the American constitutional system is to be maintained. Or is he going to ask for an appropriation and for authority each time the Russians "show signs of encroaching upon the interests of a peaceful and stable world"? If that is his plan for dealing with the maneuvers of a dictatorship, he is going to arrive at the points of encroachment with too little and he is going to arrive too late. The Russians, if they intend to encroach, will have encroached while Congress is getting ready to hold hearings.

A policy of shifts and maneuvers may be suited to the Soviet system of government, which, as Mr. X tells us, is animated by patient persistence. It is not suited to the American system of government.

It is even more unsuited to the American economy which is unregimented and uncontrolled, and therefore cannot be administered according to a plan. Yet a policy of containment cannot be operated unless the Department of State can plan and direct exports and imports. For the policy demands that American goods be delivered or withheld at "constantly shifting geographical and political points corresponding to the shifts and maneuvers of Soviet policy."

I find it hard to understand how Mr. X could have recommended such a strategic monstrosity. For he tells us, no doubt truly, that the Soviet power "cannot be easily defeated or discouraged by a single victory on the part of its opponents," and that "the patient persistence by which it is animated" means that it cannot be "effectively countered" by "sporadic acts." Yet his own policy calls for a series of sporadic acts; the United States is to apply "counterforce" where the Russians encroach and when they encroach. . . .

There is, however, no rational ground for confidence that the United States could muster "unalterable counterforce" at all the individual sectors. The Eurasian continent is a big place, and the military power of the United States, though it is very great, has certain limitations which must be borne in mind if it is to be used effectively. We live on an island continent. We are separated from the theaters of conflict by the great oceans. We have a relatively small population, of which the greater proportion must in time of war be employed in producing, transporting and servicing the complex weapons and engines which constitute our military power. The United States has, as compared with the Russians, no adequate reserves of infantry. Our navy commands the oceans and we possess the major offensive weapons of war.

But on the ground in the interior of the Eurasian continent, as we are learning in the Greek mountains, there may be many "individual sectors" where only infantry can be used as the "counterforce." . . .

Yet the genius of American military power does not lie in holding positions indefinitely. That requires a massive patience by great hordes of docile people. American military power is distinguished by its mobility, its speed, its range and its offensive striking force. It is, therefore, not an efficient instrument for diplomatic policy of containment. It can only be the instrument of a policy which has as its objective a decision and a settlement. It can and should be used to redress the balance of power which has been upset by the war. But it is not designed for, or adapted to, a strategy of containing, waiting, countering, blocking, with no more specific objective than the eventual "frustration" of the opponent.

The Americans would themselves probably be frustrated by Mr. X's policy long before the Russians were.

The policy of containment, which Mr. X recommends, demands the employment of American economic, political, and in the last analysis, American military power at "sectors" in the interior of Europe and Asia. This requires, as I have pointed out, ground forces, that is to say reserves of infantry, which we do not possess.

The United States cannot by its own military power contain the expansive pressure of the Russians "at every point where they show signs of encroaching." The United States cannot have ready "unalterable counterforce" consisting of American troops. Therefore, the counterforces which Mr. X requires have to be composed of Chinese, Afghans, Iranians, Turks, Kurds, Arabs, Greeks, Italians, Austrians, of anti-Soviet Poles, Czechoslovaks, Bulgars, Yugoslavs, Albanians, Hungarians, Finns and Germans.

The policy can be implemented only by recruiting, subsidizing and supporting a heterogeneous array of satellites, clients, dependents and puppets. The instrument of the policy of containment is therefore a coalition of disorganized, disunited, feeble or disorderly nations, tribes and factions around the perimeter of the Soviet Union. . . .

In the complicated contest over this great heterogeneous array of unstable states, the odds are heavily in favor of the Soviets. For if we are to succeed, we must organize our satellites as unified, orderly and reasonably contented nations. The Russians can defeat us by disorganizing states that are already disorganized, by disuniting peoples that are torn with civil strife, and by inciting their discontent which is already very great. . . .

There is still greater disadvantage in a policy which seeks to "contain" the Soviet Union by attempting to make "unassailable barriers" out of the surrounding border states. They are admittedly weak. Now a weak ally is not an asset. It is a liability. It requires the diversion of power, money, and prestige to support it and maintain it. These weak states are vulnerable. Yet the effort to defend them brings us no nearer to a decision or to a settlement of the main conflict. Worst of all, the effort to develop such an unnatural alliance of backward states must alienate the natural allies of the United States.

The natural allies of the United States are the nations of the Atlantic community: that is to say, the nations of western Europe and of the Americas. The Atlantic Ocean and the Mediterranean Sea, which is an arm of the Atlantic Ocean, unite them in a common, strategic, economic and cultural system. The chief components of the Atlantic community are the British Commonwealth of nations, the Latin States on both sides of the Atlantic, the Low Countries, and Switzerland, Scandinavia and the United States. . . .

Now the policy of containment, as described by Mr. X, is an attempt to organize an anti-Soviet alliance composed in the first instance of peoples that are either on the shadowy extremity of the Atlantic community, or are altogther outside it. The active proponents of the policy have been concerned immediately with the anti-Soviet parties and factions of eastern Europe, with the Greeks, the Turks, the Iranians, the Arabs and Afghans, and with the Chinese Nationalists.

Instead of concentrating their attention and their efforts upon our old allies of the Atlantic community, the makers and the shapers of the policy of containment have for more than a year been reaching out for new allies on the perimeter of the Soviet Union. This new coalition, as we can see only too clearly in Greece, in Iran, in the Arab states and in China, cannot in fact be made to coalesce. Instead of becoming an unassailable barrier against the Soviet power, this border-land is a seething stew of civil strife. . . .

The nations of the Atlantic community are not occupied by the Red Army. They cannot be occupied by the Red Army unless the Kremlin is prepared to face a full scale world war, atomic bombs and all the rest. Though impoverished and weakened, the nations of the Atlantic community are incomparably stronger, richer, more united and politically more democratic and mature than any of the nations of the Russian perimeter.

If the Soviet Union is, nevertheless, able to paralyze and disorganize them, then surely it can much more readily paralyze and disorganize the nations of the perimeter. They are already paralyzed and disorganized. They have never, in fact, been organized and effective modern states.

Yet we are asked to believe that we can organize the perimeter of Russia, though the Russians are so strong and so cunning that we cannot consolidate the Atlantic community.

By concentrating our efforts on a diplomatic war in the borderlands of the Soviet Union, we have neglected—because we do not have unlimited power, resources, influence, and diplomatic brain power—the vital interests of our natural allies in western Europe, notably in reconstructing their economic life and in promoting a German settlement on which they can agree.

The failure of our diplomatic campaign in the borderlands, on which we have staked much too much, has conjured up the specter of a Third World War. The threat of a Russian-American war, arising out of the conflict in the borderlands, is dissolving the natural alliance of the Atlantic community. For the British, the French, and all the other Europeans see that they are placed between the hammer and the anvil. They realize, even if we do not realize it, that the policy of containment, in the hope that the Soviet power will collapse by frustration, cannot be enforced and cannot be administered successfully, and it must fail. Either, Russia will burst through the barriers which are supposed to contain her, and all of Europe will be at her mercy, or, at some point and at some time, the diplomatic war will become a full scale shooting war. In either event Europe is lost. Either Europe falls under the domination of Russia, or Europe becomes the battlefield of a Russian-American war. . . .

It will be evident, I am sure, to the reader who has followed the argument to this point that my criticism of the policy of containment, or the so-called Truman Doctrine, does not spring from any hope or belief that the Soviet pressure to expand can be "charmed or talked out of existence." I agree entirely with Mr. X that we must make up our minds that the Soviet power is not amenable to our arguments, but only "to contrary force" that "is felt to be too strong, and thus more rational in the logic and rhetoric of power."

My objection, then, to the policy of containment is not that it seeks to confront the Soviet power with American power, but that the policy is misconceived, and must result in a misuse of American power. . . .

The policy concedes to the Kremlin the strategical initiative as to when, where and under what local circumstances the issue is to be joined. It compels the United States to meet the Soviet pressure at these shifting geographical and political points by using satellite states, puppet governments and agents which have been subsidized and supported, though their effectiveness is meager and their reliability uncertain. By forcing us to expend our energies and our substance upon these dubious and unnatural allies on the perimeter of the Soviet Union, the effect of the policy is to neglect our natural allies in the Atlantic community, and to alienate them. . . .

At the root of Mr. X's philosophy about Russian-American relations and underlying all the ideas of the Truman Doctrine there is a disbelief in the possibility of a settlement of the issues raised by this war.   Having observed, I believe quite correctly, that we cannot expect "to enjoy political intimacy with the Soviet regime," and that we must "regard the Soviet Union as a rival, not a partner in the political arena," and that "there can be no appeal to common purposes," Mr. X has reached the conclusion that all we can do is to "contain" Russia until Russia changes, ceases to be our rival, and becomes our partner.

The conclusion is, it seems to me, quite unwarranted.   The history of diplomacy is the history of relations among rival powers, which did not enjoy political intimacy, and did not respond to appeals to common purposes.   Nevertheless, there have been settlements.   Some of them did not last very long.   Some of them did.   For a diplomat to think that rival and unfriendly powers cannot be brought to a settlement is to forget what diplomacy is about.   There would be little for diplomats to do if the world consisted of partners, enjoying political intimacy, and responding to common appeals.

63. Dictation From Strength *

Mr. Charles Bohlen has described the attempts of the United States to create "situations of strength" (Selection 53).   When this strength had been created, it was our intention to negotiate with the Soviet Union "from strength."   The thesis of this argument was that attempts to negotiate a settlement before the economic and military strength of the United States and its allies were brought to par with Soviet strength would be futile.   In such circumstances, the Soviets would make no compromises but merely issue demands.

Mr. Rich analyzes the psychological problems involved in the process of negotiating from strength.   In effect, Mr. Rich says that the sense of moderation and compromise tends to be weakened when a nation becomes strong enough—a tendency develops not to negotiate, but to dictate.

* Grover S. Rich, "Negotiation from Strength: The Psychological Problem," *The Antioch Review*, September, 1952, pp. 259-265. Copyright *The Antioch Review*, Inc., 1952.   The author has been an officer in the United States Foreign Service, and is Assistant Professor of Political Science, University of Utah.

The American people fervently want peace, yet ironically enough they may cause the very war they seek to avoid, simply because of their misunderstanding of American foreign policy and the vital role they must play if it is to succeed.

To begin with, what *is* American foreign policy? In the words of its major architects, we aim to "reassume a military posture" and then "negotiate from situations of strength." In essence, we seek to re-militarize ourselves and our allies, create a system of armed alliances opposed to Russian power, and then negotiate settlements which will permit the peaceful coexistence of the two camps.

The danger of war in such a policy can hardly be overestimated. It is, to use General Marshall's phrase, "a calculated risk," based on the precarious assumption that Russia will permit us to erect a series of strongholds around her borders without a fight. Yet there is another risk we take—not with the Russians but our own people; namely, will the American people be *willing* to negotiate?

The question sounds absurd at first hearing. After all, the one thing Americans *do* agree upon is their desire for peace. Moreover, there is apparently a fairly widespread fear of our armament-alliance program and its possible consequences. Opponents range from Herbert Hoover to Henry Wallace, and in view of the periodic resistance of the "economy bloc" to congressional appropriations, one might ask whether we shall even be able to adequately defend ourselves, let alone play the role of an aggressor.

Yet in spite of some opposition we continue to arm ourselves and our allies according to plan, and if we are to avoid the pitfalls of such a policy, now is a good time to re-examine the dangers inherently involved.

One of these dangers is surely the psychological unpreparedness of the American people. It must be remembered that we are being asked to do something few other people in history have been able to do—prepare for war and then sue for peace. A nation's capacity for compromise decreases as its rearmament increases, until the climate of opinion will no longer support give-and-take negotiations. It is extremely difficult for any country, once mobilized, to avoid war; the temptation to use its power is too great.

While this is true of any nation, it is especially true of democratic countries like our own, in which the government is responsive to popular will. Our avowed purpose is to "reassume a military posture," and our rearmament, if it is to be effective, must be moral and psychological as well as military. It is useless to produce tanks and ships if our people are not prepared to fight.

Yet in seeking to create the will to fight, do we not thereby destroy our ability to negotiate? We are reaching a point where "negotiation" is thought of as "appeasement" in the public mind. When this happens the danger is not merely one of chauvinistic goverment officials being unwilling to compromise, but of an aroused public demanding that they do not. Is not this the real significance of General MacArthur's popularity? A policy of "getting tough" is, at best, a dangerous proposition, if one's aim is not to fight.

In seeking to achieve "total" rearmament—moral as well as military —government spokesmen have bombarded the American people with a "hate the enemy" campaign rarely seen in our history; never, certainly, in peace time. Moreover, as Communism is the enemy, our preponderantly conservative press has readily fallen into line. This campaign, while certainly justified in most cases, is rapidly convincing the American people that the Communists are impossible to deal with; that it is useless to reason with them as they understand only one thing: force.

The degree of truth in this is not the important thing; rather it is whether any people so convinced are capable of negotiating. The term negotiation by its very nature implies compromise, and any real attempt to reach a peaceful settlement with Russia will obviously involve painful concessions on the part of both parties.

Yet any administration which determines to achieve an honest settlement will surely be accused of "appeasement." The State Department is already thought of in some circles as being the captive of its conservative opposition. "McCarthy," it is said, "not Acheson, is making our policy." Once the public's hatred of Russian Communism has reached a white heat, it will take a very brave Secretary of State indeed to even advocate—yet alone try to conduct—a compromise settlement with the USSR. The political unpopularity of such a policy may prove too great for any office holder to ignore. He would fall easy prey to our professional patriots and headline-hunting congressmen. No man these days can afford to be labeled "pro-red," "Communist dupe," or "appeaser," and expect to remain long in public service. Apparently no one is immune from such attacks, moreover. Even Eisenhower, in the New Hampshire primary campaign, was accused of "softness towards Russia." Such tactics may ultimately make it impossible for any administration to bargain diplomatically with the Soviets, and the only alternative to diplomatic negotiation is eventual war.

Our allies in particular are fearful that a combination of American blundering, bluff, and impatience will provoke a "wrong war, at the wrong time, and in the wrong place." We would do well to make a more serious effort to understand these fears. Their periodic reluctance to accept American policies and leadership with the proper enthusiasm may at times prove frustrating, but it may also provide a necessary stabilizing influence.

Now would be a good time for Americans to dip into the history books and review the story of our entrance into the Spanish-American war. It illustrates amply how an aroused public opinion, whipped up by an irresponsible press, can readily push a reluctant government into war. Who can say at what point today's chauvinism and McCarthyism will get out of hand? I for one do not want to fight a "Holy War" brought on by mass hysteria.

Those who guide our present psychological and military rearmament bear a terrifying responsibility. They not only take a "calculated risk" with the enemy, but with their own people. They do not control the process of molding public opinion, yet they are accountable to it.

It is time that the term "negotiation from strength" be more clearly spelled out for the American people. There is a decided difference between "negotiation" and "dictation." Any attempt to dictate to the Russians could lead to only one conclusion, for big powers of relatively equal strength simply do not dictate to each other; they fight. Unless the necessity of compromise is made clear to our people we may needlessly cause a war we seek to avoid.

Our policy is predicated on the assumption that the Russians will permit us to arm an anti-Soviet coalition without a fight. This makes it all the more necessary to make our intentions clear, for surely they cannot be expected to sit idly by and watch us rearm if they are convinced we intend to wage a war against them. If either our intentions or our ability to negotiate peacefully is questioned, the Soviets will have little choice but to strike when it best suits them.

Meanwhile our more irresponsible newspapers talk of preventive war, an American airman publicly advocates the atomic bombing of Russia, and an American general writes in his diary: "War! As soon as possible! Now!"

All the while the Politbureau is skeptically trying to determine our real intentions. "It is perfectly true," they might argue, "that the Americans claim they want only to create a more favorable balance of power; but when will a 'balance' of power become a 'preponderance' of power? They say they seek only to negotiate from strength; but how much strength, and when will 'negotiation' become 'dictation'? They say the door is always open to a reasonable settlement of our differences; but what is 'reasonable,' and when will they slam the door?

"Surely the Americans know that the balance of power is a British myth. No nation wants a real balance; they all seek an imbalance in their favor. What the Americans really want, then, is to bargain with us from a position of superior power. Surely they are political realists enough to realize that this is impossible, however. We shall never permit ourselves to become unarmed as they did following World War II. So they probably know that they will have to deal with us on fairly even terms some day. What is important to us, then, is whether they will be *able* to negotiate. The present administration may mean what it says, that it intends to bargain diplomatically; but in the end the U.S. government is a creature of what the Americans like to call 'public opinion,' which is molded by forces increasingly hostile to compromise."

We Americans, however, do not have a monopoly on recalcitrance. There is a very grave danger that Russia will also reach a point where she is unable to negotiate. She may well have reached it already. Russia's leaders may be the cool and calculated schemers they are usually pictured to be; on the other hand, they may be merely a handful of desperate men with their backs to the wall, willing to take any step, however drastic, which might save them from destruction.

It is true, of course, that any dictatorship is capable of sudden shifts in policy while democracies are not. It has taken the United States five years, and nearly as many Secretaries of State, to swing from cooperation to a "get tough" policy with Russia. At each step of the way—Truman Doctrine, Marshall Plan, NATO, German Rearmament—the government has had to pause and wait for reluctant elements of press and public to catch up. In contrast, the USSR went along blandly professing its hatred of Nazism for years, only to make a military alliance with Hitler overnight. In a sudden reversal of policy, Stalin recognized the Badoglio Government in Italy at a time when our own State Department, fearing public reaction, didn't dare. Russia broke dramatically with Tito in 1949, yet our own government is still unable to take full advantage of the break.

In brief, Russian foreign policy is dictated by a handful of men who control opinion, rather than reflect it. It may not seem unreasonable to assume, therefore, that the USSR is capable of reversing itself and negotiating a settlement with us.

The situation is not this simple, however. Few of Russia's apparent policy reversals in the past have involved a significant loss of territory or other power elements vital to her national interest; rarely has she lost even prestige. Yet on practically every major issue on which the United States and Russia are in disagreement, effective settlement will involve the most fundamental concessions on the part of both. In every geographic area and upon every principle where there is conflict, neither party can back down without a severe loss of prestige, military and territorial advantage, or both. Can either side permit the other to unify and rearm Germany? Will we get out of Japan, or they out of East Europe? Will we abandon NATO, and can they permit a rearmed Western Europe?

Assuming the improbable, if Stalin should announce tomorrow that he is sincerely ready to negotiate a world-wide settlement of our differences, what could we say? What are we prepared to give up? And if we confess the inability of our own statesmen to compromise on these vital issues, we must also recognize the difficulties facing the Kremlin.

The danger of war is compounded by the fact that the Soviets and Americans are not the only ones playing this game of Russian Roulette. The United States is passing out aid to all takers, garnering allies from every corner of the globe, and doing everything possible to bolster their resistance to Russia. Meanwhile the USSR is conducting a ruthless purge of the leadership of its satellites and fomenting a vitriolic anti-American campaign on its side of the iron curtain. The result is inevitable: diplomatic "incidents" occur daily which not long ago would have resulted in hostilities. In 1739 a few over-enthusiastic Spaniards cut off the ear of an English Sea Captain and His Britannic Majesty promptly declared war. Today such an incident wouldn't even rate a by-line in the daily press. Diplomacy has admittedly sunk to new depths, but how many American planes can be shot down and how many American correspondents jailed before a war is provoked?

Historians conclusively agree that one of the major weaknesses of alliance systems is the danger of irresponsibility on the part of the lesser countries of the alliance. Backed by a big power, they are prone to take actions they would not otherwise dare to take, actions which often involve the major powers in a war they would prefer to avoid. Our refusal to arm South Korea before the Communist attack was predicated on this fact. In view of the outcome of that policy, we are now proceeding under full throttle to arm all potential allies—even against the apparent wishes of some of them, as in the case of West Germany.

Yet, as Korea itself proves, big wars are started by small countries. It is perfectly true that the most powerful nations can cause a major conflict by miscalculation, as Hitler did in 1939; more often, however, wars begin inconsequentially with the assassination of an Austrian Archduke or some other minor incident between lesser countries.

Goaded on by one or the other of the present "Big Two," a belligerent Turkish diplomat or Hungarian army officer could easily by some irresponsible act begin a chain of events which would lead us all into the morass of World War III, if the attack on South Korea has not already done so.

The lesson of all this should be clearly understood: Events have forced us to adopt policies which are completely foreign to our nature and ideals as a people—policies which, at best, must overcome great odds to succeed. The results of armament races, alliance systems and power balancing in the past prove this only too well. History is on the side of the skeptic.

We hardly need be reminded, however, that even though the odds are against us, the alternative to measured resistance is national suicide; history is equally clear in this regard. Refusal to meet the challenge would not only mean war but defeat. Our policy is not wrong, therefore, but only dangerous—far more so than the public has yet realized.

If this policy is to succeed, the psychological preparation of the American people is a prime requisite. As a nation we are entering a sort of "psychological no-man's land," quite unlike anything we have ever known before. At best we face a twenty-year war of nerves, and the only foreseeable alternative to armed war is an armed stalemate. This situation is unique to Americans, one in which history provides few guideposts. Past experiences leave us totally unprepared to meet the problems we must face—many of them as yet unknown. Our national habit of assuming that there is always a quick and easy answer, our characteristic impatience, and our traditional ideas about what we continue to miscall "war" and "peace," are perhaps as dangerous to us as Stalin himself.

The victory of our foreign policy may ultimately depend upon the American people. Steel nerves, calm persistence, and continued political maturity on their part could easily spell the difference between success and failure; between peace and war. This is assuredly no time for cold feet; but cool heads will help considerably.

64. POINT FOUR PROPAGANDA AND REALITY *

Mr. Vogt contends that the objectives of the Point Four Program cannot be realized. He doubts that "the shotgun wedding of

* William Vogt, *American Perspective*, Spring, 1950, pp. 122-129. The author has been Chief of the Conservation Section of the Pan American Union.

Economics and Technology" will produce the food required to eliminate "hunger and misery." Increases in population, shortages of land, skills, tools and fertilizers, lack of "socio-economic flexibility," and other factors will defeat our efforts to improve conditions to any significant degree in the underdeveloped areas of the world.

Mr. Vogt suggests that the United States establish a system of estimates of demand based primarily upon population trends, and an inventory of resources also indicating trends. This system would be set up by agreement with the governments of underdeveloped countries and would be given "the widest possible publicity" so that "the people of the areas involved may know what to expect, and why they cannot expect more." In this way, he believes, the people will be spared the cruel disappointment which will surely follow from the inability of the United States to fulfill its Point Four promises.

At no period in the history of the human race has the power of the lie been so great as it is today. This is a simple effect of exponential increase in human communication facilities. The untruth need not be malicious, nor even understood by its originator. It is enough that it can be transmitted to human beings who have not the wisdom to evaluate it; and wisdom has not begun to keep up with the techniques of communication.

The influential groups in world society, whether they be the American hucksters or the international Cominform, depend on this power of the lie to peddle their particular product. If the listeners can't read, their sales resistance will be lower. You can't fool all of the people all of the time, but you can fool an appalling number of them long enough to create extremely dangerous situations.

The fault is in no sense intrinsically that of the people. When they have enough facts their collective judgment is sound. Hitler knew this well, and concealed or perverted the facts. The same thing is true of Stalin. And the same thing, unhappily, is true of the State Department of the United States. We have adopted the policy of trying to outlie the Communists, apparently with the hope that our falsehoods will be more acceptable than those of the Communists.

In a sense, the fault is not that of the State Department. They were pushed out on the end of a rotten limb by the President when he promised a "bold new program" to provide "triumphant action . . . against hunger, misery and despair" and "growing abundance." Obviously the Department couldn't repudiate the President, and some of them have been trying to figure out how to climb off that limb ever since.

Others, suffering from delusions, have sincerely espoused the President's proposals and are busily trying to create substance out of void, order out of chaos. Their alchemy, they believe, will not only achieve the objectives stated by the President. The benefits that will accrue to the people of the world will be so great that they will no longer be beguiled by the promises of Stalin.

The first wave of enthusiasm, which set the Treasury Secretaries of all the "backward" countries drooling, was dashed when the Truman administration announced that it would ask for $35 million to initiate Point IV in the entire world. But the bullish trend was somewhat reestablished with the more recent suggestion that the American people put $50 billion on the black, as a bet against the red.

What are these various people—from the President down—talking about? Can triumphant action against despair be achieved, in fact, by the shotgun wedding of Economics and Technology? What, aside from words and other symbols, do economics and technology have to work with? What processes are involved, and how are they to be set in motion and directed to the desired ends? More space than is available would be needed to give approximately complete answers, but we can throw some of the more important ones into relief.

Triumphant action against hunger and misery, which we may assume to be antecedent to triumph over despair, at least in the minds of President Truman and other leaders both in our government and in international organizations, depends upon the access of every human being to an adequate supply of certain substances. These include, in the first instance, between 1000 and 2000 pounds of food a year, and food in sufficient variety to provide more than calorie-bearing carbohydrates; there will be required the proteins that provide energy, protective foods, such as green fruits and vegetables, minerals, and vitamins. Some of our technologists have seemed to imply that the food problem could be solved with hybrid corn, but although it is true that rats get along fairly well on such a diet, it is not likely to satisfy the human animal.

Will the people of the world be fed—through a Point IV program, or any other that is likely to be developed? Since food is basic to any plan of human betterment, this is a fair question. And it should be answered as it is asked—not in terms of the subjunctive mood and conditional tense. What the agronomists and economists *might* do, in an ideal situation, or even under American conditions, has nothing to do with the actual processes that are going on—and will continue to go on —in the soils of the world, and in the churning stomachs of children and women and men.

My own answer to the question is based on more than six years of actual field work in so-called backward countries, plus more years of study of scientific reports on other areas. And, much as I regret it, my answer has to be in the negative. Many people who know the backward areas agree.

"Can you tell me," I asked a very knowledgeable agronomist on the staff of FAO, "of a single one of the so-called backward countries of the world, where the increase in food production is even beginning to keep pace with the increase in population?"

His answer was a reluctant, "No." Such increase as there has been in food production has, of course, taken place mostly in the technologically advanced areas that do not need it. The backward peoples of the world, by and large, simply do not have enough of land, skill, tools and fertilizers, and—above all—socio-economic flexibility, to increase their production as fast as is necessary. Where, in backward areas, there is no large outlet for cash crops, farmers cannot secure the means of filling these needs. Years of costly, high power extension work and agricultural education in the literate United States have made good farmers out of only a small fraction of our farm population; some who know the situation place the estimate as low as ten per cent. It is utterly unrealistic to talk about meeting the demand for an adequate diet within a decade or two; and since people live and suffer in a real world, not in the promised world of technicians and bureaucrats, making promises that cannot possibly be kept seems to me downright cruel and vicious.

The United Press recently reported on a United Nations survey stating that the production of a number of basic commodities, including wheat, potatoes and barley, in 1947 was below the 1928 level. Meanwhile, of course, the world population had grown enormously—probably by more than 300 million of those churning stomachs. And while we are failing—and failing miserably—in our efforts to meet the world demand for food, we are not trying to reduce the demand. We are actually expanding it. There is grim humor in the fact that on this policy the Cominform and the Catholic Church agree—even in Italy.

Nor is food the only problem. In the long run, it may not even be the most important. In this world of accelerated communication, where people give words a hard-currency value, it is difficult to see how democracy can survive unless men and women everywhere are able to evaluate those words. And few of us in this country doubt, I think, that the fall of democracy would be tantamount to the beginning of a new Dark Ages.

If people are not to be made mere captives of the words of the Cominform, or the Hitlers of tomorrow, they must be able to distinguish fact from fiction, sound inference from delusion. This requires an irreducible minimum of education.

Yet education costs money. Teachers must be paid. Schools must be built. Books must be available. And these books must be based on scholarship and research. There must be good teachers and good books, or only negative literacy will be developed.

In the rice bowl economy, there is not enough surplus wealth to provide these indispensables. There is not even enough in Mississippi and Louisiana, some Fair Dealers tell us; the deficit must be made up by New York and California. How, then, is there likely to be enough in Haiti, where the income is seven cents a day, in India where it is five cents—in China and Borneo and Africa where, if it is any more, the increase is not significant?

When in the relatively simple matter of food production we are not keeping up with the demand, how can we hope to provide the water (where and when it is needed), the timber for hundreds of uses from railroad ties to the paper for the printing of books and newspapers? How are we to find the surplus wealth to build the roads that permit the integration of economies, the shipment of raw materials? Where we start with populations that are 50-90 per cent illiterate, how are we to educate not only the masses of the people, but their leaders? Where are the teachers, the scientists, the technicians, the doctors, the newspapermen, coming from? These, too, are the product of wealth above and beyond the mere subsistence level.

Approximately every second and a half the world population increases by one of these empty stomachs. By far the biggest proportion of this increase takes place in the so-called backward countries. Most of them have geographic limitations that combine into far more resistant environments than ours. In nearly all of them, farmers, lumbermen, cattle-, sheep- and goat-men are reducing the productivity of the environment that exists. Nor are they likely to stop—even if we offer our assistance. For few of these countries are in the hands of the people. They are, by and large, controlled by colonial powers—or by oligarchies of powerful business groups and big landowners, operating through the instrumentality of armies and police forces. Unless Point IV aid by-passes these groups—which means by-passing governments—the people of the world are not likely to profit by our efforts. In much of Latin America, for example, any successful effort to end the misery and despair of the people would have to be preceded by social revolution. It is not without reason that many Latin American leaders fear democracy more than they do Communism.

Unless we establish such controls over the use of American capital, and other developmental forces, Point IV activities are likely to benefit chiefly those who are already comfortably situated in the backward areas. And unless we control the exploiters of natural resources—both Americans and nationals of the countries involved—the net result is likely to be something approaching permanent destruction.

The chances of "triumphant action against misery and despair" are minute. The possibility of success within a period shorter than a number of decades is virtually non-existent. Yet we are largely relying on promises of such progress as our answer to Communism.

Communism is not going to solve the problems of the peoples of the world—and they will eventually find it out. Neither will democracy solve these problems, in the terms stated by the United States government and its President. Unless production is rapidly increased *on a long range basis,* of which there seems to be no likelihood at the present time, and the demand is effectively reduced, increasing poverty and not prosperity will be the lot of the people. As Walter Lowdermilk has expressed it, we are engaged in a race between food and population. And population is drawing steadily ahead.

We are also involved in a race between truth and lies—two lies. Our lie, with Freedom up, may for a time outrun the Communist lie. But there is no possibility that we can provide abundance for burgeoning populations in 25, or 40 or 50 years. Perhaps the Communist lie will become the favorite as, in the next decade or so, the futility of our efforts becomes patent. Whatever happens, in the home stretch, Truth is sure to be ahead. And in a world whose exploding populations insist on making impossible demands on a resistant environment, Truth is virtually certain to be a bony steed with a bony rider, scythe in hand.

Few words in history have been more foolish than President Truman's Point IV remarks. It is, perhaps, not too late to correct the harm they have done. We shall lose face in doing it; but this, it seems to me, would be far preferable to leading hundreds of millions of people through the Valley of Despair to ultimate destruction. Faith among the people of the world in the integrity of the United States has been deteriorating since the latter days of President Roosevelt's administration. The Point IV hoax will not improve the situation. Nor, parenthetically, will the logorrhea that seems to be a chronic American disease.

I do not mean to suggest that we should withdraw from the world, in a Wherry-like retreat to the womb. We have so much to give the world that we really don't need to present it as though it were the Hollywood version of a soap opera. It is of critical importance, both to other countries and to our own, that we do not make impossible promises. We have been going "to make the world safe for democracy," establish "freedom from want and fear," abolish "hunger, misery and despair" so often, during the past 35 years, it is a wonder that even the non-Communist countries have not begun to give us the Bronx cheer.

Secretary Acheson, wiser than most of his critics, has stated that our foreign policy must be adjusted to particular circumstances and particular times. Development, operation, and expectation under the Point IV program must be similarly adaptable. But there are, it seems to me, certain requirements and yardsticks that should be set up in agreement with the governments controlling the respective "backward" areas; furthermore, these requirements and yardsticks should be given the widest possible publicity, especially within the areas concerned. They should include:

1. *An estimate of demand.* This should be based, primarily, upon expected population trends, and should be revised annually. It should also include estimates of the amounts and kinds of foodstuffs required to meet the demand: educational facilities, housing, water-supplies, hospitalization, etc. In other words, the best possible approximation of what will be needed to provide a stated standard of living, within given periods, for expected numbers of people.

2. *An inventory of resources, showing trends.* This will show what the cooperating agencies have to work with (including human resources) and will keep before the people of the world the potentials and limits of resources for any area—either within the area, or by exchange; will show whether or not resources are being utilized on a sustained-yield or destructive basis; and will indicate whether or not production can be expected to keep up with demand. News reports that Spain was seeking hundreds of millions of bushels of wheat failed to remind their readers that, a fortnight or so previously, publication of the Spanish budget had shown only one per cent of the total devoted to agriculture. Obviously, before aid is given to any area, it should be required to take reasonable steps to help itself. Spain, it seems to me, in the face of this irresponsibility deserves no outside help.

3. *Full and free dissemination of these estimates, or inventories,* both in publications and over the radio—so that the people of the areas involved may know what to expect, and why they cannot expect more.

Spot-checks must frequently be made of the estimates by independent, technical groups. Obviously, since the State Department, Institute of Inter-American Affairs or Office of Foreign Agricultural Relations must come to heel when the Administration whistles, they cannot be depended upon for honest evaluation. The United Nations, the FAO and Organization of American States, are at even more of a disadvantage; they have a plethora of masters, some of them statesmen, but many who are unfortunately pipsqueak politicians who cannot permit the organizations they control to say anything that might offend national prestige or sensibilities. Evaluations might be made under a non-political National Science Foundation, if one can be established; or, failing this, by scientific committees drawn from outside government and responsible directly to Congress.

Such bilaterality will shock those who put their faith in international bodies; unfortunately, when facts may be suppressed or perverted because of political expediency, it is impossible to maintain faith in the capacity of international bodies to deal with facts. And, whether they are palatable or not, those facts stay with us.

In every case—accepting Secretary Acheson's formulation—we must make sure, before we undertake it, that the people and governments of the various areas will want strongly enough what we consider development to do their part. Incredible though it may seem to large numbers of Americans, not all the people in the world want the education that we have made a shibboleth; not all of them want our material standard of living enough to accept the hard work and self-discipline on which it must be based; nor will many governments be willing to jettison such waste and extravagance as corruption and useless military organizations in the interest of citizen welfare. These are limiting factors powerful enough to wreck any "development" program.

The nub of the matter is facts. They go on—such facts as 55,000 more people in the world every day, in the face of wasting soils, water, and forests—and words either do not change them or else change them only with glacial slowness. No matter how fast we talk, the facts remain. If we do enough talking, the people of the world will finally see through our verbalizing, and realize that empty bellies are not filled with words, nor even dollars.

One need not travel very far beyond our borders to realize that some of them already realize it. When that understanding sweeps the world, it will be too late for us to do anything about it.

65. THE UNITED STATES AND THE UNITED NATIONS *

Mr. Ernest A. Gross has described the policy of the United States in the United Nations and cited several reasons for American adherence to the U.N. (Selection 56). Of course, Mr. Gross dealt in general principles of policy, principles with which the author of this selection would presumably agree. Mr. Fleming's article is

* D. V. Fleming, *The Annals of the American Academy of Political and Social Science,* November, 1951, pp. 73-82. The author is Professor of Political Science, Vanderbilt University.

primarily concerned with specific American actions in the U.N.—
and he does not believe that the United States has always acted
wisely there. Mr. Fleming concludes, however, that our leadership
in the U.N. "has been as good as might be expected." The role
of the U.N. he says, is "to make a sustained, devoted, even sacrificial
effort to join together again in some tolerable relationship the two
halves of a world . . ."

What is the role of the United States in the United Nations, six
years after its creation? To what extent has the United States been
able to obtain agreement to its views? What limitations in our leadership have developed? How successful have the lesser democracies been
in modifying our attitudes? What concessions have been made to the
views of the Soviet bloc? Will the Soviet-Western conflict end in the
breakup of the United Nations?

BACKGROUND OF U.N.

The United Nations is founded on the principle of co-operation among
the great powers. President Roosevelt originally favored the application
of this principle without another league of nations, but after it became
clear that the American people wanted to repair their error of 1918-20
he worked faithfully with Secretary of State Cordell Hull to create U.N.
before the end of the war should lessen or disrupt the unity among the
victors—a timing which history has amply vindicated.

The Soviet Government would greatly have preferred a great-power
control of the world, because of its dictatorial nature and its unhappy
experience with the League of Nations. However, the Soviet leaders
co-operated loyally with the Americans in creating U.N. The Union
of Soviet Socialist Republics made ten concessions at San Francisco
which "contributed greatly to the liberalizing of the Dumbarton Oaks
proposals." She also cast her votes for locating the meeting place of
the United Nations in the United States—a step she would not have
taken had she anticipated the antagonisms which developed later.

Then on August 6, 1945 the first use of the atomic bomb completely
transformed the power prospects of the great powers. It was followed
by a strong Anglo-American diplomatic campaign in the Balkans and
complete deadlock in the London Council of Foreign Ministers in
September.

This is the atmosphere of conflict which has dominated the life
of U.N. since its organization in early 1946. Instead of being an
organ to preserve the peace made by the great powers, U.N. has become
a battleground between giant governments unable to make peace. Given

the cleavage between the U.S.S.R. and the United States, this was inevitable; but the fact makes it exceedingly difficult to write a useful article on this subject. Only an account which defends the American position throughout can be acceptable to most Americans. Yet the use of U.N. by both sides of the power conflict merely as an area of conflict and as a place for justifying national acts would seem to doom it to eventual disruption.

A great many Americans ardently desire to push the Communists out and convert the United Nations into a military alliance against them. Since it is my belief that this would probably be the prelude to a war which would largely destroy western civilization, I shall try to review our record in U.N. with the objective of its mission to hold the world together, in some fashion, constantly in mind.

SUBSTANTIVE ISSUES

From this starting point, what has been the record of our leadership of the United Nations?

Armaments

In the field of atomic energy control we have convinced the non-Communist world of the generosity of our proposal for world control, made in June 1946—a great moral success. On the practical side our plan never had a chance of the acceptance after the Truman-Attlee-King declaration of November 15, 1945, which sought the control of atomic energy through a U.N. commission whose work "should proceed by separate stages, the successful completion of each one of which will develop the necessary confidence of the world before the next stage is undertaken." The chance was infinitesimal that the Soviet Union, immensely proud of its role in World War II, would enroll in the American atomic school and faithfully complete each grade, proving its reliability in every lesson. It would prefer to stall, while making its own atomic bombs and power plants.

Similarly, the Soviet effort to submerge the atomic issue in a drive for general disarmament was successful from the standpoint of world opinion when the General Assembly adopted the resolution of December 14, 1946, but we were able to nullify progress in that direction as effectively as Moscow did on atomic energy.

The result was stalemate and no arms control of any kind. We chose to have perfect controls or none.

Iran

In the Iranian dispute in 1946 the United States and Britain successfully prosecuted the Soviet Union for overstaying her leave in Azerbaijan, and recovered that province for Iran. In the aftermath, the U.S.S.R. lost her oil concession. Nothing effective was done to remedy the abysmal conditions in which the Iranians live. Then in 1951 Iran's feudal rulers rewarded her benefactors by seizing the great British oil fields.

These events suggest (1) that in such a situation police action is insufficient unless followed by deep-seated remedial measures, and (2) that the western monopoly of the vast oil wealth of the Middle East rests on a very unstable basis.

Warmonger Charges

The Soviet drive to convict individual Americans and interests of warmongering was a considerable success. The generalized Assembly resolution of November 17, 1947 registered the conviction of delegates who had been listening to our radio and press that there was too much inflammatory talk of war.

Berlin

In the Berlin crisis the United States failed to persuade the smaller states on the Security Council to introduce a simple resolution calling for the lifting of the blockade, but achieved a resolution including that point.

This success was somewhat dimmed by the Evatt-Lie proposals for immediate four-power conversations to settle the dispute.

The United Nations maintained a mediating personality of its own throughout its consideration of this dispute in October-November 1948.

Palestine

The many changes in American policy on Palestine—from partition to trusteeship, partition, mediation, delay, the Bernadotte plan, and mediation again—were due to divisions of opinion between the White House and influential groups in the State and Defense Departments; the President generally favored the Zionist cause, and his opponents concentrated on preserving our interest in Arab-controlled oil. Enforcement of U.N. resolutions was also blocked by the fear that action would necessitate the use of Russian troops in the area.

Franco Spain

In the long story of the U.N.'s ostracism of Franco Spain, our government went along reluctantly at first and finally exerted persistent leadership to revoke the ban, under the pressure of American cotton interests, military arguments, religious groups, and strong conservatives.

The argument that recognition did not imply approval was strongly developed, but reversed in the case of Communist China.

Indonesia

In the Indonesian conflict there was an important exception to the general rule that the United States supported postwar governments of a conservative or reactionary character as bulwarks against communism. In the case of Indonesia, resentment against the highhanded efforts of the Dutch to reconquer their lost colonies combined with a realization that the Dutch course would turn Indonesian nationalism toward communism, to produce by degrees an American policy of strong pressure on the Dutch, both in the Security Council and diplomatically, which finally eventuated in independence for Indonesia.

The result is that the Indonesians, though cautiously neutralist, may be counted on to incline to the side of the West in emergencies.

Korea

In Korea the United States secured a 1947 Assembly resolution creating a commission which supervised an election in South Korea. The rightist government which resulted was accepted by the General Assembly on December 12, 1948, as the only legal Korean government, and a permanent commission was set up to seek the unification of Korea.

There was accordingly a strong legal basis for the action of the United Nations in forcibly repelling the attempts of the North Koreans, in June 1950, to unify Korea by force. Though South Korea was not a member of the United Nations, she was its ward. On broader grounds, also, there was ample justification for the decision of the American Government to lead the United Nations in forcibly repelling the North Korean invasion. If this aggression were not turned back, there was every probability that U.N. would never be more effective in fulfilling its essential function than the League of Nations was, and the decline of U.N. would permanently end mankind's hopes for collective security.

These considerations were reinforced by the dynamics of the power-ideological struggle. If Communist aggression succeeded in Korea, it would succeed in Indochina and other places. The Truman Doctrine had been a dismal failure in China, and if it were not defended in Korea it would go the way of an impotent U.N., to the great profit of the Truman administration's domestic opposition. No principle is more fixed in the American mind than that appeasement of totalitarian aggression does not pay. Moreover, our position in Japan might quickly become untenable.

Crossing the 38th Parallel

When in October 1950 the aggressors were thrown back across the 38th parallel, the basic factors of world politics counseled moderation and restraint.   The conflict had turned out to be, among other things, a genuine civil war.   The Russians had not backed their protégés with the little air power which apparently could have swept us off the Korean toe before the Inchon landing.   China had not intervened, though her interests in Korea were much more immediate and intimate than ours. The Korean-Manchurian border, with its great Yalu power installations, was probably the most sensitive frontier in the world.   If we held it, the strategic-political position of both China and the Soviet Union would be imperiled.   They would be as certain to react to our approach to the Yalu as we would be to cross the Rio Grande if a Russian-led U.N. army were advancing through northern Mexico.   Apart from strategic considerations, they could no more permit us to conquer the North Koreans than we could allow them to communize the South Koreans by force.

Clearly, we would be pushing the other side too far if we insisted on more than the repulse of aggression, in a region many thousands of miles from our frontiers and actually on a critical frontier of both China and the Soviet Union.   Nevertheless, we yielded to the natural American impulse to make the victory complete.   General MacArthur's impatience was a factor, but the entire western world became somewhat intoxicated with victory.

The Asiatic members of U.N., led by India, pleaded in vain for restraint at the 38th parallel.   Sir Benegal Rau argued repeatedly that

it would impair faith in the United Nations if we were even to appear to authorize the unification of Korea by the use of force against North Korea, after we had resisted the attempt of North Korea to unify the country by force against South Korea.

This was reasoning which it was very difficult to evade.   Using force to *compel* the unification of Korea, after using force to defeat that same objective, strained the moral fiber of U.N. to the utmost.   The argument, too, that the 38th parallel boundary was completely artificial went far toward justifying the claim of the North Koreans to be fighting a civil war in their own country, especially since the moral authority of U.N. was nonexistent in the vast area between Seoul and Stettin.   In the case of the Chinese, especially, the rankling memory of a century of Western imperialism enabled them to believe passionately that the U.N. forces in

Korea threatened to impose the old hated shackles upon them again, and it did not help matters that the U.N. army was advancing under General MacArthur, who was known to favor the eradication of the Communist revolution in China.

These deep-seated factors were ignored, and the U.N. forces rolled on toward the Yalu, until they were driven back across the 38th parallel by the Chinese, who thereupon became "dizzy with success" and decided to sweep the Americans out of Korea.

Branding China

This development produced a fierce demand in the United States for branding China as an aggressor, to be followed by sanctions against her. If North Korea was an aggressor, so now was China. On January 5 the United States sent notes to twenty-nine governments warning that the United Nations might collapse unless China was branded, and our delegates brought similar pressure on the delegates of the twenty-nine nations at Lake Success.

However, the desire of the other U.N. members for another cease fire effort was too strong to be denied, and the United States felt compelled to await the attempt, especially since we were sure that the Chinese would reject it. The U.N. proposal, submitted on January 11, 1951, called for the withdrawal of all foreign troops "by appropriate stages," and a conference of the United Kingdom, the United States, the Soviet Union, and Communist China to work out a settlement, including the Formosan question and China's representation in the United Nations.

The news that the United States had accepted this proposal in the Assembly produced an outcry in the Congress, which was not lessened by China's counterproposal of a seven-nation conference and the withdrawal of the United States Seventh Fleet from the Formosan Straits. Secretary Acheson promptly denounced it as unacceptable, demanding further U.N. action. Most of the Arab-Asian bloc and some of our European allies held that the Chinese reply was not a rejection, but a bargaining step. Prime Minister Nehru of India warned that to brand China as an aggressor would be "to bolt and bar the door to a peaceful settlement in the Far East." But the United States would not be denied. A terse resolution branding China and demanding further action against her was introduced in the General Assembly on January 20 and pressed to swift passage.

In the debate, Sir Benegal Rau denied that China's reply was a rejection; it was "partly acceptance, partly nonacceptance, partly a request for elucidation, and partly a set of counterproposals." On January 22

Rau presented some further modifications of the Chinese reply, and the United States was unable to block a 48-hour adjournment to consider these points.

On January 19 the United States House of Representatives passed a resolution demanding branding, with only two dissenting votes.   It was timed to confront the United Nations Political Committee when it met at 3:00 P.M. on the same day.   On January 23, the Senate unanimously passed a demand that China be branded, and a declaration that she should not be "admitted" to U.N.   Two days later the Senate sidetracked for four months India's request for two million tons of wheat urgently needed for famine relief.   On the same day President Truman issued a statement giving his preference for "calling an aggressor an aggressor," and the branding resolution passed the General Assembly on January 30, after amendments to placate the stout opposition to sanctions and to alleviate fears that it would close the door to peaceful settlement.

The entire episode gained no credit for American leadership in U.N. The extreme tactics used to force the branding resolution through had employed everything in our arsenal of pressure weapons, short of steaming a couple of battleships up the East River and training their guns on the U.N.'s new headquarters.   The forcing of our will upon many friendly and reluctant governments left them in the frame of mind described by James Reston when he wrote that the United Nations would have taken pleasure in passing a resolution that it was the sense of the members that the United States had been "undiplomatic, unwise, emotional, contradictory and slightly hypocritical in its handling of the Chinese Communists for more than a year now."

The branding resolution inflicted a searing wound on the national pride of revolutionary China and made it certain that the Korean war would go on at least until a frightful mountain of casualties compelled negotiation.   Thereafter, we had no choice but to pursue what we ourselves labeled the policy of "Operation Killer," slaughter without end, until Chinese pride could be smothered, temporarily at least, in a sea of blood—killing, also, which "lost us what we cannot afford to lose, the mind of man in Asia."

Stalemate

The recall of General MacArthur precipitated a national decision not to expand the Korean conflict into a world war, and high official expressions of willingness to accept a cease fire at or near the 38th parallel, leaving our ideal of a unified Korea to be pursued by political means.

These means are no more likely to be successful than they were before June 25, 1949.   It is unrealistic to suppose that Korea can ever belong to "our side." Neither China nor the Soviet Union "will endure in Korea a government that is anti-Communist and pro-American," any more than we would endure in Mexico the setting up by the East of a government which was pro-Communist and anti-American. Politically, the best arrangement we can hope for is a neutralized Korea under the U.N., with its Asiatic members doing most of the supervision. Otherwise, Korea would seem doomed to remain a nation divided, for the convenience of the great powers, after she has been devastated more thoroughly than even Germany was during the late war, and after infinite loss, privation, and death inflicted upon both halves of the Korean people.

The Koreans have been crucified even worse than the people of Spain and Czechoslovakia were in the days when fascist aggression was not opposed. Yet their tragedy may enable the two opposing blocs of nations to realize what a real death struggle between them would be like. The Russians may be convinced that their satellites can win no easy victories, and the Americans may learn that the containment of Communism by force of arms around the vast Eurasian perimeter is an uncertain business.

ORGANIZATIONAL QUESTIONS

The great-power conflict has naturally been fought also on the plane of the internal life of U.N.

Admission of New Members

In the matter of admitting new members, it has largely paralyzed a vital function of U.N. Afghanistan, Iceland, and Sweden were admitted by consent of both sides on November 9, 1946, and Siam, Pakistan, Yemen, Burma, and Israel were admitted later. Deadlock has prevented the election of Albania, Mongolia, Jordan, Eire, Portugal, Hungary, Italy, Rumania, Austria, Bulgaria, Finland, Ceylon, Nepal, and the two Korean republics—a total of fifteen states.

The West has consistently opposed the admission of the Soviet satellites—Albania, Mongolia, Hungary, Rumania, and Bulgaria—and the Soviet Union has vetoed the others in retaliation. The protégés of the West have repeatedly received nine votes in the Security Council. The Soviet entries have sometimes received several votes, but have been defeated by abstentions. Thus, at the 206th meeting of the Council, Hungary received five votes and there were six abstentions. On other occasions the United States and others have voted "no" to the satellite applications, though these votes are never spoken of as vetoes.

Efforts to override the Soviet "vetoes" began in November 1946. The Russians frankly said that they had no objections to admitting Finland and Italy, but that they would not be admitted unless others were. The 1947 Assembly adopted a resolution asking the International Court of Justice for an advisory opinion on the legality of that position. The Court ruled, by a 9 to 6 vote, that this was illegal. Two of the majority submitted separate opinions.

Actually, the legal requirements of the Charter offer plenty of justifications for rejection, when rejection is desired. The requirement that the applicant must be (1) a state, (2) peace loving, and (3) able and willing to carry out the obligations of the Charter, gives enough leeway.

Thus the United States has not been able to believe that Mongolia is independent, or that Bulgaria and Albania should be admitted while they aided the Greek guerrillas, or until they observed the provisions of their peace treaties "by abolishing the oppressive, tyrannical practices of their governments."

On its part, the Soviet Union has doubted that Ceylon is independent, has derided the idea that Jordan is, and has charged the United States with supporting the applications of fascist states like Portugal, while rejecting those of states like Mongolia which aided in the fight against fascism.

Admission en Bloc

Repeated admonitions by the Assembly to the Security Council to reconsider the applications have been fruitless, as was the offer of the Soviet Union on June 16, 1949, to admit all of the twelve states whose applications had repeatedly been examined by the Security Council. This offer was rejected by our Representative Austin, who insisted that each applicant be considered individually. This was a reversal of our stand in 1946 when our delegate had proposed the en bloc admission of eight disputed states and the U.S.S.R. refused. In 1949 the U.S.S.R. pressed an en bloc admission resolution, which was defeated in the Assembly on November 22.

If all the waiting applicants were admitted, the Soviet bloc in U.N. would be increased by five members in the General Assembly. No additional clients of Moscow would be added to the Security Council. This would mean, from our viewpoint, that in the Assembly there would be five more people to argue and obstruct and take up time. That would be annoying to us, but it is not easy to see that any real loss would be involved. Most of the ten new anti-Communist members would be unassailably anti-U.S.S.R. There would still be left, also, our own huge bloc of twenty votes in Latin America, plus our numerous allies in western Europe and the British Dominions, not to mention Liberia, Iceland, and the Philippines.

One who reads the records is impressed by the almost monotonous regularity of the 40 to 6 votes by which nearly all resolutions are passed —a result due largely to the violence of the Soviet attacks upon the West. If the dozen states who have so long been awaiting admission come in, the majorities would be about 47 to 11, with the usual number of abstentions.

From the position of the United Nations there would seem to be everything to gain by an agreement to increase its membership from 59 to 71, or 74, especially if the present small Soviet bloc felt a little less lonely and moderated its intransigence. The alternative is to move in the direction, already endorsed by the United States, of depriving the Soviet Union of its right to block admissions, that is, to gain the admission of Communist states. This road would seem to lead toward the secession of the Soviet bloc, and perhaps others, from the United Nations.

Election of Officers

Two elections have sharply reflected the great-power conflict. In October 1949 Yugoslavia became a candidate for the Security Council with American support, though her split with the other Communist states of eastern Europe made her incapable of representing that area. The Soviet representatives waged a tense campaign for Czechoslovakia, and the United States sent instructions to its diplomatic missions throughout the world. High officials of the United Nations Secretariat worked unsuccessfully for a compromise. When the vote was taken, on October 19, 1949, there was a crisis atmosphere, some fearing that the issue might "tear the world organization apart," while "many delegates resent [ed] having to make such a choice at this time." Yugoslavia won, 39 to 19, with one vote more than the necessary two-thirds.

Her election may be justified from the standpoint of the great-power struggle and of Yugoslavia's exposed position. From the viewpoint of preserving the U.N., there was no gain in the complete isolation of the U.S.S.R. in the Security Council, the votes against her now being changed from 9-2 to 10-1.

In 1950 a similar crisis occurred when the Soviet Union vetoed the re-election of Secretary General Trygve Lie. The United States demanded his re-election on the ground that failure to re-elect would punish him for his strong stand on Korea, and rejected three other candidates who had been second to none in supporting the U.N. in Korea. Representative

Austin, speaking with "great emotion," threatened to veto any other candidate, and the other delegates reluctantly voted an extension of his term for three years.

The Little Assembly

As one means of circumventing the Soviet Union's veto, the United States proposed, on November 12, 1947, the creation of a permanent committee representing all members to consider and report on any dispute or "situation," to recommend special Assembly sessions, and to conduct investigations. The proposal had been watered down considerably on the insistence of the smaller U.N. members. It was still opposed totally by the Soviet bloc, which argued that the prohibition against considering questions which were on the Security Council's agenda was meaningless, since there was always a Western majority of seven which could remove questions from the agenda at any time. The Soviets also pointed out that the West seldom needed to veto anything, since it always had the required majorities to advance or defend its position.

In practice, the Little Assembly has been a useful though not very important organ, without superseding the Security Council.

The Acheson Plan

The North Korean aggression led the United States to propose a comprehensive plan, which was adopted on November 3, 1950, for by-passing the veto. It was recognized that the accident of Soviet absence from the Security Council could not be counted on again. Therefore to enable the Assembly to deal with future aggressions, the resolution conferred upon seven members of the Security Council the authority to call the Assembly into session if the Security Council, "because of lack of unanimity of the permanent members," fails to deal promptly with "a threat to the peace, breach of the peace, or act of aggression."

The "Uniting for Peace" resolution further established a Peace Observation Committee and a Collective Measures Committee, urged the members of U.N. to have armed forces ready and waiting for the Assembly's disposal, and amended the Assembly's rules of procedure to prevent Soviet obstruction of action there.

The arguments for thus by-passing the Soviet Union's veto power are appealing. The U.S.S.R. has vetoed too much. Only its self-imposed absence enabled U.N. to resist aggression in Korea. We must now make sure that the Soviet Union can never veto enforcement action in the future. The primary purpose of U.N. is to restrain aggression, and it must have the right to change its basic law by usage in order to fulfill this primary aim.

The logical circle seems complete. Yet it has been questioned by one of the foremost American authorities on collective security. In his study of "The Development of the General Assembly," Leland M. Goodrich points out that the aggrandizement of the Assembly's powers is not a "development in terms of the democratic process," nor does the Assembly offer any special advantages as an organ for keeping the peace. On the contrary, the Assembly is not as representative as the Security Council of the power necessary to keep the peace. Because of the Soviet bloc boycott of all its peace-enforcing activities, it may find itself unable to carry out the resolutions passed by a two-thirds Assembly vote, most of the voters possessing little means of implementation. This is "a somewhat unrealistic position" for the Assembly to be in, and the attempt so to use the Assembly becomes "a divisive rather than a unifying influence within the United Nations." Goodrich further observes that

the use of the veto by the Soviet Union, often deliberately invited by those against whom it has been directed, has been evidence of an unwillingness on the part of the Great Powers, and more particularly the United States and the Soviet Union, to make important concessions from positions initially taken.

Faced with impasse in the Security Council, two alternatives were open: to make concentrated efforts to improve great-power relations, or to develop the functions of the General Assembly as they have been during the past two or three years,

with the result that the United Nations loses much of its initial character as a universal peace organization and assumes, in fact, the character of an organization to protect the "free world" against the threats from behind the Iron Curtain.

TOWARD THE FUTURE

The United States might well pause to consider now whether this evolution should be pushed farther. To do so might mean the early crossing of a 38th parallel in the life of U.N., beyond which the membership of the Communist states would seem to them to be useless.

Would it not be wiser to remember that the Soviet vetoes, taken as a whole, are a symptom, rather than the cause, of the deep conflicts of interest in the power struggle? There is much to be said for the belief that "the veto was precisely the one mechanism in the U.N. machinery which made it fit to serve as an instrument of conciliation rather than coercion."

The United Nations was created to alleviate the world's tensions and ills. It was not created to develop ideal situations, legally or on the battlefield, but to hold together a world in which the disequilibriums and disharmonies can be adjusted only approximately. Rather than pass "the point of no return" in converting U.N. into a Western military alliance, may it not be better policy to expand its membership to universality and then push mightily the ameliorating, life-giving side of U.N.'s mission?

It would be irksome to us to let the United Nations administer a greatly expanded Point Four program, but the people of Asia will fear and distrust any development program administered by us alone. It would also doubtless be still more deeply irritating to us to have any of our funds spent for constructive purposes by U.N. behind the Iron Curtain. Yet the costs and the mental suffering would be microscopic when compared to those involved in a third world war.

We can proceed, if we choose, on the theory that "only one rogue government, the Soviet Union," has barred the way to the success of the U.N. This is an attitude of mind which can only lead to the breakup of U.N. Only if there is at least an appreciable return, on both sides, to the assumption of great-power negotiation and compromise upon which the Charter was written can U.N. achieve its indispensable function, the prevention of another world war.

The United Nations is our only hope of averting a permanently divided world, with the odds heavily in favor of a final struggle for world domination between the two sides. Nor will it help us greatly to have the law always on our side, if the result is still the destruction of the highly urbanized civilization of the North Temperate Zone.

Thus far the leadership of the United States in the United Nations has been as good as might be expected, in a highly fallible world, from an inexperienced world power suddenly thrust into leadership. We have apparently led U.N. through its first great crisis successfully. Can we now lead in developing its creative mission for the long pull?

On their part, the Russians could afford to avoid the barbed word occasionally and to modify their dogma that we will boom-and-bust and arm-and-fight ourselves into oblivion. We are not obliged to do either. The Communists must learn, too, and be taught, that conspiratorial revolution is not the only way to change outmoded and unjust social orders. The West has ample techniques and means of keeping the stream of orderly reform and progress moving, if it will only use them.

What is the role of a United Nations which has successfully survived

the first real, and very bloody, test of collective security ever made on
this planet? Surely it is to make a sustained, devoted, even sacrificial
effort to join together again in some tolerable relationship the two halves
of a world which so desperately needs a truly global exchange of commerce in the goods and services of peaceful intercourse.

Selected Bibliography

Selected Bibliography

Chapter One

Carr, E. H., *The Twenty Years' Crisis* (London: Macmillan, 1940). A survey of international relations. An early attempt to apply the methodology of political science to the study of international relations.

Gurian, Waldemar, "The Study of International Relations," *Review of Politics,* July, 1946. An analysis of some of the intellectual problems inherent in the study of international relations.

Kirk, Grayson, *The Study of International Relations* (New York: Council on Foreign Relations, 1947). A treatment of the general problems involved in the study of international politics.

Morgenthau, H. J., *Politics Among Nations* (New York: Knopf, 1954). A popular text in international politics illustrative of the realist point of view.

Russell, F. M., *Theories of International Relations* (New York: Appleton, Century, Crofts, 1936). Describes how various peoples have viewed the problems of international relations throughout history. Contains an historical survey of political theory in the international field.

Schwartzenberger, Georg, *Power Politics* (New York: Praeger, 1951). An interpretation and analysis of international politics as power politics.

Chapter Two

Bailey, T. A., *A Diplomatic History of the American People* (New York: Appleton, Century, Crofts, 1950). One of the classic histories of American diplomatic relations especially noteworthy for its readability and wit.

Beard, C. A., *The Idea of National Interest* (New York: Macmillan, 1934). Still one of the best studies of the concept of the national interest.

————, *American Foreign Policy in the Making, 1932-1940* (New Haven: Yale University Press, 1946). A well documented study of the problems of American foreign policy during the years 1932-1940. Defends the isolationist position.

————, *President Roosevelt and the Coming of the War, 1941* (New Haven: Yale University Press, 1948). An analysis of the problem of re-

541

sponsibility for American involvement in World War II. Defends the isolationist position and blames the President for our involvement.

Bemis, S. F., *A Diplomatic History of the United States* (New York: Henry Holt, 1950). A thorough survey of diplomatic history.

Cook, T. I., and Moss, Malcolm, "Foreign Policy: The Realism of Idealism," *American Political Science Review,* June, 1952. A defense of idealism as an approach to American foreign policy.

————, "The American Idea of International Interest," *American Political Science Review,* March, 1953. Another defense of idealism in American foreign policy and an attack on the advocates of power politics and the balance of power.

————, "Hinderances to Foreign Policy: Individualism and Legalism," *Journal of Politics,* February, 1953. A thoughtful analysis of the origins and nature of legalism and individualism in American foreign policy.

Kennan, George, *American Diplomacy, 1900-1950* (Chicago: University of Chicago Press, 1951). A study by a prominent foreign service officer. Suggests that American foreign policy would be more successful if based upon a realistic assessment of world politics.

Langer, W. L., and Gleason, E. S., *The Challenge to Isolation, 1937-1940* (New York: Harper, 1951). A survey of American foreign policy during the years prior to 1941. Unusually rich in documentary materials.

Morgenthau, H. J., *In Defense of the National Interest* (New York: Knopf, 1951). A provocative treatment of the concept of the national interest. A realist analysis of past American policy and a prescription for the present and future.

Perkins, Dexter, *The American Approach to Foreign Policy* (Cambridge: Harvard University Press, 1952). One of the best balanced presentations of the theoretical aspects of American foreign policy.

Taft, R. A., *A Foreign Policy for Americans* (New York: Doubleday, 1951). An example of the neo-isolationist viewpoint in American foreign policy by the late leader of the Republican Party.

Tannenbaum, Frank, "The American Tradition in Foreign Relations," *Foreign Affairs,* October, 1951. An analysis and defense of "idealism" in foreign policy.

Tucker, R. W., "Professor Morgenthau's Theory of Political Realism," *American Political Science Review,* March, 1952. A point-by-point attempt to refute the realist theories of Hans J. Morgenthau.

Wright, Quincy, "Realism and Idealism in International Politics," *World Politics,* October, 1952. Another defense of idealism in American foreign policy.

Chapter Three

Almond, Gabriel, *The American People and Foreign Policy* (New York: Harcourt, Brace, 1950). A valuable treatment of American foreign policy in terms of public opinion, national character, and political behavior.

Angell, J. W., *Financial Foreign Policy of the United States* (New York: Council on Foreign Relations, 1933). A reasonably unbiased account of the expansion of American financial interests into the foreign field.

Bell, P. W., "Colonialism as a Problem in American Foreign Policy," *World Politics,* October, 1952. A contemporary assessment of American foreign policy problems that derive from the pressures of colonialism and imperialism.

Bolles, Blair, "Influence of Armed Forces on U. S. Foreign Policy," *Foreign Policy Reports,* October 1, 1946. A reminder of the influence of the military establishment upon the formation of American foreign policy.

Browder, R. P., *The Origins of Soviet-American Diplomacy* (Princeton: Princeton University Press, 1953). An analysis of the influence of domestic politics and the actions of foreign governments upon the decision to recognize the Soviet Union.

Cottrell, L. S., and Eberhart, Sylvia, *American Opinion on World Affairs* (Princeton: Princeton University Press, 1948). A compendium of American public opinion on important questions of world affairs.

Eliot, G. F., "Science and Foreign Policy," *Foreign Affairs,* April 1945. A review of the impact of scientific developments upon American policies by a military affairs analyst.

Feis, Herbert, *Sinews of Peace* (New York: Harper, 1944). An account of the trade, monetary, raw materials, and investment problems of the post-war world.

Feuerlein, Willy, *Dollars in Latin America* (New York: Council on Foreign Relations, 1941). A treatment of American economic relations with Latin America.

Fifield, R. H., and Pearcy, G. E., *Geopolitics in Principle and Practice* (New York: Ginn, 1944). A standard text on geopolitics.

Flanders, D. P., "Geopolitics and American Foreign Policy," *Political Science Quarterly,* December, 1945. An attempt to view post-war American foreign policy from the perspective of geopolitics.

Leith, C. K., Furniss, J. W., and Lewis, C., *World Minerals and World Peace* (Washington: Brookings Institution, 1943). The relevance of mineral resources to foreign-policy problems. Includes statistical and graphic representations.

London, Kurt, *Backgrounds of Conflict: Ideas and Forms of World Conflict* (New York: Macmillan, 1945). An examination of the influence of ideological factors upon world politics.

Markel, Lester, *et al., Public Opinion and Foreign Policy* (New York: Harper, 1949). A symposium on the roles of the President, Congress, the State Department, and the Military in the formation of public opinion on foreign policy.

Masland, J. W., "Pressure Groups and American Foreign Policy Preceding

Pearl Harbor," *Public Opinion Quarterly,* Spring, 1952. A survey and analysis of pressure group activity in the period prior to 1941.

Mikesell, R. F., *U. S. Economic Policy and International Relations* (New York: McGraw-Hill, 1952). A comprehensive analysis of the influence of domestic economic interests upon American foreign policy.

Perkins, Dexter, *Hands Off: A History of the Monroe Doctrine* (Boston: Little, Brown, 1941). An analysis of the influence of the tradition of the Monroe Doctrine throughout the history of American foreign affairs.

Schattschneider, E. E., *Politics, Pressure and the Tariff* (New York: Prentice, Hall, 1935). A classic study of pressure group influence upon American tariff policy.

Spykman, N. J., *The Geography of the Peace* (New York: Harcourt, Brace, 1944). A view of the geographical problems of American security and foreign policy.

Wright, Quincy, *A Study of War,* 2 vols. (Chicago: University of Chicago Press, 1942). An analysis of the causes of war through classification and description of war curatives, peace movements, and war causes.

Chapter Four

Brookings Institution, *Governmental Mechanism for the Conduct of United States Foreign Relations* (Washington: Brookings Institution, 1949).

————, *The Administration of Foreign Affairs and Overseas Operations* (Washington: Government Printing Office, 1951).

Cheever, D. L., and Haviland, H. F., Jr., *American Foreign Policy and the Separation of Powers* (Cambridge: Harvard University Press, 1952). An analysis of the constitutional framework and administrative organization of American foreign policy, with special reference to the interaction of the executive and legislative branches of the government.

Cohen, B. C., "Foreign Policy Making: Modern Design," *World Politics,* April, 1953. A discussion of the study of American foreign policy with critical comments on recent works in the field.

Commission on Organization of the Executive Branch of the Government, *Foreign Affairs: A Report to Congress* (Washington: Government Printing Office, 1949). The report of the Hoover Commission assessing the foreign policy functions of the executive branch of the government. Contains recommendations for changes in methods of operation.

Crandall, S. B., *Treaties—Their Making and Enforcement* (New York: New York University Press, 1948). Valuable as a basic inquiry into the treaty-making process.

Dahl, R. A., *Congress and Foreign Policy* (New York: Harcourt, Brace, 1950). A study of the role of Congress in the formation of foreign policy, with emphasis on Congressional behavior patterns.

Dangerfield, R. J., *In Defense of the Senate* (Norman: University of Oklahoma Press, 1933). An attempt to rescue the Senate from its reputation as "treaty-wrecker."

Dennison, E. E., *The Senate Foreign Relations Committee* (Stanford: Stanford University Press, 1942). History and procedures of this important committee.

Elliott, W. Y., *et al., United States Foreign Policy: Its Organization and Control* (New York: Columbia University Press, 1952). An inquiry into the means of strengthening the constitutional and institutional framework within which American policy is formulated and executed.

Grassmuck, G. L., *Sectional Biases in Congress on Foreign Policy* (Baltimore: Johns Hopkins University Press, 1951). A statistical analysis of sectionalism in Congressional votes relating to foreign policy.

Herring, E. P., *Public Administration and the Public Interest,* Chapter V on "The State Department and the Public" (New York: McGraw-Hill, 1936). The effects of public opinion and other public pressures on the State Department.

Lay, J. S., "The National Security Council's Role in U. S. Security and Peace Program," *World Affairs,* 1952. A study of the political functions of this foreign policy planning agency.

London, Kurt, *How Foreign Policy Is Made* (New York: Van Nostrand, 1949). Insight into the details of the foreign policy process.

Mann, F. K., "The Government Corporation as a Tool of Foreign Policy," *Public Administration Review,* October, 1943. A brief consideration of the role of this administrative entity in the conduct of American foreign policy.

McCamy, J. L., *The Administration of American Foreign Affairs* (New York: Knopf, 1950). A survey of the administrative apparatus of American foreign policy with special emphasis upon the role of administration in the policy-making sphere.

McClure, Wallace, *International Executive Agreements* (New York: Columbia University Press, 1941). An analysis of the problems and processes involved in the making of executive agreements.

Nigro, Felix, "Senate Confirmation and Foreign Policy," *Journal of Politics,* May, 1952. An historical survey and analysis of Senate confirmation of foreign policy appointments.

Perlman, P. B., "On Amending the Treaty Power," *Columbia Law Review,* November, 1952. A discussion in legal terms of the issues raised by the Bricker Amendment's proposed revision of the treaty-making process.

Plischke, Elmer, *Conduct of American Diplomacy* (New York: Van Nostrand, 1950). An analysis of institutions and processes.

Sutherland, A. E., Jr., "Restricting the Treaty Power," *Harvard Law Review,* June, 1952. More about the legal and constitutional problems raised by the Bricker Amendment.

Westphal, A. F., *The House Committee on Foreign Affairs* (New York:

Columbia University Press, 1942). A study of a Congressional committee of constantly increasing importance.

Wright, Quincy, *The Control of American Foreign Relations* (New York: Macmillan, 1922). A compilation of the legal and institutional characteristics of the control of American foreign policy.

Chapter Five

Bartlett, J. R., *The Record of American Diplomacy* (New York: Knopf, 1947). A well-selected collection of the basic documents of American foreign policy.

Documents on American Foreign Relations (Princeton: Princeton University Press for World Peace Foundation, 1939 *et. seq.*). A valuable yearly publication covering all functions and areas of American foreign policy.

Malloy, W. H. (ed.), *et. al., Treaties, Conventions, International Acts, Protocols and Agreements between the United States of America and Other Powers (1778-1937)* 4 vols. (Washington; Government Printing Office, 1910, 1923, 1938). A definitive compilation of all treaties to which the United States was a party, 1778-1937.

Richardson, J. D., *Messages and Papers of the Presidents* (New York: 1911). The standard work for presidential pronouncements before the twentieth century. In addition, a varied collection of the speeches and public papers of all the presidents is available.

United States Statutes-at-Large.

REGULAR GOVERNMENT PUBLICATIONS

Department of State Bulletin (weekly).

Documents and State Papers (monthly).

Serials:

Arbitration Series (1929 *et seq.*).

Commercial Policy Series (1929 *et seq.*).

Conference Series (1929-1946).

Executive Agreement Series (1929 *et seq.*).

Papers Relating to the Foreign Relations of the United States (1861 *et seq.*). Special issues of this series have occasionally been produced; such as: *Japan, 1931-1941* (2 Vols.) and *The Lansing Papers*, 1914-1920 (2 Vols.).

Treaties and Other International Acts Series (1946 *et seq.*).

Treaty Series (1929-1946).

The New York Times is notable for its practice of printing the full text of many important foreign policy pronouncements, speeches, statements, etc.

Chapter Six

American Friends Service Committee, *The United States and the Soviet Union* (New Haven: Yale University Press, 1949). A presentation of the Quaker position on American foreign policy.

American Perspective (Washington: Foundation for Foreign Affairs). A quarterly containing symposiums devoted to the presentation of alternatives in American foreign policy with points of view from a variety of experts.

Baldwin, Hanson, *The Price of Power* (New York: Harper, 1948). A discussion of the larger implications of the post-war power position of the United States.

Brookings Institution, *Major Problems of United States Foreign Policy* (Washington: Brookings Institution, 1947 *et seq.*). A summary of the major designs of American foreign policy issued yearly by a staff of experts.

Brown, N. W., *The United States and India and Pakistan* (Cambridge: Harvard University Press, 1953). An analysis of United States' relations with the important "third force" nations of Asia.

Byrnes, James, *Speaking Frankly* (New York: Harper, 1947). An authoritative account of the problems and formation of American post-war policy from the personal experience of the participating American Secretary of State.

Department of State Bulletin (Washington: Government Printing Office). An indispensable weekly revealing the design of American foreign policy as published by the State Department in speeches, documents and special articles.

Dulles, F. R., *The Road to Teheran* (Princeton: Princeton University Press, 1944). An historical account of Russian-American relations, 1781-1943.

Dulles, J. F., *War or Peace* (New York: Macmillan, 1950). A critique of Soviet-American relations and other foreign policy problems by the present Secretary of State.

Ellis, H. S., *The Economics of Freedom* (New York: Harper, 1950). A treatise on the Marshall Plan and other current developments in American economic foreign policy.

Foreign Affairs (New York: Council on Foreign Relations). A journal containing articles dealing with the problems and conduct of American foreign policy and international relations in general. Especially valuable because many of its contributors hold official and authoritative positions in the United States government and other governments.

Guerrant, E. B., *Roosevelt's Good Neighbor Policy* (Albuquerque: University of New Mexico Press, 1950). An account of American relations with Latin America under the Good Neighbor program by a former State Department political analyst.

Hoffman, P. G., *Peace Can Be Won* (New York: Doubleday, 1951).

Suggestions for U. S. leadership in the post-war world by the former director of the Marshall Plan.

Lippman, Walter, *The Cold War* (New York: Harper, 1947). An incisive criticism of the policy of containment and the Truman Doctrine.

Latourette, K. S., *The American Record in the Far-East* (New York: Macmillan, 1952). An evaluation of American policy in the Far East.

Oppenheimer, J. R., "Atomic Weapons and American Policy," *Foreign Affairs*, July, 1953. One of the few appraisals of the effects of atomic weapons upon American foreign policy.

Perkins, Dexter, *The United States and the Caribbean* (Cambridge: Harvard University Press, 1947). A survey of the role of the United States in the "American Mediterranean."

Rostow, W. W., "Notes on a New Approach to U. S. Economic Foreign Policy," *World Politics*, April, 1953. Some new thoughts concerning the role of the United States in world economic affairs.

Sherwood, R. E., *Roosevelt and Hopkins* (New York: Harper, 1948). An authoritative account. Offers insight into the origins and conduct of American foreign policy during the Roosevelt era.

The United States in World Affairs (New York: Harper, 1947 *et seq.*). An analytical summary of important American foreign policy actions.

Vandenberg, Arthur H., Jr. (ed.), *The Private Papers of Senator Vandenberg* (Boston: Houghton Mifflin, 1952). An account of the Senator's role in the formation of postwar American policy with special reference to the establishment and implementation of the bipartisan foreign policy.

Vinacke, H. M., *The United States and the Far East, 1945-1951* (Stanford: Stanford University Press, 1952). An analysis of the position of the United States in the Far East in the half dozen years following the end of the war.

World Politics (New Haven: Yale University Press). Interesting for its presentation of new research in the field of American foreign policy.

Index

Index

551